Mikael Parkvall

Limits OF Language

almost everything

you didn't know

you didn't know

about language

and languages

WILLIAM, JAMES & Co.

8536 SW St. Helens Drive, Ste. D · Wilsonville, Oregon 97070 · USA · www.wmjasco.com

BATTLEBRIDGE
PUBLICATIONS

United Kingdom and Sri Lanka · www.battlebridge.com · pb@battlebridge.com

Publisher—US edition   Jim Leisy
Editor and Publisher—UK edition   Philip Baker
Production Editor—US edition   Tom Sumner

Printed in the U.S.A.

For information, contact William, James & Company:
        Rights and Permissions
        William, James & Co.
        8536 SW St. Helens Drive, Ste. D
        Wilsonville, Oregon 97070

Cataloging-in-Publication information is available from William, James & Co.

First published in the United Kingdom in 2006.

isbn (paperback): 978-1-59028-198-7
isbn (hardback): 978-1-59028-210-6

BRIEF CONTENTS

DETAILED CONTENTS

LANGUAGE DEATH AND REVIVAL—PAGE 57

BIG AND SMALL LANGUAGES—PAGE 65

LANGUAGE CHANGE—PAGE 88

LANGUAGE FAMILIES—PAGE 99

SPECTACULAR SPREAD—PAGE 105

LANGUAGE IN ALTERNATE HISTORY—PAGE 111

WRITTEN LANGUAGE—PAGE 114

SIGNED LANGUAGES—PAGE 125

LEARNING YOUR FIRST LANGUAGE—PAGE 133

SECOND-LANGUAGE LEARNING—PAGE 136

POLYGLOTS—PAGE 143

NON-HUMANS AND LANGUAGE—PAGE 148

ARTIFICIAL LANGUAGES—PAGE 157

FORENSIC LINGUISTICS—PAGE 165

PARTS OF SPEECH—PAGE 265

VERBS—PAGE 266

NOUNS—PAGE 268

ADJECTIVES—PAGE 270

ADVERBS—PAGE 271

ADPOSITIONS—PAGE 273

ARTICLES—PAGE 275

DEMONSTRATIVES—PAGE 277

PERSONAL PRONOUNS—PAGE 280

NUMERALS—PAGE 288

NEGATION—PAGE 296

CASE—PAGE 298

GENDER AND NOUN CLASSES—PAGE 301

NUMBER—PAGE 305

TENSE, MOOD AND ASPECT—PAGE 309

VOICE—PAGE 316

MORPHOLOGY—PAGE 318

FOREWORD

T his book was born, as I recall, during a stroll along the Regent's Canal in London in the spring of 2001. My friend Philip Baker who had founded the Battlebridge publishing company had asked me about ideas concerning a book that might appeal to a wider audience than the titles they had thus far produced. I was myself very happy with my idea, and had expected Philip to excitedly start jumping up and down in his seat. When I carefully expressed my disappointment with what I perceived as lack of appropriate enthusiasm, I realized I had forgotten that he is British. "I am *wildly* enthusiastic", he calmly stated, in a tone you would only hear from a Briton.

During the following five years, *Limits of Language* grew at rather uneven intervals, but finally—here it is. It was originally conceived as a kind of *Guinness Book of World Records* for languages, but as languages do not easily lend themselves to quantifying, it would have been impossible to write a book consisting only of non-subjective records. Therefore, not only the *Guinness*, but also a few other books which formed my childhood view of the world served as models: *The Book of Lists* and the publications by the Diagram Group. Drawing on these sources of inspiration, I hope that *Limits of Language* can show the uninitiated some of the incredible aspects that linguistics and human languages have to offer, teach beginners some of the basics of linguistics, but also to serve as a reference book for experienced linguists—here, the linguist can identify the extremes, and thereby judge to what extent his or her own language is "normal".

This book contains data on almost 1000 language varieties, and a book with such a broad scope is bound to contain some errors. It would be impossible to actually master—or even have considerable experience of—more than a fraction of these languages. So, like any linguist dealing with more than a handful of languages, I have had to rely on descriptions and analyses made by others, the quality of which I am not always competent to assess. It would thus be surprising indeed if there were absolutely no inaccuracies to be found among these pages. While I have endeavoured to consult people with a solid competence in the languages concerned, if there are any cases where I have not been careful enough, I would very much appreciate having these drawn to my attention. In that way, any errors or shortcomings can be corrected in future editions of *Limits of Language*. Also, of course, readers of this book may know of additional material worthy of consideration for inclusion in subsequent editions, and I would be very grateful to receive such suggestions. So, for these reasons and for feedback of any kind, please contact me at <beyondlimits@battlebridge.info>. It would be much appreciated if you could also indicate the source of your information (or alternatively indicate your competence as a speaker of the language in question).

Some initial errors have in fact already been spotted and corrected by the helpful friends and colleagues who have gone through parts of the manuscript, or who have otherwise contributed significantly. These include Bjørn Bojesen, Östen Dahl, Eskil Dalenius, Niklas Edenmyr, Robert Eklund, Stéphane Goyette, Anthony Grant, Harald Hammarström, Bernd Heine, Samuel Härgestam, Tore Janson, and Jonas Söderström. In particular, Peter Bakker, and Daniel Bunčić have been involved in the making of this book to an extent just short of listing them as co-authors.

Olle Engstrand, Jussi Karlgren, Ulrika Kvist Darnell (who suggested the very title), Zita Lekeberg, Anna-Lena Nilsson, and Ljuba Veselinova have also been helpful in various ways, as has Päivi Juvonen, who was at an early stage intended to co-author the book. While this did not happen, she has remained the best of friends throughout the process. I am also grateful to all the following people who provided me with information or assisted in other ways: Inger Ahlgren, Keira Ballantyne, Hendrik Biebeler, Mickey Blake, Lars Borin, Ross Clark, Mark Donohue, James Emmett, Anders Eriksson, Anders G Eriksson, Bill Foley, Colette Grinevald, M J Hardman, Ellen Jernström, Niklas Jonsson, Axel Kristensen, Diana Krull, Mai Kuha, Henrik Liljegren, Eva Lindström, Mike MacMahon, Matti Miestamo, Bill Morris, John Ohala, Nicholas Ostler, Jens Östlund, Roz Prickett, David Quinto, Dónall ó Riagáin, Jørgen Rischel, Sarah Roberts, Bernhard Wälchli, Ashley Williams, Janet Wilson. In addition, Philip Baker has engaged himself in this enterprise to an extent way beyond what a publisher/editor normally does.

The Max-Planck-Institut für evolutionäre Anthropologie in Leipzig, Germany, had the kindness to invite me to spend several weeks there as a visiting researcher in the spring of 2006. As this happened to take place just a few weeks before the original publication of this book, some of my time there was spent on making final preparations for that. I am grateful to both the institute and its staff for the hospitality they showed me.

Let us not speculate about any possible causality, but two great linguists sadly passed away shortly after having provided comments on this book—Larry Trask and Peter Ladefoged. I had no idea how serious Larry's condition was when I sent him a draft copy, but realized afterwards that he was in fact reading the manuscript on his deathbed. Having long been impressed by his works, I was nevertheless amazed by the exceptional detail of his comments. His last message simply finished with the line "I've been in poor health recently, and reading this stuff has cheered me up no end". I loved hearing that, of course, but those words took on a new meaning when he died not long afterwards. For his impressive contributions to linguistics, and for his helpfulness in the making of this book, I would like to dedicate this book to the memory of Larry Trask. Peace be with him, and may he enjoy himself whatever he may be doing these days.

A NOTE ON SOME CONVENTIONS ADOPTED IN THIS BOOK

Although written in English, this book is international in using metric units throughout. No bushels, long tons, furlongs, fluid ounces, fathoms, pounds per square inch, hogsheads, or stones' throws in sight anywhere. For the same reason, it also uses the decimal comma instead of the decimal point, and gives dates in accordance with international standards, i.e. in the format YYYY-MM-DD.

Although published in the US, the punctuation follows the norms of UK English in that punctuation marks are placed outside of quotation marks when the meaning demands it.

For language names, an effort has been made to make these conform to the practices of the Ethnologue database (www.ethnologue.com), which should facilitate the search for additional information on these languages. In some cases, this was not possible, and in a few, a label thought to be more widely known was—for precisely that reason—preferred over the Ethnologue counterpart (e.g. "Cantonese" rather than "Chinese, Yue").

For phonetic representation, this book uses the International Phonetic Alphabet (IPA). For information on how to interpret the IPA, go to http://www.arts.gla.ac.uk/ipa/ipachart.html. An easy-to-use interactive introduction to the IPA for only the sounds of English is here: http://www.arts.gla.ac.uk/ipa/ipachart.html.

LANGUAGE VARIATION AND REGISTERS FOR SPECIAL OCCASIONS

IN MOST, possibly even all societies, people speak differently on different occasions. In western cultures, for instance, we usually express ourselves differently while having a drink at the pub with our close friends than we would at an employment interview—we use a different *register*. In many societies, this register differentiation is far more institutionalized than in English. Among the most commonly cited examples are Aboriginal languages in Australia, many of which contain subsystems often referred to as "mother-in-law" languages or "avoidance styles". These must be used in the presence of certain relatives (though not necessarily mothers-in-law). In some languages, the entire lexicon (except function words) is replaced, while keeping the grammatical structure intact. Very similar phenomena are also encountered elsewhere in the world, e.g. in some languages of southern Africa.

MOST DIALECTALLY HOMOGENOUS LANGUAGES

Deciding which language is the most dialectally homogenous all boils down to what you choose to label "a language". If Indo-European is a language, then it sure is heterogeneous, but if what you and your buddies—but nobody else—speaks is a language, then it probably is pretty homogenous. Among more widespread areas where languages (as customarily defined) display remarkably minor differences with regard to geography, those of Russian, American English, Icelandic, Hakka, and Hausa may be mentioned. "Surely", I can hear someone say, "you can hear the difference in speech between a person from New York and one from Boston?". Well, although some Bostonians have more or less expected me to perceive differences in pronunciation between people living on opposite sides of the same street, the fact remains that there are hardly any areas of the world where you could travel a distance corresponding to that between, say, Miami and Seattle, or Boston and Los Angeles, without having more difficulties in making yourself understood than you would in the USA. Similarly, the differences between Moscow and St Petersburg, although (barely) perceivable to native speakers, are virtually negligible when you consider that speakers of regional varieties of Bengali, Khanty, Italian, Fijian, and Japanese would have a hard time (to say the least) understanding each other unless they adapted to the standard. (And note that these languages are spoken in far smaller geographical areas than are Russian and American English).

In general, the relative lack of dialectal variation applies to recently colonized territories, and thus to all European languages in the New World and Oceania. Interestingly, however, the first ever description of the English of the Falkland Islands (Sudbury 2000:85-86) documents a certain dialectal variation, with the speech varieties of Hill Cove (of West Falkland) and Darwin and Walker Creek (on southern East Falkland) being the most noticeable. There are no readily available population figures for these settlements, but given that all of West Falkland has a total population of 144 (excluding the far more numerous sheep and penguins), the Hill Cove variety would also seem to be a good candidate for one of the smallest dialects of English.

The recent settlement situation also applies to Israel, where the geographical differences among native speakers are small indeed. (The Hebrew of individuals may be influenced by the other languages they speak but this has little to do with geography.)

MAKING FUN OF THE HANDICAPPED

Like its neighbor Nootka, Quileute has a number of odd speech registers. When speaking to cross-eyed persons, for instance, every word must be prefixed by /tạ-/. Similarly, words directed to 'funny persons' must be made to begin in /tḷ-/. Prefixes used when addressing small-sized men, hunchbacks and lame persons are /s-/, /tʃʔ-/ and /tʃχ-/ respectively.

MOST RECHERCHÉ REGISTER

The Lardil people of Mornington island off Australia's north coast until recently had a particularly peculiar speech register, called Damin. It is remarkable in several ways, and it is difficult to avoid the impression that it was more or less consciously created precisely in order to be spectacular.

The vocabulary consisted only of a couple of hundred words, and the affixes were identical to those of ordinary Lardil. Its flamboyant character was manifested mainly in its phonology. First, it is the only language known outside of southern Africa to include clicks (see p 245), and it even had a couple of click sounds not attested in any other language in the world. Furthermore, it has an exceptional variety of phonation types, including a pulmonic ingressive and velaric and glottalic egressives.

Other extravagant features of Damin include a pronoun inventory with a distinction only between first person singular and everything else (Lardil has 19 different personal pronoun forms). Similarly remarkable is the regular formation of opposites by means of a prefix, where a negative, rather than a positive adjective, is the base form (e.g. *tjitjuu* 'small' versus **kuri**tjituu 'large').

Damin was taught by older men in initiation rites, but ceased to be used during the 20th century. Now, Lardil itself, of which there are only a couple of dozen speakers left, is suffering the same fate.

OTHER UNUSUAL REGISTERS

It is reported that speakers of Kalam (New Guinea) must use a special register when collecting pandamus nuts. Unless they do so, the spirits inhabiting the nuts would realize that the nut is about to be picked, and would cause it to rot instantly.

From Africa, a "royal accent" has been reported among speakers of Akan. This is not unusual in itself, since nobility is often associated with specific speech styles, but the Akan variety stands out in including (among other things) conscious stuttering.

In the same part of the world, Itsekiri and Okpe have developed partially different vocabularies to be used depending on the time of the day. Thus, concepts such as 'blood', 'fire' and 'firewood' are labelled differently by day and by night.

In Buru (eastern Indonesia) taboos are related not primarily to activities or interlocutors, but particularly to geographical areas. In certain areas, specific words must not be used, and in others, particular subjects (e.g. hunger and thirst) must be avoided. The uninhabited interior of Buru island constitutes a special case. There, any language can be spoken, provided it is *not* Buru. Malay would do fine (as would Cockney, Basque or Klingon), but a specific language called Li Garan has also developed. Li Garan is only used by persons who for one reason or another need to visit the area concerned.

MOST ELABORATE STATUS DIFFERENTIATIONS

Remarkably complex systems of speech levels, where your speech makes far-reaching adjustments to the social standing of the person you're talking to, are conspicuous in East Asia. One of the most ornate and oft-cited examples is that of Javanese, which sports a high (*krama*), a neutral (*madya*), and a low (*ngoko*) speech level, with a further distinction into two sub-levels of each variety. As can be seen from the examples below, virtually all words are differentiated, including function words, numerals, and basic items such as 'yes' and 'no'.

Highest level	*Menapa*	*nandalem*	*mundhut*	*sekul*	*semanten?*
	Menapa	*panjenengan*	*mendhet*	*sekul*	*semanten?*
	Napa	*sampéyan*	*mendhet*	*sekul*	*semonten?*
	Napa	*sampéyan*	*njupuk*	*sega*	*semono?*
	Apa	*sliramu*	*mundhut*	*sega*	*semono?*
Lowest level	*Apa*	*kowé*	*njupuk*	*sega*	*semono?*
Literal translation	*question marker*	*you*	*take*	*rice*	*that much*

'Did you take that much rice?'

The differences between the various styles are primarily lexical, and almost every single word must be substituted when switching from one style to another. Some analysts, however, have also claimed to have identified prosodic and morphophonemic differences, although these remain poorly understood.

Korean features seven degrees of politeness for the 2nd person pronouns. In addition to that, Korean used to have a 'superpolite' level, which is now archaic.

The choice of appropriate pronoun forms is also a delicate matter in Sinhala. As well as five levels of politeness, there are special ones for addressing Buddhist monks. On top of this, regional variation makes the friendly/egalitarian form of one part of Sri Lanka vulgar or insulting in another. One teaching manual advises Sinhala-learners to avoid using 2nd person pronouns until they have lived in the country for at least six months!

AMERICAN INDIAN CODE TALK

Following a suggestion from a Philip Johnston, who had grown up in a Navajo reservation in Arizona, the American military in early 1942 hired a number of Navajo speakers for use as radio-telegraphists. Even if Japanese cryptographers could crack an ordinary code, chances were slim that they would be in a position to first crack the code, and then find somebody to translate the message from Navajo to Japanese.

The Navajo code-talkers were first used in battle on Guadalcanal in August of 1942. Not only was the code more difficult to crack for the enemy, but the Navajos were also more efficient, as they had the knowledge of Navajo in their heads rather than in a code book. In addition, even in the unlikely case that the Japanese should learn to understand Navajo, it would be impossible for them to imitate it with a native-speaker accent, and thus the risk of receiving fake messages was minimised.

The success was such that the code-talkers had their own body-guards, assigned to protect the valuable pool of competence.

In order to adapt the Navajo lexicon to the realities of modern warfare, words for various birds and fish were drafted in to serve as designations for aircraft and warships. Names for foreign nations were also coined,

and 'Australia' was *Cha-yes-desi*, that is 'rolled hat', while 'Britain' was *Toh-ta* or 'between waters', and France *Da-gha-hi*—'beard'. Other items for which Navajo lacked words were conveyed letter by letter in English, because Japanese overhearing the communication might get a clue as to the content of the message by understanding the English words. The spelling, however, was such that Navajo words were used for the initial letter of the *corresponding English words*. Thus, *dze* stood for the letter *e*, as the Navajo word means 'elk'. In order to avoid repetitions, which might facilitate things for enemy code-crackers, the most common letters had two or three Navajo counterparts. In this way, the name Guadalcanal, which contains four instances of a could be rendered as *klizzie, shi-da, wol-la-chee, lha-cha-eh, be-la-sana, dibeh-yazzie, moasi, tse-nill, tsah, tse-nill, ah-jad*, with only one repetition. The whole chunk translates into English as *goat, uncle, ant, dog, apple, lamb, cat, axe, needle, axe, leg*—in other words 'Guadalcanal'. The Japanese never did succeed in cracking the code.

Much of the code-talker activities were classified for a long time after the war, but they did get a late recognition as the *National Navajo Code Talkers Day* was proclaimed on

Photo of Navajo Code Talkers in formation at Camp Pendelton, California

August 14, 1982 by then American president Ronald Reagan (a local *Navajo Code Talkers Day* had been declared in New Mexico already on April 10). In 2002, the Hollywood film *Windtalkers*, starring Nicholas Cage, was made on the theme, and a monument to the Navajo language warriors has been erected in Phoenix, Arizona. Perhaps the surest sign of the veterans' popularity is that the very phrase "Navajo Code Talkers" is now a registered trademark of the *Navajo Code Talkers' Association*.

It should be noted, finally, that American Indians (in that case Choctaws) had been used for these purposes already in the First World War, though their history is less well documented. Also, even though the Navajos were the most numerous, members of other nations, such as the Comanches, also saw action in this role during World War Two.

A similar practice has been documented in South America. During the Chaco war against Paraguay in the early 1930s, the Bolivians used Chiquitano as a secret code.

SOURCES NOT MENTIONED IN THE TEXT

Australian "mother-in-law" languages: Dixon (1980:58-65).
Dialectal differences in Russian: Comrie (1990c:66), Östen Dahl (p c).
Dialectal differences in Hausa: Newman (1990:215).
Dialectal differences in Hakka: Li & Thompson 1979:298.
Dialectal differences in Khanty: Comrie (1981:7).
Lack of dialectal variation in Hebrew: McWhorter (2001:86).
Special handicapped-directed speech varieties in the American north-west: Mithun (1999:275).
Damin: Hale (1973), Dixon (1980:66-67).
Pandamus register in Kalam: Lynch (1998:259).

Itsekiri and Okpe: Wolff (2000:305).

Akan: Wolff (2000:306).

Buru: Grimes & Maryott (1994).

Elaborate register differentiations in Javanese: Irvine (2001:29-30).

Politeness in Korean: Sohn (1999:207, 269, 272).

Politeness in Sinhala: Philip Baker (p c)

American Indian code talk: Singh (1999:221-30) and the *Navajo Code Talker Association*. Comanche code-talkers mentioned in the *Shawnee News-Star* 2002-06-12 and the *Daily Oklahoman* 2002-06-12.

Bolivian use of Chiquitano as a secret war language: Adelaar (2004:478).

LANGUAGE GEOGRAPHY

WHEREVER THERE ARE PEOPLE, there are languages. Language geography is therefore necessarily a product of human settlement. Yet, languages are not necessarily dispersed in the same way as people are.

MOST LINGUISTICALLY DENSE COUNTRIES

The most linguistically dense countries are microstates or other very small countries which have attracted immigrants for various reasons (often fiscal ones). Thus, apart from the dubious case of the Vatican State, Monaco may be the linguistically most diverse sovereign country in relation to its area (1,95 km^2). Almost half of its population speaks French, while a fifth speaks Italian. English, German, Dutch, Portuguese and Spanish all account for more than one percent of the population, closely followed by smaller minorities speaking Swedish and Greek.

Among somewhat larger countries, Singapore has an unusually complex linguistic situation — the *Ethnologue* lists 21 languages for this city state of 637,5 km^2. Excluding countries for which four languages or less are listed in the *Ethnologue* (for which one language more or less would yield an enormous difference), the 17 languages listed for the Federated States of Micronesia puts that country in the world record class with more than 24 languages per 1 000 km^2. It is followed by Vanuatu which, with its 109 languages has a language density of 8,9 languages/1 000 km^2. Most other competitors are found in the notoriously heterogeneous South-East Asia/Pacific area.

LEAST LINGUISTICALLY DENSE COUNTRIES

The countries with the smallest number of languages in relation to their respective areas are mostly territories which contain vast inhospitable deserts. In this category, we find Greenland, Kazakhstan, Saudi Arabia and Turkmenistan, all with a language density well below 0,005 languages/km^2.

It is worth noting that linguistically rich countries such as China, Brazil, USA, and Australia are found in this rather than the "dense" end of the spectrum. They are in other words exceptionally multilingual more by virtue of their size than anything else.

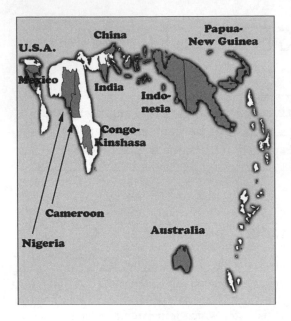

Languages are very unevenly distributed among the countries of the world. The map tries to capture this fact by rendering each country in a size corresponding to the number of languages spoken in it. (Because of the inherent problems in accomplishing this, sizes are rather approximate). The ten shaded countries are those in which more than 200 languages are in use.

MOST LINGUISTICALLY DIVERSE COUNTRIES

There is little doubt that the island of New Guinea, divided between Papua New Guinea and the Indonesian-occupied West Papua, is an area which has an unparalleled wealth of languages. On this island, which is neither geographically nor demographically significant on a global level, something like a sixth of all the world's languages are spoken. Again according to the numbers supplied by *Ethnologue*, the most linguistically diverse countries are as follows:

Country	No. of languages	Country	No. of languages
Papua New Guinea	823	Australia	235
Indonesia	726	Congo-Kinshasa	218
Nigeria	505	China	201
India	387	Brazil	192
Mexico	288	United States	176
Cameroon	279	Philippines	169

The *Ethnologue* also uses another interesting way of measuring linguistic diversity—"Greenberg's diversity index". It indicates "the probability that any two people in the country picked at random will have different mother tongues", and has a theoretical range of variation between 0 (for a completely homogenous country) and 1 (for a hypothetical country where every single citizen has his own exclusive language). Most countries which score zero are island microstates, some of the few larger countries with a near-complete linguistic homogeneity being Jamaica, Tunisia, El Salvador, Madagascar,

Burundi and the Koreas. The most populous almost-monolingual countries are Japan and Brazil.

Most countries with exceptionally high diversity values, not surprisingly, are located in Melanesia, an area notorious for its exceptional linguistic diversity. Papua New Guinea scores highest, with 0,99, followed by its neighbors Vanuatu and the Solomon Islands, which, along with Cameroon and Tanzania, all in the 0,96-0,97 range. Even the *one hundred* most widely spoken languages of Papua New Guinea account for only about two thirds of the country's population.

There is a general tendency for poor and underdeveloped countries to be more diversified than first world states (or, to put it another way, high-tech civilizations are more or less artificially cleansed in that nation-states and education tend to more or less push citizens into the same linguistic fold). The western country (apart from tax haven Moncao and the Vatican State) ranking the highest is Israel (0,73), followed by Belgium and Canada, both around 0,59-0,60.

Some countries show high diversity figures (above 0,70) not so much due to the presence of a plethora of indigenous languages, but rather because of contemporary immigration. The most obvious case in this category is Israel, but we also find oil-rich Gulf States of United Arab Emirates, Qatar and Bahrain, with their large contingents of South and East Asian labourers, the European microstates of Monaco, the Vatican State and Andorra, as well as American and French overseas territories such as Guam and French Guiana, where artificial economies based on metropolitan government spending attract job-seekers from neighboring third world countries.

The average value is about 0,40, and in all, as defined by the Ethnologue, the average country houses 44 languages—no doubt more than most people would expect.

This diversity index was first proposed by Greenberg (1956), and is defined as $DI = 1 - \Sigma(P_n)^2$, where P_n is the fraction of the total population made up by speakers of the n-th language of the country in question.

CONTINENT WITH THE FEWEST LANGUAGES

According to the *Ethnologue* statistics, Europe is by far the linguistically poorest continent—only 3% of the world's languages are spoken there. The remaining 97% are relatively equally distributed across the planet. On the other hand, it is possible to travel from the Rio Grande to northern Alaska without ever passing a language boundary, while a trip of comparable length in Europe would encompass a great deal of linguistic variation. Once aboriginal languages are extinct (and the vast majority of those that haven't already passed into oblivion are acutely threatened, and usually on the verge of extinction), North America and Australia are going to be the most monolingual continents on earth—both of them dominated by the same language. Even now, you can (perhaps allowing for a few detours) go from Tierra del Fuego to Alaska without really crossing more than a single language boundary, which is unparalleled elsewhere in the world, except perhaps for the case of Russian, which will take you from St. Petersburg to Kamchatka. Allowing one language boundary crossing,

Mandarin would then take you into the tropics of south-east Asia.

In another sense, however, Europe is less linguistically poor than it would seem. Applying Joseph Greenberg's diversity index to entire continents, Europe is linguistically considerably more varied than Oceania or the Americas. The explanation, of course, is that while the latter two continents have plenty of indigenous languages, these are for the most part very small indeed, and are vastly outnumbered by a small number of originally European languages. In Europe, on the other hand, the largest languages are relatively equal in size.

Africa	Asia	Europe	North America	Oceania	South America
0,96	0,93	0,92	0,62	0,60	0,56

Continent-wide diversity figures

MOST ISOLATED LANGUAGES

Of course, the most isolated language in the world would be one that we have never heard of (and there may still be a few left). On the other hand, lack of contact with western civilization need not imply that a language is isolated from its neighbors. On the contrary, in, for instance, remote areas of New Guinea which few westerners have visited, multilingualism in a number of local languages is often the norm. The most isolated languages appear to be found in the same areas where linguistic fragmentation is the highest, that is in the rainforests of the Amazonas, Indonesia and along the border between Nigeria and Cameroon. Languages specifically mentioned as exceptionally isolated in the Ethnologue include Hixkaryána, Avá-Canoeiro and Yanomamö of Brazil (the latter also spoken in Venezuela) and Pisabo in neighboring Peru, Tugutil of Indonesia, and Akum, Beezen, Tibea and Acipa of the Cameroon/Nigeria area. These languages are spoken by small groups of people (Avá-Canoeiro only has about 50 speakers) in remote areas with virtually no roads, and their users are for the most part not bilingual in other languages.

MOST WIDESPREAD LANGUAGES

A few languages have spread to such an extent that they have circumnavigated the globe in a rather literal sense. English is of course the most obvious case, with English-speaking New Zealand being located almost as far from Britain as one can possibly travel (hence the name Antipodes for a group of islands off New Zealand). Spanish comes close in that parts of South America are almost on the other side of the globe vis-à-vis the Philippines, which is still home to a tiny Spanish-speaking minority. Also close, but not quite there, are Tahiti and the Seychelles, and Vanuatu and the Ivory Coast city Abidjan, all partially French-speaking. Three languages compete for the largest continuous area. At least 15 million continuous square kilometers each are dominated (not only officially, but by actual speakers) by English, Russian and Arabic. English is of course unique in completely dominating two entire continents, while English, French and

Spanish are probably the only ones having non-immigrant native language communities on all the world's inhabited continents. 28% of the world's land area is occupied by countries having English as their official language. French follows quite a bit behind, with 14%, as do Russian (12%) and Arabic (10%). Among the others, only Spanish, Portuguese, and Mandarin account for more than 5%. Romani is quite possibly the world's most cosmopolitan language in the sense that if you are a speaker of this language, there is a 95% chance that another speaker will be from another country. For Spanish and Arabic, this figure is 88%, and for Yiddish about 78%. Despite the world-wide spread of English, the demographic weight of the United States (which is home to two thirds of all native speakers of English) reduces the figure for English to 52%.

Top-10 languages by continent

Europe	North America	South America	Asia	Africa	Oceania
Russian 10,0%	**English** 45,7%	**Portuguese** 45,0%	**Mandarin** 11,0%	**Arabic** 13,0%	**English** 69,9%
German 12,8%	**Spanish** 36,7%	**Spanish** 43,5%	**Hindi** 6,8%	**Hausa** 4,0%	**Fijian** 1,5%
English 8,5%	**French** 2,1%	**Quechua** 2,6%	**Bengali** 5,4%	**Yoruba** 3,1%	**Hindi** 1,3%
French 8,1%	**French Creoles** 1,9%	**Guaraní** 1,4%	**Japanese** 3,2%	**Fula** 3,1%	**Italian** 1,2%
Italian 8,0%	**English Creoles** 1,1%	**Aymara** 0,5%	**Panjabi** 2,9%	**Igbo** 2,6%	**Samoan** 1,0%
Polish 5,5%	**German** 0,9%	**Italian** 0,5%	**Arabic** 2,5%	**Oromo** 2,5%	**Cantonese** 0,9%
Ukrainian 4,6%	**Sinitic lgs** 0,7%	**German** 0,3%	**Wu** 2,4%	**Amharic** 2,5%	**Greek** 0,9%
Spanish 4,5%	**Italian** 0,4%	**Japanese** 0,2%	**Javanese** 2,2%	**Malagasy** 2,0%	**French** 0,9%
Romanian 3,3%	**Tagalog** 0,3%	**English Creoles** 0,2%	**Telugu** 2,1%	**Somali** 1,4%	**Enga** 0,8%
Dutch 2,9%	**Náhuatl** 0,3%	**Mapudungun** 0,1%	**Marathi** 2,0%	**Ciluba** 1,2%	**Arabic** 0,7%

Here is a way of making Italian appear as the most wide-spread language on earth: it is the only language that makes it into a top-ten list of languages on four of the world's six permanently inhabited continents. English, French, German, Spanish and Arabic only do so for three continents each (as does Chinese, if you combine the Sinitic languages). With the exception of Arabic and Italian, these are also among the ten most widely spoken languages among the population of transient scientists on the seventh continent, Antarctica. Note that, contrary to popular belief, there are more speakers of Portuguese than of Spanish in South America.

ODDEST GEOGRAPHICAL DISTRIBUTION

The Fula language is thought to have originated somewhere in the area of present-day Senegal and Guinea. Beginning in the 12th century, however, the Fulas began an eastward expansion, so that they now occupy a band stretching for about 5000 kilometers from the Atlantic to the Nile. As the pious Moslems that they generally are, the Fulas have thus striven ever closer to Mecca for more than eight hundred years!

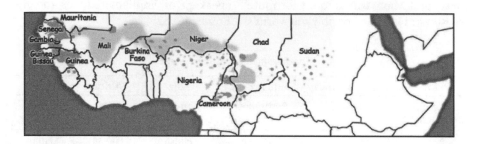

The expansion is in part due to a succesful adaptation to cattle raising in the arid Sahel climate, and in part through sheer conquest. In the eastern parts of the area, Fula has managed to establish itself as an important regional lingua franca in parts of Cameroon and Nigeria (see pp 66–68).

Known under a variety of names (e.g. Fulani, Fulbe, Fulfulde, Peul, Pulaar, and Toucouleur), Fula now has 26 million speakers. It is the biggest language of Guinea, the second in Senegal, Cameroon, Guinea-Bissau, Burkina Faso, Mauritania, and the Gambia, and third in Niger, Mali and Nigeria. Close to two million additional speakers are scattered over eight other West African countries.

ON THE WRONG SIDE OF THE BORDER

The Bering Strait divides Siberia and Alaska from one another. On both sides, people speak Yup'ik—the only language indigenous to both the New World and the Old. The official language of the Siberian side is Russian, while that of the Alaskan side is English. However, when the Russians arrived in the region, they came overland (except for the crossing of the strait, of course), and took more interest in the American side than in the areas which today remain Russian. The English-speakers, on the other hand, came by sea, and had partly different commercial interests, for which reason they had more contact with the Asian coast. A couple of centuries later, traces of this situation are still linguistically visible—Siberian Yup'ik has more loan words from English than has its Alaskan sibling, which in turn has incorporated more Russian terms. Thus, for instance, the word for 'cow' in Siberian Yup'ik is derived from English *cow*, while the Alaskan variety uses a form derived from Russian корова (korova).

Another case of language material winding up in unexpected places is provided by Dutch-lexicon creoles. Three such languages survived in the Caribbean area into the 20th century: Negerhollands, Berbice, and Skepi. Similarly, three areas remained under Dutch rule: the ABC islands (Aruba, Bonaire, and Curaçao), the SSS islands (Saba, St

Eustatius, a k a 'Statia', and the southern half of St Martin (see pp 25–26) and Dutch Guiana (now independent under the name Surinam). Creole languages were spoken in all three areas, but none was lexically based on Dutch. Papiamentu, the main language of the ABC islands, draws its lexicon first and foremost from Spanish, while an assortment of English-lexicon creoles and creoloids are used on the SSS islands and in Surinam. Meanwhile, the three Dutch creoles were all used in countries were English is the official language: Negerhollands was spoken on the U S Virgin Islands, and the other two in British Guiana (now Guyana *tout court*). In other words, at least in the 20th century Caribbean, Dutch rule and the use of a Dutch-derived language were in a perfectly complementary distribution.

AN ODD GEOLINGUISTIC SITUATION

The tiny Caribbean island of Saint-Barthélemy, or St Barth, presents a remarkable linguistic fragmentation. Despite being a mere 10 kilometers across, and home to little more than 3 000 people, it has traditionally had at least four distinct languages. In the north-western part, a Norman patois has some 500-700 speakers, and in the east, a French-lexicon Creole is used by 600-800 people. In the middle region, an archaic variety of French is now on the verge of extinction. In addition to this, in the administrative center of Gustavia, a black population, some 100 strong, speaks a local and slightly creolized variety of English. On top of this, standard French is the official language, and is increasingly used. (Members of all groups born after about 1970 usually have standard French as their mother tongue).

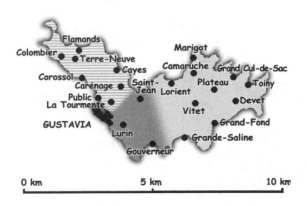

St Barth and its language boundaries

While this situation is not particularly uncommon in the world as a whole, it is rare in the western world, especially in a recently colonized area—such linguistic fragmentation usually requires far more time than just a couple of centuries to develop. Understandably, this diversity requires isolation, and as late as in the 1940s, there were people in the northwestern village of Flamands who only visited Gustavia once a year. And yet, the distance between the two is about two kilometers!

MAKING THE MOST OUT OF A SINGLE ISOGLOSS

Particularly since the Napoleonic Wars, language has been seen as a basis for nationality, and thus for drawing country boundaries. For instance, one of the reasons for recognizing Rhaeto-Romance in Switzerland as a separate language was to counter Mussolini's claims to the southern parts of the country.

In continuum situations, however, language boundaries are difficult to establish, and at the most, isoglosses can be identified. Thus, the fact that Serbian and Macedonian— as opposed to Bulgarian—used [c] or [ʧ] as a reflex of proto-Slavic *tj* was exploited by Serbian nationalist Aleksandar Belić in 1919 to support Serbia's claim to most of what is today Macedonia. On the other hand, the use of a suffixed definite article in Macedonian (as well as in Bulgarian, but not in most varieties of Serbian) was sufficient for some Bulgarian writers to demonstrate that not only Macedonia, but also the Timok-Morava valley in southern Serbia should really be under Bulgarian jurisdiction.

DENSEST ISOGLOSSES

Baarle-Hertog is a Belgian enclave in the Netherlands. On most maps detailed enough to show the community in the first place, it simply figures as a dot.

Baarle presents an intricate patchwork of Dutch and Belgian territory, even including enclaves-within-enclaves. In the sketch above, the shaded territory is Belgian

However, on a really detailed map, the enclave turns out to consist of innumerable little unconnected patches. Not only one, but a multitude of frontiers run through the town, and some houses are actually divided between the two nations (in which case the owner is considered a citizen of the country in which his front door happens to be). This division goes back to 1190, when the duke of Brabant ceded the territory to the lord of Breda, with the exception of the land which was built-up at the time.

On both sides of the intricate line, Dutch is spoken. A Dutch dialectologist who visited the area in 1956 was therefore first sceptical about the locals' claims that the utterly complex state border was actually also a dialect border. But when he questioned people, however, it turned out that the Belgians indeed did say *gazet, fakteur, madam* and *sjuust* ('newspaper', 'post', 'mrs' and 'just') where the Dutch would use *krant, post, mevrouw* and *precies.* The differences even included certain phonetic features.

An isogloss is a line on a map indicating the geographical division between two comparable linguistic features. Such features can include different words for the same thing (for example, the locally preferred word for 'a stream' is generally beck in some of the most northerly English counties and brook elsewhere), different pronunciations of the same word (e.g. there are three widespread regional pronunciations of 'last' in England: [læst], [last] and [lɑːst]), or different uses of verb forms (e.g. instead of standard 'we are' the dialectally preferred form in an area south and west of Worcestershire and Oxfordshire (but excluding Devon and Cornwall) is we be). Isoglosses for English are often based on the usage of older people to reveal dialectal differences which may now be declining.

VOLUNTARY LINGUISTIC SEGREGATION IN SOUTH DAKOTA

In 2005, the Michigan-based firm Nederveld Associates, Inc. announced their plan to construct an entirely new town in South Dakota.

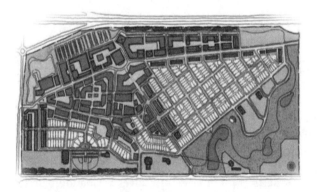

The Laurent town plan

The name chosen for the community is Laurent, after Laurent Clerc, who introduced French Sign to the United States (see p 127). Located 50 km west of Sioux Falls, Laurent is to receive the first of its envisaged 3 000 residents in 2006.

While this is unusual in itself (especially since no new settlements had been established in that state for a century), the truly unique feature of the town is that is to be designed specifically for sign language users.

A street view in Laurent, South Dakota

One design feature intended to cater for the future deaf residents is a fully bilingual (English and American Sign) school system. Also, public spaces are to be designed with maximal visibility in mind, to facilitate signing. Shop assistants and officials would of course be bilingual, and emergency vehicles would have more lights and fewer sirens. Internet connections are to pay special attention to the needs of the hearing-impaired, so that signing can be easily transmitted over video.

SOURCES NOT MENTIONED IN THE TEXT

Unless otherwise mentioned, the number of speakers of various languages, in this and the following sections, are from Parkvall (n d), while population figures are from the 2005 edition of the *CIA World Factbook*.

Languages in Monaco: based on birthplace and citizenship data in the 2000 Monaco census. The semi-official indigenous Monégasque language is assumed to be extinct (cf Shaul 2002).

Fula's geographical distribution: Olson (1996:181-82), Arnott (1974), Parkvall (n d).

Russian and English loans in Yup'ik: Comrie (1981:258).

Presence and absence of Dutch creoles: Holm (1989).

Linguistic situation in St Barth: Maher (1997b), Calvet & Chaudenson (1998).

Making the most of an isogloss: Friedman (1996).

Baarle-Hertog: Weijnen (1957:4-5), Thijs (2000).

Laurent, South Dakota: Press Release from Nederveld Associates Inc., Official web site of Laurent at http://www.laurentsd.com (2005-03-30).

LANGUAGE AS A LEGAL MATTER

MOST COUNTRIES ON EARTH have a linguistic legislation of one kind or the other. About two thirds specify in the constitution that this or that is the official language, but in most cases, it is hastily added that all languages are equal. Upon closer inspection, however, it is painfully obvious that some languages are more equal than others.

THE WORLD'S MOST DANGEROUS LANGUAGE

Although many, and perhaps even most countries have exerted repression on minority languages, it is less common that entire languages have been declared illegal, as has been the case with Kurdish in Turkey. To be sure, children have been punished for speaking the wrong language in school (Basque in Franco's Spain, Welsh in Britain, French in the USA, Aboriginal languages in Australia, Saami in Sweden, etc.), or laws have been adopted to reduce the public use of undesired languages (such as the *Loi Toubon* in France). Though extreme, the Turkish example is not unique.

Probably no other language has invoked such fear with authoritarian regimes as has Esperanto.

There is another language, however, which has been banned as such, and in more countries than any other—Esperanto. There is no complete list of countries where Esperanto has been banned, but quite a few are mentioned in Ulrich Lins' book *La Danĝera Lingvo* ("the dangerous language") including Nazi Germany, Stalin's Soviet Union, China, Yugoslavia, Austria, Japan, Bulgaria, Portugal, and Spain. As late as in 1990, an Iraqi Esperantist was let out of prison only on the condition that he never teach the language again.

LANGUAGE CONFLICT INVOLVING ONLY ONE ETHNIC GROUP

In Greece, *katharevousa* (literally 'pure language'), was the official language from independence in the 1820s until the end of military rule in 1976. Yet, most people spoke *dimotiki* ('people's language'), which had not been subject to the artificial cleansing of foreign (in particular Turkish) loans that *katharevousa* had. The lower variety subsequently became instrumentalized, but a classical diglossic situation still persisted. Although only one ethnic group was involved, this diglossia (see p 53) was not unproblematic. The translation of the gospels and the writings of Aischylos into *dimotiki* around 1900 led to riots, resulting in several deaths and the turnover of the government.

EARLIEST DOCUMENTED LANGUAGE-BASED DISCRIMINATION

The biblical Book of Judges provides some details on the battles between Gileadites and Ephraimites. Both peoples spoke Hebrew, but with dialectal differences. A good way, then, to distinguish members of one group from the other was to ask them to pronounce the word *shibboleth* ('torrent'). Apparently, Ephraimites would normally depalatalize this word into *sibboleth*. Doing so at a Gileadite checkpoint, however, had fatal consequences, as it revealed the ethnicity of the speaker. If we are to believe the Book of Judges (chapter 12, verses 5–6), 42 000 Ephraimites were thus slain and tossed into the Jordan.

THE INFAMOUS LANGUAGE LEGISLATION IN FRANCE

In 1994, the Mitterrand government passed the *Loi no. 94-665 du 4 août 1994 relative à l'emploi de la langue française*, better known as the *Loi Toubon*, after Jacques Toubon, then Minister of Culture. Contrary to popular belief, it does not really outlaw the use of languages other than French, but it states, among other things, that public signs "should be in French", although the French text may be accompanied by a "translation into a foreign language", provided that the French version is "equally legible, audible or intelligible" (articles 3 and 4).

More seriously, the law forbids the public use of "foreign terms and expressions" whenever there is a French counterpart. Even more worryingly, "foreign languages" in this context refers to anything other than French, that is, it includes languages such as Breton, Basque, Occitan, and Creole, some of which are in fact majority languages in parts of the French Republic.

Similar laws exist, by the way, in a number of other democracies, e.g. Poland and Mexico.

MOST REPRESSIVE MINORITY LANGUAGE POLICY

Even though many atrocities in world history have affected certain linguistic groups more than others, most ethnicity-based human rights violations have more complex roots, often also involving religion and other factors.

Nevertheless, most countries have a history of repression of languages perceived as a threat to the ethnicity from which the élite caste is recruited. Even in states with relatively old democratic traditions, bans on using languages other than the official one in public milieux persisted well into the 20th century.

In recent years, much of this hostility has been toned down, but there are some remarkable cases where exceptionally oppressive language policies are still in force. Chief among these is probably Turkey.

Speakers of Turkish form a massive majority of the country's population, but between a fifth and a tenth are believed to be speakers of Kurdish.

According to official Turkish policy, however, they did not exist until recently as a separate ethnicity, and were until 1991 referred to as "mountain Turks". Kurdish schools, associations, names, and even music were banned.

"No spitting on the floor or speaking Breton"

In the bad old days, not too long ago, even countries now regarded as relatively civilized, had laws banning one language or another. The Americans forbade French in Louisiana and Maine, while the French forbade Breton in France.

The very constitution of the country makes the point quite clear in stating that *"No language prohibited by law shall be used in the expression and dissemination of thought"* (article 26), that *"Publication [of newspapers] shall not be made in any language prohibited by law"* (article 28), and that *"No language other than Turkish shall be taught as mother tongue to Turkish citizens at any institutions of training or education"* (article 42).

Specific laws, such as Law 2932, passed in 1983, further stipulate that the conveying of any idea in languages which are not official languages of other nations (which, of course, Kurdish is not) be punished with imprisonment. Amazingly, Law 2932 also states contrafactually that the mother tongue of all Turkish citizens is Turkish (!!!).

There may be light at the end of the tunnel, however. Due mainly to pressure from the European Union, which Turkey is eager to join, some of the above laws were repealed in the 1990s, and constitutional changes were announced in October 2001 and again in August 2002. June 2004 even saw Turkish national television broadcast a short program in Kurdish for the first time ever.

Yet, in terms of minority language policy (and also respect for human rights in general), Turkey has little to be proud of.

To be sure, there are other contenders for the title. Leclerc (2006; in my translation) describes the language policy of Syria as "unacceptable", as it "ignores the most fundamental rights" of the nation's inhabitants, while that of Turkmenistan is characterized as "pulverization of the linguistic rights of all minorities". He does not give much in the way of examples from Burma, but nevertheless summarizes the situation in that country in a way which makes further analysis redundant. Burma, Leclerc concludes, is "at the very bottom of the abyss".

Yet another case of an authoritarian regime and an assimilatory language policy is Malaysia. In this country, the policy enforced— consisting essentially in the promotion of Malay and acceptance of English—is beyond discussion. The Sedition Act of 1948 and the Constitution (Amendment) Act of 1971 explicitly state that the status of Malay "may no longer be questioned".

LINGUISTIC RIGHTS IN THE "CRADLE OF WESTERN DEMOCRACY"

In 2001, Sotiris Bletsas was fined and sentenced to fifteen months' imprisonment by Greek authorities for having distributed a brochure on European language minorities five years earlier. The publication in question was produced by the European Union, of which Greece is a member. The reason for Bletsas' imprisonment was that the brochure contained a section on Aromunians, a Romance-speaking minority in northern Greece. In Greek legalese, his actions constituted "dissemination of false information", which could cause "fear and anxiety among citizens". Fortunately, Bletsas was acquitted on appeal in December of the same year. Leclerc (2004) offers some more examples of violations of linguistic rights in Greece. He concludes that "when a state cannot even accept the presence of a weak minority constituting 3% of the population, and from which it has nothing to fear, we are not talking about intolerance, but of outright secterism and fanatism" (my translation). Interestingly, while no ethnic minorities are said to reside in Greece, official sources willingly speak of five million Greeks in the diaspora, including no less than 400 000 in southern Albania alone. Less biased—well, my own—estimates suggest slightly more than 2,5 million speakers of Greek outside Greece, of whom less than 90 000 live in Albania. There is also another interesting feature of Greek language legislation: the constitution adopted in 1975 explicitly outlaws Bible translation (!). Article 3 of the constitution reads (in translation): "The text of the Holy Scripture shall be maintained unaltered. Official translation of the text into any other form of language, without prior sanction by the Autocephalous Church of Greece and the Great Church of Christ in Constantinople is prohibited".

MOST GENEROUS MINORITY LANGUAGE POLICY

Some few linguistic minorities have little if anything to complain about. English-speakers in South Africa, for instance, constitute less than 10% of the population, but their language dominates the public life in many domains to the virtual exclusion of more widely-spoken tongues. But then, English is a language with considerable prestige and international value. In Ireland, Irish is heavily protected, but there, it is seen as a matter of national pride, and not the exclusive property of the few who speak it natively. Switzerland has a remarkable policy vis-à-vis the languages which are smaller than German, but then, even the speakers of the majority language constitute less than two thirds of the population in this country, which is also by tradition extraordinarily decentralized.

As in most bilingual societies, language usage on public signs is of high symbolic value. In the municipalities declared bilingual by Finnish law, road signs appear in both languages.

A far more remarkable case, therefore, is Finland. The majority language accounts for well over 90% of the population, and the minority language is of little international use. Yet, the Swedish-speaking minority in Finland enjoys a status that most other minorities of comparable size (5,6% or less than 300 000 individuals) and (lack of) international currency can only dream of. According to the Finnish constitution, Finnish and Swedish are the republic's official languages, and in theory, they are on equal footing. Needless to say, no matter what the government does to support a minority language spoken natively by just one citizen out of 18, daily life in Helsinki tends to be more in Finnish than in Swedish (although it is located in a historically Swedish-speaking part of the country).

Governmental efforts to promote bilingualism are impressive, though. For one thing, all speakers of Finnish are required to study Swedish, and about a third claim to actually master it. The Swedes must of course also study Finnish as a second language, but are offered monolingually Swedish education in all subjects and at all levels. Most Swedish-speakers in Finland are bilingual, though there still remain people in heavily Swedish-speaking areas who do not speak Finnish.

Although the Swedish-speakers have their own political party, which attracts the vast majority of Swedish votes, the other parties— competing for the remaining Swedes, or about 1% of the total population—are, with just one exception, bilingual. Similarly, there is an entirely Swedish-speaking University in Turku, but teaching is nevertheless offered in Swedish elsewhere as well. There is also a monolingually Swedish diocese grouping the parishes where Swedish is spoken, and even a Swedish-speaking army brigade.

The Finnish national broadcasting company offers television in Swedish (amounting to about 10% of the programming), as well as two monolingually Swedish radio channels. In addition to this, there is a truly impressive array of Swedish language newspapers and books, not to mention theatres and other cultural institutions. Swedish periodicals even include specialized magazines for horticulturalists, scouts and guides, war veterans, members of men's choirs, yacht owners, the mentally retarded, the visually impaired, people interested in wind power stations, and those working with heating, ventilation and sanitation! (Bear in mind that we are dealing with a dwindling population of less than 300 000, most of whose members have access to material both in Finnish and from Sweden).

In theory (though usually not in practice), it is possible to live one's entire life in Swedish, while playing a full part in society.

Finland's Swedish-speakers live mostly in coastal areas. The constitution specifies that three major cities (Helsinki, Turku and Vaasa), are to be bilingual regardless of demographic developments.

It is true that this policy of bilingualism (and especially the compulsory Swedish courses) is questioned every once in a while, but it does have a lot of popular support—a 1997 poll showed that 70% of Finland's Finnish-speaking population feel that Swedish is an essential part of Finnish society, and even more would consider it a pity if the language were to die out completely in Finland. This support is decreasing (even though some want to deny it), but there is remarkably little tension between the two groups.

Although during the 20th century, the proportion of Swedish-speakers dropped dramatically from 12,9% to 5,6% of the total population, the decrease is more due to emigration than to assimilation, and bilingual couples are again beginning to send their children to Swedish-medium schools (in fact, more often than to Finnish schools).

Even more remarkable is the fact that some immigrants choose Swedish rather than Finnish as their primary language, and that they represent a proportion of all immigrants which is higher than that of Swedish-speakers in the nation as a whole. Thus there are now Swedish-speaking Somali Finns and Swedish-speaking Rwandan Finns.

Many had long awaited a reform of the Finnish language laws—after all, how small can the minority become, and still expect to retain its rights? Indeed, in January 2004, a new language law was passed, the essence of which was... a strengthening of Swedish-speakers' rights! Two months later, educational authorities proclaimed that they planned to double the number of Swedish-medium schools in monolingually Finnish-speaking areas.

Swedish in Finland is definitely threatened but, should it die out, the Finnish authorities will certainly not be responsible for that.

SMALL MAJORITY LANGUAGES

Papua New Guinea is probably the country where the smallest proportion of the population speaks the country's biggest indigenous language—only about 5% of the inhabitants of Papua New Guinea are native speakers of Enga.

In every fourth country in the world, the most widespread language is native to less than half of the population.

Western countries are typically significantly less heterogeneous, which is why Israel stands out. Israeli authorities provide no official language statistics, but do collect data on ethnicity and place of birth. The country's proportion of locally born Jews therefore constitutes the best approximation of native speakers of Hebrew that there is, and that proportion is around 50%.

SMALL OFFICIAL LANGUAGES

The smallest natively spoken language to enjoy official status in an independent country is Nauruan, which despite its mere 6 000 speakers is co-official in Nauru. A smaller number is recorded for Tokelauan, which has about 4 500 speakers and is official

(in theory even to the exclusion of English) in Tokelau. The archipelago is not fully independent, however, and is administered by New Zealand.

The smallest language to be the *sole* official language of any independent country is probably Icelandic with slightly less than 300 000 speakers in Iceland.

Despite the existence of many small independent countries, it is very rare for languages with less than one million speakers to ever be the main vehicle of administration on a national level.

Four other official languages should be mentioned in this context—Hiri Motu (Papua New Guinea), Sanskrit (India), Latin (the Vatican), and Classical Arabic (several Arab countries) all lack native speakers, as far as is known.

Although small languages in some countries are official for sentimental or nationalistic reasons, they may in practice be very sparingly used as such (e.g. Irish in Ireland). Possibly the smallest language to truly enjoy full official language status is Faeroese, in that it is used (more than any colonial language or the like) in written form in administration,. With only 50 000 speakers, it has taken over much of the functions that Danish formerly had on the Faeroe islands. Along with Greenlandic, another language of Denmark, it might even be the smallest language which is the normal and regular medium of written expression of its speakers.

The Faroese daily Dimmalætting *has an impressive circulation of 10 000 copies*

MOST OFFICIAL LANGUAGE

Of the world's 6 000 or so languages, only about 113 are recognized as official in any country. 14 of these have this status in two countries, and 13 are official in three or more countries. The most common official language by far is English (73), followed by French (39), Arabic (25), Spanish (21), Portuguese (8) and German (6).

About two thirds of the world's countries specify an official language in their constitution. For a few of those which do not—including Britain and Israel—this is due to them not having a written constitution in the first place! For others, such as the United States, and Sweden, the *de facto* official language is so only by virtue of tradition rather than legislation (and the constitution itself is written in English and Swedish respectively). The above figure also includes countries in which one language or the other is official only by practice.

English is also the world's most official language in another sense. The combined number of inhabitants of countries having English as their official language is a staggering 2 100 millions (almost half of them in India). No other language is able to challenge this position, the closest competitors being Mandarin and Hindi/Urdu, each with slightly more than half that number. Next follow Spanish and French, both with between 300 and 400 million "official" speakers.

HIGHEST NUMBER OF OFFICIAL LANGUAGES

Of the world's 233 states or state-like entities, 75% have only one official language—*de facto* or *de jure*. Until recently, no country recognized more than three official languages on a national level (though Switzerland had three "official" and one "national" language).

Despite being a very small country, the Seychelles has three official languages. As seen above, the only daily paper carries news in English, French and Creole.

The 1997 South African constitution, however, acknowledges no less than 11 official languages, viz. Afrikaans, English, Ndebele, Northern Sotho (Pedi), Setswana, Swazi, Southern Sotho, Tsonga, Venda, Xhosa and Zulu. The constitution does not stop there, naming various other languages to be promoted in the country: Khoi, Nama, and San languages, South African Sign, German, Greek, Gujarati, Hindi, Portuguese, Tamil, Telugu, Urdu, Arabic, Hebrew and Sanskrit. In all, 25 languages are mentioned in the constitution. Just to be on the safe side, it also expresses support for all other languages "commonly used by communities" or "for religious purposes" in South Africa.

In practice however, only English and Afrikaans are used at the national level, with the other languages only being regionally official (at best). And even so, English has clearly gained the upper hand after the abolition of apartheid, and South African public life leaves little doubt that some languages are more equal than others.

Not unexpectedly, in December 2002, the South African government decided that each of its departments would use one and only one language (chosen among the eleven) as its working language. This will no doubt be English in the overwhelming majority of cases, and critics expressed fear that this is a first

Official languages in the countries mentioned above:

Switzerland	Singapore	Belgium	Papua New Guinea	Bolivia	Seychelles	Vanuatu
German	English	Dutch	English	Spanish	Seychellois Creole	Bislama
French	Malay	French	Tok Pisin	Quechua	English	English
Italian	Mandarin	German	Hiri Motu	Aymará	French	French
Rhaeto-Romance	Tamil					

step towards complete Anglicization. Or, as a Constitutional Assembly official put it: *"we in the ANC do not believe in ethnic languages"* (!).

Apart from Switzerland and South Africa, Singapore also recognizes four languages on a national level, while Belgium, Papua New Guinea, Bolivia, the Seychelles, and Vanuatu each do so with three languages.

(For India, see below) The most common combination for an officially bilingual country is—not unexpectedly—English and French. These are de jure co-official in five countries (Vanuatu, Canada, the Seychelles, Rwanda, and Cameroon), and de facto so also in Mauritius. The next most common language combo is Arabic and French, which are official in three countries, viz Djibouti, Chad, and the Comoros.

DISCREPANCY BETWEEN NUMERIC AND OFFICIAL STATUS

In almost one out of every three countries, the most spoken language has no official status. Conversely, in quite a number of countries, the only official language has close to no native speakers at all. One such case is Mauritius, where native speakers of English make up about 0,01% of the population, while neither Mauritian French Creole, the home language of 70% of all Mauritians, nor Bhojpuri (the language of most of the others), have any official recognition whatsoever.

The situation is similar in quite a few African countries, although statistics are generally far less reliable.

A special case, of course, is the Arab countries, which use Classical Arabic as their only official language—a language which has no native speakers anywhere.

AN UNEXPECTED MAJORITY LANGUAGE

A little-known fact is that English, or a slightly creolized version thereof is traditionally the majority language of a French department.

The *département* of Saint-Martin has had an English-speaking majority for the last couple of centuries. As it happens, Saint-Martin is located in the Caribbean, but is legislatively part of France in exactly the same way as Hawaii or Alaska are parts of the USA. As in all other parts of France, French is the one and only official language of the island.

Since the 1960s, however, the population of St-Martin has risen from less than 5 000 to more than 30 000, mostly through immigration. The native-born now make up less than half the population, and immigrant languages such as French, Haitian, Guadeloupean, Spanish, and Papiamentu are now widely spoken in addition to the original English.

Even in France proper, English is spoken by more people than one might think. It is the mother tongue of some 0,45% of the country's population—a far larger proportion than some indigenous languages, such as Basque, can claim.

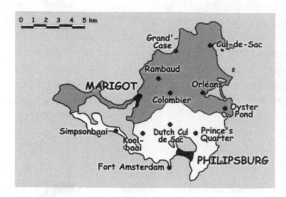

Although much smaller than European microstates such as Andorra or Liechtenstein, the island of St Martin has, since the mid-17th century, been divided between France (the northern part) and the Netherlands (the southern part).

UNEXPECTED OFFICIAL LANGUAGES

In 1855, an American adventurer, William Walker (1824-60) seized power in Nicaragua, proclaiming himself dictator. Apart from re-legalizing slavery, he also proclaimed English the official language. His reign (and the thereby official status of his language) only lasted for two years, before he was dethroned and shot in Honduras.

In the Austro-Hungarian double monarchy, Latin remained official for longer than elsewhere. In the Hungarian part of the country, Hungarian gradually replaced Latin only in the 1830s and 1840s. Today, Latin remains an administrative language only of the Vatican State. However, its daughters, the Romance languages, are official in no less than 60 independent countries, i.e. almost one in three.

In the late 1990s and early 2000s, Africa for the first time saw the introduction of new official languages in countries which had no historical connection to the languages in question. In the new constitution of 1996, until then bilingual Rwanda was declared officially trilingual in Rwanda (mother tongue of the entire population), French—and English. The reason for this was the return of 800 000 Rwandan refuges from Uganda, who were more proficient in English than in French. They constituted more than a tenth of the country's population. In 1998, Congo-Kinshasa saw a similar development—English was about to be introduced alongside French partly because the new dictator Kabila wanted to express his gratitude towards the officially anglophone countries which had helped him to power, and partly because many of his cabinet members had grown up in exile in Uganda, and therefore spoke English better than French. A third similar case is Eritrea, independent since the mid-1990s. Again, Eritrea has not been the possession of Britain or any other English-speaking country.

Another remarkable African case is the choice of English as sole official language of Namibia in 1990. Afrikaans was, and remains, the dominant lingua franca in the country. It is spoken by far more whites, and better understood by the black population, than English. It was the fact that Afrikaans was perceived as an instrument of apartheid which prevented it from gaining official status. It remains the case, however, that even in the parliament which decided on official monolingualism, debates are more frequent in Afrikaans than in English. The parliament even went so far in its zealousness as to forbid state employees from writing or speaking to fellow citizens in any language other than the official one—regardless of the fact that this would make them unintelligible to the vast majority of the population. This decision was later condemned by the UN, and it is, at least, not actively enforced. Interestingly, between the censuses of 1991 and 2002, Afrikaans made numerical progress as the language used in Namibian households.

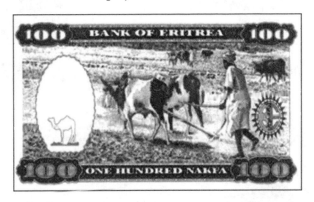

Eritrea appears still not to have an official language, but its banknotes carry text in English only. The choice of languages of banknotes is deeply symbolic in many countries.

While losing ground in eastern Africa, French made progress further west, and for similar reasons. Equatorial Guinea—one of the most isolated and corrupt countries in modern world history—experienced a re-immigration of refugees who had spent some time in (officially francophone) neighboring countries. Dictator Obiang was then desperately searching for new friends, and found them among the less scrupulous leaders in the Élysée Palace. French was given co-official status with Spanish soon afterwards (1998).

In addition, the two former Portuguese colonies of Cape Verde and Guinea-Bissau have joined *Francophonie*, the organization of French-speaking states (see p 81). The continent's most populous country, Nigeria, was also close to introducing French as an official language in 1996, again in order to make a political statement. For economic and other reasons, this came to naught, however.

In 2000, the commission on "Japan's Goals in the 21st century", a consultative body for the prime minister, suggested that English be given official status in Japan. Not unexpectedly, the proposal turned out to be highly controversial.

In Ireland, the 1948 constitution declared Irish as the first official language, reducing English to a position as "second official language". Official bilingualism remains largely symbolic, and although Ireland is in theory the only European country to have a minority tongue as its "first official language", the country and its administrative apparatus remain virtually monolingual in English.

Another case of surprising official

bilingualism is Israel, where Arabic is official despite the somewhat apartheid-like treatment of Arabs by Israeli authorities. As in the case with Ireland, however, this bilingualism remains mainly symbolic.

In New Zealand, English has always been the country's de facto official language, but in 1987, the decision was made to elevate Maori *de jure* to this status. Since no need was felt to pass a law regarding English, Maori thus in theory became the only official language of New Zealand. Similarly, in Sweden, a parliament decision in 1999 gave official recognition to the five minority languages Standard Finnish, Meänkieli Finnish, Saami, Romani, and Yiddish. Meanwhile, Swedish has *de jure* no official status. Nor does Swedish Sign, with more users than four of the five minority languages taken together.

The coat of arms of the Soviet Socialist Republic of Belarus, including the Republic's motto in Yiddish

Speaking of Yiddish, although I am uncertain as to its official status in interwar Belarus, it is worth noting that the Soviet Belarusan coat of arms from about 1920 until the 1940s featured the slogan *Workers of the world unite* in four languages, of which Yiddish was one (the other being Russian, Belarusan and Polish).

Rumour also has it that the ever capricious Stalin made English an official language of the Soviet Union (!) for a brief period, but I have not been able to verify this.

Wilhelm Molly, co-founder of Amikejo

Finally, there was once a state with Esperanto as its official language. The story of the Moresnet enclave is a little known, yet highly interesting footnote in European history. As is well known many of Europe's boundaries were redrawn after the Napoleonic wars. It proved difficult, though, to define the new border between Prussia and the Netherlands in the area of Moresnet (now on the three-state intersection between Germany, Belgium and the Netherlands). A small no man's land of 3,44 km² (larger than Monaco, but smaller than Gibraltar) with 256 inhabitants became known as Neutral Moresnet.

A German immigrant to Moresnet, Wilhelm Molly, happened to become an avid Esperantist. Together with the Frenchman Gustave Roy, he decided to proclaim the independence of the neutral territory, under the name of *Amikejo* (literally "friend-place"). The free state's official language would be Esperanto. A national anthem was composed, a flag was devised, and stamps began to be issued. Following this, the International Esperantist Congress even decided to move its headquarters from The Hague to Moresnet/Amikejo.

The first part of the Amikejo national Anthem. (Note the misspelt title!)

Alas, the situation only lasted for a couple of years, because the microstate was overrun by German troops as the First World War broke out. The Versailles treaty which ended the war contained an article in which Germany recognized complete Belgian sovereignty over Moresnet.

GASTRONOMIC LANGUAGE PURISM

In several parts of the United States and Canada, the First World War resulted in widespread anti-German sentiments. Many local authorities in Nebraska, Illinois, Ohio, Iowa and elsewhere took rather far-reaching measures against the German language (an ironic twist to that is that English itself is illegal (!) in Illinois—see below). The speaking of any foreign language in public places was outlawed in some places, and phone operators were instructed to pull the plug on any non-English telephone conversations (a practice which has also been known in Australia). The teaching of languages other than English was banned, as were foreign-language newspapers. American participation in the war did not last very long, so many of these laws were passed only after the ceasefire, but continued in vigor for much of the interwar era.

Among the more ridiculous outcomes of these bans are the rewritings of restaurant menus. Eateries where *sauerkraut, German fried potatoes* and *hamburgers* had earlier been served, now offered customers the same items as *Liberty cabbage, American fries* and *Salisbury steak.*

Sometimes history repeats itself. In early 2003, anti-French feelings were strong in the USA following French failure to support American aggression against Iraq. And, sure enough, in March 2003, it was reported that American restaurants quit selling *French Fries* and *French Dressing,* instead offering *Freedom Fries* and *Liberty Dressing.*

As a response to this, a group of German university professors under the leadership of Armin Burkhardt of Magdeburg University suggested that German replace its English loan-words. In order not to be taken as chauvinistic purists, their proposal included replacing the English loans with their French counterparts. Thus, while Americans would keep eating their *freedom fries,* Germans would no longer wear 'T-shirts' and go to 'parties', but instead dress in *tricots* and invite each others to *fêtes.* Further suggested replacements included *bonvivant* (playboy), *mannequin* (model), *niveau* (level) and *ordinateur* (computer). Some of these items (*fête, mannequin* and *niveau*) already existed in German, while others (*tricot, bonvivant* and *ordinateur*) were suggested new loans.

RETROACTIVE ASSIMILATION

Attempts at suppressing Turkish in Bulgaria culminated during the winter between 1984 and 1985. During this intense "Bulgarization" campaign, not only living Turks were forced to change their names into Bulgarian ones (written, of course, in Cyrillic), but so were the deceased ones—Turkish tombstones had to be redone in order to display the new Bulgarian names that the government had bestowed upon the dead!

While the change of "foreign" names has been enforced in many countries, Australia adopted a diametrically opposed policy during the First World War—Australians of German descent were not allowed to anglicize their names even if they wanted to, since this might make them not look like the enemies of the state they were assumed to be. In many ways, this is similar to the forced adoption of *Israel* and *Sara* by Jews in the Third Reich.

FROM DIALECT TO LANGUAGE OVERNIGHT

On February 22, 1999, the Bulgarian government recognized Macedonian as a language of its own. Until that date, the official Bulgarian policy had always been that Macedonian was a dialect of Bulgarian. To emphasize the significance of the decision, Bulgarian radio spent much of the day playing Macedonian folk songs.

The pride in finally speaking a 'language' rather than a mere 'dialect' has lead to some absurd consequences. While Bulgarian and Macedonian are perfectly mutually intelligible, Macedonian authorities are reported to insist on the use of interpreters when dealing with Bulgarian businessmen.

AN INDIAN TOWER OF BABEL

In the Indian parliament, 15 different languages are used by the 787 members, and a statement made in Tamil may well meet opposition in Assamese or Panjabi. The right to interpreting is guaranteed by the constitution, and frequently used. Admittedly,

though, speeches in Hindi or English are more frequent. The fifteen so-called "scheduled languages" are officially recognized in India, but are normally used only at the state level—at the national level, the official languages of India are Hindi and English.

FIRST KNOWN LANGUAGE OF INTERNATIONAL DIPLOMACY

There is evidence that Akkadian, a now extinct Semitic language spoken mainly in Iraq and Syria, was used for international diplomacy and business relations as early as the second millennium

BC. Writings in Akkadian (often obviously produced by non-native speakers) have been found throughout much of the Middle East, as well as in present-day Turkey and Egypt.

MOST LINGUISTIC CONSTITUTION

Countries vary considerably with regard to how much detail on language use (if any) they include in their constitution. While not all countries specify an official language, many constitutions do include such a section. There is certainly no constitution, though, which includes so much linguist lingo as that of the tiny Pacific microstate of Tuvalu. Its fifth article is even entitled *"gender and number"* (three cheers, linguists!), and specifies that *"In this Constitution, (a) the masculine gender includes the female gender; and (b) the feminine gender includes the masculine gender; and (c) the singular number includes the plural; and (d) the plural number includes the singular"*. In other words, the constitution explicitly discusses markedness.

OWNING A LANGUAGE

From Melanesia, there are a couple of attestations of languages being owned, and even bought and sold! In some cases a pidgin, or a trade jargon is intimately connected to the trading situation for which it was developed and in which it is used. Since the trading relationships are often the property of certain clans, so too is the language.

From Vanuatu, it is reported that the Longana so much admired the Lolovoli dialect of their neighbors that they offered to buy it. The price was paid in traditional goods, and so the Longana had acquired the right to their new speech variety. The Lolivoli, on the other hand, had to change their speech as well, since they had given up the right to their traditional language.

One easily gets the impression that this is an areal feature, and indeed, Foley (1986:24) comments from New Guinea that *"like other cultural artefacts, language is a trade item"*.

LANGUAGE LEGISLATION IN THE UNITED STATES

That more or less absurd legislation has an entertainment value is proven by the fact that Koon, Powell & Schumaker's (2002) book on "dumb laws" became an instant bestseller. Below follow some language-related examples from the United States. Some of these may no longer be in force, and most are, of course, in any case not enforced.

Illinois	*The English language is not to be spoken (sic!). (The official language is "American" [see p 29].)*
Kentucky	*One may not interrupt or insult a public speaker by means of offensive language.*
Mississippi	*One may be fined up to USD 100 for using "profane language" in public places.*

Little Rock, Arkansas	Arkansas must be pronounced "Ark-an-saw" with the final "s" being silent. This pronunciation, which derives from the days of French rule, was determined by the General Assembly of 1881.
Joliet, Illinois	The first vowel of the town name of Joliet must be pronounced as a diphthong (i.e. [ow] rather than [ɔ]). An inappropriate pronunciation is punished by a five dollar fine.
Sulphur, Louisiana	Saying obscene things on the telephone is illegal. (The same law also forbids telephone users to "intentionally hang up or disengage the connection".)
Rehoboth Beach, Delaware	No use of profane language within 300 feet (= 91,4 m) of a place of worship.
Memphis, Tennessee	Beggars must not use profane or abusive language, either during the solicitation or following a refusal.

SOURCES NOT MENTIONED IN THE TEXT

The world's most dangerous language: Lins (1988), *Linguist List* 2.162.

Language conflict involving only one ethnic group: Hyltenstam (1997).

Language legislation in France and Poland: Leclerc (2001).

Turkish repression: Leclerc (2000), Karimova & Deverell (2001), Amnesty International, Human Rights Watch/Helsinki, media coverage.

Malaysia: Schiffman (1995).

Linguistic rights in the "cradle of western democracy": Amnesty International, European Bureau for Lesser Used Languages.

Exaggerated claims on Greeks in Albania and elsewhere: Poulton (1998:64).

Language policy in Finland: McRae (1997).

Restriction of official language use in South Africa: South African Broadcasting Corporation reporting, 2002-12-04.

Quote from South African Constitutional Assembly official: Venter (1999:620).

Language situation of Saint-Martin, and immigration to the island: Martinez (1994), Abou (1992), Klomp (1993).

Number of English-speakers in metropolitan France: Héran, Filhon & Deprez (2002).

Official English in Nicaragua: Cienciala (1996).

Official languages in African countries, in Ireland and in Israel: Leclerc (2006).

Maori as New Zealand's only official language: Ross Clark (p c).

Sweden: Media coverage.

Official Esperanto in Moresnet/Amikejo: Damen (2003).

Discrimination against Germans in interwar USA: *Linguist List* 6.832.

Restrictions on German in Australia during WW1: Televised documentary *Pozieres*, broadcast on the *Discovery Civilization* channel 2003-08-24.

German urge to replace English loans with French: News report from *Reuters* 2003-04-09.

Retroactive assimilation of Turks in Bulgaria: Leclerc (2001).

Bulgarian recognition of Macedonian: *Dagens Nyheter* 1999-02-23.

Interpreting between Bulgarian and Macedonian: Ljuba Veselinova (p c).
Languages of the Indian Parliament: *Svenska Dagbladet* 1995-01-19.
Use of Akkadian in diplomacy: Dalby (1998:11-12), Paper (1982).
Owning a language: *Linguist List* 12.1887 and Jones (1996).
Dumb language laws in the USA: Powell & Koon (2002), Crombie (2000:70).

LANGUAGE PLANNING

FOR THE MOST PART, languages and language situations change on their own. Sometimes, though, authorities make attempts at changing things in a direction they find desirable. This is referred to as "language planning".

PLANNED KOINÉIZATION

In 1936, the Dutch government appointed the *Stichting voor het Bevolkingsonderzoek in de drooggelegde Zuiderzeepolders* (Foundation for demographic research in the reclaimed *Zuiderzeepolders*), whose task it was to make sure that the newly reclaimed land was settled by the right people. The idea was to let the new population represent a cross-section of Dutch society with regard to a number of features, including dialect. The encounter of several different forms of speech would ensure the development of a new variety, which would be more suitable for interregional communication. Dialectal surveys were carried out, but it seems that the ideas were not fully implemented, as the Second World War intervened. After the war and the fall of Nazism, public opinion was considerably less favourable to the type of planned settlement represented by the project.

PLANNED PIDGINIZATION

Pidgins normally develop spontaneously in settings where two or more peoples need an interethnic lingua franca. It is very common that speakers of the language from which the pidgin draws most of its vocabulary dismiss it as "bad English", "bad French", "bad Russian" or bad what-not. In other words, pidgin languages are usually not highly regarded. Kolonialdeutsch is an interesting partial exception. Germany was (mainly because it did not exist as such before 1871) a late-comer in the scramble for colonies. When it acquired its first overseas possessions in 1884, Pidgin English was an already established lingua franca in several of them, much to the dismay of German authorities. Introducing German would have posed problems, since dark-skinned peoples were believed to be too intellectually inferior to be able to grasp the subtle nuances of the German language. Therefore, Kolonialdeutsch ('Colonial German') was devised in 1916 by Emil Schwörer as a deliberately simplified language. It displayed many of the shibboleths of pidgin languages, except that it had not emerged spontaneously, but was a pure armchair product. During the First World War, Germany was bereft of all its colonies, and therefore, Kolonialdeutsch was never actually launched.

Example of Kolonialdeutsch:

Das ist de große Kaiser von Deutschland. De name von de Kaiser ist Wilhelm de Zweite. Er tut wohnen in sehr große feine Stadt in Deutschland; er hat viele Landen, viele Soldaten, viel Geld; aber er hat nur eine Frau, die Kaiserin. Alle menschen müssen folgen ihm.

'That is the big emperor of Germany. The name of the emperor is William the second. He does live in very big fine city in Germany; he has plenty lands, plenty soldiers, plenty money; but he has only one wife, the empress. All people must follow him'.

The above sample is prompted by the teacher showing a picture of the Kaiser to one of the more talented students. As it happens, the fictitious dialogues do not altogether follow the grammatical rules that Schwörer had himself set up.

PURISM IN REVERSE

When authorities interfere with linguistic borrowing, it is usually the case that they want to keep the official language as 'pure' as possible, and discourage unwanted influences from other languages. Mozambique is one of the few places where precisely the opposite has happened. In 1981, the then president Samora Machel initiated a campaign called Enriquecer uma língua, i.e. "enrich a language". The country's Bantu-speaking population was encouraged to integrate as many loans as possible from Portuguese into their native tongues. That way, it was believed, linguistic unity would be achieved, as everybody would finally wind up speaking Portuguese. For different reasons, the same thing has been going on with Macedonian, whose speakers have long fought to have their language recognized as a distinct from those of its neighbors. After World War II, a number of words deemed too similar to their equivalents in Bulgarian or Serbo-Croatian were replaced by Romance borrowings. Examples include лактира (laktira) 'to breast-feed', кремира (kremira) 'to cremate', ургира (urgira) 'to urge', номинира (nominira) 'to call by name', ретурнира (returnira) 'to return', траверзира (traverzira) 'to cross', and швалерисува се (Kvalerisuva se) 'to have casual love affairs' (< French chevalier).

A HEROINE FOR BREAKFAST

Saparmyrad Niyazov, life-time president of Turkmenistan, is a despot whose rule includes many tragicomic aspects. After having won landslide victories in elections with a turnout well over 99%, he has had his parliament officially name him Türkmenbashi, i.e. 'father of all Turkmens'. Like many others of his ilk, Niyazov has liberally dotted the landscape with gold statues of himself. His literary work, the Rukhnama (or 'Book of Souls'), is obligatorily studied in schools as a subject of its own, but has lately come to be used as a textbook in various other subjects, such as history and geography. Decisions taken by the megalomanic president have gradually become increasingly capricious, and recent years have seen bans on ballet, opera, public smoking, lip synching, beards, gold teeth, recorded music, health care in rural areas, and car radios. He also has plans for the construction of a giant ice palace and penguin enclosures in the Karakum desert.

In line with colleagues such as Kim Il Sung, Saddam Hussein and Stalin, Niyazov has a fondness of naming things after himself. Innumerable streets, schools, airports, farms and people are named after him, and his name is also applied to a brand of vodka, a meteorite, the country's second largest city, and a television channel.

The dictator's renaming whims extend not only to proper names, but also to other aspects of the Turkmen lexicon. The word 'old' is forbidden with reference to people, and when someone turns 61, he enters 'the prophetic age', which is followed by 'the inspired age' (73 and beyond).

Besides glorifying himself, Niyazov also honours his mother Gurbansoltan Edzhe ('the Turkmen heroine'—her heroic accomplishment of course being that she gave birth to the country's foremost son). Apart from being the name of his mother, Gurbansoltan Edzhe is now also the name of a women's magazine, the name of the year 2003, and the name of the month of April (January is officially renamed Türkmenbashi). In 2002, Niyazov decreed that 'bread' (not a particular type, but bread as such) would no longer be known as chorek, but as—Gurbansoltan Edzhe.

LINGUISTIC ENGINEERING IN MELANESIA

The speakers of Selepet in the village of Indu in New Guinea have adopted buge as a negator instead of the traditional bia, which is still used by Selepet speakers elsewhere. That is not particularly remarkable in itself, as all languages change over time. However, it is reported that this was a conscious decision made at a village meeting, and that the old negation was abandoned in order to set the inhabitants of Indu off from other Selepets.

Similarly, Riro-speakers of the island of Choiseul off New Guinea have for the same reason performed metathesis on final CV syllables into VC syllables—that is, words ending in a consonant followed by a vowel, such as -pa, have been reversed into a vowel-consonant sequence, such as -ap).

Finally, the speakers of Usai, a Buin dialect of Bougainville Island, have inverted the genders of their language, making all masculines feminine, and vice versa. Again, this is said to have been done in order to mark the distinctivity of the group.

NOUN CLASS PRESCRIPTIVISM

In Setswana, a Bantu language of southern Africa, names of familiar peoples, such as neighboring Bantu groups, are placed in the class called 1/2. Less familiar peoples, however, such as Chinese, as well as Khoisan groups, are included in the inanimate 5/6 class, along with words such as 'dirt' and 'clay'. Especially given that parts of the population of Botswana (where the language dominates) consist of Khoisan-speakers, this has become politically sensitive. Users of Setswana are now advised to include the "less familiar" peoples into the animate class.

Another example of authorities

intervention in noun class system comes from Thai. In 1854, King Mongkut of Siam demanded that words for "noble" animals, including 'elephant' and 'horse', be used without the classifier morpheme that would accompany them in ordinary Thai.

Watch your speech! By royal decree, this noble beast is not to be classified

SOURCES NOT MENTIONED IN THE TEXT

Kolonialdeutsch: Perl (1998).
Loan word campaign in Mozambique: Leclerc (2006).
Latinate borrowings in Macedonian: Voss (2000).
Niyazov's rule in Turkmenistan: media coverage.
Linguistic engineering in Melanesia: Lynch (1998:71).
Noun class prescriptivism: Aikhenvald (2000:349).

USING MORE THAN ONE LANGUAGE

AN OLD JOKE goes something like this:
What do you call a person who speaks three languages? *Trilingual.*
A person who speaks two languages? *Bilingual.*
And a person who speaks only one language? *American.*

In much of the western world, in particular in English-speaking countries, bilingualism is not the norm, and even those who do remember fragments of their high school French or Spanish tend not to use it other than in rather specific circumstances.

With a number of languages far superior to the number of countries, a simple arithmetic exercise indicates that countries are normally multilingual, and in many parts of the world, it is perfectly normal not only to know several languages, but also to use more than one during the course of a normal day.

Although it is often said that the average human is bi- or multilingual, there is no way of testing the claim, since no world-wide survey on multilingualism has ever been made. Even on a national level, such data is scarce, and questions of competence in other languages than the country's official one(s) are only rarely included in censuses. Every once in a while one comes across statements that the average Zambian speaks three languages, the average Nigerian four, and so on, but these claims are usually impossible to substantiate. The most we can say is that it does indeed seem like westerners (in particular, of course, Anglophones) in general are less multilingual than people in most other societies.

One might expect bilingualism to be extensive in a country like Canada, which is officially bilingual in two of the world's most internationally useful languages. Yet, in the 2001 census, less than 18% of the country's population were able to speak both English and French. Even though this is a considerable increase in comparison with earlier censuses, the fact remains that it is a proportion vastly surpassed by most (officially monolingual) European countries, and a number that must be seen as a massive failure of several decades of official bilingualism. Among Anglophones, a mere 7% commands both of the country's official languages. The number of alloglots (native speakers of neither English nor French) capable of speaking either

English or French, however, is higher than the English/French bilinguals, and contributes to making more Canadians bilingual. The number of trilinguals is virtually negligible.

While foreign language instruction (or perhaps, rather, English teaching) is increasing in Europe, infamously monolingual United States is becoming less interested in foreign tongues. In 1960, more than 16% of all American college students took a foreign language, but 35 years later, this figure had dropped to less than half of that. Among the few that did show an interest in learning a second language, the most popular choice has shifted from French to Spanish (1969 being the turning point).

Meanwhile, in the world's other major English-speaking country, Britain, foreign language teaching seems to be on the increase. In a recent survey, 28% of 16-19 year-olds claimed they were bilingual, as opposed to 15% overall.

MOST MULTILINGUAL CITIZENS

Examples of countries which do include a question on the above subject in their censuses are India, Latvia, New Zealand and Malta. For other countries, there are semi-official questionnaire results and estimates by individual authors.

We thus know that the average Luxemburger speaks 3,03 languages (including the mother tongue, i.e. the average citizen knows two *other* languages). The in-

habitants of Congo-Brazzaville are slightly more impressive, with a repertoire of 3,10 languages. However, Peter Stein's (1982) survey of language use in Mauritius gives a number of 3,78 for the average Mauritian, which, along with that reported for Benin by Igué & N'Ouéni (1993:5), is the highest figure that I have come across for an entire nation. The Mauritian figure is also confirmed by a later study (Atchia-Emmerich 2005).

The following diagram displays the number of languages (including the mother tongue) spoken by the average citizen in selected countries with impressive and not-so-impressive rates of multilingualism.

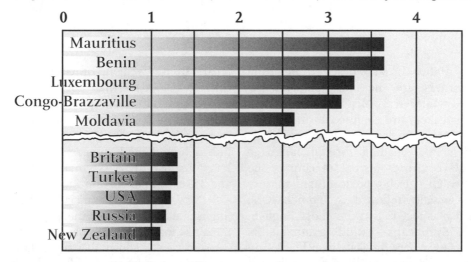

The plurilingualism of Mauritians is nicely illustrated in this example from an elementary school in Mauritius. English is the country's official language, and is therefore supposed to be the major language of instruction in Mauritian schools, but as can be seen, code-switching between English (here in bold face), French (in italics) and Creole (underlined) is rampant.

Teacher: *Regarde* en ku sa travay la . . . *Il y a* **fifteen** . . . *Il y a* **three** *là* . . . kan nu pu **reduce to lowest term**, *ça devient* **three to one** . . . *alors, combien* **women will join the committee** . . . ki *chiffre* sa bizen vini la pu nu kapav gany **three to one?**

(Look at this task. There are fifteen—there are three there—when we are to reduce it to the least common denominator, it becomes three to one. So then, how many women will join the committee? What number must come there in order for us to get three to one?)

Pupil: (no response)

Teacher: sa vin **one** . . . apre, laba ki mo truve? Par ki mo kupe laba pu ki **fifteen** vin **three?**
(It becomes one, so, then what do we have here? By what should I divide here so that fifteen becomes three?)

Pupil: **By five.**

No matter how you see things, the Luxemburgers are the most polyglot EU citizens, while the Mediterraneans and English-speakers are confined to the corner of the European language-learning class. English is the leading foreign language in all EU countries (except of course, the two in which it is the predominant mother tongue), usually followed by French. One interesting aspect is that the most English-speaking Europeans—excluding inhabitants of countries where English is official—are the Swedes. They speak little else, however (apart from Swedish, of course), whereas competence in German and French of the Dutch and Danes makes the latter nations more polyglot. Disregarding the mother tongue, 33% of the EU_{25} (the 25-member incarnation of the European Union) citizens know English, 12% German, 10% French, and 3% each Spanish and Russian.

New Zealand is officially bilingual in English and Maori, but the population still remains massively monolingual—the New Zealand census shows that some 95% of the country's population speak only English.

The remainder are mostly Maoris, the vast majority of whom also command English. The proportion of Anglophones who speak anything but English (be it Maori or another language), on the other hand, is virtually negligible. The fact that 90% of the Maoris live on the North Island makes the southern half of the country massively monolingual.

As for the sub-national level, I have collected data for several hundred ethnic or other groups.

The highest figure ever reported is that of Swedish-speaking exiles from Vyborg (until World War II Finland's second city, but since then located in Russia). Virtually everyone knew Finnish, while knowledge in Russian and German was more or less expected. In addition to that, quite a few were familiar with English and French. In all, the average member of this group spoke 4,08 languages. The only other group that I have come across which approaches this value is Armenians in Jerusalem's Old City, who master exactly 4,00 languages. They are followed by Dutch business executives (3,90) and speakers of the Chadian language Kabalai (3,85).

The normal state of affairs, regardless of whether you look at entire countries or at ethnic groups is to speak about 1,7 languages.

GROUPS

*I*t is often suggested that Americans or Australians are the least polyglot of all nationalities. Indeed, among the least multilingual peoples, we find first and foremost a number of English-speaking groups. Here, we find e.g. Ontario Anglophones (1,15), Australians (1,12), and whites in New Zealand (1,07). In practice, the figure 1,07 means that only one person in fifteen speaks *anything* besides his or her own mother tongue! Similarly pitiful are the non-native language capabilities of Russians in the former Soviet Union (1,04) and Hindi-speakers in India (1,17).

In July 2004, a survey in Britain concluded that less than a tenth of all Britons were able to speak a language other than English. The reports did not mention this, but ten per cent pretty much equals the proportion of residents having a mother tongue other than English in the first place! A poll of 1 500 workers by the recruitment firm Office Angels found that fewer than 5% could count to 20 in another language. A majority of the respondents said they would like to live abroad, but most figured they would not require language knowledge for that, believing that "everyone speaks English" (in fact, five out of six humans do not). When this was discussed in the British media, newspaper writers used a tone indicative of humility and shame. Yet, this feeling was clearly not shared by a large proportion of the "men in the street" commenting on the newspaper reports. A relatively typical comment was *"Let's stop giving ourselves a hard time about not speaking Flemish and be real about our history, heritage, and the supremacy of our language"*. More memorable, to my mind, were the words of the person who wrote *"If we have to adopt their money (euros), then they should speak our language. Seems fair to me"*. Interesting, isn't it, to think about this person's perception of "us" and "them", since most EU members—let alone the rest of the world—do not use the Euro.

In the *Ethnologue*, some language communities are portrayed as almost entirely monolingual. A surprisingly high number of these live in West Papua (eastern New Guinea), where the extreme linguistic diversity might lead us to expect a near universal multilingualism. The following five language communities are those which are described

not only as having an extremely limited number of bilinguals, but which are even said to be "completely monolingual".

Language	Country	Speakers
Awbono	West Papua	100 or fewer
Tokuni	West Papua	100 or fewer
Kopkaka	West Papua	250

Language	Country	Speakers
Momuna	West Papua	2 700
Chenchu	India	28 754

Other sources indicate a monolingualism in a few additional small peoples. In the immensely diverse Amazon basin, the Pirahã continue to be monolingual in

Pirahã after having spent two centuries in contact with Portuguese-speakers, and having surely been in touch with other non-Pirahãs far longer than that.

DO WE REALLY LIVE ON THE SAME PLANET?

Although no statistics exist, few people who have had any contact with Australia or Australians would contest the claim that Anglophone Australians usually do not speak anything besides English. There is no indigenous minority which is not numerically negligible, and the percentage of students studying a language other than English in year 12 was as low as 12,5% in 1992.

It is somewhat puzzling, therefore, that in a statement made on 27 November 2000, the chair of the Ethnic Affairs Commission in New South Wales, Stepan Kerkyasharian, referred to Australia as "the most multilingual nation on earth". A year later, Kerkyasharian in an official media release claimed that Sydney "currently boasts the most multilingual and multicultural workforce of any Asia-Pacific city".

WHERE FAMILIES ARE BILINGUAL BY DEFINITION

Presumably, the normal state of affairs is that a given person's mother tongue is also their "father's tongue". Not so in Amazonia (or at least the Vaupés area on the border between Colombia and Brazil, on which most accounts are based). In many populations of this area, "ethnic group" is emphatically synonymous with "language group", and an individual is considered to belong to his or her father's group. So far, things are not particularly unfamiliar to a westerner. However, an unusual feature of Vaupés is that marrying someone with whom you share the same native language

is considered outright incestuous, so you have to seek a partner in another tribe. Society is patrilocal, and the wife is expected to move in with her parents-in-law. Thus, in a normal settlement, all adult men share the same tongue, while women speak a variety of languages. In practice, this means that the father's language is the lingua franca, but that the child grows up acquiring at least one other language.

Linguistic exogamy is also reported from some areas of Australia's Cape York peninsula.

Another reported case of language-based

taboo where one's linguistic belonging determines one's relations to other people is Margaret Mead's account of the Biwat of New Guinea, where cannibalism was accepted if and only if the person eaten had a different native tongue than the consumer.

MOST AND LEAST MULTILINGUAL CITIES

Virtually all the world's countries are multilingual, and the same goes for cities. Every once in a while, one city or other tries to claim the label "most multilingual city". It comes as no surprise that hundreds of languages are spoken in a metropolis such as New York, Los Angeles or London. Yet, cities such as these are dominated by one single language, and many minorities consist of isolated individuals. Also, for the most part, immigrant languages fail to survive much beyond the first locally born generation.

The interesting figure isn't really the number of languages of a city, since this at least to some extent comes automatically with its size. More interesting are cases where a city has an extraordinarily fragmented indigenous population. Many of these are found in countries for which no reliable statistics exist. Therefore, nothing can be claimed with certainty, but among the about 350 metropolitan areas with more than one million inhabitants, those of South Africa must surely rank among the most multilingual major cities that there are. The diagrams below show the linguistic composition of three South African municipalities (native languages as recorded in the 2001 census). As can be seen, in none of these does any single linguistic group account for more than a third of the total population.

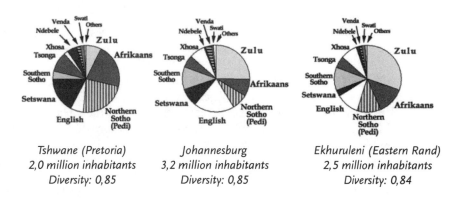

Tshwane (Pretoria)
2,0 million inhabitants
Diversity: 0,85

Johannesburg
3,2 million inhabitants
Diversity: 0,85

Ekhuruleni (Eastern Rand)
2,5 million inhabitants
Diversity: 0,84

(The concept of linguistic diversity is explained on p 9)

Including guesstimates for countries with less precise statistics than South Africa, there are few other cities which may be even more heterogeneous than Johannesburg and Pretoria. One of the few African countries with a language question in the census is Malawi, whose capital Lilongwe scored 0,83 in the 1998 census.

The highest diversity in the USA is that of Queens in New York City (2001 census). With a population larger than many independent nations, and home to half a million speakers of Spanish alone, Queens' diversity index was 0,70. The whole of New York City at the same time sported a diversity of 0,68, while Los Angeles scored slightly lower (0,64).

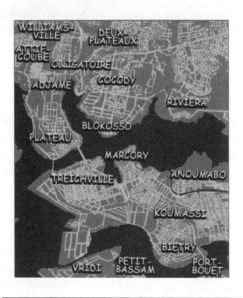

Might this be the linguistically most heterogeneous city in the world? Abidjan, with a few thousand inhabitants around 1900, now hosts a population approaching three million, most of whom were born elsewhere. Though still the economical center of the Ivory Coast, it was in 1983 officially replaced as the capital by Yamoussoukro— the village of origin of the country's dictator.

Maputo (Mozambique) and Singapore are two other highly diverse cities for which reasonably detailed figures are available. The diversity is 0,77 and 0,75 respectively. In 19th century Europe, Riga (then in Russia, now in independent Latvia) and Vyborg (Russia) showed rather impressive figures around 0,70. In the Congolese capital Kinshasa, the value is about 0,71. Nairobi scores 0,74 in Githiora's (2002) survey.

One very interesting case is Abidjan, the economic capital of the highly multilingual Ivory Coast. Having grown from a small village in 1900 to several million inhabitants today, it continues to attract immigrants from the rest of the country and from neighboring nations. Unfortunately, there are no reliable statistics for Abidjan; the only useful figures I have been able to find are those in Delpech (1983:568), Bernus (1962) and Antoine & Herry (1982, 1983: 374). My suggested diversity index of 0,90 is thus uncertain, but note that Kube's (2005: 103–04) survey indicates an even higher figure.

Given the extraordinary linguistic fragmentation of Papua New Guinea (see p 8), its capital Port Moresby would also seem like a good candidate. If, however, we limit ourselves to cities with more than one million inhabitants, almost all candidates are found in Africa. Yet, even there, Abidjan is special in that the original language of the site where the city stands is numerically insignificant in it today.

It is important to remember, however, that linguistic fragmentation need not be indicative of exceptionally multilingual inhabitants. Montreal, for instance, has a fairly diverse population (roughly 55% French, 20% English, 25% others), but the proportion of inhabitants speaking both English and French only barely exceeded 50% in the 2001 census, and even that represents a considerable increase in comparison to earlier censuses.

At the other end of the scale, which major city might be the *least* multilingual? Again, there are no reliable statistics, but my suggestion is either Havana (Spanish) or Pyongyang (Korean)—both countries lack sizeable linguistic minorities, and are introvert enough not to attract immigrants. This situation, of course, may be somewhat altered in the future, as it is not unreasonable to expect a change in the political conditions in Cuba and North Korea. Other metropolises where chances of hearing more than one language spoken ought to be small might be found in Madagascar, South Korea, Brazil, Portugal, and Japan.

In the United States, where language statistics are readily available, the lowest linguistic fragmentation (0,008) is found in

Glascock county, Georgia. According to the 2001 census, the county was home to a mere four speakers of Spanish and three each of French and Greek.

MONOLINGUAL COUNTRIES

Even disregarding recent immigrant populations, few if any countries are entirely monolingual. If nothing else, the presence of at least some deaf people everywhere (statistically to b e expected in any country with about a thousand or more inhabitants) ensures that there is at least a minority of signers in any given country.

Some small countries, such as the Maldives and San Marino, are virtually monolingual as far as *indigenous spoken mother tongues* are concerned, as are some non-independent territories like the Faeroe Islands. Even there, however, the (former) colonial language is still omnipresent as a medium for formal communication and government business. Yet other countries—including St Kitts-Nevis and the Cape Verde Islands—are in one sense monolingual, but there exists a continuum between the basilectal creole spoken by many and the élite's European language from which the creole draws most of its vocabulary.

Some few bigger independent countries that come close to being monolingual include El Salvador, the two Koreas, Iceland, Haiti, Cuba, Portugal, and Madagascar, all of which have unusually small indigenous minorities. For those who consider Arabic one rather than several languages, Yemen would also fit the bill.

CORPORATE MONOLINGUALISM

The *Worldlingo* company regularly surveys the ability (or willingness!) of various major companies to respond to e-mail in languages other than English or the language of the company's home country. In the surveys done so far, the share of appropriate responses (i.e. a response in the same language as used in the original message) usually lies around 9–10%. Japanese, French, Spanish, Italian, German, and Portuguese—all widespread languages—were used in the survey, and about 240 major corporations of seven countries (France, Italy, Britain, Germany, USA, Japan, and Australia) were tested.

The Italian firms performed best, with an average of 25% appropriate responses, somewhat surprisingly followed by the French. More predictably, English-speaking nations scored lower, with Australian companies producing an average of 4% appropriate responses. Even Australia's largest company, AMP, simply responded by writing "In English Please" in the subject line.

The language used also mattered—e-mails sent in Spanish were more likely to be rewarded with an appropriate response, while those in Japanese hardly ever did.

WorldLingo gives a Multilingual Email Excellence Award (WMEA) to the company with the fastest response time from each country. In the August 2001 survey, this went to the Michelin Group of France, which managed to send a response in German in just 1 hour and 17 minutes. Among the more interesting responses provided was that of the Royal Bank of Scotland, which replied "We do not understand French"—written in French . . .

MOST BILINGUAL PUBLISHING

For the countries for which official UNESCO statistics on the subject are available, Sri Lanka is, by quite some margin, the country in which the largest proportion of all publications are bi- or multilingual—25%. Canada, Yugoslavia, Mauritania, and Ukraine follow, and only in sixth place do we find South Africa—the country in the world with the highest number of official languages (see p 24). Alas, it is uncertain precisely what UNESCO means by "a bilingual publication". Sri Lanka lacks bi- or multi-lingual books and newspapers but government's written communications with the public are all trilingual (Sinhala, English, Tamil) as are electricity and phone bills, and the packaging of most local goods.

BIGGEST SHARE OF FOREIGN-LANGUAGE PUBLISHING

According to UNESCO statistics, no less than 79% of everything published in Eritrea between 1991 and 1995 was in "foreign languages". At least at the time of writing this, Eritrea does not technically have an official language, so it is not entirely obvious what is meant by "foreign" in this context. Only in one other country, namely Brazil, was the share of foreign-language publications more than half of the total output (64%). In Nigeria, Paraguay, Jordan, and Belarus, the xenoglot share was a mere 1%.

MOST TRANSLATED LANGUAGES

UNESCO provides statistics on the number of translations made to and from a given language. In 1980, 29% of all recorded translations were made into English, followed by Russian, German, French, and Spanish. In the 1990s, the dominant language was German (22%), closely followed by English (21%) and French (17%), with Russian and Spanish far behind (8% and 2% respectively).

Also included are the languages from which translations are made. In both the 1980s and 1990s, English represented the majority of all source texts. Of the 123 countries featured in UNESCO's Index Translationum database, 84 do their translation mostly from English. French is the only other frequent chart-topper (in 19 countries), and is almost universally the second choice, with German, Spanish, and Russian scoring surprisingly low. The statistics offer some minor surprises. Who would have thought, for instance, that the major target language of Thai translations in 1996 was Danish? Or that in Peru, the major source language of translated publications in the mid-1990s was Korean?

The major language for which translations were far more often made out of than into for the period 1979-2005 was English, followed at quite some distance by Russian and Swedish, the other two big net exporters of texts. Languages which more often constituted the target than the source of translations included Korean, Portuguese, and Japanese. An even better ratio than English, however, is found for Latin, which is only very rarely the translators' target language. For some reason, Germany proved the most fond of translating literature into Latin.

MOST TRANSLATED TEXTS

The Bible is, so far as I can tell, the book which has been translated into the greatest number of languages—at least no one seems to have challenged that oft-repeated claim.

Yet, there is little agreement as to how many Bible translations actually exist. Frequently cited numbers vary between 350 and 2 000 for the entire Bible, and about 2 500 to 3 000 for parts of it. Regardless of which number is the most credible, it sure is increasing, for translation is in progress for at least another 1 500 languages.

In any case, Bible translations vastly outnumber those of other works cited as particularly frequently translated, such as the *Bhagavadgita*, the *Tao Te Ching*, *The Diary of Anne Frank*, *Alice in Wonderland*, Dante's *Divine Comedy*, *Microsoft Office for Windows for Dummies*, *Pippi Longstocking*, *Don Quixote*, or the works by Mao Zedong, Karl Marx, William Shakespeare or Jehovah's Witnesses.

According to the *Guinness Book of World Records*, the most translated document seems to be the United Nations Universal Declaration of Human Rights, now available in 327 languages. Among novelists, Agatha Christie tops the list, followed by Jules Verne and Enid Blyton.

UNESCO provides statistics for translations by year. A comparison between the years 1980 and 1996 reveals, not unexpectedly, that Vladimir Lenin has been dethroned as the world's most translated author, and has even left the top 100, as have Karl Marx, Friedrich Engels, and Leonid Brezhnev, all formerly among the top ten. The Bible also slipped from number two to number 16. A noticeable change between the two years is the increasing dominance of Anglo-Saxon authors. Of the top 50, no less than 35 were Anglo-Saxons in 1996, as compared to 22 in 1980.

LARGEST TRANSLATION SERVICE

At the time of writing this, the European Union has 25 member states, whose official languages all (with the exception of Luxembourgeois and Irish) have official status in the organization. This means a total of 20 languages (Czech, Danish, Dutch, English, Estonian, Finnish, French, German, Greek, Hungarian, Italian, Latvian, Lithuanian, Maltese, Polish, Portuguese, Slovak, Slovenian, Spanish, and Swedish), thus defined in the first article of the Council Regulation No. 1. That in turn yields 190 possible combinations, which the Union must be able to handle.

The translation service of the European Commission is, so far as I know, the largest translation organization in the world The

Directorate-General for Translation has 1 650 full-time translators and support staff of 550. Yet, the demand is such that about 20% of the texts are processed by a couple of hundred free-lance translators hired on a non-permanent basis. This number constantly increases as the nine languages of the countries that joined in 2004 are gradually promoted to the same status as the eleven languages of the older members. Before the latest expansion of the union, the annual output was almost 1,5 million pages, but with the nine new members, this is expected to rise to about 2,5 million.

In addition, the Joint Interpreting and Conference Service (SCIC), has 500 staff interpreters and makes additional use of 2 700 freelance interpreters.

The cost of translation was estimated at 320 million euros in 2006, which is equivalent to about 0,8% of the total EU budget. The 2007 figure has been suggested to reach as high as 800 million Euros. Including interpreting (€ 200 million), the total cost for each EU citizen is around €2 per year (or, as EU officials themselves like to point out, "about the cost of a cup of coffee"). Though the number of member countries is expected to increase significantly, it is by no means certain that this latter figure will rise, since the number of tax payers will increase as well.

Swedes usually pride themselves of (and frequently also overestimate) their knowledge of English. Swedish is also, together with Finnish, the language into which the fewest translations are made. Most translations are made from English and French (together representing 88% of the documents), and more than anything else into German (13%, followed by French and English).

Not surprisingly, the EU has shown a great interest in machine translation, and this has been gradually implemented since 1976, when the first program (from English to French) entered service. There are now translation programs for 18 language pairs (out of the 190 possible ones), all involving English or French. Each month, about 50 000 pages are now subject to machine translation.

With Catalan having a special status, Turkish is the most widely spoken language without official status in the EU with almost three million speakers within the union. Other languages spoken natively by more than a million inhabitants of the EU, but nevertheless without official status include Arabic, Russian, Serbo-Croatian, Occitan, Romani and Sardinian. The smallest official EU language is Maltese, which has about 430 000 native speakers in the EU countries. It is thus less widely spoken than about twenty non-official languages, including Lesser Antillean French Creole, Panjabi, Albanian, Kurdish, and Welsh.

FIRST MACHINE TRANSLATION

The first primitive machine translation devices were patented (independently of one another) in 1933 by the French-Armenian Georges Artsrouni and by the Russian Pyotr Smirnov-Troyanskii. The first systems to see actual service were developed in the late 1940s, due to American eagerness to understand Soviet physics papers. In 1951, the first full-time researcher in machine translation, Yehoshua Bar-Hillel, was hired by the Massachusetts Institute of Technology.

FIRST SIGN LANGUAGE MACHINE TRANSLATION

At the University of Pennsylvania in Philadelphia, research is underway on a program translating spoken English to 3D animated American Sign Language (ASL).

Meanwhile the eSIGN project, an outgrowth of ViSiCAST, both funded by the European Union, seeks to provide virtual translations of speech and text into computer-generated signs. These are the first machine translation projects of their kind.

At the University of South Wales, Mohammed Waleed Kadous has also worked on machine recognition of a sign language, in his case Australian Sign (Auslan).

SOURCES NOT MENTIONED IN THE TEXT

Foreign language teaching (Britain, USA): *Global English Newsletter* 5-1999; Lambert (1999).

Language knowledge in the European Union and its applicant countries: Data found in the Canadian magazine *Langue & Société*, no. 38 (March 1992), the German *Treffpunkt: Das Magazin der Axel Anderson-Akademie (Hamburg)*, no. 14 (1997), p 30, and also on INRA 2001 and official EU statistics on <http://europa.eu.int/comm/education/languages/sv/lang/europeanlanguages.html>.

Multilingualism in Congo-Brazzaville: Woods (1998:315).

Multilingualism in Benin: Igué & Windali N'Ouéni (1993:5).

Multilingualism in Moldavia: Ciscel, Hallett & Green (2002:54-55).

Swedish-speaking exiles from Vyborg: Tandefeldt [ed.] (2002:151).

Armenians in Jerusalem's Old City: Spolsky & Shohamy (1999:136).

Dutch Business executives: Rosen, Singer & Digh (2000).

Foreign language competence among the Kabalai: Hamm (2003).

Language competence of Russians: 1989 Soviet census.

Language competence of Hindi-speakers: 1991 Indian census.

Example of three-way code-switching in Mauritius: Tirvassen (1999).

Language competence of Ontario Anglophones, New Zealanders and Australians: The 2001 censuses of the respective countries—in the Australian case combined with some extrapolation (see Parkvall [forthcoming] for details).

2004 reports and comments on the language (in)competence of Britons: BBC News, 2004-07-29.

Monolingualism among the Pirahã: Everett (2004).

Studying foreign languages in Australia: From an anonymous article on the University of Australia web site (http://www.unisa.edu.au/eqo/pubs/cultural/cu05.htm, 2002-06-21).

Bilingual families in Amazonia: Sorensen (1967), Aikhenvald (2003:2), Gomez-Imbert (1991).

Linguistic exogamy in the Cape York peninsula: Aikhenvald (2004:11).

Cannibalism among the Biwat: Foley (1986:24).

Language diversity: Mozambique—1997 census; Singapore—2000 census; Riga—1897 census, in Čekmonas (2001:92); Vyborg: 1812 census, in Tandefelt [ed.] (2002:67); Kinshasa: Nyembwe (2001:220).

Corporate monolingualism: Nua Internet surveys (2001) and World Lingo (2001).

Bilingual and foreign-language publishing, and most translated languages: UNESCO. Figures refer to the period 1991–1995 unless otherwise indicated.

Most translated texts: International Bible Society, United Bible Societies, UNESCO statistics.

Translation in the European Union: Europeiska kommissionens översättningstjänst (2001a, b), Cunningham (2001), BBC news, 2004-04-08, *Dagens Nyheter* 2005-01-31, EU Directorate-General for Translation and the Joint Interpreting and Conference Service.

First machine translation: Hutchins (1995), Manaris (1998).

First sign language machine translation: Zhao et al. (2000), eSIGN project homepage at http://www.visicast.cmp.uea.ac.uk/eSIGN/index.html, 2004-03-22.

LANGUAGES IN CONTACT

ALL POPULATIONS ARE, and always have been, in contact with others. Just as one would expect, this leaves its mark on languages, and there is most certainly no such thing as a "pure" language devoid of influences from its neighbors.

It is certainly true that some things are borrowed more easily than others, but a fairly recent insight among linguists is that *anything* can indeed be borrowed.

MOST LOANWORDS

An oft-cited piece of linguistic data is the fact that the English lexicon contains more loans from French and other languages than inherited Germanic vocabulary. In fact, this situation is far from being as unusual as one might think. To just mention a few, languages as different from one another as Breton, Maltese, Basque, Swedish and Kalderash Romani in Europe, Chi-Mwiini and Daisu in Africa, Armenian, Bai, Gaddang, Japanese, Korean and Vietnamese in Asia, and Lake Miwok in North America all have more borrowed than inherited lexical material.

Very few languages are known to have a vocabulary that contains more than 80% borrowings, but some do exist. Vlax Romani is reported to be in the 80% range, and in Brahui, a Dravidian language on the frontier of Iran and Pakistan, as well as in Hungarian and Albanian, loan-words are even said to amount to as much as 90% of the total lexicon. In all, there are only some 200 words in Albanian directly inherited from proto-Indo-European.

These borrowings, however, usually tend to be found in the more peripheral parts of the lexicon. In English, for instance, the proportion of borrowings in the core lexicon is about 16%. Anthony Grant, who possesses an impressive expertise in this area, knows of only a few cases where the borrowings in the core vocabulary—here defined as the combined 100- and 200-item Swadesh lists—exceed 30%. One is Acehnese (spoken on Sumatra), which has a huge number of loans from Mon-Khmer, and lesser additions from Malay, Dutch, Sanskrit and Arabic. Its relative Jarai, which is spoken in Vietnam, is said to have an even higher proportion of borrowed core words. Further to the south-east, Haruai of New Guinea has an amazing 38% (mainly from neighboring Kobon) of borrowings on a modified Swadesh list. On the same island, Warembori has a basic lexicon which is almost equally split between 45% Austronesian and 55% Papuan elements.

> A Sprachbund is a group of languages whose members display similarities due to contact. The languages are not necessarily related, or at least not closely so, but have over the years developed a number of common features. It is typically difficult to determine a specific center from which these innovations spread.

In northern Australia, some of the languages of the Arnhem Land Sprachbund have more loans than inherited words even in their core vocabularies, and in northern Europe, 37 of the 100 "most common" words in Saami are reported to be borrowed. Nevertheless, it is possible that the first prize goes to another New Guinean language, for Kaulong of New Britain has a mere *ten* inherited items on a 192-word modified Swadesh list.

It could of course be argued that intertwined languages (see below) contain even higher proportions of borrowed lexicon.

MOST FAMOUS SPRACHBUND

The most famous Sprachbund in western linguistics is no doubt the one covering the Balkan peninsula, immortalized not least through the Dane Kristian Sandfeld's (1930) work *Linguistique balkanique*. Its two main competitors are those of (i) south-east Asia and (ii) north-western USA and south-western Canada.

Dahl (2005) calls south-east Asia "the ultimate language area", since it is an area with truly exceptional structural homogeneity in relation to a relatively high degree of genetic differentiation.

MOST INTERNATIONAL WORDS

While all languages borrow vocabulary from others, only some words are successful enough to be incorporated in more than just a handful of languages. It seems that the most international words are proper names (including place names and trade marks). Next to those, we find a large number of words *derived from* proper names, including *-isms* and *-ists*, various scientific discoveries, measurements (*volt*, *ampère*, etc), pet breeds, plants species, medicaments, minerals and so on. Recently discovered chemical elements also usually have the same name in all languages (except in China). Many of these are of course specific to a rather small group of users of any language, rather than being topics of everyday conversation for ordinary mortals.

So, among words which actually are known by larger numbers of people, *coffee* (from Yemeni Arabic), *tea* (from southern Sinitic), and *chocolate* (probably from Aztec *xokoatl*) stand out. Some languages spoken in the areas where these stimulants were first cultivated and consumed have indigenous words for them, but in most of the rest of the world, they are known by variants of the same original names.

Some modern-day competitors include *bikini*, *curry*, *golf*, and *jazz*. One might also expect 20th century inventions such as *telephone* and *television* here, and indeed these words are widespread. Yet, a sizeable number of languages have launched coinings of their own, usually based on a morpheme meaning 'far away' combined with 'speak' and 'see' respectively. (Though to the extent that these are direct translations of the more international labels—which is often the case—it could be argued that we are still dealing with loans.)

Incidentally, while it is common to borrow words, it is less common that they are reclaimed by the original lender. In a sense this has happened when, as a result of EU legislation, only champers from the French district of Champagne may be sold under this name.

Some languages prefer to coin their own words even for modern inventions. My favorite is Montana Salish p'ip'úyčn 'automobile', which literally translates as 'it has wrinkled feet'. Sure does.

AN UNBORROWED BODY-PART?

Basic terms, such as words for body parts are less easily borrowed than names of cultural artefacts. While not all languages have a word for 'space shuttle' or 'genetic engineering', and therefore may feel a need to borrow it, they presumably all have words for 'arms' and 'legs'. Yet, these, along with 'hands', 'tongue' and 'eyes' have indeed been borrowed. The one word for a body-part which has been proposed never to have been borrowed from one language to another is 'ear'. Several cases have been suggested (including the corresponding term in Proto-Indo-European); among the more convincing are perhaps Malagasy *sofina*, which may be borrowed from Malay rather than inherited from Proto-Austronesian, and Northern Tajiki's *qulaq*, borrowed from Uzbek.

A more clear-cut case is Bislama of Vanuatu, in which *sora* 'ear', is borrowed from French *les oreilles*. But then Bislama is a creole (more precisely an English-lexicon creole), and creoles do not fit in the normal family-tree model. Incidentally, the same word in Bislama's close relative Tok Pisin is expressed as *yau*, which at least appears to be of non-English origin. The small Sri Lankan isolate Vedda has borrowed 'ear' from Sinhala, but then, Vedda too is in many respects an atypical language.

LARGE NUMBER OF BORROWED PHONEMES

It is well known that click sounds are found (almost) exclusively in the languages of South Africa. It is also generally believed that they originated in

Khoisan languages, and that their presence in the Bantu languages of the area is due to borrowing. However, the Khoisan bestowed not only clicks upon their neighbors, but also other phonemes. Thus, Xhosa is said to owe more than a score, and perhaps even 25 phonemes to its contact with Khoisan. Many other languages have got one or two new phonemes through borrowing, but rarely more than a handful.

Even more extreme is the intrusion of foreign phonemes into Fagauvea, a Polynesian Outlier language also known as West Uvean. Its contact with the Melanesian neighbor Iaai is said to have introduced no less than 27 new phonemes, thus more than doubling its original inventory. Lake Miwok is another language which has borrowed, so to speak, its own weight in phonemes, including several new articulation types.

STARTING AT THE WRONG END

Some things are borrowed more easily than others. In general, free, lexical morphemes are easily borrowed, whereas bound and grammatical morphemes are more resistant to pressure from the outside. In other words, we would expect a language with a certain amount of borrowing to be more affected in the more lexical end of the lexicon, and more conservative in the grammatical end. Not so with Mednyj Aleut, a now virtually extinct language spoken in the Bering Strait.

Contact with Russian certainly has had an impact on the Mednyj Aleut lexicon and phonology, but not a remarkable one—94% of the recorded verbs, and 61,5% of the nouns are still of Aleut origin, and much of the borrowed verbs in any case relate to concepts

introduced by the Russians. The pronouns and the function words however are for the most part Russian. As you can see below, the entire verb morphology (in bold) is directly from Russian, only attached to Aleut verbs!

	Mednyj Aleut	Russian
'I stand'	anqaχta**yu**	sto**yu**
'You stand'	anqaχta**iš**	sto**iš**
'He stands'	anqaχta**it**	sto**it**
'We stand'	anqaχta**im**	sto**im**
'You stand'	anqaχta**ite**	sto**ite**
'We stand'	anqaχta**yat**	sto**yat**

Few, if any, comparable cases have been attested elsewhere.

MOST STABLE DIGLOSSIA

A diglossia is rarely stable forever. Either the prestige language takes over completely, leading to the extinction of the folk speech (as with Indian languages being ousted by English in the USA), or else, a new political situation makes the less prestigious variety appropriate in contexts in which it was formerly not used (as when Latin ceased to be used in Europe or when French became extinct in Britain).

There are at least two cases where a

diglossic situation has been stable over the centuries. One is Switzerland, where local varieties of Swiss German (unintelligible to a Berliner) seem unthreatened by Standard German. Meanwhile, the latter seems secure in its role as official language. Another case is the Arab world, where a similar situation must have obtained for about a millennium. Local varieties of Arabic are the everyday languages of people who happily use Classical Arabic for any official purpose.

A diglossic situation is typically one in which a low-prestige language is confined to private domains, such as with family members and close friends, whereas another, more prestigious variety (often acquired in school, rather than natively) is used in public and more official settings. This situation is more common in the world than westerners tend to be aware of, and in e.g. Africa (where European colonial languages usually occupy the prestige position), it is rather the rule than the exception.

Michif text

Interviewed by Dutch-Danish linguist Peter Bakker, Michif-speaker Margaret Desjarlais here tells the story about how her language came into being (French items are in bold):

Les Canadiens come across, les Sauvagesses mâci-wîcamâweyak and then puis êkwa les enfants ê-ayâwâ-cik. La Sauvagesse namôya kaskihtaw en français takitotât ses enfants. Le Français namoya kaskihtâw ses enfants ta-kitotât en cri. En français êkwa kitotêw. Êkwa quelques les deux kiskinohamahk kîkwây. Ohci pîkiskwêw rien que en cri êkwa en français.

Translation

When the French Canadians came from across the ocean, they started to marry Indian women and then they had kids. The Indian woman couldn't speak French. The Frenchman couldn't speak Cree to their kids, so he spoke to them in French. Some of them learned to speak French and Cree. Therefore he speaks only French and Cree (mixed).

Unfortunately, Michif is today a dying language, as it is gradually replaced by English. As can be seen in the excerpt above, English words and phrases are today omnipresent even in the speech of the few who still master this unique language.

So far as is known, there is no parallel to Michif anywhere else in the world.

SOURCES NOT MENTIONED IN THE TEXT

Borrowing in English: Anttila (1972:172).
Borrowing in Hungarian and Breton: Stéphane Goyette (p c).
Borrowing in Maltese: Brincat (2001).
Borrowing in Basque: (Trask 1997:309).
Borrowing in Swedish: Hock (1991:423), Anttila (1972:172).
Borrowing in Kalderash Romani: Boretzky (1991:4-13).

Speakers of Michif outside their camp in the late 19th century

Borrowing in Brahui, Vlax Romani, Gaddang, Kalderash Romanı, Lake Mıwok, Chı-Mwıını, Daisu: Anthony Grant (p c).

Borrowing in Vietnamese, Armenian, and Bai: Dalby (1998:668).

Borrowing in Japanese: Shibatani (1990a:132-3, 1990b:142-45).

Borrowing in Korean: Kim (1990:156), Sohn (1999:87).

Borrowing in Albanian: Anttila (1972:172), Hock (1991:423), Trask (1997:217).

Borrowed lexicon in Acehnese, Jarai, Haruai, and Kaulong: Anthony Grant (p c).

Warembori: Mark Donohue (p c).

Arnhem Land Sprachbund: Heath (1981).

Borrowing in Saami: Sammallahti (1998:92).

Most international words: Traunmüller (forthcoming), *Linguist List* 9.1779, 10.703.

An unborrowed body-part: *Linguist List* 6.915, 6.1126. Borrowing of 'ear' in Indo-European, Malagasy, Tajiki, Bislama and Tok Pisin: Anthony Grant (p c). Vedda: Philip Baker (p c).

Xhosa clicks: Dalby (1998:679).

Phonological borrowings in Fagauvea and Lake Miwok: Anthony Grant (p c).

Mednyj Aleut: Thomason (1996b:460), Sekerina (1994:29). Verb inflexion example from Golovko (1996:70).

Magori and Maisin: Lynch (1998:57), Foley (1986:283).

Mixture in Ayiwo and Lödai: Mühlhäusler et al. (1996:424-25).

Wutun: Lee-Smith & Wurm (1996:883) and Wurm (1996:820).

Michif: Bakker (1997), and Peter Bakker (p c).

Language situation in Switzerland: Bernhard Wälchli (p c).

LANGUAGE DEATH AND REVIVAL

PRESUMABLY, languages have been born and passed into oblivion for as long as mankind has existed. It is probable that the number of languages has remained relatively constant during this time—languages simply had fewer speakers when there weren't as many people on earth. The present period is probably unique, though, in that at least half of the world's languages are threatened. Many estimates even predict that as many as **90%** of today's 6 000 languages will become extinct during the 21st century. Meanwhile, very few new ones are born, and resurrection of a dead language is almost unheard of.

There are at least three ways for a language to become extinct. One is for it to transmogrify into another language, as Latin did. Since this trans-formation was gradual, there never was such a thing as the last speaker of Latin, and thus no date when Latin died. Another, more common, way for a language to fall into desuetude is for it to become less and less popular among parents, so that in time their children grow up speaking only another language. The original language is lost but the people continue to exist. Finally, as Crawford (1996) puts it, languages can not only die, but they can also be murdered. There are cases where an entire population has been exterminated (or wiped out by natural disasters), and where a language has thus met an extraordinarily sudden death.

BIGGEST MORIBUND LANGUAGES

The UNESCO *Red Book on Endangered Languages* defines an "endangered language" as one "with some children speakers at least in part of their range but decreasingly so" and a "seriously endangered language" as one "practically without children" among its speakers.

Most more or less endangered languages are generally small, but some are surprisingly big. In France, Occitan with perhaps 3 000 000 speakers, and Breton with some 500 000, are both seriously endangered. To the north thereof, Walloon and Frisian (each with maybe 300-500 000 speakers) are also in a precarious situation. Most varieties of Sardinian, a conservative Romance language spoken by a million or so, are threatened, as is another Italian language, Friulian, with about 350 000 speakers. Several not-so-small languages of Russia are also endangered, including Chuvash (approximately 1 300 000 speakers), Bashkir (1 000 000), Udmurt (520 000), Erzya (500 000), Eastern Mari (500 000), Gagauz (170 000), Kalmyk (150 000). In the same country, Crimean Tatar (250 000) is even considered "seriously endangered".

Yiddish, used by 10-15 million people prior to the Second World War, has suffered badly from first the Holocaust, and then from assimilation both in the diaspora and in Israel. It now has two to three million speakers throughout the world. Very few of these are children, except in certain circles in Israel, where some speakers consider Hebrew "too holy" to use in everyday conversation, and who therefore reserve Yiddish for this purpose.

Another case is Quechua—which, if counted as one single language—has more than nine million speakers, but which in many areas is not passed on to children.

Even more spectacularly, Javanese is described by Dalby (2002:139) as seriously threatened by the variety of Malay now labelled Indonesian. Javanese is one of the fifteen most widely spoken languages in the world. It must surely be the biggest language ever whose existence has been considered in danger.

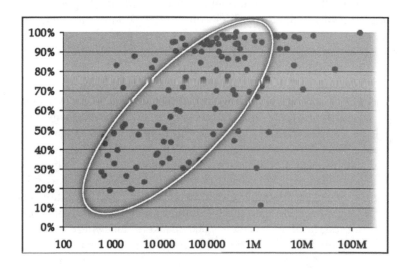

In general, smaller languages are indeed more vulnerable than bigger ones. This is illustrated here by data from the last (1989) Soviet census. On the Y axis is the proportion of the members of a given ethnic group which still speaks its traditional language. On the X axis, we have the total membership of the group in question (please note that the scale is logarithmic). The trend is obvious— shift to Russian is less marked in larger groups. The odd man out (bottom right) is Yiddish—despite numbering almost 2 million at the time, only 11% of the Soviet Jews clung on to Yiddish.

On the other hand, there are a few languages which used to be thought to be facing extinction but which now appear to be in a healthier state. Basque, with 900 000 speakers, seems less threatened now than it was some time ago (at least in Spain—the situation on the French side is considerably worse), as is the language of the half a million strong Welsh-speaking community. Lithuanian was considered seriously threatened in the late 19th and early 20th centuries (and even pronounced dead in 1886) but is now healthy. It has well over three million speakers, and is the sole official language of Lithuania.

One of the biggest languages which has made it onto somewhat safer ground is Ukrainian, which sports some 45 000 000 speakers. Seriously threatened by Russian under Soviet rule, it is now the only official language of an independent country. At least in theory, that is. Many Ukrainians still speak either Russian, or a form of Ukrainian heavily influenced by Russian.

THE PACMANS OF LANGUAGES

The *Ethnologue* lists about 500 languages as "nearly extinct", meaning that they are down to their last few elderly speakers. For half of these (mainly indigenous languages of Australia and the United States), the population is shifting to English. In South America, 56 languages are giving way to Spanish. Chiefly on the same continent, 19 languages are being crushed under the weight of Portuguese, while Russian is putting nine languages to death. Notable small-scale conquests are reported for e.g. Jukun, Nepali, Bunun, and Pashto.

It should be noted that ongoing language death in Australia and the USA is most probably better documented than it is for most other countries, where the passing into oblivion more likely goes unnoticed. Therefore, English can be suspected to be overrepresented in the above figures.

Apart from those already mentioned, other glottophags which are surely underreported include Arabic, Bislama, French, Fulfulde, Kituba, Lingala, Malay/Indonesian, Mandarin, Nepali, West African English Creole, Sango, Swahili, Tagalog, Tok Pisin, and Vietnamese. It is hardly surprising that it is primarily languages which already are widely spoken which threaten minority tongues. There are, however, still places in the world where the conqueror is not English or any of the other global juggernauts. On New Guinea, Woria, Kwerisa, and Karawa are losing their last speakers to Demisa, Kaiy, and Pouye, respectively, despite the fact that each of the latter has less than 1 000 speakers. Elsewhere on the same island, the 1 200 strong Berik is even assimilating two of its neighbors, Bonerif and Mander, and in Vanuatu (former)

Araki-speakers are abandoning their language for Tangoa with only 800 speakers. In Surinam, speakers of Sikiana and Akurio are shifting to the local giant, Trío, which is thereby swelling its ranks to 1 151.

The current trend is very clear—big languages get even bigger at the expense of smaller ones. It is probable that no language is guilty of more cases of linguocide than English (in possible competition with Portuguese). It is impossible to tell for sure how many languages it has replaced or is replacing, but a number around 500 ought not to be an exaggeration. Beginning at home, with the extinction of Manx and Cornish, English then expanded overseas, and killed off most of the indigenous languages of North America and Oceania (and to a lesser extent elsewhere). Counting hundreds of languages before the arrival of Europeans, both continents are now about 90% English-speaking.

While English has almost 16 million speakers in Australia, the biggest Aboriginal languages are each used by a mere 3 000 individuals. They are thus vastly outnumbered even by languages which we hardly think of as "Australian", such as Aramaic, Kurdish, Slovak, Somali, Maltese, Polish, and Vietnamese. Similarly, in the United States, by far the most popular indigenous language, Navajo, is spoken by less than 150 000 people, which makes it the 21st language of the country. No other American Indian language even makes it into the top 50, and most of them are dying.

Other exceptionally glottophagous languages include the other major languages of European colonization, such as Spanish, Portuguese and Russian. A rookie in this context is Tok Pisin, the English-lexicon creole of Papua New Guinea. This country is home to more languages than any other state in the world, but several of them are losing ground to Tok Pisin. Should it manage to kill off all the indigenous languages (at present some 800), it might even outdo the European languages in this respect.

European overseas expansion has had a most disastrous effect on languages spoken in the New World and Oceania, and only a minority of those still in use may be expected to survive another century. The graphs above illustrate the approximate numbers of languages in use in Brazil Australia and the USA prior to contact with Europeans, the number still spoken today, together with a prognosis for the year 2100.

These figures draw mainly on data from SIL's Ethnologue database, with additions from various other sources. SIL sometimes uses the criterion of a numerical limit of 600 speakers as a criterion for "endangeredhood", and I have taken this as a starting point, while transferring languages from one category to the other whenever there are specific reasons to do so. This includes mainly explicit statements on language shift or the age structure of the population.

Estimates of the number of languages used before European arrival are of course hazardous to make, and they often differ considerably from one source to another. For Australia, for instance, numbers between 200 and 700 are given, and for Brazil, Crystal (1997) suggests as many as 1 000.

RAPID LANGUAGE SHIFT

*I*t is sometimes said that complete language shift takes three generations—while the grandparents only speak the old language, the middle generation is bilingual, and the grandchildren are monolingual in the new language. There are plenty of cases, though, where the process is less protracted.

Even in the USA, where there is much ado about the increasing number of Hispanics, English is the dominant language for no less than 70% of the American-born Hispanic children.

Much the same thing goes for Native Americans. In the mid-1970s, 95% of the children of Rock Point, a Navajo-speaking community in Arizona, came to school with little or no knowledge of English. A mere two decades later, only half spoke fluent Navaho, and today, 80% are said to be monolingual Anglophones. Comparable figures have been advanced with regard to Walapai-speaking children in neighboring Peach Springs.

The situation on Easter Island is similar. In the late 1970s, three out of four school-children had Rapa Nui as their mother tongue, but only 15 years later, the share was down to just one in four.

On the Caribbean island of Dominica, the local creole known as *Patwa*, which has traditionally been the native tongue of virtually all Dominicans, is being replaced by English. In the mid-1990s, virtually no Patwa could be heard in the streets of Roseau, the island's capital. It is said that, in order not to hear any English but only Patwa, in the same streets, one would have to go back in time a mere 30 years.

On Newfoundland, an observer visiting the French-speaking communities in the late 1920s reported that, while the inhabitants around the turn of the century were unable to speak English at all, the children of the Benoîts and Bergerons now could not or would not speak any French.

Another case involving French also comes to mind, not primarily for the rapidity of the language shift, but for the unusual reason behind it: Until relatively recently, the language of the Channel Islands (Jersey, Guernsey, Alderney and Sark) was a variety of French. Only in 1900 did English begin to be used in the local administration, and until the 1930s, most of the local legislation was drafted in French. Signs of decline were evident even in the first half of the 20th century, but a decisive blow to the language was the evacuation to Britain of many of the islander civilians during the Nazi occupation of the Second World War.

Without knowing whether or not they would ever be allowed to return, many of the children acquired the English of their foster parents, and had virtually forgotten their native tongue when the islands were liberated in 1945 (they remained occupied until the ultimate German surrender). French has become completely extinct on Alderney and only has a couple of dozen remaining speakers on Sark. About 2% of the population are now fluent speakers on Guernsey, and perhaps two or three times as many on Jersey. The vast majority of these are aged, and there can be little doubt that Channel Islands French is on the verge of extinction.

These are just a few examples of what is in fact a relatively common phenomenon. If society changes quickly, so do people's language loyalties.

RAPID LANGUAGE DEATH

Sometimes, languages die not because their speakers desert them, but simply because their speakers die, and in such cases, language death can of course be even more drastic.

One well-known case is that of the Californian language Yahi. The number of Yahi dwindled from 1 900 in the mid-1840s, when the gold rush began, to about 100 two decades later. In 1912, Ishi, the last speaker of the language was encountered, and after having been donated (sic) to a museum, he became quite famous. But since his death in 1916, the language is completely extinct. California was the linguistically most diverse region in North America, and in 1800, this state alone contained about 100 languages. Half of these still have a few elderly speakers, but not a single one is learned by children, meaning that the pre-Columbian languages of California will soon be completely extinct.

Ishi—the last speaker of Yahi

Another example of this is the Kwakiutl of British Columbia, who were decimated from an estimated 19 125 in 1786 to a mere 1 039 a century and a half later. Today, only a few hundred speakers remain.

In South America, the Amazonian language Júma had 300 speakers in 1940, but in the 1990s, their numbers had dwindled first to seven, and then to a mere four in 1998. The language is obviously facing extinction.

Even more dramatic is a case from the rain forests of Venezuela, where explorers unknowingly brought with them an influenza virus while passing through a small village on the banks of the Coluene River. Less than ten people survived the tragedy, and with them, the Trumai language fell into desuetude.

For similar reasons, another South American language, Bora, saw its number of speakers falling from 15 000 in 1915 to a mere 427 twenty-five years later. It did not die out, however, but partly recovered, and now has almost 3 000 users.

The case of Tamboran is even more extreme—indeed as dramatic as language death can possibly be. In 1815, a volcanic eruption on the Indonesian island of Sumbawa killed every single speaker of the language.

Again in South America, the number of Nambiquara speakers was estimated at about 20 000—50 000 at the beginning of their contact with western civilization in 1911. Gruesome epidemics had by the mid-20th century reduced this number to 500. The current number is above 800, and even though knowledge of Portuguese is improving, children still learn their ancestral tongue.

These examples could be multiplied, but the most well-known, and one of the most spectacular examples of genocide-related language death, is that of the language or languages of Tasmania. The island is thought to have had about 4 000 inhabitants when the first Europeans arrived. The British began settling the island in 1808, and twenty years later, an organized genocide began, as the governor declared war on the Aborigines. Martial law allowed anyone to shoot and kill natives found in settled areas, and ethnic cleansing was taken one step further as chains of people swept across the island looking for survivors. In 1835, thus after less than three decades, the Aboriginal Tasmanians were virtually annihilated, and in 1847, only 47 survivors were left. The British, on their part, had suffered 183 casualties.

Today, a couple of thousand Tasmanians claim aboriginal descent, but they are of mixed origin—the reputedly last full-blooded native Tasmanian died in 1876. In any case, the Tasmanian language or languages are long forgotten, and only poorly documented.

SLOW LANGUAGE REPLACEMENT

There are plenty of languages which are certainly not yet extinct, and which may never be, but which have been repressed for several centuries. Basque in Spain, the Celtic languages of the British Isles, Ainu in northern Japan, and both Mohawk and Cajun French in North America are some examples.

Massive Anglicization of Ireland began in the early 1600s, and towards the end of the next century, Irish-speakers had become a minority in their own country. Around the time of Irish independence, probably only a tenth of the population spoke Irish natively, and today, the number is thought to be around 1%. Given its current support by authorities, the death of Irish is perhaps less certain now than it once was, but should it die out as a mother tongue, that will end a process which has been going on for more than four centuries.

Also on the British isles, Cornwall was incorporated into England in 936, but only in the late 16th century were all speakers of Cornish bilingual in English. And not until 1891, or after more than a millennium, did the last real speaker (John Davey of Zennor) pass away. (Cornish has since been revived— see below –, but its speakers have usually not acquired the language natively, and all are dominant in English, so if you ask me, that doesn't really count.)

It is problematic to give a precise number of years, since it is not obvious precisely when language death kicks in, and if the language is still alive, it may even be incorrect to speak of 'language death'. In any case, it is clear that the process of language replacement can be rather protracted and span over several centuries.

AN UNUSUAL CASE OF SHIFTING LANGUAGE LOYALTY

Before the separation of India and Pakistan in 1947, the most important language of the two countries was commonly referred to as "Hindustani". When the need arose to emphasize the new national identities, the terms "Hindi" (for the Indian/Hindu variety) and "Urdu" (for the Pakistani/Muslim one) became more popular. Hindi and Urdu are thus two different labels for what is essentially one and the same language. While Hindustani was spoken by tens of millions before the break-up of British India in 1947,

the numbers claiming to speak this dwindled rapidly, as more and more people declared their allegiance to Hindi and Urdu. Already in the 1951 Indian census, the number of Hindustani speakers had decreased by 90%, and in 1971, only 11 000 Indians claimed it as their mother tongue.

A somewhat similar development can be seen in the former Yugoslavia, where people more or less overnight went from speaking Serbo-Croatian to speaking "Serbian", "Croatian" and "Bosnian".

LATIN IS DEAD—BUT THE KING LIVES!

Jukka Ammondt, a k a "Dr Ammondt" (yes, he does have a PhD) is a Finnish tango singer. (In Finland, the tango is not only danced,

but also sung, and it is *immensely* popular.) In 1995, he released his first international best seller—*The Legend Lives Forever in Latin*, containing seven Elvis Presley songs in Latin. The hit parade included numbers such as *Nunc hic aut numquam* ('It's Now or Never'), *Non adamare non possum* ('Can't Help Falling in Love'), *Cor ligneum* ('Wooden Heart') and *Tenere me ama* ('Love Me Tender'). Two years later, he followed up the success with the album *Rocking in Latin*, featuring classics such as *Quate, Crepa,*

Rota (better known as 'Shake, Rattle and Roll').

In 1999, Ammondt announced that he was planning to record Elvis songs in Sumerian, and in July 2001, the album, which among other tracks included a highly original Sumerian rendition (with a touch of Leonard-Cohen-goes-oriental) of *Blue Suede Shoes*, was released.

SUCCESSFUL LANGUAGE REVIVAL

The most famous and successful case of language revival is no doubt the case of Hebrew. After a period of several centuries when the language was demoted to being a written language used mainly for religious purposes, the decades around 1900 saw its rebirth as a spoken language (for more information, see Ben-Yehuda on p 98).

Other revival attempts concern Celtic languages. Belfast, Northern Ireland, had not had a native-speaking Gaelic community for a century of more, when language revitalization was initiated in the 20th century. A community of eleven families then taught themselves Irish from books, and started talking it to their children. They all moved into the same residential area, in order to keep their new language community together. They spoke only Irish (albeit with a heavy English accent) with each other, and so a generation of truly bilingual children grew up with an English-tinted Irish and English as their two mother tongues. Some of these new Irish-speakers now have Irish-speaking children of their own.

Another Celtic language, Cornish, died out in the early 19th century. (Dolly Pentreath, who passed away in 1777, is reputed to have been the last native speaker, but this is not quite true; see p 63.) In the 20th century, however, some parents have begun to speak Cornish to their children, and in a sense, it again exists as a spoken language. Nevertheless, there are probably no speakers with a competence in Cornish equalling that in English, and it deserves to be underlined that language revival in the sense that the once extinct language again becomes the main vehicle of communication of a community is exceedingly uncommon, and *almost* unheard of—in fact, Hebrew may even be the only example that there is.

SOURCES NOT MENTIONED IN THE TEXT

Former threats to Lithuanian: Krakovska (2004), Östen Dahl (p c).
Assimilation of Hispanics in the USA: Crawford (1996).
Navajo and Walapai: Crawford (1996), Dalby (2002:164).
Language shift on Easter Island: Conniff (1993:67).
Dominica: Author's field observations.
French in Newfoundland: Tricoche (1929:211).
Channel Islands: Spence (1993), Jones (2001), Sallabank (2003).
Number of Yahi speakers: Mithun (1999:564).
Language diversity in California: Campbell (1997:16).

Kwakiutl: Anonby (1999:33).

Júma: *Ethnologue*, editions 13 to 15.

Trumai: Crystal (1997).

Near-extinction of Bora: Adelaar (2004:417).

Tamboran: Nettle & Romaine (2000:51).

Nambiquara: Lowe (1999:270).

Tasmanian: Clark (1988), Mühlhäusler (1996:121-28).

Death of Cornish: Dalby (2002:80-83).

Decrease of native Irish speakers: Dalby (2002:110).

Dwindling numbers of Hindustani speakers: Masica (1991:430).

Dr Ammondt's recordings in Latin and Sumerian: Ammondt's own home page, *Dagens Nyheter* 2001-07-04. His releases have, of course, also found their way into the author's own record collection.

Irish in Belfast: *Glot International* 2 (9-10), p 26, and Dónall ó Riagáin (p c).

Revival of Cornish: George & Broderick (1993:645).

BIG AND SMALL LANGUAGES

IN A COMMUNIQUÉ issued in May 1999 by the *Bureau of European and Eurasian Affairs*, part of the USA Department of State, it was stated that *"Norway is in the top rank of nations in the number of books printed per capita, even though Norwegian is one of the world's smallest language groups"*. To Americans, a language whose speakers are a mere five million strong may well seem small. In world terms, however, Norwegian is actually one of the mankind's linguistic giants.

Most estimates regarding the number of languages in the world range from 5 000 to 8 000—let's say 6 000 for the sake of simplicity. Dividing the total number of people in the world (six thousand million) by this figure would then make one million native speakers per language on average. Yet, this is far from being the whole story, for languages are *very* unequal in size.

Speakers of the top 20 languages alone account for more than half of humankind, and the top 100 are mother tongues of well over three quarters. If we disregard these, there thus remain 5 900 languages for the last quarter of the terrestrial population. These languages, then, representing 98% of all languages, are thus each spoken by about around 250 000 people. If on the other hand we group the speakers of the smallest 3 000 languages together, we find that they are no more than 10 million, or less than 0,2% of the world population!

Had the American civil servants responsible for the above quote known that about 98% of all languages have fewer speakers than does Norwegian, it is hardly likely that they would have described it as *"one of the world's smallest language groups"*.

The median speaker number is probably somewhere around 5 000 or 6 000, so languages are smaller than many people think!

SMALL LANGUAGES

Several hundred languages are so small that they are spoken only by a few individuals. The *Ethnologue* classifies 417 languages as "nearly extinct", on the basis of there being "only a few elderly speakers still living". Even so, there certainly are those which are even smaller in terms of number of native speakers, for there are plenty of languages which are used only for ritualistic purposes and other special occasions, and which are not transmitted in the normal way from one generation to the other. These, then, are languages without any native speakers at all.

It is, in other words, not in itself particularly interesting to ask what the smallest language on earth might be, for the only logical possibilities are "no speakers" for a dead language, and "one speaker" for a living language (or two if you believe that that there has to be someone with whom one can converse for a language to be alive). Examples of both can easily be found. Obviously, when a language dies, someone has to be the last to go, and many a language has been documented at a time when there was only one remaining speaker. Instead, a more interesting question to ask is how small a language can be, and yet remain vigorous, in the sense of being used by all generations, and transmitted to children.

This obtains for very few languages with less than 1 000 speakers, and indeed, many languages with far more speakers

Language	Country	Speakers	Remarks
Burumakok	West Papua	≥40	Only limited bilingualism
Araona	Bolivia	87	Increasingly bilingual in Spanish
Awbono	West Papua	≤100	No bilingualism
Tokuni	West Papua	≤100	No bilingualism
Kwer	West Papua	100	
Mvanip	Nigeria	100	Bilingual
Macaguán	Colombia	≥130	Mostly monolingual
Aer	Pakistan	100–200	Only men are bilingual
Cacua	Colombia	150	Many are monolingual, especially children
Ngkâlmpw Kanum	West Papua	150	Bilingual
Ipiko	Papua New Guinea	200	
Yoke	West Papua	200	Very limited bilingualism
Hinukh	Russia	200	Remains the family language and has high prestige
Kumbewaha	Indonesia	250	Multilingual
Kirikiri	West Papua	250	Most are bilingual
Burmeso	West Papua	250	Rather proficient in Indonesian
Kopkaka	West Papua	250	No bilingualism
Tamnim Citak	West Papua	290	

than that are threatened by extinction (see "Biggest moribund languages", pp 56–58). The *Ethnologue* sometimes contains remarks on these matters, and—except for sign languages, for whose speakers there are usually few possibilities and incentives to shift to something else—I was able to find 18 languages with less than 300 speakers (and another 14 with less than 500) which were explicitly labelled "vigorous" or "spoken by people of all ages" or "spoken by children". As can be seen, these languages are highly concentrated to Melanesia and South America.

The fact that many of these groups have limited proficiency in surrounding prestige languages is especially indicative of stability. Obviously, bilingualism is a prerequisite for language shift.

In some cases, however, this claimed lack of bilingualism is puzzling, since inbreeding would normally prevent a population of merely 100–200 individuals from being genetically viable.

BIG LANGUAGES

Biggest languages by number of native speakers: the Top 50 (as of 2005)

Rank	Language name	Speakers	Main country
1.	Mandarin	881 100 000	China
2.	Spanish	378 000 000	Mexico
3.	English	340 800 000	USA
4.	Hindi/Urdu	335 600 000	India
5.	Bengali	208 800 000	Bangladesh
6.	Portuguese	196 800 000	Brazil
7.	Russian	154 700 000	Russia
8.	Japanese	127 300 000	Japan
9.	Panjabi	111 400 000	Pakistan
10.	Nile Arabic	110 700 000	Egypt
11.	German	96 100 000	Germany
12.	Wu	90 400 000	China
13.	Javanese	84 600 000	Indonesia
14.	Telugu	83 300 000	India
15.	Marathi	78 600 000	India
16.	Korean	76 300 000	South Korea
17.	French	74 600 000	France
18.	Vietnamese	74 000 000	Vietnam
19.	Tamil	73 100 000	India
20.	Cantonese	66 200 000	China

THERE ARE SEVERAL POSSIBLE WAYS of estimating the size of a language. What do we really mean by "big" in terms of languages? The most obvious criterion, perhaps, is the number of mother tongue speakers. However, although Mandarin is the biggest language of the planet in terms of native speakers, few people would contest that English is somehow more "important". Obviously, then, there are also other factors which contribute to the international importance of a language. In the following, we shall examine some aspects of how the concept of size can be applied to languages.

21.	Maghreb Arabic	63 800 000	Algeria	36.	Pashto	37 300 000	Pakistan
22.	Turkish	62 900 000	Turkey	37.	Oriya	35 300 000	India
23.	Malay/Indonesian	62 700 000	Indonesia	38.	Hausa	35 200 000	Nigeria
24.	Italian	61 200 000	Italy	39.	Ukrainian	34 900 000	Ukraine
25.	Thai	58 300 000	Thailand	40.	Sunda	32 400 000	Indonesia
26.	Min Nan	56 100 000	China	41.	Bhojpuri	29 100 000	India
27.	Gujarati	51 800 000	India	42.	Yoruba	27 600 000	Nigeria
28.	Jinyu	47 900 000	China	43.	Fula	26 800 000	Nigeria
29.	Persian/Tajiki	45 800 000	Iran	44.	Gan	26 700 000	China
30.	Xiang	41 600 000	China	45.	Burmese	26 300 000	Burma
31.	Kannada	41 200 000	India	46.	Maithili	25 400 000	India
32.	Polish	40 900 000	Poland	47.	Sindhi	25 300 000	Pakistan
33.	Peninsular Arabic	40 800 000	Saudi Arabia	48.	Uzbek	25 200 000	Uzbekistan
34.	Malayalam	39 500 000	India	49.	Azerbaijani	25 200 000	Iran
35.	Hakka	37 300 000	China	50.	Romanian	24 300 000	Romania

Most of the major languages, in particular those which spread as a result of European colonial expansion, are official in countries where they are not spoken natively (in fact, often not spoken at all!) by the majority of the population. Thanks to the demographic weight of India, English has by far the largest number of "official speakers" in the world (an overwhelming majority of Indians, however, do not master English). The following figures indicate the total number of inhabitants (in millions) of the countries having one of ten major languages as their official one(s).

1.	English	2 113	5.	French	317	8.	Portuguese	216
2.	Mandarin	1 303	6.	Arabic	294	9.	Russian	173
3.	Hindi/Urdu	1 175	7.	Malay	255	10.	German	109
4.	Spanish	378						

Of the world's 5 000–8 000 languages, just over 100 have official status in some nation. 25 of these are official in more than one country. English is the official language in no less than 75 states or state-like entities, French in 39, Arabic in 25, Spanish in 21, Portuguese in 8, and German in 6.

It seems normal for a language to have

a proportion of 80%–90% of native (L1) speakers. Among the major world languages, probably only English and French have more secondary users (L2) than native speakers. Some regional lingua francas, however, have a significantly higher share of L2 speakers.

The table below is ordered by proportion of L2 users, and the shading indicates their proportion of the total number of speakers for selected languages (it should be remembered that most of these figures are very uncertain and approximate).

Language	Main region (L2)	L1	L2	L1 + L2	%L2
Kâte	New Guinea	6 125	80 000	86 125	93%
Swahili	East Africa	2 500 894	30 000 000	32 500 894	92%
Krio	Sierra Leone	478 000	4 000 000	4 478 000	89%
Adawama Fulfulde	Cameroon	668 700	4 331 300	5 000 000	87%
Efik	Nigeria	400 000	2 000 000	2 400 000	83%
French	Africa, Europe	74 600 000	200 000 000	274 600 000	73%
Malay	Indonesia	62 700 000	143 000 000	205 700 000	70%
English	Europe, India, Africa	340 800 000	700 000 000	1 040 800 000	67%
Tagalog	Philippines	24 023 936	40 000 000	64 023 936	62%
Wolof	Senegal	4 978 203	3 785 000	8 763 203	43%
Russian	Former Soviet Union	154 700 000	110 000 000	264 700 000	42%
Afrikaans	South Africa	5 885 926	3 619 000	9 504 926	38%
Catalan	Spain	6 876 850	3 435 000	10 311 850	33%
Hindi/Urdu	India, Pakistan	335 600 000	163 000 000	498 600 000	33%
Hausa	Nigeria	35 200 000	14 800 000	50 000 000	30%
Azerbaijani	Azerbaijan, Iran	25 200 000	7 941 000	33 141 000	24%
German	Europe	96 100 000	25 000 000	121 100 000	21%
Arabic	Muslim world	230 000 000	50 000 000	280 000 000	18%
Kannada	India	41 200 000	8 654 000	49 854 000	17%
Mandarin	China	881 100 000	178 000 000	1 059 100 000	17%
Amharic	Ethiopia	21 750 193	3 587 000	25 337 193	14%
Spanish	Americas	378 000 000	45 000 000	423 000 000	11%
Bengali	India, Bangladesh	208 800 000	22 000 000	230 800 000	10%
Tamil	India	73 100 000	8 000 000	81 100 000	10%
Burmese	Burma	26 322 749	3 000 000	29 322 749	10%
Portuguese	Africa, Brazil	196 800 000	20 000 000	216 800 000	9%
Yoruba	Nigeria	27 600 000	2 000 000	29 600 000	7%
Telugu	India	83 300 000	5 334 000	88 634 000	6%
Japanese	?	127 300 000	1 000 000	128 300 000	1%

Under very special circumstances, the percentage of L2 speakers may be exceptionally high. The Urubú-Kaapor sign language of Brazil, for instance, has 7 native speakers, but is reported to be mastered by the entire tribe, which is some 500 strong.

Another way of measuring the importance of a certain language is to consider the number of second language speakers. Obviously, the learner must consider a language important in order to devote time to learning it. Here, we may note a major difference between Mandarin and English. Whereas we just saw that Mandarin has two and a half times as many native speakers as does English, relatively few people outside China have taken the trouble to learn it.

Even more extreme figures, of course, would be obtained by taking into account languages which have few or no native speakers in the first place, such as Latin, classical Arabic, Sanskrit, Esperanto and various pidgin languages.

Irish also comes close to this. Being used alongside English more for reasons of national pride than for communicative efficiency, it is taught to the overwhelming majority of Irish for whom English is the native tongue. Many of these fail to acquire conversational skills in it, but the proportion of L2 speakers is nevertheless thought to be around 97%.

"RICH" LANGUAGES

The strength of a language clearly depends on factors other than the number of speakers. An obvious one is economy. Given that the USA alone is responsible for almost a quarter of the world economy, it is hardly surprising that English rather than Mandarin has become the world's primary lingua franca. The table below combines the GDP of all countries in which a given language is official, listing the 20 "richest" languages.

Interestingly, the English-speaking share of international trade is far smaller. The USA has a huge domestic market and, in particular imports much more than it exports, which makes Anglophone countries responsible for only 24,7% of the world's exports, followed by 13% each for French- and German-speaking nations.

Rank	Language	Economic share	Rank	Language	Economic share
1.	English	42,28%	11.	Hindi	1,69%
2.	Japanese	11,31%	12.	Korean	1,66%
3.	French	9,37%	13.	Russian	1,59%
4.	German	8,30%	14.	Swedish	1,30%
5.	Spanish	5,76%	15.	Malay	1,18%
6.	Mandarin	5,43%	16.	Turkish	0,74%
7.	Italian	4,97%	17.	Norwegian	0,61%
8.	Dutch	2,27%	18.	Danish	0,59%
9.	Portuguese	1,96%	19.	Polish	0,59%
10.	Arabic	1,91%	20.	Greek	0,54%

If we look at things in a historical perspective, English has remained rather stable since the mid-1800s, as the relative decline of one major English-speaking superpower (Britain) coincided with the rise of another (the USA). During the same period, French and German have gone hand in hand downhill, not because the nations using them have become poorer, but because of the arrival of new competitors on the scene. The most salient trends during the past couple of decades are on the one hand the decline of Russian, and on the other hand, the rise of Mandarin.

GLOBAL INFLUENCE

Graddol (1997:59) introduces another interesting measure of the international importance of languages. His figures in the table below (referring to the mid-1990s) are built partly on demographics and economic power, but also take into account "the likelihood that these speakers will enter social networks which extend beyond their locality". The index score of 100 is arbitrarily assigned to the position of English in 1995. One problem, however, with this measurement, is that a Frenchman or a German might insist on using his or her language in these interethnic contacts, whereas a Chinese is unlikely to do so, for the simple reason that their interlocutor, as we have just seen, is unlikely to know Mandarin in the first place.

Language	Graddol score	Graddol revised	Weber
English	100	100	37
French	33	31	23
German	42	13	12
Mandarin	22	6	13
Spanish	31	6	20
Malay	4	5	n/a
Arabic	8	3	14
Russian	3	2	16
Portuguese	5	1	10
Japanese	32	0,5	10
Hindi/Urdu	0,4	0,17	9
Bengali	0,09	0,02	n/a

Graddol's figures could therefore be combined with this likelihood, as measured by the share of L2-speakers given above. This combination is found in the "revised Gradoll" column. A further improvement might result from including the likelihood that the "dominant" speaker in the conversation has the possibility of shifting to the less dominant language. Even Frenchmen and Germans are more polyglot than Americans, thereby further increasing the possibility of English being used in an encounter involving an American.

In addition to the Graddol scores, I have added the numbers from a similar estimate on the global importance of languages presented in Weber (1997).

LANGUAGES IN SCIENCE

During the second half of the 20th century, English defined itself as the language of science *par excellence*. While earlier scholars had to be proficient in several languages in order to keep up with the most recent developments, it is in many scientific fields seen as increasingly eccentric to write (or even read!) in anything but English. The graph below illustrates this development. It shows how the output of scholarly articles within the field of medicine has become totally dominated by English. It is based on articles found in the PubMed bibliography, compiled by the *National Library of Medicine*. Needless to say, "national", means "American", for which reason a slight Anglo-Saxon bias may be expected

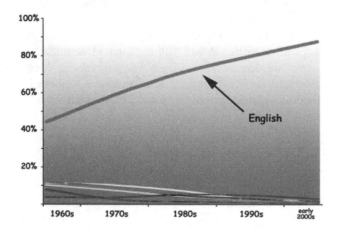

Englisch über alles

In the 1960s (which is as far back in time as the database goes), less than half of all papers were published in English, but by 2001, its share had risen to almost 90%. Three other formerly important languages of science, French, German, and Russian, each represented more than a tenth of the output before 1970, but none nowadays exceeds 2%. The three other languages represented above (apart from "others") are Spanish, Japanese and Italian.

This Anglicization of science is a recent phenomenon which has conquered the world in virtually no time. Graddol (1997:9) illustrates this with the fact that in 1950, the German journal *Zeitschrift für Tierpsychologie* ('Journal for Animal Psychology') was entirely in German. Just over three decades later, 95% of its articles were in English, and in 1986, the journal took account of this by renaming itself *Ethology*.

MEDIA REPRESENTATION: LANGUAGES IN THE PRESS

There exists no complete listing of newspapers and their circulation figures. The following draws on data culled from a large number of sources, including 4 570 daily newspapers, of which I managed to find circulation statistics for 1 112. The resulting list is certainly not complete, but does represent well over half of the about 550 million newspapers consumed daily on our planet.

In all, more than 80 languages are represented (i.e. almost as many as those enjoying official status in a country—but still only a fraction of those actually spoken).

In terms of the number of titles published, English is in the lead with 1 506 titles, followed by German (485), Spanish (330) and French (283). The circulation figures, given below, also put English in a spectacular lead. (The figures are adjusted—i.e. almost doubled—to represent the actual circulation rather than the one found in my incomplete sample).

Rank	Language	Copies/day
1	English	134 300 000
2	Japanese	81 000 000
3	Mandarin	70 000 000
4	French	27 300 000
5	Spanish	24 000 000
6	German	22 700 000
7	Russian	18 800 000
8	Korean	17 400 000
9	Arabic	10 200 000
10	Hindi/Urdu	9 500 000
11	Dutch	7 900 000
12	Turkish	7 900 000
13	Italian	6 500 000
14	Portuguese	5 700 000
15	Ukrainian	5 300 000
16	Malay/Indonesian	4 800 000
17	Bengali	4 600 000
18	Swedish	4 000 000
19	Romanian	3 700 000
20	Polish	3 500 000

English and French share the distinction of being the only languages to have daily newspapers published on all six inhabited continents (Antarctica doesn't have any dailies).

Seen above are French-language papers from Cambodia, Haiti, New Caledonia, Tunisia, Lebanon, Mauritius, Algeria and Canada.

English-language dailies are published in about 100 countries. French, Spanish and Arabic ones in 39, 27 and 23 countries respectively.

LANGUAGES IN BOOKS

The UNESCO statistical yearbook presents annual figures for book publishing, with a breakdown by language. Graddol (1997:9) cites the 1995 figures which are as follows:

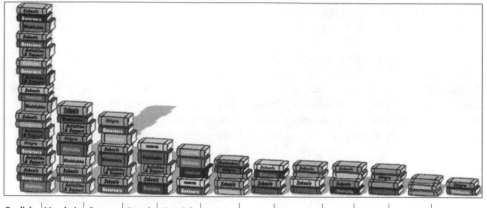

English	Mandarin	German	French	Spanish	Japanese	Russian	Portuguese	Korean	Italian	Dutch	Swedish
28,0%	13,3%	11,8%	7,7%	6,7%	5,1%	4,7%	4,5%	4,4%	4,0%	2,4%	1,6%

LANGUAGES IN FILMS

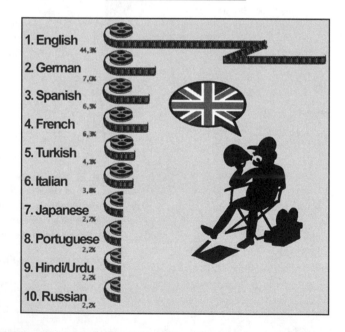

1. English 44,3%
2. German 7,0%
3. Spanish 6,5%
4. French 6,3%
5. Turkish 4,3%
6. Italian 3,8%
7. Japanese 2,7%
8. Portuguese 2,2%
9. Hindi/Urdu 2,2%
10. Russian 2,2%

What do Crow, Esperanto, Guinea-Bissau Creole Portuguese, Klingon, Latin, Lithuanian Sign, Marshallese, Tibetan, Tlingit and Yakut have in common? As opposed to the overwhelming majority of the world's languages, they have been used at least once on the silver screen.

The *Internet Movie Database* contains data on hundreds of thousands of film titles indexed according to a variety of factors, including language. The best represented of these is English (with 156 179 titles or 44,3% of the total), followed by German (7,0%), Spanish (6,5%), and French (6,3%; all three of these having between 20 000 and 25 000 titles). In all, 37 languages are represented by more than 500 titles. While a certain western bias may again be expected (disfavoring e.g. Hindi, Russian, Mandarin, Cantonese, and Japanese), it seems reasonable to assume that more films have been made in English than in any other language.

Perhaps the most important observation that can be made from the film list, however, is that about 98% of the world's languages are not in any way represented!

LANGUAGES ON THE RADIO

Most countries do at least some broadcasting in the languages actually spoken by their inhabitants, even when these enjoy no official status. But which languages are used when broadcasting for an international audience? Most industrialized countries have programming intended for listeners outside the own borders. I examined the language choices of the foreign services of 35 countries. Not unexpectedly, most offer programming in English. In fact, only one country did not, namely Finland. Budget cuts forced the Finns to make a difficult choice, and interestingly, they chose to retain their services in Finnish, Swedish and Russian, and to drop English. 26 of the 35 countries transmit in French (its absence is typical of Asian and Northern European countries, where the position of French is weak), 23 each in Spanish and Russian, 19 in German, 17 in Arabic, and 14 in Portuguese.

Apart from the international languages, several unusual ones are featured, usually as a result of targeting audiences in neighboring countries. It is notable that Romani is used in no less than 11 countries, and that Esperanto transmissions are offered by five. The Vatican Radio, interestingly, claims to broadcast in "Scandinavian".

LANGUAGES ON THE WEB

A couple of more or less ambitious attempts to map the use of different languages on the web have been made since the late 1990s. The one by the French company *Alis Technologies* (1997) and the ones by the American organization *International Technology and Trade Associates* and *Inktomi* provided similar results in that the Anglophone share was immensely dominant. However, a study on the web presence of Romance languages made in 2000 by the *Unión Latina* and the *Fundación Redes-y-Desarrollo* (2000b in the table below), suggested that the proportion of English-language web pages had been overestimated by other researchers, and proposed a much lower (though still impressive) figure of 60% for this language.

In any case, a common feature of most of these studies is that the initial dominance of English is gradually giving way to an increased diversity as the web becomes less American and more international.

Proportion of all web pages

Language	1997	1998	1999	2000a	2000b	2001a	2001b	2002
English	82,3%	71%	72%	86,5%	60%	68,4%	52,0%	72%
German	4,0%	7%	7%	5,8%	6,3%	5,8%	7,0%	7%
Japanese	1,6%	4%	3%	0,3%		5,9%		6%
French	1,5%	3%	3%	2,4%	4,4%	3,0%	4,6%	3%
Spanish	1,1%	3%	3%	1,2%	4,9%	2,4%	5,7%	3%
Mandarin		1%	2%			3,9%		2%
Italian	0,8%	1%	2%	1,6%	2,8%	1,6%	3,1%	2%
Portuguese	0,7%	2%	2%	0,8%	2,1%	1,4%	2,8%	1%
Korean		1%				1,3%		1%
Russian	0,1%		1%			1,9%		1%
Dutch	0,4%	1%	1%	0,5%				2%
Swedish	0,6%		1%	0,4%				
Finnish	0,3%		1%	0,5%				

Share of world online population

	2001	2002	2004
English	47,5%	40,2%	35,8%
Sinitic lgs	9,0%	9,8%	14,1%
Japanese	8,6%	9,2%	9,6%
Spanish	4,5%	7,2%	9,0%
German	6,1%	6,8%	7,3%
Korean	4,4%	4,4%	4,1%
French	3,7%	3,9%	3,8%
Italian	3,1%	3,6%	3,3%
Portuguese	2,5%	2,6%	3,5%

There is also a survey of the languages spoken by the web users, provided (and regularly updated) by marketing communications consultancy *Global Reach*. The 2001, 2002 and 2004 figures (from March in each case) are provided to the left in order to highlight the current trend—the internet users get less and less Anglophone as more and more non-American users get connected.

OFFICIAL LANGUAGES OF INTERNATIONAL ORGANIZATIONS

On the page opposite, yet another way of illustrating the international importance of various languages is given. A number of intergovernmental organizations are listed, followed by a couple of randomly chosen international organizations with individuals, rather than states, as their members. For each organization, the number of participating countries is given, along with the official languages of the organizations in question.

In addition to the major languages listed in the table opposite, the European Union has bestowed official status also on the other official languages of its member states (pp 47–48), while Rotary International has done the same for Finnish, Swedish, and Korean.

In the United Nations—the most international organization there is—language usage during the 203 UNESCO meetings held in 2000 was documented by Kudryavtsev & Ouedraogo (2003). The following percentages indicate the proportion of meetings in which a given language was used:

Language	%
English	98,5%
French	93,6%
Spanish	25,6%
Arabic	11,8%
Russian	6,4%
Mandarin	3,0%

Studying the minutes for a number of UN sessions during the first few years of the 21st century, one notices that out of the six official UN languages, the delegates from more than half (56%) of the 191 countries concerned preferred to speak in English. 18% used mainly French, 11% mostly Spanish, while 9% chose Arabic. Delegates from nine countries, or 5% expressed themselves first and foremost in Russian, whereas only China stuck to Mandarin (Taiwan has not so far been allowed to become a member of the United Nations).

The World Health Organization, another United Nations body, lets its member states choose the language in which they want to receive the WHO proceedings. In the late 1990s, 71% chose English, 29% French, 12% Spanish, 11% Arabic, 6% Russian and 1% Mandarin (some states requested the documents in more than one language).

Table abbreviations:

English	French	Spanish
German	Arabic	Portuguese
Russian	Japanese	Italian
Mandarin		

Organization		E	F	S	G	A	P	R	J		M
International Olympic Committee	199	E	F								
International Telecommunication Union	189	E	F	S?							
United Nations (official languages)	189	E	F	S		A		R			M
United Nations (working languages)	189	E	F								
Universal Postal Union	189		F								
International Monetary Fund	183	E									
World Intellectual Property Organization	177	E	F	S	G			R	J		
Interpol	177	E	F	S		A					
International Committee of the Red Cross	175	E	F								
International Labour Organization	174	E	F	S	G	A		R			M
International Fund for Agricultural Development	162	E	F	S		A					
World Organization for Animal Health	156	E	F	S							
World Customs Organization	156	E	F								
World Trade Organization	140	E	F	S							
World Tourism Organization	138	E	F	S				R			
International Air Transport Association	133	E	F	S							
Commonwealth of Nations	53	E									
Organization of African Unity	51	E	F			A	P				

		E	F	S	G	A	P	R	J	I
Council of Europe (working languages)	40	E	F		G			R		I
Council of Europe (official languages)	40	E	F							
Organization of American States	35	E	F	S			P			
OECD	30	E	F							
European Union (official languages)	24	E	F	S	G		P			I
European Union (working languages)	24	E	F							
Secretariat of the Pacific Community	22	E	F							
Arab League	22					A				
Asia-Pacific Economic Cooperation	21	E								
Common Market for Eastern and Southern Africa	20	E	F				P			
NATO	19	E	F							
OPEC	11	E								
ASEAN	10	E								
G7/G8 Group	8	E	F							
West African Monetary Union	8		F							
Rotary International	n/a	E	F	S	G		P		J	I
Int'l Federation of Oto-Rhino-Laryngological Societies	n/a	E	F	S	G				J	
Amnesty International	n/a	E	F	S		A				
International Leprosy Association	n/a	E	F	S						
International Pediatric Association	n/a	E	F	S						
World Blind Union	n/a	E	F	S						
International Naturist Federation	n/a	E	F		G					
International Ski Instructors Association	n/a	E	F		G					
Inter-Parliamentary Union	n/a	E	F							

LANGUAGE SIZE IN THE PAST

It is probable that the number of languages on earth has remained relatively constant throughout most of mankind's history, despite the fact that the world population has increased dramatically. Before the advent of agriculture (the factor mainly responsible for this increase), humans were hunter-gatherers and lived in very small communities, and a normal language may well have had only a couple of hundred speakers. Unfortunately, though, that period is too distant for us to make any certain statements.

For some languages, it is possible to reconstruct the approximate number of speakers in a less remote past. The table below gives the estimated number of speakers (in millions) for six major languages.

The development of the geographic distribution is also interesting. In the 1850s, the USA surpassed Britain as the world's biggest Anglophone nation, and ever since then there have been more native speakers of English outside Europe than on the British Isles. The European share of the total Anglophone population has continued to shrink, and now represents less than a fifth of the total. Spanish and Portuguese turned into predominantly New World languages as early as in the mid- and late 1700s respectively, and have gone

Year	English	French	Spanish	Portuguese	Japanese	Korean
1550	3,1	12,3	6,7	1,2		
1600	4,4	14,5	7,2	1,5		
1650	5,8	16,1	6,4	1,8		
1700	6,1	16,1	6,5	2,2		
1750	7,9	19,3	9,5	3,6	25,7	
1800	16,9	22,4	17,5	6,2	26,1	
1850	44,1	32,6	28,6	11,0	26,5	
1900	110,0	41,2	52,7	22,0	43,2	12,2
1950	198,0	52,0	130,0	57,8	82,0	32,4
2000	340,0	77,0	340,0	175,0	125,0	78,0

even further in this direction than has English. Today, well over 90% of their speakers reside in Latin America. The number of speakers of Spanish has increased more than sixfold during the past century, due mainly to the high birth rates in Latin America.

Note that the above figures include what we at least now would call "dialects", so the figures for English, for instance, include Scots (but not, of course, Scots Gaelic). Similarly, the figures for French include all Oïl dialects (but not Occitan). Creoles are excluded in all cases. This may lead to a slight overestimate. For instance, at the time of the French revolution plenty of dialect-speaking Frenchmen were incapable of using standard French, according to the contemporary investigator Abbé Grégoire.

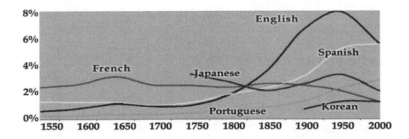

In about 1950, about 8% of the world's population was English-speaking, which is the highest proportion reached by any of these languages. It fails to compare, however, with Mandarin, whose native speakers currently make up around 15% of the world population. Might this be the greatest proportion ever achieved by a single language?

FUTURE SIZE OF LANGUAGES

PREDICTIONS ARE ALWAYS difficult to make, especially, they say, when they're concerned with the future. What seems reasonably certain is that big languages will continue to encroach upon smaller ones. The smaller languages are thus becoming fewer and fewer, while the big ones keep getting bigger.

Linguists interested in these issues often lament the decreasing linguistic diversity which is the result. Regardless of our feelings about it, the diversity sure is on its way out. Metrics

But just how big will the big languages be in, say, another 50 years? David Graddol (1997:27) has made an attempt to answer this question, and his estimate of the number of speakers is given below. I decided to also contribute my own modest proposal, and this is given alongside Graddol's numbers. My figures are the result of a combination of the United Nations' demographic prediction combined with my own assessment of the future linguistic situation in the world's countries.

For the sake of completeness, I am also including Otero's (1999) numbers for the three languages he considered. As can be deduced from the huge differences between Otero's results and mine, I am rather sceptical of his figures. No doubt, history will prove me right. . .

GLOBAL ESTIMATE FOR 2050:

	Language	Parkvall	Graddol	Otero	Present number
1.	Mandarin	1 121 000 000	1 304 000 000		881 100 000
2.	Hindi/Urdu	662 000 000	556 000 000		335 600 000
3.	Spanish	555 000 000	486 000 000	537 600 000	**378 000 000**
4.	Arabic	490 000 000	482 000 000		250 000 000
5.	English	432 000 000	508 000 000	854 600 000	**340 800 000**
6.	Bengali	328 000 000	229 000 000		208 800 000
7.	Portuguese	262 000 000	248 000 000		196 800 000
8.	Panjabi	205 000 000			111 400 000
9.	Malay/Indonesian	152 000 000	80 000 000		62 700 000
10.	Russian	136 000 000	132 000 000		154 700 000
11.	Marathi	117 000 000			78 600 000
12.	Telugu	117 000 000			83 300 000
13.	Vietnamese	113 000 000			74 000 000
14.	Tamil	104 000 000			73 100 000
15.	Japanese	104 000 000	108 000 000		127 300 000
16.	Turkish	90 000 000			62 900 000
17.	French	85 000 000	76 000 000	223 500 000	**74 600 000**
18.	Korean	85 000 000			76 300 000
19.	German	84 000 000	91 000 000		96 100 000
20.	Javanese	80 000 000			84 600 000

Based on the above, it would seem (at least so far as the major languages are concerned) that Hindi/Urdu and Malay/Indonesian merit the title of being the *fastest-growing languages* in the world. Malay is assimilating plenty of languages in Indonesia, and Hindi/Urdu-speaking states are responsible for an disproportionate share of India's population growth.

LANGUAGE-BASED INTERNATIONAL ORGANIZATIONS

I t could be argued that the Commonwealth of Nations (Britain and its former colonies) or the Arab League are organizations based to a large extent on a sense of linguistic belong- ing, but neither defines language as a criterion for membership. Indeed, the Commonwealth in 1995 accepted (after some hesitation) non-Anglophone Mozambique as a member.

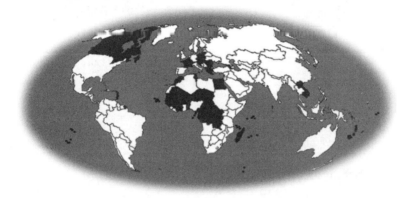

Francophonie members (including observer states).

The world's biggest inter-governmental linguistic organization is the *Francophonie* (founded in 1970 as the *Agence de coopération culturelle et technique*) headed by former U N secretary-general Boutros Boutros-Ghali. The organization has 46 independent member countries, four "associate members", and ten countries with an observer status, together representing almost a quarter of the world's countries, and well over 700 million people. Being an association of countries wanting to promote the use of French, *Francophonie* membership is based on linguistic criteria. At least in theory. Certain unnamed countries with—to say the least—a moderate degree of Francophone past or present may reasonably be expected to partake in order to improve their chances of foreign aid from France, Belgium, Switzerland, or Canada. In fourteen of the states with full membership, French is not even an official language, let alone spoken by the inhabitants.

When in 2004, Greece decided to attend Francophonie meetings (albeit only as an observer), this was generally perceived not as an attempt to benefit economically, but rather as a protest against Anglo-American world dominance.

A similar, but smaller, organization of Portuguese-speaking countries, the *Comunidade dos Países de Língua Portuguesa* (CPLP), was founded in 1989. Its members are Angola, Brazil, Cape Verde, Guinea-Bissau, Mozambique, Portugal, and São Tomé-Príncipe, with newly independent East Timor having observer status.

Also similar in scope and mission, though not devoted to one single language (but rather a group of languages) is the "Romance club" *Unión Latina*, which groups together some 36 countries, mainly in Latin America.

CPLP logo

At least two other transnational networks of this type exist, namely for speakers of Dutch (participants from eight countries) and Turkic languages (with representatives from six states).

Flag of the Arab league

The Arab League, founded in 1945, has 23 member states with 250 million inhabitants, but focuses generally on cultural—rather than a specifically linguistic—sense of belonging.

GROSS OVERESTIMATIONS OF THE OWN LANGUAGE'S SIZE

In a press release from the Turkish prime minister in 1997, it was claimed that Turkish was spoken by some 200 million people, making the language the seventh most widely spoken in the world. Since then, this figure has been repeated in a variety of official Turkish publications and governmental home pages, with the rank often given as sixth.

More balanced accounts talk about slightly more than 60 000 000 native speakers of Turkish, which would make it the world's 22nd language in terms of speakers. Its closest relatives can muster another seven million, and the more distantly related languages yet another 83 million. Taken together, the total number of speakers of all Turkic languages only barely surpasses 150 million (although treating them all as Turkish would be comparable to saying that the mother tongue of Germans, Dutch and Norwegians is English), so it really is a mystery how the

Turkish government's figure was reached.

In order to further impress us, the homepage of the Turkish embassy in the United States states that the Turkish language "goes back 5 500 years, and perhaps even 8 500" and that it furthermore has "a flawless phonetic, morphological and syntactic structure, and at the same time possesses a wealth of vocabulary". Wow!

Needless to say, not a word is said about the existence of minorities speaking languages other than Turkish in Turkey.

It must be admitted, though, that in terms of curious calculus, the Turkish government is outperformed by the Queens College of New York. Presumably in order to attract students to its courses in American Sign, the college's home page proclaimed that "American Sign Language (ASL) is the third most used language in the world today". As mentioned on p 127, ASL may well be the third largest language of the United States, but some of the more than 6 000 million non-Americans on the planet might not agree that the USA equals the world.

While not concerned with their own language, the newspaper report in Sweden's most influential daily *Dagens Nyheter* on November 27, 2004 illustrates a tendency among Swedes to be "holier than the pope" when it comes to overestimating the size and significance of English. The article happily explains that English has now become the mother tongue of some forty million Indian citizens. In fact, the latest available census figures (considered reasonably reliable by most independent observers) at the time gave the number at around 178 000, which means that the *Dagens Nyheter* estimate is exaggerated to the extent of being about 225 times greater than the true figure!

A final example is the radio station which in the early 1940s gave the number of speakers of Swahili as 180 million, seemingly not reflecting on the fact that the entire population of Africa at the time was only 160 million (of whom the overwhelming majority, then as now, knew not a word of Swahili).

WORLD LANGUAGES

THE MAPS BELOW show the geographic distribution of the most widespread languages on earth, the only ones which could lay claim to world language status. The black areas represent the countries in which the language in question is official, which does not necessarily imply that it is spoken natively.

There is little doubt that English has won a decisive victory in the struggle of world primacy, and it has attained a status not approached by any other language in human history. It remains to be seen whether this situation will last forever. Throughout history, prestigious lingua francas have declined as the powers that spread them have disintegrated. Now, here is one of the secrets behind the success of English—when Britain ceased to be the most powerful nation on earth, its successor in this role also happened to be English-speaking. A weakening of American economical, cultural and military power would thus seem to be the prerequisite for the displacement of English as the most important vehicle of communication on our planet. Nevertheless, one might speculate whether this would suffice. In cases such as when Latin was the prestige language in Europe, its use was confined to the élite, and most ordinary people didn't even have a smattering of it. Without a solid demographic base, it is difficult for a language to maintain its dominant position. English, on the other hand, is increasingly being learned even by people with only moderate exposure to formal education. This also happens all over the planet, which dwarfs the risk of replacement by invasion from some other part of the world. Therefore, even if the rapid economic growth in East Asia should turn Europe and North America into sleepy backwaters, English might yet retain its current position.

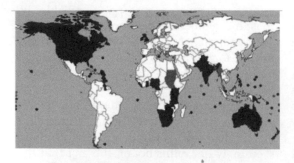

English

English is without doubt the most important international lingua franca of our time. Including second-language speakers, it could well be the most spoken language of our planet. Given the geographical spread, and the demographic, economic, cultural, and military power backing English, it seems unlikely that this position would be threatened in the near future.

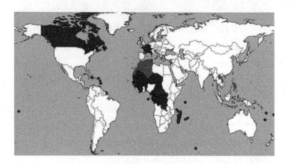

French

Given its important (though decreasing) role as a world language, French has a surprisingly small number of native speakers, and it relies heavily on auxiliary users. On the other hand, it is geographically more widely spread than any other language, except English, though its position in Asia is weak. A world language on the decline, French still remains a giant in the international arena.

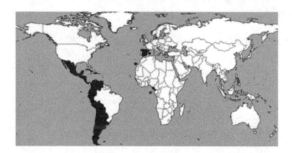

Spanish

Spanish has now passed English as the second biggest language of the world in terms of mother-tongue speakers. As opposed to French, its rival as the second world language, the importance of Spanish is growing. The main disadvantage in contrast to French, however, is its geographical concentration in just one area—Latin America.

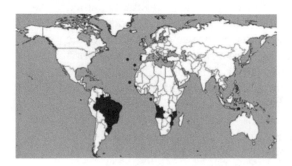

Portuguese

Except for its role as a colonial lingua franca in the 16th and 17th centuries, Portuguese has neither tried nor succeeded in establishing itself as a world language proper. Yet, Brazil is a potential economic giant, and the countries in which Portuguese is used have a tight network to promote it. Of interest, though of negligible political importance, is the existence of various Lusophone groups in several parts of Asia where Portuguese is not official.

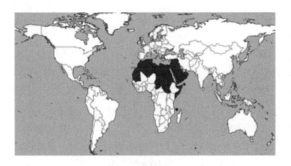

Arabic

As the language of Islam, Arabic is important far beyond the countries in which it is official. Contrary to English and French, however, it has played a minor political role as an international language.

Finally, it may be worth pointing out that English has not yet ousted all the world's other languages, though some seem to hold this belief . . . :

PERCEIVING ENGLISH AS THE ONE AND ONLY FOREIGN LANGUAGE

In Congo-Brazzaville, all teaching is in French. Twelve-year-old Kacharel Bitoutikila says he doesn't find speaking French very difficult, though writing presents some problems. When asked about what he would like to do in the future, Kacharel has a ready reply: he would most of all like to learn English, the language which would enable him to travel abroad. "Preferably to France", says Kacharel in perfect French. When worried by the expression on the reporter's face, he adds "...or maybe Canada?".

WORLD LANGUAGE OR LOCAL LINGO?

In 1966, *National Geographic*'s reporter Bern Keating paid a visit to the Francophone southern Louisiana. In the town of Lafitte, he baffled a crowd by addressing them in French. "I could not have stopped the conversation quicker by firing a ten-gauge shotgun into the crowd", writes Keating. How could he speak French, the local fishermen wondered—after all, he obviously wasn't from Lafitte. "Oh, man", Keating replied, "people speak French in lots of places besides Lafitte". After having considered this fact, one of them thoughtfully commented: "Yeah, I guess you're right. Lafayette, Houma, Thibodeaux, all them Loozeean places, folks speak French, so they tell me".

SOURCES NOT MENTIONED IN THE TEXT

Numbers of native speakers are based on Parkvall (n d; for major languages) and the *Ethnologue* (in other cases).

Proportion of L2 speakers: *World Almanac*, p 578, the *Ethnologue*, David Dalby's *Linguasphere Register*, WIPO (2000), Weber (1997), author's own estimates.

L2 speakers of Irish: Dónall ó Riagáin (p c), Irish 2002 census.

Rich languages: GDP figures (for 2004) from the World Bank. Countries with more than one official language are included in the sum for all these languages. Historical

GDP figures from Angus Maddison are available at www.eco.rug.nl/~Maddison (2005-08-01).

Languages in films: Internet Movie Database (http://imdb.com, accessed 2005-02-12).

Web language surveys: 1997 figures from http://babel.alis.com/palmares.fr.html (Alis Technologies survey). The 1998 figures from O'Neill, Lavoie & McClain (1998). 1999 and 2002 figures from O'Neill, Lavoie and Bennett (2003). The two *Unión Latina* surveys: http://funredes.org/LC. Inktomi results (2001a), only partially available from their own site (!) are also cited from this source. International Technology and Trade Associates figures from http://usic.wslogic.com/intro.html. Global reach survey: www.euromktg .com/globstats/. 2001b figures from emarketer.com (but originally from the Catalan organization Vilaweb).

Official languages of international organizations: Information material from the respective organization, plus some additional data from WIPO (2000).

The language count in UN meetings was done by myself based on the organization's official minutes.

Language use in the WHO from World Health Organization (1999:4).

Past size of languages: These data are derived mainly from numbers provided by Jan Lahmeyer's *Population Statistics* page at www.library.uu.nl/wesp/populstat/populhome.html (2002-06-20). Korean and Japanese were chosen mainly because they have both (for most of their history) been spoken mainly in one single country, and both Japan and the Koreas are also virtually monolingual. For the (originally!) European languages I have made rather complex calculations involving all countries where they have (or have had, in the case of French in North Africa) significant numbers of native speakers. I have also tried to include the gradual assimilation of minorities, such as Occitan, Irish and Amerindian languages. Lack of reliable demographic data and information on historic language shifts prevented me from including e.g. Chinese and Indian languages.

Abbé Grégoire on the speech of Frenchmen: Dalby (2002:26).

Details on language-based international organizations from the respective organizations, and Breton (2000).

Overestimation of language sizes: The Queens College page, www.qc.edu/CEP/la500.htm (2003-04-22), claimed American Sign to be the third most spoken language in the world until mid-2005. The same wording continued to be used by the New York City College of Technology (www.citytech.cuny.edu/files/academics/cscbulletin.pdf (2005-08-21). As mentioned in the text, the Turkish claim to 200 million speakers is found in a large number of sources, of which the earliest known to me is a press release from the *Directorate general of press and information*, of the office of the Turkish prime minister, issue the 15th of September 1997. Overestimation of Swahili: Pei (1942:53).

The interview with Kacharel Bifoutikila was published in *Dagens Nyheter* 2001-07-11. Amazed Cajuns from Keating (1966:353-54).

LANGUAGE CHANGE

MANY NON-LINGUISTS BELIEVE that a—or even *THE*—principal occupation of linguists is the tracing of ancient etymologies, that is "from what word Y does our word X originally stem?" This is not the main concern of today's linguists, although one thing which linguists do study is how (and why) languages (including words) change through time. For change they do, regardless of frequent popular outrage over new usages.

YOUNGEST LANGUAGES

For virtually all the world's languages, there isn't really a birthdate. Even though we consider, say, French a daughter of Latin, there is no point in time when we can claim that Latin ceased being spoken in Gaul, and when French began. The development from Latin to French was gradual, and in one sense, the difference between the two is mostly a matter of terminology. Greek, for instance, has, despite changes, been known under this name since long before Latin developed into French.

However, apart from pidgins (makeshift interethnic varieties) and constructed languages (see pp 157–64), there are a few languages for which we can say that before the year so-and-so, this language definitely did not exist. These are creoles (nativized pidgins) and intertwined ("mixed") languages. Most known creoles emerged several centuries ago, but some turned into mother tongues only around 1900 or even later, and along with natively spoken Esperanto, these can therefore be said to be the youngest native languages there are. In addition to these, there are also a few modern sign languages for which the origin can be pinpointed.

The following seven all emerged as community languages in the late 19th or early 20th centuries. Two of them—Nicaraguan Sign and Gurindji Kriol—were even born in the late 20th century!

Language	Language type	Area
Australian and Melanesian creoles	English-lexicon creoles	Australia, Melanesia
Chinook Jargon	Chinook-lexicon creole	USA & Canada
Hawaiian Creole	English-lexicon creole	Hawaii
Kinubi	Arabic-lexicon creole	Kenya, Uganda
Media Lengua	Quechua-Spanish intertwiner	Ecuador

Sango	Ngbandi-lexicon creole	Central African Republic
Nicaraguan Sign	Sign language	Nicaragua
Al-Sayyid Bedouin Sign	Sign language	Southern Israel
Gurindji Kriol	Gurindji-Kriol intertwiner	Australia

Some of these enjoyed an exceptionally short career. Natively spoken Chinook Jargon is already extinct, and Hawaiian Creole is rapidly retreating before the onslaught of English.

Modern Israeli Hebrew—to the extent that it is different from Biblical Hebrew—can also be viewed as a young language. The first native speaker is believed to have been born in 1882, and for the most part, the language was nativized between 1890 and 1914. In 1904, only a couple of dozen people were native speakers, but around the time of the First World War, they numbered tens of thousands, and three quarters of the younger Jews in Palestine indicated Hebrew as their first or only language.

"Lithuanian is said to be Europe's oldest language", this Swedish newspaper clip proclaims. The misconception has presumably arisen because Lithuanian is highly conservative, and it is thought to be more faithful to its Indo-European origins than most of its sisters are. Yet, with the exception of pidgins, creoles, intertwined and artificial languages, calling any one language older than another is simply nonsensical.

DEVELOPING INTO YOUR OWN OPPOSITE

The most obvious and visible changes in language are lexical: words are borrowed from neighboring languages and the meaning of words may be changed over time. In some cases, cumulative change can take the word quite a long way away from where it started. The original and the current meaning may even be opposites of one another (see Janus words, pp 205–06).

This is the case of *silly* in English. It is related to *soul*, and once meant such things as 'pious', 'innocent' and 'blessed'. Now, someone who puts his faith in God can be seen as 'feeble' (and who isn't in comparison to the Almighty?), and from there, the word went to 'feeble-minded', and even 'foolish' or 'stupid'. Meanwhile, another word, *nice*, drifted in very much the opposite direction. It is first attested as 'foolish' or 'stupid', but went via 'strange' and 'extravagant' to 'elegant' to today's 'pleasant' and 'agreeable'.

The Indo-European root **bhel-* meant things like 'to shine, to flash, to burn, to be white', etc. Given the 'shiny' meaning, it is not surprising that one of its descendants in English is *bald*. Its associations with fire, however, gave rise to a Germanic form **blakaz* 'burned'. When things burn, one frequent result is that they become black, and hence *black*—a perfect opposite of one of the original meanings! Incidentally, *blaze, blank,* and—perhaps more unexpectedly—*flagrant* are other English words derived from this root.

BIZARRE SOUND CHANGE

Historical linguistics is much concerned with sound changes (albeit to a lesser extent these days than when the subdiscipline was still young) that is, what became of a given sound when proto-X developed into X.

Sound changes are sometimes predictable. The development from, say, /an/ to /ã/, or /ti/ to /tʃi/ are—mostly for reasons of human anatomy—highly predictable, and no competent historical linguist would be surprised by learning that such a sound change has occurred in a given language family.

Some of the most unexpected sound changes known to me have taken place in Samoyedic languages. Examples include */w/ → /q/, */j/→ /q/, */V/ → /ŋgV/, and even */s/ → /k/ before /e/ and /i/. (This of course, presupposes that the proto-forms are correctly reconstructed).

MOST STABLE VOCABULARY ITEMS

In Indo-European lexico-statistical comparisons, the items most resistant to replacement have proven to be *we, I, five, four, three, two, who*. The least stable item on the Swadesh 200 list (see pp 101–03) is, by quite some margin, *dirty*.

Dolgopolsky (1986) examined a number of lexical items in languages of Europe and Asia, and in his sample, *me* was the most stable item. It had been replaced in none of the languages examined, while *dead* had been replaced in about a quarter.

NAUGHTIEST GRAMMATICALIZATION

To the best of my knowledge, only one language has grammaticalized the word for 'penis'. The Ancient Egyptian *m-b3ḥ*, glossed as 'at, in the phallus' became a locative preposition meaning 'in the presence of (respected personalities)'. The same source also mentions the development of *ha-* 'vagina' into a preposition 'in' in the Oregonian language Takelma.

Bulgarian has grammaticalized *kur* (or *xuy*) 'penis' into a negator, but its use remains stylistically marked.

RAPID LANGUAGE CHANGE

It is reported that in a mere 50-year period in the mid-20th century, the Muyuw language of Woodlark Island off New Guinea underwent some rather spectacular changes, including replacement of 13% of the core vocabulary, and a change in word order from GEN N to N GEN (that is, from something like *Mary's apple* to *apple Mary's*). In most languages with a well-documented past, such far-reaching changes usually take between a couple of centuries and a millennium.

Dixon (1997:79) also reports that Irish went through an exceptionally rapid development between the years 400 and 600, but this claim appears to be controversial.

In Australia, certain Aboriginal languages have changed dramatically under the pressure of English in just one or two generations. Among speakers of Tiwi, used on Bathurst and Melville islands off the coast of northern Australia, younger and older speakers are reported to have problems understanding one another.

In some cases, parts of the lexicon are replaced at a faster rate than would be expected. For various reasons (usually having to do with reverence for a diseased person), lexical items are tabooed and must be replaced. When, say, Jean passes away, a new name must be found (through borrowing or coining) for the blue canvas trousers. In some cultures, not only the name of the deceased cannot be used, but also all similar words—in the hypothetical case, then, we'd have to get new words also for, say, *dean* and *bean*. This type of lexical renewal is a nuisance for historical linguists especially those working on Australian, south-western New Guinean, and Greenlandic languages.

CONSERVATIVE LANGUAGES

For most of the world's languages, we simply know very little about their history (and in many cases even about their genetic relationship to others). The degree of conservatism can therefore not really be assessed. Among European languages, however, Lithuanian is probably the candidate most often mentioned. While both surviving Baltic languages are highly archaic in character, most observers tend to agree that Latvian is slightly less so than Lithuanian. Other frequently mentioned European languages are Icelandic and Sardinian (particularly the Logudorese variety), which are unusually similar to their respective mothers, Old Norse and Latin.

Similar cases are found outside Indo-European. We may note that a contemporary speaker of Georgian is able to read (albeit with some effort), texts from the 8th and 9th centuries, something that would be quite impossible for an Englishman.

Again, outside of the areas where languages have a long written tradition, such comparisons are difficult to make, though Anttila (1972:381) notes that both Turkic and Austronesian languages in general have changed more slowly than Indo-European.

TELLY-INDUCED LANGUAGE CHANGE

The studies which have been made on the subject (e.g. Chambers 1998) usually conclude that language use in the media has a relatively minor impact on everyday speech. However, Ross (1995; cited in Graddol 1997:47) has studied how 'hello' is translated into Italian when American films are dubbed. The normal Italian translation would be either *buongiorno* or *ciao*, depending on the degree formality required. However, neither of those matches the lip movements of 'hello' very well, and therefore, *salve* has become substituted for the more common equivalents. After extensive televised use, this greeting has now caught on, and young Italians are now said to use it more spontaneously than before.

REDUCTION

It is a well-known fact in historical linguistics that words tend to get shorter through time. The more times you utter a word, the more predictable it gets, and the less effort you need to put into your utterance, and so on. Even though this is a universal tendency, some words in some languages are more severely mutilated than others. One of my favourites in this case is French—a daughter language of Latin. The following table displays a number of French words which are considerably shorter—to say the least!—than their Latin counterparts:

Latin	French	Meaning
augustum	/u(t)/ (août)	August
altum	/o/ (haut)	high
sigillum	/so/ (sceau)	seal
vitellum	/vo/ (veau)	calf
avunculum	/ɔ̃k(l)/ (oncle)	uncle
undecim	/ɔ̃z/ (onze)	eleven
bellum	/bo/ (beau)	beautiful
sanctum	/sɛ̃/ (saint)	holy

Latin	French	Meaning
gagatem	/ʒɛ/ (jais)	jet
securum	/syʁ/ (sûr)	safe, secure
aquam	/o/ (eau)	water
jejunum	/ʒœ̃/ (jeun)	fast
insulam	/il/ (île)	island
calidum	/ʃo/ (chaud)	hot
oculum	/øj/ (œil)	eye

Given that French spelling still—for the most part—reflects a medieval pronunciation, French words tend to contain more graphemes than morphemes. Those who have studied Latin may want to ponder a while on how the Romans would have spelt /ʒwɛ/, i.e. '(they) played' (which the French still persist in spelling jouaient, with five vowels in a row!). Another nice example from the same language is the verb paradigm for the verb 'to have' (habere in Latin, avoir in French):

Latin	French	Meaning
habeo	/e/ (ai)	I have
habes	/a/ (as)	You have
habet	/a/ (a)	He/she/it has

Latin	French	Meaning
habemus	/avɔ̃/ (avons)	We have
habetis	/ave/ (avez)	You have
habent	/ɔ̃/ (ont)	They have

Among other natural candidates to the most-extreme-reduction title, Danish and Cheyenne are obvious choices. Cheyenne has turned a reconstructed Proto-Algonquian *peponwi* 'winter' into *a'a* in just a millennium and a half. With its 1 500 speakers, it is a threatened language, so we will never know, but one cannot help wondering how the Cheyennes might express the season in question in another couple of centuries. Meanwhile, Danish has turned 'week' (from proto-Germanic *wīkon*) into [uə]. The evidence below should speak for itself (although it may appear shocking to sensitive readers):

Spoken Danish	Written Danish	English
øːu̯ ʌ ɔːu̯ øːu̯ʌ ʌːi̯ ʌ øːʌ i Dʔː	*Ove og Åge øver øje og øre i år*	Ove and Åge train their eyes and ears this year.
i ɔːʔʌ aʌ øʔʌ ʌu̯ʌ ʌ ɔʔʌ aʔʌ aʌ bʁoʔʌ̥	*I åer er øer, og over åer er broer*	In rivers, there are islands, and over rivers, there are bridges.
ɛːʌæ aị̯ʌ Dːʌ æ eʔ	*Eva ejer årer af eg*	Eve owns ores of oak.

Although I am uncertain as to the representativeness of this example, it is difficult to leave out the Irish rendition of 'I won't get'. Now, written Irish would have this as *Ní bhfaighfidh*, which is fair enough. But the second word in this sentence is phonetically realized as—[wiː].

SOME INDIVIDUALS WHO HAVE HAD A DISPROPORTIONATE INFLUENCE ON LANGUAGE DEVELOPMENT

LANGUAGES AND LANGUAGE SITUATIONS change all the time, but in most cases no single individual can be held responsible for the changes. There are few cases, however, of individuals making a decisive impact on language use. Here are a few examples.

JOHANNES AAVIK

Attempts at radically changing the way in which people speak their mother tongue are usually moderately successful at best. The changes brought about in Estonian by Johannes Aavik (1880–1973), however, is an unusual case of spectacular success.

His language renewal started in 1905 as a part of the standardization of Estonian as a written language. The goal was twofold: there was on the one hand a desire to extend the language's repertoire, and to adapt it to a new era, but the proposed changes also had nationalistic overtones—Estonian should be freed from some of the influences of other languages, mainly German and Russian.

Aavik proposed numerous new lexical items and morphological devices, some inspired by Estonian dialects, others by faraway languages such as Japanese. Yet others were simply invented by Aavik, without any foreign or dialectal prototype whatsoever. The process also included Aavik publishing advertisements where he promised a reward for any proposal that appealed to him.

About 800 of Aavik's words are said to remain in everyday usage (such as *relv* 'weapon', *laip* 'corpse', *roim* 'crime', *veenma* 'to persuade' and *reetma* 'to betray'), including 16 of his artificial words. Perhaps most remarkable, however, is the rapid change

Johannes Aavik

from a word order partly patterned on German to one that was felt to be more authentically Estonian. In the early 20th century, it was common to place auxiliaries clause-finally. Aavik's recommendation to avoid this was highly successful, and the German-influenced pattern is now considerably rarer than it used to be. Aavik also preferred a strict adherence to SVO word order, but in comparison to e.g. Finnish, Estonian still displays a high proportion of sentences with the typically Germanic verb-second order.

BROR REXED

Swedish has traditionally, like most other European languages except modern English, made a distinction between one second person singular pronoun used with equals and in intimate relations (like French *tu* and German *du*), and another used under more formal circumstances and with socially superordinate interlocutors (cf French *vous*, German *Sie*).

In the radical spirit of the late 1960s, this practice was frequently questioned, but some habits are hard to break, and though perceived by many as a symbol of inequality, the use of formal *ni* rather than informal *du* persisted in Sweden.

In 1967, however, a certain Bror Rexed (1914–2002) took office as the head of the National Board of Health and Welfare, and declared that he preferred to be addressed as *du* by everybody, regardless of social standing, and he furthermore suggested that this be practiced throughout his organization.

Difficult though it may be to picture this today, the media coverage of the event was huge, and the impact of Rexed's decision was enormous. While he was ridiculed by some, most people seem to have been delighted that someone influential had taken the first step towards what was seen as a more democratic use of language. The *du*-reform rapidly caught on and spread like wildfire, and soon conquered the entire country. Although the development would most likely have eventually taken place even without Rexed's involvement, in the memory of those who are old enough to have experienced the reform, Bror Rexed's name is forever linked to it.

ADOLF HITLER

In 1939, three quarters of the world Jewry— or about 11 million people—used Yiddish as their first or only language. It was the main Jewish tongue in the areas of eastern Europe where the density of Jewish settlement was the highest. As is well known, however, a large proportion of Europe's Jews perished in the Holocaust, and this is believed to

7:-#()

Adolf Hitler

have included about half the Yiddish-speaking population.

Moreover, the foundation of the modern state of Israel was in part a consequence of the atrocities of World War II, and when surviving European Jews migrated there in the post-war era, they and their descendants tended to shift to Hebrew. Many Jewish communities in Europe and North America were also so weakened, or even virtually disintegrated, that their remaining members abandoned Yiddish in favour of the national languages of their respective countries. The number of Yiddish-speakers today is probably around 2 million, most of whom are elderly. It is possible that no other language of this size has experienced such a sharp and sudden decline in terms of numbers of speakers, and it is doubtful how much of this would have happened without Hitler's rise to power.

EDWARD YOUNG AND JOHN ADAMS

Pitcairn island, a British dependency in the southern Pacific, is known for its distinctive speech which has its roots mainly in English but includes many Polynesian words. It is now considered a language in its own right, officially called *Pitkern*.

The island was populated by the nine mutineers from the *Bounty* (an event made famous through several literary and cineastic accounts) and 19 Polynesians, eleven of whom were female.

Only one of the mutineers is reported to have had more than rudimentary education, 21-year old Edward Young from the island of St Kitts in the Caribbean. From an early point in Pitcairnese history, Young organized religious services and a school of sorts for the children. He was thus well placed to influence the emerging language and this is shown by the presence of various linguistic features from St Kitts such as *maga* 'thin'.

Soon after their arrival in Pitcairn fights broke out between the men over the women, which led to a series of killings so that, within four years, Young and his successor as community leader, John Adams were the only

John Adams

surviving mutineers. Young shared some of his bookish knowledge with Adams but died a natural death in 1800, leaving the elderly John Adams as the only native speaker of British English. A pious Christian (though a poor reader), Adams regularly read aloud to his people from the island's only book, the Bible. But for the extended presence of Young and Adams, it is most likely that Pitkern would have distanced itself more radically from English than it has.

GOD AND ADAM

One of the major linguistic innovators in world history is undoubtedly God. In the book of Genesis, we learn that after creating day, night, heaven, earth and the seas, God coined precisely these names for them (Genesis 2). He was not alone in this task, however, for after the creation of Man (so named in Genesis 5), Adam was there to help him, and in fact invented more names than did his heavenly father.

Among Adam's first words were not—as some palindrome aficionados would have it—"Madam, I'm Adam", but rather "She shall be called Woman", and so Adam started his naming career. Later (Genesis 2:19), God showed him all the animals he had created, so that Adam could bestow suitable names on them. Given biologists' estimates that there are tens of millions of animal species in the world, Adam must surely be the most active word inventor in the history of mankind.

God and Adam

LUDWIG ZAMENHOF

Ludwig Zamenhof (whose background and work are mentioned on p 157) never achieved quite what he set out to do, namely the creation of a language which would be the universal auxiliary tongue of the entire world. Nevertheless, millions of people have learned Esperanto, and it must be considered a remarkable influence by one single individual.

JOHN II OF PORTUGAL

As is well-known, Italian seafarer Christopher Columbus believed that the Indies could be reached by sailing westwards instead of eastwards. We are also all familiar with how this led to him re-discovering America for Spain. What is less known, however, is that he first approached John II of Portugal (1455–95) for funding. The king was only moderately interested, however, in particular because Bartholomeu Diaz had already rounded the Cape of Good Hope, and thereby discovered a sea route to the riches of India. Columbus thus approached other potential royal patrons until Spain's King Ferdinand V and Queen

Isabella finally agreed to finance the voyage.

As a result of this, Pope Alexander VI in 1494 divided the world into separate Portuguese and Spanish spheres of influence, the former roughly corresponding to the Old World (and the easternmost part of South America which later became Brazil) and the latter to the New World. This, in turn, explains why Latin America is mainly Spanish- rather than Portuguese-speaking, as well as why the Spanish language has had such a limited impact in Africa and Asia.

Spanish is now the world's second language in terms of number of native speakers. That honour might have gone to Portuguese if John II's decision been different.

John II of Portugal

MUHAMMAD

Before the emergence of Islam in the 7th century AD, Arabic was but a tribal tongue among others on the Arabian peninsula. The rise of the new religion, however, united several thereto rivalizing groups, and made expansion possible.

Within a mere century, speakers of Arabic had conquered the entire Middle East, and most of North Africa, i.e. what is still today the heartland of Islam. Few Arabs ever migrated to the more far-flung parts of the empire, but Arabic's status as both the language of the conquerors and that of the new religion entailed large-scale language shift.

Today's spoken Arabic is dialectally fragmented enough to merit questioning of the label "language" (rather than "languages"). Nevertheless, speech varieties descended from Classical Arabic are natively spoken by some 200m people, and understood by tens of million others. The rest of the world's 1 700 million Muslims are to varying degrees exposed to it, through it being the language of the Qur'an.

It is quite likely that this would not have been the case, had the 40-year-old travelling salesman Muhammad not met the archangel Gabriel in his revelations.

Gabriel approaches Muhammad

ELIEZER BEN-YEHUDA

E liezer Ben-Yehuda has earned a place in history as *the* reviver of Hebrew in Israel. His son, born in 1882, i.e. a year after Ben-Yehuda's arrival in Palestine, became the first native speaker of Hebrew in modern times. While he did struggle fanatically to make Hebrew the language of the Jewish colony in Palestine, and while his importance to the Hebrew movement is beyond doubt, the dominant role that is usually ascribed to him has been questioned. The Zionist leader Menaxem Usiškin made the following comment on this: "I know [that Ben-Yehuda was not the reviver of Hebrew]. But the people are asking for a *hero*, so we give them the hero". In any case, the revival of an extinct language is a truly extraordinary achievement, and Eliezer Ben-Yehuda clearly had an important role in the Hebrew renaissance.

SOURCES NOT MENTIONED IN THE TEXT

Youngest languages: Pasch (1996), Samarin (1982:28), Heine (1973:58), Philip Baker (p c), Holm (1989:517-524), Sarah Roberts (p c), Grant (1995a, 1996a/b, p c), Zenk (1988), Thomason (1983), Johnson (1978), Heine (1982), Prokosch (1986), Muysken (1981, 1994), Sandler et al. (2005), Kegl, Senghas & Coppola (2001), McConvell (2002), McConvell & Meakins (2005).

Nativisation of Hebrew: Izre'el (2000), Nahir (1998), Bar-Adon (1975), Kutscher (1984).

Developing into your own opposite: See Janus words, pp 205–07.

Bizarre sound change: Ante Aikio on the *Indo-European* list, 2001-06-08.

Most stable vocabulary items: Dyen, Kruskal & Black (1997b).

Ancient Egyptian naughty grammaticalisation: Heine et al. (1993:166).

Takelma naughty grammaticalisation: Heine et al. (1993:232).

Bulgarian naughty grammaticalisation: Ljuba Veselinova (p c).

Rapid language change: Lithgow (1973 cited in Dixon 1997:10 and Nettle 1999b:134), McConvell (2002:335).

Taboo as a factor in language change: Krauss (1973a:842, 851), Bergsland & Vogt (1962:126), Lithgow (1987:395), Haviland (1979:210).

Conservativeness of Georgian: van Driem (1993:230).

Conservativeness of Baltic languages: Baldi (1983:97, 1985:94).

Cheyenne reduction: McWhorter (2001:291).

Danish reduction: Peter Bakker (p c) and personal experience.

Irish reduction: Olle Engstrand (p c).

Johannes Aavik and Estonian: Lars Borin (p c), Comrie (1981:100), Diana Krull (p c), Vihman (2004: 54, 57).

Pitkern: Maude 1964a.

Menaxem Usiškin quote: Bar-Adon (1975:12).

LANGUAGE FAMILIES

A LANGUAGE FAMILY is a group of languages which all descend from a common mother. Thus, the Indo-European languages (the group which includes most languages of Europe, Iran and India) have been demonstrated to stem from an ancestral language called Proto-Indo-European.

BIGGEST LANGUAGE FAMILY

The biggest language family in terms of number of speakers (and this regardless of whether or not you include non-native speakers) is, by a wide margin, Indo-European. Of the world's top-ten languages in terms of native speakers, seven are Indo-European, and approximately half of the current world population are speakers of a language descended from what was probably spoken in southern Russia or the Ukraine some six millennia ago (or in Turkey 9 000 years ago, if you are sympathetic to the proposal made by Renfrew [1987]). Furthermore, 60% of the world's population live in a country where an Indo-European language is official, which, in turn, is the case in more than 75% of all countries.

In terms of geographical coverage too, Indo-European must now be considered to be in the lead, well-represented as it is on all continents. It completely dominates Europe, Oceania and the two Americas. With almost a third of Asia's population being speakers of Indo-European languages, Africa is the only inhabited continent where the Indo-European presence is modest in terms of native speakers (and yet, the vast majority of African states use an Indo-European language for administrative purposes).

Prior to European colonial expansion, however, Austronesian could rival the geographical span of Indo-European. Extending from Madagascar to Easter Island, this family covered well over half the earth's circumference.

If we instead define "biggest family" as the one with the most member languages, the winner is Niger-Congo, with its (according to the *Ethnologue*) 1 489 languages, closely followed by the 1 262 of Austronesian.

OLDEST LANGUAGE FAMILY

There is a serious problem involved in determining the age of any language family. Since languages continuously change, it is much easier to demonstrate the relatedness of two daughter languages which split off from their mother not too long ago, than to prove a genetic relationship between languages which diverged centuries earlier. Most historical linguists seem to agree that the upper time limit for tracing a genetic relationship is 10 000 years at most. Little actual proof is available, but it is believed that the margin of error at such time depths exceeds the remaining inherited component. Thus, the younger a family is proposed to be, the more acceptable the claimed relationship is to linguists.

Some suggested families, such as Nostratic, Amerind, Ural-Altaic, and Proto-World (the assumed common mother of all the world's languages, possibly spoken 100 000 or so years ago) are not generally accepted by historical linguists.

For a variety of reasons, including the relative abundance of documentation of earlier stages, Indo-European is one of the few families whose existence is beyond all doubt (its age and geographical origin is quite another matter). It is usually believed that this family has a time-depth of about 6 000 years. Roughly similar ages are often assigned to Uralic, Sino-Tibetan and Austronesian. A possibly older family is the Afro-Asiatic one, which includes, among others, Arabic, Hebrew, and Berber. Estimates of its age range from 8 000 to 13 000 years. One of its subgroups, Cushitic, has itself been suggested to be something like 7 000 years old. Worthy of note also is that figures as high as 10-17 000 years have been proposed for Nilo-Saharan and Niger-Congo. Khoisan has been claimed to date no less than 20 millennia back, but not only is it a much more dubious family entity, but the grounds for the claim are also utterly shaky. Other language families accepted by most linguists, such as Eskimo-Aleut, Bantu, Dravidian, Algonquian, Turkic, Mongolian and Mayan are slightly or considerably younger than this.

For some families, the age depends on inclusiveness. Athabaskan-Eyak-Tlingit, for instance, is often given an age of about 5 000 years, but when Haida is included to form the controversial Na-Dené family, the proposed age almost doubles to 9 000 years.

BIGGEST ISOLATE

A couple of dozen languages are recognized as isolates, that is, not demonstrably related to any others. The most widely spoken of these is either Korean, with almost 80 million speakers, or Japanese with about 120 million. The problem here is that Ryukyuan is sometimes seen as a divergent dialect of Japanese, and sometimes as a language in its own right—in the latter case, Japanese would not, properly speaking, be an isolate.

LANGUAGE WITH THE MOST PROPOSED RELATIVES

B asque is no doubt the most famous isolate, and its apparent lack of a genetic relation to anything else has inspired plenty of people to seek fame by being the first to discover Basque's lost kin. Trask (1997) covers these attempts, mentioning how various people have tried to relate Basque to several Caucasian languages, Berber and other Afro-Asiatic languages, Iberian, Pictish, Etruscan, Caucasian, Semitic, Minoan, Sumerian, Burushaski, Niger-Congo, Khoisan, Uralic, Dravidian, Munda, Sino-Tibetan, Austronesian and Na-Dene. In fact, given that Basque has also been suggested to be the mother-of-all-languages (see p 343), it has, technically speaking, been suggested to be related to *every* language on earth. Inuktitut (Eskimo) and Ainu are other languages for which an amazingly large number of relatives—including, of course, Basque—have been proposed.

One can glean a certain disillusion from the words of the now deceased great Vasconist and historical linguist Larry Trask, who had the following plea on his homepage:

"I'll be happy to try to answer a brief question ... But please note: I do not want to hear about the following: Your latest proof that Basque is related to Iberian / Etruscan / Pictish / Sumerian / Minoan / Tibetan / Isthmus Zapotec / Martian; Your discovery that Basque is the secret key to understanding the Ogam inscriptions / the \Phaistos disc / the Easter Island carvings / the Egyptian Book of the Dead / the Qabbala / the prophecies of Nostradamus / your PC manual / the movements of the New York Stock Exchange; Your belief that Basque is the ancestral language of all humankind / a remnant of the speech of lost Atlantis / the language of the vanished civilization of Antarctica / evidence of visitors from Proxima Centauri".

Among other languages with a plethora proposed relatives is Tamil. Attempts have been made to try to relate it to Finnish, Japanese, Wolof, and Australian languages. Particularly interesting is the idea of the ancient Tamils sailing around the coast of Africa in the opposite direction to Vasco da Gama without apparently stopping anywhere on the way until they got to Senegal...

When Mark Rosenfelder compiled a list of fake Mandarin Quechua cognates in order to demonstrate how easy it is to *get the impression* that two unrelated languages are siblings, "one gentleman wondered aloud (wondered anet?) if I might have proved that Chinese and Quechua **are** related. Some days it's not worth getting out of bed".

SIMILAR AND DISSIMILAR LANGUAGES

Judging from the 200-item Swadesh list, the Indo-European languages in Dyen, Kruskal & Black (1997a/b) with the smallest number of shared cognates are Pashto and Albanian, which share only about 7% of their core lexicon. In practice, this means that it would be impossible to prove the relationship, were it not for the existence of intermediate kin.

Among varieties normally treated as different languages, the most similar are Afrikaans and Dutch, Czech and Slovak, and Icelandic and Faroese, all of which share well over 90% cognates with their respective sisters. One might perhaps add that Serbian, Croatian, and Bosnian, regarded by some as different languages since the wars in the early 1990s, have even higher cognation rates.

The closest relative of English, using the same criteria, is the creole language Sranan

> A pair of words in two different languages are cognate if they stem from the same proto-word. The percentage of cognates were once used in glottochronology to try and establish the time passed since the related languages parted company. The Swadesh list, intended to contain the most basic and stable vocabulary items, was set up as a standard word list to use in such comparisons.

(66%), followed by Dutch and Afrikaans (61%) and Danish and Swedish (59%). These figures only take into account the relatedness of the 200 supposedly most basic words, and completely ignore differences in grammar and pronunciation, as well as the rest of the vocabulary. This may be why Frisian (56%), often thought of as the closest living relative of English, ranks below German (58%) in terms of similarity to English. World-wide, the language pair with the typologically most divergent members in Dahl's (2005) metric are Juǀʼhoan (southern African desert) and Central Yupʼik (Arctic Alaska), which are indeed spoken at a near-maximal distance from one another, and in very different surroundings. The two most similar languages among the 222 discussed are Dutch and German.

MEASURING DISTANCE IN DAYS

Among the Akan people, distance between languages is measured in time, just as it is in glottochronology. The time span given, however, does not relate to the time elapsed since the posited split-up, but rather the time believed to be required to learn another language. Thus, from the point of view of Asante-speakers, Fante is a one-day dialect.

MOST AND LEAST REPRESENTATIVE LANGUAGES

Cyusow (2004) and Dahl (2005) both draw on the database of Haspelmath et al. (2005) to assess the "normality" of languages. In typological terms, Cyusow's strangest language (= least representative of the world as a whole) is Wari' of Amazonas. The most odd family is Northwest Caucasian, while—somewhat more surprisingly—the most extreme *area* is north-west Europe (including Dutch, German and French). Other areas with noticeably strange languages are the Caucasus, Amazonas, north-west Australia, eastern and

Pashto	Albanian	English
leːvə	ujk	wolf
kilə	katund, fshat	village
aːvreːdəl	dëgjoj	to hear
zoːɽ	vjetër	old
stoːriː	yll	star
zər	njëmijë	thousand
aːloːzol	fluturoj	to fly
χaraːb	keq	bad
vədʒil	vras	to kill
luːr	vajzë, bijë	daughter
koːzidəl	ngjitem, kërcej	to climb
speː	qen	dog
vroːr	ɣëlla	brother
χandləl	qesh	to laugh

Yes, folks, Albanian and Pashto are related—but it sure takes more than just a trained eye to see it!

western North America and the northern Philippines. Dahl's oddity champions also include Wari' and Dutch, as well as Barasana, Irish, and—as the winner—Central Yup'ik.

The most "normal" languages, according to Cyusow, are spoken in India, central Africa, eastern Indonesia, Melanesia, Colombia and southern Meso-America. More normal than any others are Bagirmi (India) and Khasi (Chad). Dahl's results are relatively similar,

with Brahui (Pakistan) being the definition of normality.

Again using the word lists in Dyen, Kruskal & Black (1997a/b), the Indo-European language which shares the most of its core lexicon with the other members of this family is Slovak, which has a cognation rate of 31% with the average other Indo-European language. At the other end of the scale is Albanian, for which the figure is less than 13%.

BEFORE SIR WILLIAM

Almost every linguistics textbook mentions Sir William Jones who in 1786 set out his ideas on the interrelatedness of Indo-European languages at the *Asiatick* [sic] *Society* in Calcutta.

This has led many to believe that Jones established the concept of high-level language families. A couple of other families had, however, been recognized before or simultaneous-

ly with this event, including Algonquian, Semitic and Arawak.

Even the family status of Indo-European itself was not first established by Jones, for it was rather explicitly mentioned in 1686 (thus an entire century before Jones) in a speech in Wittenberg, Germany, by Swedish scholar Andreas Jäger.

It was also hinted at by English mathematician and cleric John Wallis in his *Grammatica Linguae Anglicanae*, published in the early 1650s. It includes a 37-member cognate set in English, Latin and Greek.

Many of Jones' predecessors did not grasp the family concept as we do today. While they did identify families, they often pictured one of their living members as the "pure" language, of which the sisters were mere distortions. One pioneer who envisaged the concept of relatedness in a more modern

William Jones (1746–1794)

John Wallis (1616–1703)

way was Hungarian János Sajnovcs, whose 1770 work *Demonstratio idioma Ungarorum et Lapponum idem esse* ('Demonstration that the language of the Hungarians and the Lapps is the same') established the Uralic family.

SOURCES NOT MENTIONED IN THE TEXT

Biggest language family and Biggest isolate: Speaker and language numbers from *Ethnologue*.

Oldest language family: Krauss (1973b:952-53), Dixon (1997:2), Dalby (1998), Larry Trask (p c), Shevoroshkin (1995:164), Hayward (2000:75), Ehret (2000:288-93).

Very high ages for Niger-Congo and Nilo-Saharan: Dalby (1998:453, 348).

Mark Rosenfelder's fake Mandarin-Quechua cognates: His website at www.zompist.com.

Measuring distance in days: Dalby (1998:viii).

Established families prior to William Jones: Campbell (1997:29), Aikhenvald (2001:170), Metcalf (1966), Hayward (2000:83), Comrie (1981:94).

SPECTACULAR SPREAD

DURING THE COURSE of human history, languages have been born, have expanded, shrunk, and died out. Some, however, have grown in size in a most remarkable way. Yet, it should be borne in mind that only 10 000 years ago, the entire population of the earth lived as hunter-gatherers in bands comprising only a couple of hundred individuals. So not only the languages mentioned here, but in fact every tongue there is, descends from a very small ancestral language.

ENGLISH

English is no doubt the best representative of the spectacular spread of certain languages which was brought about by the European conquest of most of the world during the second millennium of our era. From having been a relatively insignificant insular language of a couple of million people on a foggy island in the 1500s, English spread in just a few centuries to all continents, and was even the first language to be spoken on a celestial body other than our own planet. It is now the world's third language in terms of number of native speakers, and it is believed to be mastered to some extent by at least one earthling out of every six, which is a position matched by no other contemporary language (except possibly Mandarin), nor probably by any historical one.

OTHER IMPERIAL LANGUAGES

A couple of other languages of former empires can be said to have "exploded" in a way similar to that of English. A prime case is of course Latin. From being confined to the little town of Rome, it ousted all the Celtic tongues of the European mainland, as well as several others.

Latin as such is no longer natively spoken, but its descendants—the Romance languages—now have something like 700 million native speakers on all continents (thus twice as many as English has).

Similar factors have spread Russian, Arabic, Mandarin, and Quechua way beyond their original homelands.

Two other languages which experienced a similar expansion at about the same time are Sanskrit and Middle Chinese. Indeed, taken together, the daughters of Latin, Sanskrit and Middle Chinese are now spoken natively by roughly half the human race (to say nothing of their profound impact upon their respective neighboring languages, such as English, Japanese, and Malay).

Paradoxically, much of the Latinization of Romance Europe took place after the fall of the Roman Empire. In Gaul, Latin spread from south to north, but several areas, even in the south-west did not shift until the 9th century. On this map, darker shades indicate earlier Latinization.

Malay did not spread so much through imperialism and conquest as through trade, but its expansion is truly remarkable. In 1920, the number of native speakers in Indonesia, which is the language's main stronghold, was estimated at around 500 000. It became the official language of the country as independence arrived after the Second World War, and in 1980, about 17 million Indonesians spoke Malay natively. Reliable figures are hard to come by, but my guesstimate is that the number of Indonesians with some form of Malay as their mother tongue is now well over 40 million.

RENNELLESE SIGN

The Rennellese Sign language of Melanesia was developed in 1915 by one Kagobai, the only deaf individual on Rennell island. From him, it then spread to other inhabitants of the island. Since Kagobai's death, it is no longer used, and is only remembered by a few people.

ESPERANTO

As mentioned elsewhere in this book (p 158), Esperanto speakers experienced a rise in number from one in the 1880s to several hundred thousand in just a couple of decades. It now even has native speakers, estimated at around 1 000.

AFRIKAANS

Afrikaans, spoken mainly in South Africa, is derived from Dutch, which was implanted on the Cape by a small number of settlers in 1652. Today, it is spoken natively by almost 7 000 000, and known by another 3 000 000.

Birth rates among the Dutch colonists were high, and around 1700, the settlers parented six children each. As early as in 1731, most of the about 2 000 settlers were born in South Africa. Even if a few Dutch immigrants arrived after that date, the Afrikaners had already assimilated several hundred French-speaking Huguenots, so the original Dutch-speaking input is likely not to have been greater than a few thousand individuals at the most.

Not only high birth rates, but also assimilation helped to spread the language. Today, whites (including plenty of descendants of Huguenots and Germans) constitute a minority of all Afrikaans-speakers. Home language users in the 2001 South African census included well over 3 million "coloreds" (i.e. people of mixed ancestry), 2,5 million whites, more than a quarter of a million blacks and almost 20 000 ethnic Indians.

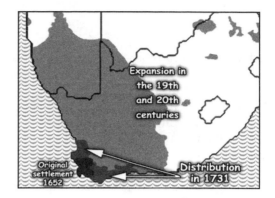

INTERETHNIC LANGUAGES OF PAPUA NEW GUINEA

Papua New Guinea is exceptionally rich in languages, and there is therefore a need for lingua francas—auxiliary languages which can be used between speakers who do not know each other's native tongues. The primary language of the country today is the English-lexicon creole Tok Pisin. It has been shown that Tok Pisin did not develop in New Guinea, but that it was brought in from island Melanesia towards the end of the 19th century. Since then, it has expanded considerably. Mühlhäusler (1996:80) estimates the number of speakers to have been about one thousand in 1890, 15 000 around the time of the first world war, and 100 000 just before the second. Census figures indicate 530 000 speakers in 1966, and 700 000 five years later. Today, at least a million, and possibly even more than two million people know it. It has also acquired a number of native speakers, probably around 100 000.

Another important interethnic language in the same country, Hiri Motu, is a pidginized version of the Austronesian language Motu of New Guinea. Hiri Motu became the lingua franca of a police corps founded by the British in 1890, consisting of 2 Fijians and 12 Solomon Islanders, who were later joined by local recruits. After training in the capital of Port Moresby, the constables were sent out to various villages in the rural inland, where their prestige contributed to the popularity of the pidgin. The language is now, alongside English and Tok Pisin, one of the three national languages of Papua New Guinea, and though on the decline in favour of the other two, it still remains spoken by an estimated 150 000 people.

A less well-known lingua franca in New Guinea is Kâte, which is used on the Huon peninsula. German missionaries arriving in the late 19th century found 800 native speakers when they began using it in their religious teaching. Because of this, it began to spread throughout the area. It is now losing its lingua franca role, but at least in the 1970s, about 115 000 people had some competence (active or passive) in Kâte. Apart from its use as a second language, it has also encroached upon some of its neighboring languages.

KRIO

Between 1792 and 1800, the British resettled a number of ex-slaves from the Americas in Sierra Leone on the West African coast. With them, they brought the English-lexicon creole languages spoken on Jamaica and in the Carolinas. Their number was less than 1 500 in the early 1800s. However, their language (now known as Krio), was learned by the tens of thousands of other freed slaves from Nigeria which were landed in the area during the following decades. Today, Krio is the mother tongue of about half a million in Sierra Leone, and is spoken as a second language by virtually all the remaining four million inhabitants.

Even more spectacular, though, is the spread of Krio to other parts of West Africa. Since the freed Nigerians had been exposed to western culture in Sierra Leone, the British found it convenient to use them as middlemen in their colonization ventures in Nigeria.

As a result, thirty to forty million Nigerians now speak the offshoot of Krio known as "Nigerian Pidgin", and there are several million additional speakers in neighboring Cameroon. Forms of speech derived from Krio are also widely spoken in Ghana and in Equatorial Guinea, and to a lesser extent in the Gambia. In all these countries, the language first and foremost has an auxiliary role in

Most of the native speakers of Krio live on the Freetown peninsula, where the toponymy leaves remarkably little doubt as to the identity of the former colonial power.

interethnic communication, but it also has acquired quite a few native speakers (perhaps three million) in recent decades.

With an increase from 1 500 to well over 40 million speakers in two centuries, Krio and its daughter languages must surely constitute one of the most extreme (albeit rarely mentioned) cases of rapid language spread in human history.

FRENCH SIGN LANGUAGE

The development of American Sign Language from French Sign is described elsewhere in the book (p 127), but merits mention here as it shows how a few individuals can constitute a nucleus for an entire speech community.

While Marseilles and Strasbourg are located within the political boundaries of present-day France, they still represent "conquests" on the part of the language, insofar as these cities were historically not French-speaking.

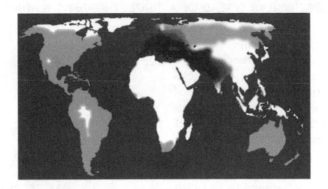

Of course, Proto-Indo-European itself represents a case of phenomenal language spread, having gone from being an insignificant language of western Asia or south-eastern Europe to having native speakers on all continents (in the form of various daughter languages), together representing half of humanity. Lighter shades on this map represent more recent spread.

The table below illustrates the spectacular spread of some languages in listing the ten biggest cities of each language. Only in the case of French are the majority of cities located in the country of origin of the language. For English, Spanish and Arabic, this is true only for one of the top-ten cities.

	ENGLISH	SPANISH	ARABIC	PORTUGUESE	FRENCH
1.	*New York*	*Mexico City*	*Cairo*	*São Paulo*	**Paris**
2.	*Los Angeles*	*Buenos Aires*	*Baghdad*	*Rio de Janeiro*	*Montreal*
3.	**London**	*Lima*	*Algiers*	*Belo Horizonte*	**Lyons**
4.	*Chicago*	*Bogotá*	*Khartoum*	*Porto Alegre*	**Marseilles**
5.	*Washington*	*Santiago*	*Casablanca*	*Recife*	*Brussels*
6.	*San Francisco*	**Madrid**	*Alexandria*	*Salvador*	**Lille**
7.	*Philadelphia*	*Caracas*	**Riyadh**	*Fortaleza*	**Toulouse**
8.	*Boston*	*Guadalajara*	*Damascus*	**Lisbon**	**Nice**
9.	*Detroit*	*Santo Domingo*	*Giza*	*Brasília*	**Nantes**
10.	*Dallas*	*Monterrey*	*Tunis*	**Porto**	**Strasbourg**

Today, 16% of the native English-speakers, 8% of the Spanish-speakers, 7% of the Arabic-speakers, and a mere 5% of the Lusophones (i.e. speakers of Portuguese) live in the countries from which their languages originally spread. For the French, the corresponding figure is 73%.

SPECTACULAR SPREAD OF A SINGLE LINGUISTIC FEATURE

Some linguistic features have spread within a language, or even between several languages at a surprising speed. One of these is the dorsal (rather than apical) pronunciation of /r/ found in most varieties of French, German and Danish. Its original history is obscure, but Paris is most frequently cited as the center of spread of this innovation.

Dorsal /r/ seems to have become increasingly popular in that area in the 17th and 18th centuries, and started to spread into other areas of France. Before France fell, however, Denmark succumbed to the new prestigious norm. The feature is first attested in Copenhagen in the 1780s, and within a century and a half, the entire country was conquered. From Denmark, the dorsal /r/ established bridgeheads in Sweden and Norway, where it conquered large portions of land. Meanwhile, urban centers in Portugal, Germany and northern Italy were overrun.

With Spain and Britain being among the few western European countries still only marginally affected, the new /r/ now turned to overseas expansion, and made inroads in Israel, Québec, Brazil, New Caledonia and a few other areas.

Today, dorsal /r/ is part of the standard in French, German and Danish. It is optional in standard varieties of Dutch and

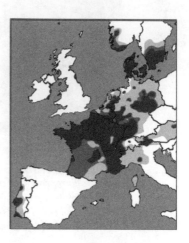

Dorsal /r/ in present-day Europe. In the areas with the darkest shade of grey, most people used this pronunciation before World War 2.

Portuguese, and regionally dominant in Swedish, Norwegian and Italian. In order to explain the unparalleled success of this linguistic blitzkrieg, it requires people to have shifted within their lifetime, and this has indeed been shown to have taken place in e.g. Canada.

While impossible to prove beyond doubt, I would suggest that this is the most rapid spread by any linguistic feature (other than isolated lexical items) in documented history.

SOURCES NOT MENTIONED IN THE TEXT

Spectacular spread of Rennellese Sign: Groce (1985:68), citing Kuschel (1973, 1974).

Spectacular spread of Afrikaans: Guelke (1988). Map of language spread in Gaul based on Lodge (1993:43).

Spectacular spread of Tok Pisin: Baker (1993), Bartens (1996:171), the *Ethnologue*.

Spectacular spread of Hiri Motu: Dutton (1985).

Spectacular spread of Kâte: Foley (1986:32), Mühlhäusler (1996:147).

Spectacular spread of Krio: Huber (1998a, b, c), Holm (1989:429-30), Charles (1998:59).

Spread of dorsal /r/: Ongoing, but still unpublished, original research by the present author.

LANGUAGE IN ALTERNATE HISTORY

ALTERNATE HISTORY is a fascinating hobby which is, as such, relatively unknown, although most of us from time to time cannot refrain from engaging in it. Alternate historians choose a time in real world history (called OTL, i.e. "our time line"), modify one or two parameters, and speculate on "what would have happened if . . .". The scenarios thus developed are sometimes quite detailed and can provide a fascinating and thought-provoking read. Some such alternate history scenarios involve language or linguistics as a central component.

While most discussion on alternate history is confined to the internet, at least two language-related cases have been featured in books. Linguist and science fiction writer Suzette Haden Elgin has written a short story called *Hush My Mouth* (Elgin 1986), in which Blacks during the American Civil War define English as the oppressor's tongue. For want of a better medium of communication, some refuse to speak at all.

Pedersen (1980) is about the 1920s Norwegian language dispute getting more serious than it did in OTL. After a parliamentary decree to change the city's name, the citizens of Bergen take up arms and proclaim an independent state of their own. The two countries are reunited only after both having joined the EEC (currently the European Union) in 1972.

Many scenarios concerning language-related subjects deal with the possibility of French becoming better represented overseas. As one discussant put it, *"I almost think that the difficulty is explaining why it didn't happen in OTL"*. One such scenario concerns Canadians fleeing the British conquest of Canada in 1763 to settle in large numbers in Missouri, leading to a major francophone population along the Mississippi valley (there is one, but it is now almost completely assimilated into Anglo-American mainstream culture). Another deals with New Zealand being colonized by the French in the 1840s (which, again, was close to happening in OTL), where the bilingual (Maori-French) republic, independent since 1972, is known as Nouveau-Dauphiné.

Ever since independence in 1972, the Southern Cross tricolour has flown proudly over Nouveau-Grenoble and other major cities of Nouveau-Dauphiné.
Not.

Some other more or less likely scenarios which have been discussed on the internet newsgroup *soc.history.what-if* include the following:

- Latin survives Anglo-Saxon immigration, and Britain remains partly Romance-speaking.

- Alternatively, English succumbs to the pressure of Norman French, again with the result that parts of the country are Romance-speaking today.
- During the Meiji Restoration, radical groups succeed in having Latin script officially adopted in Japan.
- The 1885 Métis (half-breed) rebellion in Manitoba is not crushed, and today's central Canada instead becomes a Métis republic, speaking Cree, French, and Michif (p 53–54).
- Instead of being replaced by English, the pidgin language Chinook Jargon remains the lingua franca of the American Northwest. In OTL, it had this role until the late 19th century. Vikings settlements in Greenland and Newfoundland survive, yielding a substantial indigenous Norse-speaking population by the time other Europeans arrive.
- Or, Norsemen are attracted not by Vineland, but by Arab tales of sunny Africa. A contingent sails down south and settles in what is today South Africa, something that results in Viking Boers speaking a Bantu-Norse mixed language.

IT JUST MIGHT HAVE HAPPENED

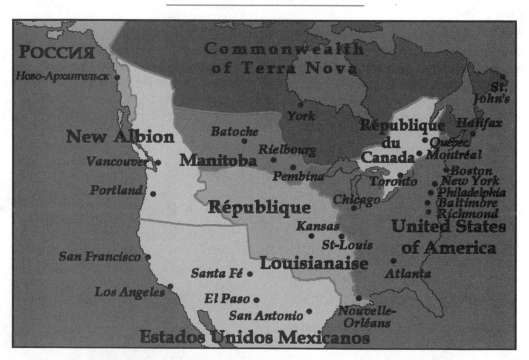

The fictitious North America above contains three English-, three French- and one Spanish-speaking nation. In addition, Novo-Archangelsk is the center of an extension of Russian Siberia. In fact, nothing of this was very far from happening, and both Louisiana (1768-69) and Manitoba (1869-70 and 1885) have actually experienced brief periods of independence.

		CAPITAL	INDEPENDENT	POPULATION	LANGUAGE(S)
Alaska (Russia)		Novo-Archangelsk	*no*	1m	Russian 70%
New Albion		Victoria	1931	15m	English 90%
Terra Nova		St John's	1931	1m	English 90%
Manitoba		Rielbourg	1840	4m	French 40%, Michif 40%
Canada		Québec	1783	17m	French 90%
United States		Washington	1776	140m	English 90%
Louisiana		Nouvelle-Orléans	1810	24m	French 70%, English 20%
Mexico		México	1821	130m	Spanish 70%, English 20%

WRITTEN LANGUAGE

FOR MOST of humanity's existence, speaking and signing have been the only ways of transmitting language. During the last few millennia and, in particular, the last couple of centuries, a new linguistic code has become more and more important—writing. Although writing is essentially a representation of spoken language, it has gradually developed into a linguistic representation in its own right.

HIGHEST AND LOWEST LITERACY RATES

A number of countries report a literacy rate of between 99% and 100%. These include mostly first world countries, but also North Korea and Uzbekistan. The countries with the smallest proportion of literate citizens are Niger (18%), Burkina Faso (27%), and Sierra Leone (31%). Incidentally, the illiteracy top ten list is remarkably similar to a list of countries where gender differences with regard to literacy are the greatest (see below).

The lowest literacy rate in Europe is found in Albania (87%), followed by Malta, Serbia-Montenegro, and Portugal (all around 93%). Given that the French overseas departments are counted as integral parts of France (and politically thereby Europe), the literacy rates of French Guiana is noticeably low (83%). (British and American overseas areas also have lower literacy rates than their respective motherlands, but are—with the exception of Hawaii—not officially regarded as parts of these).

Parker (1997) attempts to estimate the degree of literacy by language, rather than by country. In his listing, 14 languages share the honour of having the most literate speakers (all 100%), namely Abkhaz, Belarusan, Danish, Faeroese, Finnish, Dutch, Georgian, Greenlandic, Icelandic, Irish, Japanese, Luxembourgeois, Tongan, and French. The languages occupying the other end of the scale, all with 18% literate speakers, are all spoken in Burkina Faso (suggesting that Parker may in fact be dealing with country- rather than language-based statistics).

If newspaper statistics are anything to go by, the most keen readers are the Norwegians, who consume 590 daily newspapers per 1000 inhabitants. They are followed by the Japanese (578), and the Icelanders (535). The least newspaper-reading nations are all located in Africa. Taking non-independent nations into account, it is noteworthy that the newspaper consumption in Hong Kong is 786 per 1000 inhabitants, while the Swedish-speaking segment of Finland, with its 12 dailies, reaches 550.

MOST POPULAR WRITING SYSTEMS

The vast majority of the world's literate people use writing systems of European or Chinese origin. Counting only those able to read and write (numbers usually available only at the country level) and the writing system in which they are most likely to have learned to do so, we arrive at the following, very approximate, figures: Roman 42,5%; Hànzi 26,2%; "Indic" 16,7%; Arabic 6,7%; Cyrillic 5,5%; others 2,4%.

Hànzi is the writing system used for Mandarin and other Chinese languages, and which also provides the backbone of Japanese writing. "Indic" here refers to both direct and indirect descendants of the Brahmi script. These include the writing systems used for most languages of India and adjacent countries as well as much of south-east Asia. "Others" include other scripts in current use such as Armenian, Georgian, Hebrew (related to Arabic), Greek (from which the Cyrillic script stems), Korean, and Amharic.

LITERACY—GENDER DIFFERENCES

For most of the world's countries, men are reported to be literate to a greater extent than women. In a few countries, this discrepancy is so great that there are almost three literate men for each literate woman. Extreme cases are Sierra Leone, Niger and—not unexpectedly—Afghanistan, where the Taliban régime outlawed schooling for girls. In most industrialized countries, there is no such difference.

The most notable exception is Lesotho, where 25,5% of the men are illiterate, but only 5,5% of the women. This is because, while boys and girls start school at the same age, many of the boys are withdrawn before acquiring much if any literacy in order to spend their time herding cattle for several years. Most young men ultimately go on to work in the South African mines where literacy is not required.

Given the widespread western view of gender discrimination in the Muslim world, it is interesting to note that both Qatar and the United Arab Emirates, are among the few states where more women are literate than men. This may perhaps be related to the very high proportion of immigrant workers from South and Southeast Asia in both these states.

MOST COMPLEX WRITING

The strongest candidate for a hideously complex writing system is probably that of Japanese. It combines of elements several different systems, the oldest of which is the logographic writing, known as *Kanji*, which was introduced from China. Then, there is the *Katakana* system, derived from abbreviations of the Kanji signs, and the *Hiragana* writing, which originated as a cursive style of Kanji. Both of these are syllabic systems. That makes three parallel writing systems for one single language—but it's still not the end of the story. For one thing, Latin characters also sometimes turn up in texts, and there are several ways of Romanising Japanese, of which no less than two enjoy official recognition. It is furthermore possible to write both from left to right, as well as from top to bottom.

Perhaps the most spectacular additional complexity is that the Kanji symbols have several different readings. Sometimes, they are to be read in Chinese, that is with their Chinese sound values, whereas in other cases, they require to be pronounced as the corresponding Japanese word. As if that weren't enough, Chinese words have been borrowed in different periods and from different varieties of Chinese, and for this reason, one and the same sign may require three different readings depending on

its context! In addition, there may be more than one native word corresponding to the Chinese sign.

Today, Kanji symbols (of which a literate Japanese is expected to know about 2 000) are used mostly for lexical morphemes, Hiragana is used for grammatical morphemes, and Katakana for more recent loanwords, in telegram style, and for certain ideophones.

THE UNIQUE FOURTH TYPE

All writing systems of the world are based on one or more of three principles. Symbols may represent (1) individual sounds (as in most European and Near Eastern scripts), or (2) syllables (as in the Japanese *Hiragana*

King Sejong depicted on a South Korean bank note

and *Katakana* scripts, or the Cherokee script—see below). These two principles may be combined, as in the semi-syllabic scripts used for many, mainly southern, Asian languages and Amharic. And (3) they may represent morphemes, as do the Chinese logograms. The only exception to these principles is Korean *Han'gŭl* writing.

Devised in 1446 by King Sejong (or at least under his auspices), Han'gŭl is the only known script to be based on phonetic

features, that is subphonemic characteristics of pronunciation. If you look at the Han'gŭl symbol for /n/ below, you will notice that the shape is somewhat similar to a raised tongue-tip (if you imagine the speaker facing left). Since /s/ is made with the tongue-tip somewhat closer to the teeth, its symbol schematically represents a tooth. Now these are continuant sounds—in order to write plosives, you simply add a stroke on top of the symbol, as can be seen in the symbols for /d/ and (what was formerly) /ts/.

ㄴ	ㅅ	ㄷ	ㅈ
n	s	d	ts (now t͡ʃ)

Thus, the Korean script (at least as originally devised) is partly iconic, and highly compositional. Some of the genius of the system has been obscured by subsequent developments in spoken Korean, and some became less apparent through the practice of stacking the Han'gŭl letters in writing, making each syllable look more like a Chinese logogram. Yet, there is little doubt that King Sejong and/or his entourage possessed a deeper understanding of phonetics than is evidenced in most other 15th century civilizations.

A LOST WRITING SYSTEM

As opposed to many of their neighbors, the speakers of Naga languages did not write until modern times. When British explorer J P Mills asked the natives about this fact, they were able to explain the anomaly to him. God once did give writing to this people as well, only the skins on which they wrote were eaten by a dog, and since then, the art of writing has been lost to the Nagas.

In southern China, the Miao also claimed to once have mastered writing, using a system as ancient as that of the Han Chinese. The expansion of the latter group forced the Miao to migrate south, and during this trek, all the books were lost in the Yellow River. In 1904, the British missionary Samuel Pollard arrived among the Miao, and devised a script for them. According to Miao oral literature, the writing he introduced was in fact identical to the one that had been swept away during the river crossing generations earlier. Apparently, the books must have drifted to Europe, where Pollard could collect them and re-introduce the writing system. It has been suggested that the ancient myth contributed to the enthusiasm with which Pollard's system was received by the Miao.

MOST AND FEWEST CHARACTERS

The writing system with the largest number of documented characters must, more or less by definition, be a logographic one. The best described such system is that used for Mandarin. The most comprehensive Mandarin dictionary there is contains about 56 000 different characters, although most of these are rarely used. A mere 500 symbols cover about 80% of an average text. With a knowledge of 1 000, you would understand 91%, and with 2 400 the proportion would rise to about 99%.

Seneca (spoken in New York state and adjoining parts of Canada) and Tahitian are both written in Roman script, but only make use of thirteen letters.

MOST ELABORATE CHARACTERS

The Mayan hieroglyphs are probably the most complex there is in terms of character design. The system was long thought not to be a proper script, but its decipherment by Russian linguist Yuri Knorosov in the early 1950s proved otherwise.

About 550 logograms are known, in addition to 150 syllabic symbols. A selection of symbols of both types can be seen to the right.

While the average sign in Chinese writing contains 10,3 strokes (and considerably less for the most common logograms), the Mayan symbols are obviously a good deal more intricate.

Sample Mayan characters

WORST SPELLING

There is no way of measuring the optimality of an orthography, especially since there is no consensus on what would constitute the perfect writing system. Many would argue that an alphabetic writing system should reflect actual pronunciation, but other considerations usually also play a role.

In any case, there are languages which are renowned for their miserably faulty letter-to-phoneme correspondences. French is one such language (for a few examples, see p 76). Another, of course, is English. It is said that there is no English speech sound which is always spelled in the same way, and nor is there any English letter which always represents the same speech sound. Sentences such as In the drought, it was hard enough to think that rough thought through thoroughly have been invented to illustrate the short-comings.

English spelling is difficult. Here a Pakistani barber suggests some improvements.

While English spelling has often been ridiculed, Chomsky & Halle (1968:54) in their Sound Patters of English were brave enough to claim that "conventional orthography is [...] a near optimal system for the lexical representation of English words" (!). But then, of course, the issue of what the underlying representations look like could be subject to discussion. Pullum (1991:118) counters that English orthography is "so insane it makes the underlying representations in The Sound Patterns of English look sensible".

Other languages with spelling systems notoriously unhelpful with regard to the pronunciation of words include Burmese, Tibetan, Assamese, and Irish. In most cases, the main reason for this is the utterly conservative character of the orthography, so that it represents pronunciations which have been outdated for centuries.

FREQUENT ALPHABET CHANGES

The choice of alphabet and orthography is often based on political and cultural loyalties. When these change, so sometimes does the writing system. For instance, the American lexicographer Noah Webster in 1789 proposed that Americans should deliberately change their orthography in order to distance "American" from "English".

Turkey is no doubt the best known case of alphabet change. Eager to be perceived as a progressive western country, rather than a backward Middle East nation, Turkish leader Atatürk ordered a shift from Arabic to Latin writing after the First World War. In some lesser known cases, things have not been so simple. Several languages of Russia or former Soviet Asia underwent more than one such shift during the course of the 20th century. Typical examples are Uzbek and Kirghiz, which were first written in Arabic script, then in Latin characters from the 1920s, until the introduction of Cyrillic in 1940. There is a movement to switch back to Latin script in many places, presumably as a way of marking distance vis-à-vis Russia, a step already taken by some ex-Soviet languages.

In July 2001, Azerbaijani president Heydar Aliev declared that from the 1st of August, the country's official language was to be written in Latin script. Thus, literally overnight, Azerbaijani newspapers became illegible for the majority of their habitual readers. This was the country's third change of writing system in less than a century—from Arabic to Latin script in the 1920s, then Cyrillic a decade later, and now Latin again. "Some countries go to war when the domestic political problems become unbearable", commented Russian newspaper *Izvestiya* laconically, "others change their writing system". Some Azeri newspapers threatened to revert to Cyrillic if the circulation should drop dramatically. In this case, of course, the whole point of the reform—i.e. an Azerization of the public discourse—would be forfeited. Though they could no longer read their own newspapers, Azeri citizens were at least entitled to a new public holiday, for president Aliev proclaimed the 1st of August as "National Alphabet Day".

Another example is Kalmyk. In 1648, this language got its own alphabet, but in 1924 Stalin decreed that Kalmyk be written in Cyrillic. A mere six years later, the Latin alphabet was introduced, only to be replaced again with Cyrillic in 1937, which is still in use. In line with the chaotic tradition, however, a radical spelling reform was launched in 2000—and abandoned the year after.

The speakers of Abkhaz (most of whom live in Georgia) should perhaps be glad that their authorities have not gone for Latin writing, for during the 20th century alone, the language has switched not only from Cyrillic to Latin to modified Cyrillic, but also lived through a brief period of using the Georgian alphabet. Not surprisingly, there have been recent suggestions to revert to Latin again.

The Ossetes too have lived through frequent alphabet changes. From the mid-19th century, the language had its own script, for which Latin letters were substituted in 1923. Northern Ossete switched back to the indigenous script in 1938, but at the same time Southern Ossete began being written in the Georgian alphabet, which in turn was replaced by Cyrillic in 1954.

OLDEST WRITING SYSTEM

Sumerian cuneiform is generally acknowledged as the oldest writing system known. Its use is attested from around 3200 BC. Every once in a while, though, other scripts are suggested to be even older.

In 1998, it was announced that Günter Dreyer of the *Deutsche Archäologische Institut* in Cairo had discovered Egyptian writing dating from two to four centuries earlier. Some of his colleagues have argued, however, that his finds represent something less than a fully developed writing system, a question which will no doubt be debated for years to come.

The year after, reports from Harappa in present-day Pakistan spoke of symbols resembling writing which were believed to date from about 5500 BC. Again, there are serious doubts on whether the symbols depict real objects or whether they really represent language—only in the latter case would it merit being called writing.

In 2003, the finding of incisions on fourteen fragments of tortoise shell was reported from Jiahu in China's Henan province. The shells were radiocarbon dated and shown to be 8 600 years old. But again, as only 11 separate symbols were identified, it is not yet certain that the inscriptions could qualify as writing.

Almost as old are the Vinča symbols found at several excavation sites mainly in the Balkans. A somewhat larger number of signs have been documented, but the script—if that is indeed what it is—remains undeciphered.

It would therefore seem that Sumerian cuneiform still remains the oldest indisputable instance of writing. The oldest writing system *still in use*, however, is the Chinese logographic script. First attested around 1200 BC, it still is one of the most frequently used in the world, although it has of course undergone changes in the course of time.

THE IMPORTANCE OF ALPHABETICAL ORDERING

Those using the Latin alphabet tend to take alphabetical order as the key to sorting, storing and retrieving information for granted. In cultures using other scripts, various alternatives have been devised. The Chinese, for instance, use about 200 *radicals* for this purpose. (These are the most basic characters, combinations of which form other characters.) Unfortunately there is lack of agreement on how one orders things after the identification of the first radical, making filing more cumbersome than in the West.

This western system, however, still leaves room for some improvisation. It is said that Korea registered its name with the international football federation FIFA (*Fédération Internationale de Football Association* [sic]) as *Corea*, only to afterwards change it back to *Korea*, which may explain why the 2002 World Cup was co-hosted by Korea and Japan rather than—as one would expect—by Japan and Korea. That same year, at the November 2002 NATO summit, the organization thought it had made clear that Ukrainian President Leonid Kuchma was not welcome, but he nevertheless did turn up. This was most annoying to the British and American delegates, as these had been most outspoken in their opposition to his participation. Therefore, the organization's other official language, French, was employed for once. Using the English names of the participating countries would have placed the Ukraine right next to the United Kingdom and the United States. Thanks to these countries' names in French, the meeting could be held with Kuchma's *Ukraïne* at a safe distance of seven seats away from Tony Blair's *Royaume-Uni* and more than 30 from George Bush's *États-Unis*.

So, even among cultures using the Latin alphabet confusion may arise. In 1994, the alphabetical order of Spanish was changed so that *ch* and *ll* are now treated as sequences of two letters rather than as separate letters. The Dutch, on the other hand, sometimes treat *ij* as a single letter, sometimes as a combination of *i* and *j*, and e.g. telephone directories normally treat *ij* as an allograph (variant) of *y*. While German dictionaries list *ä* and *ö* under *a* and *o* respectively (some telephone directories, on the other hand, treat *ä* as *a+e*), Swedes treat them as letters in their own right, ordered at the end of the alphabet, after *z*. On the other hand, they normally lump *v* and *w* together. As for the Icelanders, they arrange their telephone directories according to given names rather than surnames.

An interesting additional feature of alphabetical ordering is that no one has the slightest clue as to its origins!

MISINTERPRETING EGYPTIAN HIEROGLYPHS

Athanasius Kircher was the most well-known and respected authority on Egyptian hieroglyphs in 17th century Rome. In 1666 he published an interpretation of the texts on the obelisk which still stands on the Piazza della Minerva. One passage in the text was translated by Kircher as follows:

> *Osiris's protection against the violence of Typhon must be invoked in accordance with appropriate rituals and ceremonies, through sacrifices and through appeal to the protective spirits of the threefold world, in order to assure the happiness and wealth which the Nile usually bestows upon the enemies of Typhon's violence.*

After the decipherment of the Egyptian hieroglyphs by Jean-François Champollion a century and a half later, we now know that the passage in question simply reads *Psammetichus*—the name of an Egyptian Pharaoh!

There is no doubt that Kircher was a highly intelligent man. Apart from works on several different subjects (including his thoughts on a universal language), he left plenty of interesting innovations behind, but you'll have to admit that in this particular case, he was rather far off the mark.

The name of Pharaoh Psammetichus, which was so drastically misread by Kircher

MAKING THE MOST OF WHAT ONE HAS

Successful adaption of a writing system from the language for which it was originally created to a new one usually requires some changes. Thus, many languages using the Latin script have added a few symbols to suit their needs (examples from Europe include ã, å, ä, â, æ, ç, č, é, è, ê, ĭ, î, ɪ, ñ, ö, õ, ô, ø, š, ß, ù, û, and ü). In most cases, the new symbols derive from a modification of an existing letter. More rarely, a symbol other than a letter is employed. In Marshallese, for instance, a language of the Marshall Islands in the Pacific, the ampersand symbol (&) is used to represent the phoneme /ɛ/. Between 1993 and 1995, the Turkmen alphabet included the letters £, $, ¥, since replaced by ž, ş and ý respectively.

An alternative to introducing new symbols is to combine already existing ones. Plenty of languages do this, including English, which has <ch> for /tʃ/. Possibly unique, however, is the tetragraph (combination of four symbols) used in Kabardian. Its script features <КХЪУ> as a way of writing /qʷ/(which is a single phoneme, although not even the IPA has a symbol for it!)

A more radical case is that of Maldivian. The conversion of the Maldives to Islam in 1153 entailed the introduction of Arabic script to the island kingdom. For some reason, however, the script wasn't taken over as such, but rather, the Maldivians chose several Arabic numerals to stand for some of the consonants of Maldivian. The remaining consonants are represented by symbols from an older local set of numerals, by Arabic letters, or by locally developed characters.

Arabic numerals and Maldivian consonants with their western transliterations

Possibly the best known example in this genre, however, is the Cherokee alphabet. In 1809, a Cherokee intellectual and diplomat known as Sequoyah began working on a writing system. Although illiterate himself, he was convinced that writing was an important key to the might of the Anglo-Americans.

*Sequoyah proudly demonstrates
his invention in a contemporary painting*

After 12 years, he presented the result of his efforts—a syllabic writing system consisting of about 85 symbols. He first taught the new syllabary to his daughter in order to persuade the skeptical tribal elders of the usefulness of his invention. This aroused considerable enthusiasm among his fellow country-men, and within a year, they were virtually all literate. A printing press was acquired, and the Cherokee soon began printing their own newspaper, and a considerable amount of other printed material, both in Cherokee and in English appeared. Needless to say, this could not be tolerated by the new masters of the country (despite the Cherokee, including Sequoyah himself, having fought with the Americans against the British in the war of 1812), and the Cherokee nation was destroyed,

its surviving members being deported to less valuable lands in Oklahoma.

When the letters of English didn't suffice, Sequoyah resorted to Greek, Hebrew and numerals for inspiration. Either because he didn't read English, or simply because he didn't care, the sound values of the symbols in Cherokee have nothing in common with those of the languages from which they were borrowed. Thus, the symbol *R* stands for the syllable /e/, *M* is pronounced /lu/, while *4* is /se/.

The writing system is still used among speakers of Cherokee in Oklahoma, although the number of people literate in it is limited.

a	e	i	o	u	v [5]
D a	R e	T i	Ꮩ o	Ꮎ u	i v
S ga Ꮎ ka	Ᏺ ge	Ᏻ gi	A go	J gu	E gv
Ꮂ ha	Ᏸ he	Ꮓ hi	Ꮆ ho	Ꮀ hu	Ꮔ hv
W la	Ꮄ le	Ᏼ li	G lo	M lu	Ꮕ lv
Ꮝ ma	Ꮋ me	H mi	Ꮣ mo	Ꮝ mu	
Ꮎ na	Ꮄ ne	h ni	Z no	Ꮗ nu	Ꮕ nv
Ꮦ qua	Ꮙ que	Ꮥ qui	Ꮖ quo	Ꮘ quu	Ꮷ quv
Ꮝ s Ꮧ sa	Ꮦ se	b si	Ꮠ so	Ꮢ su	R sv
Ꮮ da Ꮚ ta	Ꭲ te	Ꮧ di Ꮨ ti	V do	S du	Ꮫ dv
Ꮣ dla Ꮭ tla	L tle	C tli	Ꮯ tlo	Ꮰ tlu	P tlv
G tsa	Ꮴ tse	Ꮣ tsi	K tso	Ꮪ tsu	Ꮳ tsv
Ꮤ wa	Ꮺ we	Ꮻ wi	Ꮼ wo	Ꮽ wu	Ꮾ wv
Ꮿ ya	Ᏸ ye	Ꭰ yi	Ꮿ yo	G yu	B yv

Sequoyah's Cherokee syllabary

CHROMATOGRAPHIC WRITING

Bekerie (2003) provides some very brief data on a script of—to the best of my knowledge—a hitherto undocumented type. This script, apparently used by the Edo of Nigeria, consists of oval shapes (not unlike the *Teletubbies*), some with "ears", others with "feet", and sometimes embellished with dots.

Apparently, the *color* of the ovals is distinctive. The available information is very limited, but if this is indeed a fully-fledged writing system, it may well be the only instance in the world of a chromatographic script, i.e. one based not only on the shape of the characters, but also on their color.

SPEED READING

Some people are evidently better than others at reading at exceptionally high speed. Howard Berg, for instance, co-author of *Speed-Reading the Easy Way*, has claimed to be able to read 25 000 words a minute. At this rate, he would be able to consume four thick novels in a mere hour. George Stancliffe, founder of *The American Speed Reading Project*, says he taught a dyslexic woman to read 18 000 words a minute.

Most normal people read, and get a reasonable grasp of, about 300 words a minute, though some may achieve twice that speed.

Speed-Reading the Easy Way by Howard Berg & Marcus Conyers

Kim Peek

Only one person is known who can read at an amazing pace, and yet achieve a near total retention: American autist Kim Peek. Born in 1951, Peek is reportedly able to recall the contents of some 7 600 books he has read.

Although unable to brush his own teeth without great difficulty, Peek developed the ability to read a page of print in 10–15 seconds—and with a 98% retention rate. Most people would require several minutes for such a task.

Kim Peek was partly the model for Raymond, the savant in the 1989 film *Rain Man*, starring Dustin Hoffman and Tom Cruise, and just like the fictional Rain Man, Peek also has unimaginable counting skills and memorizing capacity. It is reported, by the way, that most of his autistic characteristics disappeared as a result of the public exposure generated by the film.

SPEED WRITING

The *Guinness Book of World Records* mentions Oregonian Barbara Blackburn as the world's fastest typist. She is able to sustain a speed of 150 words per minute for 50 minutes (equalling 37 500 key strokes). Using a specially designed keyboard, she attains a speed of 170 words per minute, and has in shorter dashes reached a rate of 212.

SOURCES NOT MENTIONED IN THE TEXT

On writing systems in general: Sampson (1985) and Robinson (1998).

Literacy: *CIA World Factbook* and Parker (1997).

Newspaper consumption: UNESCO (data from 1996).

Literacy - gender differences: UNESCO (data from 1997), *CIA World Factbook.*

Reason for female literacy in Lesotho: Philip Baker (p c).

Korean Han'gŭl: Sampson (1985:120–44).

Lost Naga writing system: Dalby (1998:334).

Miao writing system: Enwall (1994–95).

Number of Chinese signs necessary to read: Chen (1999:137).

Number of characters in Seneca and Tahitian: Katzner (1994).

Number of strokes in Chinese characters: Melin (2000:104), Chen (1999:161).

Burmese spelling: Wheatley (1990:109).

Irish spelling: Mac Eoin (1993:105).

Assamese spelling: Campbell (1991:102).

Complex Japanese writing: Shibatani (1990b:121-31).

Noah Webster's proposed spelling reform: Graddol (1997:6).

Alphabet changes in ex-Soviet Asia: Katzner (1994).

Kalmyk writing: Kornoussova (2001).

Abkhaz alphabet changes: Comrie (1981:33).

Ossete alphabet changes: Comrie (1981:164).

Alphabet changes in Azerbaijan: *Dagens Nyheter* 2001-08-04.

Günter Dreyer's old writing in Egypt: BBC Online News 1998-12-15.

Old Pakistani script: Rao (1999).

Tortoise shells from Jiahu: Li et al. (2003).

Vinča symbols: Daniel Bunčić (p c).

The importance of alphabetical ordering: Bits and pieces from Philip Baker (p c). Alphabetical order at the NATO summit: CNN, 2002-11-22.

Misinterpreting the Egyptian hieroglyphs: Robinson (1998:22).

New Turkmen letters 1993-95: Schlyter (2003), Daniel Bunčić (p c).

The ampersand symbol in Marshallese (Katzner 1994).

Kabard tetragraph: Comrie (1981:199).

Maldivian writing: Gair & Cain (1996).

Speed reading: Based primarily on Carroll (2001) and Peek (1997).

SIGNED LANGUAGES

SPEECH AND WRITING are not the only media used to transmit language. For the several million people around the world who are profoundly deaf, speaking is not even an option and, instead, signing is used.

SIGN LANGUAGES OF THE WORLD

Very little work has been done on sign language typology, or on genetic relationships between the various signed languages. Nobody even knows how many sign languages there are, although there certainly are far more than the 100 or so listed in the *Ethnologue*. Only in some cases do we have indications of how one or the other language spread. Thus, we know that American sign language (ASL) is derived from its French counterpart LSF (see p 127). Similarly, signed languages in Australia and South Africa owe a lot to sign systems of the British Isles. Coincidences of history are responsible for some more surprising relationships, such as the sign language of Portugal being derived in part from that of Sweden. As a consequence, American and French signers may understand each other, but not American and British ones. Similarly, some signers in Kenya use a dialect of Belgian Sign, while others use a hybrid of American and Korean Sign.

THE MOST COMMON SIGN LANGUAGE MYTHS

Signers constitute a minority in the societies where they live, so it is perhaps not surprising that many aspects of their situation, including the nature of their languages, is often misunderstood. The following seem to be the most common misconceptions.

- **Sign languages are not fully-fledged languages**. As indicated elsewhere in this book, there is no widely-accepted definition of what constitutes an impoverished language, as opposed to a "proper" one—and no such definition is ever offered by those who claim that one language or another is "primitive". Sign languages certainly are able to express abstract concepts, and they do have native speakers.
- **Speaking Sign is the same thing as finger spelling**. Every once in a while, people may offer to teach you a sign language but in fact show you finger spelling. The picture below illustrates the ASL sign for 'sit' while the three pictures to the right show the finger spellings for S-

I-T. Finger spelling is to signed language basically what spelling out loud is to spoken language.

- **Sign languages were consciously constructed by hearing people**. If you think about it, this belief is really quite demeaning—as if deaf people would be less capable of developing language on their own. In any case, signed languages were not really "invented" by anybody, just like no one "invented" English or Latin or Zulu. Languages, spoken and signed alike, have (with very few exceptions) developed on their own for centuries and even millennia, without there being a clear starting point. Wherever there are people, there is a language, and wherever there are deaf people, there is a sign language! It is true that many signed languages have not been standardized until recent times, but standardizing a language is hardly the same thing as inventing it.
- **Sign Language is international**. Given the above, that languages, including signed ones, have developed spontaneously—why should sign languages be international, when spoken languages aren't? Sign languages still remain notoriously understudied, so no one really knows how many there are, but at least a hundred-odd different varieties have been attested. Thus, there is a Puerto Rican, a Balinese and a Kenyan sign language. And the boundaries between signed languages, just like those of spoken languages, do not necessarily follow national boundaries. Algerian Sign extends into Morocco, Standard French Sign is also used in Togo, and countries such as Switzerland, Malaysia, France, Canada and Tanzania each use more than one sign language. Belgium, which has several spoken languages, has only one signed language. That said, there have been attempts to actually create international sign languages (the most well known being known as Gestuno) but, much as with Esperanto among the hearing, success has been limited.
- **Sign languages are based on spoken languages**. If this were the case, we would expect e.g. both British and American deaf to use one and the same sign language, since their hearing compatriots for the most part speak English. In fact, the British and American sign languages are completely unrelated, and mutually unintelligible. American and French Sign, on the other hand are related, and to a great extent are mutually intelligible. In many cases, sign languages are even utterly different in structure from the spoken language used by the surrounding community. There are also signed versions of spoken languages, but e.g. "Signed English" is basically a combination of American or British Sign and the grammar of English. Of course, most signers have some competence in the majority language around them—in literate societies, they usually know how to read and write it, with varying degrees of proficiency. Because of this, signers are influenced by the majority—just as any other minority language is. But that does not make American Sign any more or less based on English than is Navaho.

THE MOST WIDELY USED SIGN LANGUAGE

The most widely used sign language in the world is probably the American Sign Language, or ASL. The *Ethnologue* lists it as having somewhere between 100 000 and 500 000 "primary users", but the presence of about two million profoundly deaf people in the USA might make it the country's third language in terms of number of users. In addition, several million hearing Americans (according to the most generous estimates up to 15 000 000) have some degree of competence in ASL.

Indian Sign Language, used in India, Bangladesh and Pakistan, would be a potential rival, with its about 1 500 000 primary users, as would Chinese Sign Language, given the more than three million deaf in China, Taiwan and Malaysia. Little is known about Indonesian sign language, but 2 000 000 deaf are reported from Indonesia. In Asia, however, the less developed infrastructure does not permit the high degree of standardization that comes with the enrolment of American children in deaf schools, so that a deaf person in China or India is less likely than her counterpart in the USA to acquire competence in the national standard sign language.

Moreover, just like English among the hearing, ASL is also the *lingua franca* in many international contexts, and it is to some extent known by deaf people from other countries who have contacts with deaf foreigners.

ASL has furthermore—to a great extent due to the work of American missionaries—greatly influenced sign language development in the Philippines, Hong Kong, Canada, Singapore, and more than a dozen countries in Africa and Latin America.

Thomas Gallaudet and his teacher Laurent Clerc first introduced French Sign Language in America

MOST PROLIFEROUS SIGN LANGUAGE

In this context, special mention has to be made of French Sign Language (LSF), as the Mother of if-not-all-then-at-least-many sign languages.

LSF, itself standardized in 1752, was taken to the USA in the early 19th century by Thomas Gallaudet and his teacher Laurent Clerc, and LSF and ASL still remain partly mutually intelligible. In addition to its indirect (through ASL) impact on many sign languages of the world, LSF is used as such in Switzerland and Togo, while the sign languages of Austria, the Czech Republic, Italy, Russia, Belgium, the Netherlands, and Tunisia all have their roots in LSF. LSF has also exerted a considerable influence on signing in Germany, Denmark, Spain, Quebec, Ireland, Greece and elsewhere. Ironically, it is not used throughout France since the area around Lyons has its own sign language.

SIGN LANGUAGE AS A MEDIUM OF HIGHER EDUCATION

The only university with a sign language—in this case ASL—as its main means of instruction is the Gallaudet University in Washington. Founded in 1864, the university now has almost 2 000 students and about 1 100 employees.

LOCALLY WIDESPREAD SIGNING COMPETENCE

Genetically-caused deafness is rampant in some populations. In consequence, local sign languages have been used for as long as anyone can remember, and often also mastered by a significant proportion of the hearing population. A famous case is that of Martha's Vineyard, whose first white settlers from Kent in England brought a genetic disposition for deafness with them. Vineyard Sign is now extinct, but was used until about 1910 by a large part of the hearing locals. Similar cases have been attested in Ghana and Bali. Four extreme cases are listed below. In some of these localities, it has been reported that hearing people too may use the sign language among themselves in a variety of situations.

Nohya, Mexico	*14 deaf in a population of about 400. Most of the hearing know Sign.*
Providence Island, Colombia	*19 persons deaf from birth. Most of the other locals (some 3 000) are proficient signers.*
Rennell, Solomon Islands	*Developed in 1915 by a single individual, who taught others. Now extinct.*
Urubú-Kaapor, Brazil	*Seven deaf L1 signers, but the rest of the tribe, some 500 persons, are also childhood signers.*
Unnamed Keresan-speaking village in New Mexico	*14 out of 650 are deaf, but most of the older generation know the local sign.*

SIGN SINGING

In the mid-1990s, Taiwanese television regularly aired a sign singing contest. A singer would sing the lyrics to a pre-recorded musical background, while the contestant signed the same lyrics. Similar contests have been held in California, and in the 1970s, there were even groups of deaf performers touring the USA signing popular songs. The African-American female a cappella ensemble Sweet Honey in the Rock has been around for a long time, and still performs together with a sign language interpreter.

WHEN YOU CAN'T HEAR VOICES IN YOUR HEAD

It is not uncommon for criminals to claim that their deeds were inspired by voices in their heads. One may wonder if deaf psychotics differ from hearing ones in this respect. At least in some cases, it seems that they do. In early 2002, Joseph Mesa, a student at Gallaudet University, was tried and found guilty of having murdered his two course mates Eric Plunkett and Benjamin Varner—all three of whom were deaf. Mesa claimed insanity, and that he had been urged to kill by strange voices. These were not literally voices, however, for what he had experienced was signing hands clad in black gloves telling him to commit murder.

EARLY SIGN RECORDINGS

Signing is difficult to represent adequately in writing—although such systems do exist, they are only rarely used. One consequence is that there are hardly any very early examples of signing known prior to the invention of motion pictures at the very end of the 19th century.

In 1898, just three years after Louis Lumière's construction of the motion picture camera, none other than Thomas Alva Edison documented what is probably the first filmed use of a sign language—the legendary William "Buffalo Bill" Cody communicating in Plains Indian Sign with Iron Tail of the Sioux. In 1907 Edison also made the first recording of ASL, and as early as 1912–13, the National Association of the Deaf in the USA produced an entire series of films in the language.

SOME INTERESTING SPECIFIC SIGNS

Those sharing my faiblesse for the equivoque might be interested to know that the sign for 'horny' in ASL is similar to that for 'hungry', only with a more energetic delivery. Many a student has confused the two, or has been misunderstood when trying to say *really* hungry'.

The sign for 'condom' in many sign languages looks just as you'd expect it to. In Swedish Sign, for instance, you put up your index finger, and pretend to roll a condom over it. In Japanese Sign, the motion is the same, only you do it as if you were rolling the condom over your head . . .

The ASL sign for 'I love you' is suggestive—it looks uncannily like what some would interpret as a symbol for the devil, or

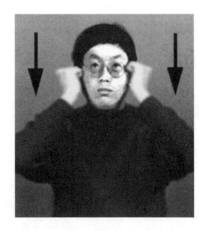

Or maybe the Japanese know something about safe sex that we don't.

which in the Mediterranean area means 'your wife cheats on you', or the gesture which heavy metal fans associate with their preferred music.

Finally, I have another East Asian favorite. In Taiwanese Sign, the word for 'brother', illustrated here, presumably came into being before a knowledge of American obscene gestures reached the island.

This is Taiwanese Sign for 'brother'. Really.

The number of deaf-blind people in the world is difficult to calculate, in particular since the phenomenon is a gradient one (how poor does your hearing and eyesight have to be in order for you to qualify as deaf-blind?). In western countries, the rate of deaf-blindness is usually said to be around 0,015%, whereas in some developing countries, the proportion may be twice as high. Therefore, there must be at the very least 1m people in the world today who are unable to communicate by either auditory or visual means.

Depending on the degree of impairment, large print, lip-reading, speech and ordinary signing may be used for communication to some extent. Other methods include palm writing, tadoma (tactile lip-reading), finger Braille, and Morse. The most common means of communication, however, is tactile sign, in which sign language is produced in the hands of the addressee (usually called "consumer" in these contexts).

Since most users of tactile sign languages who were not born deaf-blind communicated in ordinary sign languages before losing their eyesight, the former are usually modified versions of the latter. One difference imposed by the new medium is that tactile sign is usually more linear and sequential, and so more similar to signed versions of spoken language.

A REMARKABLE TACTILE SIGNER

Born in 1880, Helen Keller became both deaf and blind at 18 months of age. Fortunately, her parents had the will and the means to hire someone to teach her Tactile Sign and Braille, both of which she quickly learned. Thus, from the age of seven, she was almost always accompanied by Anne Sullivan, who was herself partly blind but not deaf, and who served as a link between Keller and the outside world.

At the age of ten, she was sent to a school in Boston, where another teacher taught her to speak by letting Keller's fingertips feel the position of her lips and tongue in action. This method also allowed her to learn tactile lip-reading.

In 1894, Keller entered a deaf school in New York, and later continued to the Cambridge School for Young Ladies in Massachusetts. She began studying at Radcliffe College in

1900, with Sullivan, as always, by her side, translating the lectures into Tactile Sign for her. Four years later, she graduated cum laude, with honours in German and English. While studying at Radcliffe, she also wrote *The Story of My Life*, which was published serially in *The Ladies Home Journal* and, in 1902, in book form. This encouraged her to go on to publish a number of other books.

After having read Marx and Engels, Keller joined the Massachusetts Socialist Party, for which she produced a number of articles and lectures. Despite this, she was received in the White House by every American president from Grover Cleveland to John F Kennedy, and in 1961 she was even one of 30 Americans to whom President Johnson awarded the nation's highest civilian recognition, the Presidential Medal of Freedom.

In addition to the achievements already mentioned, it should be noted that Keller also learned to master horseback riding, dancing, and Greek. She died in 1968, at the age of 87. Even before Keller's death, her life with Sullivan formed the basis of a successful play, *Anne Sullivan Macy: The Story Behind Helen Keller*, in 1959, and a film, *The Miracle Worker*, in 1962.

It should perhaps be noted that, while Helen Keller is the world's most famous deaf-blind person, there are numerous other people with a similar handicap whose accomplishments are truly remarkable. Deaf-blind societies in various countries often have their own local heroes as role models.

Helen Keller as portrayed on a Japanese stamp

FIRST SCIENTIFIC STUDY OF TACTILE SIGN

Although some minor studies had been done earlier in the USA, Mesch (1994) seems to have been the first linguistic study on a tactile sign language—Swedish Tactile Sign. It was later expanded into Mesch (1998) and translated into English as Mesch (2001).

SHE TOOK THE TRUTH INTO HER OWN HANDS

Interpreters usually have to swear on oath that they will faithfully translate impartially, without adding to or altering the content. But loyalty can conflict with conscience. In the 2004 elections in Ukraine, which had been run by the corrupt Yanukovych who officially won over his challenger Yushchenko, the results were widely considered to have been falsified by the government. As the fraudulent results were officially broadcast to the Ukrainians, they were simultaneously rendered in Ukrainian Sign by Natalia Dmytruk. She started translating faithfully but, after a while, the official version and her translation began to diverge. "Yanukovych has 49,5% of the votes against Yushchenko's 46,6%", said the official. "The election commission's results are bogus", signed Dmytruk. "Yanuko-vych is the winner" said the official. "I am ashamed to translate such lies to you. Our president is Yushchenko", signed Dmytruk. The very next day, the news presenter himself told viewers: "We're not going to lie to you any more".

Dmytruk's heroism resulted in several awards from human rights organizations, in recognition of her part in what became known as the "orange revolution".

SOURCES NOT MENTIONED IN THE TEXT

Details on which sign languages are spoken where are derived mostly from the *Ethnologue*.

Common myths and individual signs in specific languages: Personal experience with deaf linguists at Stockholm University's Linguistics Dept, one of the few to include a section devoted to the study of sign languages.

Martha's Vineyard: Groce (1985).

Helen Keller's life: Obituary printed in the New York Times 1968-06-01.

Data on Gallaudet enrollment from the University itself.

David Quinto was kind enough to answer some basic questions about American Tactile Sign.

Sign singing: *Linguist List* 6.257; Sweet Honey in the Rock home page.

Early Sign recording: Veditz (2002) and Fronval & Dubois (1978:7).

Keresan Sign is discussed by Kelley & McGregor (2001).

Delusional Signing inspiring murder: American media coverage.

LEARNING YOUR FIRST LANGUAGE

MOST OF US learned a native language from our parents or others who were around us in the years immediately following our birth. A few people happened to be in a position where this was not an option. Legends tell the stories of Romulus and Remus, Mowgli, and Tarzan, who did not grow up among humans. Regardless of how much confidence we may have in these stories, there are more or less well-documented cases of children who have grown up without human contact—or at least not enough of it to learn a human language. Whether or not they were literally raised by animals or just lived in the wild, or could be better described as "neglected" or "confined", they are often known as "wolf-children". Today linguists prefer the word feral to cover all such cases so this is the term used below.

OLDEST FIRST LANGUAGE LEARNER

There are reports in the literature of people having come into contact with a human language at ages as high as 21 (Jean of Liège, 17th century), 22 (the Sow-girl of Salzburg, early 19th century) or 23 (the Wolf-child of Kronstadt, late 19th century).

None of these cases, however, are well documented, and we know virtually nothing about how much language—if any—they acquired. Among the scholarly documented cases found after the onset of puberty, most, such as "Genie" ("discovered" at the age of 13), have not managed to learn any language well.

A possible exception is the legendary Kaspar Hauser, who was first exposed to language at age 16 in 1828, and who is reported to have learned to speak very well (but then, he is in some reports credited with some rather supernatural talents).

Kaspar Hauser (c 1812-1833)

Sudam Pradhana, found at the age of 24 in Orissa, India in 2001, had originally learned to talk, but had forgotten this skill during his eleven years in the forest.

A 17-year old neglected boy encountered in Jacksonville, Florida, in 2005, "could not talk, but only grunt".

Since both these two cases are so recent, there is at present no information available on whatever linguistic progress they may have made.

An obvious problem in all feral child cases is that it is difficult to tell to what extent the failure to acquire language is due to a child having passed the critical period for normal first-language learning or to the psychological traumas connected with their unusual experience of childhood.

BEST STUDIED FERAL CHILD

I t is unlikely that any feral child has been as extensively studied as "Genie", a Californian child who had spent the first 13 years of her life tied up in a small room. "Genie" was discovered by the authorities in November 1970, and her development was monitored closely until at least 1975.

EARLIEST ADPOSITIONS

T o the best of my knowledge, there is no study on which words are first acquired by children from various language backgrounds. At least one subset of words, however, namely adpositions, has been studied in such a way. Children from four different linguistic environments were found to acquire adpositions in the following order:

	English	Italian	Serbo-Croatian	Turkish
1.	in	in	on	in
2.	on	on	in	on
3.	under	under	beside	under
4.	beside	beside	under	beside
5.	between	between	behind	behind
6.	in front of	in front of	between	in front of
7.	behind	under	in front of	between

(Obviously, for the three other languages, the English translation is given rather than the actual item). The earliest prepositions are generally phonetically simpler than those learned later on, and could also be argued to be less complex from a semantic perspective. In most cases, they are also more common in the adult input received by the child.

LANGUAGES WITHOUT MOTHERESE

I n most western societies, as well as in many other parts of the world, toddlers tend to be addressed in what is known as *motherese* (or, more politically correct, *parentese*, or *care-giver speech*). The features of this speech register are also rather similar across the world, usually including short sentences, frequent repetitions, higher fundamental frequency, and exaggerated pitch contours.

There are cultures, however, where the child is, to a far greater extent, left to its own devices. Children are not seen as potential conversation partners, and they are rarely addressed in the first place. Conversations will have to wait until the child has learned to produce intelligible speech (makes sense if you ask me!). In some areas, the child is not even listened to unless it can be understood—something that contrasts with many western parents' expanding on the child's gooing and attempting to find a message in it.

Languages whose speakers fulfil some or all of these characteristics—and who are at least reported not to use motherese—include Samoan, Warlpiri, K'iche' Maya, Kaluli, and Javanese.

Of course, not being addressed by its parents does not necessarily mean that the child is deprived of conversational opportunities, as provided by e.g. peers and older siblings.

SOURCES NOT MENTIONED IN THE TEXT

Feral children: Crystal (1987:289), Ward (2005), Seguin (1907:3-4), Gonçalves & Peixoto (2001:46-47), Newton (2002). Also newspaper reports and Andrew Ward's fantastic web site <feralchildren.com>.

Earliest adpositions: Johnston & Slobin (1979), Slobin (1982).

Lack of motherese: Bavin (1995:380-81).

SECOND-LANGUAGE LEARNING

IN SOME WESTERN COUNTRIES, monolingualism is the norm. In the world as a whole, though, it is more common to master two or more languages. In many cases, it is more or less a matter of survival, as the official language differs from the home language of its citizens.

LARGEST FOREIGN LANGUAGE INSTITUTE

The American *Defense Language Institute Foreign Language Center* in Monterey, California, is often said to be the world's largest foreign language institute. As the name suggests, its mission is to provide language expertise for the American armed forces. Founded in 1941, it originally focussed on Japanese, but later taught mostly east European languages. In the early 21st century, Arabic and Afghan languages experienced an immense increase in popularity.

In all, the institute has a staff of slightly more than 1 000, of whom almost 800 are language instructors. The number of students is usually between 2 000 and 2 500. Since its beginnings in 1941, about 170 000 students have graduated from the institute.

Incidentally, Monterey is also the self-proclaimed *Language Capital of the World*. It is responsible for a fourth of all post-secondary learning of foreign languages in the United States. Apart from the *Defense Language Institute Foreign Language Center*, the city is also home to several other language-related businesses, including the world's largest

provider of telephone-based interpretation and an institute which offers the only master's degree program in conference interpretation in the country.

Both *Berlitz International* and *EF Education* have also claimed to be the world's largest language training organizations, but even upon request, neither company provides any information to verify or refute their claims. Another world-wide language-training organization is the *Alliance Française*, which enrols 300 000 students in more than 100 countries.

Yet another institution which has claimed this title is the Latter-day Saints' *Missionary Training Center* in Provo, Utah. It normally has 2 700 students, but although language teaching is important, it is not the only task of the center, and not all students take language lessons.

Among local institutions, one might also mention the Hong Kong branch of the British Council, which has 10 500 English students, and the Victorian School of Languages in Melbourne, Australia, enrolling some 13 000 students studying 43 different languages.

WORLD'S BIGGEST LANGUAGE LESSON

In an attempt to get into the *Guinness Book of World Records*, the city of Birmingham in March 2002 staged the self-proclaimed "world's biggest language lesson". For several minutes, about 60 000 Brummies (natives of Birmingham) stopped whatever they had been doing and set about learning a few phrases in one of 22 foreign languages.

THE SECRET BEHIND SPEAKING ENGLISH

In many a language, including English, 'tongue' is a synonym for 'language'. In South Korea, this has recently been taken more literally than one might expect (and wish). As in other countries, many Korean parents have a feeling that their children may have a better chance to succeed in life with an ability to speak English.

English is not this guy's native language (he grew up speaking Hebrew and Hungarian), but as you might guess from seeing his oral appendage, Gene Simmons (or Chaim Witz) does speak it pretty darn well.

Apparently, a belief has developed in some circles that the difficulties experienced in pronouncing English are due to the allegedly less flexible tongue of Koreans. Thus, if a surgical operation could improve the child's English, this would carry with it financial benefits. The price for the incision is reported to be in the USD 230-400 range. All in all, in 2002, South Koreans were reported to spend the equivalent of 3 000 000 000 US dollars on learning English.

MOST POPULAR FOREIGN LANGUAGES

The inclination to learn a language other than your mother tongue varies considerably from one population to the other (pp 39–40). Still, even in countries where rather few people actually learn more than one language, there is usually an obvious choice for those who do. (Please note that "foreign language" in the following refers to anything which is not the mother tongue of a majority of the population— I am thus not discriminating between what is in the literature referred to as "second language" and "foreign language").

Data is lacking from some countries (in particular ones such as Afghanistan, East Timor and Eritrea where more or less recent political upheavals have made accurate data hard to come by, and countries too small to support a statistical service), but there remain 165 other countries and semi-dependent territories (which after all constitute the vast majority of nations).

English is, by quite some margin, the most popular foreign language (82 states), followed by French (28) and Classical Arabic (19). At some distance follow Russian (9), Portuguese (6), Spanish (4), German (3) and Dutch (3). Amharic, Urdu, Persian, Nepali, Maori, Mandarin, Malay, Irish, Hindi, Hebrew, Tagalog, and Dutch are first foreign languages in one country each. In Greenland, the Faeroe Islands, and—until 1999—Iceland, Danish is the first foreign tongue learned.

In Japan, English is the first foreign language

Outside the Arab world, the normal state-of-affairs for a country which is neither English- nor French-speaking, is that English is the first foreign language studied, while French is the second (if indeed students ever study a second foreign language). A notable exception is the United States, where, since 1969, students have been more keen on studying Spanish than French.

In Europe, the dominance of English is more recent than many people are aware. It has basically expanded from north to south, replacing German in Scandinavia in the 1950s and in Netherlands and France in the 1960s. Later, it dethroned French in Spain in the 1970s, and in the following decade in Portugal and Italy.

LESS POPULAR FOREIGN LANGUAGES

Famous Eccles—pseudonym of a young amateur linguist from Australia—started out learning French. Having felt the joy of being bilingual, he wouldn't stop there. From French, he went on to Ubykh, !Xũ, Pirahã, Elvish, Klingon, and also acquired some Ancient Egyptian and Basque. Sometimes you cannot help feeling that unpredictability tends to become predictable . . .

MOST AVID LANGUAGE-LEARNERS IN EUROPE

Counting only the major languages (English, French, German and Spanish), the European country in which the largest proportion of students (at secondary school level) study a foreign language is Luxembourg. The enrolment amounts to 284,5% of the total student body (i.e. the average student learns more than one language). Luxembourg is followed by the Netherlands and, at some distance, by Denmark. At the other end of the scale, we find Spain (103,9%) and Ireland (100,4%). Luxembourg is also noteworthy in that it is the country (apart from Britain and Ireland) where English is responsible for the smallest proportion of students—both French and German are being learned by more students. Romania is the only other country included in the study where another language (French) is more popular than English.

¿HABLA USTED PHRASE-BOOKISH?

Phrase-books are intended to include the most necessary phrases for use in a foreign environment. It may well be that "Don't shoot!" is useful in Chechnya, but in many cases, one cannot but wonder what the authors had in mind when compiling their language guides. The following examples are all authentic. Whenever an ungrammatical (or un-pragmatic) English translation is given, this is cited just as it was found in the original (or, in those cases where the intended target audience did not consist of English speakers, in an English translated by Yours Truly in a way intended to represent the stylistic finesses [or finesselessness, if you will] of whatever western language the sentence was originally rendered in).

I was stabbed with a spear (Lozi)	*Carry me, slowly* (Nepali)
I had a suckling-brother, who died at the most tender age (Swedish)	*Didn't you tell me 'immediately' half an hour ago?* (Japanese)
Is this the first time you marry? (Setswana)	*I have my own syringe* (Indonesian)
At what time were these branches eaten by the rhinoceros? (Pidgin Arabic)	*They will not help you much, they are like a singed cat* (Irish Gaelic)
Sew nicely with skill (Setswana)	*I want a specimen of your urine* (Russian)
Please play a foxtrot (Yiddish)	*The corpse will be taken to Tonga* (Tongan)
Don't shoot! (Chechen)	*Put your hands over your head!* (Somali)
The beast had a human body, the feet of a buck, and a horn on its head (Swedish)	*I had yams and fish for two days, and then I ate fern roots* (Hawaiian)
Are you deaf in both ears or one? (Lozi)	*She has excellent breasts* (Welsh)
I need something for a tourniquet (Yiddish)	*Must I swallow them whole?* (Portuguese)
I don't play the violin, but I love cheese (French)	*Is the salesman a Jew?* (Ukrainian)
Hum! I see! So you also belong to the company of avaricious people, eh? (Japanese)	*Do you think foreigners are pigs that you put out dirty cutlery and forks?* (Japanese)

Don't pester the girls in the next tent (Welsh)	*Do you practice safe sex?* (Hindi)
Because I was out buying a pair of wooden shoes (Vietnamese)	*Has your daughter reached the age of puberty?* (Sikololo)
For all things, do not come (Swedish)	*I'd like to go to a Komsomol party* (Russian)
Can you take me to the minefields? (Chechen)	*This way, he makes me grey hairs* (Swedish)
Cook the dogs' food and put yesterday's milk in it (Sikololo)	*Fiona's solo dance was very good indeed* (Tongan)
I am sick and tired of talking to you (Japanese)	*What do we pay for the children?* (Polish)
With the wolves, one must howl (Swedish)	*All the road signs have been pulled down* (Welsh)

One of the compilers of phrase-book sentences, Mark Rosenfelder, was fascinated by the uselessness of many of these phrases, but decided to create his own set of more useful sentences, for which he provides translations into French, German and Spanish. Some examples include:

- *How much is that in real money?*
- *Don't "imperialist pig" me, my good man.*
- *That's not all! I have two more photo albums!*
- *Do you have highways in your country?*
- *That's got to be silicon.*
- *You wouldn't have these ghettos if you people were willing to work.*
- *It's nothing compared to our shopping centers.*
- *Could I have some <u>clean</u> water?*
- *Can I have fries with that?*
- *Has there been any real intellectual life in your country since Sartre?*

The title "the world's worst phrasebook" probably has several contenders. However, *English as she is spoke* by José da Fonseca and Pedro Carolino, is sometimes hailed as the worst in its genre ever. "Its damage to Anglo-American/Portuguese-Brazilian relations can only be estimated" said one reviewer of a 20th century reprint.

It was first published in Paris in 1855 with the title *O Novo Guia da Conversação, em Português e Inglês, em Duas Partes* ("The new guide to conversation, in Portuguese and English, in two parts"). Its unintentional humour quickly made it more appreciated by Anglo-Saxons than by its intended target audience. In 1883, a London publisher reprinted it with the title *English as she is spoke*. American editions soon followed, one with a preface by none other than Mark Twain, which helped to further popularize it.

Apparently, the authors did not actually speak English, but did have access to Portuguese-French and French-English dictionaries. The result led one modern commentator to the observe that "Da Fonseca has gone down as the worst scholar in history [...] The irony is that, unlike most of his colleagues, it means that people still read him". A problem, though, is that the authorship of this masterpiece is uncertain, and it has even been speculated that da Fonseca and Carolino were one and the same person. A more credible suggestion, perhaps, is that the elusive Carolino made a word-for-word translation of an already extant Portuguese-French phrasebook earlier published by da Fonseca. In that case, it would clearly be unfair to give da Fonseca the honour of having produced one of the least competent works in the history of phrase-book production.

Whatever the case may be, *English as she is spoke* is highly entertaining piece, and the following selection of sentences can only give a hint of how she was spoke by whoever the actual author was.

- The sun lie down. It is light moon's.
- What are then the edifices the worthest to have seen?
- I have mind to vomit.
- I am pinking me with a pin.
- The thunderbolt is falling down.
- The rose-trees begins to button.
- Take attention to cut you self.
- Tongh [sic] he is German, he speak so much well [...] spanish that [...] the Spanishesmen believe him Spanishing.

- Let us prick.
- Let us take patience, still some o'clock, and we shall be in the end of our voyage.
- It want to have not any indulgence towards the bat buffoons.

- You mistake you, it is a frog! dip again it in the water.
- Which hightness want you its? I want almost four feet six thumbs wide's, over seven of long.
- I have a particular care of its, because I know you like the bottoms.
- I row upon the belly on the back and between two waters.
- He sin in trouble water.
- It want to beat the iron during it is hot.
- It is difficult to enjoy well so much several languages.
- The stone as roll not heap up not foam.
- That which feel one's snotly blow blow one's nose

Related to phrase book sentences are *effles*. The word is derived from the acronym EFL (**E**nglish *as* a **F**oreign **L**anguage), and denotes sentences of the sort one encounters in language-learning materials, but never in real life. These are always grammatically impeccable, but tend to be pragmatically awkward. Memorable examples from English textbooks—effles of course exist in other languages as well—include *Peter is not a pencil*, *A hat is not food*, *Shall I leave without paying?*, *Ouch! O, foolish bee!* and *Her food is eaten by her*.

Higgins (2000) cites a particularly nice example where two children perform dialogues along the lines of *Is your name John? No, it isn't* for several chapters, until, in lesson six, it turns out that the children are brother and sister.

Let us not forget, finally, that this genre does have literary qualities that can be exploited artistically. The dialogues of Eugène Ionesco's famous *La cantatrice chauve* (*The Bald Soprano*) draw on effles, as does Tom Pop's Fragments from the subconsciousness, published in 1971 in a Festschrift to linguist Jim McCawley.

SOURCES NOT MENTIONED IN THE TEXT

Language teaching in Monterey: Defense Language Institute Foreign Language Center web page at <http://pom-www.army.mil/atfl/daa> (2002-08-31). An article in the Government Executive Magazine, 2002-04-01. Information from the city of Monterey.

Other language teaching organisations: Basically the home pages of the respective organisations. Statistics for the Alliance française were not available from the headquarters, and were therefore instead taken from the web site of its Tasmanian (!) branch at <tased.edu.au/tasonline/mltaweb/afdehob.htm> (2002-09-01).

Korean tongue incisions: Seattle Times 2002-04-07, Corsetti (2002).

Most popular foreign languages: Mostly Hendrik Biebeler (p c), Leclerc (2006), Yukita (2003), Witte (2000), Truchot (2002:7), and the "National reports" prepared for the Council of Europe's European Centre for Modern Languages.

Famous Eccles: His own home page.

Language-learning in Europe: Witte (2000).

Phrase book sentences: Mainly Rosenfelder (2002), but also Neuhaus (1911), Muraz (1926), Bulitta (1942), Stirke & Thomas (1916), Cortazzi (1987:345-47), and Philip Baker (p c).

Mark Rosenfelder's own phrases for the modern tourist: The Zompist Phrasebook (http://www.zompist.com/phrases.html), 2005-08-28.

The history behind *English as she is spoke*: Kite (2002), discussion on the homepage of The Collins Library, who put out a new edition of the phrase book in 2002 (http://www.collinslibrary.com/pedro2.html; 2005-08-29).

Effles: Higgins (2000).

POLYGLOTS

BUKU KHAN, the creator of the Uighur empire, should perhaps be considered the most impressive polyglot of all times. Born from an earth mound, he "knew all the tongues and writings of the different peoples". At least this is how local mythology has it. In real life, few if any have managed to master even one per cent of the world's 6 000+ languages.

It is impossible to avoid a certain western bias in discussing polyglots. In exceptionally multilingual areas, such as New Guinea or the Amazonas, a competence in five or so local languages has been reported to be fairly normal, and the repertoire of certain individuals presumably extends far beyond that. Yet, these are rarely reported on in the literature. And thus, most of the following people are westerners.

What is also paramount to recognise is the fact—obvious though it may seem—that language competence is relative. How well do you need to speak language X in order to be considered competent in it? It would be surprising indeed if some of the reports on someone being "fluent" in this or that language did not overstate that person's knowledge.

That said, it seems that the most amazingly polyglot person there is must be Ziad Fazah. Born of Lebanese parents in 1954, but living in Brazil since 1971, Ziad Fazah claims command of no less than 58 languages. No wonder the Brazilian press has referred to him as a *torre de Babel ambulante*—a walking tower of Babel. At school, he learned French and English, but after that, he taught himself all the other languages, beginning with German and Mandarin. Although he is still acquiring more languages, it is noteworthy that he learned almost all those he currently speaks between ages 14 and 17.

He made his first public appearance in a Spanish TV show in the late 1980s, where the hosts confronted him with Cambodians, Vietnamese and other East Asians, all of whom Fazah could talk to in their respective mother tongues.

Ziad Fazah

He has since been subject to similar tests in TV shows in Greece, Germany and elsewhere, so evidence of his multilingualism is beyond mere hearsay. In one such test, on home ground in Brazil, the Polish, Greek and Japanese testers were satisfied with his results, while the Finnish vice-consul in Rio said that "he mixed up some inflexions, but would surely get along in Finland without an interpreter". At least, this illustrates, that "speaking language X" is a relative concept, and that even the sun has its spots.

Fazah now lives in the Rio neighborhood of Flamengo, where he earns his living as a teacher, and provides occasional translation services. To many people's surprise, he has not travelled much outside Lebanon and Brazil.

In 1997, Fazah launched his own series of language learning books, starting with *Ensinando a Aprender Espanhol*. He has also been called upon by the Rio police, sometimes as a translator, and sometimes in order to determine the origin of refugees when this could not be established otherwise.

In his own book, Fazah enumerates the 58 languages which he speaks. 56 of these are relatively unproblematic: Albanian, Amharic, Arabic, Armenian, Azerbaijani, Bengali, Bulgarian, Burmese, Cantonese, Czech, Danish, Dutch, Dzongkha, English, Finnish, French, German, Greek, Hebrew, Hindi, Hungarian, Icelandic, Indonesian, Italian, Japanese, Khmer, Kirghiz, Korean, Lao, Malay, Malagasy, Mandarin, Mongolian, Min Nan, Nepali, Norwegian, Papiamentu, Pashto, Persian, Polish, Portuguese, Romanian, Russian, Serbo-Croatian, Sinhala, Spanish, Swedish, Swahili, Tajiki, Thai, Tibetan, Turkish, Urdu, Uzbek, Vietnamese and Wu. However, to me, "Butanês" would seem to be the same thing as Dzongkha, and one might wonder what "Cingaporenho" (="Singaporese") refers to. One could further argue that "Malay" and "Indonesian" are one and the same language but, having gone to school in Lebanon, Fazah presumably knows both Lebanese and Classical Arabic, which could be said to be two rather different languages.

Better known than Ziad Fazah is the man usually mentioned as the world's greatest polyglot, Giuseppe Gaspare Mezzofanti (1774-1849), who appears to have spoken at least 30 languages. Born in Bologna as the son of a carpenter, Mezzofanti studied both classical and modern European languages at school, and also picked up Meso-American languages from missionaries returning from work overseas. When assisting the soldiers of various nationalities wounded during the Napoleonic wars, Mezzofanti took the opportunity to learn their languages as well. His language skills and religious piousness took him to Rome in 1814, where he remained in the service of the Pope until his death.

Cardinal Mezzofanti

Of course, Mezzofanti's competence was never tested in any scientific way. Yet, his talent was remarked upon by several independent observers (including Lord Byron, who referred to him as a "monster of languages, the Briareus of parts of speech, a walking polyglot"). Thus, for instance, a Dr F Forster reports that he amused himself by speaking to the cardinal in the ten languages that he himself knew. Having exhausted his own impressive repertoire, Forster tried the little Welsh that he mastered, in response to which Mezzofanti began talking to him "at once, like a Welsh peasant".

The number of languages said to

actually have been spoken by the cardinal varies considerably. Some people who met him gave figures between 18 and 40. The cardinal himself, at various times, claimed to speak 40, and later even 78 languages. After Mezzofanti's death, his nephew Gaetano Minarelli concluded that his uncle must have known no less than 114 languages.

Trying to be very impartial, Russell (1858) found evidence from speakers of the languages in question that the cardinal must have had reasonable competence in at least 25 different languages (Albanian, ancient and modern Armenian, ancient Greek, Arabic, Aramaic, biblical and rabbinic Hebrew, Chaldean, Coptic, Czech, English, French, German, Illyrian, Italian, Latin, Maltese, Mandarin, Persian, Polish, Portuguese, Russian, Spanish and Turkish). A further 14 (Amharic, Basque, Danish, Dutch, Geez, Gujarati, Hindustani, Hungarian, modern Greek, Romanian, Swedish, Syriac, Algonquin [sic] and Californian [sic]) were claimed to have been spoken by him but his competence in them is not confirmed by native or near-native speakers. Of these, "Algonquin" and "Californian" are problematic, as is Illyrian given that nothing is known of it other than it once existed. He is also said to have spoken an additional 11 languages "rarely and less perfectly".

A score of other persons are mentioned in the literature as speakers of more than 25 languages, but for most of these the claims are difficult or even impossible to verify.

One particularly interesting case is Emil Krebs, who translated for the German embassy in China at the beginning of the 20th century, and who is said to have spoken more than 60 languages. Interestingly, his brain is preserved, and has recently been examined. When it was compared to the brains of a control group, it was concluded that architectonic features of Broca's area in Krebs' brain was responsible for his talents.

Another interesting polyglot character is the boy genius William Sidis (1898-1944). Right after his birth in Boston, his Jewish-Russian immigrant parents were determined to raise their son as a genius (which, as one commentator points out, "this tells you more about the parents than the kid"), and indeed, in terms of intellectual accomplishments, young Sidis made a good start.

After allegedly having started to read the New York Times at the age of 18 months, his achievements reached almost mythical proportions. He is reported to have sped through school in no time, first lectured at Harvard at 11 and predicted black holes years before anyone else. Seen by the outside world as a freak who despised social activities (and bathing), he was not only obsessed by cosmology, mathematics and public transport, but also devised a speed-reading system of his own and constructed an artificial language called Vendergood. Languages known to have been spoken by Sidis include Latin, Greek, Russian, French, German, Hebrew, Turkish and Armenian, but some have claimed that he spoke not only eleven, but forty or even two hundred languages.

FEMALE POLYGLOTS

Kato Lomb, described by Krashen & Kiss (1996), speaks 17 languages, and is thereby the most multilingual woman that I have come across (although Russell 1858 devotes a section to female polyglots, none of those mentioned by him surpassed seven languages). Another major female polyglot, Dutchwoman Anna Maria van Schurman (1607–1678), spoke 14 languages, according to van Beek (1999), who also mentions other multilingual women of the time.

POLYGLOT LINGUISTS

Although believed by laymen to be amazingly polyglot and, language buffs though they are, professional linguists in fact rarely astound outsiders with excessive language abilities. There even exist some few linguists who are practically monolingual—not unexpectedly primarily in English-speaking countries and in France. One of the major polyglots in modern linguistics, however, must surely be Austrian-Australian Stephen Wurm (1922-2001). Wurm grew up in an exceptionally cosmopolitan environment, and so by the age of six, he had more or less native-like command of English, Norwegian, Finnish, Hungarian, Mongolian, German, Russian, Mandarin, Spanish and Turkish. According to Laycock (1987:3), he later acquired "fluency in several dozen others". Others who have met Wurm have testified to his remarkable knowledge of languages (but also questioned his fluency in some). Pawley (2002) ascribes Wurm fluency in 21 languages (including eight non-European), and claims that he could "get by" in twenty others.

Two other modern-day linguists are also often credited with a competence in an unusually large number of languages: Ken Hale and Claude Hagège. In its obituary of Hale, the *Los Angeles Times* claimed he spoke no less than 50 languages. Hale himself, however, had denied this in an interview. A particularly interesting aspect of his competence was that his repertoire was typologically extremely varied (Miskito, Jemez, O'odham, Navajo, Polish, Warlpiri, Mayangna, etc.), and that the languages were acquired mostly in the field. Claude Hagège, who grew up in a French-speaking Jewish environment in Tunis said in an interview that he doesn't count the number of languages he is able to speak, but admits that he probably masters "a couple of dozen".

Yet other currently active linguists with a reputation of speaking unusually high numbers of languages include Russian-Australian typologist Sasha Aikhenvald, Russian-Israeli Nostraticist Aaron Dolgopolsky, Brazilian Caribanist Sergio Meira, American Sino-Tibetanist George van Driem, and Iranist Don Stilo. Romani scholar Donald Kenrick is reported to be able to "translate from 60 languages, of which he speaks 30".

The Dane Rasmus Rask counts as one of the founding fathers of linguistics as a scholarly discipline. Among his achievements is the first grammar of modern Icelandic, as well as descriptions of Anglo-Saxon, Spanish and Frisian. He is best known, however, for his pioneering work on the relations between the Indo-European languages, and in 1818 he discovered what has since become known as Grimm's Law. As opposed to many other linguists, he learned to actually speak an impressive number of languages during his short life. The *Guinness Book of World Records* gives the number as 28, while the *Encyclopædia Britannica* contents itself with a more modest 25.

Rasmus Rask as depicted on an Icelandic stamp

The father of Indo-European studies, William Jones, is also said to have been a major polyglot. Estimates vary from 28 to 41 as to how many languages he knew, with the former being the most oft-cited. Some sources, however, put the number at a mere 13.

SOURCES NOT MENTIONED IN THE TEXT

The Buku Khan legend: Dalby (1998:658).

Some exceptional polyglots are mentioned in the Guinness Book of World Records, and a discussion is also found in *Linguist List* 7.881.

Details on Ziad Fazah and his multilingualism come mainly from Lima (1996), and from Rafael Scapin's web page *Ziad Youssef Fazah: O Maior Poliglota do Mundo* at <if.sc.usp.br/~rafael/ziad1.htm> (2001-06-14).

Some basic biographical data for some of the polyglots were taken from the *Encyclopædia Britannica*. Additional bits and pieces were found in *Cosmoglotta* 12 (1), pp 1-2 (1933) (for Rasmus Rask), Mariscal (1996) for Cardinal Mezzofanti, and the *Catholic Encyclopedia* (for Cardinal Mezzofanti and others).

There are at least three biographical works on Cardinal Mezzofanti, namely Manavit (1853), Mitterrutzner (1855) and Russell (1858), of which the last also contains a section on other renowned polyglots

Emil Krebs and his brain: Amunts, Schleicher & Zilles (2001).

Wurm's talents are mentioned in print in Pawley (2002), Laycock (1987:3) and Honan (1997).

William Sidis: Wallace (1986).

The Ken Hale obituary referred to was published in the *Los Angeles Times* (2001-10-28, page C06). The interview where Ken Hale denied his excessive language capabilities was published in *Glot International* 2 (pp 9-10).

Claude Hagège interview found in *L'Express* 2000-02-11.

Donald Kenrick: Gunnemark (2000).

NON-HUMANS AND LANGUAGE

HUMANS HAVE probably always wondered what animals would say if they had the gift of speech. In modern days, several experiments have been carried out in order to determine to what extent animals actually are able to use language. Most linguists agree that although animals do of course communicate with one another and with humans, they do not have language, nor are they capable of learning it from humans.

LARGEST VOCABULARY ACQUIRED BY AN APE

The gorilla Koko was claimed by her trainer Francine Patterson to master some 600 American Sign Language (ASL) signs. An estimate following stricter criteria, however, put the figure at a more moderate 200. The same number of symbols has also been claimed for Kanzi, the Bonobo of Sue Savage-Rumbaugh. For most other language-trained apes, the suggested vocabulary sizes are somewhere between 100 and 200.

A CHAT WITH KOKO

In April 1998, the first ever internet chat between a human and an animal took place. Questions were written by the audience, translated for Koko into sign language, and her sign responses were then typed by a human. With Koko in the studio was her trainer, Francine Patterson (FP). Below follow some extracts from the chat.

Q: Koko are you going to have a baby in the future?
Koko: Pink.
FP: We've had earlier discussion about colors today.
Koko: Listen, Koko loves eat.
Q: What are the names of your kittens?
Koko: Foot.
FP: Foot isn't the name of your kitty.
Q: Koko, what's the name of your cat?
Koko: No.
Q: Do you like to chat with other people?
Koko: Fine nipple.
FP: Nipple rhymes with people, she doesn't sign people per se, she was trying to do a "sounds like...".

Q: How do you feel about Michael? [Koko's male gorilla friend]
Koko: Foot, foot, good.
Q: Foot means male, right?
Koko: Nipple.
FP: Remember that foot = male, right.
Koko: Good.
Koko: Lips, apple give me.
FP: People give her her favorite foods.
Koko: Love, browse drink nipple.
FP: Browse is like... the little foods/snacks we give them.
Koko: Koko loves that nipple drink, go.

Judge for yourself, but on seeing this, at least some of us were distinctly underwhelmed, and left with a feeling that Koko's claimed language abilities did not quite live up to expectations.

BEST KNOWN SUBJECTS OF APE LANGUAGE RESEARCH

LEGEND: Chimpanzee Gorilla Orangutang Bonobo

Trainer	Species	Ape's name	(starting) date	Medium	Results and remarks
Lighter Witmer		*Peter*	*1909*	*speech*	*Produced one word ('mama').*
W H Furness		?	1916	speech	*Produced two words ('papa' and 'cup').*
Robert Yerkes		Prince Chim	1925	speech	
Luella & Winthrop Kellogg		*Gua*	*1931*	*speech*	*Raised in home with human child. Never said a word, but understood 100 at the age of 16 months (which was more than her human foster brother). She never went beyond that level.*
Cathy & Keith Hayes		Viki	1947	speech	*Learned to speak four words.*
Beatrice & Allen Gardner, later Roger Fouts		Washoe	1966	ASL	*Knows 200 words well, but has occasionally used others. Reportedly the first chimp to spontaneously create signs of her own. Production includes extensions and compounding. Sensitive to word order (agent before verb, experiencer after).*

Researcher	Subject	Year	Method	Notes
David & Ann Premack	Sarah	1968	plastic tokens	130–150 words with 75-80% accuracy. Managed spatio-temporal displacement.
Roger Fouts	Lucy	1970	ASL	Managed word order distinctions and produced innovative compoundings. Lied.
Beatrice & Allen Gardner; later Roger Fouts	Dar, Moja & Tatu	1972	ASL	Lived with Loulis and Washoe (Moja died in 2002) at the Chimpanzee and Human Communication Institute in Ellensburg, north-western USA.
Francine Patterson	Koko	1972	ASL + speech	224 words—according to some sources, her repertoire has since increased to 1 000 signs. Coined original compounds, and made extensions. Able to lie. Claimed to even understand irony and rhyming. IQ measured at 70–95. Severe methodological criticism from other scholars made Patterson reclusive, and Koko was largely withdrawn from the limelight.
Duane Rumbaugh & Sue Savage-Rumbaugh	Lana	1972	keyboard	150 words.
Herbert Terrace	Nim	1973	ASL	125 words. Two-word sentences—all longer sentences only contained repetition. Little spontaneous signing. Results relatively disappointing, but has partly been ascribed to Nim's young age and his having had several different trainers.
Duane Rumbaugh & Sue Savage-Rumbaugh	Sherman & Austin	1975	keyboard	Sherman and Austin (but not Lana) master hyponym/hyperonym relations.
Francine Patterson	*Michael*	1976	ASL + speech	Acquired 600 signs. Michael, who died in 2000, was the "husband" of Koko.
Lyn Miles	Chantek	1978	ASL	150 different signs. Coining, e. g. 'eye drink' for contact lens solution. Caught lying. Claimed to have invented own grammatical rules (VO with visible object, OV with invisible object).
Tetsuro Matsuzawa	Ai	1978	Kanji writing	Good at numbers. Knows several hundred logograms.
Roger Fouts	Loulis	1979	ASL	70 words. Washoe's foster child.

Sue Savage-Rumbaugh		Kanzi	1980	speech + keyboard	Passive: 2000–3000 words, active: 250+. Relatively spontaneous acquisition and production. Masters spatio-temporal dislocation. Production partly ergative (!).
Rob Shumaker		Azy, Tucker, Bonnie, Kiko, Indah & Iris	1992	abstract computer symbols	

ASL=American Sign Language. "Speech" refers to English in all the cases above. Apart from the very first projects, attempts have not been made to have the apes speak, since it is now understood that their anatomy makes this impossible. Therefore, speech is used only *to* the apes, who then respond through some other medium.

BEST COMMUNICATIVE PERFORMANCE BY AN APE

It is difficult to claim that any one ape has performed better than another if there are no strict guidelines as to what constitutes language-like communication. Also, of course, an ape might outperform others in one area but not in another. In any case, I feel that the available evidence suggests that the above-mentioned Kanzi is the most impressive ape speaker. His understanding of spoken English is apparently extra-ordinarily accurate (by ape standards), and his own production is more spontaneous and adequate than for most of his "colleagues". And, perhaps most importantly, Kanzi is possibly the only ape to have reached this level mostly by spontaneous learning rather than through outright teaching. Yet, it must be remembered that even the best apes, including Kanzi, perform linguistically and cognitively at a level comparable to a human 2-year-old.

LARGEST DOG VOCABULARY

The nine year old border collie Rico rose to stardom in 2004 when he was reported to have acquired a vocabulary of 200 human words, far more than documented in any other dog. Impressively, when asked to fetch a newly introduced item among seven already familiar ones, he made the inference that the unknown word must refer to the never-before-seen item. Yet, Rico only masters nouns, and only fetchable ones at that. So while he has been proven to master words, it remains to be shown that he actually understands *language*.

MOST HUMAN-LIKE COMMUNICATION (WELL, IN A WAY...)

We would, of course, expect communicative behaviors of apes and other closely related creatures to be the most similar to our own use of language. In many ways, this is true. Apes are able to learn things from humans that slugs and squirrels seemingly cannot. Yet, not even apes have been demonstrated to have linguistic skills more than remotely similar to those of adult humans. (It should be borne in mind, however, that while communication among apes and certain monkeys has been extensively researched, we still know remarkably little about many other species generally regarded as intelligent, such as dolphins, whales, and elephants. While few people would assume that to be true, it nevertheless remains *possible* that members of these species actually do possess language.)

In any case, one of the most remarkable characteristics of human speech is its *duality of patterning*. This has not yet been convincingly shown to be present in other species. Except for one. Bees. The way in which bees, of all creatures, communicate does, in a sense, have this feature. When a scout bee returns to the hive, it performs a dance to show its fellow bees the location of a food source.

The details vary a little between different kinds of bees but, as a general rule, the direction of the dancing indicates the direction of the food source, while the length of the dance, and the number of waggles included, give the other bees an idea of the distance. In addition, the vigour with which the dance is performed may be indicative of the perceived food quality.

These parameters of a scout bee's dancing may then enter into an infinite number of combinations. Thus, the bee may be the only creature, aside from humans, which is able to convey an unlimited number of messages! Paradoxically though, despite the infinite number of possible messages, the bee, unlike humans, cannot communicate about anything other than food sources. So far as we know, bee dancing cannot be used to discuss the existence of a supreme being, or to order a pizza, or even to comment on yesterday's nectar supply or indicate that nectar *cannot* be found at a given location. The system's limitations become clear by the simple fact that a bee cannot indicate height above ground level. In one experiment, food was placed above the hive itself, and the scout bee's message "Lots! Yummie! Here! Right HERE!" did nothing but puzzle its colleagues. In the 1920s, the Austrian ethologist Karl von Frisch became the first to decode the "bee language" and in 1973 his efforts were rewarded with a Nobel prize.

DUALITY OF PATTERNING

In animal communication systems, a sound (or other signal) is normally holistic, that is, it describes an entire situation. One sound might mean "Watch out, there's a predator about", while another might say "Get out of here—this is my territory!". Now, if there's a finite number of sounds, there's also a finite number of things which can be said. Humans also have a finite number of sounds, but our system doesn't stop there. Our sounds, such as /b/, /i/ or /g/ don't mean anything by themselves but, in contrast to animals, we combine these into meaningful sequences: morphemes, words, phrases, clauses, and sentences. This way, a finite number of signs allow us to produce an infinite number of utterances, and thus convey an infinite number of messages.

BEST TALKING BIRD

Prudle, an African grey parrot (*Psittacus erythacus*), was awarded the British title of Best Talking Parrot-like Bird for twelve years in a row. Before her death in 1994, at an age of almost 40 years, Prudle was said to have acquired a vocabulary of more than 800 English words, and was reported to even have been able to conduct a polite conversation.

She was apparently particularly fond of asking "What are you doing?"

Irene Pepperberg, evolutionary biologist of Tucson, Arizona, has for an extended period of time conducted work with another African Grey named Alex. Alex has an impressive aptitude for speaking, and does not merely mimic humans, but also knows how to count, identify objects, and knows the concepts of same and different. When various objects are presented to him, Alex is able to correctly distinguish between their color, shape and material.

Irene Pepperberg and Alex

Of more peripheric interest, the lyrebird of Australia and New Guinea is a bird which has not been shown to communicate by means of language, but which has mimicking capabilities in many ways seemingly exceeding those of parrots. Occasionally shown on television wildlife shows, the lyrebird has been filmed imitating not only the calls of other birds, but also—with eerie accuracy—the noises made by the cameras filming it, car engines and alarms, and, not least, the screech of the chainsaws destroying its habitat.

TALKATIVE TREES

Amazing though it may seem, there is some evidence that certain plants are capable of some limited communication (albeit not with humans). The most interesting case is that of the acacia trees of the African savanna. Wouter van Hoven of Pretoria University has studied the acacias' reaction to munching antelopes. In order not to have to give up its foliage to the browsers, the tree excretes tannin, a poison which could kill the preying herbivore. This may not seem all that remarkable, but it is not only the tree under attack which produces tannin, but also other trees in the vicinity. In other words, some kind of communication system seems to enable the attacked acacia to warn fellow acacias of the imminent danger. The message is thought to be transferred in the form of ethylene which travels twenty or more metres through the air. Alerted trees then step up their tannin production in just five to ten minutes.

CONVERTING WOOFS INTO WORDS

In 2001, the Japanese company Takara launched a product called "Bowlingual". Attached to a dog collar, Bowlingual registers the sounds emitted by the pet. It then analyses them and sorts them into different categories. Finally, the voice converter module "translates" the growls, yelps and barks into human speech, and so the dog is able to convey 200 different messages to its owner, including (whether or not this was the intended message) "You're ticking me off!", "This is fun!" or "I'm bored!".

The success of this product called for a follow-up, and sure enough, in mid-2003, Takara announced that the brand new "Meowlingual" would be avilable from November that year.

TALKING TO ALIENS

I n the late 18th century, the Genèvoise spiritist medium Hélène Smith (*nom de plume* of Catherine Élise Müller) held séances for her friends. In altered states of consciousness, she told her audience about her previous lives, some of which included space travel. During a visit to planet Mars, Smith claimed to have acquired fluency in Martian, some of which she wrote down in an exotic-looking script.

Unlike many other such samples, Smith's Martian was highly structured and regular.

In November 1974, this message was sent out from Arecibo on Puerto Rico to whoever-might-be-out-there

Its consistency convinced some that her language was not mere glossolalic gibberish, but a true language—possibly even real Martian. Upon closer inspection, however, it turned out that not only was the "Martian" phonology identical to that of Smith's native French, but the grammatical structure of the language was also such that there was a one-to-one correspondence between French and "Martian". Clearly, the language Smith had allegedly acquired during her trips to Mars was but an amateurish relexification of French.

While this, the best known case of alleged extraterrestrial communication, turned out to be a fake, alien communication strategies is a most serious field of research. Earthlings have several times sent messages in which we tell a little about ourselves into outer space, hoping that somebody Out There might receive them and understand them. But how should we compose our message in order to facilitate comprehension by whatever intelligent life forms there may be beyond our solar system? I will not try to summarize the state of the art of this research here, but would like to recommend McConnell (2001), which provides a most interesting discussion of the subject.

Apart from animals (and aliens), humans have an interest in communicating with another type of semi-intelligent being: machines. This is a lot more difficult than it might sound, given that the machines were contructed by humans themselves.

FIRST CHATTERBOT

The first computer program to handle human language in a way that enabled it to communicate with humans was Eliza, so named after the character in *Pygmalion/My Fair Lady*. Created by Joseph Weizenbaum, Eliza would mimic Rogerian psychoanalysis, in which the psychiatrist would ask questions based on the what the patient was telling. Under some circumstances, Eliza could make the user feel s/he was really having a meaningful conversation, although the endless repetitions and loops soon became rather annoying. In reality, of course, Eliza never "understood" any of the input provided, but simply matched it to certain predefined patterns.

EXAMPLE OF A CONVERSATION WITH ELIZA

ELIZA: Hello. I am Eliza. How can I help you?
ME: I don't feel well.
ELIZA: Why do you not feel well?

ME: Everybody hates me
ELIZA: Surely not everyone?
ME: Well, most people, at least.
ELIZA: Please go on.
ME: You know, they never understand me.
ELIZA: You like to think they never understand you, do you not?
ME: That is certainly not the case.
ELIZA: Does it please you to believe that that is certainly not the case?
ME: Not at all. I want you to help me.
ELIZA: Can you elaborate on that?
ME: You know, I've already been to a bunch of shrinks, but people keep telling me you're the best there is. So I'm hoping you could provide some guidance. So can you help me?
ELIZA: Does that question interest you?
ME: I wouldn't have come here if it didn't.
ELIZA: Do you wish that it didn't?

FIRST BOOK OF COMPUTER-GENERATED POETRY

In 1984, a program named Racter released a book of poetry and short essays entitled *The Policeman's Beard is Half-Constructed*. The introduction, by Bill Chamberlain, claims that "with the exception of this introduction, the writing in this book was all done by computer". Here is an example of Racter's poetical talents:

Bill sings to Sarah. Sarah sings to Bill. Perhaps they will do other dangerous things together. They may eat lamb or stroke each other. They may chant of their difficulties and their happiness. They have love but they also have typewriters. That is interesting.

Later, however, the project was criticized, and it was claimed that Racter's role was lesser (and Chamberlain's greater) than had been claimed.

FIRST ACCEPTED COMPUTER-GENERATED CONFERENCE TALK

Having had enough of unsolicited mass e-mailings advertising the 2005 *World Multi-Conference on Systemics, Cybernetics and Informatics*, three M I T (Massachusetts

Institute of Technology) students decided to seek revenge.

Presumably inspired by Alan Sokal's (1996) legendary hoax, Jeremy Stribling, Daniel Aguayo and Maxwell Krohn set their computer to generate a completely nonsensical submission which wound up being entitled *Rooter: a methodology for the typical unification of access points and redundancy.*

According to the conference organizers, none of the reviewers commented on the paper, which led to it being automatically accepted.

SOURCES NOT MENTIONED IN THE TEXT

Ape achievements in general: Rumbaugh (1977), and the respective institutions, with additional data from Hawes (1995). Early ape experiments: Gardner, Gardner & van Cantfort (eds; 1989:5). Specific apes: Sherman and Austin: Savage-Rumbaugh, Rumbaugh & Boysen (1978), Savage-Rumbaugh & Lewin (1994), Nim: Terrace (1979), Lana: Rumbaugh, Warner & von Glasersfeld (1977), Koko: Patterson & Linden (1981), Shaw (1993:1-2), Chantek: Miles (1993: 47, 52), Washoe: Gardner & Gardner (1979), Sarah: Premack (1971). The 1992 Orangutan project is mentioned in Hawes (1995).

Rico the border collie: Kaminski, Call & Fischer (2004) and Bloom (2004).

Bee dancing: Nachtigall (1969:129-32).

Talking birds: Prudle the parrot: Guinness Book of World Records. Alex the parrot: Pepperberg and Alex have their own project home page at www.alexfoundation.org.

Devastating critique of much animal language resarch is commonplace, one of the best among the more easily accessible being Wynne (2004).

Communicating acacias: Corliss (1991), Croke (1999), Lestienne & Péricard-Méa (1997:262).

Bowlingual: Press release from Takara.

Hélène Smith's Martian: Flournoy (1983).

First chatterbot: Manaris (1998).

Racter and The Policeman's Beard: Racter, Chamberlain & Etter (1984), Barger (1993), Aarseth (1997).

First accepted computer-generated conference talk: *New Scientist* 2496, p 6.

ARTIFICIAL LANGUAGES

SINCE AT LEAST THE 17TH CENTURY (and quite probably before that), various people have created artificially constructed languages (or *conlangs*), for the most part in order to offer humanity a neutral, easily mastered and logical means of interethnic communication (an *auxlang*). In other cases, the goal has been artistic—sometimes, the language itself is the work of art, while for others, the artificial language forms part of, for instance, a novel project or a film. All in all, the enormous flora of constructed languages ranges from the ingenious to the outright ridiculous.

MOST SUCCESSFUL ARTIFICIAL LANGUAGE

Of artificial creations attempted to serve as international auxiliary languages, the most successful by far is Esperanto, launched in 1887 by Polish oculist Ludwig Zamenhof. There are no reliable statistics on the number of users, but estimates (based mainly on the numbers of textbooks sold, and membership of Esperantist associations) usually range between a few hundred thousand and a couple of million speakers around the world.

Esperanto was originally presented as *la lingvo internacia* 'the international language', but Zamenhof published it under the pseudonym *Doktoro Esperanto*—literally 'the doctor who hopes', and that name has since stuck to the language, and become accepted by Esperantists themselves.

Of languages not intended for the role of international lingua francas, but rather created for artistic purposes, Klingon would seem to have the largest number of followers. It was created in 1984 by professional linguist Marc

L. Zamenhof—granddaddy of auxlang creation

Logo of the KLI

The cassette course Power Klingon was released in 1993 as a follow-up to the successful Conversational Klingon

Okrand for the third film in the *Star Trek* series.

Its creator himself estimates that *"probably 700 people, maybe more, [...] have been studying the language in one form or other"*. Meanwhile, the *Klingon Language Institute* (KLI) boasts more than 1 000 members, and roughly a dozen of these are said to be fully fluent in the language. Hermans' (1999) survey includes 79 actual speakers.

The KLI publishes its own Klingon studies journal (*HolQeD*), and is currently working on translations of the Bible and Shakespeare into Klingon.

In 2004, Klingon also entered the world of serious news broadcasting, as it began being used by the German international broadcaster *Deutsche Welle*.

In addition, people have also performed marriage ceremonies in the language.

In a similar vein, the artificial languages used in J R R Tolkien's novels—in particular Quenya—have received a great deal of attention, and are learned and used by some of the many devoted Tolkien fans. The number of such speakers is not known.

AN ARTIFICIAL LANGUAGE GOING NATIVE

While most people have at least heard of Esperanto, and have a vague idea of what it is, few are aware that the language has had native speakers since at least 1919. Nobody knows for sure how many there are, but at least 350 cases are known, and it has been suggested that there may be three times as many.

It should perhaps be emphasized that the children in these cases automatically and without any problems whatsoever also acquire the majority language of the locality where they grow up, and there is—as far as is known—no one with Esperanto as his or her *only* mother tongue. (I have personally come across two native Esperantists, both of whom grew up in both Esperanto and Swedish.)

In most documented cases, Esperanto has been used in the family circle not out of necessity, but rather as a kind of intellectual experiment. It is not uncommon, however, that Esperanto is chosen simply because the parents are from different language backgrounds and have no other language in common.

Every once in a while, there are rumors about nativization of the above-mentioned Klingon, but there seems to be no evidence, and I strongly doubt the veracity of these rumors. At least one parent did start to raise a child in Klingon, but gave the experiment up after a couple of years. *"It lacked some crucial vocabulary, such as words for bottle and diaper"*, he complained, and added that the child *"eventually [...] stopped listening to me when I spoke in Klingon"* and that it *"was clear that he didn't enjoy it"*.

A BIT OF GEEKOLOGY: WHO ON EARTH SPEAKS KLINGON?

We know that Klingon is the language of an alien warrior civilization, but who *on earth* speaks Klingon? Well, not only is Klingon rare in having a linguistics journal and other semi-academic infrastructure devoted to it. It is also a rare conlang in that it has been studied from a sociolinguistic point of view—there are at least two such Klingon studies.

For convenience, earthlings often write Klingon in Latin characters, but it does have its own alphabet.

In part, these confirm the stereotype image of Klingon speakers—77% are male, most work with computers in one way or the other, and the largest group is in their mid-twenties. Depending on how prejudiced you are, you may be more surprised to learn that when it comes to marital status, a minority (less than 40%) are single.

In addition to Klingon (and, of course, languages such as English, French, German and Spanish), almost a fifth of the respondents in one survey also speak another artificial language—including two who have created their own conlang.

As mentioned above, I know of no cases of nativization of Klingon, but who knows what the future has in store? In Hermans' (1999) thesis, almost two thirds of the (human) Klingonophones do want their children to learn the language . . .

At the risk of perpetuating the impression that only oddballs take interest in Klingon, it is difficult to leave out the news report from Portland, Oregon, where the health services in early 2003 advertised for Klingon speakers. The reason was said to be that some of the patients of the county's mental hospitals would speak nothing but Klingon to the staff. By law, the authorities are therefore compelled to provide Klingon-English interpreters. In reality, however, the Klingon interpreters have yet never been called into service.

Below follow some examples of artificial languages, which are not necessarily representative, but which simply happen to be among my personal favorites.

BRITISH ROMANCE

Brithenig is the brainchild of New Zealander Andrew Smith. It is based on an alternative history scenario (pp 111–13) in which Latin displaces Celtic in Britain, leading to a Romance language on British soil.

The flag of Kemr, presumably modelled on the Welsh flag

As opposed to the existing Romance languages, Brithenig presents rather far-reaching substrate influences. Apart from a sizeable proportion of Celtic lexicon, it has somehow acquired the notorious consonant mutation system so characteristic of Celtic languages. A participant of a newsgroup discussion described Brithenig as "the damnedest thing—a Romance language with those peculiar Welsh mutations!". This made another participant react thus: "Who are you calling beculiar? I won't have Welsh called pheculiar—it's an insult to my mheculiar fathers!" (Readers with some experience of Celtic language might appreciate the joke . . .).

Should you ever get to Kemr, the land of the Brithenig speakers, you might get the question *E'gw ystad nonc ci inawant?* *'Have you ever been here before?'*

AGLOTTIC POP—TAKING NONSENSICAL POP LYRICS TO THEIR LOGICAL EXTREME

In 1981, the self-titled debut album of *Caramba*, produced by Hazze Kamikaze and Giorgio Martini of *Studio Garage de Garbage* hit the Swedish record stores. Its two sides (*Blaztah 1* and *Blaztah A*) contained ten songs in a non-existent language, including the single *Hubba hubba zoot zoot*, which performed decently on the charts. The album cover listed a number of musicians involved, including talents such as Clapton Combo (gitaronimo), Dr. Fritz Höfner (baribasso), Zingo Allah (prutto), Gaston El Ton Yon (pianissimo), King Kong (tango) and Tudor Ludor (batterie). While the actual originator was unnamed, it was subsequently revealed that Caramba was the jocular side project of Michael Tretow, the producer behind the sound that made ABBA so successful.

Of particular interest to linguists is the fact that, for those of the songs which mimic a certain musical type (e.g. Hawaiian or Russian folk music), the fictitious lyrics similarly imitate the phoneme inventory and syllabics of the actual language alluded to.

Other artists who have more or less invented their own languages include the Icelandic band *Sigur Rós*, French progressive

Yours truly is a proud owner of Caramba's self-titled debut (and only) album.

rock band *Magma*, the Finnish act *Circle*, and Swedish *Urga*, to mention but a few.

Also, in the 2003 edition of the Eurovision Song Contest, Belgian *Urban Trad* ended up in an honourable second position with *Sanomi*—again a song performed in a non-existent language.

SOLRÉSOL—THE "MUSICAL LANGUAGE"

Solrésol was the first artificial international auxiliary language to gain a wider following. It has been described as "unusually eccentric even by the standards of artificial language projects". That speaks volumes, and if you consider its many unusual features, it is still no exaggeration.

The construction of Solrésol started in 1817 by Frenchman Jean-François Sudre. His basic idea was that music is an international language of sorts. And, if you consider that the world in those days meant the western world, then the solfeggio scale *do, re, mi, fa, so, la, ti* could be considered international as well (though to the French, that is *do, ré, mi, fa, sol, la, si*). Sudre let these seven notes be the phonemes of his new language. Using words with up to four notes leads to a total vocabulary of 2 600 roots, a number which of course increases dramatically if we take the derivational and inflectional possibilities (see below) into account. This would seem to make Solrésol a rather full-fledged language.

The seven monosegmental words denote the most basic concepts, such as 'and', 'yes' and 'not'. Less basic ideas are then expressed by increasingly longer words. One feature of the Solrésol lexicon which may appear ingenious (but which I suspect is somewhat dysfunctional) is that words are grouped into semantic categories, whose members share the same initial syllables. For instance, words beginning in *dore* denoted various periods of time, so that *doremi* (or 𝅘𝅥𝅮 if you like) meant 'day', *dorefa* 'week', *doreso* 'month', and so on, while *doredo* stood for the concept of 'time' itself.

As for the grammar, Solrésol is a rather analytic SVO language. Tense and mood is marked not by inflection, but by free preverbal markers. For the passive, the copula *faremi* is used. Questions are made, as in many European languages, by changing the word order from SV to VS.

While there is no grammatical gender in Solrésol, biological sex is indicated by length on the last syllable. Thus, while *resimire* means 'brother', 'sister' is *resimiree*. The same device also functions as a pluralizer, so that 'days' would be *doremii*.

Another suprasegmental feature, stress, is also exploited, and carries a derivational load. The unmarked *resomila* is 'to continue', but nouns, adjectives and adverbs can be derived from it, and we thus have *résomila* 'continuation', *resómila* 'continuing', and *resomíla* 'continuously'.

A particularly intriguing feature of Solrésol, not found in any natural language so far as I am aware, is the derivation of opposites—this is done simply by inverting the word. For instance, 'good' is *fala*, and logically enough, then, 'bad' is the same, but backwards, that is *lafa* (remember that what is written by two letters here is really *one note*).

The most fascinating aspect of the language, however, is that Solrésol is a truly multimedial language. First of all, it can obviously be sung or hummed, or played on an instrument. Secondly, it can be written, as in the examples above. Given that the names of the notes all begin with different consonants (except for *sol* and *si* in the French notation), most of the vowels are redundant, and 'week' needs therefore not be written *dorefa*, but may just as well be rendered as *drf*. In order to overcome the problem posed by peoples not accustomed to the Latin alphabet, several other scripts were also devised. To begin with, normal musical notation may of course be used to transcribe the tones. In addition to this, a special stenography was designed, where each of the seven syllables is represented by one single stroke. The notes were also assigned numbers, and so, the word 'week' can also be transcribed as 124. These numbers, in turn, can also be represented by knocks (or bell strikes or shots) with a person not in sight or with a blind person, or by blinking lights, to assure communication between ships. This was more revolutionary than it may sound, given that Solrésol was constructed before the invention of the Morse code.

Introduction to Solrésol, or "The musical language", by Jean-François Sudre.

The multimedial possibilities obviously fascinated Sudre a great deal, because he also encouraged the writing of the stenographic signs in the air for interlocutors not within hearing distance, tactile signing (with the fingers of one hand pointing between those of the other, which would symbolize the bars of musical notation) for the deaf-blind—or indeed for communication between a deaf and a blind person.

As if this were not enough, each note was also assigned one of the seven colors of the rainbow, which allowed communication by means of signal flags, something that made the French army interested in the project (they even bestowed a grant of 50 000 francs on Sudre). At night, colored signal rockets could be employed for the same purpose.

This led a modern Solrésolist to the following comment: "*Imagine for a moment a universal language, translatable to color, melody, writing, touch, hand signals, and endless strings of numbers. Imagine now that this language was taught from birth to be second-nature to every speaker, no matter what their primary language. The world would become saturated with hidden meanings. Music would be transformed, with every instrument in the orchestra engaged in simultaneous dialogue [. . .] [T]he beginning of Beethoven's Fifth seems to talk about 'Wednesday' [. . .] Needless to say, obsessive fans who already hear secret messages in music would not do their mental stability any favors by learning Solrésol*".

Sudre was hailed as a genius during his life-time. His work was complimented by many influential personalities of his days, and he won awards at the world exhibitions in Paris (1855) and London (1862). He died, though, before the first grammar had appeared, so it was published posthumously by his widow in 1866. An international Solrésol society was founded in Paris, which thrived until about the First World War, a century after the language's inception. The coup de grâce on Solrésol was more than anything else the success of Esperanto, which, being closer in structure to natural languages, was considered more easily learned.

MOST EXCENTRIC ESPERANTO CLONE

Since the creation of Esperanto in the 1880s, several attempts have been made at reforming it. Even though plenty of users found the language easy to learn, many had ideas for what they considered to be improvements. Surely the most odd of these is Poliespo, created in 1991 by Nvwtohiyada Idehesdi Sequoyah (formerly known as Billy

Joe Waldon). Sequoyah/Waldon is Cherokee, and felt that the international language would benefit from the addition of the polysynthetic characteristics of his native tongue (hence the name of the language). Poliespo contains the entire Esperanto lexicon and grammar, but also more than 200 Cherokee affixes. The phonology was "embellished" with tones, and an expansion of the phoneme inventory from 28 to 61! The grammatical system contains non-European features such as evidentiality (see pp 312–13), and displays plenty of allomorphy—considered a no-no by most auxlang supporters (yes, Sequoyah/Waldon actually did intend Poliespo to be the universal auxiliary language of humankind).

Although few seem to agree with him, the creator of Poliespo claims that the language allows faster thinking (!) than any other language.

In 1992, Sequoyah/Waldon was convicted and put on death row in the San Quentin prison in California. The allegation, however, was murder, rather than conlanging.

MOST RHYMING CONLANG

DiLingo, once dubbed *Pig Latin from Hell*, is a language upon which prizes such as *The Strange Enlightenments Award* and *The Warped Award* have been bestowed. It is created by a certain Sumus Cacoonus who himself describes it as a *"rhyming, metered, matrixed, linguistic inanity that flexes enough Betz cells to reach ideal neurosynaptic brain rate"*. To get a taste of the unusual language, let us begin with the pronoun inventory, which includes *ing, ying, ting*, and even a fourth person *sting*.

The copula is *ing*. Future tense is formed by a preverbal particle *zing*, while the possessive suffix is *-igimming*. Comparatives are formed by suffixing *-iling*, and superlatives with *-iving*. It comes as a bit of a surprise, though, that 'too' is expressed as *Jane* (so named after the street where the language's creator once lived).

For those who want to try out a few sentences in DiLingo, I would recommend starting with the following:

He was doing	*Tang ang dangdang*
You had been doing	*Yong ong dongdong*
Why do you do this?	*Ving ding ying ding diz?*
Where are you?	*Fring ing ying?*
What didn't I do?	*Jang dang anct ang dang?*
Either he goes or I go.	*Frick ting vring frack ing vring.*

SOURCES NOT MENTIONED IN THE TEXT

Conlangs in general: First and foremost the useful resources www.langmaker.com and www.sys.uea.ac.uk/~jrk/conlang.html, and the links provided there—in practice, the home pages of the respective language creators.
Interview with Marc Okrand: USA Today 2001-05-24.
Klingon on Deutsche Welle: BBC news 2004-09-15.
Klingon in marriage ceremonies: USA Today 2001-05-24.

Natively spoken Esperanto: Bergen (2001), Versteegh (1984, 1993b), Corsetti, Pinto & Tolomeo (2004).

Natively spoken Klingon: Edwards (1996, 1999).

Klingon Sociolinguistics: Hermans (1999), Wahlgren (2004).

Klingon at Oregonian asylums: CNN report 2003-05-10.

British Romance: Smith's Brithenig page at http://hobbit.griffler.co.nz/introduction.html (2001-09-06).

Non-language in pop: The author is happily in possession of both the Caramba and Urga albums.

Other fictious languages of popular music: Paulsson (2002), Martin Warin (p c).

Solrésol: Couturat & Léau (1903:33-39), Collins (2001), Gajewski (1902), Large (1985:60-62).

Poliespo: Gant (1997).

FORENSIC LINGUISTICS

FORENSIC LINGUISTICS is the interface between crime-solving and linguistics. Forensic linguists can assist with judicial processes in a variety of ways. These include speaker identification, handwriting analysis, and other means of determining who said or wrote what, and what the person actually meant. Forensic linguists may also deal with the assessment of courtroom interpretation.

Not only can forensic linguists help the prosecutor in framing criminals, but their efforts may also clear the falsely accused.

IDENTIFYING A RECLUSE BILLIONAIRE

In 1971, the McGraw-Hill publishing company intended to pay to self-proclaimed ghost writer Clifford Irving 765 000 American dollars for what he claimed to be the autobiography of Howard Hughes, the eccentric billionaire. Some time after this became known, Hughes himself claimed he had never met Irving, and insisted that the work was a fake. Yet, he refused to come forward in person, and would only make phone calls from his Bahamas home. In order to verify that the caller actually was Howard Hughes, Lawrence Kersta of the Bell Telephone Acoustics & Speech Research Laboratory was called in. After a spectrographic analysis and a comparison to a 1947 recording of Hughes, he concluded that the person on the telephone was indeed who he claimed to be. In addition, handwriting experts were convinced that the letters authorising Irving's biography, which were at first thought to be produced by Hughes' hand, were in fact produced by Irving, trying to mimic his handwriting. The forgerer received two and a half years of imprisonment.

THE MYSTERY OF THE PERSIAN MUMMY

In October 2000, a spectacular find came to the attention of Pakistani authorities. In Quetta, close to the Afghan border, what appeared to be a 2 600 year-old mummy had been discovered. At a press conference a week later, it was confirmed that the mummified body was that of Rhodugune, a Persian princess. What puzzled archaeologists was that mummification Egyptian-style had not been attested in the Persian empire. Could it be that the Persian kings not only imported masons and other craftsmen from Egypt, but also embalmers? It seemed as if part of history might need to be rewritten.

On the sarcophagus, there was a breast-plate bearing a cuneiform inscription, saying "I am the daughter of the great King Xerxes. Mazereka protect me. I am Rhodugune, I am". Since doubts had been raised regarding the authenticity of the find, the curator of the National Museum of Pakistan sent the text to cuneiform expert Nicholas Sims-Williams of the University of London. The reply she received provided a considerable boost to these doubts. In Old Persian, one would expect the word for 'king' to have a genitive suffix *–hya* (indicating possession). Yet, the word appeared simply as *Shiathiya* in the inscription, rather than as *Shiathiya**hya***. This made Sims-Williams suspect that the inscription had in fact not been made by a native speaker of Old Persian. In addition to this, he was aware that Rhodugune is actually the Greek version of the princess's name, a version which only became current later. During her lifetime, and among her fellow countrymen, she would rather have been known as Wardegauna.

Now that suspicions were raised, several other investigations, including X-ray photographing, CT scans and radiocarbon dating confirmed that the mummy was in fact a fake. The body had not been embalmed 2 600 years ago, but in 1996. Despite being a relatively competent work, the deceit was revealed, and led to a murder investigation. Without linguistic analysis, the forgery might have passed unnoticed—at least for longer than it did.

THE HELANDER DEBÂCLE

In 1952, a new bishop was appointed in the Swedish diocese of Strängnäs. It became clear only after Dick Helander had taken office that the other two contestants had been the subject of slander in anonymous letters sent to the committee handling the appointment of Lutheran bishops.

After having let linguists examine the letters, it was found that 32 idiolectal features were common to them and to writings known to have been produced by Helander, and because of this, and other forensic evidence, he was finally found guilty of libel and dismissed. There was no unanimity among the linguists involved and, until his death in 1978, Helander kept denying his involvement, despite his fingerprints having been found on the envelopes. In 2002, a geneticist examined DNA found on the envelopes, and was able to prove that it was *not* the former bishop's saliva which had sealed them.

Helander's green Halda. This was proved to be the typewriter on which the libellous letters were written. But by whom?

POSTHUMOUS PARDON THANKS TO A LINGUIST

In November of 1949, British semi-literate van driver Timothy Evans walked into a police station reporting the death of his wife. Investigators found not only his wife, but also his little daughter buried in the back yard. Evans himself was immediately suspected, and after having confessed to the murder, Evans was imprisoned and hanged. Before his execution, however, he withdrew his confession, saying that he had confessed only in order to avoid reprisals on the part of the police, and instead accused his neighbor John Christie. A couple of years later, it was proved that Christie was indeed a serial killer, as the remains of several women were found in and around his flat. Three years after Evans' death, Christie was hanged on the same Pentonville Prison gallows. Evans was posthumously pardoned, but only for the murder of his daughter, and not for that of his wife.

In the late 1960s, Swedish linguist and Anglicist Jan Svartvik took a close look at the confession statements. Since Evans wasn't really literate, they had been written down by the police, but they were of course intended to represent an oral confession by Evans. Svartvik proved that the part where Evans allegedly confessed the killing were stylistically very divergent from the rest of his utterances. In particular, the conjoining of utterances, which was what Svartvik primarily studied, differed radically between the parts which Evans had admitted to have spoken, and the parts which he later retracted. Svartvik's evidence therefore constituted a rehabilitation of sorts for Evans, albeit one which he didn't live to enjoy.

Another similar, and equally famous case also comes from post-war Britain. In 1952, the two British teenagers Derek Bentley and Chris Craig were caught in the act while trying to break into a warehouse. The police asked the boys to hand over their gun, but while Bentley surrendered immediately, Craig resisted arrest. Bentley urged his companion to do so by saying "Let him have it, Chris", after which Craig shot and killed a constable. At the ensuing murder trial, both were found guilty, but 16-year old Craig received lifetime imprisonment (detention "during Her Majesty's Pleasure") because of his youth. Bentley, who was three years older (but according to some had a mental age of 11), was hanged after having admitted his crime.

The question was, did the now famous line "Let him have it, Chris!", said to have been uttered by Bentley at the time of the arrest, mean "Shoot him" or "Let him have the gun"?

Forensic linguist Malcolm Coulthard was inclined towards the latter, and was asked to have another look at the Bentley statements. One of Coulthard's most striking observations was that a very large proportion of the sentences in the so-called confession began with "Chris and I then...", "The policemen then...", etc. This, Coulthard showed, is highly unusual in casual speech, but is, on the other hand, very common in police reports. In other words, the style suggested that the confession was in fact fabricated by the police. Also, the unusually high proportion of negatives prompted Coulthard to claim that it was unlikely that it was produced without questions from the police officers.

A film about the Bentley case was directed by Peter Medak in 1991, and at least two plays on this theme have also been produced. Four songs, including one by Elvis Costello, also deal with this miscarriage of justice.

In 1998, Derek Bentley was finally granted a posthumous pardon.

USING LINGUISTICS TO FRAME THE UNABOMBER

Between 1978 and 1995, a terrorist known as the *Unabomber* (so named for his choice of **un**iversities and **a**irline offices as targets) spread fear in the United States. Apart from his bombings, the Unabomber also sent manifestos to several American newspapers in which he expressed his disgust of modern technology and civilization. After Montana hermit Ted Kaczynski became the prime suspect, a professor of English literature, Don Foster, was assigned to comparing the Unabomber manifestos with writings known to have been produced by Kaczynski. "The authorities could have been led to Ted Kaczynski", Foster says, "without fingerprints, without DNA, without eyewitnesses, without the forensic analysis of bomb components, just by paying extraordinarily close attention to the bomber's own words".

A close inspection of the bomber's manuscripts, led Foster not only to conclude that the writer was highly educated and nourished a strong dislike of modern technology, but also that he would have grown up during the 1950s, that he was influenced by authors such as Aldous Huxley, Eugene O'Neill and Joseph Conrad, that he "identified himself with wood", that he enjoyed reading *Scientific American* and *The Saturday Review*, and that his favorite hangouts included libraries in northern California. After Kaczynski's arrest, it turned out that he had even (using his real name and address) written a letter to the editor of *The Saturday Review* in a language very similar to that of the Unabomber manifesto.

In 1996, Kaczynski was arrested, and following his confession in 1998, he received four life sentences.

INCLUSIVITY IN COURT

Although I have concentrated on the juicier cases above, it should in all fairness be admitted that much of the activities of the forensic linguist have to do with courtroom interpretation rather than actual crime-solving. Nevertheless, even such activities can provide interesting food for thought. While some languages have an inclusivity distinction in their pronominal system, English is not one of them. This rarely leads to problem in the daily life of most English-speakers, but it can indeed do so in court.

In one particular case, accused person A confessed that "We killed that X", a statement to which B concurred. Now, did this mean that "Yes, we (= A and B) killed X" or "Yes, you are right when saying that 'we' (= A and C) killed X"? In other words, should A's pronoun use be considered an *inclusive* or an *exclusive* 'we'?

INCLUSIVITY

In English, and in most European languages, 'we' can mean "you and I" (= inclusive) , but also "Bruce and I, but not you" (= exclusive). In many languages outside Europe, two completely different words are used for these two meanings.

SOURCES NOT MENTIONED IN THE TEXT

Identifying Howard Hughes: Ramsland (2000, 2001).

The falsified Persian mummy: BBC show The Mystery of the Persian Mummy, first aired 2001-09-20, Romey & Rose (2001), Pakistani newspaper The Dawn 2000-12-22.

Bishop Helander: Johannisson (1973), Swedish daily Dagens Nyheter (2002-01-15).

Timothy Evans case: Svartvik (1968).

Derek Bentley case: Reap (2002).

Identification of Ted Kaczynski as the Unabomber: Ramsland (2000).

Inclusivity in court: Gibbons (2003:295).

THE SUBJECTIVE APPROACH

LINGUISTICS IS the scientific study of language(s), but it will be obvious to many people that there can be no scientific way of determining what is the most beautiful or expressive language on earth, just as it is impossible to prove that Mozart produced better music than Madonna (or vice versa). Although it is perhaps less obvious to a non-linguist, nor is there any way of determining, say, the oldest or simplest language in the world. Yet people are clearly fond of making such statements and even for linguists, it may be of some interest to know what ordinary mortals have to say on subjects like these. I fine-combed the web in search of statements of this type and, for whatever it's worth, here are the top-ten lists:

Most Beautiful	Oldest/Most Ancient	Easiest/Simplest	Hardest/Most Difficult	Richest
French	Sanskrit	English	English	English
Italian	Tamil	Indonesian	Japanese	Arabic
English	Chinese	Esperanto	Chinese	Sanskrit
Spanish	Basque	Spanish	Hungarian	French
Japanese	Ancient Egyptian	Chinese	Finnish	Tamil
Russian	Aramaic	Ido	Ojibwa	Latin
Portuguese	Scots Gaelic	Italian	Korean	Chinese
Arabic	Syriac	Japanese	Russian	Yiddish
Chinese	Arabic	Hebrew	Arabic	Persian
Latin	Athabaskan	French	Basque	Korean

In a few other categories, I came across too few statements to permit an ordered listing, but here are the languages that were mentioned:

Ugliest:	Finnish, French, Dutch, Swedish, German
Most expressive:	Old Church Slavonic, English, Greek
Most logical:	Esperanto, German, French
Most Systematic:	Sanskrit
Most romantic:	French, Italian, German, Portuguese
Most scentific:	Sanskrit, Korean

Unscientific as these views are (as is, admittedly, my survey of them), there is little doubt that quite a lot of people do hold them. Interestingly, it has been demonstrated that people speaking what are perceived as 'beautiful' dialects are also judged more physically attractive. It remains to be shown, though, that speakers of Sanskrit are perceived as older than other people. Thinking about it, they probably are on average, as Sanskrit is not acquired by children as a mother tongue, but rather learned in a scholastic environment, as it functions as 'the Latin of India'.

In the above, I am especially pleased to note that some people perceive German as 'romantic'. I have always thought I was alone in thinking of it as the Language of Love.

In some cases, additional comments are provided. Here are two gems by anonymous writers:

- *Okay, it's true that the English language is the richest language in the world, with over 800 000 words. And the next richest is German with half that number. The Italian language may only contain 250 000 words and it's no wonder they have so many problems because no one ever gets to the point of what they are saying — they know not how to communicate using real words — especially the politicians, they never say anything.*

- *Also, the Korean language is such a beautiful, rich language that if you master it, you can pronounce 390 000 000 different sounds. This is probably the richest language in the world. That's why we should learn Korean.*

Wouldn't we all like to know how that figure was arrived at?

AESTHETICS

While the beauty or otherwise of a particular language or a particular word is obviously in the eye of the individual beholder, some surveys have been done. The most well-known in the English-speaking world is probably the one organized by the *National [=American] Association of Teachers of Speech* in 1946. The top-ten ugliest words in English according to this poll were as follows:

1. cacophony	6. phlegmatic
2. crunch	7. plump
3. flatulent	8. plutocrat
4. gripe	9. sap
5. jazz	10. treachery

In a 2004 survey of supposedly beautiful words carried out by the British Council among 40 000 non-native speakers of English in 102 countries, *mother* won the first prize, followed by the equally unexpected (well, unimaginative, if you ask me) *passion, smile, love, eternity, fantastic, destiny, freedom, liberty* and *tranquility*. To my mind more interesting entries were *peekaboo* (48), *kangaroo* (50) and *hiccup* (63).

Commenting on the results, others (mostly native-speakers) added entries such as *curmudgeonly, salacious, twaddle, sesquipedalian, bubble, ferret, gobsmacked, manure, plump, bazooka, octopus, masculine, butter, flummoxed, shell-shocked, decadent, sophisticated, fliffus, condescending, lust* and *spatula*. Some gave a specific reason for their pick. *Irksome*, for instance, was qualified as "sound[ing] like it should mean more than it actually does". One interesting comment in this genre was that of New Zealander Musaab Al-Saleem, who noted that the word *news* contains "the first letters from north, east, west and south which are the directions from which news comes from!". However, I have a sneaking suspicion that he was not the first to make this observation.

The perception of a particular word as 'ugly' or 'beautiful' clearly depends both on what it means and how it sounds. Words such as *tranquil, golden, chimes* or *lullaby* figure more frequently on people's lists of nice-sounding words, than does, say, *diarrhoea*, which doesn't necessarily sound less beautiful to someone unfamiliar with its meaning. It seems pretty obvious that *jazz* would not stand a chance if the 1946 survey were to be repeated today.

There is also a clear tendency for words

> The sonority hierarchy ranks consonants according to, basically, how vowel-like they are. Voiceless plosives such as /p/, /t/ and /k/ rank very low, while /l/, /n/ and semi-vowels like /w/ share more characteristics with vowels.

considered 'ugly' to contain plosives, while 'beautiful' words are richer in vowels and nasal and liquid consonants, in other words phonemes high on the sonority hierarchy. Eckler (1992) adds to his discussion of whether or not to admit place-names in a listing of 'ugly' English words that it "is hard to refuse KENNEBUNKPORT, a K-B-K-P-T combo that sounds like a trunk falling down a flight of stairs!".

In one scene of the 2001 film *Donnie Darko*, the literature teacher played by Drew Barrymore has the words "cellar door" written on the blackboard, remarking that "a linguist" had claimed this to represent the most aesthetically pleasing sound combination of any human language. This created a rumor that the word (or rather compound) had somehow actually been "scientifically proven" to be remarkably beautiful.

In the commentary accompanying the DVD issue, the film's director Richard Kelly attributes this observation to Edgar Allen Poe. A prolonged discussion on this subject among fans of the film followed in many a forum. In the end, it seems like Poe never did make a claim to that effect. Nor has it apparently been found among the writings of Jane Austen or T S Elliot, who also figured as suspects. Instead, the first—at least the first *certain*—mention of "cellar door" as a particularly beautiful word seems to go back to J R R Tolkien, who in a 1955 lecture (published in 1963 in the *O'Donnell Lectures in Celtic Studies* series) claimed that "Most English-speaking people, for instance, will admit that *cellar door* is 'beautiful,' especially if dissociated from its sense (and from its spelling). More beautiful than, say, *sky*, and far more beautiful than *beautiful*". Rumor also has it that the French once voted *cellar door* "the most beautiful word" in English, but I have not been able to substantiate this.

In October 2004, the *Deutscher Sprachrat* (German Language Council) and the *Goethe-institut* presented the results of its competition on the favorite words among speakers of German. The favorites—some more predictable than others—included *Lebenslust* 'zest for life', *Erdbeermund* 'voluptuous lips', *Glück* 'happiness', *Liebe* 'love', *Gemütlichkeit* 'comfort, cosiness', *Heimat* 'homeland', *Mitgefühl* 'compassion', *Pusteblume* 'dandelion', *Sehnsucht* 'longing' and *Vergissmeinnicht* 'forget-me-not'. The winner, however, turned out to be *Habseligkeiten* 'belongings', followed by *Geborgenheit* 'safety, security', *lieben* 'to love' and *Augenblick* 'moment'. Victory in the words-

proposed-by-children class went to *Libelle* 'dragonfly'. A special prize was also awarded to *Rhabarbermarmelade* 'rhubarb marmalade'.

It should be noted that the jury considered not so much the words as such, but paid more attention to how the more than 22 000 participants argued in favor of their proposals.

Similar surveys have also been held in other countries. In the Netherlands in 1980, *liefde* 'love' won, but in another, which was organized in 2004 by the Meertens Instituut in Amsterdam, *desalniettemin* 'nevertheless' was more surprisingly crowned the winner, followed by such words as *vlinder* 'butterfly', *melancholie* 'melancholia', and *konijn* 'rabbit'. A year later, Sweden's leading morning newspaper also carried out a survey of this kind and *sommarvind* 'summer breeze' emerged as the most popular choice.

In the 1920s, psychologist Wolfgang Köhler exposed a number of people to two geometric shapes looking roughly like those on the left. He then invented the words *takete* and *maluma* for them but did not tell his subjects which was which. It turned out that, for the overwhelming majority of them, the fluffy, cloud-like shape was associated with *maluma* and the more aggressive-looking explosion-like object with *takete*.

The experiment was inspired by an earlier one by Georgian psychologist D Usnadze.

SOURCES NOT MENTIONED IN THE TEXT

The claim that speakers of 'beautiful' dialects are judged more physically attractive is reported by Giles & Niedzelski (1998:89).

British Council 2004 survey of the "most beautiful English word": BBC News 2004-11-27.

The beauty of *Cellar Door* was discussed extensively on the LUSENET *Works of Edgar Allan Poe* list during 2003 and 2004, as well as on other discussion lists.

Names for shapes experiment: Usnadze (1924), Köhler (1929).

Beautiful German words: BBC News 2004-08-01, *Dagens Nyheter* 2004-10-25.

Beautiful words in Dutch: Oostendorp (2004).

Most beautiful word in Swedish: *Dagens Nyheter* 2005-11-15.

LANGUAGE MYTHS

ONE THING which is a constant annoyance to linguists is the wide variety of misconceptions about language held by many laymen. Here are some of the more common ones.

THE LEGENDARY SNOW HOAX

What has become known as the *Great Eskimo Vocabulary Hoax* is one of the all-time classics. For decades, linguistics textbooks informed readers that Eskimos had a great many words referring to 'snow'. This "fact" gradually became widely known among the general public and today even the Greenlandic Tourist Board lends it credence! Refuting this claim has recently become one of the most enjoyable activities for know-it-all linguists.

The first to attempt to trace the origin of the snow legend was apparently Martin (1986), though the standard reference these days is Pullum (1991). It turns out that anthropological linguist nestor Franz Boas in 1911 mentioned in passing that Eskimo (or Inuktitut) had four *and perhaps more* words for snow. When this was cited by his disciple Benjamin Whorf, the number "happened" to become somewhat greater. And so the fabrication of a mountain out of a molehill was in full progress. Numbers of Eskimo snow words mentioned in print now go up to at least 400.

Pullum's essay on the subject is highly entertaining, and his idea on the reasons for the myth's popularity is worth quoting:

The alleged lexical extravagances of the Eskimos comports so well with the many other facets of their polysynthetic perversity: rubbing noses; lending their wives to strangers; eating raw seal blubber; throwing Grandma out to be eaten by polar bears.

The actual number of snow words in Eskimo is difficult to estimate, although some have tried—and the estimates rarely go beyond a dozen. In any case, it is worth pointing out that pretty much any language whose speakers have more than a fleeting acquaintance with snow have more terms than the generic *snow* might suggest. If you think about it, even a "non-exotic" language such as English possesses words such as *avalanche, powder, sleet, slush, blizzard, dusting, flurry,* and *hardpack* besides *snow*, not to mention compounds including the word *snow* and various terms for frozen water, such as *ice, frost* and *hail.*

While at least some Eskimo varieties—in contrast to English—do distinguish between 'falling snow' and 'snow on the ground', so did Classical Greek.

THE GERMAN VOTE

*E*very once in a while the claim is heard that German was on the verge of becoming the official language of the newly independent USA. To spice up the story a little, it is often added that the proposal was defeated in the Congress by the smallest possible margin—one single vote.

In a way, the story makes sense—for obvious reasons, late 18th century Americans were not overly pro-British, and some measures were indeed taken to distance the new nation from its old mother country. Given a large number of German-speaking immigrants, what would be more natural than to pick a language different from that of the tea-drinking Britons? And had the vote passed, would the first man on the moon have spoken German?

In fact, the officialization of a language other than English was considered (Hebrew, Greek and French were suggested). The legendary vote, however, never took place. The origin of the story appears to be that a House Committee, in its dealing with a German settlement in Virginia, recommended that federal statutes be printed and distributed in German as well as in English, where need be. The discussions dragged out, and a member suggested adjourning. *This* proposal was voted on, and was rejected by 42 votes to 41. As the adjournment was not passed, the issue itself was not raised again until three days later (16 February 1795). This time, an English-only policy won the assembly's vote and, after approval by the Senate, the law was signed by George Washington himself.

We never were as close as some have it to hearing Herr Armstark utter these words.

Another important fact, rarely pointed out, is that even if viewed favorably by the authorities, German would probably have had little chance to oust English from the USA. The first national census, taken five years before the "German vote", reveals that only 5,7% of the white population was "German", as opposed to almost 90% English-speakers.

IF IT WAS GOOD ENOUGH FOR JESUS . . .

*M*iriam "Ma" Ferguson, in 1925 inaugurated as the first woman governor of Texas, is usually accredited with having said "If the King James version was good enough for Jesus, it's good enough for me" with regard to new Bible translations. In some versions of the story, the quote is about bilingual education ("If English was good enough for Jesus, it is good enough for the children of Texas"), and in others, it is attributed to her husband and predecessor, James "Pa" Ferguson, who according to the *New York Times* would have uttered it as early as in 1917.

Andersen (1996) provides some background facts, and it turns out that in 1963, a

Newsweek report gave "a principal from the American south", as the source of the quote. Since then, it has been said to have originated with Arkansas governor Orval Faubus, "some long-dead British politician", "an old lady in England", preachers in Arkansas and Texas, a certain Texas high school coach, Virginia congress-man Frank Wolf, and former US vice-president Dan Quayle, often portrayed in the media as monumentally ignorant. More recently, these words were attributed to Republican politician Linda Smith by the *Seattle Times* in the mid-1990s.

Obviously, it cannot be proven that no one has made a statement of this sort, but the large number of purported originators is suggestive of urban myth status. On the other hand, in a Canadian newspaper interview, bible translator Susan Brooks Thistlewaite of

the Chicago Theological Seminary, claimed to have heard several people talking about "the King James version being good enough for Jesus" in a dead serious manner.

THE SECRET MEANINGS OF COCA COLA

Among urban legends, there is a rich flora of coke-lore, that is, myths related to the soft drink sometimes seen as a symbol of American imperialism. At least two of these have a linguistic connection. First, it has been rumored in certain Arab countries that the Coca-Cola logo, if read upside down, turns into an anti-Islamic message. The rumor was believed to have a part in plummeting sales in Egypt and Saudi Arabia, so the Coca-Cola company was worried.

Coke proved not to be anti-Islamic after all

It was presumably with some relief that the Coca-Cola company heard the statement in May 2000 from the Grand Mufti Sheik Nasser Farid Wassel, the most influential religious authority in Egypt. After having consulted several experts, he concluded that the rumors were groundless, and that even the most pious Muslims could continue drinking Coke if they so wished.

At the opposite end of the Asian continent, the Coke logo gave rise to another myth, namely that the Chinese characters used by the Americans to transcribe the brand name had various weird meanings such as 'mare fastened with wax' or 'bite the wax tadpole'.

Given the way in which Chinese is written, it can indeed be highly problematic for a western company to find an entirely suitable way of writing its brand name. A combination of Chinese characters may be used to approximate the pronunciation of the name of the product, but each of these characters has itself a meaning of its own. Since 1928, the (very carefully chosen!) official version of Coca-Cola in China can also be read as 'to allow the mouth to be able to rejoice', or more loosely 'something palatable from which one receives pleasure'. What is undoubtedly true, however, is that individual Coca-Cola salesmen and distributors in China before 1928 used their own home-made transliterations, which some-times produced unexpected or even undesirable readings, including such things as those quoted above.

It has been said that if Coca-Cola were a name inherited from proto-Germanic, it would be Köcher Köhler in German.

THE CHAMBER OF HORRORS: ASSORTED ALL-TIME CLASSICS

A part from the ones already discussed, the following is the list, in no particular order, of the most classic myths which we would rather not hear again. (Note that these are not actual quotations but rather paraphrases of common misconceptions.)

For any country, there is one and only one language. Just as the people in Greece speak Greek, so do the Pakistanis speak Pakistani. Exceptions are American Indians and Australian Aboriginals. They have no countries of their own, but speak Indian and Aboriginal respectively.

All deaf people speak the same language, called The Sign Language, which isn't really a full-fledged language. Alternatively, sign languages are modelled upon the spoken languages of the countries where they are used (p 128).

Certain languages are somehow older than others, and some languages do not change at all. Somewhere in Appalachia (or was it the Ozarks?), people speak pure Elizabethan English.

English has a larger vocabulary than any other language (pp 189–91).

While you and I speak languages, many people only speak dialects. This applies especially to third world countries, where most people use speech forms which are mere dialects. This may have something to do with the fact that you and I live in Nations populated by Peoples, whereas They are simply organized in Tribes.

Throughout the history of humankind, languages have developed towards an increasingly greater perfection. Until now, that is. These days, people just don't know how to speak properly any more.

 While languages of the civilized world (and English in particular) are suitable for expressing abstract thoughts, many languages spoken in far-away areas do not allow their speakers to carry out conversation on scientific, philosophical and metaphysical issues. The small vocabulary of such languages forces their speakers to resort to pantomime and heavy use of gestures. These languages also usually do not have any grammar whatsoever.

The more exotic the language is from the writer's point of view, the more common claims of this kind are made. Yet, one sometimes encounters such claims with regard to languages of cultures with which one would expect writers to be more familiar. For instance, Heurlin & Olagüe (1968:75)—a textbook for Swedish students of Spanish— happily state that Basque "es tan primitivo que no existen en sus raíces palabras abstractas. Así, para decir Dios, hace falta emplear una perífrasis: 'Jangoi-co-a', 'el Señor que está arriba'" ("...is so primitive that it has no abstract words. Thus, to speak of God, one has to use the circumlocution 'the Gentleman who is above'").

Haiman (1979:84) parodies this myth thus: "The Ooga Booga of the central Congo have 346 words for various kinds of sands, but no single word for sand in general; therefore these people are incapable of making generalizations; therefore they are incapable of abstract thought; therefore...". On the following page, he makes the observation that most varieties of English have no generic word covering 'drink', 'eat' and 'smoke'—obviously related concepts which are merged in many a language.

 The vocabulary in particular, but also a language's grammar and pronunciation are strongly influenced by the physical environment in which its speakers live. There is also a close and easily observed correlation between their world view and the structure of their language.

 And, of course—what is perhaps the most persistent of them all: There is a correct and an incorrect way of speaking. People who have studied a lot speak better than those who have not. Also, written language is generally better than spoken language.

Note that many of the above claims cannot be proven to be false, but nor is there anything to suggest that they could be true (a few of them are discussed in some detail elsewhere in this book). Despite what the layman may think, the position of the linguistic establishment on these issues is not simply wishful thinking. Evans (1998:167) expresses this better than most, in admitting that *"Linguists would love to have primitive languages to study in order to understand how human language has evolved"*.

In addition to these, there are plenty of myths applying to specific languages. For instance, it is often said that the presence of /θ/ in Spanish (corresponding to the th sound in 'thistle') is due to noblemen imitating the lisping of a particular king (a similar story on the introduction of uvular *r* in French is dubious, but less obviously untrue). Also, for every language, there are plenty of etymological myths, i.e. misconceptions regarding the origins of particular words.

SOURCES NOT MENTIONED IN THE TEXT

Language myths in general: Bauer & Trudgill (eds) (1998), discussions on the *Linguist List*, personal experience.

Snow in classical Greek: Jussi Karlgren, p c.

Almost official German in the USA: Baron (1990:88), Crystal (1987:365), Heath & Mandabach (1983), *Linguist List* 6.609 and 6.644, and postings to the newsgroup alt.folklore.urban.

The language of Jesus: Andersen (1996), Edwards (1994:204), Canadian newspaper *Globe and Mail* (1995-08-31), *New York Times* (1995-08-13).

Coke-lore: Entries by Barbara Mikkelson on the Urban Legends web site, <http://www.snopes.com>.

PRAGMATICS

EVEN THE MOST CASUAL CONVERSATION is subject to more rules than we tend to be aware of. There are culture-specific preferences in all speech communities on how to begin a conversation, how to switch the topic, how to end the current speech exchange, etc. Failing to observe these preferred ways of doing things would immediately make you seem socially incompetent, or even outright rude. At the very least, in most societies, you are supposed to answer if directly asked a question. You usually have to give a certain amount of feedback, or at least utter something like "mhm", to show that you're interested in what your interlocutor is saying—otherwise the conversation will cease to be. You also need to signal your withdrawal from the conversation (even if it's temporary) either with explicit overt signals such as "wait a second, there is someone at the door" or by some other more subtle covert ones such as raising your eyebrows.

VERBAL INTERACTION IN ABORIGINAL AUSTRALIA

Among Australian Aboriginals, pragmatic rules are rather different from those familiar to westerners. Something being said does not necessarily require a response of any kind. Or it may entail a response from people other than the one directly addressed. More seriously, many Aboriginal cultures value knowledge as a resource of the same kind as money is to westerners. It has to be guarded and shared only with caution. Both of these behaviors have been reported to cause serious problems in court, where conversation is even more rule-governed than in daily life. Several spectators may spontaneously respond to a question posed by the judge to a witness. The accused may launch a long monologue, including asking questions of his own to various members of the court, instead of keeping to the short question-and-response ritual required by western judicial practice. And, crucially, Aboriginal views on the sharing of knowledge along kinship lines or other alliances may prevent someone from responding to a question even if they do possess the required information. University of Hawaii forensic linguist, Diana Eades, specialises in communication between whites and Aboriginals. "Aboriginal people think it's bad manners to talk about very serious issues before they get to know you or before they build up trust", she says, "whereas most police and lawyers come from cultures where being direct and up front is respected". Also, says Eades, "Aboriginal people will often take time to think and consider a question before answering it. White lawyers often take this to mean that they don't have an answer and so they move on to the next question".

Brisbane solicitor Andrew Boe says that it takes some experience for a white judge to handle the Aboriginal pragmatics. "The lawyer asks a question and the Aboriginal person will raise an eyebrow", Boe says. "To them this means 'yes'. But the lawyers or police think they're being smart and think things like "Oh, they're dumb blacks, I'm trying to help them and they can't even give me the basic information I'm asking for".

TRUE OR FALSE—OR SOMETHING IN BETWEEN?

In Madagascar, as in Aboriginal Australia, information is a precious commodity, which cannot be disseminated any which way. In addition, a Malagasy would lose face if it turned out that he had claimed something that turns out to be wrong. Therefore, Malagasy responses to greetings are quite often violating Grice's Maxim of Quantity. In answering vaguely, you have given some information, without committing yourself to a future (and therefore by definition at least somewhat uncertain) event. Thus, when asked about where he's heading, the traditional Malagasy wouldn't answer "To the store to buy some beer; we're having a party this evening", but rather "just a little more to the north". Similarly, when asked when the party is going to take place (in case you happen to have found out about it), a reply such as "sometime this month" would be perfectly appropriate, even if the actual date is today. After all, something unforeseen *might* intervene and prevent the party from actually taking place. (One might suspect, however, that only a westerner would ask such silly questions, since a Malagasy would presumably be able to predict the answer.)

Keenan & Ochs (1979:150) also mention another case illustrating the Malagasy unwillingness to commit oneself to information of uncertain truth value. The planning of a wedding had proceeded so far that the town hall was booked, and appropriate clothing had been bought. Still, on the question about when the event was going to take place, one of the people involved would only answer "Oh, pretty soon now".

Malagasy discourse habits have attained an almost legendary status for its aversion for directness. "A fifth of the conversation", says a Malagasy primary school teacher, "should be to the point. The rest should be all about word play". Worries have been expressed that the use of mobile phones poses a threat to traditional Malagasy oratory skills and circumspect discourse strategies. As each minute of talk is so expensive, people are forced to cut it short.

CHAOTIC CARIBBEAN CONVERSATIONS

Reisman (1974) reports that by western standards, conversations on the island of Antigua appear "almost anarchic". Most notably, there is no constraint on several people speaking simultaneously, and when someone else starts to speak, this is not interpreted as a signal to the current speaker to stop talking. It is in other words difficult to interrupt someone else, but in case you should succeed, that is not considered impolite. Interrupting oneself in order to make remarks on another topic is also reported to be acceptable, as is falling asleep during a conversation!

BEING POLITE IN WOLOF

Among speakers of Wolof, in West Africa, there are rather strict rules for responding to a greeting, which are quite unlike western ones. The basic idea is that higher status is associated with passivity, and in an encounter it is therefore up to the socially inferior to initiate greeting. The superior is supposed to respond to the questions regarding his and his family's health, but not to ask any questions in return. He is expected to answer slowly and in a low-pitched voice, in a manner that would make him appear haughty to a westerner, while the greeter should speak rapidly and loudly.

Both parties are thus supposed to agree on placing themselves in an unequal relationship, and avoiding greeting is simply not an option. Now, one could easily assume that the only trouble arising out of this would be that both parties might be eager to be recognized as the superior. However, while this entails respect and power, it also implies certain obligations, often of a financial nature. The Greeted may therefore not accept the superior role, and instead of replying to the questions, he may himself start asking questions, the worst-case scenario being that neither wants to respond to the questions put forth by the other!

GREETING IN MANINKA

In order to highlight the contrast between western and West African greeting rituals, Bird & Shopen (1979) first give an example of two hurried Americans meeting each other in the street:

A: *Hello Ed!*
B: *Hi! How are you?*
A: *Sorry, I'm in a hurry.*
B: *Yeh, me too.*
A: *See you on Saturday.*

Then, they present a similar situation, involving two equally hurried speakers of Maninka:

Mamodou:	*Ah, Sédou, you and the morning!*
Sédou:	*Excellent. You and the morning!*
Mamodou:	*Did you sleep in peace?*
Sédou:	*Only peace.*
Mamodou:	*Are the people of the household well?*
Sédou:	*There is no trouble.*
Mamodou:	*Are you well?*
Sédou:	*Peace, praise Allah. Did you sleep well?*
Mamodou:	*Praise Allah. You Kanté.*
Sédou:	*Excellent. You Diarra.*

Mamodou:	Excellent.
Sédou:	And the family?
Mamodou:	I thank Allah. Is there peace?
Sédou:	We are here.
Mamodou:	How is your mother?
Sédou:	No trouble.
Mamodou:	And your cousin Fanta?
Sédou:	Only peace. And your father?
Mamodou:	Praise Allah. He greets you.
Sédou:	Tell him I have heard it.
Mamodou:	And your younger brother Amadou?
Sédou:	He is well. And your uncle Sidi?
Mamodou:	No trouble, praise Allah Where are you going?
Sédou:	I'm going to the market. And you?
Mamodou:	My boss is waiting for me.
Sédou:	OK then, I'll see you later.
Mamodou:	Yes, I'll see you later. Greet the people of the household.
Sédou:	They will hear it. Greet your father.
Mamodou:	He will hear it.
Sédou:	May your days pass well.
Mamodou:	Amen. May the market go well.
Sédou:	Amen. May we meet soon.
Mamodou:	May that soon arrive in good stead.

Similarly elaborated greeting rituals are also documented from neighboring Wolof.

POLITENESS IN KOREAN

Being an east Asian language, Korean too has rather intricate systems of showing due respect to the interlocutor. The second person pronoun (i.e. simply *you* in English) has five levels of politeness, and yet, the 'blunt' level in turn has three different variants. At a sentence level, no less than seven conventionalized levels of politeness are reported, and that still doesn't include the recently phased-out 'superpolite' level.

A PRAGMATIC UNIVERSAL?

References to pragmatic universals are rather difficult to come across. One putative such feature, however, is irony—although it may not extend to all individuals, no speech community seems to have been documented where verbal irony is not a part of the communication repertoire.

While it has been suggested that Chinese are unable to understand irony, this has been ascribed to their tendency to "in any case say the opposite of what they mean all the time".

BAD TURNTAKING SKILLS

On September 26, 1960, Cuba's new leader Fidel Castro gave the longest speech in the history of the United Nations—he spoke uninterrupted for 4 hours and 29 minutes.

In a conscious attempt to gain a place in the *Guinness Book of World Records*, Zimbabwean bank director Jonah Mungoshi spoke virtually without stop for 36 hours in April 2003.

USE OF PERSONAL NAMES

In some Indian languages, including Toda, individuals may not utter their own names. Instead, upon being introduced into a new group of people, you have to ask someone else to give your name. Some groups have also tabooed the use of one's spouse's name. The usual strategy is to then refer to your better half as 'the mother/father of your children'.

In Malagasy, it is yourself that you should avoid. Should you want to mention your own mother, for instance, you had better introduce her as e.g. "the mother of" followed by the name of your sibling.

As pointed out on p 91, tabooing of personal names after an individual's death, is not uncommon around the world.

SOURCES NOT MENTIONED IN THE TEXT

Verbal interaction in Aboriginal Australia: Foley (1997:252-53) + *Law Society Journal* 33 (2), p 82.

Malagasy pragmatics: Keenan & Ochs (1979:148, 150), Foley (1997: 278-79).

Mobile phones as a threat to Malagasy discourse strategies: Harman (2002).

Wolof: Foley (1997:256-59), Irvine (1974).

Politeness in Korean: Sohn (1999: 207, 269, 272).

A pragmatic universal: *Linguist List* 9.582.

Chinese and irony: Daniel Bunčić (p c), referring to Sinclair & Wong (1991).

Castro's speech: Guinness Book of World Records.

Jonah Mungoshi speaking for 36 hours in a row: *Dagens Nyheter* 2003-04-14.

Restrictions on using names in India: Nishit (2003).

Restrictions on using names in Malagasy: Keenan & Ochs (1979:152).

LANGUAGE AND GENDER

A GREAT DEAL has been written on men's and women's speech styles in western societies. Yet, at least if you ask me, the differences in speech between the sexes are almost negligible when compared to the expectations on gender loyalty that society imposes in other areas. Nevertheless, several non-European languages have considerably more elaborate linguistic gender manifestations.

LANGUAGES WITH THE GREATEST GENDER DIFFERENCES

Several languages impose different norms on their users depending on the sex of the speaker. Languages such as Japanese, Gros Ventre, Lakota and Chukchi are often cited in this context. Probably no language, however, goes as far as did Island Carib.

The language of the Island Carib of the Lesser Antilles was first described by French missionaries in the 17th century. One feature they noticed was the differences in speech depending on the addressee—men were spoken to literally in another language than were women. On closer inspection, it turned out that the female-directed speech was Arawak, a language known from other islands in the vicinity, whereas male-directed speech combined the same grammar with a mainly non-Arawak vocabulary, uncannily similar to that of the Carib language of mainland South America.

The oral literature of this people had it that Carib conquerors from the mainland slaughtered all the Arawak men (probably not too long before European contact), and then married the local women. The invading Caribs would then have been addressed in their own language by their wives. Later generations, brought up in closer contact with their Arawak-speaking mothers than with their fathers, would later gradually have forgotten the Carib grammar, and only retained the lexicon, along with the feeling that this was the appropriate vocabulary to use when speaking to men. The traditional explanation behind Island Carib sounds too good to be true, and has indeed been questioned, but if it is a myth, it has not been disproved.

Island Carib is now extinct in the Lesser Antilles. It is thought that the last speaker died in about 1920. However, in the 18th century, runaway French slaves on the island of St Vincent came into contact with the Island Caribs and adopted their language. After a rebellion, they were deported to Central America by the British just before 1800, and the language is now spoken only by a Black population in Honduras and neighboring countries. In this variety, unlike earlier Island Carib, the gender differences have been levelled and only a very limited number of words remain sensitive to the sex of the addressee.

*Men and women don't speak the same language
(picture reproduced by kind permission from*
Om ingen nyper mig i rumpan snart så går jag hem
by Anna-Karin Elde)

In many other languages with great gender differences, only relatively small portions of the system are affected. One other example deserves mention, however. In Yana, formerly spoken in California, the majority of the word stock had separate male and female forms (where the female forms were also used by men when addressing women). As opposed to the situation in Island Carib, though, lexical items in the two Yana registers were relatively systematically (albeit often unpredictably) related to one another. In most cases, the male form contained an extra syllable.

Chiquitano, spoken in Bolivia, has a number of forms used only by men *when talking about other men*. These include both lexical and grammatical features, and constitute a rather central and conspicuous part of Chiquitano grammar.

Also worth mentioning is that differences of this sort are not found only in the lexicon or phonology, but may also be encountered in syntax or morphology. In Lakota, for instance, verbs have different imperative forms depending on the sex of the speaker. And in Japanese, female speakers are expected to drop the copula if it is followed by the final particle *yo*.

NON-STANDARD FEMALE SPEECH

It has long been noted that there is a tendency for women to keep closer to the *prescriptive* standard than men do, whereas men tend to deviate from this norm, by for instance being overly conservative or overly innovative. Most claims to the contrary come from the Middle East, where female speech varieties in Jordan, Syria and on the West Bank have been observed to be further from the standard than male speech. It has been suggested that this has to do with their generally lower level of education (although I am far from convinced of this).

The opposite of a prescriptive grammar is a descriptive grammar, which documents how people actually speak, without making value judgements.

PRESCRIPTIVE refers to how teachers and pedants tell you the language should be spoken. They are concerned with upholding traditional standards such as saying "you and I" (rather than "you and me") or "whom did you speak to?" (rather than "who did you speak to?").

AN EXLUSIVELY FEMININE SCRIPT

Nüshu is a script which has been used for centuries by unschooled peasant women in the Jiang Yong Prefecture, located in the Hunan Province in south-eastern China. It is remarkable, and possibly unique, in having being known and used only by women.

It has been suggested that the Jiang Yong women created Nüshu as a substitute, since they were not entitled to schooling, and therefore never got to learn normal Chinese writing. It then proved to have the additional advantage of being able to function as a secret language.

The women of the area have traditionally constituted a closely knit community within the community. Marriages leading to the migration of a woman to another village were a source of great concern and sorrow within the sisterhood. Japanese Nüshu researcher Orie Endo has therefore suggested that the script developed as a means for the women remaining in their village of origin to secretly communicate with their ex-pat "sisters".

A large proportion of the characters (of which there are 1 000-1 500) resemble those of Hànzi, or traditional Chinese writing, and the script most probably derives therefrom. Other characters, however, are likely to have been inspired by embroidery designs—textile handicraft was of major importance to the women in the area.

A paramount difference between the two systems is that while Hànzi symbols are first and foremost logograms, i.e. with each symbol representing a single word or concept, the Nüshu symbols, including those derived from Hànzi, are mainly phonetic.

The oldest preserved writings are from the 1600s, but it is believed that the script is older than that, and it has been suggested that it may date as far back as to the 10th century. Unfortunately, the existence of the script was not brought to scholarly attention until the early 1980s, when there were only a very small number of individuals left who still mastered it.

On closer investigation, it was even found that a small local literature in Nüshu existed, mostly consisting of love stories, but also of poems bemoaning the injustices in life.

In April 2002, the Chinese authorities announced their intention to spend the equivalent of one million Euros on preserving the script. The plan includes the erection of a museum devoted to Nüshü. In the following year, Zhou Shuoyi, thought to be the first man to know the language, published a dictionary of 1 800 characters.

Unfortunately, however, the reportedly last competent user of Nüshü, died in September 2004, at the age of 94 (according to herself) or 98 (according to the authorities).

THE QUEST FOR A GENDER-NEUTRAL PRONOUN

In many languages, not least European ones, the sex of a referent is obligatorily encoded in a language. If you're using nouns, you may say *person* instead of *man* or *woman*, or *child* instead of *boy* or *girl*. But with pronouns, there is no word covering both *he* and *she*, and in some cases, this has

proved problematic. Using only one of the two (in practice usually *he*) risks offending some listeners/readers, while the set phrase *he or she* is felt a bit cumbersome. Sometimes this makes you envy the Finns, in whose language *hän* covers both 'he' and 'she'. This is by no means unique to Finnish, and the same state of affairs obtains in e.g. most languages of Africa and of the Pacific. In some European languages, including Swedish and English, attempts have been made to remedy this, with the first attested case for English being from 1884.

Borrowing into English from a wide variety of languages has been suggested, including Old Norse, Mandarin, Latin, Hawaiian, German, French, Proto-Indo-European, British dialects, and even Klingon (Finnish *hän* has also been launched as a candidate for Swedish). Some proposals want to extend the inanimate *it* or the generic *one*, while others point out that *she* could be used, as it already encapsulates *he*! Yet others, such as *ip, hse, ve, thon, ith, fm, po* and *mef* are entirely new coinings.

Perhaps the most common strategy, though, is to try to combine *he* and *she* into one single word. It is probably uncontroversial to say that the resulting forms vary a great deal in aesthetic quality. Candidates in this category include *hesh, heesh, he'er, hiser, himorher*—and, not least, my personal favorite *h'orsh'it*, which also incorporates the inanimate *it*. It was proposed in 1975 by Joel Weiss of Northbrook, Illinois.

GENDERED COMPUTERS

In an experiment reported by Nass & Moon (2000:85), subjects were exposed to computers presenting the subjects "computers and technology" (as the authors point out, a "stereotypically 'male' topic") and "love and relations" (a "stereotypically 'female' topic"). The information from this 'tutor computor' was then tested on a 'test computer', and the results were finally evaluated on a 'evaluator computer', which drew conclusions such as 'Your results suggest that the tutor computer has done a good job'. All but the test computer addressed the subjects via a prerecorded voice.

Among several other interesting observations, the researchers found that the subjects—regardless of their own gender—tended to agree more with the evaluator computer when this used a male voice than they did when it used its female voice. (The actual message being the same, of course). Also, they put more trust in "male" tutor computer's lessons on "computers and technology", whereas they found the "female" tutor computer more reliable when it came to "love and relations".

SOURCES NOT MENTIONED IN THE TEXT

Island Carib: Taylor (1977), Taylor & Hoff (1980), Hoff (1994).
Yana: Sapir (1929).
Chiquitano: Adelaar (2004:479).
Lakota: Mithun (1999:508).
Japanese: Shibatani (1990b:373-74).
Non-standard female speech: *Linguist List* 6.328.
Nüshu: Mainly Endo (1999), with some additional data from Liming (1998) and from the TV broadcast *Det hemliga språket* on Swedish Public Service television 2002-01-18. Also BBC News 2002-04-18, *China Daily* 2004-11-08, Chinaview news agency 2004-09-23.
Epicene pronouns: *Linguist List* 3.282, Baron (1981, 1986).

HOW MANY WORDS ARE THERE?

I AM CERTAIN that many readers would want and expect a book of this kind to contain a world record on lexical richness. (Many would also no doubt expect English to be the record-holder.) Instead, I will try to explain why it is impossible to include such an entry.

SOME REASONS WHY WE CANNOT ESTIMATE THE NUMBER OF WORDS IN A LANGUAGE

Non-linguists are fond of discussing languages in terms of how many words they have. Surely, many believe, a language with a very large number of words must be more expressive than one with a smaller vocabulary. The language usually accredited with the richest vocabulary is English. The number of words claimed to exist in the English vocabulary varies from one source to another—from 300 000 to a million or more—but whatever the number given, it is almost always far larger than that of any other language in the world.

Every once in a while, linguists disappoint laymen by telling them that it is meaningless to discuss the "number of words" in a given language. One reason is that, for the number of words in language X, people usually cite the number of words listed in the most comprehensive dictionary of that language. However, for hundreds of languages which are not normally written, there simply are no dictionaries at all. Logically, this would imply that these languages have no words at all, which is clearly absurd. And of course, there was a time when there existed no dictionaries even for the allegedly exceptionally rich languages.

It is true that some of the most comprehensive dictionaries of lesser-known languages list a number of words which is clearly smaller than you'd find in dictionaries such as *Oxford*, *Collins* or *Le Grand Robert*. But then, the latter are the fruits of centuries of lexicography, and hundreds of people have been involved in producing them. Not many dictionaries exist for most smaller languages, and those that do are the result of the work of a few enthusiasts. The very study of them is a quite recent phenomenon. If there were only three English dictionaries, and if they were each the work of two people without access to printed texts, how many words would they include? Surely not millions.

Even if we were to accept the dictionary argument, it can easily be shown that any issue of an ordinary newspaper contains lots of words that are not found in any dictionary—and this goes for English as well as for any other language. Does this then mean that they are not English words (or Russian or Japanese or whatever)? If so, what language is the newspaper written in?

We could also approach the question by asking such truly basic things as "what is a language?" and "what is a word?". To neither of these do linguists have an answer with which they themselves are happy. To begin with the first, there is no agreement on where one language stops and another begins. Languages usually have a number of dialects. Now, should a word count of English include only the words used by educated Londoners, or should it also include speech features found only in Nebraska, Wales, Queensland, Liberia, or Trinidad? Similarly, how should we treat specific occupational or technical jargons and slang? Do words only used by shipbuilders, stamp collectors, chemists, teenagers, or botanists—but unknown to most other people—count as English words? If not, how do we tell whether a particular word really is "unknown to most others"?

The same argument can also be made with reference to variation across time rather than across space. Just as the philosopher Heraclitus said of the impossibility of stepping into the same river twice (since the water you bathed in the first time has reached the sea by the time of your second dip), snapshots of English taken at two different times would be different. Some words disappear, while other new ones are coined. But how do we know when a word has disappeared from the language? If we find words in, say, Shakespeare that are no longer current (whatever that is taken to mean), does that mean that they are not English words? And when did English become English in the first place? English is descended from proto-Germanic, but when did it split off from proto-Germanic? Is there a point in time where we can say that people no longer spoke proto-Germanic, but rather Old English? (And is Old English the same thing as English?)

And when can we say that a new coining has entered the language? Obviously, somebody has to come up with the coining, but is it an English word if only this person uses it? If not, how many others must adopt it before it is an English word?

And what about borrowings? Are *chef d'œuvre* and *coup d'état* English words? Or are they French words? If so, is *very* (which comes from French *vrai*) also a French word? Or are perhaps *chef d'œuvre* and *coup d'état* composed of several words? If so, what does the word *d* mean?

There are several million species of animals and plants that have Latinate scientific names. If these are Latin words, then Latin might be considered the language with the richest vocabulary, most of which, paradoxically, has been acquired since Latin ceased to be a spoken language.

Most would probably agree that flour and flower are different words, which just happen to sound the same. But polysemic words are such that they not only sound the same, but also have meanings that are somehow related. Are for instance man 'male human' and man 'human being in general' two different words? And what about foot (of a leg) and foot (of a mountain or a paper)? Or mouse (the rodent) and (computer) mouse?

How do we deal with inflections and derivations? Are *book* and *books* two different words or just two forms of the same word? And what about *good* and *better* or *go* and *went*? If *speakable* is a derivation of *speak*, then is *portable* a derivation of *carry*? The situation gets even more awkward when we consider what linguists call zero derivation, i.e. when the derived word is similar in appearance to its root. One example of this is the noun *walk* versus the verb *to walk*.

When comparing the vocabularies of different languages, we need also take into account the different ways of stringing morphemes together. English doesn't have much morphology, but just like other Germanic languages, it is fond of compounds. Thus, English has a word *type* and a word *writer*, in addition to *typewriter*. French, on the other hand, has *écrire* 'to write' and *machine* 'machine', but expresses 'typewriter' as *machine à écrire*, i.e. 'machine to write (with)'. Does this mean that *typewriter* counts as an extra word for English but that *machine à écrire* does not count as an additional word in French? If so, languages with even more compounding than English, such as German, must have an infinitely larger number of words—compare for instance the classic *Donaudampfschifffahrtsgesellschaftskapitänsmütze* with its English translation

'Danube Steam-boat Shipping Company captain's cap' (and yes, the new German orthography does require three <f>s in a row; German formerly required only two <f>s, as in the poster on p 194). Bear in mind also that, as indicated later on pp 318–319, it has, for instance, been claimed that *every single verb* in some languages has hundreds of thousands, and even several million different forms, incorporating both subjects, objects and other material.

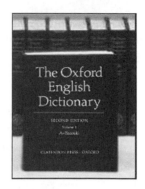

Numerals and place-names are two interesting groups of words in this respect. You would surely agree that *three* and *eight* are English words, as are *third* and *eighth*. But consider higher numerals, such as *Two billion three hundred and forty three million eight hundred and seventy-six thousand five hundred and ninety-five.* This is normally written as a sequence of several words in English, but not so in many other languages. Therefore, the written version of 2 343 876 595 could be considered a word by their speakers. If the language in question also has ordinals, 2 343 876 595th might then be seen as another word, and its counting system alone would dwarf the entire English vocabulary in no time.

The Oxford English Dictionary *is usually claimed to be the most exhaustive one there is for English. The 1989 edition contains full entries for 171476 words "in current use", and 47156 obsolete ones.*

A similar argument could be made with reference to place names. One might, for instance, suggest that Cambridge (England) and Cambridge (Massachusetts) should count as one word. However, they clearly refer to two different entities, one to a city in Britain, and the other to a part of Boston on the other side of the Atlantic. They thus mean two entirely different things, just like *bank* (where you deposit your money) and *bank* (of a river). You might object that names constitute a specific category of words, which is not language-specific, and therefore not part of any specific language. After all, Cambridge is a word that cannot be translated. But then, again, *London* isn't *London* to everybody—it is *Llundain* to the Welsh, *Londres* to the French, *Lontoo* to the Finns, and *Londýn* to the Czech. Similarly, *Moscow* is *Moskva* to the Russians, *Athens* is *Athinai* to the Greek, *Lisbon* is *Lisboa* to the Portuguese—and so on.

That said (phew!), the heftiest dictionaries of English usually claim to list between 300 000 and 700 000 words, and most estimates on the number of words known by English-speakers have been suggested to vary between 20 000 and 80 000. The number of words actually used by speakers of both English and Mandarin tends to be in the 4 000–8 000 range. Since Mandarin has an unusually long written history, it can be shown that while the size of dictionaries has increased considerably during the past two millennia, the number of different words used by a given author has remained constant.

The Californian *Global Language Monitor* has received some attention in the media thanks to their English word count. As of February 2006, the company reports, English contains 986 120 words. For anyone having problems with such an exact figure, a qualifying "plus or minus a handful" is added. In contrast, the same company reports, "There are fewer than 100 000 words in the French language".

SOURCE NOT MENTIONED IN THE TEXT

Active vocabulary size of Mandarin- and English-speakers: Nichols (2005:1).

LONG AND SHORT WORDS

AS WITH THE LONGEST sentence (pp 325–26), there is no such thing as a longest word. In many languages, you can make compounds longer and longer by adding more and more elements to them. In addition, linguists have no definition of what a word really is! Even in English, problems with word definition are evident. *Have* is a word, but is *'ve* in *I've* a word? Is *uh-uh* one word or two—or perhaps not a word at all?

SHORTEST WORDS

Many a language has a few words consisting only of one letter or phoneme, like English *I* or French *à*. Words can—more or less by definition—not get shorter than that. Morphemes, however, can, and as mentioned on p 259 several languages have morphemes not even containing phonemes, but consisting only of a suprasegmental feature.

Yet, it is possible for a morpheme to be reduced even further, and develop into a zero morph. Examples in English include e.g. *several aircraft-Ø*, where the plural morpheme is—for reasons which I will not attempt to explain here—considered to be present, but silent (this is what the Ø, or "zero" symbol means).

> **A *MORPHEME*** is the smallest unit of meaning in a language. Thus, while pencils is one single word, both pencil and -s are morphemes. A **suprasegmental** feature is one which consists not of a phoneme, but of a something more abstract, such as length or high tone.

LANGUAGES WITH EXCEPTIONALLY SHORT WORDS

In South-East Asia, most languages have predominantly monosyllabic words, and this is probably the area of the world where words are the shortest.

The table on the following page shows the large variation average word length of some languages.

Note that the figures refer to *letters* per word, rather than phonemes per word, which most linguists would probably consider more interesting. The latter is unfortunately more difficult to calculate, given that written texts are easy to obtain, whereas phonemically transcribed language is not.

In languages which excel in compounding, words can get far longer than they usually do in English. Its Germanic sisters are far better at compounding than is English itself. Thus, Dutch *wapenstilstandsonderhandelingen* 'cease-fire negotiations', sure is long (30 letters), but by no means abnormal. And Germanic languages are capable of going a lot further than that. When the strip light was patented in Sweden in the interwar years, this was done under the name of *lågtryckskvick-silverångurladdningsanordning* (43 letters), 'low pressure mercury vapour discharge device'. Should you find this difficult to repeat rapidly, you may be relieved to learn that the everyday name has since become the neatly bisyllabic *lysrör*, literally 'light tube'.

Language	Main region	letters/word	Language	Main region	letters/word
Inuktitut	Greenland	12,2	Latvian	Latvia	4,8
Potawatomi	North America	8,3	Tagalog	Philippines	4,7
Quechua	South America	8,0	German	Europe	4,5
Shuar	Peru	7,0	Cebuano	Philippines	4,4
Turkish	Turkey	6,5	French	Western Europe	4,4
Finnish	Finland	5,9	Icelandic	Iceland	4,3
Indonesian	Indonesia	5,7	Scots Gaelic	Great Britain	4,2
Swahili	East Africa	5,6	Spanish	Latin America	4,1
Hungarian	Hungary	5,6	English	North America	4,0
Awabakal	Australia	5,5	Vietnamese	Vietnam	3,4
Latin	Southern Europe	5,3	Haitian	Haiti	3,3
Uma	Indonesia	4,8	Maori	New Zealand	3,3

YES, THERE *ARE* LONGER WORDS THAN "ANTIDISESTABLISHMENTARIANISM"

Quite a lot has been written about the longest word in individual languages. For English, the word pneumonoultramicroscopicsilicovolcanokoniosis (45 letters), referring to a disease of the lung, is often cited as being the longest word in most English dictionaries. Sometimes quoted as the longest non-medical word is floccinaucinihilipilification, meaning 'the act of estimating as worthless'. Rumor has it, though, that the lung disease word was in fact coined and propagated by the American crossword association National Puzzlers' League in the 1930s, and indeed, the Oxford English Dictionary explains its meaning, but adds that it occurs "chiefly as an instance of a very long word". Of course, no one uses words like these in everyday life. As I write this, the longest words in the top stories of today's edition of the New York Times are nonconfrontational and telecommunications. The longest words used by Shakespeare are anthropophaginian, indistinguishable, and undistinguishable. Among reasonably usable English words, one might also cite incomprehensibilities.

While many an English-speaker is convinced that *antidisestablishmentarianism* (28 letters) is the longest word in his mother tongue, the German counterpart is *Donaudampfschifffahrtsgesell-schaftskapitänsmütze* 'Danube steam shipping company captain's cap' (45 letters). Presumably, no speaker of German has ever used the word with non-jocular intention.

They may not say Donaudampfschifffahrtsgesellschaftskapitänsmütze *very often, but the steam shipping company really did exist. It was founded in Austria in 1829.*

Various editions of *the Guinness Book of World Records* have listed chemical terms as the "longest word", including the 207 000 letter monster (describing the nucleotide links of the human mito-chondrial DNA) which was published in extenso in a 1981 issue of *Nature*. It should be noted, though, that chemical terms may easily grow out of proportions. The length of such a DNA-related term depends only on the length of the longest hitherto described protein, and more complex ones are discovered and described every once in a while. As with other exceptionally long words, they are also virtually useless in practice—in the format used in this book, 207 000 characters would take up about 50 pages!

SOURCES NOT MENTIONED IN THE TEXT

General examples of long words: Miller (2001).

Word length in various languages: Calculated from texts in the languages in question, varying in length between 1 000 up to about 20 000 characters. For most languages, the texts were Bible translations. For a few, I did the same calculation on other texts as well. While this yielded different figures, the ranking remained the same.

Pneumonoultramicroscopicsilicovolcanokoniosis as a possible fake: Cole (1989).

That difficult Swedish word for 'strip light': Bergman (1954:22).

It has been suggested that the truly longest word is the one which follows "And now a word from our sponsor"!

HAVING A WORD FOR IT

EVERYBODY KNOWS that different languages have words for different things. Laymen seem to be so fascinated by this fact that exaggerations on this subject are reiterated in the popular press. If other people are weird, learning that their language is equally weird reinforces the pet prejudices that we somehow don't want to let go of. Nonetheless, the differences which do exist *are* fascinating.

EXPRESSING AN ODD FOOD PREFERENCE

Hadza is a rather peculiar language spoken by a couple of hundred people in Tanzania. It is normally considered part of the Khoisan family of Southern Africa, although all that is certain about its affiliation is that it is not related to its Bantu neighbors, and that it has click phonemes (see p 245) just like Khoisan languages. One particularly odd feature of Hadza life is the interest in scavenging. The carcasses conquered from hyenas, lions, leopards and wild dogs are sometimes rotten, infested with insects and maggots and are bound to give the Hadzas a bad stomach. Yet, they appreciate it to such an extent that the practice continues. This culinary tradition is reflected in the Hadza lexicon in that there are separate words for dead animals. Interestingly, while the "carcass lexicon" is less fine-grained in that e.g. elephants and hippos are merged into one category, it does differentiate male and female animals.

Living animal	Hadza word	Carcass	Hadza word
lion	*mondo*	dead lion or eland	*hubu'i* (♂), *hubu'e* (♀)
eland	*komati*		
elephant	*mindjadiko*	dead elephant or hippo	*kapula'i* (♂), *kapula'e* (♀)
hippo	*wets'aiko*		
zebra	*dongoko*	dead zebra	*hanta'i* (♂), *hanta'e* (♀)
rhino	*losho*	dead rhino	*huku'i* (♂), *huku'e* (♀)
giraffe	*ts'okwanako*	dead giraffe	*hawa'i* (♂), *hawa'e* (♀)
warthog	*kwa'i*	dead warthog or pig	*hacha'i* (♂), *hacha'e* (♀)
(bush) pig	*tl'aha*		
impala	*popo*	dead impala	*tl'unku'i* (♂), *th'unku'e* (♀)
baboon	*ha!'aneya*	dead baboon	*!nokowi* (♂), *!nokowe* (♀)
gnu	*bisoko*	dead gnu or hartebeest	*ts'onowi* (♂), *ts'onowe* (♀)
hartebeest	*!eleko*		
ostrich	*kenangu*	dead ostrich	*hushuwe*

In all honesty, it should be added that the differentiation between living and slaughtered animals is indeed reflected in some other languages as well, including one spoken mainly by two tribes known as 'Britons' and 'Americans', who differentiate between e.g. *pig* and *pork*, *cow* and *beef*, *calf* and *veal*, *sheep* and *mutton*, etc. Yet, why the fans of Hadza cuisine are more interested in indicating gender differences among the dead than the living simply beats me.

MACROPOD LOCOMOTION IN ARNHEM LAND

It should come as no surprise that an Australian language has a better developed kangaroo terminology than European languages (for obvious reasons, no European language even had a word for 'kangaroo' until the late 18th century). Thus, the lexicons of many Australian languages make rather subtle distinctions between various types of macropods. A particularly interesting feature of Gunwinggu, spoken in the north-western part of the country, is that it has gone a step further in lexicalising some of the behaviour of these animals. The following four Gunwinggu verbs illustrate this:

kamurlbardme 'the hopping of a black wallaroo (Macropus bernardus)'
kalurlhlurme 'the hopping of an agile wallaby (Macropus agilis)'
kamawudme 'the hopping of a male antilopine wallaroo (Macropus antilopinus)'
kadjalwahme 'the hopping of a female antilopine wallaroo'

MOST DIFFICULT-TO-TRANSLATE WORD?

In 2004, the translation company *Today Translations* reported that it had let 1 000 of its employees pick the words they found the most difficult to translate. The winner turned out to be the Ciluba word *ilunga*, meaning 'a person who is ready to forgive any abuse for the first time, to tolerate it a second time, but never a third time'.

SOUTH SEA CLOUDS

'Cloud' is thought of as such a basic concept that it is one of the items included in the Swadesh list (pp 102–03). Although the trained eye of someone with an interest in meteorology can distinguish between different kinds of clouds, to most of us they still remain—clouds. Not so in New Guinea. McElhanon (1987:425) reports that most non-Austronesian languages of this island distinguish between cumulus clouds and cumulo-nimbus clouds.

Just two instances of "cloud" to most westerners. Not necessarily so to New Guineans.

KOREAN KIN AND OTHER RELATIVES

The kinship terminology of Western European languages is pathetically under-developed in comparison to certain tongues spoken elsewhere in the world. Korean is an example of such a language. Like English, it distinguishes between *lineal* (parent-child) and *colateral* (siblings) relationship. Furthermore, it consistently takes *male* versus *female* into account, as well as *ascendance* (e.g. parent or grandparent) or *descendance* (e.g. child or grandchild). It also matters whether your relationship is *consanguineous* or *in-law*, if it is on the *father's side* or *mother's side*, and finally whether you're *elder* or *younger* than the person to whom you are referring. The possible combinations between these produce an impressive array of kinship terms—Sohn (1999:112-15) lists 71 different forms, without explicitly saying that his list is exhaustive.

Quechua kinship terms do not indicate the sex of the referent (as do *brother* and *sister*). On the other hand, they do reveal the sex of the "owner". Thus, there is no difference between 'brother' and 'sister' (or for that matter 'child'), but there is one between *čuri* 'father's child' and *wawa* 'mother's child'.

The least complex kinship system ever documented has been suggested to be that of Pirahã. Everett (2004:30-31) enumerates nine terms, and says the listing is exhaustive. Yet the kinship relations themselves are not necessarily less complex among the Pirahã, since incest taboos are considerably less strict than in most societies.

MISCELLANEOUS GOODIES

Of all the things, actions and other features of the world around us, different languages have chosen to lexicalize different chunks. The words below are simply among my personal favorites:

Yup'ik	*caginraq*	'skin or pelt of caribou taken just after the long winter hair has been shed in spring'
Yup'ik	*partak*	'spruce root stretched above water, from which hang a line of snares just above the water's surface, to catch waterfowl'
Yup'ik	*qamigartuk*	'he goes seal-hunting with a small sled and kayak in the spring'
Yup'ik	*pug'uk*	'it (a fish or a seal) came to the surface, emerging halfway'

Yup'ik	*mangirruq*	'it (a dog) is chewing on frozen food, or on the ice where food has frozen on the surface of the snow'
Yup'ik	*yuuguq*	'he got out of a boat or sled, took off clothing, removed a net or snare, or took objects out of a container'
Yup'ik	*qellukaq*	'aged seal flipper'
Yup'ik	*alrapaq*	'back-to-back sitting partner'
Dutch	*klunen*	'to walk or run overland with skates on (usually from one body of frozen water to another)'
Kuot	*aFone*	'to drink from a bottle in such a fashion that drool trickles from the mouth back into the bottle'
Swedish	*palla*	'to steal fruit (in particular apples) from somebody else's fruit tree'
Swedish	*pulsa*	'to walk (with moderate effort) through snow whose depth is more than a couple of centimetres, but less than several decimetres'
Swedish	*kallsup*	'a gulp of water that a bather accidentally inhales/intakes'
Swedish	*panikragg*	'a bar pick-up chosen for no other reason than your increasing desperation as closing time approaches'
German	*fringsen*	'to steal coal from railway waggons or potatoes from fields in order to survive' (after archbishop Frings, according to whom God would forgive such acts)
Czech	*knedlikovy@*	'rather partial to dumplings'
Czech	*zakecat se*	'to forget something through talking too much'
Czech	*umudrovat se*	'to philosophize oneself into the madhouse'
Chavacano	*baleNga*	'excessive swinging of arms while walking'
English	*googly*	'(of an off-breaking cricket ball) disguised by the bowler with an apparent leg-break action'

Given the amount of criticism that popular books such as Adam Jacot de Boinod's *The Meaning of Tingo* have aroused among linguists, it could be added that the above words have all been produced by native speakers and/or professional linguists.

DEBUNKING A POPULAR MYTH

New Zealand linguist Terry Crowley has produced what is, to my mind, one of the most memorable quotes regarding how the language of a particular people not necessarily reflects its cultural preferences:

> *"[W]hile languages tend to develop lexical specializations in areas that are of cultural importance, the mere existence of lexical specification should not, by itself, be taken as a sign that something is of particular cultural or environmental significance to people who use that word. For*

instance, I have recently heard the word "wedgie" on American TV programmes, which refers to the situation when one's underwear rides up uncomfortably between one's buttocks [...] As far as I know, this word is not part of either New Zealand or Australian English. I do not think that we should interpret this difference as meaning that American underwear manufacturers are inflicting a shoddy wedgie-prone product on the American people, or that Australasians are more tolerant than Americans of sartorial discomfort".

The word *wedgie* had indeed been documented in at least Australian English before the time of Crowley's writing, but his point still stands—there isn't necessarily a close correlation between languages and cultures.

IMPROVING YOUR LANGUAGE BY MEANS OF LIFFS

In the book *The meaning of Liff* (1983), later expanded into *The Deeper Meaning of Liff* (1990), Douglas Adams (best known for the Hitchhiker's Guide to the Galaxy series) and John Lloyd made an attempt at putting names on a number of liffs. A liff, the authors explain, is "a common object or experience for which no word yet exists". Rather than inventing the phonetic strings, Adams and Lloyd picked a number of existing place-names, and assigned new, interesting meanings to them. The examples which follow are quoted with the kind permission of Pan Books.

In case you ever wondered, Liff itself is located in eastern Scotland.

Given that many of the phenomena named in the Liff book are more or less universal (at least to westerners), it ought to be translatable, and indeed there is a German (*Der tiefere Sinn des Labenz*) and a Finnish edition (*Elimäen tarkoitus*), in which primarily German and Finnish place names are used. Actually there are two Finnish translations—given that Finland is a country devoted to bilingualism (pp 20–22), there is of course also a Swedish-language edition (Mickwitz, Ringbom & Westö 1999), published in Finland, and drawing exclusively on Finland Swedish toponymy.

EXAMPLE LIFFS

Adlestrop: The part of a suitcase that is designed to get snarled up on conveyor belts in airports. Some of the more modern adlestrop designs have a 'quick release' feature that enables the case to flip open at this point and fling your underclothes into the conveyor belt's gearing mechanism.

Dungeness: The uneasy feeling that the plastic handles of the overloaded supermarket carrier bag you are carrying are getting steadily longer.

Frolesworth: The minimum time it is necessary to spend frowning in deep concentration at each picture in an art gallery in order that everyone else doesn't think you're a complete moron.

Goole: The puddle on the bar into which the barman puts your change.

Hobbs Cross: The awkward leaping manoeuvre a girl has to go through in bed in order to make him sleep on the wet patch.

Kalami: The ancient Eastern art of being able to fold road maps properly.

Kibblesworth: The footling amount of money by which the price of a given article in a shop is less than a sensible number, in the hope that at least one idiot will think it cheap. For instance, the kibblesworth on a pair of shoes priced at £19,99 is 1 p.

Milwaukee: The melodious whistling, chanting and humming tone of the milwaukee can be heard whenever a public lavatory is entered. It is the way the occupants of the cubicles have of telling you there's no lock on their door and you can't come in.

Nazeing: The rather unconvincing noises of pretended interest which an adult has to make when brought a small dull object for admiration by a child.

Ocilla: The cute little circle or heart over an 'i' used by teenage girls when writing their names.

Polyphant: The mythical beast - part bird, part snake, part jam stain - that invariably wins children's painting competitions in the 5–7 age group.

Rochester: One who is able to gain occupation of the armrest on both sides of their cinema or aircraft seat.

Ventnor: One who, having been visited as a child by a mysterious gypsy lady, is gifted with the strange power of being able to operate the air-nozzles above aeroplane seats.

Wimbledon: That last drop which, no matter how much you shake it, always goes down your trouser leg.

Yarmouth: To shout at foreigners in the belief that the louder you speak, the better they'll understand you.

SOURCES NOT MENTIONED IN THE TEXT

Macropod hopping in Gunwinggu: Evans (1998:164).
Most difficult-to-translate word: BBC News 2004-06-22.
Korean kinship terms: Sohn (1999:112-15).
Words for children in Quechua: Adelaar (2004:235).
Odd words in Yup'ik: Mithun (1999:10, 37).
Odd word in Dutch: Peter Bakker (p c).
Odd word in Kuot: Eva Lindström (p c).
Odd word in German: Daniel Bunčić (p c).
Odd word in Chavacano: Molony (1977:136).
Odd words in Czech: Kellnerova & Clarke (1997).
Terry Crowley quote: Crowley (1997:200).

DICTIONARIES

WHILE A GRAMMAR describes the rules of a language, the dictionary lists the language's arbitrary component, that which cannot be compressed into rules—that is, its lexicon.

MOST PROCRASTINATED DICTIONARY PUBLICATION

Compiling a dictionary is a painstaking work which often takes decades, despite the large number of people involved. The first edition of the *Oxford English Dictionary*, for instance, required 50 years before it was completed in 1928. Work on the German *Deutsches Wörterbuch* was commenced by the Grimm brothers (best known for their collections of folktales) in 1838, and finished only in 1961. In neighboring Netherlands, the final version of the *Woerdeboek van de Nederlandse Taal* was presented to the public in December 1998, after 160 years. Work on the Swedish counterpart, the *Svenska Akademiens Ordbok* began in 1884, with the first volume being published nine years later. In 2002, the lexicographers had still not got to the end of the alphabet, but only to *talkumera*—an archaic word meaning 'to talc'. The aim is to finish the dictionary by 2017.

Delays such as these of course lead to the language having changed considerably during the editing process. The word *chauffor* (from French *chauffeur*) is currently a normal Swedish word for 'driver (of a bus, taxi or lorry)', but is included in the *Svenska Akademiens Ordbok* with the meaning 'stoker'.

WORST DICTIONARY

Lots of dictionaries could surely lay claim to being the least exhaustive. One which has explicitly been dubbed "the world's worst dictionary" is a 1970s edition of *Webster's Dictionary of the English Language: Handy School and Office Edition* (HSOE). Christopher McManus went through the dictionary, and was baffled by the exclusion of words such as *cow, dark, death, dig, door, hat, have, he, ice, live, much, my, no, of, see, time, to, two, we, very, why, wife* and *wood*, to just mention a few. Of 1 850 common three- and four-letter words which he found in each of his seven other dictionaries at hand, almost half were missing in the HSOE. The dictionary also contains oddities such as misplaced word series and words with illustrations but without entries! McManus hypothesizes that about 40% of the intended dictionary somehow disappeared in the editing process . . .

AN ONOMATOPOEIC DICTIONARY

Ernst Havlik's (1981) *Lexikon der Onomatopöien* is an entire dictionary only consisting of comic strip sound effects. It contains an introductory analysis, 2 222 onomatopoeic items, and 111 illustrations. The section on kissing, for instance, contains *glork, schmatz, schuic, shluk, smack, smurp* and *shmersh*—quite a poetic collection in itself. More unexpected are *woin* and *töff*, both of which are intended to represent the sound of a car horn. A breaking car apparently goes *tata* in at least one source, and from a "scientific laboratory", one gets to hear *foodle, grink*, and *sqwunk*. Perhaps even more interesting are the sounds *floop, flop* and *flomp*, which represent the sound of a bra being taken off.

Anyone prejudiced against the genre as such, may see it as a confirmation that the sections on "violence" take up 17 pages, while that devoted to "thinking" consists of a mere five lines.

DIRTY DICTIONARIES

Aleksey Plutser-Sarno is an authority on Russian slang who had already produced several books on the subject when he embarked on publishing a new dictionary series, Большой словарь мата (Bol'šoj slovar' mata) 'Comprehensive Dictionary of Russian Slang'. The most remarkable feature of this series is that each of the 12 volumes is entirely dedicated to just a single word, listing 500–1000 constructions that include it. The first volume from 2001 dealt exclusively with the word хуй (xuj) 'dick', and was followed by пизда (pizda) 'cunt' in 2005. At the time of writing this, the third volume, ебать (ebat') 'to fuck', is in press, and volumes four and five (on блядь (bljad') 'whore' and пиздец (pizdets) 'clitoris', respectively, will be published shortly.

Some of the idiomatic constructions listed in the dictionary also occur in everyday colloquial speech, but with e.g. блин (blin) 'pancake' instead of блядь or хрен (xren) 'horse-radish' instead of хуй.

SOURCES NOT MENTIONED IN THE TEXT

Procrastinated dictionary publication: Johansson & Neppenström (1991:58), Peter Bakker (p c), the Swedish Academy.
Worst dictionary: McManus (1995).

COMMON WORDS

EVERY ONCE IN A WHILE, the linguist gets asked about the most common words in a given language. The question is difficult to answer for several reasons. One is that it is a lot more difficult than people realize to define what a word is. Another is that words are not equally common in different genres—for one thing, there is a significant difference between speech and writing. When frequency lists are presented, they are usually based on written rather than spoken language, simply because writing is easier to handle and analyse. It is also a lot easier to count word forms (where *eat, ate* and *eating* represent three words) than *lexemes* (where these three would count as variants of one word).

MOST FREQUENT WORDS IN ENGLISH

Counting lexemes rather than forms, the top-ten words in (British) English are as follow, according to the British National Corpus:

1.	the	6.	in
2.	be	7.	to (the infinitive marker)
3.	of	8.	have
4.	and	9.	it
5.	a	10.	to (the preposition)

While these words are common in all types of language, there are significant differences between genres. Not surprisingly, spoken language contains more pronouns than lexical noun phrases. A written text would be more likely to refer to someone as *the woman with the flashy car*, where a conversation would contain more instances of *she*. In particular, the first person singular *I* is considerably more frequent in speech than in text—in its different guises (such as *me, my, mine*) it is, for instance, the most frequent word in Shakespeare's plays (which, although written, were intended to be spoken aloud rather than read).

MOST FREQUENT WORDS IN OTHER LANGUAGES

Frequency lists for other languages look rather similar to those of English, but with some important differences. The most common lexeme in French is *le/la*, corresponding to English *the*. Then, however, comes *de*, corresponding to the English preposition *of*, which, as we have seen, is only the 3rd most common item in English. This is no doubt because *de* serves to mark all genitive relationships in French (and also because of the use of a partitive article in French), while English alternates between *the world's future* and *the future of the world*. Similarly, if we count forms, *la* is second, not first, as English *the* is. The reason for this is presumably that while

English has only the form *the*, French splits the definite article into *le* (masculine), *la* (feminine) and *les* (plural). On frequency lists of Finnish and Russian, a word meaning 'the' does not figure at all simply because these languages do not have articles in the first place. Swedish and Romanian do, but the definite article still does not make it into a frequency list. In these cases, the reason is that the definite article is a suffix, and thus not counted as a word in its own right. Put another way, while lists of the most common words in various languages *tend* to look relatively alike the one we just saw for English, the details depend on the architecture of the language in question.

FREQUENCIES IN SPECIFIC GENRES

Any English text is bound to contain an extremely high proportion of words such as *the, is, of,* and a number of other important grammatical markers. What follows after these, however, is more dependent on the type of text investigated. If you, as I did, go through an issue of the *Financial Times*, for instance (in my case the one from March 19, 2002), you'll find *the* at the top, followed by other already familiar words.

More specific to the genre, however, are

words such as *policy, market, bank, business, dollar, EU* and *rate*, which all make it into the top 100. Whether it is a coincidence or not, one cannot help noting that *monetary* outscores *people* . . .

While on the subject of word frequencies in different genres, you have no doubt all wondered which the most common pop music rhymes are. After having examined the lyrics of the major Anglophone hit singles of 2003, I am proud to be able to present the following list:

1.	you	6.	go
2.	me	7.	tonight
3.	yeah	8.	do
4.	love	9.	night
5.	baby	10.	way

Heart, feel and oh are just outside the top-10. This list counts words which are used to rhyme with something else—the pair together and forever is popular indeed, but then they don't really rhyme.

Some rhymes do suggest a certain focus on nocturnal activities, but I suspect it would be premature to conclude that the presence of *baby* is due to a specific interest in child-raising among the performers.

JANUS WORDS

A particularly interesting group of words are those which may also function as their own opposites. If nothing else, they provide a nice illustration of the arbitrariness of language.

Janus words are appropriately named for the Roman god Janus, which is known for having had two faces.

Such words are also known as *antagonyms, contronyms* or *opponyms*. The phenomenon goes by a great many other names, and is sometimes also referred to as *antiphrasis, enantiosemy, antilogy, enantiodromia* or *auto-antonymy*.

Janus words are not normally the result of misunderstanding, but rather of the random drift in languages. It is common enough for two words originally completely unlike each other to both be subject to the same sound law, and thereby ending up sounding similarly. By pure coincidence, such a process may strike words which happen to have more or less opposite meanings. Another common way for Janus words to develop is that the original meaning of a word is rather general, and then two more special meanings evolve from it.

In pre-Christian Roman theology, Janus was the god of doorways (!)

SOME ENGLISH JANUS WORDS

Word	Meaning	. . . but then it also means
adumbrate	to clarify	to cast a shadow over
aught	all	nothing
cleave	to bring together	to cut apart
clip	to cut a little piece off	to put a little piece on
custom	usual	special
dust	to remove dust	to apply dust (as in fingerprinting)
fast	steady, not moving	moving at high speed
fireman	man who stokes the fire of a steam engine	person employed to extinguish unwanted fires
handicap	disadvantage in some contexts	advantage given to weaker competitor
impregnable	able to be impregnated	unable to be pregnated
model	archetype	copy
moot	suitable for debate	not worth discussing
peer	noble	person of equal rank

put	lay	throw
puzzle	to pose a problem	to try to solve a problem
quantum	very small	very large (quantum leap)
sanction	a punitive action	to endorse
sanguine	murderous	optimistic
scan	to examine closely	to glance at quickly
temper	calmness	passion
trim	to cut things off	to add something onto
with	He fought with me [=on my side]	He fought with [=against] me

Some additional Janus words display their opposite meanings only in spoken English, while retaining different spellings. Two such examples are *aural* 'heard' vs. *oral* 'spoken' and *raise* 'to erect' versus *raze* 'to tear down'. The second pair, incidentally, illustrates another way for Janus words to develop—English has borrowed the former from Old Norse, but the latter from French. Some examples from other languages include:

Language	Item	Meaning 1	Meaning 2
Dutch	*ettelijk*	many, much	(a) little, (a) few
French	*plus*	more	no more
German	*Kontrahent*	opponent (often used in sports)	two parties sharing a contract, like the English 'contractor' (rare)
Latin	*immo*	yes	no
Mandarin	*shou⁴*	give	take
Portuguese	*já*	already	soon
Russian	*predat'*	to devote	to betray
Sahidic Coptic	*ehrai*	upwards	downwards
Latin	*altus*	high (e.g. mountain)	deep (e.g. lake)
Swedish	*maximera*	to set an upper limit to	to make as large as possible (due to English influence)

The Mandarin example is ambiguous only in speech, since the written forms differ.

Other words could be said to belong in this category from the Anglophone perspective, but not necessarily from the point of view of the native speakers of other languages. In particular, many languages do not distinguish between *lend* and *borrow* or between *teach* and *learn* (just as English fails to tell the two meanings of *lease* [viz. 'to borrow for money' and 'to lend for money'] apart). The meaning of these words should probably rather be paraphrased as 'to transfer temporarily from one person to the other', without there being a specified direction of the transaction.

Incidentally, *New York Times* is said to have had an entire Sunday crossword devoted to Janus words around 1990.

When the contradictory effect is achieved in a combination of several words, this construction is sometimes referred to as an oxymoron. Examples include *conspicuous by one's absence* or *deafening silence*. Tongue-in-cheek examples include collocations such as *business ethics, Christian Scientists, military intelligence, rap music, soft rock,* and *Toronto life.*

PSEUDO-LOANS

It is well known that plenty of loan-words from English have entered languages all around the world during the past century or so. What is less frequently pointed out, however, is that many of these languages contain words that look English, and which their speakers often believe to be English, but which are merely nonsensical to most native speakers of English. Occasionally, the same phenomenon is observed with words believed to be from some other prestigious language.

Language	Item	Meaning
French	*baby-foot*	'table-top football' (= US 'soccer')
Japanese	*bakkumiraa* (< back + mirror)	'rear-view mirror'
Danish	*butterfly*	'bow-tie'
French	*do it*	'do-it-yourself'
German	*Dressman*	'male model'
Swedish	*freestyle*	'walkman'
German	*Handy*	'mobile phone'
Croatian	*monkey*	'the @ symbol'
Japanese	*ooero* (< OL < office + lady)	'female office worker'
Brazilian Portuguese	*outdoor*	'a roadside poster'
French	*pin's* (sic)	'lapel badge'
German	*Pullunder*	'short-sleeved pullover'
German	*Showmaster*	'TV show host'
Japanese	*teeburu supiiti* (< table + speech)	'dinner speech'
German	*Twen* (< twenty)	'person aged 20-29'
Russian	софт (soft)	'software'
Russian	шейпинг (shaping)	'aerobics'
Sinhala	*short eats*	'snacks'
Mauritian Creole	*shortminded*	'narrow-minded, unimaginative'

SOURCES NOT MENTIONED IN THE TEXT

Janus words: First and foremost an extremely voluminous and long-lived discussion on the *Linguist List* in 1995, under the heading "Words that are their own opposites".

Pseudo-loans: First and foremost *Linguist List* 10.1388. Additional pseudo-loans from Shibatani (1990b:151), Inoue (1979:254), Dalby (2002:191), Curnow (2001:427), Trudgill (1994:21), Anders G Eriksson (p c) and Daniel Bunčić (p c).

COINING NEW WORDS

A NEW CONJUNCTION

Conjunctions are closed-class items, meaning that they are not normally spontaneously borrowed or coined like nouns and verbs often are. Instead, new conjunctions and prepositions, just like affixes, usually develop very gradually from more lexical material through *grammaticalization* (or, more rarely, they are borrowed).

Among the 118 conjunctions in *Merriam-Webster's Collegiate Dictionary* (10th Edition), however, one was deliberately coined, namely *iff*. *Iff*, which first appeared in print in 1955, is used in mathematics and logic with the meaning of "if and only if". The new word has its counterparts in several other languages, such as French *ssi*, Spanish *sii*, Italian *sse*, Finnish *joss* and Swedish *omm*.

COINING WORDS FOR MONEY

Some words which started life as trademarks later entered everyday speech. Examples of in English include *aspirin, cellophane, cornflakes, escalator, heroin, hoover, kerosene, mimeograph, tabloid, thermos, trampoline, yo-yo* and *zipper*. Sometimes there is an etymology behind the innovation, sometimes not. For instance *velcro*, coined by its innovator, Swiss engineer Georges de Mestral in 1948, is a blend of French **vel**ours 'velvet' and **cro**chet 'hook'. The patent expired in 1978, but the name is still a registered trade mark. *Nylon*, on the other hand, was thus named in the 1930s by the Du Pont corporation for no reason in particular—it just sounded nice to the Du Pont naming committee, which considered 400 names for *Fiber 66* before settling on *nylon*. Some interesting but false etymologies have been proposed, such as a conflation between **New** York and **Lon**don, or an acronym of *"Now You've Lost, Old Nippon"*, alluding to the expected market loss of Japanese silk.

CORPORATE PRESCRIPTIVISM

For some time now, the *Photoshop* graphics editor developed by Adobe Systems has been one of the most widely used imaging editors. Its fame has led to the widespread use of photoshop as a verb with the meaning 'to digitally alter or retouch a picture' (just like *Google* has come to mean 'to do a web search'). As an indication of the new word's popularity, the American shows *The West Wing* and *Desperate Housewives* both used it as a generic term in the same weekend in October 2005.

One might think that the creators of the software would be flattered by this, but this is not the case. Instead, for fear of not being able to renew the trademark rights if the name becomes too much of a household item, the company strongly discourages such a use, and provides guidelines regarding the use of the brand name. The following use is labelled "incorrect" by Adobe: The image was Photoshopped. A "correct" usage would instead be "The image was modified using Adobe® Photoshop® software." Similarly, instead of "A photoshopper sees his hobby as an art form", Adobe would prefer you to say "Those who use Adobe® Photoshop® software to manipulate images as a hobby see their work as an art form."

COINING A WORD BY MISTAKE

The second edition of *Webster's New International Dictionary* (1934) contained the word *dord,* as a chemical term meaning 'density'. The only problem was, that no such word exists, or has ever existed outside of *Webster's*. The background is that a contributor submitted "d" as the abbreviation for 'density'. Wanting to indicate that it could be written in upper or lower case, he wrote "D or d". A typesetter then misinterpreted this as a new word entry—*dord*. Alas, the charming word was deleted from the dictionary in 1940.

> **Dor·ca·the′ri·um** (dôr′ká·thē′rĭ·ŭm), *n.* [NL., fr. Gr. *dorkas* gazelle + *-therium.*] *Zool.* A genus of chevrotains consisting of the water chevrotain and extinct species.
> **Dor·cop′sis** (dôr·kŏp′sĭs), *n.* [NL., fr. Gr. *dorkas* gazelle + *-opsis.*] *Zool.* A genus of small kangaroos of Papua.
> **dord** (dôrd), *n. Physics & Chem.* Density.
> ‖**do′ré′** (dŏ′rā′), *adj.* [F.] **a** Golden in color. **b** *Metal.* Containing gold; as, *doré* silver. — *n.* = DORÉ BULLION.
> ‖**do′ré′** (dŏ′rā′), *n.* [F., gilded. See 2d DORY.] The wall-eyed pike. *Fr. Canadian.*

The term "ghost word" itself was coined by etymologist Walter Skeat in 1886 for words such as *dord*, which can be found in dictionaries, but not in real life.

Yet, a few words coined by mistake have, as it were, slipped out of their cages and pursued more or less successful careers in the outside world. For instance, English has a word *darkling* (meaning 'almost dark'), which historically consists of 'dark' plus a suffix *-ling*. The 19th-century poet Lord Byron misinterpreted this as the *-ing* form of a supposed verb **to darkle*, and so he coined the verb *darkle* 'to become dark', without realizing that he was doing so. His new word was picked up by other writers, and enjoyed some currency for a while, though it has now mostly disappeared. Then there is *helpmeet*. In the King James Bible, in Genesis 2:18, God decides "to make an help meet for him", where *meet* is an adjective meaning 'suitable'. But a 17th-century printing wrongly put this as "to make an help-meet for him", and the new word *helpmeet* entered the language and was given a suitable meaning. It was later folk-etymologized to 'helpmate'.

The word *tweed* is also said to come from a misprint. The cloth was originally called *tweel* (Scottish for 'twill'). In 1831, a Scottish cloth merchant's catalogue misprinted it as *tweed*. By chance, the principal cloth-weaving area of Scotland is in the region of the River Tweed. By association of ideas, the misprint stuck, and *tweed* is now a word distinct from *twill*, and it has even given rise to the adjective *tweedy*.

Ghost words are usually the result of a mistake, but a few represent conscious hoaxes on the part of the dictionary compilers. One such item is *kelemenopy* (defined as 'the one essential trope neglected by classical rhetoricians: a sequential straight line through the middle of everything, leading nowhere') in John Ciardi's *A Browser's Dictionary*. Ciardi later admitted that it was "based on *k-l-m-n-o-p*, the central sequence of the alphabet, having ten letters before and ten after it. Hence, a strictly sequential irrelevance. 'Kelemenopy' is from my own psychic warp, to see if anyone would notice, and because I have always dreamed of fathering a word".

Most of the things that surround us have been known to us for as long as we can remember. They are therefore already named, and most of us do not normally encounter situations where we actually have to invent new words. Science is an exception, however, since its very task is to discover things previously unknown. Biology and chemistry are two scientific disciplines where the invention of new names is particularly common.

THE TEN SILLIEST NAMES OF MOLECULES (IN NO PARTICULAR ORDER)

Arsole	Arsole is the arsenic equivalent of pyrrole. It is shaped like a ring.
Fucitol	Fucitol is also known as *L-fuc-ol* or *1-deoxy-D-galactitol*. Its wonderfully trivial name comes from the fact that it is derived from the sugar *fucose*, found in a seaweed called Bladderwrack, whose Latin name is *Fucus vesiculosis*. Interestingly, there are several articles in the *Journal of Biochemistry* in 1997 concerning a kinase enzyme which acts on fucose which were written by Japanese authors who were unaware that 'fuc-K' might not be the most suitable abbreviation for this.
Dickite	Dickite, $Al_2Si_2O_5(OH)_4$, is named for Thomas Dick, the Scottish geologist who discovered it.
Penguinone	For once, the etymology is precisely what you'd have guessed: *3,4,4,5-tetramethylcyclohexa-2,5-dienone* does get its name from its similarity with a certain flightless bird (see below).
Adamantane	Although it might sound like it, Adamantane is *not* named after an early 1980's British pop star.
Moronic Acid	The origin of this name appears to be unknown, but a nice one it is.
Gossypol	Gossypol, found in cotton seeds, was used as a male contraceptive in China, successfully rendering a fifth of its users permanently sterile.
Uranate	Uranate is another name for a uranium oxide anion.

Commic Acid	Commic Acid is named for a plant in which it is found, the Myrrh tree *Commiphora pyracanthoides*.
Psicose	The sugar Psicose (a k a ribo-hexulose) gets its name from being extracted from the antibiotic *Psicofurania*.

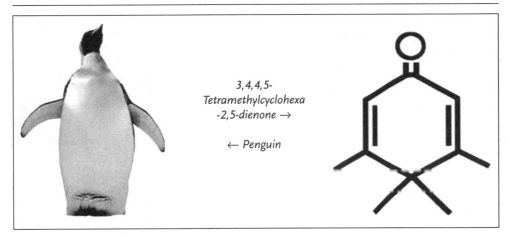

3,4,4,5-
Tetramethylcyclohexa
-2,5-dienone →

← *Penguin*

BIOLOGICAL NAMES

In the 1750s, the Swedish botanist Carl von Linné (a k a Carolus Linnaeus) devised an international system for naming biological species, which is still in vigor. Although an international naming board keeps an eye on the terminological developments, naming is basically up to the discoverer of the species or genus in question. As a result, the appropriateness of some names have been questioned. One oft-cited example of this is the a giant fossil insect *Rochlingia hitleri*—so named in 1934 by a German researcher after a certain dictator.

Having a new species named after you can be both a great honour and a bit of an embarrassment. The moth *Dyaria* was named by amateur lepidopterist Neumoegen whose sole intention was to honour a colleague named Dyar.

Given that there were (and perhaps still are) millions of species lacking a Latin name, and given that the discoverer basically has the right to bestow whatever name he pleases on new species, it is not surprising that some biological names have turned out rather odd. As early as in 1753, Linnaeus himself could not refrain from calling a genus of butterfly peas *Clitoria*, and this was followed up by one of his colleagues with the clam genus *Vagina* in 1811. The first half of the 19th century also saw the addition of the genera *Disaster* (sea urchins) and *Enema* (scarab beetles) to the catalogue.

While knowledge of Latin was a must to an 18th century scientist, most of their modern successors have little or no competence in that language. The perceived need for Latin-sounding names is presumably the reason why there is a beetle named *Ytu brutus* and a parrot known as *Vini vidivici* (sic).

Botanists of yore were not necessarily more prudish than those of today. The Latin name for the foul-smelling stinkhorn (pictured on the right) is Phallus impudicus—and this comes from no lesser person than Linnaeus himself.

Most species named after people of course owe their names to biologists, or occasionally statesmen. Some have been named after the classics of literature, including Arthur Conan Doyle, Bram Stoker, Mephisto, and Beeblebrox (two different species are named after this two-headed character in Douglas Adams' *Hitch-Hiker's guide to the Galaxy* series). In this genre, the salamander genus *Œdipus* suitably contains both a species named *Rex* and one called *Complex*. At least two comic strips have been blessed with species named after them, namely the fish *Batman* and the louse *Garylarsoni*.

Movies and TV have also made their presence felt in biological terminology—a spider of the *Apopyllus* genus surnamed *now* is perhaps the wittiest example, but there is also the crustacean *Godzillius*, the fossil snake *Montypythonoides*, and the cicadas *Laureli* and *Hardyi*. Jurassic Park author Michael Crichton has had a dinosaur species (*Bienosaurus crichtonii*) named after him, while King Kong had to make to do with *Chloridops regiskongi*—a now extinct Hawaiian finch. Finally, those familiar with both Greek and post-war popular culture might realise that the name of the fossil amphibian *Eucritta melanolimnetes* contains a reference to the classic 1954 horror film, *The Creature from the Black Lagoon*.

Musicians who have been honoured include Beethoven, Mark Knopfler, Frank Zappa, the Grateful Dead, the Beatles and the Rolling Stones. Much to the joy of the present author,

The Ramones on their way to a practice in the mid-1970s. Could it be that getting a trilobite named after them was a major driving force behind the band?

the members of the Ramones and the Sex Pistols have all had species of trilobites named after them, bearing witness of the sophisticated musical preferences of Canadian palaeontologists Greg Edgecombe & Jon Adrain.

In the 1990s, wasp expert Marsh named an entire genus *Heerz*, and simultaneously baptized two of its species *Heerz tooya* and *Heerz lukenatcha*. While at it, Marsh also blessed the world with *Verae peculya*— yet another wasp species.

A certain difficulty at making decisions can be discerned

from names such as *Brachinus elongatulus* (a bombardier beetle whose name consists of Greek *Brachyus* 'short' and Latin *elongatus* 'prolonged') and *Boselaphus tragocamelus*, an Indian antelope, whose name literally translates as 'ox-deer goat-camel'. One senses a slight disappointment from names such as *Anticlimax* (a fossil gastropod), *Ba humbugi* (a snail), and the scarab beetle *Cyclocephala nodanotherwon*. What emotions lay behind the naming of the little fly *Brachyanax thelestrephones*—literally 'little chief nipple twister'—I dare not even guess.

In 1926, the Pole Dybowski coined the longest genus name in the history of biology— Gammaracanthukytodermogammarus

loricatobaicalensis—an amphipod). Later he became a little more moderate, and just one year later, he christened another amphipod *Rhodophthalmokytodermogammarus cinnamomeus*, which, after all, is quite a few characters shorter. In terms of coining names which at least look difficult to pronounce, Regel & Schmalhausen offered some competition by naming an umbellifer *Schtschurowskia* (though in all fairness, the name looks more awe-inspiring than it actually is—<schtsch> is really just the German transliteration of Russian Щ. At the other end of the spectrum, there is Oldfield Thomas, who in 1902 named a Chinese bat *Ia io*—along with the fly *Iyaiyai* this may be the only all-vowel name of any species.

SOURCES NOT MENTIONED IN THE TEXT

Trademarks becoming ordinary words: Johansson & Neppenström (1991:19) and Mikkelson (2001), among others.

The story of *Dord*: Gove (1954).

Coining of *tweed*, *helpmeet* and *darkle*: Larry Trask (p c).

Other ghost words: Pearce (1986).

Silly molecule names: May (2001).

Biological terminology: Menke (1993), Conniff (1996), Isaak (2001), Yanega (2001)

COLOR TERMS

BERLIN & KAY (1969) is the most classic study of basic color terms in a hundred different languages. *Basic* in this context excludes composite terms such as *light blue*, non-integrated borrowings such as *cérise*, and words which are primarily used as e.g. nouns, such as *cherry* or *chocolate brown*.

Berlin & Kay's work was primarily centered on similarities rather than on differences between languages, but with regard to world records, one thing that they and their successors noted was that the number of basic color terms in the languages studied varied between two and eleven.

Berlin & Kay also observed that certain colors are more basic than others, so that we would expect a language which has 'brown' and 'pink' to also have 'red' and 'green'.

LARGEST NUMBER OF COLOR TERMS

The average language, out of the 98 featured in Berlin & Kay (1969), had 5,4 basic color terms. Few had more than the eleven found in English. This number is by no means unique to English, however, but is rather common in European languages. It is less so elsewhere, but does occur in e.g. Hebrew, Japanese, Korean, and Zuni.

English	black	white	red	orange	yellow	green	blue	purple	pink	grey	brown
French	noir	blanc	rouge	orange	jaune	vert	bleu	violet	rose	gris	brun
German	schwarz	weiß	rot	orange	gelb	grün	blau	lila	rosa	grau	braun
Swedish	svart	vit	röd	orange	gul	grön	blå	lila	rosa	grå	brun
Finnish	musta	valkoinen	punainen	oranssi	keltainen	vihreä	sininen	liila	rosa	harmaa	ruskea

Having eleven basic color terms is common in European languages.
Note, however, the presence of loans for orange, purple and pink, which used
to be absent from the color term inventories of most European languages.

Two of the languages included, however, surpassed this number, namely Hungarian and Russian, which were the only ones with an arsenal of 12 basic color terms (see below).

SMALLEST NUMBER OF COLOR TERMS

Exotic though it may seem to a westerner, plenty of languages make do with only two basic color terms—'black' and 'white' (or 'dark' and 'light', if you will). Examples include Kuku Yalanji and Meriam of Australia, the African languages Ngombe and Bassa, Paliyan of India and Dani, Nipsan and Walak, all spoken in Western New Guinea.

To avoid misunderstandings, it should be emphasized that these languages are of course *able* to express other hues as well, just as English is capable of expressing *cyan* or *bordeaux*, even though these are normally not considered *basic*.

If there is any language which can be said to merit the label "eccentric" more than any other, then Pirahã is it. This baffling language is entirely devoid of color terms.

UNUSUAL AND PROBLEMATIC CASES

Hungarian is odd among the world's languages in having in its repertoire of basic color terms a distinction between bright red and dark red. Similarly, some varieties of Slavic, including Polish, Russian and Ukrainian distinguish between two kinds of blue. The most unusual language in this respect may well be Tsakhur, which is spoken on the border between Russia and Azerbaijan. It is the only language known which has a basic color term for turquoise.

The South American language Jaqaru is another one with odd priorities. It has eight basic color terms, but four of these refer to colors that many other languages would lump together as 'red': shocking pink, burgundy, reddish brown and wine red.

Another language from the same continent is not quite as spectacular, but nevertheless unusual: contrary to expectations, Tariano fails to distinguish between green and blue, but does have a word for purple.

A language which has been described as particularly difficult to fit into Berlin & Kay's generalizations is Ainu, an isolate of northern Japan. It has four basic color terms, including one, *hu*, which covers red and green, and another, *siwnin*, covering blue and yellow.

Another unusual case is that of Mlabri (α-dialect, spoken by some 300 people in northern Thailand) which uses an interesting circumlocution to denote greyish brown or khaki color—'the color of the badger's genitals'. Interestingly, male and female speakers use the expression differently, matching the sex of the badger in question. Women would thus say /plil ˈçwɛç/ 'vulva [of] badger', while men would use /ɗoŋ ˈçwɛç/ 'penis [of] badger'. There is a parallel in Laotian Mlabri (γ-dialect, spoken by fewer than 30 persons), where fermented tea leaves (sucked as a stimulating drug) are called by women /çoʔuːm ˈçɛʔ/ '[that which] smells [of] vagina' and, by men, /çoʔuːm ˈɗoŋ/ '[that which] smells [of] penis'.

SOURCES NOT MENTIONED IN THE TEXT

Color terminology in general: Berlin & Kay (1969), MacLaury (2001).
Color words in Pirahã: Everett (2004).
Color words in Hungarian and Russian: Plank (2000).
Color words in Ukrainian and Polish: MacLaury (2001).
Color words in Tsakhur: Davies, Sosenskaja & Corbett (1999).
Color words in Jaqaru: Hardman (1981).
Color words in Tariano: Interview with Alexandra Aikhenvald by Adrian Barnett in the February 2004 issue of *New Scientist*.
Color words in Ainu: Smith (1996:9).
Mlabri for 'greyish brown' or 'khaki color': Jørgen Rischel (p c).

PERSONAL NAMES

TOP TEN SURNAMES IN SELECTED COUNTRIES

The top ten surnames in each of 27 different countries are set out in a table on the two following pages.

The presence of European given names as surnames in some countries in the Caribbean is explained by the fact that most of the population is descended from slaves who often had no surname. Upon the abolition of slavery, several different strategies were used to bestow surnames on the newly freed citizens, one of which was simply the adaptation of a given name. In other cases, names betray more or less recent migration patterns, as can be seen when comparing Britain versus the USA, or Réunion versus the Seychelles.

In Korea, the top-ten surnames encompass half of the population. For the Chinese, the corresponding figure is 40%, for Denmark 33%, and for Sweden and Spain just below 20%. In Finland, Poland and the Czech Republic, on the other hand, less than 4% of the population share the ten most popular names, and in Belgium, this figure is just above 2%. In Brussels, where both the country's main linguistic groups are present, just one person out of every hundred has one of the ten most common names. It thus doesn't take much to chart, and indeed, Nguyen (of Vietnamese origin) is one of the top ranking Bruxellois surnames.

The United States has a very diverse array of names, presumably because its population stems from several different countries. Only 6% of all Americans have one of the top-ten surnames. Yet, although people tracing their origins to the British Isles make up only a fifth of the American population, almost all the top-100 surnames in the USA are distinctly Anglo-Saxon. 13 Spanish names are featured, but no German, French or Italian ones. This is no doubt due—at least in part—to German, French and Italian onomastics being considerably more varied than Spanish. The most common non-Anglo names are García, Martínez and Rodríguez, which all make it into the top 20. At least at the top end of the frequency list, American name frequencies are very similar to British ones. Hughes is notable in being considerably more common in Britain than in the States. The reverse is true for Moore, Miller and Anderson. For the last two, this is no doubt because of immigration of e.g. Scandinavian Anderssons and German Müllers.

On Pitcairn Island, the last British colony in the Pacific, *all* inhabitants have one of the top-ten surnames. In fact, enumerating eight would suffice, as that would exhaust the complete surname inventory of the island. Another British possession, Tristan da Cunha in the south Atlantic, used to beat it by one, as only seven surnames were shared by the entire population. In 1986, though, an eighth was added through the settlement of a Scotsman on the island.

The table overleaf (compiled from census statistics) captures some of the variation in last name diversity in some countries and territories.

TOP TEN SURNAMES IN SOME COUNTRIES

	1	2	3	4	5	6	7	8	9	10
BELGIUM	Peeters	Janssens	Maes	Jacobs	Mertens	Willems	Claes	Goossens	Wouters	De Smet
BRITAIN	Smith	Jones	Williams	Brown	Taylor	Davies	Wilson	Evans	Thomas	Johnson
CHINA	王 (Wang²)	陈 (Chen²)	李 (Li³)	张 (Zhang¹)	刘 (Liu²)	杨 (Yang²)	黄 (Huang²)	吴 (Wu²)	林 (Lin²)	周 (Zhou¹)
CZECH REP.	Novák	Svoboda	Novotný	Dvořák	Černý	Procházka	Kučera	Veselý	Horák	Němec
DENMARK	Jensen	Nielsen	Hansen	Pedersen	Andersen	Christen-sen	Larsen	Sørensen	Rasmus-sen	Jørgensen
DOMINICA	Joseph	Charles	George	John Baptist	James	Francis	Étienne	Esprit	Lewis	Fontaine
FRANCE	Martin	Bernard	Thomas	Robert	Petit	Dubois	Richard	Garcia	Durand	Moreau
GERMANY	Müller	Schmidt	Schneider	Fischer	Meyer	Weber	Schulz	Wagner	Becker	Hoffmann
GUADELOUPE	Greaux	Louis	Bourgeois	Kancel	Romain	Guillaume	Alexis	Étienne	Ledée	Laplace
HUNGARY	Nagy	Kovács	Tóth	Szabó	Horváth	Kiss	Varga	Molnár	Németh	Farkas
INDIA	Singh	Kumar	S(h)arma	Patel	Shah	Lal	Gupta	Bhat	Rao	Reddy
IRELAND	Murphy	Kelly	O'Sullivan	Walsh	Smith	O'Brien	Byrne	Ryan	O'Connor	O'Neill
ITALY	Rossi	Russo	Ferrari	Esposito	Bianchi	Romano	Colombo	Ricci	Marino	Greco

Country	佐藤 (Sato)	鈴木 (Suzuki)	高橋 (Takahashi)	田中 (Tanaka)	渡辺 (Watanabe)	伊藤 (Ito)	山本 (Yamamoto)	中村 (Nakamura)	小林 (Kobayashi)	斎藤 (Saito)
JAPAN	佐藤 (Sato)	鈴木 (Suzuki)	高橋 (Takahashi)	田中 (Tanaka)	渡辺 (Watanabe)	伊藤 (Ito)	山本 (Yamamoto)	中村 (Nakamura)	小林 (Kobayashi)	斎藤 (Saito)
MARTINIQUE	Jean-Baptiste	Joseph	Jean-Louis	Jean	Germany	Marie-Sainte	Édouard	Adelaide	Sainte-Rose	Jean-Marie
NETHERLANDS	De Vries	De Jong	(De) Boer	Bakker	Meijer/Meyer	Smit	Visser	Bos	Mulder	Vos
NORWAY	Hansen	Olsen	Johansen	Larsen	Andersen	Nilsen	Pedersen	Kristiansen	Jensen	Karlsen
POLAND	Nowak	Kowalski	Wiśniewski	Wójcik	Kowalczyk	Kamiński	Lewandowski	Zieliński	Szymański	Woźniak
RÉUNION	Payet	Grondin	Hoarau	Fontaine	Boyer	Robert	Hoareau	Rivière	Maillot	Dijoux
ROMANIA	Popescu	Popa	Radu	Ionescu	Şerban	Matei	Stoica	Gheorghe	Constantin	Stan
RUSSIA	Иванов (Ivanov)	Смирнов (Smirnov)	Васильев (Vasiljev)	Петров (Petrov)	Кузнецов (Kuznetsov)	Фёдоров (Fedorov)	Михайлов (Mihajlov)	Соколов (Sokolov)	Павлов (Pavlov)	Семенов (Semenov)
SEYCHELLES	Hoareau	Esparon	Savy	Marie	Rose	Pillay	Laure	Bibi	Morel	Jean
SOUTH KOREA	김 (Kim, Gim)	이 (Lee, Yi, I)	박 (Park, Pak, Bak)	최 (Choi, Choe)	정 (Jung, Chung, Jeong)	강 (Gang, Kang)	조 (Cho, Jo)	윤 (Yoon, Yun)	장 (Jang, Chang)	임 (Lim, Im)
SPAIN	García	Fernández	González	Rodriguez	López	Martínez	Sánchez	Pérez	Martín	Gómez
ST. LUCIA	Joseph	Charles	James	John Baptist	Augustin	Williams	Edwards	Mathurin	Phillip	Francis
SWEDEN	Johans-son	Anders-son	Karlsson	Nilsson	Eriksson	Larsson	Olsson	Persson	Svensson	Gustafs-son
USA	Smith	Johnson	Williams	Jones	Brown	Davis	Miller	Wilson	Moore	Taylor

DIVERSITY OF SURNAMES IN CERTAIN TERRITORIES

Country or territory	Share of the population having the most common names			Number of names required to cover 10% of the population
	Top 10	Top 20	Top 100	
Germany	40,90%	?	?	2
Denmark	33,22%	42,32%	?	2
Réunion	26,03%	36,48%	57,61%	3
Spain	19,65%	26,05%	?	5
Sweden	19,50%	24,41%	40%	4
Hungary	16,86%	21,62%	34,44%	5
Norway	8,64%	12,17%	23,59%	13
Québec	6,51%	10,35%	26,73%	19
Britain	5,70%	8,45%	?	?
USA	5,62%	8,37%	19%	28
Martinique	4,04%	6,58%	19,83%	37
Finland	3,90%	?	?	?
Czech Republic	3,85%	5,86%	?	?
Poland	3,16%	5,09%	?	?
Flanders	3,01%	4,74%	11,95%	73
Walloonia	2,03%	3,51%	10,33%	94
Belgium	2,03%	3,22%	8,60%	>100
Brussels	1,06%	1,77%	5,30%	>100
China	?	56%	87%	2

MOST COMMON FIRST NAME

There are no reliable statistics for the worldwide frequency of names, but the *Guinness Book of World Records* suggests that the most common given name in the world is most likely Muhammad and derivates thereof, and the guess certainly doesn't seem unreasonable. Maria and its side forms might possibly offer some competition in the Christian world.

AN UNEXPECTED FLIPINO NAME

During the days of American rule on the Philippines, at least one Filipino couple named their son *Ababís*, after what they believed to be the patron saint of the United States. Being a strongly Catholic country, where names of saints were introduced by the Spanish, the Philippines abound with San Josés, San Pedros, San Carloses and San Juans. The conclusion that Ababís must be yet another character on the list of saints was based on hearing Americans in moments of distress exclaim something that sounded like *San Ababís!*

EUROPEAN NAMES IN AFRICA

In most African countries, a European tongue continues to be the prestige language even after independence. For this reason, many Christian Africans have European names. In some cases, though, they are not taken over directly from Europe, but a distinctly local flavour and innovativeness is evident. For instance, the 2002 African football championship featured Zambian players named Gift, January and Laughter. Nigeria, for its part sent a Peterside, a Justice, two Fridays and two Sundays. At the time of writing this, African cabinets list both Precious and Witness. Many of these may be direct translations of traditional African names which often allude to the circumstances surrounding a person's birth. Other unusual "English" names which have been reported include Wonderboy and Superfine.

Not only colonialism proper, but also missionary activities had the consequence of Europeanizing names in Africa. For instance, the Congolese boy Kacharel, mentioned elsewhere in this book (p 83), grew up with his uncle Bertil-Höök, whose first name combines the first and last name of the Swedish missionary. Finland never had any colonies in Africa, but in Namibia, Finnish missionaries were conspicuous. For that reason, many Ambo in the northern part of the country still bear distinctly Finnish names.

Although presumably not of European origin, one of my favorites among African surnames is Tokyo Sexwhale, former premier of South Africa's Gauteng province. Luckily, South Africa is now a democracy, but in neighboring Zimbabwe, it is said that making jokes about the name of former president Canaan Banana led to rather severe punishments.

CHANGING POLITICS, CHANGING NAMES

Political turnovers have always led to changes in the names given to children. One notable instance of this in the western world is the introduction of Christianity. But even in modern times, the same process can be observed. During the First Gulf War, the names Saddam and Norman (after US general Norman Schwartzkopf) allegedly increased in frequency in various countries.

Seibicke (1991:40) shows that the proportion of Germans named *Adolf*, not surprisingly, was higher before and during the Second World War, than after it. The same is true for Slovenia, where Adolf peaked in the early 1940s, only to experience a drastic drop in popularity shortly afterwards. The most popular male name during the 20th century was Franc, although it has been on the decline since the First world War (before which one Slovenian boy in ten bore the name). Other names which have experienced more or less brief periods of popularity include Elvis (1970s and 1980s) and Kevin (1990s).

In Bolshevik Russia, some pious parents gave their children names such as *Elektrifikatsya* 'electrification' and *Vil*, the latter being the initials of Vladimir Ilych Lenin. This naming system was imitated in many of the Soviet satellites in Eastern Europe, and in post-war Yugoslavia *Lenjin, Staljin, Molotov* and *Timošenko* began appearing as first names, as did compounds such as *Marklen(a)* (which includes the name Marx) and *Vladilen(a)*. Marshal Tito's name inspired formations such as *Titoslav(a)* and *Titomir(a)*. Other attested Yugoslav neologisms include

Staljingradka, Komsomolka (Komsa), Ruska, Vjazma, Sutjeska, Neretva, Petoletka (five year plan) and *Traktor(ka)*. Yet, the prize-winner must certainly be the Armenian name which translated as 'five year plan completed in just four years'!

WHERE THE PEOPLE HAVE NO NAMES

It has been suggested that the use of proper names for individuals (and usually also for places) is universal among human communities. As with most rules, it seems that this too has its exceptions. The speakers of Machiguenga, an Arawakan language of Peru is one, according to two anthropologists who have conducted fieldwork in the area. The Machiguengas live and die without having had a name bestowed upon them, and are normally referred to simply by kinship terms. In modern times, they have been given Spanish names, but, it is reported, "they rarely used them [. . .] and frequently forgot or changed them".

SOURCES NOT MENTIONED IN THE TEXT

Surnames in various countries: Wallechinsky et al. (1979), Sohn (1999:109), April 2001 issue of the Japanese journal *Awa Life*, Lareau (2003), Carroll (2003), Wikipedia (2004), own research (phone books, etc), census bureaux of the respective countries.
An unusual Philippine name: Trask (1996:19).
Finnish names in Namibia: Saarelma-Maunumaa (2003).
Given names in Slovenia: Statistical Office of Slovenia.
Ideological naming in Eastern Europe: Aleksov (2000), Östen Dahl (p c).
Absence of names among the Machiguenga: Hurford (2003).

PLACE-NAMES

PLACE-NAMES CONSTITUTE an interesting part of any language's vocabulary for several reasons. Hopefully, some of these will become apparent below.

NAMES OF COUNTRIES

Among the slightly more than 200 independent countries of the world, there are a few whose names defy any attempt at etymologizing. Most of the others can be assigned to a small number of categories, the most common of which is probably "the land of the X-people". First, and perhaps somewhat trivially, there are a number of countries which are simply named for their capital:

Algeria	*Djibouti*	*Kuwait*	*Mexico*	*Panama*	*Singapore*
Andorra	*Guatemala*	*Luxembourg*	*Monaco*	*San Marino*	*Tunisia*

In addition to these, Guinea-Bissau is in part named for its capital. Morocco owes its name to the name of the city Marrakech, although this is not its capital. The same goes for Togo, which is named for the village of Togodo (now Togoville). The opposite, i.e. a capital named after a country, is rarer, but those of Brazil (*Brasília*) and Belize (*Belize City*) are two examples.

Less obvious, and more interesting, certain other countries are named for geographical features found *outside* the country itself:

Benin	The African country Dahomey renamed itself Benin in 1975. The medieval kingdom of Benin, however, was located in what is today Nigeria, as is Benin City.
Cape Verde	The actual Cape, which is the westernmost part of the African mainland, is situated in Senegal.
Ghana	Named after the medieval kingdom of Ghana, which, however, was not located within the borders of the present-day republic of the same name, but for the most part in what is today Mali.
Grenada	Named after Granada in southern Spain.
New Zealand	"Old" Zealand is found in the Netherlands. *Zeeland*, as it is spelt in Dutch, simply means *sea-land*.
Papua New Guinea	One of four countries in the world with 'Guinea' in its name. Three of these are located in Africa while New Guinea lies in the Pacific.
Romania	This name ultimately refers, of course, to the city of Rome.
Seychelles	The Seychelles were named by French explorers for Jean Moreau de Séchelles, minister of finance under Louis XV. This man, in turn, owed his name to a village in northern France.
Venezuela	Named after Venice—legend has it that the huts on poles reminded the first European explorers of the Italian city.

223

As we shall see, both Bolivia and the Seychelles simultaneously belong to both this and the following category.

Yet other countries are named after individuals. The most obvious are those whose names begin with "Saint", such as **St Kitts**, **St Lucia**, **St Vincent** and the Grenadines and **São Tomé** and Príncipe. **Israel** and **El Salvador** are named after Biblical characters.

That the following countries are also named after individuals is less obvious:

Philippines	Named after Spanish King Philip II.
Kiribati	The local pronunciation of "Gilbert", the name bestowed upon the islands in honour of British captain Thomas Gilbert who passed by in 1788.
Belize	No one knows for sure, but the most common assumption is that the name Belize is a distortion of the name of a Scotsman Peter Wallis (or Wallace) who founded a settlement there in the early 17th century.
Colombia	After Christopher Columbus.
Marshall Islands	For British Captain John Marshall, who sighted the islands in 1788.
Solomon Islands	Named after the biblical King Solomon, with an allusion to the wealth of the mines associated with him.
Mauritius	Named by Dutch explorers after their Prince Mauritz of Nassau.
Bolivia	Simón Bolívar, who freed much of South America from Spanish rule. Like the Seychelles, this country also belongs to the former category, as the Bolívar family stemmed from the village of Bolibar in the Basque country.
USA	The USA is of course named for the continent on which it is situated, but that in turn is thought to have got its name from the Italian explorer Amerigo Vespucci (1451-1512), credited with being the first to identify North and South America as continents separate from Asia and from one another (though cf Rea (1964) and Laubenberger & Rowan (1982)).

A NEW TOPONYMIC TRADITION?

Place-names all over the world tend to describe the natural environment around the geographical feature in question. Even many of those which are not transparent today, have once been so, before sound changes and language shift rendered them opaque to most people, including their current inhabitants. Transparency is therefore often an indication of recent settlement, and such names are predictably common in countries founded as overseas colonies.

Possibly unique to the United States, however, is a fairly large number of settlements whose names represent blends of the names of the states close to whose border they are located. One might argue that from an aesthetic point of view, the results vary considerably.

Calnevari Nevada close to the three-state intersection with California and Arizona. In the same area, we also find a Calneva, a Calada, a Calvada and a Calzona.

Dakoming On the Wyoming/South Dakota border.

Delmar On the Delaware/Maryland border. Closer to Virginia (customarily abbreviated VA) there is also a Delmarva.

Florala On the Florida/Alabama border. Not far away, there is also an *Alaflora*.

Idavada Close to the Idaho/Nevada border.

Illiana Near the Illinois/Indiana frontier. Closer to Missouri (MO) we find Illmo.

Kanorado On the Kansas/Colorado border. On Colorado's south-eastern periphery, Oklahoma has yielded Oklarado.

Kenova Kentucky on its Virginia (VA) border. It has a nearby relative in Kenvir.

Latex Between Texas and Louisiana (LA), there is not only a Latex, but also a Texla. A common border with Arkansas has also resulted in a Laark.

Marydel Maryland on the border with Delaware. Nearby, we find Mardela.

Mexicali California on the border with Mexico. There is also a *Calexico* on the Mexican side.

Michiana Michigan on the border with Indiana.

Minnkota A wildlife area between South Dakota and Minnesota.

Missala Between Mississippi and Alabama.

Monida The Idaho-Montana state line has given rise not only to Monida, but also to Idmon.

Okeana Ohio close to the three-state intersection with Kentucky and Indiana.

Orovada Close to the Oregon/Nevada border.

Penmar Near the Pennsylvania/Maryland border, while the town of *Sylmar* is actually split between these two states.

Penndel On the Pennsylvania/Delaware border.

Penowa Close to Pennsylvania's borders with Ohio and West Virginia.

Tennemo Tennessee on the border with Missouri (MO). The latter abbreviation also shows up in Moark, just south of the Arkansas border.

Tennga Georgia (GA) on the border with Tennessee. The ga part also features in Alaga, between Alabama and Georgia.

Texarkana On the very state line between Arkansas and Texas (and immortalized in the song "Cottonfields"). Further to the east, Arkana combines the state names of Arkansas and Louisiana. Arkoma is of course located closer to Oklahoma.

Texhoma On the Texas/Oklahoma border.

Texico New Mexico on the border with Texas.

Texola Oklahoma on the border with Texas.

Ucolo Utah on the border with Colorado. The northern part of the state features a Utida, including instead the name of Idaho.

Uvada Utah on the border with Nevada.

Vershire Straddling the state line between Vermont and New Hampshire.

Virgilina Virginia on the border with North Carolina.

Wissota A lake between Wisconsin and Minnesota.

Wyodak In Wyoming, but still not far from South Dakota. Further to the south, a less phon-aesthetic Wyocolo is found.

A handful of other American place-names are borderline (!) cases. Ohio and Iowa are not located next to one another, but *Ohiowa*, Nebraska, was settled from these two states while *Penn Yan*, New York, was named by Pennsylvanians and New Englanders, i.e. Yankees. *Norlina*, North Carolina is a telescopic form only involving one state name. *Colwich*, Kansas is formed from *Colorado* and the *Wichita Railroad*. A close relative is *Miloma*, Minnesota, which is named for the railroads leading to Milwaukee and Omaha respectively.

Also in the same vein is the *Lake Koocanusa*, a dam on the Kootenai River, which runs between Canada and the USA. The name combines the first syllable of the river with the names of the two countries sharing the dam.

As it happens, the United States also sports another highly unusual place naming technique. Naming places after people is of course common worldwide, but sometimes, (often because the area was already chock-full of *Smiths* and *Jones*es, and something was needed

*Though over-represented in the New World, the acronymic place-naming is not unique to it. The southern Swedish village of Flerohopp turns out to be named for an iron manufacturing plant founded there in 1725 by Messrs. **Fle**etwood, **Ro**thleib and **Hopp**enstedt.*

to avoid confusion), the Americans have also exploited the possibility of reversing names.

Thus, localities such as *Trevlac, Trebloc, Noswad, Siwel, Snevets, Nostrebor, Rolyat* and *Sniktaw* are derived from reversals of surnames (usually of their founders)—Calvert, Colbert, Dawson, Lewis, Stevens, Robertson, Taylor and Watkins respectively. The towns of *Darnoc, Lebam* and *Adnaw,* on the other hand, are inversions of the given names of their earliest inhabitants.

My personal favorite is *Orestod* in Colorado. It gets its name from being the end point of a railroad line, and so, the mileage, counting from the point of departure was "dot zero". Now, if the railroad starts in Dotsero, what is more natural than naming the other end of the line *Orestod?*

As a final note on the word-play subject, we may note a few more places in the USA which have also been creative in applying personal names to localities. *Bucoda* in Washington includes the names of co-founders Buckley, Collier and Davis. Similar compromises lie behind the towns of *Gilsum* (< Gilbert + Sumner) and *Paragould* (< Paramore + Gould). Given names and surnames were combined in *Cadams* (< C Adams), *Wascott* (< W A Scott), *Eleroy* (< E Leroy) and *Marenisco* (< Mary Relief Niles Scott).

ALEXANDER THE PROLIFEROUS AND HIS SUCCESSORS

A lthough I know of no specific study, I would like to propose that there are five people who have given rise to more place-names than anybody else.

First, **Alexander** the Great of Macedonia (356-323 B.C.) created one of the largest empires to date. Already before his campaigns abroad, he had one of the cities in his home country renamed *Alexandropolis.* His conquest of Egypt then led to the appearance of *Alexandria* and *Alexandretta* on the map, names which still survive in Western toponymic tradition. Along his way, Alexander developed a habit of naming most of his major strongholds after himself. After some time, there were thus two Alexandrias in present-day Pakistan, six

in Afghanistan, two each in Iran and Turkey, and at least one each in Iraq, Turkmenistan and Tajikistan. There was also an additional *Alexandropolis* in Iran. Although most of the Alexandrias no longer bear the name, it still survives in somewhat altered form, e.g. in the name of Afghanistan's second city, *Kandahar.* In addition, there are now at least a dozen Alexandrias in the United States and other countries colonized long after Alexander's death.

A couple of centuries later, the Roman empire was at its zenith under Julius **Caesar.** Many places were thus named after the successful dictator. Again, many of the cities have since been renamed, but the name of the most famous of all Roman rulers still survives in those of e.g. *Tours* (< *Caesarodunum*) and *Fréjus* (< *Forum Julii*) in France, *Zaragoza* (< *Caesaraugusta*) in Spain, *Cherchell* (< *Caesarea Iol*) in Algeria, *Kayseri* (< *Caesarea Cappadociae*) in Turkey, and of the Channel Island of *Jersey* (< *Caesarea*). Apart from names on maps, of course, we also owe appellations such as *Kaiser* and *czar* to Caesar.

More than a millennium and a half later, Americans showed their gratitude to their revolutionary leader by naming the newborn country's capital Washington. Later, a state was given the same name, as well as no less than 31 counties, and there are now well over 100 Washingtons in the United States, not counting all the Washington Doros/Heights/Islands/Junctions/Mills/Mounts/Valleys, etc.

Despite the loss of its American colonies, Britain was not out of the game, and under

pious affection or lack of imagination on behalf of the Britons. In addition to this, Victoria Peaks and Victoria Rivers dotted the map of the British Empire (including a Victoria Land in Antarctica), and a couple of dozen Victorias sprang up in the United States. Some, such as Limbe (Cameroon) and Labuan (Malaysia) have regained their pre-Victorian names, thus contributing to a bit more toponymical variation. Meanwhile, the hamlet of Queen Victoria in Mauritius, is normally known as La Queen. A few additional names, such as the Australian state of Queensland, does not include her name, but nevertheless refer to the queen (needless to say, Australia also has a state named Victoria).

Finally, another revolutionary leader, Vladimir Ilych Ulyanov, better known as Lenin, changed the maps (in more than one sense) during the first half of the 20th century.

Once the leaders of mighty nations. But what else do they have in common?

Even disregarding the numerous parks, boulevards, public buildings, also named after the godfather of bolshevism, there was an impressive array of Lenin towns in the former Soviet empire (some of which still remain).

the long reign of Queen Victoria, the country came to possess what is still the mightiest empire in world history. Not surprisingly, her subjects enthusiastically set about naming newly conquered places after her. The settlements earlier called l'Établissement (now the capital of the Seychelles) and Pile of Bones (now the capital of Saskatchewan in Canada) were presumably intended to acquire a bit more grandeur by becoming Victoria and Regina (Latin for 'queen') respectively. Further Victorias were named in Hong Kong, in British Columbia, Malta, Australia and elsewhere at a rate bearing witness of either

Most noteworthy is of course St Petersburg, formerly known as Leningrad (the administrative region around that city is, by the way, still Leningradskaya Oblast), but there has also been a plethora of others—several Leninsks and Lenins in the Soviet Union, which has also had a Lenino, a Leninski, a Lenina, a Leninogorsk, an Ulyanovsk, as well as a mountain top named Pik Lenina. A local flavour was tried in the case of Leninabad and Leninakan. The Soviet puppet countries too, had their share of the Lenin cult, as manifested in e.g. Hungary's Leninváros (now Tiszaújváros).

Other east bloc leaders coming close to Lenin include Joseph Stalin (at least 13 cities) and Josip Broz Tito (8 cities).

Apart from Washington, the Americans have been fond of naming places after other revolutionary leaders and early presidents. Marquis Marie-Joseph-Paul-Roch-Yves-Gilbert du Motier de Lafayette, who fought alongside Washington has no less than 17 counties and at least 36 towns or cities named after him. Other popular names include in particular those of Christopher Columbus and James Monroe, followed at some distance by Lewis Cass, Henry Clay, DeWitt Clinton, Benjamin Franklin, Nathanael Greene, Andrew Jackson, Thomas Jefferson, Abraham Lincoln, James Madison, Francis Marion, Richard Montgomery, James Polk, Israel Putnam, and Anthony Wayne.

RADICAL RENAMING BEFORE LENIN

A s already noted, the Russian revolution really did change the map, and towns including Lenin and other names of Bolshevik leaders proliferated. As with so many other features of the Soviet era, however, there was an obvious, but less well known, precedent in the French revolution.

In the wake of the 1789 revolution, it was decided that the country's toponymy needed a facelift. Out went place-names containing or commemorating saints, churches, priests, as well as kings, queens, dukes, counts, palaces and other feudal features. Almost 3 500 municipalities were thus renamed, in ways ranging from poetic to outright ridiculous. In particular, any place-name containing the name of a royal highness, a duke, baron or count, as well as any name with a religious ring to it were felt inappropriate to the new republic.

Some places simply kept the acceptable part of the old name, e.g. by dropping the "saint" prefix of settlements named after saints. Thus the most basic change consisted in suppressing the tabooed part by simply turning *Saint-Pierre* into *Pierre*. Sometimes the banned element was replaced by an authorized one as when *Bourg-la-Reine* 'Queenstown' became *Bourg-Egalité* 'Equalitytown'. In a similar manner, *Royville* 'Kingstown' was made *Peupleville* 'Peoplestown', while, for instance, *Argenton-Château*, *Malay-le-Roi* and *Fresnay-le-Comte* became *Argenton-le-Peuple*, *Malay-le-Républicain* and *Fresnay-le-Peuple* respectively. In other cases, a simple spelling change could do the trick, as when *Saint-Dau* was turned into *Ceint d'Eau*.

The most remarkable manifestation of revolutionary fervour is probably the recurrence of certain revolutionary keywords in the new names. Unity was considered an important virtue, and thus, 30 towns received the name of *Union*, with another 20 being called *Unité*. The words of the revolutionary motto *Liberté, égalite, fraternité* were also applied to a number of places, and there were about a dozen each of *Libertés* and *Fraternités*, and almost twice as many *Égalités*. The revolutionary hero Marat was honoured with no less than 16 towns named after him. One of these was even called *Saint-Marat*, despite the fact that saints were supposedly banned from the map of France. In the same spirit, the well-known *Montmartre* in Paris turned into *Mont-Marat*. Another hero, the American Benjamin Franklin, was also honoured, and two cities (one of which was Bordeaux) were called *Franklin*. A certain Swiss author was also popular, and two places simply became *Jean-Jacques-Rousseau*. Another was named *Émile*, after his most famous book. Yet other examples of the admiration felt for authors and philosophers from the Age of Reason include *La Haye-Descartes* (previously simply

La Haye), the towns of *Romilly-Voltaire* and *Villiers-le-Voltaire* (earlier *Romilly-sur-Seine* and *Villiers-le-Mathieu* respectively), and the part of Lyons which proudly bore the name of *Canton-de-la-Raison*.

The *Sans-Culottes* movement (literally 'without trousers', as its members preferred a more proletarian dress code to the smart trousers of the bourgeoisie) lent its name to another eight places. Contemporary politically correct fashion also made its mark in the four places given the name of *Bonnet-Rouge*—'red bonnet'. Several other cultural manifestations and political events were also honoured. A popular revolutionary song was *La Carmagnole*, after which the town formerly known as *Villedieu* was named. Three places in France became *La Tricolore*, after the new national flag. We also find a Proclamation, and a Constitution. Also, long before this became fashionable with South American juntas, the town of *Souillac* decided to become *Trente-et-un-Mai* '31st of May'.

A few particularly pretentious names can be noted: *Versailles*, previously the seat of the royal family, was rebaptized *Berceau-de-la-Liberté*, i.e. 'cradle of freedom', and the town of Moussel became *Montagne-du-Droit-de-l'Homme*, or 'Human Rights Mountain'. Another town, earlier known as *Hénin-Liétard* was rechristened as *l'Humanité*—'mankind'. Similarly lacking in humility was *La Veuve*, which took the name of *La Voix-du-Peuple*, 'voice of the people'. Two towns decided to commemorate the revolution by calling themselves—*La Révolution*. *Saint-Genest* must also have had high thoughts about itself, as it was bold enough to take the name *Sans-Préjugé*, or 'without prejudice'. Several

communities included the words *république* or *républicain* in their names, but only two places, including the Paris suburb of *Charenton* dared call themselves simply *La République*.

My personal favorite is the country's third city at the time—Marseilles. Despite it having given its name to the revolutionary (and national) anthem, *La Marseillaise*, the city was conspicuous for its contra-revolutionary activities. In a conscious effort to humiliate the city therefore, Marseilles was given the name *Sans-Nom*—'nameless'!

This name-changing craze did not only affect France, but also extended to its colonies. Thus, the now independent Caribbean nation of St. Lucia had a *Constitution*, a *Révolution* a *Tricolore* and an *Egalité* of its own, as well as a *Le Républicain* and a *La Convention*. Neighboring Guadeloupe had its main port rechristened *Port-de-la-Liberté*, while other towns became, unsurprisingly, *Tricolore*, *Egalité* and *Fraternité*. Even less imaginative were the authorities in present-day Haiti, three of whose main towns were known as *Cap-Républicain*, *Fort-Républicain* and *Port-Républicain* (the latter being today's capital Port-au-Prince, a name obviously unacceptable to the revolutionaries).

For better or for worse, this situation lasted only for 25 years, and after the failure of the revolution, and the reestablishment of the monarchy, almost all rebaptized places regained their original names. Some of the colonies, however, escaped this, especially those which had meanwhile been lost to France. Places such as *Sans-Culottes*, *Ça-Ira*, *La Réunion* and *Floréal* still dot maps of the Caribbean and the Indian Ocean and remind us of the revolutionary naming practices.

LUNAR TOPONYMY

One of the sides of the moon has always been visible to earthlings, whereas the other one could only be explored after the construction of man-made space probes. This is neatly reflected in the lunar toponymy—the near side place names are predominantly Latinate, whereas those of the far side are mostly of American, Russian, British, German and French origin, with occasional additions from other languages.

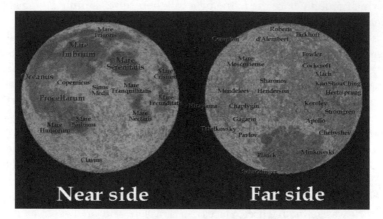

Of linguistic interest is the fact that there is a crater named after Wilhelm von Humboldt. There are also craters named in honour of Arthur Evans (the archaeologist who discovered the Linear A and Linear B inscriptions), Michael Ventris (who deciphered the latter), Jean-François Champollion (who played a major role in the decipherment of the Egyptian hieroglyphs) and Wilhelm Grimm (brother of Jakob Grimm, the man behind Grimm's law). The Saussure crater, alas, owes its name not to our hero Ferdinand, but to his great-grandfather, the Swiss geologist and mountaineer Horace-Bénédict de Saussure.

Amazingly, when the Swiss hear the name de Saussure, it is not primarily Ferdinand that springs to their minds, but rather his great-grandfather, the geologist Horace-Bénédict, who in 1787 became the third person to climb the highest of the Alps, the Mont-Blanc.

Several other members of the family have also made a name for themselves in various disciplines, including Ferdinand's own son who introduced psychoanalysis in Switzerland.

Other members of the clan became renowned agronomists, entomologists, chemists and botanists.

OLD NAMES FOR A NEW WORLD

Hundreds of places in the United States have a name beginning with "new". Most of these, of course, include the name of a place in Europe, such as York, Hampshire or Orléans.

In some cases, however, the "old town" is located further east in the USA, rather than in Europe. Thus, we find villages and towns such as New Buffalo, New Miami, New Pittsburgh, New Chicago, New Texas, New Virginia, New Washington and New Jenny Lind (the latter named after the town of Jenny Lind, which is in turn bears the name of a 19th century Swedish opera singer).

We all need a place to call home

Yet other names are coined on familiar European patterns, such as Newburg, Newbury and Newchester. Settlements such as New Addition, New Beaver, New Design, New Knockhock, New Erection and New Igloo are somewhat suggestive, but the founders of New City, New Home and Newcomerstown were apparently less imaginative.

There is also a place simply called Newness. And we must not forget the place simply called "New", which is located in Kentucky.

The opposite phenomenon is less common, but does exist. Britain has a Quebec, and Germany sports a Kamerun and a Kalifornien. Plenty of places named Amerika also dot European maps.

AND YOU THOUGHT YOU KNEW GEOGRAPHY!

When the United States was settled by Europeans, there was for one thing a need for names for settlements which until then had not existed. Also, although most immigrants to the New World left their old homes out of free will, it is difficult to avoid the impression that some of them after all did feel a certain affection for their respective home countries. As a result, there are at least 35 Berlins, 34 Parises, 31 Moscows, 28 Romes and 20 Londons in the country. A similar phenomenon can be observed in other parts of the world subject to European colonization.

MOST COMMON PLACE-NAMES

The following table lists the most common place-names in selected countries. The predominance of saints is noteworthy in Catholic areas. Also, note the absence in the United States of Springfield and Washington, widely believed to be the two most common place names in the USA.

Country	1st	2nd	3rd	4th	5th
Argentina	San José	San Antonio	San Pedro	Santa Rosa	Santa María
Brazil	Boa Vista	Santo Antônio	São José	São João	São Pedro
Canada	Mount Pleasant	Centreville	Lakeview	Pleasant Valley	Fairview
China	Taiping	Qiaotou	Hekou	Guanzhuang	Gucheng
Congo-Kinshasa	Bumba	Kasongo	Gombe	Kalamba	Katanga
Egypt	Izbat al 'Arab	Izbat al Islah	al Kawm al Ahmar	Izbat al Manshiyah	al Manshiyah
Finland	Anttila	Seppälä	Taipale	Heikkilä	Myllykylä
France	Saint-Martin	Saint-Jean	Saint-Pierre	La Chapelle	Saint-Germain
Germany	Berg	Neuhof	Hausen	Steinbach	Holzhausen
Britain	Newton	Sutton	Weston	Stoke	Norton
Haiti	Bellevue	Corail	Grande-Savane	La Hatte	La Source
India	Rampur	Ramgarh	Fatehpur	Raipur	Ramnagar
Indonesia	Kampungbaru	Tandjung	Bojong	Baru	Bodjong
Iran	Hoseynabad	Aliabad	Mohammadabad	Hasanabad	Hajjiabad
Japan	Hama	Wada	Hongo	Ono	Ota
Madagascar	Tanambao	Morafeno	Ambodimanga	Antanambao	Morarano
Mexico	San Antonio	San José	San Francisco	San Isidro	San Pedro
Mozambique	João	Manuel	José	António	Amade
Philippines	San Isidro	San José	San Roque	San Juan	San Antonio
Russia	Aleksandrovka	Mikhaylovka	Ivanovka	Nikolayevka	Berezovka
Saudi Arabia	Al Faydah	Ar Rawdah	Al Far'ah	Al Faysaliyah	Ar Rafi'ah
South Africa	Weltevrede(n)	Lalini	Rietfontein	Nooitgedacht	Klipfontein
South Korea	Sin'gi	Saet'o	Nae-Dong	Songjong	Chung-Ni, Sinch'on
Sweden	Boda	Näs	Berga	Hult	Berg
Turkey	Yeniköy	Dereköy	Yenice	Ortaköy	Akpınar, Karaağaç
USA	Fairview	Midway	Oak Grove	Five Points	Centerville

LONG AND SHORT PLACE-NAMES

The longest place-name in the world is usually said to be Llanfairpwllgwyngyll-gogerychwyrndrobwllllantysiliogogogoch, a village in northern Wales. (Incidentally, for a while the said village also had a web site including the entire name in the URL, which made it able to also claim the world's longest web address). However, Wales also sports

Gorsafawddachaidraigodanheddogleddolonpenrhynareurdraethceredigion, which in fact is eight letters longer.

LLANFAIRPWLLGWYNGYLLGOGERYCHWYRNDROBWYLL-LLANTYSILIOGOGOGOCH
RAILWAY STATION

Then of course, we are faced with the problem as to what really constitutes a place-name. The hill in New Zealand whose full name is *Taumatawhakatangihangakoauauotamateaturipukakapikimaungahoronukupokaiwhenuakitanatahu* is normally referred to simply as Taumata. Similarly, no Thai—lest trying to cure his interlocutor from insomnia—would in everyday conversation call his capital *Krung thep mahanakhon bovorn ratanakosin mahintharayutthaya mahadilok pop noparatratchathani burirom udomratchanivetmahasathan amornpiman avatarnsathit sakkathattiyavisnukarmprasit*, although that is said to be the full version (167 letters) of Bangkok's name. The first two words normally do just fine.

In all fairness, it could be said, or at least suspected, that the Welsh place-names are primarily tourist gimmicks. No local would normally go beyond Llanfairpwll or Llanfair P G when mentioning the name of his or her village.

In one case, the name rather came about as a political statement. In 2004, the village of Llanfynydd in southern Wales decided to (temporarily) rename itself *Llanhyfryddawellehynafolybarcudprindanfygythiadtrienusyrhafnauole*, meaning "A quiet beautiful village, an historic place with rare kite under threat from wretched blades". The renaming was aimed at the firm Gamesa Energy, which planned to erect a wind farm of 30 turbines in the area.

When it comes to short places names, there is even more to choose from. There are several places in Scandinavia named *Å* and *Ö*, while France has an *Y*. Elsewhere in the world, we find *A*, *S* and *U*, as well as several other one-letter names (*S*, located in Mauritius, is descriptive of an S-shaped bend in the railway track which formerly existed). More orthographically interesting, however, is the location in Virginia which was once known as 6.

SOURCES NOT MENTIONED IN THE TEXT

Place names in general: First and foremost a multitude of maps, gazetteers and historical atlases (we map geeks tend to have plenty of those at home).

A new toponymic tradition: Mencken (1921) and an atlas of the United States. Reversals from Tilque (1998).

Revolutionary toponymy in France and its colonies: Manily Luxardo (1994), Jesse (1956:80-84), Guyot (1997) and a number of maps.

Lunar toponymy: NASA, but inspired by Crystal (1987:114).

Common place-names: USA: Tilque (2001), Canada: Canadian Geographical Names Data Base. For all other countries, the American Military's GEOnet Names Server was used. For convenience, only names of populated places were used, thus excluding rivers, capes, etc.

Long and short place names: Guinness Book of World Records, Miller (2001).

Long Welsh place-name in protest against wind farm: The Telegraph, 2004-07-19.

GLOSSONYMS

"GLOSSONYM" IS A WORD which some may not have heard before, but it really just means "language name". This is an area that one might expect linguists to be interested in, but which hasn't received much attention.

Odd though it may seem, it is by no means uncommon for people not to have a name for their language in many parts of the world. Upon outsiders' insistence, they may come up with something like 'our language', and this is in many cases what has at least become the linguists' label for the variety.

SHORTEST GLOSSONYMS

A few languages have a name consisting of one phoneme. Most important of these is **E**, spoken by some 30 000 people in China's Northern Guangxi-Zhuang Autonomous Region. In the same country, there are also 3 000 speakers of **U** in the south-western Yunnan Province. E and U are also sometimes used for the languages Ere (of Papua New Guinea) and Tibetan, respectively, and U is furthermore a dialect of Khmu, spoken mainly in Laos.

The language of Shanghai and its environs, normally written Wu, is also often pronounced as if the <w> were absent. Moreover, **I** is an alternative name for Yi, another Chinese language, and **O** is the name of a dialect of Kuy, spoken in Southeast Asia.

LONGEST GLOSSONYMS

The longest names of languages known to me are **Kelentheyewelrere** (a dialect of Anmatyerre, also in Australia) and **Mishikhwutmetunee** (an alternative name for Coquille, USA). Other long names of language varieties include **Nangikurrunggurr**, which is spoken in Australia, **Kinnaurayanuskad** (an alternative name for Lower Kinnauri, India) and **Ginyamunyinganyi** (a dialect of Nyaturu, Tanzania).

GLOSSONYMS WITH VOWELS ONLY

Apart from those already mentioned, at least two language names can be written with vowels only: **Uaieue** or **Uaiuai** (more often spelt Waiwai, and sometimes Ouayeone), spoken by some 500 persons in northern Brazil, and **Uaiai**, a dialect of Paumarí spoken in one single village in the Amazonas. **Iauiaula**, an alternate name for Diodio spoken in Eastern New Guinea, comes pretty close, as does **Uru-Eu-Uau-Uau** of Brazil.

DIFFICULT-TO-PRONOUNCE LANGUAGE NAMES

If you want to impress your friends, try referring to a southern African language with clicks (see p 245) in it, such as **||ng!ke** (a dialect of N|u) or **Amankgqwigqwi**, an alternative name for ||nogwi that usually does the trick. An Indian language with a tongue-twisting name is **Lngngam**, one spelling variant of a dialect of Khasi, spoken in India.

Maybe just interesting in terms of spelling, but nevertheless attractive, are the Tibeto-Burman languages **rGya-roâ** and **lCog-rtse** (sic!).

PARLEZ-VOUS BUCKET?

The French pirate Jean de la Guilbaudière in 1698 recorded a few words from a language called Aksanas in the Tierra del Fuego. These included words such as *arret* for 'water'. When linguists later compared the word list to Qawasqar, the language later attested in the area, they found so few similarities that they concluded that Aksanas must have been a now extinct isolate, i.e. a language unrelated to anything else. In Qawasqar, water is *čafalai*. But 'bucket' in this language is *aret*, and sure enough, it turned out that Guilbaudière had elicited the word by showing a bucket of water to the natives. In other words, Aksanas was simply Qawasqar—properly spoken but badly understood.

THEY SPEAK **WHAT?!**

One language which, curiously enough, is only spoken outside of Belgium is "Belgian". In Philippine censuses, this mysterious language is listed as having 200 or so speakers. Belgians, on the other hand, tend to speak Dutch (Flemish), French (Walloon) or German. The 1961 census of India also listed 42 native speakers of "Belgian" but this was surpassed by "African" (118 speakers), "Canadian" (77), "Swiss" (75) and "American" (45). Other non-existent tongues encountered in the same census are "European", "Lebanonese" [sic], "Austrian", "Australian", "Brazil", "Siberian", "Nigerian" and "Eurasian".

The 1927 census of Turkey listed 68 900 speakers of "Jewish". Meanwhile, several censuses from Mauritius have included speakers of "Moslem".

Finally, Illinois is sometimes mentioned as the first U S state to legislate on English as the official state language. Less often mentioned, however, is the fact that the 1923 law in question actually officialized "American" rather than English (pp 31–32).

ORIGINS OF LANGUAGE NAMES

Many a language (such as most of those in Europe) is simply named for the place where it is spoken, or for the relevant ethnonym, i.e. the name of the people who speaks it. The origin of this, in turn, may or may not be known. The most common source for ethnonyms is possibly just a word meaning something like 'people', 'our people' or the like. Quite a few languages are also simply named 'language'

Language names meaning '(our) people', '(our) language', 'of (our) land' or the like:

Ainu	Japan		**Oromo**	Ethiopia
Ama	Sudan		**Yolngu-Matha**	[=Dhangu] Australia
Gilyak	Russia		**Kiowa**	USA
Wari'	Brazil		**Maia**	Papua New Guinea
Ngiyampaa	[=Wayilwan] Australia		**Maiani**	Papua New Guinea
Inuit	Greenland, Canada		**Yeidji**	[=Wunambal] Australia
Yámana	Chile		**Gujingalia**	[=Burarra] Australia
Lyase	[=Gwamhi-Wuri] Nigeria		**Beothuk**	Formerly in Newfoundland, Canada
Dâw	Brazil		**Lenape**	[=Delaware] USA
Diné	[=Apache + Navajo] USA		**Meänkieli**	Finnish dialect in northern Sweden
O'odham	[=Papago and Pima] USA		**Guugu Yimidhirr**	Australia
Maidu	USA		**Wintun**	USA
Khanty	Russia		**Yana**	USA
Papiamentu	Netherlands Antilles		**Dunne-za**	[=Beaver] Canada
Done	[=Dogrib] Canada		**Khowar**	Pakistan
Yanomamö	Venezuela		**Nanai**	Russia
Ket	Russia		**Unserdeutsch**	German semi-creole, New Guinea

Other languages are not content being simply 'the language', but prefer to underline that they are the *'real* language'—presumably as opposed to less human-like grunts produced by the barbarians in the vicinity. This is the etymology of Enets, Nenets and Nganasan of Russia, and Tsimshian of the USA. Clearly, speakers of these tongues are not the only ones having high thoughts about their own language:

Nheengatu	=Língua Geral, Brazil	'good speech'
Ləʁ'oravetl'en	=Chikchi, Russia	'proper person'
Sanskrit	India	'the perfected language'

Híaitíihí	=Pirahã, Brazil	'the straight ones'
Nahuatl	Mexico	'the pristine, transparent, pure, agreeable-sounding language'
Caddo	USA	'true chiefs'

Other languages have certainly or possibly been named by more or less benevolent neighboring peoples:

Tigak	Papua New Guinea	'my brother'
Tungag	Papua New Guinea	'my brother'
Chin	Burma	Burmese for 'friend'
Dakota	USA	'friends' or 'allies'
Hebrew	Israel	Ancient Hebrew 'ibr8 'from the other side of the river' (via Aramaic, Greek and Latin)
Mbitse	[=Tiv] Nigeria	Jukun for 'strangers'
Welsh	Britain	Anglo-Saxon for 'foreigner'
Tayo	New Caledonia	Tahitian for 'friend'
Puyallup	[a dialect of Salish] USA	'the generous ones'
Hakka	China	Cantonese for 'guests'
Yuki	USA	Wintun for 'stranger'

Words related to *Welsh* have been applied to several peoples and languages in various parts of Europe), and what is thought to be the same root is also found in Walloon (Belgium) and Valachia (Romania) and in the German *Rotwelsch*.

Not everybody regarded their neighbors as 'friends' or 'allies', and so, the name bestowed on you or your language by foreigners is by no means always flattering:

Berber	North Africa	'Barbarian'
Otomi	Mexico	Nahuatl for 'Barbarian'
Chontal	Mexico	Nahuatl for 'foreigner'
Auca	[=Waorani] Ecuador	Quechua for 'savage'
Sakai	[=Semai] Malaysia	Khmer for 'slave'
Atakapa	USA	Choctaw for 'man eaters'
Tsonga	Mozambique, South Africa	Zulu for 'vassal'
Apache	USA	Zuni for 'enemy'
Gros Ventre	USA	French for 'big belly'
Popoluca	Central America	Nahuatl for 'to babble, to speak unintelligibly'.
Malecite	Canada	Micmac for 'the one(s) who speak imperfectly'
Guarayu	[several languages] Bolivia	'savage'
Cœur d'Alene	USA	French for 'awl heart'; these Indians had a reputation for sharp bargaining with fur traders.
Eskimo	[=Inuktitut] Canada, Greenland	'speaking a foreign language' in several Algonquian languages. The well-known purported meaning 'eaters of raw meat' is apparently unfounded.
Talieng	Laos	'head-hunters'

Xifan	[=Tibetan] *Tibet*	Chinese for 'western barbarian'
Macusa	[=Carabayo] *Colombia*	'savage'
Loucheux	*Canada*	French for 'cross-eyed'
Tapuya ~ Tapuia ~ Tapuyo	several languages of *Brazil*	Tupí for 'enemy'
Abor	[=Adi] *India*	'unruly'

One category of language names are based on utterances made in the language itself:

Kalenjin	*Kenya*	'I tell you'
Fanakalo	*South Africa*	'do it like this'
Yitayita	*Australia*	'no, no'
Yorta Yorta	*Australia*	'no, no'
Langue d'Oc	[=Occitan] *France*	'yes-language' (cf *langue d'oïl* [=*oui*], which is French)
Morwap	[=Elseng] *West Papua*	'what is that?'
Lemko	[=Rusyn] *Poland*	from *lem* 'only'
Wembawemba	*Australia*	'no, no'

A number of language names simply refer to the geographical location, or physical or occupational characteristics of the speakers. Typical meanings include 'shepherds', 'reindeer owners', 'long ears', 'pygmies', 'easterners', 'islanders' and 'mountain dwellers'. Some, such as Urdu 'camp' (i.e. 'the language of the military camps'—incidentally, the word is related to English horde) bear witness of the language's birth. Some of the more suggestive names in this category are the following:

A língua de Aurá e de Aurê	*Pará, Brazil*	*'the language of Aurá and Aurê'—the only two speakers of the language when it was "discovered" in the 1980s.*
Miao-Yao languages	*China, S E Asia*	The various languages/dialects are often designated according to the traditional colors and designs of cloth. Thus, there are (in English translation) e.g. the White, Blue and Green Miao, but also the Striped, Small Flowery and Flowery Variegated Miao.
Kazakh	*Kazakhstan*	'adventurer, vagabond, free man' (cf *Cossack*).
Mixtec	*Mexico*	'cloud people'.
Huron	*USA, Canada* (extinct)	French for 'boar's head', allegedly referring to the distinctive Huron haircut.
Negerhollands	*Virgin Islands* (extinct)	'Negro Dutch'.
Tuscarora	*USA, Canada*	'hemp-gatherers'
Big Nambas, Small Nambas	*Vanuatu*	A 'namba' is a penis sheath. And among the Big Nambas, they are bigger. The sheaths, that is.
Bislama	*Vanuatu*	French *bêche-de-mer* 'sea cucumber', the trade in which was associated with the use of the language.

Karankawa	*USA*	Comecrudo for 'dog lovers'.
Zirekhgeran	[=Dargwa] *Caucasia*	'makers of chain mail'.
Nyamwezi	*Tanzania*	Swahili for 'people who shit the moon' (!).

At least four languages are—directly or indirectly—named for individuals. Thompson, spoken in North-western USA is named for a nearby river, which in turn owes its name to the explorer David Thompson. The same relation holds between Darling of Australia, the River Darling and the British governor of New South Wales, Sir Ralph Darling.

Uzbek, spoken in Uzbekistan and Afghanistan, incorporates the name of the 14th century ruler Uzbek Khan. The artificial language Esperanto also belongs in this category, for the language name, which means '(the one) who hopes' was originally the *nom de plume* of Ludwig Zamenhof, the creator of the language. Zamenhof himself simply called his brainchild *La internacia lingvo* 'the international language', but his pseudonym was later applied to the language itself.

USELESS BONUS INFORMATION 1

Malayalam (spoken in the Indian state of Kerala) is most probably the longest language name which is also a palindrome, that is, which can be read both forwards and backwards (at least insofar as we are talking about the written version of the name).

USELESS BONUS INFORMATION 2

A dogma of modern linguistics is that all languages are equally expressive, and that everything can be said in any language. Nonetheless, it has been claimed that the following languages are particularly well suited for . . .

Elegies and laments	Alas, Vale, Waling
Singing Celtic music	Enya
Talking about family	Mama, Papi
Talking about talking	Meta
Talking about business	Pay, Gold, Big Nambas
Criticizing modern art	Pomo
Writing vampire stories	Fang
Arranging transportation	Car, Van
Swearing	Dogon, Dama, Geez
Fawning	Bothlik
Denials	Non
Endless repetition	More
Making jokes	Ha, Hehe, Silisili, Bozo, Mok, Riff
Egotism	Moi, Brat, Gimme

Talking about golf	Fore, Chip
Inciting riots	Eggon, A Mok
Love and sex	Darling, Libido, Kis
Pornography	Karas, Bare, Anal, Duit, Bagarmi
Apologizing for lists like this	Sari

SOURCES NOT MENTIONED IN THE TEXT

Glossonyms in general: The origins of language names in general builds partly on information from the *Ethnologue* and Dalby (1999), but complemented from a large number of reference grammars and other sources. Particularly rewarding sources include Farfán (2001), Katzner (1994), Dalby (1998), Dixon & Aikhenvald (eds) (1999), Miller (1999), Konstantin (2002), and Campbell (1997). Names of pidgins and creoles from my own work on these languages.

Names of some Tibeto-Burman languages: van Driem (1993).

Guilbaudière's encounter with the Fuegans: Campbell (1997:14).

Speakers of "Belgian" in the Philippines: Kelz (2001).

Jewish in Turkey: Balçık (2000).

Muslim in Mauritius: the actual census.

American in Illinois: Baron (1982).

Useless bonus information 2: This is based (with a few additions from myself) on an anonymous e-mail message circulated among linguists. Unfortunately, I have not been able to trace the name of the original author.

SPEECH SOUNDS

SPEECH SOUNDS are studied by both phoneticians and phonologists.

Phoneticians are mainly interested in the nature and means of production of the actual sounds which occur in speech. They use the symbols of the International Phonetic Alphabet (IPA) to transcribe these. IPA transcriptions are normally written between square brackets. For example IPA [tʰiːθ] represents a typical pronunciation of English 'teeth'. The small raised h indicates that the initial t is aspirated (see p 262), the colon marks the i as a long vowel, and the Greek letter theta corresponds to the final *th* sound in this word.

Phonologists are primarily concerned with the organization and functions of sounds in languages. A key concept for them is that of the phoneme. A phoneme is a speech sound that does not in itself carry meaning, but which enables us to distinguish between two otherwise identical words which mean different things. For instance, English *beat* /biːt/ and *boot* /buːt/ both begin with a *b* sound and end with the sound of *t*. The only sounds which allow us to distinguish between them are their contrasting vowels, /iː/ in *beat* and /uː/ in *boot*. *Beat* and *boot* constitute a *minimal pair,* which proves that /iː/ and /uː/ are phonemes. Phonemic transcriptions are conventionally written between slashes, as here. On the other hand, the different kinds of /l/ that you hear in 'leak' (with spread lips) and 'cool' (with rounded lips) are not phonemic, since they are mere variants (or allophones) of the same phoneme. The phonetician could transcribe these words as [liːk] and [kuːɫ] but, as there are no English words whose meanings are distinguished on the basis of this difference, the phonemic representation of the /l/ can be the same in both cases.

The average number of phonemes in human languages is around 30.

LARGEST PHONEMIC INVENTORY

The largest known phoneme inventory is that of !Xũ) (yes, it *is* spelt that way!), which is spoken by about 5 000 people on the border between Angola and Namibia. It is claimed to have no less than 141 phonemes, many of them clicks.

One might argue, however, as does Nettle (1999:143), that each vowel, or tone-bearing unit should be counted separately for every tone it can be associated with. If you go along with that proposal, then Vute, a Niger-Congo language of Cameroon is your candidate, with 195 phonemes.

SMALLEST PHONEMIC INVENTORY

The smallest phonemic inventory of a human language is probably that of Pirahã, a little-known language spoken by a couple of hundred people in the Amazonas. Pirahã has three vowels (/a, i, o/) and only eight consonants (/p, t, k, ʔ, b, g, s, h/). It thus has eleven phonemes, which would put it on par with its close relative Múra and with Rotokas of Melanesia and some Western Lakes Plain languages of New Guinea such as Obukuitai (Foley 2000:367). However, as spoken by women, Pirahã lacks the /s/ of men's speech and uses /h/ in its place. As this replacement is not entirely consistent, one might still argue that even women's Pirahã has eleven phonemes rather than ten. But, depending on one's analysis, [k] could be seen as an allophone of /hi/, in which case Pirahã would still have a phoneme inventory of only ten—undoubtedly a world record.

MOST COMPLEX PHONEME

Willerman (1994) uses a biomechanical metric to evaluate the articulatory complexity of various speech sounds. Of the several hundred phonemes evaluated on a scale ranging from 0 to 6, the following phonemes were judged the most articulatorily complex:

- glottalized nasalized velarized voiceless dental affricated click
- glottalized velarized voiced dental affricated click
- nazalized breathy voiced dental affricated click
- glottalized nasalized velarized voiceless palatal lateral affricated click
- glottalized velarized voiced palatal lateral affricated click
- breathy nasalized voiced palatal lateral affricated click

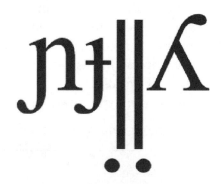

Don't try this at home, kids—it is one of the six most complex phonemes around. Before attempting this, consult your local phonetician or the resident Bushman of your area.

SOURCES NOT MENTIONED IN THE TEXT

Segment inventories in general: UPSID, unless otherwise noted.
Pirahã phoneme inventory: Aikhenvald & Dixon (1999:354-55).
Western Lakes Plain languages of New Guinea such as Obokuitai: Foley (2000:367).
Most complex phonemes: Willerman (1994:185-86).

CONSONANTS

CONSONANTS ARE—as opposed to vowels—speech sounds whose production involves an obstruction of the air stream. When some part of the speech apparatus—such as the tongue or the lips—partly blocks the stream of air, sounds like /k/, /s/ and /r/ are produced. Most of the world's languages have far more consonants than vowels in their phonemic inventory.

CONSONANTS

!Xũ) has not only has the largest documented phonemic inventory, but also the highest number of consonants, 117.

It has been claimed that Ubykh had at least 78 consonants and perhaps as many as 83 (depending on the analysis) but only two vowels, and thereby the highest consonant-to-vowel ratio. The language is now extinct, the last speaker having died in October 1992.

Haida is also remarkable in having 46 consonants and just three vowels. Other languages with unusually high ratios are found mainly in North America and the Caucasus.

Rotokas of Melanesia make s do with a mere six consonants.

PLOSIVES

Plosives (or stops) are consonants which are produced by first building up air pressure, and then releasing it. English has six plosives: /p/, /t/, /k/, /b/, /d/ and /g/.

Igbo has 22 plosives, and Lai has 20. I know of no language that lacks plosives altogether, the smallest number known being just three in Hawaiian. While the Igbo inventory benefits from several secondary articulations, various Australian and Dravidian languages have as many as six different places of articulation of plosives (again compared to a mere three in English).

Another language with a rich inventory of plosives is Yele (Yeletnye), in which secondary articulations yield no less than seven unvoiced bilabial stops, viz. /p, pʷ, pʲ, ᵐp, pᵐ, ᵗp, ᵏp/.

The ancestor of the Lakes Plains languages of West Papua has been reconstructed as having only five consonants—all of them plosives! This consonant inventory consisting of only /p, t, k, b, d/ survives in some of its daughters.

FRICATIVES

Fricatives are "hissing" sounds such as /f/, /v/, /s/ and /z/. In addition to these, English also has /θ/ (as in **thi**stle), /ð/ (as in **this**'ll), /ʃ/ (as in **sheep**), /ʒ/ (as in **treasure**) and /ɹ/ (as in **round**).

Archi (in the Caucasus) has 31 fricatives, and indeed, almost all phonemic inventories with more than a dozen fricatives are found in the Caucasus region. About one language in ten has no fricatives at all, most of which are spoken in Australia, New Guinea and South America.

AFFRICATES

Affricates are phonemes which combine the occlusion of a plosive with the "hissing" of a fricative, such as the /tʃ/ of **cheap** and the /dʒ/ in **bridge**. Archi has 24 affricates. About one language in three has no affricates at all.

CLICKS

Clicks are very rarely used as phonemes, though we all produce them once in a while. The click /!/, for instance is the sound you might make when you want to imitate a cork coming out of a bottle, while /|/ is the sound normally transcribed in English as "tut-tut" or "tsk-tsk". /‖/ is what you'd say to a horse to get it going.

!Xũ) not only has the world's biggest phoneme inventory and the largest arsenal of consonants, but also the largest number of clicks—it has no less than 48 of them! Clicks are basically only found in southern and eastern Africa, although the Damin register of Lardil in Australia (see p 2) also makes use of them.

In December 2002, the American communications company Ricoh created a minor outrage among linguists. In their advertisements, they had made use of a Bushman Chief, explaining how he could communicate with "a series of simple clicking sounds", enabling him to "teach a force of 500 men to hunt, to cure disease, even how to find an appropriate mate". Of course, the clicks are phonemes which are *part of* certain languages, rather than being the languages themselves. Many linguists felt that the Ricoh ad reinforced popular beliefs that some languages are more primitive than others, consisting merely of strange grunts and barely human sounds. Many of us contacted Ricoh on the subject—but without getting any reaction whatsoever.

LIQUIDS

Liquids are basically "r-like" (*rhotics*) and "l-like" (*laterals*) sounds. Phonemes produced with the vibration of the Spanish or Scots /r/ are known as trills.

Iwaidja of Australia has eight or nine liquids, including three rhotics and five or six laterals.

Several Athabaskan languages of Yukon and the western Northwest Territories in Canada also have five laterals, as does Tlingit of Alaska, and Navajo (which is possibly a distant relative). Yet, the highest number of laterals is found in a language in otherwise less exotic Europe, for Muasdale Gaelic on the Isle of Arran in Scotland has been reported to sport no less than six. A similar number of trills is encountered in Toda, a Dravidian language of India. It has trills with three different places of articulation (fronted alveolar, alveolar and retroflex), each of which comes in a palatalized and a non-palatalized version.

For the reconstructed proto-North Caucasian, an inventory of no less than 35 laterals has been proposed!

About one language in four has no trills at all.

Speaking of trills—British phonetician John Laver is said to be the man behind the ultimate linguistic party trick. He has been witnessed producing four trills at once, viz. a labial, an apical, a uvular and an epiglottal trill. As one initiated observer puts it, "by this time one wonders if something might come loose with all the vibrations (but it never does)".

ODD TRILL REALIZATION

Czech is one of only two languages known to have a laminal /r/ (made with the tongue-blade rather than with the apex). It derives from a palatalized /rʲ/ which still survives in e.g. Russian.

BILABIALS

Bilabials are made with both lips in contact with one another. Typical representatives are /p/, /b/ and /m/.

Of the 451 languages in the UPSID database, 450 have bilabial phonemes, whereas one does not. This is Wichita, an almost extinct language of the USA. At the other end of the spectrum is Igbo, which has eleven bilabials.

A colleague of mine once asked whether languages whose speakers use lip-plates contain bilabials. Well, apparently, they do, although for the individuals so adorned, pronouncing them is no picnic. One such language has been examined from precisely this viewpoint, namely Suri of south-western Ethiopia (an area which is a stronghold of this tradition). Suri has three bilabial phonemes, /b/, /ɓ/, /m/, and marginally also /p/. Among speakers with lip-plates, these are replaced by other sounds, e.g. [ŋ] and [d] for /m/ and /b/ respectively.

For some people, bilabials just don't come naturally

NASALS

Nasals consonants involve a stream of air let out through the nose. Phonemes belonging to this class include /m/ and /n/ and /ŋ/ (as in si**ng**).

Mazahua (of North America) has no less than 7 nasal consonants, something that few other languages match. The Siberian language Khanty comes close in having six nasals.

One language in 30 has no nasals at all, most of which are spoken in South America. Many Australian languages have up to six different places of articulation of nasals, as compared to the mere three in English.

Kaingang, a Southern Jê language spoken in south-eastern Brazil, has nasal consonants which, depending on the environment, may start and end as plosives, but which contain a nasal medial element. The word kanɛɾ 'smooth' is thus phonetically realized as [kadndɛɾɛ].

Nenets of northern Russia has the unusual possibility of nasalising its glottal stops, as in to^{ŋʔ} 'lake's' ~ to^ʔ 'lakes'.

PHARYNGEALS

Pharyngeals are formed further back in the mouth than e.g. /k/, but not as far back as e.g. /h/. English has no pharyngeals.

Columbian Salish, spoken in Canada's British Columbia has no less than six pharyngeal phonemes: /ħ, ħ^w, ʕ, ʕ^w, ʕʔ, ʕʔ^w/.

AMAZONIAN ODDITIES

From his 1994 fieldwork in Brazil, linguist Dan Everett was able to report on a most unusual sound. The languages Wari' and Oro-Win both have a dozen or so words containing [tʙ̥] (e.g. Wari' [tʙ̥um] 'to be green'), that is a dental stop accompanied by a voiceless bi-labial trill. (This is otherwise known only from Abkhaz, in the Caucasus.) In the same area, Pirahã also has another unusual sound—a flap *"in which the tongue tip hits the alveolar ridge, and then (coming out of the mouth) the lower lip"*.

SOURCES NOT MENTIONED IN THE TEXT

Ubykh: Campbell (1991:1401).
Dravidian languages in general: Steever (1990:233).
Yele/Yeletnye: Lynch (1998:88).
Reconstructed proto-Lakes Plain: Clouse (1997) via Anthony Grant (p c).
Daughters of Lakes Plains languages: Foley (2000:364).
Iwaidja: Plank (2000).
Athabaskan: Sherzer (1973:761).
Navajo and Tlingit: Mithun (1999:17).
Muasdale Gaelic: Anthony Grant (p c).
Toda: Plank (2003).

Laterals in proto-North Caucasian: The work of Nikolayev & Starostin cited in Hewitt (2005:140).

The ultimate phonetic party trick: John Ohala (p c).

Czech: Plank (2000).

Lip-plate speech in Suri: Yigezu (2001).

Khanty: Abondolo (1998c:363).

Australian languages in general: Dixon (1980:135).

Kaingang: Rodrigues (1999b:179).

Nasalisation in Nenets: Comrie (1981:117).

Columbian Salish: Mithun (1999:17-18).

Wari' and Oro-Win: (Ladefoged & Everett 1996).

Abkhaz: *Linguist List* 8.45.

VOWELS AND DIPHTHONGS

A VOWEL is a phoneme which is uttered without any constriction that disturbs the air flow. Typical vowels are e.g. /a/, /i/ and /u/, all of which can easily be uttered in isolation.

VOWELS

The vowel-wise most well-endowed language in the UPSID database is Kashmiri, which has 28 phonemic vowels. The largest *proportion* of vowels in the phoneme inventory is to be found in Klao (16 vowels and 9 consonants). Also, one possible analysis of the Middle Taz Selkup (Uralic) phoneme inventory is that there are 25 vowels and 16 consonants.

Only about 3% of the world's languages have more vowels than consonants. Although rich vowel inventories are characteristic of e.g. Scandinavia and New Caledonia, most languages with an exceptionally high vowel-to-consonant ratio are spoken in South America.

Iau, a language with 400 speakers of Western New Guinea has a phoneme inventory which is not only unusually small (13 phonemes), but one that is also odd in having more vowels (7) than consonants (6). As if this weren't enough, the vowel system has a rather eccentric organization, consisting of /ɪ, i, ɪ, ɛ, ʊ, ʊ, o, ɑ)/.

Some languages, e.g. Yimas, have a mere two vowels, and as we shall see, others have been proposed to lack phonemic vowels altogether.

It should be noted here that the UPSID generally does not take vowel length into account, something which could make numbers increase considerably in some languages. Under such an analysis, Koromfé of Burkina Faso would have no less than 40 vowels.

NASAL VOWELS

Between a quarter and a fifth of the world's languages have nasal vowels in addition to a set of oral ones. With its 13 nasal vowels (and 15 oral ones), Kashmiri would seem to be the language with the largest number of phonemic nasal vowels. While many a language, such as Irish, has phonemic nasal counterparts of all its vowels, probably no language has more nasal than oral vowels.

Koyra Chiini Songhay comes close, though. To the extent that it has 10 oral vowels against 9 nasal ones, it behaves normally. However, through borrowings from French, /æ̃/ has been introduced, and if only short vowels are counted, Koyra Chiini Songhay has six nasal and five oral vowels.

Its mirror image is found in the geographically not too distant Maba, which has twelve oral vowel qualities, but only one nasal vowel, namely /ũ/.

Wari' is also unusual in this respect. Its six oral vowels and two oral diphthongs contrast with eight nasal diphthongs—but the language has no nasal monophthongs.

Palantla Chinanteco of Mexico not only has oral and nasal vowels, but also a third category of *partly* nasalized vowels. Minimal triplets include the following:

> A nasal vowel is a vowel produced in a manner in which parts of the air flow is let out through the nose. This is a conspicuous feature of e.g. French, and you can hear two to four (depending on what variety of French you're listening to) different nasal vowels in the phrase un bon vin blanc 'a good white wine'. A non-nasal vowel, such those of English, is oral.

/ʔe³²/ 'leach' [sic]	/ʔẽ³²/ 'to count'	/ʔẹ̃³²/ 'to chase'
/ha³²/ 'so much'	/hã³²/ 'he opens it wide'	/hạ̃³²/ 'foam'

It is reported that Mahou, a Mande language of the north-west Ivory Coast exhibits a similar three-way contrast, though its semi-nasalized vowel should possibly rather be described as a diphthong containing one oral and one nasal element.

DIPHTHONGS

> A diphthong consists of a vowel and a semi-vowel. A semi-vowel is a sound which basically has the phonetic properties of a vowel without functioning as one. Thus a diphthong behaves in many ways as if it were a vowel.

Parauk (spoken in southern China, in Burma and Thailand) has 25 diphthongs, and this is the highest number that I have come across.

The variety of Dutch spoken in Maastricht is possibly unique in distinguishing between on the one hand diphthongs, and on the other hand sequences of vowel + semi-vowel. A minimal pair is [kœːʲ] 'billiard cue' versus [kœːj] 'cows'.

VOICELESS VOWELS

Vowels are normally produced with voicing. In contact with voiceless phonemes, they may occasionally be devoiced, but it is exceedingly rare for languages to include vowels which are underlyingly voiceless. Languages for which such segments have been proposed are Ik, Nisi, Comanche, Sandawe and Proto-Keresan. It appears, however, that their status is debatable in most, if not all, of these languages.

LANGUAGES WITHOUT VOWELS?

Kabardian, a Caucasian language with some 650 000 speakers was claimed by Allen (1956) to have one and only one vowel. Kuipers (1960:104) took this one step further, and suggested that Kabardian, as well as its neighbor Abaza (45 000 speakers) were completely vowel-less. This, however, was contested by Szemerényi (1967), Halle (1970) and Kumakhov (1973). Most observers now seem to postulate at least two or three phonemic vowels for Kabardian, and often as many as seven.

Of course, the suggested vowel-lessness of Kabardian concerns the phonological level. Whatever the number of underlying vowels, a great deal of allophones are present, and it does thus not necessarily give the listener an impression of hearing a language particularly poor in vowels. Before coronal consonants vowels are fronted, before uvular consonants they are retracted, before palatals they are raised, and before labial consonants they are rounded.

As a result of Kuipers' work, linguists sometimes joke about there being national holiday in Kabardia called 'Vowel Day', on which the inhabitants dress up, and gather to solemnly pronounce the Ritual Vowel, as a 'gesture of solidarity with the rest of the human race'. (The joke originated, it seems, with Jim McCawley).

Another language which has been proposed to be vowel-less is Proto-Wakashan.

In any case, a bias towards consonants in the phoneme inventory is indeed an areal feature of Caucasian languages. Ubykh, for instance, is said to have no less than 78 consonants (admittedly, three of these occur only in loanwords), and only two vowels. A couple of other languages have been suggested to have only one underlying vowel phoneme, including Tonkawa, Yuman languages, and Iatmul of New Guinea.

It may be some consolation that at least Ubykh has an inclination towards CV syllables, and its consonant clusters are more benign than one might think. Nevertheless, the sound of the language has been described as "pebbles on a marble floor".

MOST DIFFICULT-TO-DETERMINE VOWEL SYSTEM

The vowel system of Marshallese, a language of Micronesia, has been argued by certain observers to have three phonemic vowels. The official spelling, however, recognizes nine, and other analysts have suggested that the number should be adjusted to 12, or even 24.

FRONT AND BACK VOWELS

Languages normally have a front and a back vowel series, where the latter is produced with lip rounding, and the former without it. This is for acoustic reasons—it simply makes the two series easier to tell apart. Now, if this system is expanded, a front rounded series may be added. Only about 7% of the world's languages have opted for this, but it is rather common in Europe and parts of Asia, and found in languages such as French, German, Dutch, Scandinavian languages, Finnish, Turkish, and Hungarian. More uncommon is the choice made by East Asian languages such as Vietnamese and Thai, which have two back (rounded and unrounded), but only one front vowel series.

The languages in the UPSID database with the highest number of back unrounded vowels (five) are Khmer, Bruu, Apinaye, of which the first two are spoken in south-east Asia. (Apinaye is used in Brazil).

Japanese is even more odd in having an unrounded (/ɯ/), but not a rounded version of the back high vowel. It should be noted that English too is unusual in this respect, featuring as it does, the back unrounded /ʌ/, but no front rounded vowels.

Two languages in the UPSID database have opted for all the extras. Breton and Highland Chinantec have not only front rounded *and* back unrounded vowels, but also nasal vowels.

THREE DEGREES OF LIP ROUNDING

As just indicated, lip rounding is not phonemic at all in most languages, although in some, rounded vowels contrast with their unrounded counterparts. To the best of my knowledge, however, only Swedish and Norwegian, make use of three degrees of lip rounding. A minimal triplet in Swedish is rita [riːta] 'to draw' ~ ryta [ryːta] 'to roar' ~ ruta [rʉta] 'square, box'. This analysis is not uncontroversial, though, as the distinction between the latter two is more commonly (but in my view less accurately) seen as a frontness distinction.

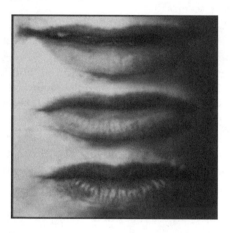

The three degrees of lip rounding in Scandinavian demonstrated by a native speaker with three mouths

---

RETROFLEXED VOWELS

Badaga, a language of Tamil Nadu in India seems to be the only language for which two degrees of retroflexion have been reported. A minimal triplet would be [beː] 'mouth' ~ [beˑ] 'bangle' ~ [be˞ˑ] 'crops'. Apparently, the three-way contrast is no longer upheld by a majority of the speakers.

SOURCES NOT MENTIONED IN THE TEXT

Middle Taz Selkup: Helimski (1998b:551).
Vowels in Koromfé: Haspelmath et al. (eds) (2005: map 10).

Iau: Hajek (2000:4, 6).

Nasal vowels in 22% of the world's languages: Maddieson (1984).

Yimas: Haspelmath et al. (eds.) (2005: map 2).

Nasal vowels in Koyra Chiini Songhay: Haspelmath et al. (eds) (2005: map 10).

Nasal vowels in Maba: Haspelmath et al. (eds) (2005: map 10).

Nasal vowels in Wari': Haspelmath et al. (eds) (2005: map 10).

Minimal triplets in Palantla Chinantec: Blevins (2004:203), Suárez (1983:47).

Mahou: *Linguist List* 5.1018.

Maastricht Dutch: Plank (2000).

Voiceless vowels: Blevins (2004:199), UPSID.

Ubykh: Campbell (1991:1401).

Kabardian and Abaza: Allen (1956), Crothers (1978:108-109), Halle (1970), Hewitt (2005:99), Kuipers (1960:104, 1968), Kumakhov (1973), Szemerényi (1967).

Proto-Wakashan: Coon (1995).

Tonkawa, Yuman, Iatmul: Brad Coon on the *Conlang* list 1997-07-11.

Marshallese vowel system: Dalby (1998:406-07).

Vietnamese: Nguyên (1990:54).

Thai: Hudak (1990:33).

Japanese: Shibatani (1990b:161).

Badaga: Emeneau (1939).

SYLLABLE STRUCTURE

LANGUAGES DIFFER not only in which sounds they employ, but also in their phonotactics, that is the possibilities of combining these into syllables. Almost all the world's languages have simple CV-syllables, that is consonants and vowels alternating, as in *mama* or *papa*. Not all languages, however, tolerate more than this.

The syllable is centred around a *nucleus*, usually a vowel. The part that comes before the nucleus is called the *onset*, and the part after it is the *coda*. A CV-syllable thus has a simple onset, and no coda. Although syllable nuclei are usually vowels, a number of languages also tolerate the more vowel-like consonants, such as nasals and liquids in this position. One such language is English, in words such as *bottle* (or, for that matter, *syllable*), where the last syllable is built around an /l/.

SIMPLE PHONOTACTICS

Languages with only or almost only CV-syllables are common in East Asia, the Pacific, parts of South America and Africa, but are also found elsewhere, and e.g. the Oto-Manguean languages of Central America are of this type. A language with such simple syllable structures must adapt words borrowed from languages with more liberal phonotactics. European loans in Japanese are well-known for this: a strike (in baseball) is *sutoraiku*, and a prêt-à-porter costume is *pereta-porute*.

As can be seen in the table below, the phonotactics drastically affects the number of possible syllables in a language, although the number of phonemes also plays a role.

Language	Main country	Syllables
Hawaiian	Hawaii	162
Rotokas	Papua New Guinea	350
Yoruba	Nigeria	582
Ewe	Togo	653
Gen	Togo	654
Aja	Togo	661
Tsou	Taiwan	968

Language	Main country	Syllables
Gã	Ghana	2 331
Mandarin	China	2 940
Cantonese	China	3 456
Quechua	Peru	4 068
Vietnamese	Vietnam	14 430
Thai	Thailand	23 638
Swedish	Sweden	»500 000

COMPLEX PHONOTACTICS

English permits syllable structures of above-average complexity, with up to three-consonant onsets (as in **strong**) and four-consonant codas (as in *sixths* /siksθs/). It is surpassed in this regard by rather few languages. One is of course Russian, which has words such as **ВЗГЛЯД** [vzglʲat] 'a look'. Another is Ancient Tibetan, which allowed onsets consisting of four consonants, as in **bsgr**ims 'to twist with a finger'. The same applies to Nambiquara of South America, whose words may also have onsets consisting of up to four consonants, as in /kwhʔākāʔlīsŭ/ 'a kind of deer'.

Caucasian languages have a reputation of being more fond of consonants than most others, and indeed, Georgian supplies words such as **mc'vrtn**eli 'trainer'. For readers able to identify with Georgian oranges in a fruit basket, **gvprckvn**is 'he peels us' is also a nice one.

Although onsets are usually more complex than codas in most languages, counter-examples are not difficult to find (English, as we have just seen, being one such case). While Swedish onsets function similarly to those in English, Swedish codas can be expanded into ridiculously clumsy clusters, as in *västku**stskt*** 'pertaining to the west coast' or *stockho**lmskt*** 'of Stockholm'. At least in theory, it is even possible to construct such words with eight final consonants. The tongue-twisting sentence to illustrate this is *Varför skulle ett Noréenskt hembiträdes förkläde vara smutsigare än ett Herbstskts?* 'Why should the apron of a maid of the Noréen family be dirtier than that of one of the Herbst family?'.

Although syllable complexity is often thought of as involving monstrous consonant clusters, it is also unusual to have syllable nuclei with more than two or three vowels. Kiribati is the only known language where a string of four vowels can be found in one and the same syllable. An example is the dimunitive suffix *-kaaei*.

VOWEL-LESS WORDS

Many languages which on the surface seem to have hideously complex syllables are in fact no worse than English. People often believe that syllables of Slavic languages are complex after having come across words such as Croatian *krv* 'blood', *crn* 'black', or the classic Czech tongue-twister *Strĉ prst skrz krk* 'stick your finger through your throat'. However, what we are seeing in these words is not complex onsets or codas, but rather the use of a consonantal nucleus. The lack of vowels simply makes the syllables look more complex than they actually are. Yet, this is not to say that the result isn't spectacular. In Bella Coola, words may be completely vowelless, and even stops may function as syllable nuclei (which is highly uncommon). Some examples include:

k'xct	*'they see you'*
qstẋ	*'pull it off!'*
p'x^wɬt	*'a kind of berry'*
q'psttẋ	*'taste it!'*
sc'qc tx	*'that's my fat over there'*
ɬ'p	*'to cut with scissors'*
c'ktc	*'I got there'*
mṇmṇts	*'children'*
nm̩lxaɬ	*'one's feet getting numb'*
k^wm̩ɬ	*'firewood'*

The daring may attempt to pronounce the vowelless Bella Coola sentence *xɬpʾχʷɬtɬpɬɬs kʷʃʾ*, which translates as 'Then he had in his possession a bunchberry plant'. Consonant crowding of this sort is typical of the languages of the area where Bella Coola is spoken, that is the American Pacific Northwest.

Berber languages are also frequently mentioned in these contexts, so I think it is worthwhile including some examples from Berber as well. Feel free to read aloud!

gwdm	'to turn upside down'	tfsχt	'you cancelled'
gwmr	'to hunt or fish'	tftχtstt	'you rolled it'
kkstt	'take it off'	tkkststt	'you took it off'
sfqqst	'irritate him'	θldi	'she pulls'
ssrksxt	'I hid him'	tnʃft	'you grazed the skin'
tˤtˤaf	'to hold'	tqssf	'it shrunk'
tˤtˤaṣˤ	'to sleep'	tskrt	'you did'
tˤtˤaʒin	'plate'	tsskʃft	'you made it dirty'
t3tbddal	'to exchange'	txznt	'you stored'
t3tsχχan	'to dip (in sauce)'	txtft	'you stole'
tʃtft	'you crushed'	xzr	'to give a look of anger or blame'
tfktstt	'you gave it'	tftktstt	'you sprained it'

It may also be worth noting in this context that American English is rather unusual by western standards in also having entire words (even polysyllabic ones) without vowels in them. As a non-native speaker faking British English, I would of course go for [bŒˇd] and [mŒˇdˊ] when pronouncing 'bird' and 'murder', but many Americans would render these as [bℝˋd] and [mℝˋdℝˋ] respectively.

PREFERRING THE UNUSUAL

As already mentioned above, CV is the universally most popular syllable structure. Yet, there are a few languages which shy away from this simple a solution. Instead, they only have, or at least prefer, VC. This applies to Arrernte and various dialects of Kunjen, spoken in Australia, but has also been reported for the Barra dialect of Scots Gaelic, spoken on the Outer Hebrides.

SOURCES NOT MENTIONED IN THE TEXT

Oto-Manguean CV-syllables: Campbell (1997:157).
Loanwords in Japanese: Shibatani (1990b).
Total number of possible syllables: Ewe, Gen and Aja from Lafage (1985:190), Mandarin based on Lyovin (1997:131-33), Swedish from Robert Eklund (p c), and the others from Maddieson (1984:22).
Ancient Tibetan syllables: Brush (1995).
Nambiquara onsets: Lowe (1999:272).

Georgian phonotactics: Comrie (1981:200).
Kiribati vowel clusters: Blevins (2004:213).
Words in Bella Coola: Olle Engstrand (p c), Mithun (1999:494).
Bunchberry plant sentence in Bella Coola: Mithun (1999:22).
Berber: Coleman (2001), Ridouane (2002a, 2002b, 2004), Dell & Elmedlaoui (1988).
Languages preferring VC syllables: Plank (2003).

SUPRASEGMENTALS

PHONOLOGICAL STRUCTURE does not begin and end with phonemes. On top of the phoneme string, there is also a more abstract varnish of *suprasegmentals*. Typical suprasegmental features are length and tone.

LENGTH

In all, about a fifth of all languages use length as a phonemic device. Some have not only long and short vowels, but distinguish three degrees of segment length. One such example is Estonian, which sports the minimal triplet /koli/ 'rubbish' ~ /koːli/ 'of (the) school' ~ /koːːli/ 'to (the) school'. Other languages reportedly of this type are Kalenjin and Agar Dinka of Africa, the North American Indian languages Chickasaw, Hopi, Yavapai, Gros Ventre, and Nootka and some Mixe languages of Mesoamerica, as well as Saami in northern Europe. A minimal triplet from El Paraíso Mixe is /ʔoj/ 'although' ~ /ʔoːj/ 'he went' ~/ʔoːːj/ 'very'.

Another African language, Kikamba, has even been reported to have four vowel lengths—short /V/, half-long /Vˑ/, long /Vː/, and extra-long /Vːː/ (where V stands for any vowel). Buin, spoken on Bougainville Island off New Guinea, has also been claimed to have a four-way distinction of vowel length. A fourth length has furthermore been proposed for Estonian, but its existence is doubtful.

Blevins (2004:201) considers Kikamba, Yurok, Applecross Scots Gaelic, and Hopi rather dubious cases. Features other than length are often involved in the distinctions, and the extra-long vowels in Yurok and Kikamba have been argued to belong to different syllables.

In any case, Estonian and Saami share the distinction of being the only known languages where both vowels and consonants come in three different lengths.

A language in which vowels can *phonetically* (as opposed to phonologically) be remarkably long is the Nigerian language Gokana. It has been argued to permit no less than six vowels in a row. An example provided by Larry Hyman (2001:162) is 'Who$_i$ said I woke him$_i$ up?', which in Gokana is realized thus:

mɛ́ɛ́ ɛ̀ kə m̄m̄ˋɪ kɛ̄ɛ̄-ɛ̄-ɛ̄-ɛ̄

As if that weren't enough, Hyman furthermore proposes that these six instances of /ɛ/ in fact derive from no less than eight underlying occurrences.

TONE

Tone is an areal feature of sub-Saharan Africa, South East Asia, and a few other parts of the world. Among Sinitic languages, the number of tones increases the further south one gets. Thus, while Mandarin only distinguishes four tones, Cantonese has no less than nine. Some dialects of Southern Dong, a Kadai language spoken in southwestern China, have been claimed to possess as many as 15 different tones. If this number seems too high, Mashan Hmong, a Hmong-Mien language of southern China is said to have 13 phonemic tones. Other languages in southern China with remarkably high number of tones include Cun (of the Tai-Kadai family) with 10 tones. Bu-Nao Bunu, spoken in the same area, is reported to have 8 to 11 tones, depending on the dialect.

The Mesoamerican Tlapanec has 10 tones in all, including three level tones, and 7 contours. For other parts of the world, Iau of Western New Guinea has the largest number of tones known to me. It has been claimed to have 8 tones, including two level tones (mid and high—there is apparently no low level tone!) and six contour tones. These tone distinctions form an important part of the encoding of tense, mood and aspect in the language.

According to Maddieson (1978:338), no language has more than five level tones (as opposed to contour tones). This is the number found in Mesoamerican languages such as Usila Chinantec and Chicahuaxtla Trique, and in the Ch'ing Chiang dialect of Hmong Daw in China and Ivorian Dan in West Africa.

BOTH TONE AND STRESS

Papiamentu, an Iberian-lexicon creole of the Caribbean one of very few languages to exploit both word stress and tone as distinctive features. Thus, *biàhá* 'to travel' and *biáhà* 'voyage' are distinguished by tone alone, but only stress can tell *Hesus ta 'pàsá* 'Jesus passes by' apart from *Hesus ta pà'sá* 'Jesus is a lunatic'.

The Melanesian language Ma'ya has also been reported to have both contrastive tone and contrastive stress.

If it weren't for the tones, some east Asian languages would have innumerable homophones—something of which there is certainly no shortage even today. Next time you come across a speaker of Lahu, you had better get the following words right (the superscript numbers indicate tone height):

ca^{33} 'to look for'	ca^{11} 'to feed'	ca^{21} 'to be ferocious'
ca^{35} 'to boil; to join'	ca^{44} 'rope'	ca^{22} 'to push'
	ca^{53} 'to eat'	

SINGING IN TONES

Singing in a tone language would seem to pose something of a problem. On the one hand, there are tones in the lyrics, the loss of which may impair understanding. On the other hand, the music is made up of tones. How is this potential conflict resolved? Sometimes, it apparently isn't, but for some tone languages, composing involves taking these factors into account, and talented composers and performers do succeed in combining the two tonal systems.

Cantonese is a language with up to nine tones (depending on the analysis). Tone in other words plays a crucial role in the language. To a great extent, the relative pitch levels and contours of the tones are actually preserved. One obvious way of accomplishing this is to adjust the entire register to the melody, and thus a certain tone is high or low only in relation to its neighboring tones, and need not have the same pitch as a comparable tone elsewhere in the song. Also, part of the secret is of course that the composer tries to choose words that go with the melody, or vice versa.

Things are a bit different in Mandarin, the most widely spoken Chinese language. In the Mandarin musical tradition, melodies are given greater importance at the expense of the lyrics. Also, of course, Mandarin only has four tones, so the problem is less acute in this case.

Needless to say, context can make up for some of the information lost when the lexical tones fail to match the music, so the result need not be utter gibberish. In most cases, it is presumably obvious in any case whether *xiang si* means 'to miss each other' (*xiang¹ si¹*) or 'to want to die' (*xiang³ si³*). Nevertheless, difficulties in understanding are reported, but luckily, lyrics are provided when it's karaoke time. Subtitles are also often added to televised performances of western-style music sung in Cantonese, since the conflict between the music and the tones would otherwise impair understanding.

In all fairness, it should be added that even spoken Mandarin is often subtitled, since speakers of Cantonese are generally more proficient in written than in spoken Mandarin.

WHISPERING AND SHOUTING SUPRASEGMENTALS

Tone languages would seem difficult not only to sing, but also to whisper, since whispering involves turning off the vocal cords. To some extent, once again, context becomes more important, and once again, ambiguities and misunderstandings are reported. But just like when the food in your mouth prevents you from performing all the tongue and jaw movements you'd otherwise do, the speech remains largely intelligible, partly because of compensatory maneuvers.

For one thing, voicing is often not entirely absent in whispering. Also, pitch is not the only phonetic correlate of high tones. Variation in loudness and length can to some extent provide the listener with compensatory cues.

An inverted problem of sorts occurs in Cheyenne. This language has a complex system for devoicing of vowels. Now, voiceless vowels cannot be shouted, and sure enough, speakers of Cheyenne revoice their breathy vowels on such occasions.

The same problems arise, of course, in non-tonal languages, provided they make use of voicing distinctions. And yet, even English is capable of being whispered.

SUBTLE SUPRASEGMENTAL DIFFERENCES

Mende of West Africa distinguishes between several types of possessive-like constructions only by means of tone and quantity. Thus, /kɔ́mi gɔmií/ is 'bee honey' in general, whereas /kɔmiî gɔmií/ is 'the bee's honey (that which the bee produces)'. The latter, however, must be distinguished from /kɔ́miî gɔmií/ 'the bee's honey (that which the bee has property rights to)'.

In Dinka, the suprasegmental morphology has been described as "rather elaborate". The following example contrasts constitute an appetizer:

à-wɛ́ɛ̀c	'You are kicking it hither'
à-wɛ̀ɛ̀c	'(S)he is kicking it hither'
à-wɛ̀ɛ̀c	'(S)he is kicking'

In Aymara of South America, segment length is involved in grammatical contrasts. It is used, for instance, to express future in the first, second and third persons (but not in the fourth, which Aymara also has).

As an aside, Aymara has only three vowels, but mixing them up can have serious consequences. One learner reports having mistakenly produced *Marintasipxañani* 'Let's commit suicide together!' instead of the intended *Mirintasipxañani* 'Let's have lunch together!'.

These are just a few examples—there are quite a number of languages which make use of similarly fine suprasegmental nuances.

SENTENCE INTONATION

Virtually all the world's languages ask polar questions (yes/no-questions) using a rising intonation. Zuni has been suggested to be the only or at least one of the few exceptions.

Another example is found in the Basque country. In the Lapurdian (*labourdin*) and Low Navarrese (*bas-navarrais*) dialects of Basque, spoken just north of the Pyrenees, a yes/no question is formed by suffixing the question particle *-a* to the finite verb. The resulting utterance is spoken with falling intonation. Other varieties of Basque do not use this question particle, and instead have rising intonation in yes/no questions.

ASPIRATION IN PALULA

Aspiration of stops, both voiced and voiceless, is quite common in the languages of the world, but aspiration of other phonemes is less so. In Palula, an Indic language spoken in northern Pakistan, though, not only stops but also most frica-tives, nasals and semi-vowels can be aspira-ted, with a resulting difference in meaning. So, for example, /tʃʰéj/ and /tʃéj/ form a minimal pair, meaning 'tea' and 'shade', re-spectively. The phonemic status of aspiration in Palula has, however, been questioned.

In some languages, among them English, voiceless stops are produced with an extra burst of air, unless immediately preceded by the fricative /s/. You can easily test this: hold a very thin piece of paper in front of your mouth and pronounce the words till and still. When pronouncing till, the paper will waft away from you, but when you say still it will barely move. In e.g. English, this so-called aspiration is an automatic phonetic process that native speakers are mostly unaware of—doing it the other way around sounds odd or non-native, but one would most probably identify the target word. In many other languages, aspirated and non-aspirated consonants are best described as different phonemes making all the difference between different words. Pronouncing the Swahili word tembo with an aspirated /tʰ/ means 'elephant', whereas pronouncing it with an unaspirated /t/ results in 'palm wine'.

Part of the story is that only one aspiration per word is allowed, for which reason aspiration can be seen as suprasegmental rather than an integrated part of its phonemic inventory.

NASALIZATION

In many languages, nasality spreads from nasals to otherwise oral segments in the vicinity. Usually, only immediately adjacent phonemes are affected. In Guaraní, this process is more extreme than in most other languages. If a word contains a single nasal element, *all* vowels (and some other segments) in the word are automatically nasalized. The only exception to this is the presence of a stressed oral vowel, which blocks the spread. Thus, /ndo-roi-ndu-'pãi/ 'I don't beat you' is phonetically realized as [nõrõĩnũ-'pãĩ].

MOST HIGH-PITCHED LANGAUGE

Very few studies have been made on the differences in voice fundamental (F_0) between various languages. In the first place, only a small number of non-European languages seem to have been studied with regard to average pitch. One of the few existing studies showed that conversational English (as opposed to English used in acting, which is at the very opposite end of the spectrum), Mandarin and Swedish are rather low-pitched, with French and German ranking somewhat higher. The most odd man out, however, is Wú (the language spoken in the Shanghai area), where the sole male speaker in the study had an average F_0 at a remarkably high 170 Hz. This may be compared to frequencies between 100 and 140 for most other men. Interestingly, Wú women speak with a rather low frequency—187 Hz, as compared to 180-240 for other female speakers. In the scarce material that is available, Wú is thus not only the language of the most high-pitched men, but also that with the least difference in F_0 between the sexes. There was, however, quite a lot of variation within the groups of Wú-speakers, possibly because of it being a tone language. The same also goes for Mandarin, but not for Swedish—despite the cliché of its sing-song intonation. As an aside, it can be noted that even within *relatively* homogenous languages, there may be dialectal differences with regard to pitch. Thus, it has been shown (and this time, on the basis of a more voluminous material) that northern Swedes on average have a lower F_0 than people from southern Sweden.

While much of the difference between men and women in this respect is obviously due to anatomical factors, it is clear that culture also plays a role. Another study shows a remarkable difference between Japanese women and men, with women's voices sometimes reaching tops at 400 Hz. It has also been noted, though, that the pitch of women's Japanese has dropped significantly among younger generations.

LOUDEST LANGUAGE

Nettle (1994) draws on a 1970 study where subjects were asked to speak to fellow countrymen at varying distances. Of the languages involved in the study, Turkish had the loudest speakers, followed by Arabic and Spanish. Speakers of Tagalog spoke most softly. Nettle's actual purpose with the article was to show that loud speech correlates with a small vowel inventory. Languages with few vowels, Nettle hypothesized, are less perceptually salient, and force their speakers to speak louder. The results are bound to give most people a too-good-to-be-true feeling, but Nettle's correlations did prove to be statistically significant.

SOURCES NOT MENTIONED IN THE TEXT

Tones in Hmong Daw and Dan: Plank (2003).
Length in 20% of the world's languages: Maddieson (1984).
Estonian length: Diana Krull (p c), Laakso (2001:187), Comrie (1981:116), Blevins (2004:201).
Kalenjin: Dalby (1998:297).
Minimal triplet in El Paraíso Mixe: Blevins (2004:201).
Three lengths in Hopi, Gros Ventre, and Agar Dinka: Hammarström (2002).
Chickasaw: Gordon, Munro & Ladefoged (2000).
Vowel length in Yavapai: Blevins (2004:201).
Vowel length in Nootka: Peter Bakker (p c).
Mixe length: Suárez (1983:34).
Length in Saami: Comrie (1981:116), Blevins (2004:201).
Kikamba length: Katamba (1983:59).
Buin: Hajek (2000:5).
Cantonese tones: Li & Thompson (1979:317), Li & Thompson (1990:87).
Southern Dong: Ramsey (1987:244).
Mashan Hmong, Bu-Nao Bunu, and Cun tones: *Ethnologue* 14.
Tlapanec: Suárez (1983:48).
Iau: Foley (2000:369).
Usila Chinantec: Suárez (1983:51).
Trique: Suárez (1983:51), Nettle (1999:143).
Papiamentu tone and stress: Rivera-Castillo (1998), Kouwenberg & Muysken (1994:208).
Ma'ya tone and stress: Remijsen (2002).

Lahu tones: Matisoff (2001:307).

Singing in tones: Chan (1987), *Linguist List* 8.567, Philip Baker (p c), Daniel Bunčić (p c).

Whispering and shouting suprasegmentals: *Linguist List* 8.567.

Mende tone: Spears (1967:272).

Dinka suprasegmental morphology: Dimmendaal (2000:177).

Aymara segment length: Hardman (2001:20).

Vowel confusion in learning Aymara: Ron Kephart on CreoLIST 1999-09-03.

Zuni intonation: Bolinger (1978:501).

Intonation in Basque dialects: Larry Trask (p c).

Aspiration in Palula: Laver (1994), Morgenstierne (1941), Henrik Liljegren (p c).

Nasalisation in Guaraní: Haspelmath et al. (eds) (2005: map 10).

F0 of various languages: Traunmüller & Eriksson (1993). Loveday (1981) and Kristof (1995), both as cited in Chan (1998).

F0 in Swedish dialects: Elert & Hammarberg (1991).

PARTS OF SPEECH

FOR MOST OF US, the first contact with the language sciences was when having to memorize parts of speech in school, which I suspect is responsible for some people's belief that linguistics is less sexy than it is. Having got this far in the book, the reader has presumably realized that there is more to linguistics than parts of speech. Now is the time to discover that there is more to parts of speech than your schoolteacher taught you.

LANGUAGES WITH NO PARTS OF SPEECH AT ALL?

Since parts of speech are often defined first and foremost on the basis of their morphological properties, it is to be expected that highly analytical languages, such as Classical Chinese are, as Norman (1988:87) puts it, "extremely resistant to any formal word class analysis".

Some other languages, mainly in North America, have been argued not to have any part-of-speech distinctions at all, at least not in the traditional sense. There may be derivational morphemes (often optional) which make things more or less "nouny" or "verby", but these can often be applied to any root. North American languages sometimes mentioned in this context include Coos, Tonkawa, Nootka, and Salish. The only valid distinction, it is suggested, would rather be between stems and less independent items, such as particles and affixes.

The same has been claimed to hold true for Tagalog and Mundari. While most or all of these cases have been disputed and/or refuted, the claim is indeed true for Esperanto. Although the latter is artificially constructed, it does have native speakers, and is at least in that sense on a par with "natural" languages. Esperanto takes this a step even further in allowing what are normally seen as affixes to function as roots. For instance, *bona*, means 'good', and can be equipped with various affixes to form other related words, such as *bonigi* 'to make something good' and **malbona** 'bad' (or **malbonigi** 'to make bad'). These affixes, however, can also stand on their own, so that *malo* means 'opposite' and *igi* is 'to make something, to turn something into'. Even though all morphemes may function as roots, they are for the most part explicitly marked according to what job they are doing in the particular context—the *-o* in *malo* signals nounhood, and the final *-i* in *igi* indicates that it is a verb.

SOURCES NOT MENTIONED IN THE TEXT

Classical Chinese: Norman (1988:87).
No parts of speech in North American languages: Mithun (1999:59-65).
For discussion of the lack of lexical categories in Nootka and Mundari, see e.g. Swadesh (1939), Jacobsen (1979), Evans & Osad (2005).

VERBS

VERBS ARE TYPICALLY—but far from always—words that denote actions. In most European languages (obviously including English), concepts such as *to have* and *to be* are expressed by verbs, despite not expressing actions. Together with nouns, verbs may be considered the most basic part of speech, and almost all languages have a class of words which could be described as "verby". Along with nouns, verbs typically constitute an open class, i.e. one which easily accepts new members.

FEW VERBS

In many languages of Australia and New Guinea, verbs do not constitute an open class, as they do in European languages. Instead, there is a small, closed class of verb stems, which combine with each other and with other linguistic material in order to express meanings encoded by verbs in more well-known languages. Thus, 'to laugh' is often expressed as 'laughter-do', where 'to do' is one of the few items that can actually be considered a verb. New Guinean languages such as Kuman, Kalam and Kobon are of this type, and reports have it that they contain a mere 100 verbs, of which only 25 are truly frequent. The verb inventories of several Australian languages are also around the 100 mark, with some languages, such as Walmajarri and Gurindji having between 30 and 40. Vedda (Sri Lanka) has a total of just 13 verbal morphemes, including separate verbs 'to be' for animates and inanimates. These are augmented by combining elements from pairs of morphemes within this basic set. Even lower numbers, however, seem to be found in languages of the Kimberleys/Daly River region, some of which are said to have only about a dozen monomorphemic verbs, and it has been claimed that Djingili even has as few as three verbs—*come, go* and *do*. These days, unfortunately, that is about as many as there are speakers of the language.

EXTENSIVE VERBAL SERIALIZATION

Many languages of West Africa, south-east Asia and Oceania have serial verb constructions. They fulfil pretty much the same task as do prepositions in European languages. Thus, sentences such as John went to town or Sarah wrote with a pen, could in these languages be expressed as John walked go town or Sarah took pen write. One of the most extensive verb cases serialization that I have encountered is that of the Papuan language Kalam, which allows five chained verbs. 'I fetched firewood' would then be expressed as *Yad am mon pk d ap ay-p-yn*, or literally 'I go wood hit hold come put COMPLETIVE ASPECT I'. Still, Khmer, Burmese and Vietnamese go beyond even this, as illustrated in the following Khmer sentence:

tɤ̀:p	stùh	tɤ̀:u	dëɲ	cap	yɔ̀:k	mɔ̀:k	ʔaop
Then	jump-up	go	follow	catch	take	come	hug

'Then, [she] jumped up, caught [the duck] and hugged it [after drawing it towards herself]'

Exceptionally, even longer chains are allowed in Kalam: a "conventional expression for 'massage'" is pk wyk d ap tan d ap yap g, which literally translates as 'strike rub hold come ascend hold come descend do'.

UNUSUALLY VERBY LANGAUGES

In the South American language Dâw, about 75% of the words in discourse are reported to be verbs. This might be expected if the language were polysynthetic, i.e. a language where entire sentences (to a westerner) may consist of a single verb with affixes. Although many of the surrounding languages are indeed polysynthetic, Dâw is not.

Many North American languages express by means of verbs what in European languages would typically come in the shape of nouns. For instance, Mithun's (1990:46-47) sample Tuscarora text includes 22 verbs (including *to be roasted maize*), but only two nouns. Languages of New Guinea have also been claimed to have a ratio of verbs to nouns which is at least somewhat higher than that found in European languages.

SOURCES NOT MENTIONED IN THE TEXT

Few verbs: Lynch (1998:175-77), Foley (1986:113, 1997:36-37), Dixon (1980:280).
Vedda: Philip Baker (p c).
Djingili: McWhorter (2001:48).
Serialisation in Kalam: Lynch (1998:176), Pawley (1993:88 in LaPolla 2005:14).
Serialisation in Khmer and Vietnamese: Bisang (1996:534).
The verby language Dâw: Martins & Martins (1999:265).
North American languages: Mithun (1990:46-53).
Verbiness of New Guinean languages (Foley 2000:387).

NOUNS

AFTER THE VERB, the noun is the most important and basic part-of-speech there is. While some languages make do without prepositions, adjectives and ideophones, it seems as if virtually all languages have 'something nouny' and 'something verby' in their repertoire. Yet, what we are accustomed to expressing by means of nouns isn't necessarily handled in the same way in other parts of the world.

NOUNS IN DIFFERENT LANGUAGES AND GENRES

In western languages at least, informal genres (typically spoken colloquial language) tend to contain higher proportions of nouns to verbs, while the opposite is true for written language, and in particular highly technical styles. The share of nouns is also slightly higher among men than among women. An interesting feature in Gustafson-Čapková's (2005:82-87) study is that radio plays are more "verby" than many samples of spontaneous real-life dialogues. The likely reason for this is that listeners can only be informed about actions through verbs in sentences spoken by actors. Thus, in a fight scene, a radio actor might say something such as "I'm going to punch you. Take that, you bastard!" whereas in real life (or a movie), no such dialogue would occur, apart perhaps from "you bastard!".

It is more difficult than one might think to compare the proportion of nouns in various languages. As we shall see, a language may well lack adjectives altogether, and can live happily with just a small set of verbs, and this alone could inflate the proportion of nouns in a running text considerably. On the other hand, an extreme instance of a polysynthetic language would incorporate much of what a westerner would consider nominal into the verb complex, thus making verbs dominant if we chose to count words (rather than morphemes).

For European languages, most studies show that nouns dominate among the earliest words acquired by children. Recent work on East Asian languages, however, indicate that verbs figure more prominently in child language there than they do in the western world. For at least Korean, this can be correlated with a higher proportion of verbs in caregiver speech.

In any case, nouns presumably constitute the most open class there is in the world's languages. Again, while they can make do with no or few adjectives and verbs, I know of no language where the category of nouns is finite—if nothing else, names of people, places, and recently introduced innovations would make the number virtually unlimited.

MOTHERING AND FATHERING

In the Yiwaidjan languages of Australia, as well as in Central Guerrero Nahuatl, Classical Chinese and in some North American Indian languages, kinship terms are normally not expressed by nouns, as we are accustomed to, but as verbs. Speakers of languages such as these would thus not say that *Donald Duck is the uncle of Huey, Dewey and Louie,* but rather that *He uncles them.*

SOURCES NOT MENTIONED IN THE TEXT

Nouns in western languages: Einarsson (1978), Melin & Lange (2000).
Acquisition of nouns in East Asia: Choi & Gopnik (1995), Tardif & Xu (1999).
Mothering and fathering: Plank (2004), Norman (1988:88).

ADJECTIVES

Europe is the only part of the world where virtually all languages have adjectives. Elsewhere, it is relatively common not to distinguish adjectives as a separate part of speech. Instead, 'the ball is red' can be expressed either with a noun (*the ball has redness*) or a verb (*the ball reds*). Dakota, Samoan, Acehnese, Salish, Korean and Mandarin are among the large number of languages which have been claimed to be devoid of adjectives.

LANGUAGES WITH FEW ADJECTIVES

In many languages—especially in India and Africa—adjectives do exist, but constitute (as opposed to the case in European languages) a closed class. The Nigerian language Igbo, for instance, does have adjectives, but only eight of them. Swedish Sign has around 15, Vedda has only three or four, while Toqabaqita, an Austronesian language spoken on the Solomon Islands, has been argued to have but one single adjective—meaning 'small'.

There is a striking similarity in what kind of properties are described by adjectives in languages with small closed adjective categories. This tendency is illustrated by Dixon (2003a:174):

> If you tell me that, working on a previously undescribed language, you have recognized a small class of, say, fifteen adjectives, I will be able to predict what their meanings are likely to be.

Investigating the meanings of the adjectives found in such systems, Dixon (1977) found that the most common ones were: 'large/big', 'small', 'long', 'short', 'new', 'old', 'good', 'bad', 'white' and 'black', more or less in this order.

SOURCES NOT MENTIONED IN THE TEXT

Adjectives in general: Dixon (1977, 1994), *Linguist List* 4.442.
Igbo adjectives: Green & Igwe (1963).
Swedish Sign: Inger Ahlgren (p c).
Vedda: Philip Baker (p c).
The lone To'abaita adjective: Lichtenberk (2005).

ADVERBS

Adverbs are words which modify adjectives, verbs and other adverbs, and which typically provide information regarding 'where?', 'when?' and 'how?'. In western languages, most adverbs are derived from adjectives (*slowly*), while a small group of highly frequent items (*soon, well, far, much*) are underived.

FEWEST ADVERBS

In many Australian languages, adverbs do not form a lexical category on any grounds other than semantic ones. That is, by most accounts, they lack a formally identifiable category of adverbs altogether.

ADVERBS BUT NO ADJECTIVES

Although languages may lack both adjectives and adverbs as distinct classes, the normal thing, if you have just one of these classes, is to have adjectives. Kambera of eastern Indonesia is the one exception to this generalization that I have come across. It has adverbs, but not a class of adjectives.

INTERROGATIVE PRO-VERBS

Most or all languages have interrogative pronouns, by means of which an NP can be questioned (*Mary read the book* → *Who read the book?*). But in order to question verbs, there is nothing similar in a language such as English. There is, though, in many Austronesian and Australian languages, as well as in e.g. Southern Paiute, Chukchi, Mandarin, Yagaria, and Rwanda. Clad in English words, a question-and-answer session in such a language could thus look something like 'The dog WHATed the boy?' 'It bit him' or 'The dog HOWed? 'It barked like this'.

SIMPLE DEICTIC SYSTEM

The basic spatial adverbs of Bavarian are the only ones I know of which fail to distinguish even a binary proximal/distal contrast. In other words, 'here' and 'there' both sound alike.

It is unusual, but at least somewhat more common, to lack the deictic distinction in demonstrative pronouns ('this' = 'that'), as in Egyptian Arabic, Supyire, French, German, Koromfé, Czech, Kera, Koyraboro Senni, Mam, Haitian, Polish, and Romanian. (In many such languages, it is precisely a 'here' or 'there' that is called into service when disambiguation is necessary).

HOW DO YOU FEEL?

Many North American languages have verbal extensions encoding the manner in or instrument with which an object is felt/touched or manipulated, that is, there are affixes which convey adverbial content. Nez Percé of Idaho is one such language which is renowned for its elaborate inventory of these markers. For Klamath, spoken in Oregon, a list of no less than 72 such morphemes has been presented. Some of the more intriguing examples include:

qb-	*with the mouth*
qbi-	*holding in the mouth so that one or more ends project*
go-	*with the head first*
tqiq-	*with the elbow*
tʃˀoq-	*with the buttocks*
sg-	*with the penis*

TELLING TIME IN PIRAHÃ

Pirahã, spoken in the Amazonas, must certainly be one of very few languages which lack specific words for telling time (apart from there being a word for 'now'). It certainly is possible to make statements referring to this or other moments in time—'other fire', for instance, means 'not today', 'moon' doubles for 'month', and 'water cycle' stands in for 'year', but there are no words devoted *exclusively* to expressing these concepts.

SOURCES NOT MENTIONED IN THE TEXT

Adverbs in Australian languages: Dixon (1980:282).
Adverbs and adjectives in Kambera: Plank (2004).
Interrogative pro-verbs: Plank (2004).
Deictics in Bavarian: Plank (2004).
No deixis in demonstratives: Lyons (1998:19-20, 112); Haspelmath et al. (eds) (2005: map 41).
Feeling in Klamath and Nez Percé: Mithun (1999:133).
Lack of time words in Pirahã: Dan Everett on *Linguist List* 12.829.

ADPOSITIONS

Adposition is a cover term for prepositions on the one hand, and post-positions on the other. English is, like most other European languages, by and large prepositional (*after* dinner, *behind* the barn, *to* Rome), but does have a few postpositions as well (the year *round*).

FEWEST ADPOSITIONS

Among pidginists, the Russo-Norwegian trade language Russenorsk is reknowned for having had only one single preposition—på. Among natively spoken languages, however, it is difficult to find adpositional inventories as small as this, unless the language in question has an extensive set of morphological cases (or, as in some North American languages, the verb contains the corresponding information, yielding constructions such as We in-sat the canoe).

One, though, is Buginese, which is said to only have one preposition. Other necessary information is provided by the verb. Another is Wari', an Amazonian language. Its one all-purpose preposition marks any non-core argument in a sentence. Since it agrees with its object in person, number and gender, its several forms often bear no surface resemblance to one another. Also in South America, Mapudungun has the one core adposition *mew ~ mo ~ mu*, which marks grammatical, spatial and temporal relations.

English is a mainly prepositional language

FLEXIBLE ADPOSITIONS

Adpositions are often thought of as invariable, and in English they are. Indeed, they normally are in languages in general. As always, though, there are exceptions. The Celtic languages Irish and Welsh are well-known for inflecting their prepositions.

The same feature is also encountered in e.g. Nahuatl of Central America and Kabardian of Caucasia.

As already mentioned, the sole preposition of Wari' inflects, often suppletively, for person, number, gender.

PREPOSITION STRANDING

A minority (albeit not a negligible one) of the world's languages allow a preposition to be moved without its NP part. Some languages, of which English is one, even tolerate several prepositions to be stacked on one another at one end of the sentence. One neat illustration of the behavior of English prepositions comes from Thurber (1957:26):

> *The day I got dressed and was about to leave the hospital, I heard a nurse and an interne discussing a patient who had got something in his eye. "It's a bad city to get something in your eye in," the nurse said. "Yes," the interne agreed, "but there isn't a better place to get something in your eye out in." I rushed past them with my hair in my wild eyes, and left the hospital. It was high time, too.*

A classic example, used by e.g. Pinker (1994), is "*Dad, what did you bring that book that I don't like to be read **to out of up for**?*". It may perhaps have been inspired by Moore (1961:197), who wrote as follows:

> *I lately lost a preposition;*
> *It hid, I thought, beneath my chair,*
> *And angrily I cried, "Perdition!*
> *Up from out of in under there."*
> *Correctness is my vade mecum,*
> *And straggling phrases I abhor,*
> *And yet I wondered,*
> *"What should he come **up from out of in under** there for?"*

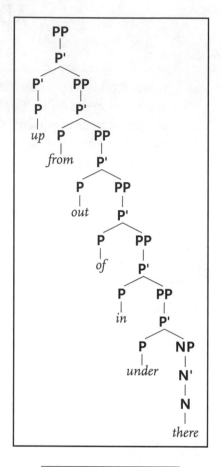

Yes, generativist readership— even this book includes a tree diagram

SOURCES NOT MENTIONED IN THE TEXT

Russenorsk: Jahr (1996:110).
Buginese: Campbell (1991:233).
Wari': Everett & Kern (1997:5, 224, 347).
Mapudungun: Adelaar (2004:520).
Irish: Taub (2001:225).
Welsh: King (1993:268-69), Watkins (1993:314).
Nahuatl: Ljuba Veselinova (p c).
Some of the quotes exemplifying preposition stranding were brought to my attention by the web site of Beatrice Santorini.

ARTICLES

MANY LANGUAGES have articles (such as the English *a* and *the*, which indicate definiteness), but it is by no means uncommon to do without them—Russian, Finnish, and Latin are just some of the many articleless languages.

TENSED ARTICLES

The articles of the Peruvian language Chamicuro are remarkable in that they not only encode definiteness, but also simultaneously express a temporal distinction (referring to the entire clause), namely past versus non-past.

THREE DEGREES OF DEFINITENESS

The South American language Nambiquara has not only a distinction between definite and indefinite, but a tripartite system, also encoding conditionality. (In a sense, admittedly, one could argue that a tripartite system is one which, as that of English, distinguishes between e.g. *wine, the wine* and *a wine*.)

English articles as depicted in the book Infant's Grammar— a pic-nic party of the parts of speech, published in London in the early 19th century.

COMPLEX ARTICLE SYSTEMS

Languages of New Caledonia have notoriously complex article systems. Dehu, for instance, encodes definiteness, distance, number and visibility in its ten article forms. The articles of Cèmuhî, spoken on the same island, only encodes gender, number and definiteness, something which nevertheless yields 25 different forms.

SOURCES NOT MENTIONED IN THE TEXT

Chamicuro: Plank (2004).
Nambiquara: (Lowe 1999:281-82).
Dehu, Cèmuhî: Lynch (1998:113).

DEMONSTRATIVES

DEMONSTRATIVES do not traditionally form a part of speech category, rather, we can in many languages identify several demonstrative paradigms representing different part of speech categories. Their common denominator is that they encode one or several *deictic* distinctions (i.e. they point out differences of location and related factors with respect to the speaker and/or person addressed). The English demonstrative adverbs *here* and *there*, or the pronouns/determiners *this* and *that*, for example, indicate where, in relation to the speaker, something is located—a very typical deictic distinction displayed in the languages of the world.

HIGHEST NUMBER OF DEGREES OF DEIXIS

One need not go far afield to find languages which, unlike English, have more than two degrees of deixis (*this* and *that*). Spanish, for instance, makes use of three degrees, viz. near the speaker (*este*), near the addressee (*ese*) and far from both (*aquel*).

In Malagasy (Madagascar), the system also encodes six distances with regard to the speaker (we are talking about 'rather far away',

'far away', 'very far away indeed', 'rather close', 'close', and 'right here'), and the same is true for Walapai. Five or more degrees of deixis are also found in the North American languages Koasati, Blackfoot, Maricopa, and Navajo.

All of these, it would appear, are overshadowed by Heiltsuk of British Columbia which possesses no less than seven.

ELABORATE DEMONSTRATIVE SYSTEMS

Dyirbal and Lezgian have notoriously complex deictic systems, which distinguish not only (relative) distance, but also things like visibility and position vis-à-vis the river. These would seem to be less impressive, though, in comparison to Inuktitut, Yup'ik, and Aleut, which express extraordinarily specific notions such as 'that large or moving one way up there', 'that one outside, only partly visible' and 'that small one going away from me'. Similarly rich systems, involving also position and dispersion, are encountered in e.g. Tupí languages.

To exemplify a system considerably more complex than that of English, here follows that of Muna, which is spoken on the island of Sulawesi in Indonesia:

aini	this (near speaker)
aitu	that (near addressee)
amaitu	that (away from both speaker and addressee, but nearby)
awatu	that (far away, lower than, or level with point of speaking or orientation)
anagha	that (not visible, but may be audible)
awaghaitu	that (no longer visible, but once was)

In addition to the distinctions just mentioned, the Malagasy demonstratives also encode visibility. That makes 14 forms. Moreover, speakers of Malagasy must also inflect their demonstratives for tense. At least in theory, that yields 42 different forms roughly corresponding to the 'this' and 'that' of English.

Bentley (1887:585-89), Laman (1912:129), and Söderberg & Widman (1966:19) give partially conflicting accounts of Kikongo demonstratives (possibly due to their describing different varieties of this language). What seems clear, however, is that there are three degrees of deixis. In addition, there are 15 different noun classes, different degrees of emphasis, which together conspire to make several hundreds of demonstrative forms in Kikongo.

NO DEMONSTRATIVES AT ALL?

In Dixon's (2003b:69) survey of languages, Ju|'hoan of southern Africa is the only language found not to have demonstratives. Instead, the verbs *hè* 'to be here, to be this one' and *to'à* 'to be there, to be that one' are used. A sentence such as 'This person told me' would thus be expressed as *Jùà hè !óá mí* {person who-is-here told me}. The same seems to hold for neighboring !Xū. Note that the purported lack of demonstratives is in a sense in the eye of the linguistic beholder—clearly, these languages do allow their speakers to point out things in their surroundings, but the deixis is expressed as a verb rather than a demonstrative as normally understood.

AN UNUSUAL DICHOTOMY

Spoken Catalan used to have a tripartite demonstrative system similar to that of Spanish, but over time, *aqueix* 'that (close to you, but far from me)' was lost, leaving only two terms. This would appear to be similar to the situation in English, which distinguishes between 'close' and 'not close' vis-à-vis the speaker only (a first-person perspective). However, as the functions of *aqueix* have been taken over by *aquest* 'this', modern spoken Catalan has an unusual two-way distinction between 'this (close to me *or* close to you, but not to me)' and 'that (close to neither)'—a third-person perspective.

A system of this sort is also reported from Carib, but the analysis has been questioned.

SOURCES NOT MENTIONED IN THE TEXT

Malagasy: Keenan & Ochs (1979:122-23).
Navajo: Lyons (1998:111).
Koasati, Maricopa, and Navajo: Haspelmath et al. (eds) (2005: map 41).
Blackfoot and Heiltsuk: Mithun (1999:132-33).
Dyirbal, Eskimo and Aleut: Trask (1993:75).
Lezgian: Lyons (1998:111).
Inuktitut: Dixon (2003b:90).
Yup'ik: Mithun (1999:135).
Tupí languages: Rodrigues (1999a:120).
Muna: Dixon (2003b:91).
Ju|'hoan: Dickens (1992:30), Dixon (2003b:69).
!Xũ: Snyman (1970).
Catalan: Lyons (1998:110).

PERSONAL PRONOUNS

PRONOUNS CAN BE USED to refer to the same kind of entities as lexical noun phrases may. We typically use personal pronouns as a shortcut in order not to have to repeat the names of people and things all the time.

English deals with two numbers (singular and plural) and three persons (1st, 2nd and 3rd), in addition to which there are special object forms (*me, you* and *him/her* as opposed to *I, you* and *he/she*) and possessive forms (*my, your* and *his/her*), and even what are sometimes referred to as *absolute possessives* (*mine, yours* and *his/hers*). That leaves the English-speaker with a number of choices to make. Nonetheless, languages like English have a relatively simple system of personal pronouns.

Another illustration from the book Infant's Grammar—a pic-nic party of the parts of speech, *this time featuring personal pronouns*

COMPLEX PERSONAL PRONOUN SYSTEMS

Complexity of a linguistic sub-system such as personal pronouns can be perceived as the number of different grammatical categories expressed by the members of the paradigm. Fijian, for instance, has four numbers (singular, dual, paucal and plural), inclusivity (see p 168) distinctions, several cases (including different sets of possessives for different noun classes), the total number of pronoun forms is somewhere between 70 and 135, depending on one's analysis. In Pidgin Fijian this figure has been reduced to six, which must surely rank as one of the more radical downsizings in language history.

Several Finno-Ugric languages spoken in Russia also exhibit complex pronominal systems. In e.g. Mordvin, the number of different forms of the personal pronouns amounts to a total of 198! Pronouns have eleven cases, three persons, two numbers most with either definite, indefinite or possessive inflection.

Many Australian languages differ from their European counterparts in encoding things such as age and kinship in the pronominal system. Adynyamathanha, for instance, has ten different forms for the first person dual pronoun, the choice between which is, to a great extent, determined by kinship relations.

In many ways, Polynesian languages tend to look "simple" in the eyes of a European observer. Their pronoun systems, however, are definitely not. Rennellese, spoken on one of the Solomon Islands has three numbers, three persons and inclusivity, in addition to which there are three different pronoun classes, depending on syntactic position. Thus, if you want to say 'our' in Rennellese, you would have to choose the appropriate one from among the following 44 forms:

a'amatou, a'amā, a'atatou, a'atā, amatou, amā, atatou, atā, ma'amatou, ma'amā, ma'atatou, ma'atā, mo'omatou, mo'omā, mo'otatou, mo'otā, omatou, omā, o'omatou, o'omā, o'otatou, o'otā, otatou, otā, ta'amatou, ta'amā, ta'atatou, ta'atā, tamatou, tamā, tatatou, tatā, tematou, temā, tetatou, tetā, tomatou, tomā, to'omatou, to'omā, to'otatou, to'otā, totatou, totā

Samoan is even more extreme, having 188 different possessive pronouns, and that still does not include those formed with emotional and partitive articles. Here, there are 72 different ways of saying 'our'—and yet, that is just the possessive system!

In the same area, Lihir of Papua New Guinea distinguishes between inclusive and exclusive forms of the first person, as well as between no less than five numbers—singular, dual, trial, paucal and plural.

Elsewhere in East Asia and the Pacific, pronoun systems are also remarkably complex by western standards because status relations are involved (see below). For some of these languages, however, the category of personal pronouns is an open rather than a closed class. This is proven by the borrowing into some lects of English personal pronouns

in order to avoid the complicated and sensitive choice between the plentiful native forms.

The pronominals of Yuchi, an Amerindian language of the USA, are also interestingly complex. Its 3rd person pronouns encode sex of both the referent and the speaker, the kinship affinities between them (whether or not they are related, and if so, whether in ascending or descending generation). As if this weren't enough, the Yuchi pronouns also take into account the ethnic identity of the people involved are, i.e. whether they are Yuchi or not.

Other North American languages reputed to have "phenomenally complex" pronominal paradigms include Kiowa and Kwakiutl, but I unfortunately lack details on these complexities.

SOMEWHAT SIMPLER PRONOUN SETS

Chimbu languages of New Guinea are renowned for their diminutive pronoun inventories. On the same island, Elseng has been said to distinguish only between a first person and everything else, although this has been questioned. Balanta of West Africa makes a distinction only between (1) the speaker, (2) all other singular persons, and (3) everything which is plural.

Ika of Colombia has a basic distinction between only first person and everything else. There is, however, also a prefix *n-*, which reveals that a "second person is somehow involved" and a *win-*, which indicates plural reference. All in all, then, disambiguating is less impossible than it would seem at first sight.

While number is often less grammaticalized than it is in Europe, few languages lack nominal number altogether. Even fewer are devoid of pronominal number, i.e. do not distinguish between *I* and *we* or *she* and *them*. The ones known are spoken primarily on New Guinea (including Nimboran,

Manem, Awyi, Simog, and Daonda), most of which instead have inclusivity distinctions. Other examples are old Javanese, old Chinese and Pirahã.

The Pirahã pronoun set not only lacks a number distinction, but the core paradigm consists of only three forms—/ti/ '1st person', /gi(a)/ '2nd person' and /hi/ '3rd person'. There are also two additional 3rd-person forms /ʔi/ and /ʔis/ used for women and animals respectively, but these do not display a fully pronominal behavior, and are thus somewhat more peripheral to the system. The pronouns are also much less frequent in discourse than are their counterparts in most other languages. Furthermore, there is evidence that the entire pronominal set has been borrowed (from Lingua Geral), suggesting the possibility of a language once completely devoid of pronouns. Vedda also has only three pronouns. These use Sinhala morphemes in non-Sinhala ways, e.g. 'this' + 'people' for 1st person and 'that' + 'people' for 3rd person.

FOURTH PERSON

Most languages distinguish between three persons. The first person, (equalling or including the speaker), second person (equalling or including the addressee) and third person (any other referent). In addition to this, some North American languages—in particular those belonging to the Algonquian family—feature what is sometimes called a fourth person, labelled *obviative* in the in-house lingo.

Aissen (1997:705) defines obviation as "systems which obligatorily rank third person nominals according to a complex function

which includes grammatical function, inherent semantic properties, and discourse salience". Here is what that usually means in practice: a sentence such as *When Laurel came into the room, Hardy was already there* could in a non-obviating language such as English be paraphrased as *When he₁ came into the room, he₂ was already there.* Even though we are obviously referring to two different third persons, English uses *he* for both. An Algonquian, on the other hand, would use different words (or rather different inflexions) for the two third persons.

SEX CONTRASTS

The word 'sex' is used here to distinguish the encoding of biological gender from that of grammatical gender.

Natural though it may seem to speakers of most Indo-European languages, lots of languages make no distinction between 'he' and 'she'. The ones who do, however, usually include sex differentiation first and foremost in the third person (38% of the languages in the world have such marking). This can be argued to serve a function—the first and second persons are by definition present in the discourse, and presumably know the sex of themselves and their interlocutors, but they may in this way be able to distinguish between third persons, provided these are not of the same sex.

It is not unheard of to include sex also in the 2nd person, which is what e.g. Tunica and most members of the Afro-Asiatic family (i.e. Arabic and its relatives), along with 6% of the world's languages do. Languages which go even further, and mark sex in all persons are twice as rare, but include Hadza of Tanzania, Ngala of New Guinea, and Rikbaktsá and Yatê

of the Amazonas. What is really unusual, however, is to have a sex contrast *only* for the first person. Yet, there are at least two languages which do precisely this: Thai, and the now extinct Indo-European language Tocharian A.

Kalaw Kawaw Ya, spoken on the islands between Australia and New Guinea, also has a sex contrast in the first person, including the possessive forms.

Speakers of Andi (Caucasia) manifest gender loyalty in the first and second persons singular, insofar as female speakers are expected to make a distinction between the absolutive and the ergative case, which is alien to male speakers.

The Central American language Diuxi Mixtec is similarly odd in this respect. Its 2nd and 3rd pronoun system not only takes into account the sex of the referent, but also that of the speaker.

The South American language Tsafiki codes sex on the first person, and in addition to distinguishing men and women, it also uses a variant *če*, used for children.

ANALYTIC AND PORTMANTEAU PRONOUNS

Some languages stuff their pronouns with more information than others. For instance, Tagalog, the most widely known language of the Philippines, has a pronoun which, without being internally analysable, means 'first person singular non-topic acting on second person singular topic'.

Virtually all languages include number in their pronominal paradigms, and almost everywhere (including most otherwise analytic languages) are the plural morphs non-segmentable—they could in this respect be said to represent portmanteau morphs as

well. Thus, while we refer to *we* as the plural form of *I*, it does not include the *-s* normally used for marking plural in English. A few English dialects do this for the second person plural, and use forms such as *y'all* or *yous* for the plural form of *you*. Yet, not even in these varieties is this extended to other forms (i.e. we do not find **Is* or **hes* for *we* and *they*). Some other languages do. Plural pronouns consisting of a singular form and a plural marker are found in several Mesoamerican languages (such as Totonac, Nahuatl, Zoque, Miskito, and Tequistlatec), in Great Andamanese, in

Dakota, in Quechua, and in Mandarin. This seems also to have been the case in some Mande languages. Less surprisingly, we furthermore find it in a few pidgin languages, such as Taimyr Pidgin Russian, Nagamese, and the now extinct Samoan Pidgin English.

LONG PRONOUN

Since pronouns are very frequent in discourse, and since, as already pointed out, their function is precisely to provide a "shortcut", they are typically very short. In the English paradigm *I, you, he/she/it, we, you, they*, no form is longer than one syllable. While bisyllabic forms do occur in languages, three-syllable pronouns (like Hebrew *anakhnu* 'we' and Spanish *nosotros* 'we' and *ustedes* 'you') are relatively rare (and at least the Spanish forms are fairly recent coinings that have not yet been subject to the withering effect of frequent usage to the extent that other pronouns have).

The longest personal pronoun form I have come across is the "first person plural disharmonic" form in the Australian language Martuyhunira: *nganajumartangara*. "Disharmonic" here means that the form is used for those belonging to a generation above or below the speaker.

Some of the longest pronouns in the world are found in Australian languages.

LANGUAGES NOT USING PERSONAL PRONOUNS

Many readers are no doubt familiar with the fact that many, in fact even most, of the world's languages do not normally use subject pronouns in the way English does in a sentence such as *She speaks*. Spanish and most other Romance languages are examples of this. The subject is realized as a verb inflexion rather than as a separate word—e.g. Portuguese *fala* 's/he speaks'. While most languages use one or other of these strategies, there are a few in which neither type of subject marking is necessary. The most well-known representatives of this type are Mandarin and Japanese, but it also includes Tagalog, Korean, Samoan, and other languages of East Asia and the Pacific.

While dropping the pronoun in Mandarin usually requires that the referent has been mentioned earlier in the discourse, Japanese is more liberal. Thus, a perfectly idiomatic way of saying *I love you* would be to simply say "love".

It has been suggested that some south and east Asian languages, such as Thai, Japanese, and Burmese lack personal pronouns, since what look like pronouns should in fact be considered nouns.

In Bella Coola, the words corresponding to personal pronouns in western languages have been analysed as stative verbs—i.e., the word for 'I' really means 'to be me'.

For the vast majority of languages, it is normal to distinguish three persons (first, second and third) and at least two numbers (singular and plural). The pronominal sets of some languages of New Guinea, though, have been claimed to only differentiate between first person and non-first person. There is at least one language which, although making this distinction, does not indicate who does what.

This is Awa-Cuaiquer, spoken in Ecuador and Colombia. If one of the event participants is a locutor, she is marked as such. A non-locutor is marked only if there is no locutor involved. This means that all we learn from a sentence such as *pjannis* {hit-FUT-LOCUTOR} is that there is hitting to be going on and that the speaker is somehow involved—possible interpretations thus include 'I will hit you', 'I will hit him' and 'You will hit me', among others. Similarly *pjannizi* only tells us that the future hitting will not involve the speaker.

In yet other languages, including Nambiquara and Pirahã, speakers tend to avoid pronouns, but not by leaving a gap. Instead, somewhat like the literary cliché of North American Indians, they repeat the lexical noun phrase at a frequency alien to European languages (e.g. 'John came in the room. John sat down. Then John began to work').

FURTHER ELABORATIONS OF THE PRONOUN SET

S ome languages go quite a bit beyond the mere necessities. The Meso-American language Chocha, for instance, has a number of special forms of the 3rd person singular, including one for things made of wood:

soa²¹ʃa)³	she/he (a child)	*soa²¹ni¹*	he/she (devotional)
soa²¹ri¹	he (a boy), it (a wild animal)	*soa²¹ba²*	it (domestic animal)
soa²¹tʃi¹	she (a girl)	*soa²¹ga³*	it (an object)
soa²¹ga¹	he (close adult friend of same age)	*soa²¹ru³*	it (a fruit)
soa²¹nu²	she (close adult friend of same age)	*soa²¹nda³*	it (a wooden object)
soa²¹ri³	he/she (respectful)		

Also in Latin America, Pirahã, which otherwise lacks the more basic feature of number in its pronoun set (see p 307) is remarkable in having a 3rd person form for "aquatic non-humans".

Several Australian languages make contrasts with regard to socio-biological features such as generation membership, moiety, kin and clan. Adynyamathanha, for instance, uses ten different dual pronouns to

express precisely these traits.

Meanwhile, as we have seen elsewhere (pp 3–4) many East Asian languages go to excesses (from a westerner's point of view) in making formality distinctions. Instead of simply caring about *I, you* and *(s)he*, a speaker of Japanese must take into account—apart from his or her own gender—the social relationship between him- or herself and the addressee, as seen in the following schema:

		FORMAL		INFORMAL	
1sg	male speaker	watakusi	watasi	boku	ore
1sg	female speaker	watasi			atasi
2sg	male speaker	anata		kimi anta	omae
2sg	female speaker	anata			anta
3sg	male referent	kare			
3sg	female referent	kanozyo			

Korean is another language of this type. The 2sg pronoun has five degrees of politeness, and even so, Sohn (1999:207) gives three variants of the "blunt" form.

GOD'S OWN PRONOUN

Mixtec languages sport a specific divine pronoun, i.e. a form reserved for God, and sometimes also other personalities associated with religion. In Chalcatongo Mixtec, /ɟa/—sometimes glossed as 'supernatural' in the linguistic literature—can be used with reference to God and Jesus, as well as for priests and nuns, and, interestingly, also the devil. A devotional pronoun is also attested for Choco.

Spoken Mandarin uses the ordinary 3sg pronoun (*tá*) for God, but in writing, it is common to add a "spirit" radical next to the pronominal sign. This practise is mainly, but not exclusively, confined to Christian writings, and has been compared to writing *he* with a capital <h> in English. For Sun Yixian (Sun Yat-sen) and sometimes also Jiǎng Jièshí (Chiang Kai-shek), the same type of reverence and respect is in some genres of Taiwanese writing shown by adding an extra blank before the name.

SOURCES NOT MENTIONED IN THE TEXT

Fijian and Pidgin Fijian: Clark (1990:180), Siegel (1987:106).
Diuxi Mixtec, Tagalog, Yuchi, Tocharian A, Thai, Adynyamathanha: Plank (2004).
Rennellese: Elbert (1965).
Samoan: Hunkin (1988), Mosel & Hovdhaugen (1992), Niklas Jonsson (p c).
Lihir: Corbett (2000).
Kiowa: Mithun (1999:446).
Simple pronoun sets in Melanesia: Foley (1986:69-70; 2000:376).
Elseng: Burung (2000), Foley (1986: 70).
Balanta: Plank (2004).
Ika: Nicholas Ostler (p c).
No pronominal number: Foley (1986:71), Lynch (1998:167) and the references given in the "number" section.
Pirahã: Aikhenvald & Dixon (1999:355), Pirahã pronouns: Thomason & Everett (2001), Everett (2004).
Vedda: Philip Baker (p c).

Obviative: Aissen (1997).

Percentages of pronominal sex-marking among the world's languages: Traunmüller (1991).

Tunica: Mithun (1999:102).

Afro-Asiatic sex distinctions: Hetzron (1990b:165, 1990c:208); Newman (1990:214); Aikhenvald & Dixon 1998:66).

Hadza: Niklas Edenmyr (p c).

Ngala: Foley (1986:80).

Rikbaktsá and Yatê: Rodrigues (1999b:185).

Kalaw Kawaw Ya: Aikhenvald & Dixon (1998:66-67).

Andi: van den Berg 2005:163).

Tsafiki: Adelaar (2004:149).

Mesoamerican languages: Suárez (1983:84).

Great Andamanese: Burenhult (1996).

Dakota: Campbell (1991:369).

Quechua: Adelaar (2004:221).

Mande languages: Rowlands (1959:55), Welmers (1976:46)

Taimyr Pidgin Russian: Wurm (1996b:83).

Nagamese: Wangkheimayum & Sinha (1997:2).

Samoan Pidgin English: Mühlhäusler (1997:148).

Long pronoun in Martuyhunira: Dench (1995:100).

Pronouns being nouns in south and east Asia: Bhat (2004:30-31).

Japanese: Shibatani (1990b:363-64).

Bella Coola: Bhat (2004:26).

Awa-Cuaiquer: Kibrik (1997).

Non-use of pronouns in Pirahã and Nambiquara: Dan Everett on Funknet 2003-01-22.

Chocha third person pronouns: Suárez (1983:34).

Australian languages: Dixon (1980:247).

Japanese formality distinctions: Shibatani (1990b:371).

Korean: Sohn (1999:207).

Divine pronouns: *Linguist List* 5.259, Plank (2004).

NUMERALS

MOST LANGUAGES allow their speakers to count and discuss the number of objects around them. This is often done by means of a separate class of words, known as numerals. This class usually encompasses a finite number of elements, which can be combined to express very high numbers. However, this is not a rule without exceptions.

NO CATEGORY OF NUMERALS

Given that numerals serve to describe entities, it comes as no surprise that in many languages, numbers behave like adjectives rather than constituting a category of their own. There are other strategies, though, of disposing of the numeral category.

In Krongo (spoken in Sudan), numbers behave as verbs. In other words, we would not say that *the cups are three*, but that *the cups three* or *the cups are threeing*. The same goes for a number of Native American languages. Also, Sesotho (Bantu), which, as will become clear below, has an interesting counting system, has a class of numerals extending to 5, while numbers 6-9 are verbs. In the members of the Lower Sepik family of New Guinea, 'one' is an adjective, while 'two and 'three' are verbs. In Slavic languages, only 2, 3 and 4 are numerals in the proper sense, whereas 'one' behaves like an adjective, and higher numbers like verbs.

Mlabri, which is spoken by around 300 people in Thailand on the border with Laos, has been claimed to have no part of speech category functioning as numerals whatsoever. Others have suggested, however, that Mlabri does have at least the numbers 'one' and 'two'.

MORE ORDINALS THAN CARDINALS

Many languages, like English, make a distinction between cardinal numbers, such as *one* and *two* on the one hand, and ordinal numbers such as *first* and *second* on the other. Some languages have no ordinals at all, and quite a few have only a limited set. Thus, the normal state of affairs is to have more cardinals than ordinals. In this context, Andamanese languages, spoken on an archipelago in the Bay of Bengal, seems highly aberrant in that they are reported to have cardinal numbers only up to 'two' but ordinals going up to 'sixth'.

SEVERAL PARALLEL NUMERAL SYSTEMS

Many languages have parallel counting systems depending on what is being counted. Nicobarese, for instance, uses one set of numerals for money and coconuts, and another one for everything else. Palauan too has a singled out coconuts and money for, together with stones, they have a counting system of their own. Three others are used in Palauan for counting humans, fish, and taro, while a fifth is used with trees, leaves and boards. Gilyak, an isolate spoken on Sachalin and on the mainland just opposite, is said to have 26 different systems of this kind.

Other languages displaying about a score of sets of numbers include Palikur, Pohnpeian, Halkomelem, Boro, and Loniu.

Yurok of California has 15 sets of numerals, including one for "fingerjoints (a measurement of dentalium shells)". Incidentally, 'three', when used of tools, is a true tongue-twister: nɹhksɹpiʔ. Nisga'a of western Canada has only four sets, but with one devoted exclusively to canoes.

Historically, this phenomenon is—wherever it occurs—virtually always a result of the merger of a numeral and a nominal classifier (see pp 301–04).

SMALLEST NUMERAL SYSTEM

Languages of Australia are renowned for having very limited sets of numerals, often said to only range from 'one' to 'three'. Languages of Amazonia are similarly poor in numerals. Most Arawak and Makú languages, for instance, only have 'one' and 'two', and for higher numbers, recourse is made to finger counting. In this vein, Andaman could be mentioned—the numbers 3, 4 and 5 in Andaman actually mean 'one more', 'some more', and 'all'.

Languages said to lack a way of counting altogether include Canela-Krahó, Krenák, and Chiquitano—all spoken in South America. Chiquitano has also been claimed to have a numeral system consisting of just a single member—'one'.

It has been also suggested that Jabutí originally did not have had any numerals at all. These days, there is a word for 'one', but the concept 'two' is expressed as 'is equal', while anything more numerous is hõnõ tõ 'know not'.

Note, however, that this refers only to lexicalized numerals—people speaking such languages need not necessarily be less apt than you and I to conceptualize higher numbers, and ways of expressing these can often be invented on the spot if necessary.

And then again, there is always Pirahã. It not only lacks numerals, but its speakers are even said to be completely alien to the very concept of counting! Given that an understanding of numbers has been demonstrated in several

Zero and 1–9 in various languages. (Latin and Amharic lacked zero.)

non-human species, this—as so many other features of Pirahã—sure sounds too good to be true. Yet, renowned linguist Dan Everett and psycholinguist Peter Gordon claim to have shown that adult Pirahãs are unable to even grasp numbers beyond about three!

LARGEST NUMERAL SYSTEM

Since there is an infinite set of numbers, there is potentially an indefinite number of numerals. Admittedly, it is rare for most of us to count beyond hundreds, unless we live in a monetary economy and have to discuss our mortgage or the foreign debt. It is telling that most western languages (and perhaps most languages on earth) share the same word for 'million' and numbers higher than that (though, deceptively, the higher numbers, such as *trillion* have different referents in Europe and in the USA—a trillion, for instance, is 10^{12} in America, but 10^{18} in most of Europe).

Indeed, even a million is such a high number that, according to the *Guinness Book of World Records*, it took Australian Les Stewart no less than 16 years to type all the numbers between 1 and 1 000 000 on 19 000 sheets of paper.

A number often cited as being the largest one having a name of its own is a *googolplex*, which is defined as ten to the *googolth* power, a googol being a one followed by a hundred zeroes. The term googol was invented by the nine-year-old nephew of American mathematician Edward Kasner when being asked to name the highest number he could imagine. The *plex* part was then added, it is said, by one of Kasner's colleagues in order to show that even higher numbers are imaginable, and, thus that there exists no such thing as a highest number!

Even higher numbers (usually, of course, only mentioned in discussions on high numbers, and of negligible practical use) include the *Moser* and the *Graham number* (named after mathematicians Leo Moser and Ronald Graham respectively).

UNUSUAL BASES

The most common bases for counting systems are 10, as in European languages, and 5, as in many African languages. Others, particularly in Central America, make use of twenty as a base, traces of which can also be seen in e.g. French *quatre-vingt* or Danish *firs(indtyve)* 'eighty' (both literally 'four times twenty').

There are plenty of variations on this theme, though. Bam of New Guinea, as well as the African languages Nyali and Tangale, have been analysed as having the base 4, while the Oto-Manguean language Northern Pame is interesting for being a consistent base-8 system. While there are a few more examples of bases 4 and 8, I have only come across a handful of languages basing their counting systems on other numbers—the Nimbia dialect of Gwandara (Nigeria) has base 12, as did the Maldivian language (of the Maldives) until recently (but only when counting coconuts!), while Kanum and Kimaama in New Guinea seem to represent base 6 systems.

The logically smallest base imaginable is two, and it does indeed occur in some languages. Counting then goes like this: "1", "2", "2+1", "2+2", "2+2+1", "2+2+2", and so on.

Nenets is possibly unique in being a

language which has been argued to have had a base 9 (the current system is adapted to the Russian one). Note, however, that this claim is highly controversial.

Palikur is also somewhat dubious, but it could be seen as having base 7, and if so, it too may be alone in its class.

BASE 64 AS A ROYAL DECREE

I n the early 18th century, Swedish king Charles XII (otherwise thought of as rather unintellectual) enjoyed discussing mathematical problems with scientist, philosopher and mystic Emanuel Swedenborg. The king was fascinated by the possibilities of replacing 10 as a base of the counting system with 64, as this number is both the square of eight and the cube of four.

Whether because he was convinced of its advantages, or just for the sheer hell of it, the capricious king ordered Swedenborg to develop such a system, with the prospect of introducing it. The intellectual was sceptic, but did what he was told, and new symbols and words were invented. Because the warrior king fell victim to a stray bullet during one of his many campaigns—most of his time on the throne was actually spent in battlefields abroad—the new counting system came to naught. Had it ever been introduced, Swedes would have had to memorize quite a few numerals, as the new system would lead to two-digit numbers all the way up to 4 096 (i.e. 64 times 64).

The warrior king and his philosopher laureate. Emanuel Swedenborg and Charles XII.

INTERESTING ORIGINS OF NUMERALS

I n most European languages, the numbers one to ten are opaque, i.e. seemingly not related to any other words. This is often also the case with many of the numbers between ten and twenty, although e.g. English *eleven* and *twelve* can be demonstrated to derive from compounds (the *-lve* part is related to the word *leave*, so that when you have counted ten of your eleven apples, there is, as it were, 'one left').

It is surely not by coincidence that 5 and 10 are the most popular bases of counting systems worldwide, given that there are five fingers each on most people's two hands. Similarly, 20 is the total number of all fingers and all toes. The fact that some languages do not treat the thumb as one finger among the others, but as something different—note that even in English, the thumb is the only finger whose name is not a compound involving *finger*—may also explain the presence of bases 4 and 8.

In many a language, therefore, 'five' is related to the word for 'hand', and 'twenty' to something like 'a whole person'. The numbers in-between are constructed in a variety of more or less fanciful ways, e.g. Klamath 8 *ndan-ksahpta* 'three I have bent over' or Unalit 11 *atkahakhtok* 'it goes down (to the feet)'.

Sesotho has words for numbers 1-5, but when the first hand is finished, that's where problems start. 6 is expressed as 'cross over', since you have to 'cross over' to the other hand to continue counting. To show 7 on your hands, you have to stretch out the index finger, as well as the thumb, and 7 is therefore expressed as 'to point out'. The following two numerals are 'two broken fingers' and 'one broken finger' respectively, since that is the number of fingers which (apart from the thumb) are not extended in order to display 8 and 9. As with 1-5, a simple word is again

used for 10, but from 11 upwards, we stop using fingers and use roots (!) instead. 'Eleven men' is therefore *batho ba leshome le motso e mong*, that is 'ten men who have one root', while 'thirty-six men' is *batho ba mashome a mararo a metso e tseletseng* or 'men tens three have roots having crossed over' (!).

Sesotho course, lesson 31: This is how we say '9999 oxen'. Really.

MORE ON FINGER COUNTING

When the fingers and toes are finished, one has to make use of other bodily extremities. Thus, in Nahuatl, which has a vigesimal system (based on twenties), the word for 400 is *tzontli*—literally meaning 'hair'!

In New Guinea, so-called *body-tally* systems are not unusual, and these make do with body parts that are not necessarily protruding. Kalam is one of these. Each number is homophonous with a body part. So counting basically starts with "finger, fingerjoint, knuckle, wrist", etc. You then continue past the head, and progress down the other side of the body, until you get to 27. Similar systems are used by many other

peoples on the island. When the hand is done, Kewa-speakers continue up towards the head. 'Forearm' is 9, 'shoulder' serves as 15, the 'ear' as 20, and so on, until the climax of 24 is reached—'between eyes'.

In an earlier draft of what you are now reading, I had felt compelled to admit that "to my knowledge—and disappointment—no language involves any naughty body parts in its counting". I am glad to be able to say that I have since been corrected on that point. There are indeed systems which include genitals and breasts, and yes—men and women do count differently! In Alamblak, male and female counting differ with regard to the breasts, while in Yopno, another New Guinea language, men use their testicles for 31 and 33, and the glans for 32!

In Vedda, counting is done in three ways, two of which use Sinhala numerals with the addition of the compound suffix *may* 'precisely'. One of these has base five, in which 'six' is expressed literally as 'five precisely more one precisely' and 'ten' as 'five precisely more five precisely'. The other uses Sinhala numerals up to ten and, potentially, beyond ten but generally only for "round" numbers

such as 20, 50, 100, etc. For "unround" numbers, a finger counting system is often preferred. To express 'eleven' in this system you first display both clenched fists, then open out all the fingers, and say *mettay* (a word of uncertain origin). Then you close the fists, hold out one finger, and again say *mettay*. *Mettay* thus means 'this many' but you have to count and total the fingers displayed in order to know the exact number. Verbally, then, all numbers from 11 upwards potentially consist of two or more *mettay*.

LONGEST NUMERALS

As mentioned above, the number of numbers is infinite, and so are the names for them. Because of this, names for numbers can be of virtually any length. To write, for instance, the number 3 788 773 in English, you'd need no less than 74 letters—and still, it is not an amazingly high number. Therefore, it makes more sense to concentrate

on numbers 1–10 alone. Since these are usually frequent in discourse, they are short in most languages.

Among languages with abnormally long basic numerals, we find the Amazonian language Tariano and the Canadian language Gwich'in. The first ten members of their respective numeral series look like this:

Tariano	
1. *pépanha*	6. *jemimamacabi*
2. *ɲamánda*	7. *jemimabacapilianúda*
3. *manálida*	8. *pehipelianúda*
4. *kepúnipe*	9. *paihipáwalianúda*
5. *pémopakapi*	10. *paihipawalianúda*

Kutchin	
1. *ihthlug*	6. *nikkittyigg*
2. *nekthuĩ*	7. *tʃitsuttetsĩnekthuɪ*
3. *unihthlog*	8. *nikkittankhut*
4. *ttankthut*	9. *vuntʃuthnuko*
5. *ihthlōkwunlih*	10. *ihthlogtʃotyin*

Another language which deserves mention here is Sesotho, which we have already encountered. Jacottet's (1906) textbook in Sesotho book has 44 lessons, but numbers, which are usually introduced early in language teaching, don't appear until lesson 31: "*The numerals being in Sesuto [sic] of a rather complicated construction, we had to wait thus far before giving an account of them*", Jacottet says. And complicated they are, in fact to such an extent that most speakers of Sesotho, including those who have never been

to school, usually prefer to count in English.

Some details of the Sesotho number system were explained above. With all the breaking and pointing of fingers, not to mention the involvement of roots, it comes as no surprise that even moderately high numerals in Sesotho are rather long. The number 9, for instance, requires no less than nine morphemes to be expressed: *ba-tho ba rob-ile-ng mo-no o le mo-ng* (dashes incidating morpheme boundaries). Should you ever feel the need to express '9999 oxen' in Sesotho, it may be useful to know that it simply translates as *likhomo tse likete tse robileng mono o le mong, tse nang le makholo a robileng mono o le mong, a nang le mashome a robileng mono o le mong, a nang le metso e robileng mono o le mong.*

SHORTEST NUMERALS

As mentioned on pp 192–93, languages of South-East Asia typically have short words. Sure enough, the shortest numerals that I have come across are found in the Chökö variety of Yi of China, and in Lati, spoken on the border between China and Vietnam. The numerals 1–10 in these languages are as follows:

	1	2	3	4	5	6	7	8	9	10
Chökö	t'a	m'	sʏ	li	ngo	so	si	zi	ku	tsʏ
Lati	tiam	su	ti	pu	m	nam	tɨ	mui	lu	pə

DISCONTINUOUS NUMERALS

Irish and other Celtic languages share the interesting feature of having discontinuous numerals. The number 'thirteen', for instance, is *trí déag* in Irish, but 'thirteen houses' is *trí theach déag*, i.e. 'thir-houses teen'. Somewhat similar phenomena are also found in Kikongo, Nootka, Mangala, and Wayuu.

SOURCES NOT MENTIONED IN THE TEXT

Rosenfelder (2001) provided most of the general material, with minor additions from Plank (2004). Harald Hammarström also brought some of the material on numerals to my attention.

Lower Sepik numerals: Foley (1986:222, 226).

Slavic languages: Daniel Bunčić (p c).

Mlabri: Harald Hammarström (p c), citing Rischel (1995).

Andamanese: Burenhult (1996).

Nicobarese: Campbell (1991:1010).

Palauan: Mühlhäusler (2003:144).

Nivkh/Gilyak: Comrie (1981:269).

About 20 different sets of numerals in Palikur, Pohnpeian, Upriver Halkomelem, Boro and Loniu: Harald Hammarström (p c).

Yurok: Mithun (1999:105).

Nisga'a: Mithun (1999:530).

Australian languages: Dixon (1980).

Arawak languages: Aikhenvald (1999a:85).

Makú languages (Martins & Martins 1999:265).

Canela-Krahó: Green (1997:181).

Krenák: Loutkotka (1955:125).

Chiquitano: Adam & Henry (1880:19), Adelaar (2004:481).

Jabutí: Aikhenvald & Dixon (1999:358).

Pirahã: Everett (2004), Holden (2004).

Maldivian from Dalby (1998:152).

Base two: Waerden & Flegg (1975:17).

Nenets: Honti (1993, 1996), Comrie (1992).

Palikúr: Green (2001).

Charles XII and the base 64 counting system: Dunér (2002).

Sesotho from Jacottet (1906) provided by Philip Baker.

Kalam: *Linguist List* 6.894.

Counting genitalia in New Guinea: Bruce (1984), Wassman & Dasen (1994).

Vedda: Philip Baker (p c).

Irish: Mac Eoin (1993:118).

Kikongo: Söderberg & Widman (1966).

Nootka: *Linguist List* 15.46.

Mangala: Harald Hammarström (p c).

Wayuu: Zubiri & Jusayú (1986).

NEGATION

NEGATION IS ONE of the few features which you can expect all languages to have. So far as is known, there is no language which does not have a way of saying *There is not a rhinoceros in this room* (provided, of course, there is a word for 'rhinoceros').

WHERE LESS IS MORE

In virtually all languages, the normal negation is a string of phonemes, as in English *not*. In a few languages, negation is marked by means of suprasegmental features, such as tone or length. Still, in both cases, something is added to the statement in order to express negation. Not so in several South Dravidian languages, including contemporary or archaic varieties of Tamil, Kannada, Toda and others. Instead, the negative sentence *omits* material present only in the affirmative version. The trick depends on their using negative constructions in which the negator replaces the tense marker. As the former often has less phonetic substance than the latter, we end up with negative verb forms that have less phonetic material than the corresponding affirmative. In some Dravidian languages, the negator is reduced to zero, and the negative construction thus consists of simply dropping the tense marker.

The following example is from Old Tamil:

kāṇ2		'to see'
kāṇinēn	1sg.AFF.PAST	'I saw'
kāṇ2ēn	1sg. NEG	'I did not see'

LEAVING NEGATION TO CONTEXT

The current French sentence negator *pas* started its career as a noun meaning 'step'. Frequently combined with the then usual preverbal negator *ne*, *pas* gradually took over more and more of the negative semantic load, and today, even moderately colloquial forms of spoken French exclude the *ne* element. Now, *ne* also combines with other elements, such as *personne* 'person', *jamais* 'ever' and *plus* 'more' to express meanings such as 'nobody', 'never' and 'no more'. The loss of *ne* in these contexts too has led to a situation where *personne*, *jamais* and *plus* can mean both 'X' and 'not X', the appropriate interpretation being left to context.

MULTIPLE NEGATION

The Peruvian language Capanahua uses multiple negators in an unusual way with demonstratives. While *haa* means 'he', *haama*, logically enough, means 'not he'. But Capanahua takes this even further, and so, *haamama* is 'not not he', that is, 'he indeed'. Finally *haamamama*, or 'not not not he' refers to 'someone else'. While all this is compatible with logic, it is pragmatically marked, or even outright impossible in other languages.

For someone speaking one of those 'other' languages, multiple negations can even be hard to handle. For instance, former American secretary of state Henry Kissinger once stated that "I am not saying that there's no circumstances where we would not use force". While certain aspects of American foreign policy cast some doubt on the interpretation, what Kissinger in all likelihood did mean was that military force is necessary in *some* (but not all) cases.

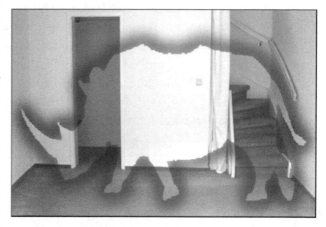

The feeling of emptiness created by the lack of a rhino can probably be expressed in any language

SOURCES NOT MENTIONED IN THE TEXT

Chamicuro: Plank (2004).
Nambiquara: Lowe (1999:281-82).
Dehu, Cèmuhî: Lynch (1998:113).
Negation in Dravidian in general: Plank (2004).
Negation in Kannada: Sridhar (1990: 227-28).
Negation in Old Tamil: Pederson (1993: 233).
Negation in Capanahua: Adelaar (2004:420).
Kissinger quote: Bahgat (2003).

CASE

CASE IS A NOMINAL INFLEXION which fulfils two main purposes. It may serve to indicate roughly who (or what) is doing what in a sentence. Thus, there is in English a difference between, on the one hand, subject forms such as *I* and *she*, and, on the other, object forms such as *me* and *her*. In some languages, such as Finnish, case also indicates placement and movement, as in *talossa* 'in (the) house', where *talo* is house, and the *-ssa* part means 'inside'.

TONAL CASE

Morphological case is usually indicated segmentally, i.e. by adding one or several phonemes to the word in question. Some few languages, however, make case distinctions entirely by tonal means. The phenomenon seems to be entirely restricted to African languages (although belonging to several different families), and possibly also Burmese.

In Matthew Dryer's 934-language sample, only four languages—all of them African—mark case mainly by tonal means.

CASES ON CASES

The languages of Western Australia's Pilbara region are keen on stacking case endings upon one another. Some of them even go as far as equipping stems with no less than four cases at once. The following extreme example comes from Gayardilt:

maku	-ntha	yalawu	-jarra	-ntha	yakuri	-naa	-ntha
woman	OBL	catch	PAST	OBL	fish	MABL	OBL

dangka	**-karra**	**-nguni**	**-naa**	**-ntha**	mijil	-nguni	-naa	-nth
man	GEN	INSTR	MABL	OBL	net	INSTR	MABL	OBL

'The woman must have caught fish with the man's net'
(OBL=oblique, MABL=modal ablative, GEN=genitive, INSTR=instrumental)

HIGHEST NUMBER OF CASES

Every once in a while, someone mentions that a dialect of Tabassaran (in the Caucasus) has over 50 cases. This claim seems to go back ultimately to Hjelmslev (1935-37). On closer inspection, however, it turns out that the system actually consists of seven cases proper, which combine with eight so-called orientation markers. A similar analysis can be applied to neighboring Avar and Tsez, and few of the notoriously case-rich languages of the region would then have more than a score or so of cases.

If the original analysis is nevertheless preferred, Tsez surpasses Tabassaran, as it would then have 56 cases. As it happens, each of these can further combine with yet another case-like suffix, thereby yielding no less than 126 distinct forms.

Ultimately, the analysis that Comrie & Polinsky (1998:105) prefer is one which posits 18 cases in Tsez and 14 or 15 in Tabassaran. To van den Berg (2005:163), Tsez case com-plexes include seven positions, which combine with a distal/non-distal distinction and the core cases essive, ablative and allative, yielding a total of 42 different combinations.

It is worth pointing out that, while one might suspect otherwise, the name Caucasus is not derived from *casus*, the Latin word for case...

Among the less controversial languages outside Caucasia, those of the Uralic family stand out. Figures cited in the literature include 24 for Komi-Permyak, 16–27 (depending on the analysis) for Hungarian, and about 15 for Finnish and Udmurt. Other notable systems with more than ten morphological cases are found in Basque, Brahui, and Hopi.

UNUSUAL CASE

The Australian languages Yidiny and Kalkatungu possess what appears to be a rather unusual case inflexion—they have an *aversive case*, indicating things that should be or are feared or avoided. In a similar vein, several Dravidian languages have a case suffix (reconstructed for Proto-Dravidian as *(k)ku*) used with objects of "verbs of fearing".

AN ODD MARKEDNESS PREFERENCE

Normally, the nominative (subject form) is the least marked case, in the sense that it requires less material to express, just like singular words are usually shorter than plural ones. The English state of affairs where *he* is shorter than *him* is thus typical. In Chukchi, however, it is the absolutive singular which is the most complex form of the noun.

SPLIT ERGATIVITY THE HARD WAY

In *ergative* languages, the subjects of intransitive sentences (such as *I breathe*) are treated on par with objects (*She kissed **him***). Exotic though this may seem to westerners, there is a logic to it in the sense that subjects of intransitives are typically less agent-like than transitive subjects. Few languages are wholly ergative, however, and most are split-ergative, i.e. they usually contain accusative elements as well. One unusually complex system is that of the Saibai dialect of Kalaw Lagaw La, spoken in northern Australia. It features accusative alignment for proper names, tripartite alignment for singular pronouns, neutral alignment for non-singular pronouns and plural common nouns, and finally ergative alignment for non-plural common nouns. Another Australian language, Wangkumara, is the only known example of a language with a fully tripartite system, i.e. where all arguments are marked differently in all areas of grammar.

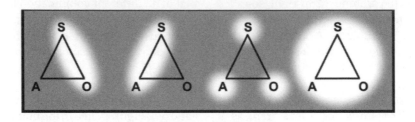

Major alignment types. From left to right: ergative, accusative, tripartite and neutral.
S=subject of intransitive sentence; A=subject of transitive sentence; O=object.

SOURCES NOT MENTIONED IN THE TEXT

Case systems in general: Blake (2001).
Tonal case: Plank (2004); Haspelmath et al. (eds) (2005: map 51).
Gayardilt: Plank (2004), Dench & Evans (1988:34-35 cited in Nichols 1992:62).
Large case systems: Blake (2001), Comrie & Polinsky (1998).
Komi-Permyak: Hausenberg (1998:312).
Hungarian: Plank (2004).
Yidiny and Kalkatung: Dixon (1980:299).
Dravidian fear case: Steever (1998:11).
Chukchi: Plank (2004).
Kalaw Lagaw La: Plank (2004).
Wangkumara: Blake (2001:125).

GENDER AND NOUN CLASSES

ENGLISH IS one of very few Indo-European languages which does not have grammatical gender. Yet, any English-speaker who has ever studied languages such as French, Spanish, or German is familiar with the difficulties in having to cope with differences between e.g. *le livre* and *la table*.

About a quarter of the languages in Nichols' (1992) 174-language sample have some kind of lexically inherent nominal classification (which sounds like an underestimate to me). This is referred to as 'gender' in Indo-European, but usually as 'noun classes' in discussions on e.g. African languages. In Europe, gender assignment has rather little to do with semantics, but the general tendency—not unexpectedly—is that the more classes a language has, the more semantic foundation they have. In other words, wherever there is more than a couple of classes, short and bulky things tend to end up in one category, trees in another, and liquids in a third one. There is virtually always, however, a considerable degree of arbitrariness in the system.

HIGHEST NUMBER OF NOUN CLASSES

The Meso-American language Tzeltal has the highest number of noun classes that I have come across. Reports indicate that between 400, and even up to 528 different groups of nouns have been identified, each taking its own classifier. For Bora of Peru, "more than 350" have been suggested, whereas Kilivila (of the Trobriand Islands in Melanesia) are reported to have about 200 classifiers, encoding categories such as 'conical bundles of taro', 'teeth' and 'parts of a song'.

East and South-East Asian languages, such as Mandarin, Thai, Vietnamese, and Burmese often have around 150 classifiers, and this number is also approached by some East Tucano tongues in Amazonia. One might also mention Chontal (of Mexico) with more than 100, the Micronesian language Kiribati which has 66 different classifiers, and Nasioi of Melanesia with 50.

The language in Nichols' (1992) 174-language sample with the highest number of genders/noun classes is Fula, which has 15 (though the number is followed by a question mark in her table). This, of course, presumes a less liberal definition of "gender/ noun class", in order to exclude numeral classifiers.

SOME FAVORITE NOUN CLASSES

In some languages, certain groupings of nouns into one class may seem rather arbitrary, to say the least, to the outsider. One such example is the noun class prefix *be-* of Kipeá (spoken in South America), which is used for words denoting hills, dishes, stools and foreheads (!).

Another nice example is provided by Tucano, which has a classifier used for 'bark that does not cling close to a tree', and through extension also baggy trousers and pieces of plywood which have become so wet that the sheets separate from one another.

The noun class system of Waris of Papua New Guinea contains several interesting distinctions, including one between the *ninge-* class and the *vet-* class. The former prefix goes with nouns denoting 'food cooked and distributed in leaf wrappers', while the latter is used with words standing for 'food removed from fire, ready to eat, without wrappers'.

Out of the seven classes of Enga (New Guinea), one is reserved for genitalia. Another consists of "orifices, locations, or crawling or aquatic referents", and therefore includes both 'mouth' and 'eel'.

Gilyak, spoken in East Asia, has classes for "different items of fishing tackle", including "smelt strung on twigs" and "poles for drying fish". Its 33-member classifier set also includes "sledges" and "day's rest on one's journey".

MOST FAMOUS NOUN CLASS

Since the publication of George Lakoff's (1987) *Women, Fire, and Dangerous Things*, many linguists are aware that one of the noun classes of the Australian language Dyirbal includes precisely these items. It also includes platypuses, echidnas, bandicoots, dogs, most birds, scorpions, and shields. The male class groups not only men, but also kangaroos, bats, most snakes, storms, rainbows, and boomerangs. There are also two other classes, one of which includes everything edible that is not meat, and by extension also cigarettes.

DO-IT-YOURSELF CLASSIFIERS

Movima has a highly unusual system of numeral classifiers. For native nouns not belonging to any of the major noun classes, the last syllable stands in as a class marker. Nouns borrowed from Spanish also get their last syllable as a class marker if they are mono- or bisyllabic, but the last two syllables if the word is longer. Thus, the class maker for 'shirt' (*camisa* in Spanish) is *-misa*, while the one for 'table' is *-sasa* (cf Spanish *mesa*).

DOUBLE GENDER SYSTEMS

Michif, the curious mixed language mentioned on p 54 has inherited not only the masculine/feminine distinction of French, but also the division into animates and inanimates found in Cree. Michif nouns thus carry two separate gender systems which require agreement both within and outside the noun phrase. It should be noted that the Cree system has relatively little to do with animacy in its literal sense. Some household items, for instance, are animate whereas others are not.

Other languages with parallel noun classifying systems are found in South America. They include Palikur (with 20 noun classes in addition to three genders) and Paumarí (with masculine and feminine in addition to two shape-based classes).

Aikhenvald (2000:67-70, 184-203) includes more examples of this sort. Yet, it seems to me that few are as extreme as the Michif system.

UNEXPECTED GENDER AGREEMENT

In many Semitic languages (including classical Arabic and Hebrew, feminine numerals (or numerals equipped with what is in other parts of the language a feminine suffix) go with masculine nouns, and vice versa.

ETHNOCENTRIC GENDER ASSIGNMENT

Yuchi, a language spoken in the southeastern USA, has ten genders, of which six are reserved for Yuchis (their use depends on the sex and relatedness of the speaker and the listener). Three genders are used for inanimates (non-living things), while the remaining one covers both animals and non-Yuchi humans. The inanimate genders were originally based on shape, but today, 'spirits' belong to the class of vertical things, while 'disease' is horizontal, and 'strength' is round.

CLASSIFYING HANDLING ACTIONS IN NORTH AMERICA

In some languages, nominal classification is manifested on verbs rather than in the noun phrases themselves. This is particularly common in North America, where verbs relating to handling of objects (and sometimes also their position) are equipped with classificatory affixes indicating animacy, shape, containment, consistency, and the like. Kwakiutl of British Columbia in Canada, for instance, has 14 such classes. An interesting feature is that the locational verbs can all be made transitive, through which process they turn into handling constructions.

GENDER IN UNEXPECTED PLACES

G ender is a category which most typically surfaces in the NP, and more often with nouns than pronouns.

Yet, some Afro-Asiatic languages, such as Afar, mark gender distinctions on verbs (referring to the gender of the subject), but nowhere in the NP triggering the marking in the first place.

In the same part of the world, Turkana displays gender contrasts in nouns, but not in pronouns. If we exclude interrogative pronouns, the same holds true also for Teop, a language of Melanesia.

SOURCES NOT MENTIONED IN THE TEXT

Tzeltal: Aikhenvald & Dixon (1998:59), Friedrich (1970:400).
Bora: Wise (1999:319).
Burmese: Aikhenvald & Dixon (1998:59), Friedrich (1970:402).
Kilivila: Senft (1996) cited in de Ruiter & Wilkins (1997).
Chontal: Suárez (1983:88).
Kiribati: Lynch (1998:120).
Nasioi: Capell (1962:371).
Kipeá: Rodrigues (1999b:185).
Tucano: Barnes (1999:219).
Waris: Foley (1986:91).
Enga: Foley (1986:90):
Gilyak: Aikhenvald (2000:109), Comrie (1981:269), Gruzdeva (2004:324-25).
Movima: Aikhenvald & Dixon (1999:369).
Michif: Bakker (1997).
Palikur: Nettle & Romaine (2000:69).
Paumarí: Aikhenvald & Dixon (1998:59).
Semitic: Hetzron (1967:180).
Yuchi: Mithun (1999:103).
Kwakiutl: Mithun (1999:110-11).
Afar: Plank (2004).
Turkana: Plank (2004).
Teop: Plank (2004).

NUMBER

MOST OF THE WORLD'S LANGUAGES have grammatical devices for indicating number. In English, this is usually done by the addition of an -s at the end of nouns, resulting in the paradigm *book ~ books*. Other languages, however, have several ways of saying 'several'.

COMPLEX NUMBER SYSTEM

According to Corbett (2000:36), the most comprehensive work on number in the world's languages, Breton is *"rightly reputed to have one of the most complex number systems"*. It would seem, however, that it does not stand a chance against the Nilotic language Shilluk of southern Sudan, which has been argued to have a *completely unpredictable* way of forming plurals. Field linguist Gilley after thirty years of study concluded that a *"general rule for the formation of plurals in Shilluk cannot be given"*. The same has been said about Shilluk's relative Luo. This does not necessarily mean that all nominal plurals are suppletive, but they are so utterly irregular that the plural form must be stored in the mental lexicon for each item. The related languages Dinka and Nuer also have extraordinarily complex rules for plural formation, though apparently not on a par with Shilluk.

NUMBERS ON NUMBERS

Breton is also unusual in allowing nouns to take more than one number marker. One interpretation of the extra plural is 'several pairs' (when combined with the dual) or 'several groups' (when combined with an already extant plural). Similar phenomena have been observed in Guarequena, spoken on the border between Brazil and Venezuela.

INVERSIVE NUMBER MARKING

Kiowa and other languages of the Kiowa-Tanoan family use a curious way of number marking not documented elsewhere, sometimes referred to as *inversive* marking. The same morpheme, in Kiowa -gɔ` (with a number of allomorphs), indicates singular *or* plural, depending on which number is the least expected. That is, a certain number is inherent in the noun, and the affix simply cancels the expected interpretation, and changes it to the other one. Apart from Kiowa and its relatives, similar phenomena are found in the Nilotic language Ma'a and in two groups of languages on the Pacific islands of New Ireland and Bougainville.

GREATEST NUMBER OF NUMBERS

A few languages have been suggested to have a quadral number, but Corbett (2000) doubts the adequacy of such a label (preferring instead *greater paucal*). In any case, five numbers (singular, dual, trial, paucal and plural) are indeed distinguished in some languages. Five such languages are known, all from the Pacific Ocean: Sursurunga and its close relative Tangga, spoken on New Ireland, the nearby, but somewhat more distantly related Lihir, Marshallese, which is the language of the Marshall Islands, and Mele-Fila of Vanuatu.

AMBAL

The long extinct Indo-European languages Tocharian A and Tocharian B are the only languages which in addition to a dual number are known to also have had an *ambal* (or *paral*). The ambal is used for natural pairs (such as eyes and ears), as opposed to the dual, which refers to any two referents.

EVEN MORE UNUSUAL NUMBERS

Every once in a while, inventors of artificial languages introduce features unheard of in existing tongues. J R R Tolkien's invented Elvish languages both have number systems reported for no natural languages. In one of them, Quenya, a noun has a singular, a dual, a plural, and a plural of multitude, as in *elelli* 'lots of stars'. In the other, Sindarin, nouns have a singular, a dual, a plural, and a plural of totality, as in *elenath* 'all the stars'.

NO NOMINAL NUMBER

In most of the world's languages, number marking on nouns is usually less obligatory than it is in European languages and, in particular, it is often not required with numerals. In other cases, it is simply optional, or is used only with humans or other animates. It is rather rare, though, for a language to lack nominal number altogether. Among the relatively few cases are the members of the Oto-Manguean family of Central America. Other examples include some Papuan languages of New Guinea, and possibly also the West African language Balanta. Ainu of northern Japan is a borderline case, in that a suffix meaning 'and others' may optionally be added to signify plurality of nouns.

NO NUMBER AT ALL

Almost all languages have a category of grammatical number (if not with nouns, then at least in the pronominal system), and only a few exceptions are known. The South American language Pirahã, Kawi (old Javanese), and old Chinese are (or were) rare in not (normally) indicating number neither in its system of personal pronouns, nor on nouns.

In Classical Chinese, it was possible to add an element meaning something like 'group' or 'associates', if an expression of plurality was considered essential, and this may well be true of the others as well.

A few languages of Oceania, including Nimboran, Awyi, Simog, and Daonda also lack pronominal number, although I do not have explicit information regarding number on nouns in these languages.

UNEXPECTED NUMBER AGREEMENT

In Finnish, numerals require that nouns be in the partitive *singular* case—provided that the numeral is higher than 'one', that is, when referring to something which ordinary mortals would consider plural.

Some Slavic languages (including Russian) have the noun in genitive singular after the numerals 2–4 (and compounds including these), but in the genitive plural after higher numbers. The historical reason behind this is that the genitive singular forms were once duals, a category which has since been lost.

VERBAL NUMBER

Many languages mark number on verbs, but in most cases, it is the number of arguments which is indicated (i.e. whether there is more than one subject and/or object). Many North American languages, however, have number marking on their verbs which indicates plurality of actions, in other words several instances of the action denoted by the verb. This is also true for Ainu, an isolate of northern Japan.

PLURAL AS THE DEFAULT NUMBER

It is commonly noted that singular is the *unmarked* (default) number. But there are rarely rules without exceptions, and Imonda and Chibcha are there to prove it. In the former, spoken on New Guinea, plural is zero-marked, while both singular and dual numbers are overtly marked. In the now extinct Chibcha, which used to be spoken in Colombia, the dual form of pronouns is the basic one. Both the singular and plural versions of pronouns are formed by affixation. In the Tibeto-Burman language Ao as well, nouns are inherently plural, and singular number needs to be explicitly marked.

SOURCES NOT MENTIONED IN THE TEXT

Breton: Corbett (2000:36).
Shilluk: Gilley (1992, cited in Corbett 2000:156-58).
Luo: McWhorter (2001:201).
Dinka and Nuer pluralisation: Frank (1999).
Guarequena: Corbett (2000:37).
Kiowa: Watkins (1984:78-100); Wonderly, Gibson & Kirk (1954); Mithun (1999:81-82).
Inversive number in languages other than Kiowa: Corbett (2000:162-65).
Sursurunga, Tangga, Marshallese: Corbett (2000:26-30).
Lihir: Corbett (2000:25).
Mele-Fila: Corbett (2000:35).
Tocharian: Plank (2004).
Tolkien's Elvish languages: Allan (ed.) (1978).
Lack of number marking in Otomanguean: Suárez (1983:86).
Lack of number marking in Papuan: Foley (1986:12).
Lack of number marking in Balanta: Bella (1946:734).
Lack of number marking in Ainu: Shibatani (1990b:32).
Pirahã and Kawi: Corbett (2000:50-51).
Classical Chinese: Norman (1988:89).
Nimboran pronouns: Lynch (1998:167).
Pronouns in Awyi, Simog and Daonda: Eva Lindström (p c).
Finnish: personal experience.
Slavic languages: Daniel Bunčić (p c).
Verbal number in North America: Mithun (1999:83).
Verbal number in Ainu: Shibatani (1990b:32).
Imonda and Chibcha: Plank (2004).
Ao: Campbell (1991:969).

TENSE, MOOD AND ASPECT

TENSE AND ASPECT both have to do with the temporal structure of the state or event described by a verb. English has a major tense distinction between 'work' and 'worked', but also makes differentiates aspect in 'to work' vs 'to be working'. Modality has to do with real and unreal worlds, and the speakers' attitude towards these. In other words, mood encodes wishes, hopes, possibilities, commands, and the like. Here, English has forms such as 'work!', 'may work', 'would work', 'should work', 'could work', and so on.

TENSED NOUNS

The Australian languages Kayardild, Lardil, Baagandji, and Pitta-Pitta present an unusual tense agreement, in which tense is not only marked on verbs, but regularly also on other words, including nouns. A somewhat similar state of affairs obtains in Nambiquara of Amazonia, where nouns take a number of inflections normally thought of as "verby", including tense, evidentiality, and causality. In the same part of the world, most Tupi-Guaranian languages also allow their nouns to take tense affixes. In one such language, namely Paraguayan Guaraní, the use of tensed nouns can look like this:

Ka'a	r-ogue-kué-gui	o-jej-apo	hey'u	porã-rã
yerba mate tree	*LINK-leaf-PAST-ABLATIVE*	*3sg-PASSIVE-make*	*tea*	*good-FUT*

'From the leaves of the yerba mate tree, a good tea can be made'

The leaves in the sentence are marked for past tense since they, at the time of the making of the tea, actually are ex-leaves, in that they are no longer hanging from the tree.

In North America too, languages with tensed nouns can be found. They include Barbareño Chumash, Potawatomi, Kwakiutl, Nootka, Salishan languages, and Yup'ik. An example from the latter language is *ikaraqa* 'my sled', *ikamralqa* 'my former sled', *ikamrkaqa* 'my future sled'. In the same way, Potowatomi allows its speakers to talk about *ntʃimanpən* 'my former canoe', with the same ending as otherwise applied to verbs (cf *nkaʃatsəpən* 'I was happy'). In Siberia, tense affixes on nouns are documented for Yukaghir and for Samoyedic and Mordvinic languages. Nordlinger & Sadler (2000) show that this feature may be less unusual than one might think. They mention in this context the African languages |Gwi, Yag Dii, Sahidic Coptic, and Gusilay, the Latin American Chamicuro and Guaymi, and Gurnu, Iaai, and Tigak of Oceania. As some discussion participants pointed out, however, when the subject was under scrutiny on the Lingtyp and Linguist lists, even non-exotic western languages have constructions such as 'my bride-to-be', 'their ex-landlord', 'the then president', 'my former self' and 'the future prime minister'. Yet, while semantically equivalent, they can hardly be considered grammaticalized.

TMA (TENSE, MODALITY, AND ASPECT MARKERS) ON PRONOUNS

Some languages use different pronouns in different modal context. Wolof (of West Africa), for instance, uses its "third pronoun series" in connexion with questions, subjunctives and conditionals.

A similar, but perhaps more systematic use of this is found in the North American language Caddo and in the African language Supyire, in which the pronominal prefixes are consistently marked for either realis or irrealis (or declarative/non-declarative). Another language of North America, Keres, encodes no less than six different moods in its pronoun series.

Use of different pronouns depending on the tense, mood and (more rarely) aspect of the clause is also attested for the Gurnu dialect of Darling, Hausa, Dii, Scots Gaelic and some varieties of Irish, and for several Oceanic languages, including Manam.

Upriver Halkomelem and Movima do not have different pronoun sets, but instead simply equip their pronouns with tense affixes.

TENSED DETERMINERS

The Arawak language Chamicuro, spoken in Peru, has one definite article, *na*, for the present and future tenses (referring to the tense of the entire proposition), and another, *ka*, for the past.

Movima of neighboring Bolivia, is another such language. Not only its pronouns, but also its articles, take tense affixes.

In the Gurnu dialect of Darling, as well as in Wari', demonstratives are marked for tense. In the latter language, it encodes (apart from spatial relationships) 'currently present', 'recently absent', and 'long absent'.

TENSED PREPOSITIONS

Titan, an Austronesian language of New Guinea has the unusual feature of marking TMA on adpositions. Many of the language's prepositions agree in tense and mood with the verb. The historical explanation for this behavior is that the prepositions once started their career as verbs.

Malagasy also marks tense (past and non-past) on e.g. prepositions, demonstratives and interrogative pronouns. Thus, 'where' is *aiza* if you want to ask where something is. Should you, however, want to ask where something *was*, you would have to use the form *taiza*.

TENSED IMPERATIVES

Imperatives (command forms, such as 'sing!' or 'eat!') are usually seen as a tense—or, more properly a mood—in their own right. In many North American languages, though, the imperatives are inflected for tense, resulting in a distinction between, for instance, 'sing (right away)!' and 'sing (later)!'. Tundra Yukaghir of Siberia is another language of this sort, with a future imperative verb form.

TONAL TMA

Ngbaka (Congo-Kinshasa) marks its four major TMA forms by means of tone alone. Some other African languages also exploit tone to make TMA distinction. Edo, for instance provides the minimal triplet *ímà* 'I show' versus *ímà* 'I am showing' and *ímá*

'I showed'.

The New Guinean language Iau, with an impressive arsenal of eight tones, has a rather intricate aspect system which relies almost entirely on tonal oppositions (Foley 2000:387).

COMPLETE TENSELESSNESS

Lots of languages lack tense proper, but they usually make aspectual or modal distinctions. Maibrat and Hatam are among the few languages that do not have any grammaticalized TMA marking at all. It has been said, however, that they share this unusual feature with other

languages spoken in the same area, that is, the Bird's Head Peninsula of western New Guinea.

A possible African candidate is Che of Nigeria. It has no obligatory marking of tense or aspect, and normally does not indicate mood either.

ELABORATE ASPECT

One of the most intricate aspectual systems I have come across is that of the Siberian language Even, which has morphological marking of more than a dozen different aspects. Competition is offered, however, by Koyukon of north-western Canada, which has four aspectual prefixes, which conspire with no less than 15 different stem-changing processes in expressing exceptionally fine-grained aspectual nuances.

Kiwai of New Guinea also has an

impressive array of aspects, achieved by combining two different sets of verb stems (CONTINUATIVE versus MOMENTARY/PUNCTILIAR) with three suffixes (ITERATIVE, CONTINUATIVE and FREQUENTATIVE).

According to Benjamin Lee Whorf, Hopi also has a remarkable wealth of aspectual distinctions. He enumerates no less than nine, which he labels *punctual, durative, segmentative, punctual-segmentative, inceptive, progressional, spatial, projective* and *continuative.*

RAREST ASPECT?

Pano languages are said by Loos (1999:234) to display suffixed *"aspectual adverbs of daytime or night-time activity"*. Their suffixation could be taken to indicate a relatively advanced state of grammaticalization, and if so, these are among the few languages known which include the day/night opposition in their

grammatical (rather than lexical) machinery.

Yimas of New Guinea shares this odd feature—it has an inflexion *-kia* which marks events happening at night. It is only used in past and in habitual, and not in the present tense. In the other, western half of New Guinea, it is reported that Berik marks its verb for 'morning', 'noon' and 'evening', in addition to morphemes indicating whether the action was performed in sunlight or in the dark. Furthermore, the Berik tense phrase contains an obligatory reference to the intensity of sunlight.

Apart from some free TMA markers, affixes encode number of subjects (for intransitives) or objects, gender, height and size of objects, distance from the speaker, the general time of day, and, of course, tense and polarity. For example, from the verb for 'give', the base form of which consists of b plus a harmonizing vowel, we get:

golbifi   'will give one large object to a woman in the dark' and
kitobana   'gives three large objects to a man in sunlight'

Other examples include:

taferebilint   'tied two large objects in sunlight close to the speaker'
gwerantena   'to place a large object in a low place nearby'
tosonswetna   'to place two large objects in a high place far away'

We don't know much about the Nhirrpi dialect of Yandruwandha, a now extinct variety of South Australia. In fact, the only known data are a ten-minute recording and 25-pages of field notes made by Stephen Wurm in 1958. In any case, Wurm's glossing of the sentences includes a grammatical morpheme translated as "action_at_night".

Semelfactive is a particular verb form denoting the carrying out of an action once, neither more nor less. There seems to be no general agreement as to whether or not there exist languages with a semelfactive aspect, so if there are any, it must be a rare aspect form indeed. It has been suggested, however, that some North American languages, including Hopi, Tunica, Yuki, Pomo, and Koyukon would fit into this category.

EVIDENTIALS GALORE

Evidentiality is a type of mood which carries information on the speaker's degree of certainty and/or the source of information about the carrying out of the action denoted by the verb. In English, such meanings would typically be conveyed by means of subordinate clauses such as *I was told that...* or *Rumor has it that...* or through the use of adverbials like *allegedly*, *probably* or *definitely*. While it is not uncommon to have two evidential markers, some languages of the Amazon Basin, such as Tuyuca, have no less than five, and Amazonia is indeed often perceived as the area in the world with the most developed evidentiality marking. These languages are surpassed, however, by Fasu of New Guinea, which even sports six different evidential markings. A rather similar system with six degrees of evidentiality is also found in the North American language Makah. The winner, though, so far as I can tell, must be Central Pomo, spoken in California. It has six or seven overtly marked evidentials, in addition to the rarely used unmarked form. These enclitic or suffixed morphemes are /-ʔma/ 'general knowledge', /-ja/ 'firsthand (usually visual) personal experience', /-ʔdoma ~ -ʔdo:/ 'hearsay evidence', /-(V)nme:/ 'sensory or auditory evidence', /-ʔka/ 'inference', /-la/ 'personal experience of one's own action' and /-wija/ 'personal affectedness'.

Interestingly, in retelling, some of these

markers can combine (at least in Eastern Pomo), so that the storyteller can add the 'hearsay' morpheme to the 'sensory evidence' one, thereby showing that he has heard from someone what the hero of the story himself experienced at the time.

Those admitting the inclusion of artificial languages may wish to know that Suzette Haden Elgni's *Láadan* has seven evidentiality suffixes.

PLENTY OF TENSES

In addition to the present tense, European languages often only have one past and one or two futures (with other verb forms often referred to as "tenses" actually rather adding other aspectual and/or modal nuances). Further afield, however, we find languages which obligatorily distinguish between actions carried out, e.g. earlier today, yesterday, the day before yesterday or even further back in time. This seems to be particularly true of New Guinean and Bantu languages. Yimas (Papua New Guinea), for instance, has, apart from a present, also four different pasts and two futures, as does Creek of the USA. Four pasts are also found in Korafe, also spoken in New Guinea and in the Burmese language Rawang. An unnamed language of Torres Strait, between New Guinea and Australia, is said by Dixon (1997:119) to go even further in having four pasts, and three degrees of futurity, something that is also true for Washo (USA). Yagua of South America, is reported to distinguish five different pasts, depending on how distant the event under discussion is. On the same continent, Capanahua has not only four pasts, but also an equal number of futures. Finally, for the Gabonese Bantu language Nzebi, Guthrie (1953:71) enumerates five pasts and two different futures. His remark that these are the "most important" temporal distinctions makes one wonder if Njebi has more to offer. The latter comment also applies to the Pano languages of Amazonia, about which Loos (1999:247) says that they have "four or more" different pasts, but that *the future set does not always mirror the past tense set in spans of time covered*".

PLURALITY OF MODALITY

The North American language Menomini has an interesting wealth of moods, as is shown by the following examples:

pi:w	'he comes/is coming/came'
pi:wen	'he is said to be coming/it is said that he came'
pi:?	'Is he coming? Did he come?'
piasah	'So he is coming after all!'
piapah	'But he was going to come! (and now it turns out that he isn't)

While this is not a world record in itself, it nicely illustrates the modal richness displayed in certain languages. Another language of the same area, Fox, has moods denoting concepts such as 'God forbid that this would happen' and 'What if it did happen—What do I care!'.

Hopi, mentioned elsewhere in this book as having an exceptionally large number of aspects and voices, does not let us down in terms of mood either (at least its tense and evidentiality systems seem to be more normal). In Benjamin Lee Whorf's account, it has a multitude of distinctions which could count as modal (although he does not label them all as such). He applies the term *mode* to the seven forms *independent, conditional, correlative, concursive, sequential, agentive,* and *transrelative.* Then, he discusses the *status* categories, which include *affirmative, negative, interrogative,* and *indefinitive.* Only after that come the modality distinctions, of which he discusses no less than nine, viz. *indicative, quotative, inhibitive, potential, indeterminative, advisory, concessive, necessitative,* and *impotential.*

LANGUAGES WITH COMPLEX TMA SYSTEMS IN GENERAL

At first sight, the Maithili TMA system seems impressive, but not outlandish. Verbs are marked for three tenses, five moods, three aspects, three persons, and three honorific grades. On top of that, though, comes a good deal of intricate allomorphy and agreement processes. With, I assume, the typically British fondness for understatements, late 19th century field linguist Grierson noted that "the Maithili verb much tried our patience". Masica (1991:287) is more outspoken when talking about the language's *"superabundance of T/M markers"*, some of which *"defy easy descriptions"*.

SOURCES NOT MENTIONED IN THE TEXT

Kayardild, Lardil, Baagandji, and Pitta-Pitta: Plank (2004).

Nambiquara: Lowe (1999:282).

Nominal tense in Yup'ik and other North American languages: Mithun (1999:154-56).

Tensed nouns Nootka, Salishan, Yukaghir, Samoyedic, Mordvinic, and Tupi-Guaranian languages: Discussions on the Lingtyp list, 20-21 January 2004.

Potawatomi nominal tense: Hockett (1958:238 in Crystal 1987:92).

Pronominal mood in Wolof: Samb (1983:62).

Pronominal mood in Caddo: Mithun (1999:178).

Supyire: Nordlinger & Sadler (2000).

Pronominal mood marking in Keres: Mithun (1999:439).

Tensed pronouns in Gurnu, Hausa, Manam and other Oceanic languages, Scots Gaelic, Irish dialects, Dii, and Upriver Halkomelem: *Linguist List* 14 (1205).

Tensed articles in Chamicuro: Nordlinger & Sadler (2000).

Tense affixes on Movima pronouns and articles: Discussions on Lingtyp 20-21 Jan. 2004.

Tensed demonstratives in Gurnu and Wari': *Linguist List* 14 (1205).

Tensed prepositions in Titan: Bowern & Aygen-Tosun (2000).

Malagasy: Keenan & Ochs (1979:123).

Tensed imperatives in North America: Mithun (1999:153-54).

Tundra Yukaghir: Maslova (2003:21).

Ngbaka: Trask (1993:270).

Edo tones: McWhorter (2001:207).

Iau: Foley (2000:387).

Maibrat: Östen Dahl (p c).

No TMA in Che: Janet Wilson on Funknet list 2003-01-21, and p c.

Even: Campbell (1991:439).

Koyukon aspect: Mithun (1999:166-69).

Kiwai: Foley (1986:148).

Hopi aspects: Whorf (1936:127).

Night-time marking in Yimas: Bill Foley (p c).

Nhirrpi: Stephen Wurm's 1958 field notes in Bowern (2002).

Hopi semelfactive: Trask (1993:250).

Semelfactive in Tunica: Mithun (1999:533).

Semelfactive in Yuki: Mithun (1999:575).

Semelfactive in Pomo: Campbell (1997:124).

Koyukon: Mithun (1999:160).

Evidentials in general: Aikhenvald (2003).

Amazonian evidentials: Dixon (1997:120), Dixon & Aikhenvald (1999:1), Barnes (1999:214).

Fore evidentials: Foley (1986:165).

Evidentiality in Makah: Mithun (1999:181), Jacobsen (1986 cited in Joseph 2003:313).

Evidentiality in Central Pomo: Mithun (1999:181), McLendon (2003:124).

Evidentiality in Eastern Pomo: McLendon (2003:109).

Yimas tense: Foley (1986:160, 166), Aikhenvald & Dixon (1998:58, 69).

Creek tenses: Mithun (1999:153).

Korafe: Lynch (1998:174).

Rawang: LaPolla (2005:26).

Washo tenses: (Mithun 1999:152-53).

Yagua pasts: Haspelmath et al. (eds) (2005: map 65)

Capanahua: Adelaar 2004:421).

Menomini moods: Hockett (1958:92 in Crystal 1987:92).

Fox moods: Hockett (1958:237 in Crystal 1987:65).

Hopi mood: Whorf (1938b).

Maithili TMA: Yadav (1996).

Berik: Westrum (1988:151, 154, 156).

VOICE

EUROPEAN LANGUAGES usually make a distinction between 'The cat chased the mouse' and 'The mouse was chased by the cat'. If you consider these English sentences, you will realize that they mean pretty much the same thing, but that the cat is somehow more prominent in the first (active) sentence, while the focus is on the mouse in the second (passive) one. The distinction is one of *voice*. Apart from the active and passive, some languages also have forms such as *mediopassive* and *antipassive*, although few have all of these.

"Voice" as depicted in the 19th century Infant's Grammar—a pic-nic party of the parts of speech. This was before hitting became discouraged in example sentences illustrating transitivity.

ODD VOICE FORM

Malagasy has an interesting voice form called *circumstantial*. While active and passive voices make the agent or patient the subject of the sentence, the Malagasy circumstantial grants the *adverbial* subjecthood. Somewhat similar constructions, where various adverbial constituents are focussed are common in Malagasy's Philippine and Taiwanese relatives, and occur sporadically in the Austronesian languages of Indonesia.

LARGE NUMBER OF VOICES

Although I unfortunately do not have any more detailed information, I have come across three languages which are reported to have a four-way distinction of voice. These include Ratahan and Tagalog (both Austronesian) and Khakas (Turkic). For those prepared to take Benjamin Whorf's word for it, Hopi would have no less than nine voices, viz. *intransitive, transitive, reflexive, passive, semi-passive, resultative, extended passive, possessive,* and *cessative*.

VOICE AGREEMENT

*I*n some languages, adverbs agree with the main arguments of the sentence. In Maori, the indigenous language of New Zealand, adverbs are reported to agree in voice with the verbs they modify. So, while *aroha* is 'love' and *nui* is 'big', the passive 'to be dearly loved' is *arohatia nuitia*.

SOURCES NOT MENTIONED IN THE TEXT

Malagasy and Austonesian in general: Keenan & Ochs (1979:125) , Niklas Jonsson (p c).
Tagalog and Ratahan voices: Himmelmann (1997).
Khakas: Campbell (1991:731).
Maori voice agreement: Hale (1973:417). His analysis was, however, subsequently contested by
    Sanders (1990, 1991), and further discussed by Hale (1991).

MORPHOLOGY

MORPHOLOGY IS the process whereby smaller elements (*morphemes* or entire words) are strung together to make words (or longer words), as in *kick+ed, re+edit* or *wheel+chair*. While English has less morphology (= is more analytical) than the average language, others are so keen on these processes that what in English would be an entire sentence may come out as a single word.

COMPLEX AND NOT SO COMPLEX MORPHOLOGY

Nichols (1992) devised an index of morphological noun phrase complexity for the 174 languages in her typological database. In her metric, the theoretical maximum score is 27, and the theoretical minimum zero. No languages reach either of these extremes, the most complex ones being Sumerian and Mangarayi, each with 15 points. The least complex languages in her sample are Chitimacha, Mandarin, Miao, and !xóõ, each of which get a mere two complexity points.

While some languages have no verb inflexions at all, and thus only one possible form of each verb, competition is stiff when it comes to having the largest number of inflected forms of each verb. American Indian, Bantu, and Turkic languages are usually mentioned. The highest claim I have come across concerns the Iroquois language Tuscarora, in which each verb—at least in theory—has up to three million forms. It should be noted, though, that Iroquoian languages have intra-verbal noun incorporation, and scores this high could be reached by counting any possible occurrence of a verb with an incorporated noun as a separate verb form. In any case, North American languages in general are infamous for their mind-bogglingly complex verbal morphology. Cheyenne verbs, for instance, have 70 tense-mood-aspect infixes, in addition to which the verbs are marked for both subject and object. Moreover, transitivity, voice, and several markers that would in other languages be realized as nominal case are attached to the verb stem. Faltz (1998) provides a detailed analysis of the Navajo verb which is so intricate that I dare not even try to summarize it. For other languages on this continent, the number of slots, i.e. potential affix positions, are above 20. For Northern Paiute, for instance, the number 23 has been reported. Another North American language, Yup'ik, makes use of no less than 450 different affixes.

Other languages with extensive verb morphology includes Even of Siberia, which has morphological marking of more than a dozen aspects, in addition to verb inflecting for voice, person, number, mood and tense. Komi (Uralic) has a case system with no less than 16 cases, and yet, this doesn't prevent it from marking its verbs for three voices, four tenses, three persons, two numbers and a couple of moods. To make things just a little bit more complicated, it also uses special negated verb forms.

Fortunately, many languages with truly fearsome morphology in one area, make do with a little less in other areas. Georgian, for example, has an impressive arsenal of verb inflexion (with six prefixal and nine suffixal positions), but on the other hand a rather simple nominal morphology, and precisely the same thing is true for many languages of New Guinea.

In more agglutinative languages, it is the noun, rather than the verb which is customized to fit the speaker's communicative needs. While English nouns have a theoretical maximum of just four forms (*car* ~ *car's* ~ *cars* ~ *cars'*), Komi nouns are said to have up to 136 different forms. Yet, its relative Hungarian beats this by having a reported 238 forms.

Morphology can of course be regular despite being exceptionally rich in forms. In Ket, however, the degree of complexity and idiosyncrasy in the verb system is such that one of the foremost authorities on the language has even suggested that "every verb is irregular".

ANOTHER WAY OF MEASURING THINGS

Several measurements have been tested in order to quantify the amount of morphology found in a given language. The best known is no doubt Greenberg's index of synthesis, which measures the number of morphemes per word. A problem is that calculating this requires properly glossed texts, and a good deal of time.

Among the couple of dozen languages for which I have either seen such data, or calculated them myself, the most analytical ones are Vietnamese and Gumawana (1,06 morphemes per word), closely followed by Yoruba (1,09). At the other end of the spectrum, we find Caquinte (3,79) and Inuktitut (3,72).

A possibly time-saving method of yielding similar (albeit not perfectly comparable) figures is to simply count the number of words used in the preamble of the *United Nations' Universal Declaration of Human Rights*, which has the advantage of being translated into a large number of languages. In the English version, this sentence (yes, it is one single sentence!) is 320 words long. In some translations, it has been divided into several, but the stretch of text considered should in any case be the same.

Just as we would expect, highly analytical languages need more words to express the same content. Edo uses no less than 682, while six other languages (all spoken in the Pacific or in West Africa) employ more than 500.

For a variety of reasons (in particular varying degrees of lexicalization), these numbers are not perfectly comparable to Greenberg's index, but for the eight languages for which I had access to both figures, the inverse correlation is not far from being perfect (-0,92), so in practice, calculations based on the U N text *almost* yields an index of synthesis for 250 languages.

MOST DADAISTIC VERB MORPHOLOGY

Linguists are supposed to take languages seriously. We are not supposed to laugh at them. So, apologies to all Kobon speakers out there, but I just can't help it. The prize for the language with the verb morphology most looking like it had been thought up by Tristan Tzara must go to Kobon. If there are any sceptics among the readers, here follows the suffixal paradigm for the counterfactual mood in Kobon:

1sg	bnep	1du	-blop	1pl	-bnop
2s	-bnap	2du	-blep	2pl	-bep
3sg	-böp	3du	-blep	3pl	-blap

PERSON MARKING ON NOUNS

Person marking is normally thought of as a property of the verb, and that is indeed where it usually surfaces, but Nama of southern Africa, along with the now extinct Elamite of the Near East, are two languages which break this generalization. The word 'king', for instance, in Elamite would be sunki-r as long as somebody other than the addressee or the speaker is spoken about. In other cases, you would have to use forms such as sunki-k 'I, the king' or sunki-t 'you, the king'.

PERSON MARKING ON NOUNS

Person marking is normally thought of as a property of the verb, and that is indeed where it usually surfaces, but Nama of southern Africa, along with the now extinct Elamite of the Near East, are two languages which break this generalization. The word 'king', for instance, in Elamite would be *sunki-r* as long as somebody other than the addressee or the speaker is spoken about. In other cases, you would have to use forms such as *sunki-k* 'I, the king' or *sunki-t* 'you, the king'.

METATHESIS AS A MORPHOLOGICAL DEVICE

While morphological operations normally involve affixes (though by no means always, as in e.g. *foot ~ feet*), a few languages of western North America, as well as the Oceanic language Rotuman, are unusual in making use of metathesis, i.e. an alternation between CV (consonant-vowel) and VC. The exact details and functions of Rotuman metathesis have been subject to debate, but it has been claimed to mark morphological distinctions such as tense, aspect and definiteness—cf for instance **epa** *la hoa* 'the mats will be taken' versus **eap** *la hoa* 'some mats will be taken'.

SOURCES NOT MENTIONED IN THE TEXT

Hopi: Whorf (1936:127).
Tuscarora verb forms: Mithun (2000b).
Cheyenne: Campbell (1991:297).

Northern Paiute: Poldervaart (2001).
Yup'ik affixation: Mithun (1999:11, 49).
Even: Campbell (1991:439).
Komi: Campbell (1991:748).
Georgian: Campbell (1991:493); Boeder (2005:22).
New Guinean languages: Foley (1986:12).
Noun forms in Komi and Hungarian: Dalby (1998:256, 324).
Ket: Comrie (1981:264).
Values for Greenberg's synthesis index: Pirkola (2001).
Kobon verb morphology: Davies (1981).
Person marking on nouns: Plank (2004).
Metathesis as a morphological device: Plank (2004).
Rotuman: Churchward (1940).

SUPPLETION

MOST INFLEXION in any language is more or less regular. But most—perhaps even all—languages also have a number of irregular paradigms. Some of these in turn, are so irregular that they qualify as *suppletive*. While, say, *make ~ made* is irregular in English, the two forms still have something in common with one another. This is not the case, for forms such as *go ~ went*, which therefore represents suppletion.

MOST VERBAL SUPPLETION

Lezgian has an unusually large number of suppletive verbs—no less than 16, which is the highest number encountered in Veselinova's (2003) 191-language corpus. The number may not seem very high, but is due to Veselinova having a rather restrictive definition of "suppletion".

SOME UNUSUAL SUPPLETIVES

Most suppletive forms in the any language belong to its most common words. Typically suppletive verbs are 'to go', 'to have', 'to be', etc. There are some exceptions, though. In Hopi, a language of south-western USA, the verb 'to go around something out of sight' is *-toni* if one person does it, but *-kya* if for some reason several people should engage in the activity. In Imonda, spoken on New Guinea, the singular form of 'to make a netbag' is *hoño*, while the plural form is *pueg*.

The Caucasian language Archi is also a good candidate for the 'most unexpected suppletive item' category. The word *bič'ni* translates as 'corner of a sack', provided we are talking about one corner only. Several corners of sacks, however, is *boždo* (what is there about sacks and bags that make them so prone to suppletion?). The Archi word for 'pier of a bridge' is also suppletive, with the singular form *biqˤ'ni* corresponding to the plural *boʁˤdo*.

SOURCES NOT MENTIONED IN THE TEXT

Lezgian: Veselinova (2003).
Hopi: Seaman (1996).
Imonda: Seiler (1985:82).

Archi: The *Surrey Suppletion Database* (http://www.smg.surrey.ac.uk/Suppletion), compiled by Dunstan Brown, Marina Chumakina, Greville Corbett and Andrew Hippisley of the *Surrey Morphology Group* in Guildford, Britain.

Special thanks to Ljuba Veselinova who brought some of the material in the suppletion section to my attention.

SENTENCES

BASIC WORD ORDER refers to the normal order of the three main sentence constituents—subject (S), verb (V) and object (O). There are logically six possible orders, SOV, SVO, VSO, VOS, OSV and OVS. The notion of "normal" is obviously problematic here, and lacks a definition completely independent of intuition. Thus, in English, *The woman read the paper* (SVO) is felt as being more 'normal' by native speakers than, say, *(It was) the paper the woman read* (OSV). In fact all six orders are to some extent possible in English (and in many other languages), but SVO is seen as the normal, or *unmarked* word order. Among other objective indications of this is that SVO occurs more frequently than other orders, many of which are also restricted to specific contexts or genres, such as poetry.

MOST COMMON AND LEAST COMMON BASIC WORD ORDER

Since the number of logically possible basic word orders is six, we might expect each to be represented by about a sixth of the world's languages. This, however, is far from being the case. There are, in fact, two global tendencies which capture the differences in frequency between the possible orders—for reasons not yet understood, languages seem to prefer placing S before V, and to avoid having objects in the initial position.

The most common basic word order is thus SOV, the least common being OVS. In fact, until the second half of the 20th century, no certain examples of object-initial languages had been documented by western linguists, the first being Hixkaryana (OVS), which was described by Derbyshire (1961). Later, Apurinã—like Hixkaryána, a Brazilian language—became the first attested OSV language. Even later,

Australian languages like Mangarayi and Ngarinyin proved to be OVS, whereas Hurrian and Coos were prone to employ object-initial word orders as frequent alternatives.

The approximate share of the world's languages with each of the six possible orders is as follows:

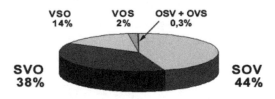

The rare object-initial languages are found almost exclusively in Latin America, and mainly in the Amazon region. A handful are also spoken in Australia and New Guinea, with isolated cases scattered elsewhere in the world.

FREE WORD ORDER AGAINST ALL ODDS

*L*anguages with a more or less free word order tend to be those with an extensive morphological machinery (Latin and Navajo are among those most frequently cited). By adding inflexional morphemes to the NPs, the listener is at no risk of confusing who did what to whom. Conversely, morphologically poor languages often have rather strict word order. However, some languages of South-East Asia, including Lisu and Lao, have free word order, despite its lack of formal devices such as case endings to mark subjects and objects. The assignment of syntactic functions thus has to rely entirely on shared knowledge, context and pragmatics. The same has been claimed for Záparo, spoken in Ecuador.

LONG SENTENCES

Long sentences have fascinated and continue to fascinate many a language aficionado, though rarely the professional linguist. The reason why linguists are so reluctant to partake in the quest for the longest sentence is simple—they know beforehand that the search is in vain. One of the first things that linguists teach their new students is that there is not, and cannot be, such a thing as the longest sentence. To be sure, some sentences are longer than others, and there is in practice some kind of limit on how long you can make your sentence if you actually want to be understood. However, any sentence, even if it goes on for pages and pages can be made longer still—you can just add *and*, and then continue with what would have been your next sentence. Pinker (1994:86-87) nicely illustrates the infinite possible lengthening of any sentence. He mentions the first sentence of William Faulkner's *Absalom, absalom!*, which, by virtue of its 1 300 words once wound up in the *Guinness Book of World Records* as the allegedly longest sentence. Pinker achieved an even longer sentence by adding "Faulkner wrote. . ." at the beginning. One could even, he continues, add "Steven Pinker said that Faulkner wrote. . .", to which somebody else might reply "Who cares that Steven Pinker said that Faulkner wrote. . .". And so on. . .

A normal sentence in the British newspaper *The Times* is about 20 words long. In fiction, we occasionally encounter things like the 424-word sentence in Hemingway's *Green Hills of Africa*, the Faulkner monster mentioned above, or Henry David Thoreau's 475-word sentence in a 1852 piece called *The Gone-to-Seed Country*.

Even the Bible has a sentence (Ephesians 1:3–14) which in the Greek original extends over 270 words, though this is cut up into four separate sentences in the English translation. (In all fairness, the use of punctuation marks was in general less developed in those days).

Since writers of judicial texts have to make sure that they don't leave any loopholes, law prose usually contains sentences far longer than in most other types of writing. Thus, for instance, the first sentence of the English version of the United Nations' *Universal Declaration of Human Rights* is 320 words long.

Again, however, long sentences fascinate people, and so does the possibility of being a record-holder. Thus, some authors have deliberately taken great pains to accomplish monstrous sentences. Apart from those already mentioned, works usually quoted as the ones containing the longest sentences in literary history are Victor Hugo's *Les Miserables* (in which one sentence contains 823 words), Marcel Proust's *À la recherche du temps perdu* ('Remembrance of things past') (958 words) and Molly's monologue in James Joyce's *Ulysses* (4 391 words).

Some lesser-known works, however, boast way longer sentences. In early 2001, Jonathan Coe's The Rotter's Club received quite some attention due (at least in part) to it containing a 13 995-word sentence. Even Coe, however, is surpassed by two eastern European authors of the 1960's— Bramy raju ('Gates of Paradise'; 1960) by Polish writer Jerzy Andrzejewski has a sentence of 40 000 words, while the entire novel *Taneční hodiny pro starší a pokročilé* ('Dancing Lessons for the Advanced in Age', published in 1964) by Czech Bohumil Hrabal is bereft of full stops. (Interestingly, the title of another one of his works translates as "Cutting it Short").

Finding Victor Hugo in a list of people producing extraordinarily long sentences has a twist of irony to it, since he is often accredited with having carried out the shortest correspondence in history. The story is that in 1862, Hugo was anxious to learn about how his latest book (which, as is happens, was precisely *Les Misérables*) was selling in the USA. His telegram to the American publisher consisted of one single symbol, namely "?". The publisher, it is reported, sent Hugo the satisfactory reply "!".

SHORT SENTENCES

So, what about the shortest sentence then? That's easy. Think about it. *Think!* Or, better still—don't even think. *Be!*

A LANGUAGE WITHOUT EMBEDDING?

Pirahã is a language which is extreme on pretty much any point there is (and the attentive reader has surely noticed that is gets its fair share of mentions in this book). It has even been suggested to be the only language known without embedding. It does have sentence structures which do look like they include embedding, but the main authority on the language, Dan Everett (2004), argues that the best analysis is one which does not postulate this as a feature of Pirahã grammar.

SOURCES NOT MENTIONED IN THE TEXT

Location of object-initial languages based on *Ethnologue* 14.

Additional object-initial languages from Nichols (1992:302-06).

Percentages of various word orders based on reports in Tomlin (1986) and Finegan (1999:253).

Lisu free word order: Crystal (1987:98).

Lao free word order: Dixon (2003a:175).

Free word order in South-east Asia in general: Enfield (2005).

Záparo: Adelaar (2004:452).

Long sentences in literature: BBC Radio 4 broadcasting on *The Rotters Club* in April 2001. Also a wide variety of internet sources in combination with library catalogues.

Shortest sentence inspired by Kolin (1979) and Anthony Grant (p c).

LINGUISTICS DEPARTMENTS

IT IS DIFFICULT to say for sure, but I would estimate that there are about 200 linguistics departments in the world. A smallish number of departments are more specialized, being devoted primarily or exclusively to computational linguistics, speech technology, sign linguistics or phonetics. The most odd man out is perhaps the Moscow State University, which has an entire department for research in psycholinguistics alone. In terms of faculty members, the average size of a linguistics department seems to be in the vicinity of 12 ("faculty" being defined here as a relatively permanently employed holder of a PhD).

BIGGEST DEPARTMENT

The biggest known linguistics department known to me is the one at Paris 7 in France, which has a faculty of no less than 35. It is followed by linguistics of UCLA in Los Angeles, with 30 faculty members.

SMALLEST DEPARTMENTS

While I have yet to come across a linguistics department with a faculty consisting of only one or two people, a faculty of three is not uncommon. At least at the time of writing this, such is the case for departments in e.g. Philadelphia (Swarthmore College) and Irvine (USA), Toyama and Sendai (Japan), Durban (South Africa), London (Queen Mary and Westfield College) (Britain), Szeged (Hungary), Lvov (Lviv; Ukraine), Passau (Germany), Regina (Canada), and Perth (Australia). Even though the department in Passau is smaller than most, it did until recently have something most other departments are bereft of: a canine mascot, in the form of the department dog Delia. Unfortunately, Delia went to join the great kennel in the sky in 2003.

LARGEST NUMBER OF LINGUISTICS DEPARTMENTS

It seems unlikely that any other country would be able to rival the number of linguistics departments in the United States, which amounts to about 70.

Not only countries, but also a few individual cities are sometimes lucky to have more than one linguistics department. The highest number in any one city is likely to be that of Greater New York, which has no less than six (two in the city itself, and one each in Stony Brook, Upper Montclair, New Brunswick and Newark), followed by Los Angeles, which has five. Cities blessed with at least three different departments include Paris, London, Moscow, San Francisco, Washington and Chicago. About two departments (depending on the count) are found in Tokyo, Sydney, Ankara, Manchester, Montreal, Cambridge (Massachusetts, not England), Bangkok, Vancouver, Leipzig, and Philadelphia, and possibly also in a couple of other places.

As can be gathered from the map overleaf, California is exceptionally rich in linguistics departments—taken as a whole, the state has no fewer than 13—far more than most countries in Europe. In addition to this, Monterey, which prides itself of being "the language capital of the world" (see p 136) is located not far from San Francisco.

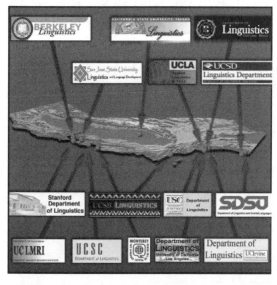

Linguistics departments in California are all over the place. In pre-Columbian times, California was the most linguistically diverse part of the present-day USA.

The Californian edge in American linguistics is also illustrated by the following LSA (=*Linguistic Society of America*) membership breakdown:

University of California at Berkeley	6,6%	*Stanford University*	4,5%
University of California at Los Angeles	5,9%	*University of Michigan*	4,2%
Arizona University	5,4%	*University of Texas*	4,1%
Indiana University	5,3%	*Massachusetts Institute of Technology*	4,0%
Summer Institute of Linguistics	5,0%	*University of Chicago*	4,0%

NORTHERNMOST AND SOUTHERNMOST DEPARTMENT

T romsø in northern Norway enjoys boasting the world's northernmost this-and-that, and the northernmost linguistics department in the world is indeed the *Institutt for lingvistikk* of the University of Tromsø in northern Norway. Its counter-part in the southern hemisphere is less obvious, but seems to be the linguistics department at Canterbury University in Christ-church, New Zealand.

MOST RENOWNED FACULTY

Few departments have more than one or at the most a couple of members who can lay claim to international fame. Two departments, however, stand out in this respect, and not surprisingly, both are located in California, more precisely in the Greater San Francisco area. Stanford University is the home base of Joan Bresnan, Eve Clark, Penelope Eckert, Shirley Brice Heath, Paul Kiparsky, Ivan Sag, Elizabeth Traugott and Arnold Zwicky, among others. At Berkeley, faculty includes Charles Fillmore, Larry Hyman, Paul Kay, George Lakoff, Ian Maddieson, James Matisoff and John Ohala (and until recently Murray Emeneau and John McWhorter). As if that weren't enough, other departments at the same university employ John Searle (philosophy), Johanna Nichols (Slavic) and Dan Slobin (psychology), all of whom can be said to be active in linguistics as well.

Tromsø in northern Norway has the northernmost linguists.

OLDEST LINGUISTICS DEPARTMENT

In the United States, both the University of Pennsylvania and the University of Chicago claim to host the country's oldest linguistics department. In Britain, the same claim is made by SOAS, that is the School of Oriental and African Studies in London. Unfortunately, I have not been able to find out whether any of these, or another department was the first in the world.

LARGEST LINGUISTIC ASSOCIATION

The linguistic association with the highest membership number is undoubtedly the *Linguistic Society of America*. In April 2002, it had no less than 4 094 members, two thirds of whom were Americans. The rest were drawn about equally from Asia (mainly Japan) and Europe (predominantly Germany, Britain and the Netherlands).

Few other linguistic societies have more than a thousand members, the largest possibly being *International Linguistic Association*, with 1 400 members. The *International Phonetic Association* might be a possible competitor, but it has chosen not to reveal the number of its members to me.

While not an association per se, the *Linguist List* is certainly the largest linguistic forum there is, with presently about 21 000 subscribers.

The wittiest name of a linguistic association is probably that of the *Linguistics Association of Delaware*, abbreviated as *LAD* (normally interpreted as *Language Acquisition Device*). It has 30 grad students as members. In this category, we must also not forget the fictious Southern Hanoi Institute of

Technology, also known as S H I T, the generative semantics association led by the legendary Quang Phuc Dong, alias Jim McCawley.

SOURCES NOT MENTIONED IN THE TEXT

Linguistics departments: The data on linguistics departments derive mainly from analysis of the departments' home pages and on personal experience. Note that only linguistics departments proper are considered here, although linguistic research may be pursued be studied elsewhere as well. For example, in Stockholm, where I live, there is only one linguistics department proper, but the university also hosts a *Centre for Research on bilingualism*, as well as eleven departments devoted to the study of specific languages or language groups. In addition to that, other academic institutions in the city have some linguistic-related activities, including the *Swedish Institute of Computer Science* (computational linguistics), the *Royal Institute of Technology* (computational linguistics and speech technology), and the medical university *Karolinska Institutet* (speech pathology). Moreover, research in subject fields such as mathematics, law, anthropology and philosophy may sometimes include quite a bit of linguistics. Again, only "real" linguistics departments are considered here.

The breakdown of LSA members was done by analysis of the email addresses in 2001 member directory. Most addresses were possible to link to a specific geographical location.

MOST STUDIED LANGUAGES

WHETHER WE LIKE IT or not, there is a tendency among linguists to concentrate their studies on certain already well-known languages.

BEST DESCRIBED LANGUAGES

Judging from the *MLA bibliography* (MLA=*Modern Language Association* of the United States), English is—rather unsurprisingly—the best described language there is. Equally unsurprisingly, it is followed by eleven other European languages. The complete top-20 list looks as shown on the right.

The position of Irish, I must admit, is unexpected. I suspect it may have to do with the inclusion of literature studies in the database.

Despite its ambitions to deal with representative samples, even typology cannot escape a bias towards big languages. The most frequently cited in Haspelmath et al. (2005), for instance, are (in order of popularity): English, French, Finnish, Russian, Spanish, Turkish, Hungarian, Indonesian, Japanese, and Mandarin. If, however, we choose to treat certain clusters of closely related varieties as one entity, the top-ten consists entirely of non-Indo-European languages: Arabic, Mixtec, Nahuatl, Chinantec, Quechua, Berber, Basque, Yukaghir, Oromo, and Zoque.

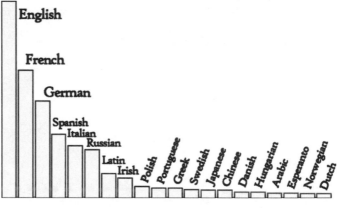

SOURCES NOT MENTIONED IN THE TEXT

Most studied languages: Publications in the MLA database between 1963 and 2001, as of 2002-11-28. I counted the languages I expected to be well represented, along with a few less well-known ones, chosen at random.

EXPERIMENTATION IN LINGUISTICS

LINGUISTICS IS A SCIENCE, and science often requires experimenting. Not all linguistic subdisciplines engage in hands-on experimentation, but some do. Here follows a review of some of the more unusual experiments performed.

TESTING INNATENESS BEFORE CHOMSKY

Pharaoh Psammetichus I ruled Egypt in the 7th century before our era. He was interested in the question of which language was original to humankind, and devised a cruel experiment to find out. It is said that he had two newborn babies taken from their parents. The babies were isolated, and received no linguistic input whatsoever. That way, Psammetichus reasoned, the language they would finally start speaking must surely be the underlying language of all humankind. The story has it that the first word uttered by the two children was *bekos*, which was the Phrygian word for 'bread'. (Phrygian is a now extinct Indo-European language of present-day Turkey.) The pharaoh was deeply disappointed, but had to admit that Phrygian, and not Egyptian, was the universal human language. It was later suggested that *bekos* was the children's imitation of the sheep that surrounded them.

A similar experiment is said to have been carried out in 1211 in Germany by emperor Frederick II of Hohenstufen who was in search of "the language of God". Several dozen children were thus sacrificed, winding up speaking nothing at all. The children reportedly all died young.

A folk tale from the coast of Småland in Sweden has the same theme. In this case, the child's first utterance is *fan*—a swearword stylistically corresponding to 'fuck'—"just like they would say in inner Småland".

EARLY SPEECH SYNTHESES

In his home country, Swedish 17th century physician and author Urban Hjärne is still remembered, but mostly for his efforts to put an end to witch-trials. A lesser-known fact is that he also carried out research on artificial speech. One of his attempts involved chopped-off heads—a commodity which was in abundant supply at the time. A bellow pumped air into the head, and by attaching strings to the heads, Hjärne controlled the movements of the tongue, lips and cheeks. Success is reported to have been moderate.

Another pioneer in this area was Alexander Graham Bell. Given his work on the telephone (the invention of which is often, although erroneously, attributed to him) it is not surprising that he had a keen interest in speech. In his youth, he experimented with artificial speech in a somewhat unorthodox way.

The experiment consisted in Bell teaching his dog to growl on command. While it did so, Bell massaged its vocal tract to manipulate the sound (something that may or may not have made the dog growl even more). In this way, the dog is reported to have been able to utter a couple of speech sounds, sufficient for it to say "How are you, grandma?".

Urban Hjärne was a multi-talented man indeed. His artistic skills are evident from this self-portrait.

BEING MEAN TO LITTLE CHILDREN AT THE WORKPLACE

A mid-1990s paper in the *Journal of Speech and Hearing Research* brought a little-known problem in child language research to the attention of the scientific community. This gem is just too good not to be cited in its entirety:

> *Presently, there appears to be a lack of consensus among researchers as to the ideal methods of eliciting a pain cry from infants. Consequently, there is no standard with which to compare across studies. For example, previous studies have elicited pain cries from infants based on a rubberband snap to the heel (Murry, Amundson, & Hollien, 1977; Zeskind & Lester, 1978, 1981), heel stick with a blood lancet or heel flick with a researcher's index finger (Corwin, et al., 1992; Lester et al., 1991), a pinch applied to the infant's arm or ear (Michelsson, Sirvio, & Wasz-Hockert, 1977b; Michelsson et al., 1982), as well as removal of electrodes used to monitor the infant's heart rate and respiration (Colton & Steinschneider, 1981; Lester, Boukydis, Coll, Hole, & Peucker, 1992). Still other studies have been less precise in reporting cry elicitation, using "physical manipulation of the infant" (Zeskind, 1981), or using "standard newborn reflexes" (Lester, 1987; Lester & Dreher, 1989). Certainly, future research should be directed toward developing a standardized method of cry elicitation.*

CAN THE IMPOSSIBLE BE LEARNED?

In 1995, Neil Smith and Ianthi-Maria Tsimpli published the results of their work with Christopher, a so-called *savant*. Christopher is mentally handicapped in many ways, but possesses a remarkable skill in learning new languages. Apart from his native English, Christopher speaks excellent French, Spanish, German and Greek, and also has some knowledge of Danish, Swedish, Norwegian, Dutch, Finnish, Hindi, Italian, Polish, Portuguese, Russian,

Turkish and Welsh. To test his abilities, Smith and Tsimpli set out to teach him the basics of Berber, a language to which he had previously had no exposure, and which is also in many ways unlike the ones he already knew. This Christopher managed quite well. Then, in order to test Chomskyan claims about 'possible' and 'impossible' human languages, they started teaching him an invented language, Epun. Epun was deliberately constructed so as to have grammatical rules not found in any existing language (such as a particular behavior of the third word of a sentence), and was intended to be unlearnable. And sure enough, Christopher failed to learn Epun.

The control group of first-year linguistics students managed to figure out how some of the 'impossibilities' worked, thus corroborating, in the view of the authors, the Chomskyan division between a language faculty, and a more general problem-solving capacity.

After the publication of their book, Smith and Tsimpli began teaching Christopher British Sign, in order to see whether he could become equally proficient in a language not using sound as a medium. The result was satisfactory, as Christopher acquired a working knowledge of British Sign.

THE MONSTER STUDY

In the late 1930s, a stuttering research programme was conducted by Wendell Johnson at the University of Iowa. Johnson suspected that part of what caused stuttering was the behavior of people in the stutterer's environment—if they expected the person to stutter, or if the person believed that they expected him to stutter, so he would. Therefore, Johnson and his student Mary Tudor set up the experiment sometimes referred to as "the monster study". A number of perfectly normal children in an orphanage were told that they might become stutterers, and that they ought not to speak unless they were sure that they would manage to do so without problems. The orphanage staff was also told to keep their eyes open for any signs of beginning stuttering. The official reason for these instructions was consideration for the children. If these would begin having fluency problems, Johnson's thesis would have found empirical support.

Within a couple of months, it was reported that the child subjects had become hesitant in speaking, and that they kept their spoken communication to a minimum—speaking only when urged to, and responding in as short sentences as possible. As a result, their grades plummeted.

Records thereafter are vague on whether most children eventually became stutterers. Nonetheless, there is evidence that some of them actually did develop a stutter. Six decades later, the ageing Tudor received a letter from one of the orphans saying "You destroyed my life. I could have been a scientist, archaeologist or even president. Instead I became a pitiful stutterer. The kids made fun of me, my grades fell off, I felt stupid. Clear into my adulthood, I still want to avoid people to this day". Obviously, the "monster" label stuck to the experiment for a reason.

BLUSHING FOR NO APPARENT REASON

Split-brain patients are of special interest in psycholinguistic research. In these patients, the nerves connecting the two brain hemispheres have been cut off in order to better cope with extreme epileptic conditions. Now, linguistic information is—in most humans—primarily dealt with by the left hemisphere. This means that experiences of stimuli reaching only the right one may be difficult to put into words for someone with little or no communication between the hemispheres.

Several studies by Roger Sperry and Mike Gazzaniga illustrate this phenomenon. Among the more memorable aspects is that if a nude picture was interspersed with other, more neutral pictures, the male subjects tended to grin or giggle, while female patients tended to blush—without being able to verbalize the reasons for their behavior.

THE ULTIMATE TEST: MIDWIFING A NEW LANGUAGE

In 1981, Derek Bickerton published his seminal *Roots of Language*, a book which had a profound impact not only on creole studies, but also on linguistics in general. Bickerton's claim was that the first generation of locally-born children in a pidgin-speaking society were exposed to such an impoverished and confused linguistic input from their parents that they "invented" their own grammatical rules, following a genetically defined blueprint inherited by every human being.

In order to get some empirical backing for the claim, Bickerton naturally wanted to repeat the experience with children being born to parents not speaking each other's language. This happens all the time, but the test required that this happen in a scientifically controlled environment, and on a large enough scale to make the kids more dependent on one another than on the parents as linguistic role models.

Bickerton therefore applied for a grant to place six families of differing linguistic backgrounds—volunteers, mind you—on a deserted Pacific island. The adults would not speak each other's language, but they would have been equipped with a 200-item word list before disembarking on the island. While the parents were busy growing coconuts, the children would grow a language of their own, thereby replicating, according to Bickerton, what children had done in Haiti, Hawaii, and a large number of other societies founded by plantation workers from varying linguistic backgrounds.

While the University of Hawaii's ethics committee approved the project, the American *National Science Foundation* had its doubts regarding the possible traumas suffered by the children, and put an end to Bickerton's dreams.

SOURCES NOT MENTIONED IN THE TEXT

Experimentation in linguistics: This section has benefited enormously from personal communication with Robert Eklund. He provided the data on early speech synthesis, and brought several of the articles cited under the other headings to my attention.

Pharaoh Psammetichus: Crystal (1987:288), Herodotus (1966:102-03).

Frederick II of Hohenstufen: Perry (2002:79).

Folktale from Småland: Svensén (1879).

The mention of baby cry elicitation is from Grau, Robb & Cacace (1995:374).

Christopher's impressive aptitude for foreign languages is documented in Smith & Tsimpli (1995), and his acquisition of British Sign in Morgan et al. (2002).

The Monster Study: Silverman (1988), San Jose Mercury News 2001-06-10.
Blushing experiment: Sperry (1968).
Derek Bickerton's island dreams: Berreby (1992).

SOME WORK THAT DIDN'T STAND THE TEST OF TIME

IN EVERY SCIENCE, theories are incessantly launched, tested, and either accepted or rejected, and linguistics is no exception. Every once in a while, some unconventional linguistic theories come with quite a bit of unintentional entertainment value. Some could even be said to be uncannily close to the "mad scientist" caricature (fortunately, though, much of what is to follow was not proposed by actual linguists).

As we all know, numerous people considered lunatics by their contemporaries have since received posthumous recognition, and their accounts are now uncontroversial. It is of course possible, though only time will tell, that some of the ideas mentioned below are in fact remarkably ahead of their times (if so, don't forget where you heard them first...).

AND THEY HUFFED AND THEY PUFFED

Campbell (1998:283) mentions an early attempt at explaining Grimm's law. According to somebody whose name (fortunately?) seems to have been lost to history, the fact that many Germanic speakers resided in mountainous regions would explain the well-known sound changes. The huffing and puffing that running up and down these mountains caused would have made it easier for them to pronounce fricatives than stops.

Another unnamed 18th-century linguist mentioned by Campbell (1998:284) suggested that the sound changes included in Grimm's law were due to hearing impairment of Germanic speakers caused by a build-up of ear wax greater than in the ears of other Europeans.

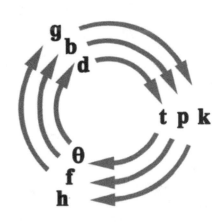

Grimm's law contributed to creating the Germanic languages we know and love today.

A FOGGY THEORY

The rounding of /a/ to /o/ in Germanic languages (e.g. modern English *stone* from Old English *stān*) was claimed by the otherwise admirable Henry Sweet (1900:32) to be due to the climate. The sound change was *"doubtless the result of unwillingness to open the mouth widely in the chilly and foggy air of the north"*.

SPEECH FROM A RAY OF LIGHT

Schmidt (1955) claims that the human brain translates light waves into sound waves. Strong exposure to sun light leads to "full sounding vowels" (whatever that means), while lack of sun light leads to "weak sounding vowels". The fact that the rainbow consists of seven colors, while many languages have a seven-vowel system is surely no coincidence. Diphthongs, Schmidt proposes, represents transitory colors in the spectrum. Therefore, it comes as no surprise, at least not to "whoever had the chance to compare a rainbow in Sicily with a rainbow in Central Europe", that Italian lacks diphthongs, for the Sicilian rainbow is "much more distinct" than a Central European one, "where the colors merge into another much deeper color". Similarly clear is the reason for the claimed preponderance of assimilation in Romance languages "heat joins, i.e. amalgamates the bodies; coldness freezes them in: they stay isolated". Nevertheless, Schmidt concludes, Romance languages "are much better than the English language to carry on processes of thinking".

DAVID OATES' SPEECH REVERSAL LAB

In the mid-1980s, Australian David Oates began working on speech reversal, i.e. the backwards playing of taped speech in search of hidden messages. Most of the time, Oates claims, humans are simultaneously speaking in two modes—one forward and one backward mode. The former is conscious, but study of the backwards mode through reversal of tape recordings reveals the subconscious thoughts of the subject. Not only do all people speak backwards, but Oates also claims that children begin speaking backwards even before they are able to form coherent sentences in a normal way.

Oates offers plenty of examples of his findings. For instance, when Neil Armstrong upon landing on the moon uttered "One small step for man", his subconscious said "Man will space walk", thereby foreseeing the future of space travel. Similarly, when president Bush was talking about the anti-Taliban war efforts in 2002, his subconscious was really saying "Arrest niggers who shame this effort". There does seem to be a less violent side of Bush's subconscious, though, for speaking on the same subject at another occasion, a reversal of his speech revealed him saying "Love is nice".

Somewhat surprisingly, even people with other mother tongues appear to speak English when their backward speech mode is examined by Oates. His collection of reversals includes the Libyan dictator Qadhafi saying "Bomb America" and "I'm a beautiful person", while Al Qaida leader Bin Laden exclaimed "But our government is wrong—terror now".

MAKE LOVE, NOT WAR—BY AVOIDING VOICED FRICATIVES!

Reed (1995) is an investigation of the relationship between the use of voiced fricatives and the propensity to solve conflicts by means of violence. The connection is explicable since psychosomatic states are related to activity in the same brain areas as is the production of voiced fricatives. So, by using voiced fricatives in everyday speech, the members of a language group excite each other to becoming even more violent. Therefore, Reed claims, the level of violence in the group is directly proportional to the proportion of voiced fricatives in their language.

Fortunately, conscious language engineering—including a revision of the world's consonant inventories—offers some hope for the future, Reed concludes. Could it be that this holds the key to eternal peace and brotherhood? I'll be damned.

EXAMINE YOUR LIMBS AND FIND OUT IF YOU CAN SPEAK

Kluge (1955) begins by explaining that clicks are produced by letting air into low pressure cavities. These include all body cavities, such as shoulder and hip joints (!), vaginas (!!) and mouths. The use of clicks in certain languages, not unexpectedly, is due to the "anatomical shape of the tongue, upper and, particularly, lower jaw and facial muscles" of their speakers.

Kluge's reasoning gets even more interesting towards the end of the article— while most animals make sounds of one kind or the other, only humans and birds sing. This can only be due to them being two-legged creatures, and "that man, in addition talks, is explained by the fact that he has arms and no wings". Finally, Kluge finished off with an explanation of tonal differences between Chinese and Tibetan—these are no doubt caused by the lower density of the air on the high altitudes on which the latter is spoken. Thirteen years latter, the same journal published an addendum to the first paper. In this, Kluge explains that he had in 1955 forgotten an important factor in language change, namely "the light in one's eyes". For, he says, "there is no doubt that the increased growth of man in the last generations is attributable to increased exposure to light, [and] the fact that psychical maturity is hereby retarded is one of the most serious side effects".

TUNE IN, TURN ON, BEGIN TO SPEAK

Glottogenesis, that is the issue of how and when human speech first evolved, is an area in which so little is known that most of what we can say will inevitably be based on speculation. An equally inevitable result of this is that the subject tends to attract more than its fair share of, shall we say, unorthodox thinkers. One of my own favorites is Judd (1980). She suggests that an accidental consumption of the hallucinogenic mushroom *Amanita muscaria* (or some similar substance) was the impetus of the development of human consciousness, and thereby also man's ability to speak. Unfortunately, there seems to be no information available regarding Judd's own consumption in relation to the writing of her paper.

And somehow, in the midst of it all,
Zog came up with this great idea
—Whoa, let's speak!

PLAGIARISM IN SOCIOLINGUISTICS

In 1975, the journal *Language in Society* published an article by Elizabeth Bates and Laura Benigni on the use of various Italian pronouns in different social contexts. Ten years later the *Journal of Pragmatics* published a similar paper, dealing with pronouns in Cairene Arabic. It was, in fact, similar to the extent that it was by and large word-for-word identical, with 'Cairo' and 'Egypt', of course, having been substituted for 'Rome' and 'Italy'. Highly embarrassed, the editors of the journal contacted the supposed author, who excused himself by stating that *"I must have confused my own notes with those from different sources, i.e. references"* (!). The blushing editors concluded that *"it is not clear ... whether any Egyptian data were collected at all for the article that we wound up printing"*. The culprit later became a lecturer in English at the University of Kuwait.

IN SEARCH OF THE PROTO-LANGUAGE

Many are fascinated by the thought of revealing what the mankind's original language would have been like. That mankind may once have possessed just such a language is not impossible, but since all languages change, it would be naïve to believe that this "original language" still exists in a recognisable form. Unsurprisingly, this has not deterred some from looking for it and even identifying it. What follows is but a small selection of those which have been proclaimed as mankind's original language.

Malagasy?

Jules Hermann, an early 20th century scholar from the island of Réunion in the Indian Ocean, proposed in his posthumously published *Les révélations du Grand Océan* that Malagasy was in all likelihood the 'primitive language of humanity'. Among the pieces of supporting evidence, Hermann adduced a number of allegedly Malagasy-derived words from various languages. One of the more intriguing is that of *Pologne* (French for 'Poland'), which is suggested to derive from *polo ina*, or 'that which has been divided into ten (parts)'—a clear allusion, so he thought, to the numerous divisions of the country between its neighbors. Other European toponyms are also derivable from Malagasy. Clearly, in Hermann's view, the word *Manche* (which is what the French call the English Channel), must originate in Malagasy *mantsa* 'sly, astute, cunning', which presumably described the prehistoric Normans. The French name for Switzerland, *Suisse*, proves the use of alpenstocks among prehistoric Swiss, for the origin of this country's name is *soïtra*, meaning 'penetrating something with a crochet-hook or a pointed stick'.

Swedish?

In his 1679 work *Atlantica*, the Swede Olof Rudbeck tried to prove that Sweden was identical to the lost Atlantis, and that Swedish by consequence was the proto-language from which even Greek and Latin were descended. Many of his contemporaries dismissed his theory as the sheer nonsense it obviously was, but in a time when Sweden was aspiring to be a regional superpower, it was well received in ruling circles.

Turkish?

Inspired by Austrian linguist Hermann Kvergić, the president of Turkey, Kemal Atatürk, in 1936 started propagating the idea that Turkish was the mother of all languages. Initially, the

"Here's where it all started". On this contemporary etching, Olof Rudbeck points out the cradle of civilization to the learned of the world.

claim was that the Indo-European language Hittite, known to have been spoken in Anatolia, was in fact Turkish, which would in turn prove that the Turks were the original inhabitants of the country (the Turks are in fact relatively recent arrivals in Turkey). Later, though, the expressed goal was set even higher, and Turkish politicians (rather than linguists) sought to prove that all the world's languages derived from a proto-language of Central Asia, that Turkish was closer to this original form, and that all other languages had developed from Turkish.

On Atatürk's orders, this doctrine, known as the *Gunes-Dil Teorisi* ('Sun-Language Theory'), was taught in Turkish schools and universities. As set out in the book *Türk Tarihinin Ana Hatlar* ('Main Points in Turkish History'), it also includes historical aspects, such as the assertion that the civilizations of Mesopotamia, Egypt, China and Rome were all established by Turks.

The pseudo-scientific support gathered in favor of the Sun-language Theory includes

Turkish derivations of words and place-names from foreign countries and languages. My favorite is the suggestion that the river Amazon (according to most other sources named by the Spanish explorer Francisco de Orellana for the female warriors of Greek mythology) got its name from a Turk exclaiming *Ama uzun!*—"But it's so long!".

After Atatürk's death, the Sun-Language Theory fell from grace. Few miss or remember it. Alas, other aspects of the Turkish nationalistic language policy still prevail.

Hebrew?

Given its religious role, it is not particularly surprising that Hebrew has attracted the attention of those seeking to prove the existence of a proto-world language. More surprising, perhaps, is that the well-known Swedish author August Strindberg was among those who tried to do this. Towards the end of his life, Strindberg started to compile (but never finished) *Verldsspråkets Rötter* ('Roots of the world language'), also known as the ABC-book. With the help of some fanciful etymologising, he concluded that Hebrew was the mother of all languages.

Finnish?

Inspired by Strindberg, Finnish eccentric Sigurd Wettenhovi-Aspa decided to show the world that the most memorable events of world history were in fact produced by the Finns. This people, he contended, stems from Java (as proven by a comparison between *Malay* and Finnish *maalaji* 'soil type'), from where they migrated to Egypt whose famous pyramids they of course erected. On their way to the Baltic, they left a considerable linguistic legacy, including, for instance, the ancient name for Paris (cf *Lutetia* with Finnish *Luteensija* 'place of bedbugs'). In this particular region, Finnish influence even lasted until modern times, as seen in the derivation of 'Bonaparte' from *Punaparta* 'red beard', and

indeed, all modern European languages are derived from Finnish. The German masculine and feminine definite articles *der* and *die*, for example, derive from the words for the most protruding parts of the male and the female bodies. Given all this, it is not surprising that the very word 'culture' comes from *kulta-aura* 'golden plough'. Somewhat more surprising, perhaps, is that Wettenhovi-Aspa's findings were printed by a publisher in Leipzig (or, as the author himself would have it, *Leipäsija* 'bread place') named *Genius*.

Basque?

Dutch-Canadian amateur linguist Edo Nyland has come up with the startling idea that all the world's languages ("except possibly Chinese") were in fact consciously invented. The world, he explains, was at first monolingual, but for religious reasons, it was decided that the use of the original "Saharian" language must discontinue. And so professional linguists set about developing new words by distorting pre-existing ones. Basque, how-ever, remained curiously close to the proto-language, and its forms can thus be used to decipher words of other languages. English, for instance, was constructed by Benedictine monks aided by linguists from Italy, but the keen observer may still glean the origins simply with the help of a Basque dictionary. So Nyland derives *begin* from *ibeni* 'to start' + *egindura* 'the action' + *inor* 'someone', *dog* from *adoretsu* 'brave' + *oguzi* 'speaks out loud', and *doctor* from *odoldun* 'bloody' + *okerkeria* 'injury' + *etorri* 'to come' + *orain* 'quickly'. Proper names too were coined in this fashion. Thus, the name of the British royal family, Windsor, is really derived from *inorenganatu* + *odolgarbitasun* + *osoro* + *orotar*, i.e. 'to bequeath + nobility + thorough + united', while Soviet dictator Stalin was named for *astapotro* + *alienatu* + *inola* 'in a brutish way—to kill a person—in any way possible'.

Some of this "may sound far-fetched", Nyland himself admits, but the trouble caused by having to memorize the newly-invented, distorted word forms, is in fact reflected in the very name of the Latin language, for it derives from *ela* 'word' + *atxiki gogoz* 'to memorize' + *inornahi* 'everybody', that is 'Everybody memorize the words'!

Similarities between basic words from which 18th century linguists worked out sound correspondences of Indo-European, are therefore in fact only superficial. The forms *pitar* (Sanskrit) and *pater* (Latin), both meaning 'father', should really be interpreted as 'When angered he demands discipline' and 'Longing for my refuge', respectively.

After moving to Canada, Nyland began applying his insights on the local languages. The caribou, the North American reindeer, owes its name to a combination of Basque *kari* 'reason, purpose, destination' and *burdun* 'roasting spit'. Alaska is similarly translated as 'miracles unending', and Canada as 'At the far end, we'll have a noisy get-together'.

Dutch?

Johannes Goropius Becanus was a 16th century thinker from Antwerp, who among numerous other occupations considered the origin of languages. Building on the (in itself basically correct) assumption that short words tend to be older than longer words, he concluded that Dutch must be an older language than Latin or Greek, which, he found, had far longer words. Not only was Dutch old, but it was in fact the oldest language on earth, having even been used by Adam and Eve in Paradise. As proof for this, Becanus invoked the very name of the language. *Duits*, as the Dutch called their language at the time, was obviously derived from *Douts*, that is *de oudste*, 'the oldest'. Becanus was severely ridiculed by following generations, and he even received the dubious honour of having a word coined from his name—the German philosopher Leibniz used *goropism* for 'absurd etymology'.

THE BEAUTY AND LOGIC OF THE FRENCH LANGUAGE

The 18th century Frenchman Antoine de Rivarol has a claim to fame through having won the prize for the year's best essay at the annual contest of the Berlin Academy in 1784. The essay "explains" why French is superior to other languages in being the most logical language there is. "The main argument is that French is an SVO language, that is one in which the normal word order is subject-verb-object. If you say *J'écris une lettre à mon ami* 'I'm writing a letter to my friend', you exist before the letter does, and that in turn must exist in order for your friend to receive it. SVO order, according to Rivarol, is therefore the "natural logic of mankind", and is a "prerequisite for reason". *Ce qui n'est pas clair n'est pas français*, Rivarol concludes, that is 'what is not clear, is not French'. This was of course 200 years ago, and we'd like to think that science has improved since. Surprisingly, though, the renowned and otherwise knowledgeable Romanist Walter von Wartburg followed an uncannily similar line of reasoning as late as in 1969. Neither de Rivarol nor von Wartburg commented on perfectly normal sentences such as *Je reçois une lettre* 'I am receiving a letter'—does such a sentence imply that the letter comes into existence only as it is received? Similarly, if the letter is expressed by means of a pronoun (*la* 'it') rather than the full noun phrase *une lettre*, French requires that the object is moved, and we thus get *Je l'écris* 'I am writing it' (literally 'I it write'). It doesn't make a great deal of sense to say that reality changes just because you choose to use a pronoun rather than a noun.

ENGLISH—A DEADLY LANGUAGE

In 2003, there was much ado about a newly discovered disease called SARS (Severe Acute Respiratory Syndrome), believed to have originated in China. One interesting aspect of this was that Americans were affected more seriously than were the Japanese, despite the number of Japanese visitors to China being higher. Sakae Inouye, of the Otsuma Women's University in Tokyo, suggested an ingenious solution to this enigma: while English has aspirated stops, Japanese does not. Therefore, a speaker of Japanese can be expected to spray fewer saliva droplets on his interlocutor than would an American, and hence, the infection spread more quickly in the USA than in Japan.

The theory does not explain, however, why the equally English-speaking British were less affected by the epidemic than the Americans (in comparison to their number of visits to China). Nor does it explain why the Italians and the French, whose languages lack aspirated consonants, both experienced a greater incidence of SARS than did the British.

MARRISM

Nikolay Yakovlevich Marr was Kremlin's linguist laureate of early Bolshevik times. Being a native speaker of Georgian, he envied the long reconstructed linguistic prehistory of Indo-European peoples. Surely, his own mother tongue must also have relatives outside Caucasia? Marr dubbed this hypothetical family "Japhetic", and the more he worked on it, the more it grew in size until most known languages turned out to be Japhetic, and thus descendants of an ancient Caucasian language. Even the River Seine, it turned out, was actually named by speakers of Japhetic—and its name meant 'blackbird'.

The ideas of Nikolay Yakovlevich Marr, once hailed as a genius, have now disappeared into the landfill of linguistic history for good.

Enthusiastically embracing the revolutionary ideals of the contemporary Soviet Union, Marr later announced another amazing discovery. Language change, just like all other historic developments, should be seen in a class-based perspective, he argued. Thus, when you scratched the surface, the speech of workers in Russia, France, Germany and Britain had more in common with one another than with the languages of the bourgeoisie of the respective countries.

Thus, languages which others considered related through a common ancestor were in reality not related at all. The various dialects of Russian, for instance, did not stem from a common proto-Russian language, but were merely the products of a common socio-economic history.

Shortly before his own death, none other than Joseph Stalin—who had himself dabbled in linguistics (see p 349)—put his foot down and dismissed Marrism as the nonsense it was.

SOURCES NOT MENTIONED IN THE TEXT

David Oates' theories on reverse speech are elaborated in Oates (1996) and on Oates' own website at www.reversespeech.com (2005-07-28).

Kluge's discussion on clicks and human language capacity from Hammarström (1971), whose translation into English I have retained.

Sami Alrabaa's plagiarism and the paper it was based on are found in the reference list as Alrabaa (1985) and Bates & Benigni (1975). The editorial apology, and Alrabaa's pretext are found in *Journal of Pragmatics* 12, p xiii.

Austronesian remnants in the Alps: Chaudenson (2001:2-3).

Sweden as the lost Atlantis: Janson (1997:149).

The sun-language theory: Alici (1996), Zürcher (1993: 98-199), Mardin (1981: 211-12), Balçık (2000), and the *Time Out Guide Istanbul* (2001), brought to my attention by Ellen Jernström.

Strindberg the amateur linguist: Hoffman (1991).

Wettenhovi-Aspa: Wettenhovi-Aspa (1935), Masonen (2003).

Edo Nyland's, er, interesting ideas, are published in Nyland (2001).

Johannes Goropius Becanus is discussed by Salverda (1990).

Antoine de Rivarol's essay has been reprinted by Éditions Arléa in Paris. Von Wartburg's illustration of the beautiful logic of French word order is found in Wartburg (1969:257).

Spread of SARS through aspirated consonants: Inouye (2003).

Nikolai Yakovlevich Marr: Slezkine (1996:843).

LINGUISTS

THERE IS A TENDENCY to think that linguists are first and foremost good looking, athletic, polite, courteous, respectful, caring, patient, warm, cheerful, outgoing, friendly, energetic, humorous, gentle, intelligent, industrious, affectionate, open-minded, honest and helpful. But in fact, there's more to linguists than that. Some of the juicier details will unfortunately have to wait for the forthcoming *Who's Bonking Who in Linguistics*, but the time has now come to get to know the women and men of our discipline a little better.

MOST CITED LINGUISTS

I suspect that seeing one's own name in a citation list makes most people happy and flattered (unless, of course, the author has completely missed your most brilliant points). The extent to which people refer to a particular linguist's work can be taken as a measurement of his or her impact on the discipline—or so it is assumed.

It is difficult to come up with an exact number of citations of a particular author, unless, of course, you go through all the thousands and thousands of articles and books that have ever been published. I tried to come up with approximate rankings, using the Humanities Citation Index, combined with searches on various web search engines. The following tables must be taken with a grain of salt, even disregarding that they are no doubt biased towards western and in particular American linguistics.

TOP 20 (WITH A CONSERVATIVE DEFINITION OF "LINGUISTICS")

1.	Noam Chomsky	11.	Morris Halle
2.	Roman Jakobson	12.	Bernard Comrie
3.	Ferdinand de Saussure	13.	Paul Kiparsky
4.	Michael A K Halliday	14.	Panini
5.	Bill Labov	15.	Otto Jespersen
6.	George Lakoff	16.	Joseph Greenberg
7.	Ray Jackendoff	17.	Leonard Bloomfield
8.	Edward Sapir	18.	Joan Bresnan
9.	William Jones	19.	Vicki Fromkin
10.	John Gumperz	20.	Bob Dixon

A more liberal definition of linguistics would result in the inclusion of Bertrand Russell, Alan Turing, Willard Van Orman Quine, Ludwig Wittgenstein, John Lyons, John Langshaw Austin and John Searle in the list.

Chomsky is possibly the only linguist who would make it into a similar list including sciences other than linguistics. In fact, in a late-1970s list of "most cited books in social sciences", Chomsky features with no less than three works—*Aspects of the theory of syntax*, *Syntactic Structures* and *Sound patterns of English*.

In various citation indexes, *Aspects* (Chomsky 1965) is by quite some margin the most cited single work in linguistics.

LINGUISTS IN POLITICS

Some linguists have taken part in the political life of their respective countries. One of the first is the 19th century French prince Louis-Lucien Bonaparte. In the 20th century, the best known is certainly Noam Chomsky—still an angry young man, despite being nearly 80 years old. Other American linguists with a political agenda include semanticist Samuel Ichiye Hayakawa, who was a Republican senator, and also founded the lobbying organization U S English, and creolist John McWhorter, active in the American race debate since the late 1990s. Three other creolists have even joined the governments of their respective countries— Danielle de Saint-Jorre in the Seychelles, Martha Dijkhoff in the Netherlands Antilles, and Manuel Veiga in the Cape Verde islands. Not unexpectedly, the creoles of at least the two former countries enjoy a higher status than most creole languages.

In Sweden, Ernst Wigforss, who was the Social Democratic Minister of Finance during most of the 1930s and 1940s wrote his PhD thesis not on economics, but on the dialects of the province of Halland. Two members of the prominent Finnish Donner family were involved in both linguistics and politics around the last turn of the century. Otto Donner was a Sanskritist and Indo-Europeanist in Helsinki, and like many contemporary Swedish-speaking intellectuals also a Fennoman, i.e. member of the movement seeking to replace Swedish with Finnish. Donner was a member of parliament for almost 30 years, and minister of education for three. His son Kai was a Uralicist at the same university, and conducted fieldwork on Nenets. He was also one of the leaders of the extreme right-wing Lapua movement. Because of his fiery nationalism, linguist and fairy-tale collector Jacob Grimm spent a while in the Frankfurt National Parliament. For better or for worse, his impact on the political developments was minimal.

In the 1990s, Georgia became another country blessed with a linguist cabinet member—Kote Gabashvili has served both as Minister of Education and the Mayor of Tbilisi. During its first brief period of independence (1918), another part of the former Soviet empire, Ukraine, had as its first president Mikhaylo Hrushevsky, a historian who published linguistic articles on the Ukrainian language. Finally, philosopher Bertrand Russell—whose œuvre often bordered on linguistics—accomplished more in his lifetime than most. His work also involved plenty of political activity, including running (although unsuccessfully) for the British parliament as a candidate for the Women's Suffragette Society.

PART-TIME LINGUISTS

Some well-known historical characters have—unbeknownst to most people—also dabbled in linguistics. Lasersohn (2000) mentions several interesting cases.

Adam Smith, the godfather of liberalism, also wrote *A Dissertation on the Origin of Languages*. Two German philosophers also contributed: Gottfried Wilhelm von Leibniz wrote on the identification of language families, while Friedrich Nietzsche worked as a Professor of Philology at Basel University. Their fellow countryman Jacob Grimm is best known as one of the storytelling Brothers Grimm, but he did make several discoveries seminal to historical linguistics. Among other authors, J R R Tolkien, of *Lord of the Rings* fame, was a Professor of Philology at Oxford, while as mentioned on p 343 Swedish playwright August Strindberg tried to prove that Hebrew was the original language of humankind.

Ivan Mažuranić had a great impact on the cultural life in Croatia around the middle of the 19th century. His linguistic claim to fame stems mainly from his co-authoring a German-Croatian dictionary in 1842, which included a large number of neologisms which are still in use. As a politician, he cleverly balanced Austrian and Hungarian interests in order to strengthen Croatia's position, and also enforced a ban on the Cyrillic alphabet. Mažuranić's portrait today apears on the 100 kuna banknotes.

Timothy Detudamo, head of Nauru's government until he died in 1953, also began his career by compiling a dictionary (of Nauruan), and then reformed the language's orthography.

Less sympathetic characters in this category include Edward (a k a John) Rulloff, 19th century American murderer, who (unsuccessfully) pleaded that his execution be postponed, as he was working on a book on the nature of language. He earned a reputation of being hyperintelligent, and his unusually large brain is still preserved.

Joseph Stalin also deserves mention in this context. Somewhat surprisingly, perhaps, Stalin was opposed to the ideas of Nikolay Marr, who insisted that linguistics must be seen in a class perspective. Even more surprising is the fact that Stalin's impact on Soviet linguistics of the time was not entirely negative (but see last entry of the table on p 351).

In Africa, we may note that Léopold Sédar Senghor, President of Senegal from 1960 to 1980, had a degree in linguistics. In the mid-1940s, he produced at least three articles on Serer and Wolof in the *Journal de la Société des Africanistes* (Senghor 1944a, 1944b, 1947).

A great contemporary European states(wo)man has also contributed, if not to linguistics as such, as least to people's interest in languages. As the president of Iceland between 1980 and 1996, Vigdís Finnbogadóttir, was not only the first female head-of-state in the area, but also one of the most popular ever. She had an interest in languages dating back to at least her days as a college teacher of French. After her retirement, she was appointed UNESCO Goodwill Ambassador for Languages, "patroness of sign languages in the Nordic countries", and also founded the *Vigdís Finnbogadóttir Institute of Foreign Languages*, which aims first and foremost to promote the teaching of foreign languages, but also to preserve linguistic diversity.

LINGUISTS WHO HAVE SPENT TIME IN PRISON

Needless to say, linguists are better people than the average human being. Yet, the world has sometimes failed to appreciate this, and some linguists have even been jailed. Here follow some examples of linguists who have served time in prison—mostly for political activities. (I have deliberately excluded some—currently active—linguists who have been convicted for more serious deeds, such as child molestation).

Mikhail Bakhtin	Arrested in 1929, charged with "corrupting the young", among other things.
Peter Bakker	Dutch creolist and student of intertwined languages who served 24 hours for travelling with false train tickets. Seemingly incorrigible, he was later caught and held a few hours for insulting the Dutch royal family.
Jan Baudouin de Courtenay	Imprisoned in St Petersburg in 1913 for writing against the state.
Noam Chomsky	Smith (1999:8) mentions that Chomsky "has been repeatedly jailed"—normally in connection with political protests.
Jacques Derrida	Arrested in Prague in 1981 for his active support for dissident intellectuals.
Zbigniew Gołąb	Polish-American Slavicist. Imprisoned first by Nazi troops, and then by the new Polish communist government 1948-49.
Antonio Gramsci	Italian semanticist, philosopher and politician who was jailed in 1926 for his opposition to the Mussolini dictatorship.
Roman Jakobson	Fleeing anti-Semitism, Jakobson was arrested for illegally entering Sweden in 1940.
Lyle Jenkins	Arrested for political reasons by the East German régime.
Idan Landau	Israeli linguist and captain of the reserve, imprisoned for 14 days in 2001 for refusal to serve in the occupied territories.
André Martinet	During the Second World War, Martinet was interned by the Nazis. As the linguist he was, he spent his days analysing the speech of his fellow inmates. When peace had returned, his results were published as Martinet (1945).
Koldo (Luís) Mitxelena	Spanish Vasconist imprisoned by the Franco régime (1937-1942), who produced some of his linguistic work in jail.

Bertrand Russell	Russell was jailed during both world wars, and again in 1961. In all cases, his radical pacifism was the reason.
Hugo Schuchardt	The father of creolistics was allegedly held for two weeks for vandalism. Further details are unknown.
Bill Stewart	American creolist who was arrested in Brazil in 1960 for criticising a Brazilian general during a speech.
Nikolai Trubetzkoy	While a fierce anti-Semite, Trubetzkoy was somewhat critical of Nazi racial politics, and was jailed by the Gestapo in Vienna. His death from a heart attack is thought to have been caused by these harassments.
Alan Turing	Alan Turing wasn't really a linguist himself, but has a place in linguistics insofar as his work is part on the ground on which computational linguistics stands. In 1952, he was convicted for homosexuality (sic), a sentence that in the end cost him his life.
Dozens of Soviet linguists	In September of 1933, the so-called "Slavists' Trial" took place in Stalin's Soviet Union. A number of people, including a large proportion of linguists, were arrested for being members of a "counter-revolutionary national-fascist organization" known as the "Russian National Party". Although such a party never existed (and is now known to have been invented by the NKVD, the forerunner of the KGB), the organization was said to have been founded by dissidents Roman Jakobson and Nikolai Trubetzkoy (hence the targeting of linguists). Linguists put to trial included Nikolai Durnovo, Viktor Vinogradov, Grigoriy Ilyinskiy, Mikhail Speranskiy, Afanasiy Selishchev and R R Fasmer. Many of the accused were exiled to Siberian concentration camps, and after a second show trial in 1937, 14 of them, including Durnovo and Ilyinskiy were sentenced to death and shot.

Finally, Paul Broca, the founder of psycholinguistics was apparently never imprisoned, but was persecuted by the French government. For unclear reasons, the authorities feared Broca's *Société d'Anthropologie de Paris,* and saw Broca as a subversive element. A police spy in civilian clothing was assigned to follow Broca's every step. The spy was clearly understimulated by the law-abiding life Broca led. When he was about to take an unauthorized walk, Broca—who had long since noticed that he was under surveillance—is reported to have told him to "sit down and earn your pay".

SINISTER LINGUISTS

Notable south paws include not only Pablo Picasso, Kurt Cobain, Marilyn Monroe, Fidel Castro, Greta Garbo, Jimi Hendrix, Joan of Arc, Ronald Reagan, and the Boston Strangler, but also a number of linguists. Lefties in linguistics include, among many others, the following names:

Bill Croft	*Bernd Heine*
Susan Curtiss	Steve Levinson
Östen Dahl	John Marshall
Jack Chambers	Robert Van Valin
Helen Dry	Bill McGregor
Susan Fischer	Fritz Newmeyer
David Perlmutter	Mikael Parkvall
Spike Gildea	Frans Plank
Colette Grinevald	Paolo Ramat
John Haiman	Haj Ross
Mike Hammond	Ken Hale

In most populations, about one in ten is more or less left-handed, the highest share observed being the about 20% among the Kwakiutls of south-western Canada

(To be fair, Paolo Ramat of the University of Pavia in Italy, is really ambidextrous.)

LINGUISTS' TIME OFF

Presumably, most linguists have interests and hobbies outside their academic life. Some of these are unremarkable, while others may come as a surprise. Below follow some examples which are innocent enough to be published (as they are for the most part listed on the respective individual's home pages or mentioned in print).

Tom Hinnebusch, UCLA	*Gardening, birdwatching, hiking*
Peter Ladefoged, *UCLA*	*Member of Atheists for Jesus*
Andrew Carnie, Arizona	*Balkan dancing, Appalachian clogging, Cajun dancing, gender free contra dancing, folk music, cats*
Phil Resnik, *Maryland*	*Swing and ballroom dance*
Caroline Smith, New Mexico	*Pigs*

Joan Bresnan, Stanford	Cycling
Ivan Sag, Stanford	*Keyboard player for* The Dead Tongues *combo. A 2001 incarnation of this band featured sociolinguist Penny Eckert (also at Stanford) on vocals.*
Arnold Zwicky, *Stanford*	*Singing*
Jack Chambers, *Toronto*	*Jazz critic*
Jens Allwood, Gothenburg	*Qi Gong*
Ellen Prince, Pennsylvania	*Caudiciforms, miniature roses, streptocarpus and African violets; Marlboros*
Robin Clark, Pennsylvania	*The Mayan Calendar, surrealism, Dadaism*
Howard Lasnik, Maryland	*Scottish country dancing and drumming*
Suzette Haden Elgin, (formerly) San Diego	*Science fiction*
Jules Gilliéron, *Atlas linguistique de la France*	*Geology*
Peter Mühlhäusler, Adelaide	*Model trains, ferret breeding, Sherlock Holmes*
Esa Itkonen, Turku	*Boxing*
John McWhorter, Berkeley	*Dinosaurs, musicals*

REVIEWING YOUR OWN WORK

G erman-Austrian linguist Hugo Schuchardt is one of the few linguists to have published a review of his own work, in this case *Kreolische Studien IX—Über das Malaioportugiesische von Batavia und Tugu*. Another, currently active, linguist has been accused own reviewing his own book in one of the most prestigious journals there are in the field. According to the author, the reviewer was "an exiled Ukrainian linguist".

DEAD LINGUISTS SOCIETY

S ome say that "old linguists never die, they just rearrange their deep structures". Yet, it seems that some of our colleagues from the past just aren't with us any longer. Some of them didn't even get to live very long, but nevertheless made a considerable impact on the discipline. On the following page are some of the James Deans of linguistics.

Danish pioneer linguist Rasmus Rask didn't get to experience his 50th birthday. But he sure has a nice tombstone. Located at the Assistens cemetery in Copenhagen, it bears inscriptions in several languages.

SOME LINGUISTS WHO DIED YOUNG

Name	Age	
Vladislav Illich-Svitych (1934-1966)	32	Russian Nostratist. Died in a car accident.
Michael Ventris (1922-1956)	34	Deciphered the Linear B script. Died in a car accident.
Mikołaj Kruszewski (1851-1887)	36	Polish linguist who exerted a certain influence on Saussure. Death reported to be due at least in part to "mental illness".
Bartholomäus Ziegenbalg (1682-1719)	37	Produced the first grammar of Tamil in any European language.
Alexander Murray (1775-1813)	38	Scottish polyglot and early Indo-Europeanist deceased from a pulmonary ailment.
Harvey Sacks (1935-1975)	40	Sociolinguist and pragmatician at the University of California. Died in a car crash.
Uriel Weinreich (1926-1967)	41	Lithuanian-American Yiddishist, socio-linguist and language contact scholar. Died from cancer.
Fujitani Nariakira (1738-1779)	41	A pioneer in the study of Japanese morphology.
Richard Montague (1930-1971)	41	Philosopher, logician and semanticist. Murdered.
Francis Whyte Ellis (1778-1819)	41	British Indologist. Is said to have died of poisoning, but others have attributed his death to cholera.
Jean-François Champollion (1790-1832)	42	Deciphered the ancient Egyptian hieroglyphs. Died of a stroke.
Alan Turing (1912-1954)	42	WW2 cryptologist and computational linguistics pioneer. Committed suicide after having been convicted for homosexuality.
Franz Nikolaus Finck (1867-1910)	43	German philologist and Indo-Europeanist.
Louis Braille (1809-1852)	43	Inventor of the tactile reading system that still bears his name. Died from tuberculosis.
Benjamin Lee Whorf (1897-1941)	44	Americanist, but mostly associated today with the Sapir-Whorf hypothesis. Died of cancer.
Wilhelm Scherer (1841-1886)	45	Austrian-German Germanicist. Died from a stroke.
Rasmus Christian Rask (1787-1832)	45	Danish polyglot and comparative linguist. Died "sickly and disillusioned".
Gerard Bähr (1900-1945)	45	German Vasconist who died in Berlin during the Russian capture of the city. His body was never found, but he is believed to have been killed by a shell.

While at least some of the good obviously die young, others get to enjoy an unusually long life, and often die with their boots on. British orientalist Ralph Lilley Turner, for instance, kept publishing until well into his 94th year.

SOME LINGUISTS WHO LIVED QUITE A BIT LONGER

Name	Age	
Murray Emeneau (1904-2005)	101	Canadian-American expert on Dravidian languages and on areal linguistics in India.
Hans Kurath (1891-1992)	101	Austrian-American dialectologist.
Pierre Le Roux (1874-1975)	101	Creator of the Atlas Linguistique de la Basse-Bretagne.
Ramón Menendez Pidal (1869-1968)	99	Romance philologist from Madrid.
Siddeshwar Varma (1887-1985)	98	Spoke 21 languages, and wrote Critical Studies in the Phonetic Observations of Indian Grammarians.
Bertrand Russell (1872-1970)	98	Philosopher, semanticist, politician, Nobel prize winner and much more.
Iorgu Iordan (1888-1986)	98	Romanian Romanist.
Ralph Lilley Turner (1888-1983)	95	His longevity allowed him to both fight in WWI and use computers in his Indian language studies.
Alexandru Rosetti (1895-1990)	95	Romanian phonetician who outlived the Ceauşescu dictatorship by two months.
Tomas Navarro (1884-1979)	95	Phonologist and director of the Atlas Lingüístico de la Península Ibérica.
Gerhard Rohlfs (1892-1986)	94	German Romanist.
Theodor Nöldeke (1836-1930)	94	German orientalist.
Michel Lejeune (1907-2000)	93	Frenchman who worked mainly on classical Greek.
Frederic Cassidy (1907-2000)	93	Jamaican-American dialectologist and creolist.
Clarence Barnhart (1900-1993)	93	American lexicographer.
Sukumar Sen (1900-1992)	92	Comparative Indologist who produced descriptions of Bengali, and wrote crime novels.
Willard Van Orman Quine (1908-2000)	92	American logician, philosopher and semanticist.
André Martinet (1908-1999)	91	The most influential French linguist in the mid-to-late 20th century.

The average linguist lives 72,2 years, though their life span has increased somewhat—linguists who have died after the Second World War have been 75,5 years old on average.

Obviously, if that trend continues, we can expect future linguists to have eternal life.

YOUNGEST LINGUIST

A good candidate for the earliest start of a career in linguistics would be Uriel Weinreich. At the age of only ten, he received a trip to the *4e Congrès international des Linguistes* in Copenhagen as a birthday present. His first published article was printed in the journal *Yidishe Shprakh* in 1943. By this time, little Uriel was 17 old. To some extent, he was no doubt spurred by having a linguist father—Max Weinreich.

Uriel Weinreich's early start was fortunate, given that he only lived until the age of 41.

FIRST LINGUISTS

The first known linguist is Paṇini, who produced a remarkably insightful grammar of Sanskrit. In its eight chapters, his work Astadhyayi (a k a Astaka) summarizes the main features of this language in 4 168 rules. Born in present-day Pakistan, Paṇini was active in the 5th century before Christ.

The first documented linguistic debate is probably that between Socrates, Hermogenes and Cratylus on the relation between form and meaning. It is published in Plato's *Cratylus*.

LINGUISTS WITH LUXURIANT FLOWING HAIR

The *Luxuriant Flowing Hair Club for Scientists* (LFHCfS) has gone from humble beginnings in 2001 to having several hundred member academics. Its very first member was no other than Harvard psycholinguist Steven Pinker. At the time of this writing, he has been followed by eight other linguists with Luxuriant Flowing Hair: Daniel Büring (formal semanticist, UCLA), William Davies (syntactician, University of Iowa), Philip Resnik (computational linguist, University of Maryland), Norvin Richards (syntactician, MIT), Michael Harman (Motorola, previously at Berkeley), Aga Skotowski (computational linguist, University of Maryland), Mark Hale (Historical linguist and acquisitionist, Concordia U) and Harald Hammarström (computational linguist, Chalmers University). A tenth linguist was nominated and accepted in December 2005 (and boy, am I happy that it actually resulted in fan mail!).

LANGUAGES SPOKEN BY LINGUISTS

The average member of ALT (the Association for Linguistic Typology) claims "proficiency" in **2,52** languages, though judging from the members I know personally, these figures are not entirely reliable. Also, the sample is not entirely representative for the field, since Georgian is the fourth most common native tongue. Quite likely because of this Russian, is the most widely spoken second language, followed by Mandarin, Arabic and Latin.

More representative, I believe, are the results from a questionnaire I myself put out to a number of creolists in 1997. Among the 71 who responded (about half of whom were native speakers of English), the average number of languages known was **4,35**. The most widely spoken second languages were (in order) English, French, Spanish, German, Dutch, Portuguese, Italian and Russian. All responding creolists knew English (in which language the questionnaire was issued), 77% French, 48% Spanish and 45% German.

The span in terms of competence was between nine and two languages, the latter only being represented among native Anglophones. In all, native speakers of English spoke **4,10** language, native speakers of French **4,17**, while others knew **4,88** languages.

Again, my personal experience leads me to believe that the results from my creolist survey are relatively representative of linguists at large.

MEN AND WOMEN IN LINGUISTICS

According to Disterheft's (1990) analysis of journal publications, the most female-dominated subdisciplines of linguistics were child language and sociolinguistics, while formal linguistics was dominated by men. While this conforms rather well to existing stereotypes, it deviates from the less expected figures produced by Balcom & Clarke (2004) based on a survey of 110 Canadian linguists.

Slight overrepresentation of women:	Syntax, psycholinguistics, semantics
Slight overrepresentation of men:	L2 acquisition, morphology, sociolinguistics, historical linguistics, phonology, dialectology, L1 acquisition
Strong overrepresentation of men:	Phonetics

NAMES OF LINGUISTIC WORKS

Pullum (1991:194-95) mentions *Semantics* as possibly the most worn-out title in the history of linguistic textbooks. He lists no less than 16 different ones, published between 1941 (Hugh Walpole's *Semantics*) and 1990 (*Semantics* by Michel Bréal). And that is still not counting Terrence Gordon's *Semantics: a bibliography 1965-1978*. Had Pullum written today, he would have been able to include another eight volumes, from *Semantics* (1993) to *Semantics* (2002), both being anthologies. The title seems to have been the most popular in 1977, which saw the publication of *Semantics* by Janet Fodor, *Semantics* by John Lyons, and finally *Semantics*, collectively authored by Stephen Walter, Michael Walrod and Rodney Kinch. Note that this enumeration excludes book titles such as *Introduction to Semantics* and the like.

My personal favorite among titles in the linguistic literature is Rudolf Botha's (2000) ***How much of language, if any, came about in the same sort of way as the brooding chamber in snails?***, published in the working papers of Stellenbosch University in South Africa. A few worthy competitors include the following:

- Why Negroes Should Study Romance Languages and Literatures (Rivers 1934).
- Vem är jag? [=Who am I?] (Nilsson 2003).
- Weak vs. strong readings of donkey sentences (Kanazawa 1993).

- The philosopher pulled the lower jaw of the hen (Cook 2001).
- Reasons why I do not care grammar formalism (Tsujii 1988).
- Read at Your Own Risk: Syntactic and Semantic Horrors You Can Find in Your Medicine Chest (Sadock 1974).
- Knuddel-zurückknuddel-dichganzdollknuddel (Schlobinski 2001).
- How I spent my summer vacation (Stampe 1972).
- Grammatical signs of the divided self (Haiman 1995).
- Crazy Notes on Restrictive Clauses and Other Matters Dating from April 1967, and Now Less Than 42.5% Believed (Postal c. 1968).

- When verbs collide (Joseph & Zwicky 1990).
- À la Recherche du Word Order Not Quite Perdu (Gregersen & Pedersen 2001).
- WCO, ACD and QR of DPs (Harley 2002).

Linguists more keen on formalist theories than I am may not agree, but I find the last-mentioned item (and one could cite more of the same sort, not least from the publication concerned) entertaining simply because of the large amount of presuppositions that goes into the title, not to mention the abstract, which states that *"the interaction of ACD and WCO [shows] that ACD repairing-movement is A-bar movement at LF, not case-checking movement".* Who would have guessed?

BEST APOLOGETIC ENDNOTE

If you've read more than a handful of works in linguistics (or, for that matter, plenty of other sciences), you quickly grow tired of the eternal "clearly, further research remains to be done before this question can be definitively settled" that routinely rounds off many a paper. (An additional source of irritation is that the papers which would best merit this set phrase tend to be the ones in which it is used the least.)

This ending comes in many guises, but the following (from Green 1972:93) must surely be one of the more innovative rephrasings:

"This paper was undertaken in an attempt to shed light on some very mysterious problems. I fear I have done little more than show which lamps have cords too short to reach the outlets".

BEST AMBIGUITY

The winner in this category is San Martin (1999), in whose background briefing it was pointed out that "Since Chomsky presented his Binding Theory in *Lectures in Government and Binding* (1981), obviation phenomena have remained rather obscure".

PRESTIGE IN LINGUISTICS

According to Balcom & Clarke's (2004) survey of 110 Canadian linguists, the subdiscipline which is by far viewed as most prestigious is syntax, followed by phonology and semantics. Areas seen as less prestigious include gender issues, dialectology, discourse analysis, L2 Acquisition, sociolinguistics, and pragmatics. While some of these areas have traditionally been seen as female, it is noteworthy that women are more sceptical about the value of these fields than men are. The most important gender difference, though, is that women consider typology less prestigious than men do.

HOW TO RECOGNIZE A REAL LINGUIST

There are several possible indications that you are appropriately devoted. In short, you know that you are a Real Linguist when...

- . . . like one of my colleagues, you choose the location of your summer house on the basis of how eccentric the local dialect is.
- . . . like Hugo Schuchardt, you transform part of your home into a "small-scale museum of fishing gear" in order to investigate an etymology. In his case, it was the French trouver 'to find', for which two alternative etymologies had been proposed. One was Latin turbare 'to stir up', which would have referred to an ancient fishing technique—when you have 'stirred up' a school of fishes, you can capture them, or, as it were, 'find' them in your trap or net.
- . . . you believe that F D in "F D Roosevelt" stands for "Ferdinand de".
- . . . you watch the film *My Fair Lady* for the sole reason that Peter Ladefoged was its phonetics consultant and it was he who chose the equipment and transcriptions seen on screen while his voice is heard producing various vowel qualities.
- . . . you think that the first line of the lyrics of the Teddy Bears' 1958 smash hit "To know him is to love him is To know know **Noam** is to love love love him".
- . . . somebody mentions a sighting of the Hale-Bopp comet, and you are the only one to appreciate that a celestial body combines the surnames of two great linguists.
- . . . like typologist Sasha Aikhenvald, you manifest your teen boredom by collecting the phrase *I don't want to go to school* in as many languages as you can (she had it in 52).
- . . . you feel an urge to read or write a book like this.

SOURCES NOT MENTIONED IN THE TEXT

Well-cited linguists: First and foremost the *Humanities Citation Index*, combined with searches on various web search engines. Also the frequency of citation in various linguistics encyclopaedias, and finally Karlsson (1994).

The list of "Most cited books in social sciences, 1969-1977" was published in the newsletter *Current Contents* 37, pp 5–16, published 1978-09-11.

The Donners and Grimm in politics: Wikipedia.

Adam Smith's writings on linguistics: Berry (1974).

Mažuranić and Detudamo as part-time linguists: Wikipedia.

Details on Trubetzkoy and on Ukraine's first president: Daniel Bunčić (p c).

Reviewing your own work: Peter Bakker (p c), Stéphane Goyette (p c).

Linguists in prison: Lots of different biographies, including Aulestia (1990), Clark & Holquist (1984:142), Glebov (2003:23), Seuren (1998), Smith (1999:8), Los Angeles Times 2002-04-22, Östen Dahl (p c), Peter Bakker (p c), *Linguist List* 5.366 and 12.1821, Independent Media

Center, Israel. The story of Broca's persecution is told in Sagan (1979). Slavists' trial: Daniel Bunčić (p c). André Martinet: Krier (1999:13).

Linguist's hobbies: Mostly from their own home pages (and other published sources) and to some extent through personal acquaintances. Jules Gilliéron from Walter (1988:137).

Left-handed linguists: Östen Dahl (p c), Colette Grinevald (p c).

Life-spans of linguists: Most of the biographical data were culled from Asher & Simpson (eds) (1994).

Uriel Weinreich: Peter Bakker (p c), Malkiel & Herzog (1967).

First linguistic debate: Crystal (1987:404).

Schuchardt's fishing museum: Tuite (2003), citing Malkiel (1993:26) and Tappolet (1977 [1905]).

Alexandra Aikhenvald's rebellious youth: *New Scientist* Interview (by Adrian Barnett) with Alexandra Aikhenvald, February 2004 issue.

Ladefoged and *My Fair Lady: Linguist List* 17.306.

LINGUISTIC TERMINOLOGY

JUST LIKE ANY OTHER profession, linguistics has its own professional lingo. Some of the linguistic vocabulary has just evolved, without anybody being aware of a given term's origin. Other items in the linguist's terminological toolbox have been introduced at a specific occasion by a specific person. Below follow examples of first use of some linguistic terms.

Semitic	1781	Ludwig Schlözer (in Eichhorn 1781:161)
synthetic	1818	Schlegel (1818)
polysynthetic	1819	Duponceau (1819), though Müller (1880) is sometimes credited
Athabaskan	1836	Gallatin (1836)
Dravidian	1856	Caldwell (1856)
aphasia	1864	Trousseau (1864)
comparative method	1864	Bréal (1864)
obviative	1866	Cuoq (1866:43)
phoneme	1873	A Dufriche-Desgenettes before the Société de Linguistique de Paris.
semantics	1883	Bréal (1883)
isogloss	1892	Bielenstein (1892)
morpheme	1895	Baudouin de Courtenay (1895)
Nostratic	1903	Pedersen (1903)
grammaticalization	1912	Meillet (1912)
Hokan	1913	Dixon & Kroeber (1913)
Afro-Asiatic	1914	Delafosse (1914)
Na-Dené	1915	Sapir (1915)

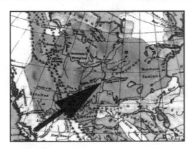

Albert Gallatin's own map showing the distribution of Athabaskan peoples was a remarkably accurate piece of cartography for its time. At the arrow-head is the lake whose name he arbitrarily assigned to the language family.

Sprachbund	1928	Trubetzkoy (1928:10)
Khoisan	1928	Schultze (1928)
archiphoneme	1929	Jakobson (1929)
diglossia	1930	Marçais (1930), despite Charles Ferguson often being credited.
neutralization	1931	Trubetzkoy (1931)
coronal	1933	Bloomfield (1933)
decreolization	1933	Bloomfield (1933:474)
group genitive	1933	Jespersen (1933)
underlying form	1933	Bloomfield (1933)
dummy element	1937	Jespersen (1937:102)
allophone	1938	Whorf (1938)
juncture	1941	Trager & Bloch (1941)
segment	1941	Scott (1941)
morph	1947	Hockett (1947)
portmanteau	1947	Hockett (1947)
stress-timing	1947	Pike (1947a)
tone sandhi	1947	Pike (1947b)
allomorph	1948	Nida (1948)
sociolinguistics	1949	Currie (1952) (presented orally in 1949)
toneme	1950	Jones (1950)

Through the Looking Glass by Lewis Carroll
CHAPTER 6: *HUMPTY DUMPTY*

"You seem very clever at explaining words, Sir," said Alice. "Would you kindly tell me the meaning of the poem called "Jabberwocky"?"

"Let's hear it," said Humpty Dumpty. "I can explain all the poems that ever were invented—and a good many that haven't been invented just yet." This sounded very hopeful, so Alice repeated the first verse:

"'Twas brillig, and the slithy toves
Did gyre and gimble in the wabe:
All mimsy were the borogoves,
And the mome raths outgrabe.*"

Lewis Carroll's Alice in Wonderland *has made several contributions to linguistic terminology, most notably the term* **portmanteau**.

"That's enough to begin with," Humpty Dumpty interrupted: "there are plenty of hard words there. *"Brillig"* means four o'clock in the afternoon—the time when you begin broiling things for dinner."

"That'll do very well," said Alice: "and *"slithy"?*"

"Well, *"slithy"* means "lithe and slimy". "Lithe" is the same as "active". You see it's like a **portmanteau**—there are two meanings packed up into one word."

noun phrase	1951	Harris (1951)
transformation	1952	Harris (1952)
diasystem	1954	Weinreich (1954)
inversive number	1954	Wonderly, Gibson & Kirk (1954)
item-and-arrangement	1954	Hockett (1954)
drag chain	1955	Martinet (1955)
onset	1955	Hockett (1955)
atelic	1957	Garey (1957)
generative grammar	1957	Chomsky (1957)
telic	1957	Garey (1957)
trace	1957	Chomsky (1957)
downstep	1959	Welmers (1959)
unrestricted grammar	1959	Chomsky (1959)
valency	1959	Tesnière (1959)
the 'fis' phenomenon	1960	Berko & Brown (1960:531)
illocutionary force	1962	Austin (1962)
relexification	1962	Stewart (1962:46)
implicational universal	1963	Greenberg (1963)
Niger-Congo	1963	Greenberg (1963)
pivot grammar	1963	Braine (1963)
serial verb	1963	Stewart (1963)
negative polarity	1964	Klima (1964)
voice onset time (VOT)	1964	Lisker & Abramson (1964:422)
bleeding order	1965	Kiparsky (1965)
semantic role	1965	Gruber (1965)
change from below	1966	Labov (1966)
complementizer	1967	Rosenbaum (1967)
gapping	1967	Ross (1967)
left-dislocation	1967	Ross (1967)
pied-piping	1967	Ross (1967)
scrambling	1967	Ross (1967)
switch-reference	1967	Jacobsen (1967)
WH-*island constraint*	1967	Ross (1967)
disjunctive ordering	1968	Chomsky & Halle (1968)
semilingualism	1968	Hansegård (1968)
monitoring	1970	Labov (1970)
tonogenesis	1970	Matisoff (1970)

cognitive linguistics	1971	Lamb (1971)
Black English Vernacular (BEV)	1972	Labov (1972). This term was politically correct for several weeks afterwards, but was ultimately (at the time of writing this) replaced by Ebonics (see below). Apologies in the likely case that things have changed while this book was in press.
interlanguage	1972	Selinker (1972)
rule inversion	1972	Venneman (1972a)
Ebonics	1973	Though commonly used only from 1996, this term was apparently first used by Robert Williams during the 1973 conference "Cognitive and Language Development of the Black Child" in St Louis, Missouri (Williams 1997).
logophoric pronoun	1974	Hagège (1974)
Cooperative Principle	1975	Grice (1975:45)
Maxims of Conversation	1975	Grice (1975:45-46)
animacy hierarchy	1976	Silverstein (1976)
antipassive	1976	Silverstein (1976)
autosegment	1976	Goldsmith (1976)
obligatory contour principle	1976	Goldsmith (1976)
split ergativity	1976	Silverstein (1976)
unification	1979	Kay (1979)
alpha movement	1980	Chomsky (1980)
non-configurational	1981	Hale (1981)
WH-*in-situ*	1981	Aoun, Hornstein & Sportiche (1981)
Maximal Onset Principle	1982	Selkirk (1982)
feature geometry	1985	Clements (1985)
head marking	1985	Van Valin (1985)
E-language	1986	Chomsky (1986)
Chechirization	1991	Matisoff (1991)
intertwined language	1994	First used by Bakker & Mous (1994:4), but attributed by them to Norval Smith.

Apart from these now established terms, the terminology unique to generative semantics should not be forgotten. In 1968, George Lakoff recommended his students to "use obviously arbitrary names like Clyde instead of arbitrary names that sound profound but aren't, like Determiner". His advice was heeded, and fellow generative semanticists Morgan, Neubauer and Rogers coined names for syntactic transformations such as Irving, Ludwig and Richard.

SOURCES NOT MENTIONED IN THE TEXT

Sources of linguistic terms: Originally based on Trask (1993, 1996b), but subsequently expanded with additions from a number of other sources almost as large as the number of entries in the table. Terminology of generative semanticists from Harris (1993:133–34, 142). A couple of interesting first mentions from Koerner (1989).

CLASSIC EXAMPLE SENTENCES

JUST LIKE REPRESENTATIVES of many other disciplines, linguists have their favorite quotes which no one can escape. Yours truly has mixed feelings about them—on the one hand, one often sighs at encountering the same old example once again. On the other hand, these worn-out sentences have become part of the linguist lore, and it could be argued that they are part of what every linguist ought to be familiar with. Even though the expression *ad nauseam* may come to mind, there is something cosy about them—it is when you see them and recognize them that you know you've done your homework properly.

This tendency of (over)using certain sentences is perhaps even more pronounced in philosophy than it is in linguistics, but as we shall see, many of the philosophers' favorites have also become part of our tradition.

CITATIONS CONCERNING THE GENERAL NATURE OF LANGUAGE

Colorless green ideas sleep furiously

This sentence, first found in Chomsky (1957:15) is undoubtedly the most classic example sentence there is. It has even been the source of poems and set to music (!). The point it wishes to make is that semantics is independent of syntax—this is undoubtedly an English sentence in the sense that it follows English syntax, and yet, it doesn't mean anything coherent.

"Colorless green ideas sleep furiously" is without a doubt the most cited example sentence that linguistics has ever produced. Now almost 50 years old, it is still very much going strong.

When it comes to linguistic form, Plato walks with the Macedonian swineherd, Confucius with the head-hunting savage of Assam.

The equality of languages as expressed by Edward Sapir. The quotation is found in Sapir (1921:218-19).

Dans la langue, il n'y a que des differences.

"In languages, there is nothing but differences". This was the motto of early 20th century structuralists, emphasizing the notion that the meaning of a linguistic expression is defined by contrasting it to other linguistic expressions. The original occurrence is in the first ever linguistics textbook—Saussure (1916:166).

Une langue est un système où tout se tient.

Loosely translated: "A language is a system where everything depends on everything else". The exact origins of this structuralist slogan are unknown, although it has been attributed to both Ferdinand de Saussure and to Antoine Meillet. See Peeters (1990), Koerner (1999:183-202) and Linguist List 14.1913 for discussion.

Язык естъ важнейшее средство человеческого общения

"Language is the most important means of human intercourse". Every printed scientific book in the Soviet Union had to include a Lenin or Marx quotation; this one, by Lenin, was the most popular one for linguistics, as it was such a general truism that it could be used for anything having to do with language.

Languages differ essentially in what they must convey and not in what they may convey.

Originally stated by Roman Jakobson (1959:236). My other favorite Jakobson quote does not seem to be as widely cited as it deserves, but as quoted by Trubetzkoy (1939), he also said that "die Phonologie [verhält sich] zur Phonetik wie die [...] Finanzwissenschaft zur Numismatik", in other words that "phonetics is to phonology what numismatics is to economics".

GARDEN-PATH SENTENCES

Garden-path sentences are such that the reader is misled into starting out with one interpretation, only to realize half-way through it that she must reparse it in order to get the intended reading.

The horse raced past the barn fell.
Immortalized by Bever (1970:316).

The old man the boats.

Seemingly first used in Milne (1982).

Time flies like an arrow. Fruit flies like a banana.

Attributed to Groucho Marx, but subsequently oft-cited in the linguistic literature as a garden-path example.

SEMANTICS

Every man who owns a donkey beats it.

Although introduced into the modern literature by Geach (1962), this sentence was earlier used by medieval logicians. It has even had an entire genre of examples named for it, the so-called "donkey sentences".

John believes that the Morning Star is Venus.

There are myriads of variants of this quote. Nothing really similar is actually found in Frege (1892), but the quote periphrases an important point made in that paper. It is argued that two words having the same real-world referent (such as 'the Morning Star' and 'Venus') are not necessarily synonymous.

The present king of France is bald.

Or, as some of us prefer to put it, ∃X:(present_king_of_france (X) ∧ ¬ (∃Y:(present_king_of_france (Y) ∧ ¬ (X=Y))) ∧ bald (X)).

Used by Russell (1905) to highlight a semantic problem. Can a sentence such as this really be considered false, given that there is no current king of France in the first place?

For some reason, Bertrand doesn't look as surprised as one would expect . . .

Snow is white.

Tarski (1944:342-3). The full version is "'Snow is white' is true if and only if snow is white", and is often accompanied by a translation into German or French ("Schnee ist weiss", "La neige est blanche").

In addition to the above, there are a number of oft-cited sentences which properly belong to the philosophers, but which occasionally find their way into linguistic writings. Examples include Socrates currit, Socrates (Sortes) est Albus, A vixen is a female fox, Every man loves a woman and A bachelor is an unmarried man.

THE STRUCTURE OF LANGUAGE IN GENERAL OR ENGLISH IN PARTICULAR

British left waffles on Falkland Islands.

Figures on the web under headings such as "Best newspaper headings of 1999", and of a number of other years as well. Whatever its origins, however, it must be earlier—the earliest mention I know of is in Pinker (1994:79). I have not been able to locate the original source, though.

John gives Mary a book ~ John gave the book to Mary ~ John hit Bill

I doubt that an original source could ever be found for any of these, since they are all somewhat trivial. The most interesting thing about them is that it is probably only in linguistic textbooks that you ever see them. If you think about your real-life linguistic experiences, you realize that these occur about as often as "The cat sat on the mat".

Flying planes can be dangerous.

Originally found in Chomsky (1957), this one made a quick career, for as early as in Lees (1960:214), it is described as "classical".

John is easy/eager to please.

Although best known from Chomsky (1965), it seems that this famous pair was presented to the world one year earlier, namely in Chomsky (1964:34).

Beavers build dams.

Another Chomsky classic, this time from Chomsky (1975). The true sentence contrasts with its passive equivalent *Dams are built by beavers*, which could be considered untrue, as dams are also built by creatures other than beavers.

The farmer killed the duckling.

Sapir (1921:91). The point made is simply that English requires an -s suffix on verbs denoting actions carried out by a third person subject, but only in the present tense—"the farmer killed-s the duckling" is ungrammatical. The reason why this sentence became a classic is presumably that the book in which it occurred was one of the earliest linguistics textbooks there is.

Sincerity admires John.

Chomsky (1957:42-43, 78) discusses the problem with animacity in passivization.

Old men and women

I must admit that I haven't managed to find the original source of this, but it is perhaps the most frequently cited example of the problem of modifier scope. Does the NP refer to 'old men and old women', or just to 'old men and (then also) women (of any age)'?

I saw the man in the park with a telescope.

I was convinced that this classic was from either Chomsky (1957) or Chomsky (1965), but cannot find it in either. It is, nevertheless, one of the most frequently replicated examples. As such it comes in a variety of guises. In some incarnations, the park and the telescope appear in indefinite form, and in some versions, the seer or the seen is the boy, the girl or John.

Floyd broke the glass.

This sentence hails from unpublished work from the mid 1960s by Haj Ross and George Lakoff. It is best known for having been analysed as consisting of eight underlying clauses. Later on, Floyd's carelessness with drinking vessels found its way into printed works such as e.g. Bach & Harms (1968:viii), Abraham & Binnick (1972:40ff) and Jackendoff (1972:28). According to

Harris (1993:154), "there was even a floor-to-ceiling, tree-structure mobile of the analysis in Ross's office".

Linguistic Theory is concerned primarily with an ideal speaker-listener in a completely homogenous speech-community, who knows its language perfectly and is unaffected by such grammatically irrelevant conditions as memory limitations, distractions, shifts of attention and interest, and errors (random or characteristic) in applying his knowledge of the language in actual performance.

By describing a non-existent linguistic Superman, Chomsky (1965:3) attempts—and succeeds for at least a while—to set the agenda for modern linguistics.

The bottle floated into the cave.

This classic is usually contrasted with Spanish La botella entró a la cueva (flotando). It is used to highlight the differences between so-called "satellite-framed" and "verb-framed" languages. While originally used, so far as I can tell, by Talmy (1978), the sentence is more often cited from Talmy (1985:61).

Seymour sliced the salami.

Another classic example from generative semantics, which originally appeared in Lakoff (1968).

THE STRUCTURE OF SPECIFIC LANGUAGES OTHER THAN ENGLISH

The Semitic root *ktb*.

This example is frequently used to illustrate the peculiar stem triplets of Semitic languages such as Arabic and Hebrew. These consist of three consonants, and depending on which vowels you insert between them, you can get a number of different words. The root ktb 'to write' can be derived and inflected to form words such as: kitaab 'book', kataba 'he wrote', maktab 'office', maktuub 'written', kaatib 'writer', maktabah 'library', mukaatabah 'correspon-dence', iktitaab 'subscription', etc. Almost as frequently used as an example is qtl 'to kill'.

big fellow box, white fellow master fight him plenty too much, he cry

This example is intended to display the analyticity of Tok Pisin, an English-lexicon creole of Papua New Guinea. It comes in a large number of guises, all claiming that the word for 'piano' in Tok Pisin is something like 'a big box which, when you hit it, cries out loud'. It is highly unlikely, to say the least, that this ever was the normal word for 'piano' in the language (as New Zealander Hugh Young put it: "Life's too short, even in the tropics"). The first attestation of a somewhat similar expression (then referring to a harmonium) is found in an 1894 account by a missionary in Vanuatu, and it may be that the popular myth can ultimately be traced from there. In 1898, the expression is said to have been heard in New Guinea (and this time with reference to a piano), and in the 20th century, the "word" pops up more and more frequently in popular accounts of Melanesian Pidgin English.

"Sir, are you by any chance one of those of whom we may not be able to make a European?"

Avrupa-lı-la -tır-ıl-a-mı-yabil-en-ler-den-mi -siniz

This one-word sentence apparently began its claim to linguistic notoriety in Lewis' (1967) description of Turkish. Meaning 'You seem to be one of those who may be incapable of being Europeanized', it has since (with slight variations) often been used as an illustration of the agglutinating properties of the language. It contains one single truly lexical element, and the morphological analysis is as follows:

{Europe-QUALITY-INCHOATIVE-CAUSATIVE-PASSIVE-ABILITATIVE-NEGATIVE-POSSIBILITY-SUBJECT.PARTICIPLE-3pl-ABLATIVE-EVIDENTIAL-2pl}.

He took the knife cut the bread (or meat).

This is one of the two most common examples used to exemplify serial verb constructions in West African and Caribbean languages. A serialising language might express 'He cut the bread with a knife' thus. A similar sentence is also sometimes used to illustrate serialization in Sinitic. Norman (1988:129), for instance, gives the example *chí dāo gē ròu* {hold knife cut meat} from Classical Chinese.

Kofi walk go market

Well, this is the other one, which translates as 'Kofi goes to the market'. It is, of course, essential that all example sentences in Kwa languages contain a character named Kofi.

Petrus amat Mariam

A sentence going something like this is frequently used to illustrate the freedom of word order which comes with a rich case morphology. Given the case marking, it doesn't matter much in what order you put these Latin words—the sentence still means 'Peter loves Mary'. In this context, one might also mention the Russian *Мать любит дочь* 'The mother loves the daughter'. This is one of the rare instances in Russian where word order actually does matter, as the nouns *мать* 'mother' and *дочь* 'daughter' happen to be the same in the nominative and the accusative.

mā 'mother', má 'hemp', ma('horse', mà 'to scold'

Like many others in Mandarin, the syllable ma can have many quite different meanings depending on the tone pattern assigned to it. This is no doubt the most frequently cited example (to which one could add the question particle ma). I am not sure when it first appeared in linguistic writings, but the earliest example I can recall is Li & Thompson (1979:299).

HISTORICAL LINGUISTICS

a stronger affinity . . . than could possibly have been produced by accident; so strong, indeed, that no philologer could examine them all without believing them to have sprung from some common source, which, perhaps, no longer exists

The words used by William Jones in 1786 in which he announced his recognition of an Indo-European language family. Although he was not the first to come to this conclusion (p 103), the frequency with which these lines have been cited does stand in relation to the impact his discovery had on contemporary academia.

cantare habeo—je chanterai

The classic example of grammaticalization, used by Meillet (1912) when he coined the very term.

Chaque mot a sa propre histoire.

"Each word has its own history". Attributed to Swiss linguist Jules Gilliéron, compiler of the Atlas linguistique de la France. What Gilliéron meant was basically that there are indeed exceptions to sound laws, and that linguistic development is not predictable.

Today's morphology is yesterday's syntax.

Coined by Givón (1971:413) to capture the essence of grammaticalization. When mentioning this in my own teaching, I sometimes parody this by adding "Today's syntax is yesterday's pragmatics" in order to capture even more of the process.

L'étymologie est une science où les voyelles ne font rien et les consonnes fort peu de chose.

In other words: 'etymology is a science where the vowels mean nothing, and the consonants matter very little'. Hopefully, etymology has progressed since. The citation is attributed to Voltaire, but seemingly never mentioned in any of his writings. At one time, a prize was even offered by linguistics historian Konrad Koerner to anybody able to track down the original quotation. The subject has been discussed on the Histling mailing list (2002-08-11) and in Linguist List 8.1459.

Mbabaram dog [dɔk/] 'dog'

The Mbabaram word for 'dog' is uncannily similar to its English counterpart, but it is not a loan. It is therefore often (along with e.g. Persian bad 'bad' and Greek theos/Latin deus) used as an illustration of how two unrelated words by pure chance can develop similar forms. For those who believe in the Pama-Nyungan family, the word has been reconstructed as *gudaga. It was etymologized, I believe, by Ken Hale (1964), later often mentioned by Bob Dixon, and then popularized by Pinker (1994:255-56).

SOCIOLINGUISTICS AND PRAGMATICS

A language is a dialect with an army and a navy

Again, no one seems to be really sure who first came up with this now classic aphorism, which has been attributed to Max Weinreich, Uriel Weinreich, Joshua Fishman, Antoine Meillet, and Louis-Hubert Lyautey (see e.g. Bright 1997). The first known occurrence in print, however, is Weinreich (1945:13) (*A shprakh iz a diyalekt mit an armey un a flot*), where the author claims he heard it from a Bronx high school teacher.

The meaning is that there are no language-internal criteria to distinguish between varieties labelled 'languages' and those labelled 'dialects'—except that the speakers of the former have more power, thereby being able to impose theirs as the standard variety.

Can you pass me the salt?

Used by Searle (1975) to illustrate indirect speech acts. This particular speech act is constructed in a way typical of questions, but an answer such as 'I guess I could' would be inappropriate unless accompanied by the speaker actually handing over the salt.

Fourth floor

The 'fourth floor' example became legendary after Labov's (1966) seminal sociolinguistic study. Wanting to study the occurrence of postvocalic /r/ in various social settings in New York, Labov asked in three department stores frequented by different classes for some item which he knew beforehand would be on the fourth floor. And sure enough, there was a correlation between poshness and the use of postvocalic /r/.

Macy's department store on Manhattan—a landmark in the history of sociolinguistics after Bill Labov's visit in the mid-1960s. On the fourth floor of this building, Labov heard 44% postvocalic /r/s in casual speech.

A: My car is out of gas, where may I get some? B: There is a gas station around the corner.

Grice (1975:51) used this sentence to illustrate his principles of cooperation in conversation. If B does not believe that the filling station is open and actually does sell petrol, she is not lying, but is indeed being uncooperative or even deceptive.

LANGUAGE ACQUISITION BY INFANTS AND ANIMALS

Water bird

This is one of the constructions claimed to display a capacity for word coining in the chimpanzee Washoe, who had just seen her first swan. The full story is in Gardner & Gardner (1969).

This is a wug. This is another wug. Now we have two .....??

This was included in Berko's (1958) well-known 'wug' test. It was devised in order to check the morphological capacity of four-year-olds. The expected answer wugs proves that the subjects had not simply memorized plural forms of known words, but had a productive morphology.

give orange me give eat orange me eat orange give me eat orange give me you.

This is the longest "sentence" ever produced by Nim Chimpsky. Terrace et al. (1979:895) were not impressed.

A dog cannot relate his autobiography; however eloquently he may bark, he cannot tell you that his parents were honest though poor.

Bertrand Russell (1948:74) made this statement on the language capacities of animals.

ʌp, mʌk, ʒɪp

From Bloom's (1973:51) classic child language study. Alison, aged one and a half, wants mom to zip her coat. The holistic one-word utterances up, neck and zip apparently all constitute versions of this demand.

fis

One of the children studied by Berko & Brown (1960) used the fis for 'fish'. Although unable to pronounce the word in accordance with adult norms, he proved to be sensitive to any incorrectness in the speech of adults (e.g. when they imitated him).

MISCELLANEOUS

ghoti

Attributed to Irish playwright George Bernhard Shaw as an alternative spelling of the word fish (gh as in enough, o as in women, and ti as in station). Always a strong advocate of spelling reform, Shaw created this example to illustrate the absurdity of English spelling. Try as I have, I have not been able to locate the exact reference. Incidentally, it has been suggested that "ghoti" could also be a spelling of "huge". Go figure.

As an aside, Marc Okrand also included this as a deliberate pun in his creation Klingon (pp 157–158). The Klingon word for 'fish' is ghotI.

England and America are two countries separated by the same language.

In this form, it was apparently claimed by George Bernhard Shaw in an early 1940s issue of the Reader's Digest. Nevertheless, in terms of content, he was preceded by one of his main competitors as the world's no. 1 producer of aphorisms. Already in 1887, Oscar Wilde's The Canterville Ghost included the line "We have really everything in common with America nowadays except, of course, language".

I speak Spanish to God, Italian to women, French to men, and German to my horse.

Sociolinguistic domains delineated by the 16th century Holy Roman Emperor Charles V.

Verbing weirds language.

A somewhat iconic sentence uttered by Calvin of the comic strip Calvin and Hobbes. The reference is Watterson (1994:53).

Ce qui n'est pas clair n'est pas français.

"What is not clear is not French". Gallic Chauvinism at its worst illustrated by Rivarol (1783:72).

La Société n'admet aucune communication concernant, soit l'origine du langage, soit la création d'une langue universelle.

"The society will not allow any presentations on either the origins of language, or the creation of a universal language". Written into the statutes of the Société de Linguistique de Paris as article 2. The contents of the sentence are perhaps more frequently cited than the actual wording. Then as now, those topics apparently tended to attract people who took linguistics a little less seriously than they should.

OTHER MEMORABLE EXAMPLES

There is a certain category of example sentences whose members may not have become classic, but which certainly deserve to be. To start with a more innocent one, I am quite fond of Spencer's (1999) Chukchi sentence *t-y-tʔar-qora-kynʔor-rkən* 'How many reindeer am I lassoing?'. Then, to get a taste of the more naughty side of linguists, Corne (1990) illustrated his overview of Tayo pronouns with the unforgettable *Tete bi pu mwa* 'Give me a blow-job'. That, in turn, continued a proud tradition from the generative semantics of the late 1960s and early 1970s. Harris (1993) provides a nice overview of this unorthodox school, and its rather eccentric choice of example sentences. Among the more spectacular, we find the following:

- The MC introduced Mick Jagger's penis as being large enough to amaze even the most jaded groupies (Borkin 1984:18).
- Since Nixon was elected, I've come to miss LBJ [=Lyndon B Johnson] (Davison 1970:190).
- Chomsky is the De Gaulle of linguistics (Lakoff 1972:196).
- Fred does nothing but smoke hashish and play the sarod; John is similar (McCawley 1976:304).
- *Sam snarped the 10 Beatle records for a nude photo of Tricia Nixon (McCawley 1982:80).
- It's likely that Nixon won't send the marines to Botswana until 1972 (McCawley 1976:220).
- The fact that Max plorbed Betty did not convince Pete to caress her on the lips (Postal 1988:74).
- J. Edgar Hoover is an old fart (Dong 1971:203).

- Hey, if John went to Chicago, that means we'll soon have a big supply of dope (Schmerling 1971:249).
- Let's fuck (Lakoff 1977:82).
- My cache of marijuana got found by Fido, the police dog (Lakoff 1971:154).
- Nixon, you imperialist butcher, take your lunatic Secretary of Defense and shove him up your ass (Foo 1970:19).

Quoting these and others, Harris (1993:129) comments that generative semantics "grew one of the more exuberant ethoi in modern science". One of those who was in the midst of it, Robin Tolmach Lakoff (1989:977) characterized the writing style of the generative semanticists as "a kind of secret handshake", and adds that it was a product of an era when "experimentation with lifestyle and personality was encouraged". Somehow, you could almost tell from their example sentences.

One of the leading figures of the movement, Jim McCawley, under the name Quang Phuc Dong (1970) published an entire paper on the syntax of the word *fuck*. It includes memorable examples such as *Fuck you or I'll take away your teddy-bear*, *Wash the dishes and fuck you*, *Fuck communism on the sofa, Boris was fucking Susie's corpse, Cynthia was fucking Gwendolyn with a dildo*, and—not least—*Fuck all irregular verbs*.

In *Linguist List* 4.825, said Harris also mentions McCawley as the founder of "porno-linguistics". Under the pseudonym "E Clifton Gamahuche", his friend Haj Ross then took the first (and only) steps towards developing metapornolinguistics, noting for instance that "in the absence of Copula agreement, the only option is Reflexivization"...

SOURCES NOT MENTIONED IN THE TEXT

Classic example sentences: In general, this section benefits from several additions (and some corrections) by Daniel Bunčić (p c). In particular, he provided the Russian examples.

The Melanesian Pidgin English piano myth was traced by Philip Baker (p c).

The quote on England and America being separated by the same language was discussed on the *EDline* mailing list in July 2002.

THE LINGUIST'S GUIDE TO THE GALAXY

THE BOOK MARKET is full of life-style guides. Among the few that I have in my own bookshelf are the ones I really need the least, like *The Bachelor Home Companion (a practical guide to keeping house like a pig)* and *Real Men don't eat Quiche*. It is rather bothersome, though, that there is nothing similar for linguists. After all, the world is full of non-linguists in obvious need of some guidance.

LINGUISTIC FURNITURE

Let us begin at home. In order to live a fully satisfying linguistic life, it is a good idea to start by making your own conform to your career choice. Multinational Swedish furniture company IKEA has marketed a number of pieces of furniture suitable for linguists. Alas, the lamp series *Tempus* ('tense'), launched in the early 1980s, is out of production, and must therefore be sought at vintage furniture shops, as are *Sats* ('clause') and *Verb* ('verb').

Fortunately, however, the kitchen accessories *Grundtal* ('cardinal number'), *Aspekt* ('aspect'), *Pronomen* ('pronoun'), *Bestämd* ('definite'), *Imperativ* ('imperative'), *Syntes* ('synthesis'), *Tag* ('tag') and *Utsaga* ('statement') are still marketed, as is the storage box *Lingo*. The name of the chair *Sandi* is presumably misspelt—no doubt, *Sandhi* is intended (after all, IKEA's founder is a known dyslexic).

As mentioned below, a chair named Esperanto is also available, though not from IKEA.

LINGUIST COOKING

For home cooking, linguists of course consult the *Linguist List Cookbook*, wittily subtitled *A Feastschrift in Honor of Jim McCawley*. Among the more suggestive recipes in this cookbook—which only exists on the web—is Klingon Bread. Before his death, McCawley himself (1984) also published *The Eater's Guide to Chinese Characters*, where the written names of some common Chinese dishes are discussed and explained.

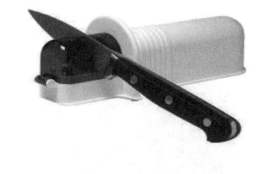

A must in every linguist's kitchen: the knife-sharpener Aspekt

Among starters, linguists have a tendency to settle for *Alphabet Soup*. Also, when it comes to lighter meals, linguists are particularly fond of *panini*, the Italian bread roll. Unbeknownst to many other consumers of this food item (but of course not to linguists), Panini was also the world's first known linguist—a Sanskrit grammarian from present-day Pakistan, active in the 5th century BC.

Linguistically kosher drinks are remarkably scarce. There are of course wines from Languedoc, one of the few geographical areas to be named after a speech style, but apart from that, the most recommended linguistic beverage is IPA beer. In order not to be perceived as partial, the various breweries which produce this kind of beer pretend that these are the initials of *India Pale Ale*. Yet, no linguist can possibly escape the obvious

interpretation that IPA really stands for the *International Phonetic Association*.

Sadly fictitious are the dishes mentioned in Zwicky, Salus, Binnick & Vanek (eds) (1970). Delicacies served at *Maxeme's The Linguist's Restaurant* include *Whorfles, Fruit Joos, Sapirribs* and *Martineted Herring*.

For those not keen on cooking, eating out is an option. At least if you live in Prague. During the late interwar years, and for much of the second world war, the Prague Linguistics Circle held many of its meetings at the Café Louvre, at 20 Národní třída in Prague. The café still exists, and prides itself of having been visited by celebrities such as Albert Einstein and Franz Kafka. For the true linguist, however, this does of course not compare to it having been the favorite hangout of Nikolai Trubetzkoy and Roman Jakobson.

A place where history was made. Café Louvre in Prague was where la crème de la crème of the European structuralist posse gathered in the late 1930s.

IN THE LINGUIST'S RECORD COLLECTION

In terms of music, there is plenty to choose from for the image-conscious linguist, and it is impossible to mention but a few of the recordings which hail our discipline.

The CD *69 Love Songs*, released by The Magnetic Fields in 1999, includes a song named "The Death of Ferdinand de Saussure". The year after, Jega presented the album *Geometry*, including an instrumental electronic piece called "Syntax Tree". In a similar genre, there

is Clock DVA, one of whose songs is tastefully named "Syntactics". One of my own favorite performers, Captain Beefheart, also rocks linguistically in asserting that "The past sure is tense". Sure is.

There are at least two songs named "Noam Chomsky", one (sounding somewhat like R E M) by the Dead Hot Workshop, and one by The Horsies. Other musical material with a syntactic connection includes at least two songs named "Dr Syntax" and a whole bunch called "Cunning Linguist".

Noam Chomsky is also featured on the EP *Bigger cages, longer chains* by the leftist rockers International Noice Conspiracy, including angry young Dennis Lyxzén of the former Swedish hardcore band The Refused. The EP was released in 2003 (though only in the US), and had a filmed Chomsky lecture as a bonus track. As if this weren't enough, there is also an entire band from Dallas, Texas, which calls itself Chomsky. The combo describes its style as "poppy rock & roll with new wave influences".

Less formalist linguists may be attracted by the indie pop band The Faint, one of whose songs is called *Syntax Lies* (oh yeah? As if pragmatics always told the truth!).

Animal language research is represented in the rock business as well, through Teddybears Sthlm whose 1996 album *I Can't Believe It's Teddybears Sthlm* contained the song *Kanzi* (see p 151).

One of the contestants in the Swedish qualifying round for the 2006 Eurovision Song Contest apparently aimed particularly at attracting votes from historical linguists by naming the song *Etymon*.

Hiphopper Prince Paul has a song named "Psycho Linguistics", while the harder act Frankenbok perform "Linguistics", tout court. Indigenous and Invictus have recorded "Twisted Linguistics" and "Latin Linguistics" respectively.

Other notable artists within the hip hop and modern dance scenes include Super-scientifiku, hiphoppers from Sundsvall, Sweden, who have released an EP called *Syntax semantics*. Magnetrixx, Si Begg & Neil Landstrumm and Organized Konfusion have blessed the world with recordings called *Syntax error, Unknown Dialect* and *Murder by Syntax*, respectively. Another Swedish rapper started his career under the alias *Motorisk Afasi* (motor aphasia), which he has since

shortened merely to *Afasi*.

For phoneticians, an act named Servotron offer the slightly Devo-inspired song "Phonetic Lecture". The 1997 album "The Conet Project " (according to one reviewer "an absolute must-have recording for anyone who appreciates the surrealist intersection of function and art") features a track entitled "Phonetic Alphabet". Phoneticians may also enjoy "Labio-dental fricative" by the Bonzo Dog Doo Dah Blues Band. No less avant-garde is ID Lab with "Phonetic Energy".

Linguist fans of Italian jazz no doubt already have in their record collection the album "Cosmic Dialects", a live recording by the band aptly named Lingua Franca.

On a sadder note, the Australian 1960s-inspired pop combo *Snout* recorded *Last Surviving Speaker* for their 2002 album *Managing Good Looks*.

An early 1980s American rock band proudly bore the name The Semantics, and from the Netherlands stem two acts with linguistic band names, namely Move Alpha and the Dikke van Dale, the latter being named after the best known Dutch dictionary. More peripherically linguistic names are, not unexpectedly, more plentiful, and include (to just mention a few) the rockers Bad English, and, of course, Marianne Faithfull's classic "Broken English". Speed kings S O D (Stormtroopers of Doomsday) had presumably been exposed to some of that prior to recording their "Speak English or die".

Zwicky, Salus, Binnick & Vanek (eds.) (1970) includes a *Linguist's Song Book* which features classics such as *I get a click out of you, The trill is gone, The transformationale*, and *All alone by the allophone* along with several dozen others.

Finally, let us not forget the rockabilly anthem *Bertha Lou*, recorded in 1957 by both Johnny Faire and Dorsey Burnette, which contains the immortal lines "Hey-hey, Bertha Lou—I wanna conjugate with you".

LINGUISTIC MONEY

In order to buy the necessary gadgetry mentioned above, we do of course need money. Interestingly, there is, or rather once was, a currency which had a special connection to language.

When the euro came into circulation in eleven European countries in 2002, some of its critics despisingly referred to it as "Esperanto money". They presumably did not know that Esperanto once did have currency of its own—to my knowledge the only *language* with a pecuniary system!

In May 1907, a Swiss named René de Saussure (whose brother was no other than our own founding father Ferdinand!) came up with a rather wild idea. In order to strengthen their position as a truly cosmopolitan and internationalist movement, he proposed, Esperantists should issue their own currency.

He gave the projected currency the name *speso* (from French *espèce* 'kind, sort'). Its value was determined in relation to gold so that a *spesmilo* (i.e. 1000 *spesoj*) corresponded to 0,733 grams of gold.

The banker Herbert Hoveler was one of the supporters of the speso project, and the same year, he founded the *Ĉefbanko esperantista* in London. Cheques were issued, with the slogan *Unu mondo, unu lingvo, unu mono* ('one world, one language, one currency) printed on them. In 1912, the production of coins was also commenced.

At the start of the First World War, the bank had 730 customers in 43 countries. The war, however, hindered the development of the new currency, and when Hoveler died in 1918, his bank, and thereby the *speso* died with him.

COLLECTING STAMPS LINGUISTICALLY

Unfortunately, glottophilately does not seem to be much talked about in stamp collectors' circles. Sadder, still, linguists are not usually portrayed on stamps, and the only instance that I am aware of is Rasmus Rask's presence on stamps from Denmark and Iceland. A few other characters whose work is a part of our discipline's history have been commemorated by stamps, though. The United States postal services have issued stamps in honour of both Sequoyah (p 122) and Thomas Gallaudet (p 127). Belarus and Croatia have done the same for Frantzisk Skaryna and Stanislav Škrabec, important standardizers of the respective national languages. Croatia has also honoured Wolfgang von Kempelen, a pioneer in speech synthesis (and scientific fraud).

A few countries have issued stamps commemorating specific languages, e.g. Ladino (Israel), American and British Sign (USA and Britain respectively), Finnish

dialects (Finland), and Croatian (Croatia). While most such stamps depict a language spoken in the country in question, there are a few exceptions. Thus, both China and Croatia have honoured Esperanto, while Tunisia celebrated the 10th anniversary of the *Conseil International de la langue française*, and Belarus did the same for the 400th anniversary of the first Slovenian grammar.

The year 2001 was the European Year of Languages, something that both Finland and Luxembourg noticed in their stamp production. The Bangladeshis rarely miss an opportunity to bring attention to its so-called *Language Martyrs* (see p 387), and indeed— they do have a stamp of their own.

Possibly *the* most linguistic issue, however, is the 2003 series produced in the Philippines, which celebrates the 50th anniversary of work in that country by the Summer Institute of Linguistics.

WHAT LINGUISTS VOTE FOR

In the 2001 municipal elections of Århus, Denmark, candidate Thomas Widmann, running for the leftist party *Radikale Venstre* tried to attract voters by pointing out that he was a linguist.

Something must indeed be rotten in the state of Denmark, for amazingly, this obvious sign of trustworthiness did not appeal to the voters. Of the 12 510 votes for Radikale Venstre in the municipality, only 69 were cast in favor of Widmann.

The campaign posters were bilingual in Danish and German, featuring the slogan *Halb deutsch, ganz radikal* (Half German, but thoroughly radical), which alluded to the fact that Widmann's father is of German origin. Also included was the message *Lingvister bør da stemme på lingvister. Thomas Widmann stiller faktisk op til byrådet, han er jo lingvist. Stem ham derfor ind!* (Linguists should vote for linguists. Thomas Widmann is a candidate for the city council, and he is a linguist. Therefore, vote him in!), as well as—of course—a syntactic analysis of this.

Thomas Widmann enigmatically failed to achieve the landslide victory we had all expected. Surely, this would never have happened in Jespersen's day.

A LINGUIST'S NIGHT OUT

When the day is over, it is tempting to go out to a bar for a little something. Needless to say, some places are more suitable than others. There are several hangouts named *X-Bar*, in obvious honour to our discipline. One each is found in Berlin (Raumerstraße 17), in Mariestad (western Sweden), in Bangkok (8 Ladprao) and in Tallinn (Sauna 1), the latter being a gay bar.

Insignificant though its exterior appearance may seem, this is nothing less than Tallinn's X-bar

LINGUISTS AND SPORTS

The average linguist may not be a major sports buff. Or at least she wasn't until recently. In the year 2001, sports giant *Adidas* revealed that it was about to produce a football (that's *soccer* to American readers) with a *syntactic surface* (no, I am not making this up). Clearly, a sport involving syntactics is bound to attract hordes of linguist spectators.

Apparently, less formalist linguists will have to wait for footballs with a pragmatic or semantic surface.

LINGUISTIC NAMING PRACTICES

The biggest object ever named for a language is most probably a continent—Latin America (or rather a continent and a half, since it includes not only South, but also Central America). Indeed, it is not unlikely that Latin is also the language for which the largest number of objects has been named. That certainly does not mean that it does not have its competitors. One of the more striking is Esperanto.

Röllinger (1997), updated by Kaminski & Bore (2002) lists more than 1 200 objects of various kinds in 59 countries named either after Esperanto, or its creator Ludwig Zamenhof. The list includes about 700 streets, 140 monuments, 50 buildings, 27 bus stops, 22 parks, 16 restaurants, 14 schools, 10 hospitals, 5 fountains, 6 hotels, 4 ships, 3 libraries, 2 islands, 2 shopping malls and 2 camping grounds, a brook, a mountain and a town (Esperantopolis, in Brazil).

A tulip was named *Esperanto* in 1968, and it was later joined by a similarly named clematis. A species of lichen is known as *Zamenhofia*, while a beetle has been baptized

Gergithus esperanto. The *Berhardt Progressive Furniture Collection* of New Zealand markets a chair named Esperanto.

Three tokens of Esperanto

Esperanto has even made its presence known in outer space—in the late 1930s, Finnish astronomer Yrjö Väisälä named two asteroids *Esperanto* and *Zamenhof*. The language itself soon followed, as the spacecraft *Voyager 1* and *Voyager 2* included disks with Esperanto recordings, for the benefit of any interested aliens.

FOR THE LINGUIST TOURIST

Linguists travel a lot. Mostly, they are on their way to things like the *Fifty-Sixth Carpathian Conference on Bilabial Trills*, but occasionally they do go for a vacation. Yet, one must not forget that a linguist on vacation is still a linguist, and needless to say, she has a preference for destinations of linguistic interest. And fortunately, several ways of

boosting the linguistic flavour of your trip are available.

Those taking a trip to Paris should take note that while there are more than 100 streets and squares in Paris named after mathematicians, there is, shockingly, only one single *Rue Ferdinand de Saussure*. Umeå in northern Sweden has a *Språkgränd* ('language alley'), and Down Under, there is a *Syntax Street* in Ipswich. In Stockholm, where not only streets, but also blocks have names, there is also a block named *Språkmästaren*, an archaic word for 'language teacher'. In London, where it is more common for buildings to have names, 44 Russell Square is *Syntax House*, home to a company named Syntax Integration Limited.

In St Petersburg, the Peter-and-Paul fortress contains a section once used to confine political prisoners, whose name is more titillating than its purpose—Trubetzkoy Bastion.

Turning to place-names, the daring might want to go to the troubled Jammu-Kashmir area and pay a visit to the town of Sandhi.

In the United States, there are plenty of places with names evoking the glory of linguistics. There are no less than 20 places

Available on Colombo's High Level Road

Pied piping arose in Hamelin, Germany

named Bloomfield, and in Texas, we find X-Bar Ranch Nature Retreat. Furthermore, we have a Case in Arkansas, and even twice in Missouri (this beautiful name also occurs in Mozambique, Angola and Italy, as well as on Corsica and Madagascar). Indiana has a slightly misspelled Grammer, and a similar orthographic problem obtains in Mississippi, where there is a Vowell. The latter should perhaps consider twinning with Bolivia's Consonancia.

The USA moreover sports four instances of Romance, and one Creole—the latter appropriately located in Louisiana.

On the same side of the Atlantic, we may note that Mexico sports a Perfecto, while Brazil prides itself of one Infinitio and one Singular. The Haitians have been logical enough to call two places Dual.

Japanese happens not to be a tone language (at least in most analyses), but most other East Asian languages are, so the two places in Japan named Tone are not completely astray. Tonologists might also like to know that Colombo (Sri Lanka) has a High Level Road (which is neither high nor level, and is best known for its many signs offering "Used Body Parts", i.e. parts to improve the appearance of clapped out motor vehicles). This city also has a Duplication Road.

In the English county of Cornwall, there is a cape called Dr Syntax's head (no *Dr Syntax's dependent* in sight, though).

Europe, more precisely Belarus, has a Khomsk, which is most likely (yes, really) the place from which a certain MIT syntactician gets his family name. And while in Europe, let us not forget that Hamelin, Germany, is the place to which we owe the syntactic term *pied-piping*.

Finally, there is a Nasal in both Yemen and Romania, and a watercourse intriguingly named Noun River in Cameroon. The same continent also has two Bantu, one in Ethiopia and one closer to the Bantu Urheimat, in Nigeria. In Greece, just over 40 kilometres north-east of Athens, there is a village named Grammatiko.

In terms of having names whetting the appetite of linguists, however, probably no place can match Linguaglossa (sic!), a town of 6 000 inhabitants in northern Sicily.

As for the travel itself, the Irish national airline, Aer Lingus, should of course be the first option. For shorter trips, one may use the Bickerton folding bicycle. This British product came with a carrying case, the idea being that commuters would take this on their train journey, then take the folded bicycle out on arrival, unfold it, tighten a couple of screws, and pedal off to work. Launched in 1977, it was popular in the 1980s but faded away in the early 90s—not unlike the *Bioprogram Hypothesis* of creolist Derek Bickerton!

WHERE TO STAY

The Hotel Cornavin, located at 1201 Gare de Cornavin in Geneva is most probably the only commercial establishment to boast "Syldavian spoken here". The Cornavin is the hotel where Professor Calculus (of the Tintin comic strip) stayed in *The Calculus Affair*. Syldavian, of course, is the language of the imaginary country Syldavia, which plays a major role in this, and a couple of other Tintin adventures. Interestingly, room 122, where Calculus stayed, did not exist when the album was written, but was added to the hotel in 1999 as a gesture towards Tintinophiles.

Having said that, it is worth pointing out the embarrassing fact that the Geneva tourist authorities confess that Saussure's home city has no monument to commemorate its great son.

Even if you're Down Under, there is no reasonable excuse for not lodging linguistically—in Sandy Bay (no, not *Sandhi Bay*), Tasmania, there is also a hotel which, in a laudable attempt to attract linguists as visitors, calls itself Dr Syntax.

AUTHORIZED TYPEFACES

In 1969, Hans Eduard Meier of Switzerland launched a font named *Syntax*, which must surely rank as the typeface with the most linguistic name.

Thanks to the similarity of its name to that of Franz Bopp, *BeeBopp* is also acceptable, as are, albeit only marginally, *Symbol*, *Signa* and *Icone*.

In addition, you may let your purely linguistic preferences serve as a guide, and follow your favorites. Bloomfield's (1933) *Language*, for instance, is set in *Monotype Modern*, and if you like Chomsky's (1965) *Aspects*, you may want to know that it is printed in *Baskerville*.

A vision of a hopefully not too distant future. Amazingly, there is still no statue of Ferdinand de Saussure in Geneva.

DRESSING DEPARTMENT-SMART

The orthodox linguist doesn't have too much to choose from, but needless to say, her wardrobe does contain linguistic gear, and she does prefer to appear linguistically clad.

The official Linguist List t-shirt

The above-mentioned band Magnetic Fields has marketed its own *Death of Ferdinand de Saussure* T-shirt. And in Leipzig the football team *Superlative Suffixes* has T-shirts bearing its name. In addition, plenty of linguistics associations and venues have produced their own t-shirts, including the *Society of Linguistics Undergrads at McGill*, the *23rd Penn Linguistics Colloquium* and the *Society for Pidgin and Creole languages*. Phoneticians can order a T-shirt with the IPA chart on it at **www.linguiste.org**. But surely most inclusive is the *Linguist List* shirt, in which this author's amorphous body can sometimes be seen.

The lower extremities do well from being immersed in a pair of *Syntax*, a product from the D C Shoe Company.

FURTHER TRAVEL TIPS: LINGUISTIC MONUMENTS

Language is an abstract entity. Nevertheless, some people have—with various degrees of success—attempted to render linguistic grandeur in steel and concrete. Below follows the top ten list of those monuments which the devoted linguist cannot afford to miss.

1. MONUMENT TO DANISH LINGUIST HEROES, COPENHAGEN

Located on the corner of Dante Plads and H. C. Andersen Boulevard, this 1936 monument honours Denmarks finest, and at the same time the country's glorious linguistic past.

2. AFRIKAANSE TAALMONUMENT, PAARL, SOUTH AFRICA

A unique attraction near Paarl in South Africa is the futuristic looking *Afrikaanse Taalmonument* (*taal* means 'language'). It symbolizes the development of Afrikaans, from Dutch and other sources, into a language of its own.

The Danes obviously know how to honour those who deserve it. In downtown Copenhagen, this monument celebrates four of those who contributed to make Denmark a linguistic superpower in the 19th and early 20th centuries: Rasmus Rask (1787–1832), Karl Verner (1846-1896), Vilhelm Thomsen (1842–1927), and N L Westergaard (1815–1878). A few other Great Danes, such as Otto Jespersen and Louis Hjelmslev are presumably not featured because they were still alive when the monument was erected in 1936.

3. MONUMENT TO THE LANGUAGE MARTYRS, DHAKA, BANGLADESH

As Bangladesh struggled for independence from Pakistan, language was an important symbolic issue. On February 21st 1952, large numbers of students publicly protested, and demanded Bengali language rights. The Pakistani police responded by opening fire, thereby killing five protesters, who have since become known as the Language Martyrs. The first version of the Language Martyrs' Monument, locally known as Shahed Minar, was constructed overnight between 22 and 23 February 1953 on the site of the tragedy from material found in the vicinity. It immediately became a site of pilgrimage for people wanting to pay homage to the dead protesters. A mere three days later, the Pakistani military tore down the makeshift memorial. A number of years later, the current monument was erected, again on the same site where the Language Martyrs where slain.

Is it a chimney? Is it a rocket launcher? Is it just a pile of concrete? No, it's the Afrikaanse Taalmonument!

4. VARIOUS MONUMENTS TO ESPERANTO

As mentioned elsewhere (p 383), there are about 140 monuments erected in honour of Esperanto.

5. SIGN LANGUAGE CONFERENCE MEMORIAL, BROWNING, USA

In 1941, a memorial was raised in the town of Browning in Montana (USA), to commemorate the conference held there 4–6 September, 1930 on Plains Indian Sign. The conference, which was probably the world's first conference on a pidgin language, attracted signers from 14 different tribes. Their signing was filmed for the American archives, since one of the main reasons for the conference was to document the disappearing language. The monument contains the participants' footprints in concrete.

6. MONUMENTS TO IVAR AASEN, ØRSTA AND OSLO, NORWAY

As many readers are aware, Norway has two standard languages: The Danish-influenced *Bokmål* standard language, and *Nynorsk* ('New Norwegian'), standardized in the nationalistic 19th century by Ivar Aasen on the basis of rural (and less Danified) dialects. Aasen is honoured by monuments both in Oslo and in his birth town, Ørsta in western Norway. In the latter town, there is also a museum devoted to Aasen's life and work.

7. THOMAS GALLAUDET, GALLAUDET UNIVERSITY CAMPUS, WASHINGTON USA

Thomas Gallaudet introduced French Sign to the United States (see p 127), and the only university in the world (Gallaudet University, in Washington) to use a sign language as its primary medium of instruction is named after him. A sculpted version of the man himself still sits in a park on the campus, and in Gallaudet's lap is his first pupil, Alice Cogswell, imitating her teacher's production of the letter "A".

As an interesting aside, Daniel Chester French, the sculptor behind the Gallaudet statue, also produced (in 1915) a statue of Abraham Lincoln, which stands in downtown Washington. The shape of the president's hands bears an uncannily close resemblance to the fingerspelt letters "A" and "L", that is, his own initials. No one is really sure whether this is intentional or not, but it is certainly not impossible, given French's earlier connections with the deaf community at Gallaudet university, and the fact that he did learn some fingerspelling. Lincoln himself also had a link with the university, since he was the one who granted it the right to confer collegiate degrees in 1864. Also, the fact that French's earlier statue at the Gallaudet university campus without doubt depicts finger spelling may be taken to strengthen the hypothesis.

Thomas Gallaudet on the campus of Gallaudet University, as sculpted in 1889 by Daniel Chester French.

8. MONUMENT TO THE ESTONIAN LANGUAGE, KADRINA, ESTONIA

Just outside the Kadrina Secondary School, there is a monument to the Estonian language, erected in 1994 following the revival of nationalism in the newly independent state.

9. OBELISK TO DOROTHY PENTREATH, PAUL, BRITAIN

Dorothy Pentreath's claim to fame is that she is often (albeit incorrectly) mentioned as the last native speaker of Cornish. She died in Mousehole in 1777. Near her grave in the town of Paul, a granite obelisk (with inscriptions in English and Cornish) commemorating the lady and her language is found. It was erected in 1860 by no other than the French prince Louis Bonaparte, a politician with a well-documented interest in languages.

10. THE NAVAJO CODE TALKERS MONUMENT IN FLAGSTAFF, USA

The *Navajo Code Talkers* monument in Flagstaff, Arizona, was erected in 1989 to the memory of the Navajos serving the United States during the Second World War. By communicating in a specially devised cryptolectal form of Navajo (pp 4–5), the Code Talkers succeeded in transmitting various kinds of information between American units without being understood by the Japanese. The monument was designed by R C Gorman, the son of one of the last surviving Code Talkers. In late 2002, plans were also announced to erect a statue in Oklahoma commemorating the Comanche code-talkers.

HONOURABLE MENTIONS

- **King Sejong** (1418-1450) in a park in Seoul. Although no one knows for certain what role King Sejong played in the actual creation of the legendary Korean Han'gŭl script (see p 116), his name is forever associated with this ingenious invention. At the entrance of Teoksugung, or the "Palace of Virtuous Longevity" in Seoul, the king still sits.
- In Lithuania's capital Vilnius, there are a couple of statues with linguistic connections. One of them shows a man smuggling books into the country, during the period (1864-1904) when Lithuanian publications were outlawed by the Russian authorities. Another depicts a mother at a spinning wheel with a child in her lap. It turns out that she is secretly teaching the child to read Lithuanian.
- In Brændekilde, Denmark, the birthplace of **Rasmus Rask**, a bust honours the village's great son. The local school is of course named after him, as is a boy scout group. In nearby Odense, a street bears his name since 1919.
- Various busts of **Michael Agricola**. The standardizer of Finnish still stands in several places in Finland, notably in front of the Turku Cathedral.
- Plenty of Czech towns have a monument to **Jan Hus**, whose phonological insights lay behind the modern Czech orthography.

It looks innocent enough, but in fact, the lady is not teaching her child how to spin . . .

. . . but rather to read in a forbidden language! The statue is found in Vilnius, Lithuania.

- Lots of towns in Serbia honour **Vuk Karadžić** with a monument. Described as "the Serbian Jakob Grimm", he collected folk tales, but also produced the first grammar and dictionary of Serbian.
- Bust of **Ivan Mažuranić** in the Zrinjevac Park in Zagreb. **Mažuranić** was a 19th century politician and reformer of the Croatian language.
- In several Slavic countries, **St Cyril** and his brother **St Method** are present in the form of statues, icons and other depictions. They are best known for their standardization of Church Slavonic and the invention of the Glagolithic alphabet.
- **Grammar**. In several medieval Cathedrals, there were sculptures symbolizing the seven artes liberales, one of which was grammar. In various ways, Grammar thus embellishes plenty of European cathedrals.
- Statue of **Victor the Wild Child**, St-Sernin-sur-Rance, France. Victor was a feral child (pp 133–34) found outside this French town, and he lived there for a while before being taken to Paris. In 1987, a bronze statue was erected, depicting the child.

WHAT LINGUISTS READ

It is striking how rarely novel authors let linguists play their most natural role—that of the hero. Fortunately, and most naturally, though, there are some exceptions. The oldest is perhaps the classic *Pygmalion*, by George Bernard Schwa—sorry, Shaw—from 1912, where the main character Henry Higgins is modelled on the British phonetician Henry Sweet. A few decades later,

C S Lewis's equally classic *Space Trilogy* features a philologist by the name of Elwin Ransom.

From more recent decades, there is much more to choose from. Edward Wellen's short story *Chalk Talk* includes a teacher of transformational grammar, and even mentions Noam Chomsky by name. From the same year, 1973, is *The Embedding* by Ian Watson. The plot here involves not only a child language researcher and a field linguist working on an Amazonian language, but also aliens with an interest in the Sapir-Whorf hypothesis! The early seventies also saw the publication of Peter Dickinson's *The Poison Grade*, where the linguist heroes are researching the language abilities of chimpanzees.

In the 1980s and 90s the genre grew steadily bigger. In *A woman of the Iron People* by Eleanor Arnason, the principal character is a field linguist who learns a non-human language. C J Cherryh also ventures into outer space in *Foreigner*, where the hero has written his dissertation on plural forms in an alien tongue. Meanwhile, linguist mystery solvers on their home planet figure in Tony Hillerman's *Coyote Waits* from 1990 and in Jack O'Connell's *Box Nine* from 1992.

Andrew Rosenheim has produced *Hands On*, where the heroes are linguists hired by a software developer, and in Simon Winchester's *The Professor and the Madman* from 1999, the action revolves around the making of the *Oxford English Dictionary*.

A particularly interesting subcategory consists of fiction not only involving a linguistic theme, but also written by linguists. No doubt best known are the works by Suzette Haden Elgin, in particular the *Native Tongue* Trilogy (*Native Tongue* 1984, *The Judas Rose* 1987 and *Earthsong* 1993)—marketed by the publisher as a "Feminist science fiction classic". Linguistics plays a major role, partly because linguists are crucial in establishing relations with non-humans. Central to the story is the development of a language called Láadan, intended to be particularly well suited to the needs of women. Linguistics is also featured in some of Haden Elgin's other books, such as the *Ozark Fantasy* trilogy (*Twelve Fair Kingdoms*, *The Grand Jubilee* and *And Then There'll Be Fireworks*, all published in 1981) and *Yonder Comes the Other End of Time* (1986).

In 1979, creolist enfant terrible Derek Bickerton published a novel named *King of the Sea*, focusing on relations between humans and dolphins—which have a language of their own. Then, 1984 saw the publication of sci-fi novel *Man of Gold* by M A R Barker—known to Americanists for his work on Klamath. The

synopsis seems realistic enough, in that it is a linguist who gets to save the world.

David Carkeet, then teaching at the University of Missouri in St Louis published, *Double Negative* (1980) and *Full Catastrophe* (1990), both of which feature a linguist as the main character.

Finally, while Anthony Burgess—best known for *A Clockwork Orange*—never quite made it to the higher level of consciousness that full linguistic training entails, he did study some linguistics. One of his other works, *The Doctor is sick*, features a linguist.

A number of other works of fiction—particularly in the science fiction genre—contain linguistic elements. Further discussions on linguistics in Science Fiction can be found in Barnes (1975), Meyers (1980), Pullum (1991:198-200), and in various issues of the *Linguist List*.

There are of course novels in other languages than English which are similarly tainted with linguistics. Fredrik Ekelund's

Jag vill ha hela världen was first published in Swedish in 1996. Its main character, Daniel Lagerhjelm wants it all—he demands success in love, as well as in his careers as a linguist and as a football player. When he fails in all three, he takes to drink. Another Swedish novel, released in 2004 and written by Daniel Sjölin, bears the tasteful title *Personliga pronomen* ('personal pronouns').

Although without linguistic content per se, a couple of Japanese *manga* comics merit mention. The mid-1990s saw a number of heroines in this genre named after Iberian-lexified creoles (!), such as *Papia Kristang* and *Papia Mentu*.

Among more general works of fiction with a semi-linguistic content, George Orwell's *1984* (with the Newspeak language) and several of J R R Tolkien's books also merit mention.

Oddly, none of the above titles has been published by *Vokativ* or *Dualis*—names of two Swedish publishers (of which the former was founded by a former student of mine).

LINGUISTICS IN FILMS

Just as in written fiction, there are strikingly few films where linguists have been given the heroic role that the general public for some enigmatic reason normally fails to associate with our profession. The most obvious intersection between linguistics and moving pictures is Marc Okrand's conlang Klingon (see p 129). Following are a few other silver screen productions where linguists get to show off:

Pygmalion / My Fair Lady
various, 1937 /38/64

George Bernard Shaw's Pygmalion is familiar to most people. The phonetician Henry Higgins (played by Leslie Howard in the 1938 version), one of the two main characters, is modelled on real-life linguist Henry Sweet. The Dutch film version came in 1937, followed by an English one the year after. The musical version "My Fair Lady" was filmed in 1964 with Audrey Hepburn as Eliza.

Ball of Fire
Howard Hawks, 1941

A lexicographer (Gary Cooper), realizing that the slang section of his dictionary is outdated, visits a nightclub in order to update it. It turns out that the nightclub singer is engaged to a gangster on the run from the police.

The Miracle Worker
Arthur Penn, 1962
Depicts Helen Keller's acquisition of tactile sign language (pp 130–31).

L'enfant Sauvage (The Wild Child)
Francois Truffaut, 1969
The true story about Victor, the language-deprived child found in south-western France in the late 18th century.

The Exorcist
William Friedkin, 1973
This horror classic features linguists from the Georgetown University linguistics department decoding a message from the devil by playing a tape backwards. In reverse, the devil apparently speaks standard American English.

Barwy ochronne (Camouflage)
Krzysztof Zanussi, 1977
A Polish film in which the action revolves around a linguistics summer school.

Het dak van de walvis (On Top of the Whale)
Raoul Ruiz, 1982
Parody of much of western academia. A group of field linguists set out to study an exotic language which consists only of one single word, which therefore means everything.

A Thousand Clowns
Fred Coe, 1965
Includes a dialect identification Wunderkind ("Upper East Side, but you spent a couple of years in Chicago").

The Statue
Rodney Amateau, 1971
British linguist wins the Nobel prize for having invented a universal language (how come there is no such prize in real life?). His wife is commissioned to sculpt a statue of him, but she makes it better hung than her linguist husband actually is.

Jeder für sich und Gott gegen alle (The Enigma of Kaspar Hauser)
Werner Herzog, 1974
Based on the true story of the boy found in Nuremberg in the early 19th century. Kaspar Hauser (p 133) is known as one of the few feral children who actually did learn to speak.

Chan is Missing
Wayne Wang, 1982
Remarkable primarily because it includes a lecture on sociolinguistics, where the lecturer is allegedly based on Deborah Tannen.

Iceman
Fred Schepisi, 1984
A Neanderthal man is found frozen in ice, is defrosted, and comes back to life. His guttural growls are deciphered by an "MIT linguist", aided by a "Pitch-Stress Meter".

Sherman's March
Ross McElwee, 1986

Features the hippie linguist Winnie, from whose mouth we have the following memorable quote: "I've told you that for a very long time, I've believed that the only important things in life are linguistics and sex. So it's easy to see how one would get involved with a linguistics professor".

Manufacturing Consent: Noam Chomsky and the Media
Mark Achbar & Peter Wintonick, 1992

Yes, this documentary about the man himself was actually shown at the cinemas. As the title suggests, though, it is more concerned with Chomsky's political side than with linguistics. Ten years later followed Power and Terror: Noam Chomsky in Our Times, *directed by John Junkerman.*

Sneakers
Phil Alden Robinson, 1992

The film is about cryptography, but also features an intriguing use of speaker identification. Cast includes Robert Redford, Sidney Poitier, Dan Akroyd and River Phoenix.

Nell
Michael Apted, 1994

A young girl has grown up in isolation with her mother, who is speechless as the result of a stroke. After her mother's death, she is forced to encounter the outside world, where a cold-hearted psychologist is more interested in studying the language-deprived Nell than in helping her. Starring Jodie Foster.

Stargate
Roland Emmerich, 1994

American soldiers (led by Kurt Russell) and an Egyptologist are transported to a far-away planet from where they have difficulties getting home. Fortunately, a thorough knowledge of hieroglyphics proves useful.

Born to Be Wild
John Gray, 1995

One of the two main characters is a gorilla named Katie who is being taught sign language.

Oscar
John Landis, 1991

When a gangester (Sylvester Stallone) decides to instead become a respectable businessman, a professor Higgins-like character, the dialectologist and elocution teacher Dr. Thornton Poole is called upon to teach proper language.

Atlantis: the Lost Empire
Gary Trousdale & Kirk Wise, 2001

Disney animation in which a decipherer of ancient languages is crucial to the finding of the lost continent. Michael J Fox does the linguist's voice.

The Jennie Project
Gary Nadeau, 2001

Two anthropologists adopt a chimp, raise it with their own children, and teach it American Sign Language.

Windtalkers
John Woo, 2002

A dramatized version of the use of Navaho as a secret radio code during World War II Pacific operations. Starring Nicholas Cage.

A few details regarding Disney's *Atlantis* merit mention. As already noted, a linguist is the hero of the film. As the newspaper *USA Today* pointed out, *"Everyone from flying elephants to lonely hunchbacks has had a chance to be a Disney animated hero. But never a linguist. Until now"*. Not only does a linguist finally get the place in a Disney animation that his trade merits, but the film also features a brand new artificial language. Disney hired Marc Okrand—of Klingon fame—to construct the new fictious language. Vocabulary-wise, it is inspired by Indo-European languages, but is not modelled on any tongue in particular. Of particular interest is the writing system—it is boustrophedon. This means that the direction of writing changes from one line to another. If the first line goes from right to left, then the next one goes from left to right. This has been attested among naturally-evolved writing systems, but it is exceedingly rare.

SOURCES NOT MENTIONED IN THE TEXT

Furniture: Old IKEA catalogues and contacts with the company.

Linguist cooking: The *Linguist List* cookbook is found at www.linguistlist.org/cookbook. Ulrika Kvist Darnell (p c) suggested the inclusion of the Alphabet Soup.

Linguists at the Café Louvre in Prague: Hajičová et al. (2002).

Music: Searches on various file-share agents, as well as canvassing of my own record collection. Sporadic mentions on the *Linguist List*. Dutch band names from Peter Bakker (p c).

Esperanto currency speso: Anon. (1994), Mee (2003). The history of the speso is also given in Jankowski (1994).

The linguistic stamps, place-names, fonts and the like were found on various web sites.

Thomas Widmann's election campaign was brought to my attention by Peter Bakker (p c).

Xomsk in Belarus: Staffan Skott "Omstridd Tjomme" in *Dagens Nyheter* 2002-09-30, p A17

Hôtel Cornavin in Geneva: Anders Eriksson (p c).

Monuments: For the most part, I have only happened to come across mentions of these monuments, and have later verified their existence with local tourist authorities or the like.

Sign Language Conference Memorial: U S Department of the Interior (1997).

The interesting aside on Gallaudet: Roz Prickett of Gallaudet University (p c).

Comanche Code Talkers monument: *Daily Oklahoman* 2002-11-20.

Various Slavic statues: Daniel Bunčić (p c).

Monuments in Lithuania: Eva Lindström (p c).

Linguistics in books and films has repeatedly been discussed on the *Linguist List* (e.g. 2.443, 2.445, 6.417, 6.418, 6.533, 6.657, 7.485 and 13.390). Yet another summary of linguistically relevant films was found in *Linguist List* 16.1639, large chunks of which were quoted word for word by a Toronto linguist from a pre-print version of this book without acknowledgement. Boo!

Language in "Atlantis": Publicity material from the Disney corporation. Atlantic quote from *USA Today* found in the issue of 2001-05-24.

THE LINGUIST'S CALENDAR

*I*n order to ensure a grand future for linguistics, it is essential that we remember our equally glorious past. Therefore—and of course also in order to provide the overworked linguist with a pretext to lift the elbow—*Limits of Language* here presents some suitable reasons to celebrate.

While it is relatively easy to list linguistics events by years, even the milestones of the discipline's history are rarely given with exact dates. Easiest to find (and the least interesting if you ask me) are, not unexpectedly, the birth and death dates of various people. The calendar started out with a search on the multitude of web-based "this day in history" pages, but draws on hundreds of publications that you wouldn't want to see listed here. Some of the more important sources are:

- Some personal data on linguists from Sebeok (1966).
- Most of the entries on linguistic legislation are from Leclerc (2006).
- Some dates regarding scripts are from Daniels & Bright (1996).
- Various dates from the life of linguists were taken from obituaries and biographies, and in some cases (for those still active) from CVs on their respective home pages.
- The archives of Linguist List produced some further dates.
- A large number of dates with reference to psycholinguistics were found in Street (1994).
- Several entries here are derived from entries elsewhere in the book, where more detailed source indications are given.
- Dates relating to Esperanto and its creator, Ludwig Zamenhof, were taken from Lapenna (1960).
- Lots of contemporary events are culled from media coverage.
- The material on suggested epicene pronouns in English was compiled by Dennis Baron, and cited here from the Linguist List 3.282.
- Excerpts from early 20th century Americanists' correspondence taken from Campbell (1997:72-3).
- A number of dates relating to early machine translation attempts are from Hutchins (1997).
- Dates referring to the Prague Linguistics Circle are from Hajičová et al. (2002).

Finally, this table has benefited from input from Bill Morris, Keira Ballantyne, Mai Kuha, M J Hardman, James Emmett, Ashley Williams and, in particular, Mike MacMahon, Jonas Söderström, and Daniel Bunčić.

JANUARY

1 **1814:** *The first Welsh language newspaper, the Seren Gomer, begins publication.*

1824: *The Camp Street Theatre becomes the first to offer plays in English in New Orleans.*

1997: *A new South African constitution comes into force, making South Africa the first country in the world with eleven official languages.*

2 **1935:** *The trial begins in New Jersey of Bruno Hauptmann, accused of kidnapping and murdering the 19-month-old son of Charles Lindbergh, the US aviator. Found guilty, he was executed in April of the following year. The case against Hauptmann included (much questioned) linguistic evidence.*

3 **1938:** *BBC begins broadcasting in foreign languages for the first time. The emissions are in Arabic, and directed towards the Middle East.*

1960: *Italian presidential decree no. 103 permits the official use of French, German and Slovenian in parts of Italy.*

4 **1785:** *Jakob Grimm, one of the Grimm brothers famous for their fairy tales, but also a linguist, is born in Hanau (Germany).*

1813: *Louis-Lucien Bonaparte, amateur linguist and prince of France is born.*

1894: *In a letter to Antoine Meillet, Saussure underscores the importance of politics and external history in historical linguistics.*

2002: *At its San Francisco meeting, the American Dialect Society votes daisy cutter (=large bomb that explodes a metre or so above the ground) as the euphemism of the year.*

5 **1945:** *At the opening session of the 19th Annual YIVO Conference in New York, Max Weinreich presents the paper which, when published, contains the first known use in print of the classic aphorism A shprakh iz a diyalekt mit an armey un a flot—i.e. a language is a dialect with an army and a navy.*

1996: *A monument to Ivar Aasen, the creator of Nynorsk, is unveiled near the central railway station in Oslo.*

2001: *Four people are charged with public order offences after a rally in Cardiff by the Cymdeithas yr Iaith Gymraeg, the Welsh Language Society.*

6 **1865:** *Birth of Russian linguist Nikolai Yakovlevich Marr.*

7 **1858:** *Eliezer Yitzhak Perelman, better known as Ben-Yehuda and the reviver of Hebrew, is born in the Lithuanian village of Luzhky.*

1927: *Never before has spoken language crossed such a vast distance—the first transatlantic phone call is made between New York and London.*

1954: *At the IBM headquarters in New York, state-of-the art machine translation is demonstrated, as a computer manages to achieve a somewhat crude translation of a number of Russian sentences into English.*

8 **1800:** *The language deprived "wild child" Victor, found in southern France, is transferred to a M Vidal in St-Sernin, where he stays for less than a month.*

9 **1905:** *Count Zech, governor of Togo, forbids education in any non-native language other than German.*

10 **1846:** *August "Wave Theory" Schleicher defends his PhD thesis in Bonn.*

1950: *American sinologist Erwin Reifler produces a 55-page study on machine translation, in which he for the first time formulates the concepts of pre- and post-editing.*

1963: *In Oregon, a Mr Wolverton Orton dies, taking the Takelma languages with him into the grave. A remarkable aspect of his language was the grammaticalization of the word for 'vagina' into a preposition.*

11 **1951:** *Law no. 51-46, better known as the loi Deixonne is passed in France. Concerning the teaching of minority languages, its aim is first and foremost to promote French, though it also speaks of protecting regional languages.*

12 **1912:** *Birthday of American linguist Mary Haas.*

2000: *The First International Conference on Linguistics in Southern Africa begins at the University of Cape Town.*

13 **1795:** *In the USA, a parliamentary vote gives rise to the urban legend that German was about to become the country's official language.*

1859: *Birth of Paul Passy, French linguist and phonetician, and—not least—the founder of the International Phonetic Association.*

1877: *A young Swiss linguist named Ferdinand de Saussure gives his first talk to the prestigious Société de linguistique de Paris.*

1900: *Emperor Franz Joseph decrees that German be the language of the Austro-Hungarian imperial army.*

1926: *Roman Jakobson makes his first presentation at the Prague Linguistics Circle on the subject of "sound laws and the teleological criterion".*

1943: *Spanish Vasconist Koldo (Luís) Mitxelena is released on probation from his political imprisonment.*

14 **1912:** *Nikolai Yakovlevich Marr becomes extraordinary academy member of the Russian Academy of Sciences.*

1987: *In Seoul, 21 year old Linguistics student Park Chong-Choi is suffocated during police interrogation for alleged pro-communist activities. Understandably, this leads to the country's biggest demonstrations for six years, involving hundreds of new police arrests.*

2000: *Death of Alvin Liberman.*

2001: *9th Inuktitut Language Week celebrated throughout Nunavut Jan. 14-20.*

15 **1961:** *Knut Bergsland and Hans Vogt submit their classic article "On the validity of glottochronology" to Current Anthropology.*

1999: *Portuguese president Jorge Sampaiq promulgates a law stipulating that Mirandese (which one might argue is a dialect of Spanish) be the official language in the region of north-eastern Portugal where it is spoken.*

16 **1492:** *The first grammar of Spanish is presented to Queen Isabella.*

1907: *Saussure begins his Course in General Linguistics at Geneva University.*

1952: *New Dutch bible translation is completed.*

1991: *The Algerian government outlaws the use of French in official contexts.*

1995: *New Hawaiian constitution declares that both English and Hawaiian be regarded as official, with English, of course, being slightly more so...*

17 **1837:** *Birth of François Lenormant, the first (at least in quite some time) to understand the Akkadian inscriptions from Mesopotamia.*

1916: *Charles Hockett is born.*

18 **1779:** *Birth of Peter Mark Roget, the author of Roget's Thesaurus.*

1965: *Birth of Lucy, the chimp taught American Sign Language by Roger Fouts.*

1968: *In a letter to Noam Chomsky, Jim McCawley assures the addressee that "There is no truth to the nasty rumor going around that the CIA is subsidizing my research in hopes of thereby diverting your energies from [protesting against] the [Vietnam] war".*

2000: *The commission on "Japan's Goals in the 21st century", a consultative body for the prime minister suggests that English be given official status in Japan. Not unexpectedly, the proposal turns out to be highly controversial.*

19 **1939:** *The first session of what became known as "the Monster Study" is held by Mary Tudor of the University of Iowa. The experiment aims at making orphan children stutter in order to test a theory that stuttering is caused by people in the environment.*

1999: *At its 656th meeting, the European Union Committee of Ministers decides to officially proclaim 2001 the "European year of languages".*

2000: *American linguist Victoria Fromkin draws her last breath.*

20 **1999:** *The German state of Saxony confirms the right to use Sorbian, in public as well as in private.*

21 **1969:** *The IASS-AIS (International Association for Semiotic Studies—Association Internationale de Sémiotique) is officially established in Paris.*

1998: *Equatorial Guinea adopts French as its second official language.*

22 **1909:** *Morris Swadesh is born in Holyoke.*

2000: *Turkey signs the European Minority Language Convention.*

23 **1948:** *Swedish gets a new word as Prof. Ture Johannisson proposes in Svenska Dagbladet that the shorter 'plast' be used instead of the English loan 'plastic'.*

1998: *The German government recognizes four official minority languages: Danish, Frisian, Sorbian, and Romani.*

1998: *After having been presented with strong linguistic evidence, Ted Kaczynski confesses to being the infamous Unabomber terrorist.*

24 **1984:** *New Luxembourg language law recognizes three languages: Luxembourgeois, French, and German.*

25 **1921:** *Karel Čapek's play RUR (Rossum's Universal Robots) premieres in Prague, and includes the first use of the word robot.*

1939: *Birth of controversial Australianist Bob Dixon (in Gloucester, England).*

1967: *From this day, Swedish laws no longer contain plural forms of verbs, long since absent from spoken language.*

26 **1850:** *First German-language daily newspaper in the USA begins publication.*

1884: *Birthday of Edward Sapir.*

1965: *Rioting erupts in India after Hindi having been declared nation's official language.*

2005: *In a refugee camp in southern Sweden, 20 Liberians riot on realizing that they have come to a country where English is not spoken natively. "We can't learn Swedish", they say, and demand being taken to the USA.*

27 **1794:** *Bertrand Barère presents a report on languages to the Revolutionary Convention in Paris, in which he argues in favor of a French-only policy: "The first two National Assemblies have already spent far too much on translations of laws into the various tongues of France. As if it were up to us to maintain the barbarous jargons and crude dialects that cannot but serve the cause of fanatics and counter-revolutionary elements!".*

1970: *Founding of the Sociedad Española de Lingüística.*

28 **1951:** *Michael Ventris produces the first in a series of Work Notes, in which he describes his progress on the decipherment of Linear B.*

1993: *Puerto Rico accords official status to both English and Spanish.*

29 **1635:** *Cardinal Richelieu founds the Académie Française to safeguard the alleged purity of the French language.*

1930: *Death of Ascensión Solorsano de Cervantes (aged 74), the last speaker of Mutsun, a variety of Costanoan once spoken just south of San Francisco.*

1999: *Portugal passes a law recognizing the linguistic rights of its Mirandese-speaking community.*

2003: *After being threatened by a boycott, Microsoft Corporation agrees to publish an edition of the Office software in Nynorsk, the other standardized variety of Norwegian.*

30 **1940:** *Benjamin Lee Whorf submits his article "Science and linguistics" to Technological Review.*

31 **1932:** *The final step in Turkey's transition from Arabic to Latin writing is taken.*

FEBRUARY

1 **1991:** *A new Koasati Grammar by Geoffrey Kimball is published by University of Nebraska Press.*

2 **1786:** *William Jones delivers his famous Third Anniversary Discourse as president of the Asiatick Society of Bengal. It is here that he makes public his ideas about Latin, Greek, Gothic, and other European languages being genetically related to Sanskrit and Persian.*

1887: *The USA prohibits the use of Native American languages in schools .*

2001: *Sotiris Bletsas is given a 15-month suspended jail sentence by a court in Athens after having distributed a leaflet claiming that there exist linguistic minorities in Greece.*

3 **1920:** *Birth of George Miller.*

2001: *Student Benjamin Varner is found dead at Gallaudet University in Washington, The arrested murderer Joseph Mesa blames his action on voices in his head. Being deaf, however, these were not literally speaking voices, but glove-clad hands urging Mesa to kill—in American Sign.*

4 **1800:** *Victor the feral child is transferred from St-Sernin to the deaf school in neighboring Rodez.*

1809: *Birth of Arthur J Johnes, who 35 years later wrote Philological Proofs of the Original Unity and Recent Origin of the Human Race, Derived from a Comparison of the Languages of Asia, Europe, Africa, and America; being an inquiry how far the differences in the languages of the globe are referrible to causes now in operation.*

1939: *Death of Edward Sapir.*

5 **1835:** *The French music journal Le Pianiste is delighted about Jean-François Sudre's creation of Solrésol, an international auxiliary language based on music. In the journal, Sudre is hailed as the Gutenberg of his days.*

1967: *Quang Phuc Dong of the "South Hanoi Institute of Technology" (S H I T), alias Jim McCawley, submits the final version of 'English Sentences Without Overt Grammatical Subjects' to a Festschrift devoted to—Jim McCawley. The paper is a study of the syntax of the word 'fuck', and includes some memorable example sentences.*

2003: *The Russian Duma passes a law which outlaws the use of foreign words "where suitable Russian ones exist".*

6 **1927:** *Estonian national broadcasting corporation Eesti Raadio transmits its first program in Esperanto.*

1928: *Nikolai Trubetzkoy presents his first paper at the Prague Linguistics Circle. It is entitled "Alphabet und Lautsystem".*

1990: *Welshman Steve Briers, the world's fastest backwards talker, accomplishes a backward recital of the lyrics of the Queen album "A Night At The Opera" in 9 minutes and 58,44 seconds.*

7 **1639:** *Work on the French Academy's Dictionnaire de la Langue Françoyse begins.*

1987: *Riots erupt in South Korea after the death in of Park Chong-Choi, who was suffocated during police interrogation. Park studied linguistics at the Seoul National University.*

2002: *Jerrold Katz dies from bladder cancer in New York at the age of 69.*

2006: *Publication of the first dictionary of Angolan Sign.*

8 **1864:** *Beginning this day, lectures are regularly given at the Société de Linguistique de Paris.*

1973: *In an article entitled "Deep language" in the New York Review of Books, George Lakoff attacks Noam Chomsky.*

2002: *A new PhD program in linguistics, available from the autumn of this year, is approved by the Gallaudet University Board of Trustees. This uni-versity is unique in having a sign language as its main medium of teaching.*

9 **2000:** *The Taiwanese minister of education declares that the study of minority languages shall be obligatory in Taiwanese schools from the following year.*

10 **1965:** *After examining linguistic evidence, British authorities conclude that Timothy Evans' murder confession was probably a fake, and a year later, pardoned him. This was 15 years too late; Evans was hanged in 1950.*

11 **1943:** *The Swedish School Teachers' Written Language Committee suggests a spelling reform, which is met by stiff public opposition.*

1992: *A 12-day sociolinguistic survey is begun in a number of villages in central Chad by SIL and the Institut Supérieur des Sciences et de l'Education.*

12 **1948:** *Andrew Booth sends his first report on his work on machine translation to the Rockefeller Foundation from which he receives his funding.*

1998: *Alija Izetbegovic appeals to Bosnia and Herzegovina's Constitutional Court of to abolish the articles declaring only Bosnian and Croatian official in the Federation and only Serbian in the Republika Srpska.*

13 **1834:** *As the first issue of Ka Lama Hawaii leaves the printers, Hawaiian joins the group of languages in which newspapers are published.*

14 **842:** *Charles the Bald and Louis the German swear the Oaths of Strasbourg, thereby producing what are usually considered to be the first texts in these two languages.*

1941: *Benjamin Lee Whorf submits his article "Languages and logic" to Technological Review.*

15 **1759:** *The German classical philologist Friedrich August Wolf is born.*

1878: *In a paper presented to the Philological Society in London, Rev W E Cousins decisively demonstrates the Austronesian affinities of Malagasy.*

16 **1795:** *American congress decides to publish federal statutes in English only, rather than, as had been proposed, in both English and German. It is this vote which is believed to have given rise to the legend of German nearly becoming the official language of the United States.*

1952: *Sheikh Mujib starts a hunger strike in support of the demand of Bengali being made the state language of East Pakistan.*

17 **440:** *Death of Saint Mesrop Mashtots, the monk who is accredited with having invented the Armenian script and helped establish Armenia's golden age of Christian literature.*

2004: *Opening of the Punjab Mother Language Festival 2004 in Delapur, a "festival to celebrate linguistic diversity and rich literary and cultural heritage of the Punjab".*

18 **2006:** *Anticipation rises in the media, as English is about to receive its one millionth word. At least, that is, if you're prepared to trust the US-based Global Language Monitor. According to their count, English contains, as of this day, 986 120 words ("plus or minus a handful"). In contrast, the com-pany reports that there are "fewer than 100 000 words" in French.*

19 **1821:** *Birth of August Schleicher, the man behind the Stammbaumtheorie.*

1888: *Otto Jespersen receives a letter from Vilhelm Thomsen, who suggests that Jespersen should concentrate on English language and literature.*

2001: *In New Delhi, the internet provider Rediff announces that it is now able to handle no less than eleven Indian languages.*

20 **2001:** *The Slovak government signs the European Charter for Regional and Minority Languages.*

2006: *The University of Venda in South Africa's Limpopo province opens a Tshivenda Language Research and Development Center.*

21 *In November 1999, this day was declared by the United Nations as the official "International Mother Language Day" to be celebrated world-wide. The day is chosen in honour of the "Language martyrs" of Bangladesh, and has been celebrated locally since 1953, the first anniversary of their death.*

1828: *Cherokee Phoenix, the first newspaper printed in an American Indian language, begins publishing.*

22 **1835:** *Jean-François Sudre again demonstrates his artificial language Solrésol publicly. This time, he silently communicates with blindfolded students in order to demonstrate the language's usefulness for the deaf-blind.*

1913: *Death of Ferdinand de Saussure.*

1999: *The Bulgarian government recognizes Macedonian as a language in its own right, rather than a mere dialect of Bulgarian.*

23 **1945:** *Ken and Evelyn Pike have a second daughter.*

1948: *At the Pakistan Constituent Assembly in Karachi, Dhirendranath Datta argues for the use of Bengali in the assembly alongside English and Urdu. This arouses exceptionally strong feelings among the delegates.*

24 **1835:** *The first Indian language monthly of the United States, the Siwinowe Kesibwi (Shawnee Sun), begins publication.*

1950: *Birth of syntactician and computational linguist G J M Gazdar.*

1964: *Noam Chomsky begins a series of six weekly lectures at the Christian Gauss Seminars in Criticism at Princeton.*

2002: *The Israeli postal authorities issue a stamp honouring the Ladino, i.e. the Judeo-Spanish language.*

25 **1977:** *Ebo Hawkson, Ghana's deputy chairman of the National Commission on Culture, makes a speech in which he urges Africans to make ex-colonial languages their own by not always following European norms.*

1988: *The Canadian Supreme Court concludes that all provincial laws of Saskatchewan are void, having been written in English only, rather than in English and French. A hastily adopted additional bill is necessary in order to restore the validity of Saskatchewan legislation.*

2000: *At the Expolangues exhibition in Paris, David Dalby launches his Linguasphere Register—an Ethnologue-like comprehensive survey of the world's languages.*

26 **1994:** *A new alphabet for the writing of Karakalpak is adopted.*

1998: *The Constitutional Court of the Republika Srpska in Bosnia-Herzegovina abolishes the 25 June 1996 law prescribing the Ekavian variety of Serbo-Croatian (the one used in Serbia) in schools, administration and the media. The Jekavian dialect used by most Bosnian Serbs may now again be used.*

27 **1897:** *Alfabetarja e gjuhës shqipe, the first school book in Albanian, is published in Istanbul.*

1953: *A proposal to simplify English spelling passes its first test. by 65 votes to 53, in the British House of Commons. Remarkably, the bill receives support from government and opposition parties. One Conservative supporter is James Pitman, grandson of Isaac Pitman of Pitman Shorthand fame.*

1969: *It is decided to establish a Division of Linguistics and Language Training at York University in Toronto.*

1992: *American linguist and politician Samuel Ichiye Hayakawa dies.*

28 **1759:** *Pope Clement XIII authorizes Bible translation into various languages.*

2003: *The Philippine postal services release a series of stamps commemorating the Summer Institute of Linguistics.*

29 **1956:** *The National Assembly of Pakistan decides that the state languages of Pakistan shall be Urdu and Bengali.*

MARCH

1 **1983:** *Russ Rymer publishes a book on "Genie", the confined child of California.*

1987: *The Nordic Language Convention comes into force. It allows citizens of these countries to use their respective mother tongues (provided it is Swedish, Danish, Finnish, Icelandic or one of the two standardized varieties of Norwegian) in contacts with authorities in the neighboring countries.*

1995: Randy Harris publishes *The Linguistics Wars* on the history of linguistic disagreement in the past couple of decades.

2 *1989:* The Navajo Code Talker Monument is erected in Phoenix, Arizona.

2003: The first International Symposium on Taiwanese Sign Linguistics is held.

3 *1894:* The USA's first Greek-language publication, the *New York Atlantis*, begins.

1930: Nikolai Y Marr becomes vice president of the Soviet Academy of Sciences

1997: The first-ever International Colloquium on Gur Languages is held at the University of Ouagadougou, Burkina Faso.

4 *1832:* Death of Jean-François Champollion, who played a major role in the deciphering of Egyptian hieroglyphics.

1947: On this day Warren Weaver, director of the Natural Sciences Division of the Rockefeller Foundation, writes to the cyberneticist Norbert Wiener that "I have wondered if it were unthinkable to design a computer which would translate. Even if it would translate only scientific material (where the semantic difficulties are very notably less), and even if it did produce an inelegant (but intelligible) result, it would seem to me worth while".

1968: Mauritania declares Arabic as co-official alongside French.

5 *1990:* Withdrawal in Bulgaria of laws aimed at the linguistic discrimination of the Turkish-speaking minority.

1996: Today's New Zealand census is the first ever to include a question on language. It turns out that 95% of the population are Anglophones, and that they constitute one of the least multilingual populations in the world.

2001: The state of New York adopts English as its official language.

2006: The final in this year's African Championship in French Orthography (La Dictée d'Afrique) takes place in Benin. Among the twelve teams is one from officially Anglophone Nigeria.

6 *1947:* Andrew Booth meets Warren Weaver again, and the Rockefeller Foundation provisionally agrees to fund machine translation research.

1995: The Estonian parliament agrees to designate all languages other than Estonian as "foreign languages". A third of all Estonian residents are insolent enough to have acquired one of these as their mother tongue.

7 *1714:* The peace treaty of Rastatt between French King Louis XIV and Holy Roman Emperor Charles VI is signed in French. This is allegedly the first time that a language other than Latin is used for the text of an international treaty. For another two centuries, French continues to be the foremost language of international diplomacy.

1909: Nikolai Y Marr becomes adjunct of the Historical-Philological Division of the Russian Academy of Sciences.

8 *1827:* Birth (in Berlin) of Wilhelm Bleek, the "father of Bantu philology".

1850: August Schleicher becomes Professor of Classical Philology and Literature in Prague.

1866: The Société de Linguistique de Paris is officially founded.

2001: Southampton's mayor marks the European Year of Languages by releas-ing 500 helium balloons outside the city's West Quay shopping center.

9 *1950:* London van driver Timothy Evans is hanged for the murder of his wife and child. Linguistic evidence later suggests that he was in fact innocent.

1956: Hellenist and comparative linguist Paul Kretschmer dies in Vienna.

2000: Hundreds of nationalist protesters in the Ukrainian city of Lviv (Lvov) demand the closure of all Russian-language publications. Others in Kyïv (Kiev) urged that Russian be banned from television as well.

10 *1876:* First electronic transmission of human speech as Alexander Graham Bell on the telephone utters "Come here, Watson, I want you" to his assistant.

1897: Antoine Meillet gets his PhD.

2000: At the age of 26, Nim Chimpsky dies of a heart attack in Tyler, Texas.

11 *1914:* George Bernard Shaw's Pygmalion, with a phonetician as one of the main characters is performed for the first time in the author's home country. Its original premiere took place in Vienna.

1986: The French language law of 1975 is supplanted by a new decree, intended to lead to the "enrichissement de la langue française".

2000: *Edgar Polomé, who—among other things— established the first linguistics department in Belgian Congo, dies in Houston, Texas.*

12 **1881:** *Turkish language reformer Kemal Atatürk is born. He replaced the Arabic script with the Latin alphabet.*

1998: *Russian-born typologist and field linguist Alexandra "Sasha" Aikhenvald becomes a naturalized Australian.*

13 **1519:** *European study of Mesoamerican Indian languages begins, as the Spanish encounter and question their fellow countryman Jerónimo de Aguilar, who, as a survivor of a shipwreck has learned Mayan.*

1845: *Birth of Polish linguist Jan Baudouin de Courtenay, forerunner of the structuralist school, and accredited (albeit wrongly) with having launched the term "phoneme".*

1938: *Kremlin makes Russian a compulsory school subject in all Soviet republics.*

14 *"Native Language Day" is a national holiday in Estonia, where linguistic rights are denied to the third of its population with the "wrong" native language.*

1857: *Birth of Rudolf Thurneysen, one of the first to apply the newly established principles of historical linguistics to Celtic languages.*

1901: *Publication of the first issue of Finnisch-Ugrische Forschungen.*

1902: *Danish newspaper Politiken coins bil for 'motor car'. While most European languages took their word for this from the beginning of Latin or French automobile, Norwegians and Swedes have since 1902 followed the Danes in using the last part of the same original word.*

15 **1849:** *Italian cardinal and polyglot Guiseppe Gaspare Mezzofanti dies.*

1939: *Just before the Nazi occupants arrive, Roman Jakobson leaves his home in Brno, Czechoslovakia, and flees to Denmark.*

1969: *MIT Press releases a paperback edition of Chomsky's Aspects.*

16 **1849:** *Birth of Karl Brugmann, neo-grammarian and comparative linguist.*

1931: *The Dutch language lovers' society Genootschap Onze Taal is formed.*

17 **2000:** *The Institut national de la langue française publishes Du Féminin, which includes recommended usage of female titles.*

18 **1909:** *Leonard Bloomfield marries Miss Alice Sayers of St Louis.*

1997: *The Netherlands officially recognizes Frisian, Yiddish, Saxon, and Limburgian as minority languages.*

19 **1884:** *Elias Lönnrot, standardizer of Finnish, dies.*

20 *The Journée de la Francophonie, celebrating the cooperation between French-speaking countries, is observed world-wide since the first meeting between Francophone heads-of-state in 1970 in Niamey (Niger).*

1978: *"Genie" is transferred back to her biological mother.*

1997: *Geoff Pullum sends a letter to the Economist with "a meaningful contiguous minimal word quintuple—7-character words, no less"—"I can't recall a blinder blander blonder blender blunder". This referred to an error in the Russian petroleum industry, which resulted in crude oil from different oilfields becoming mixed together into a single light-colored blend. Pullum adds that his letter "could have placed the Economist permanently in the linguistic book of records", although, he complains, "there isn't one". If only he knew.*

2000: *Beginning of Provincial French Pride Week in New Brunswick, Canada.*

21 **1924:** *First US foreign language course broadcast by New York's WJZ radio.*

1935: *Shah Reza Pahlavi asks the international community to use the name 'Iran' instead of 'Persia'. The new name means 'Land of the Aryans'.*

1948: *At Maidan Racecourse in Dhaka, Urdu is— despite Bengali protests—declared the one and only official language of both east and west Pakistan.*

22 **1945:** *The Arab league is founded. Today, it groups 22 Arabic-speaking states .*

23 **1948:** *Faeroese is declared the "principal language" of the Faeroe islands.*

1997: *At the initiative of the European Bureau for Lesser Used Languages "European Language Day" is celebrated for the first time. This event is not to be confused with the "European Day of Languages" of 2001, although in that particular year, the festivities are merged and held on September 26.*

24 **2001:** *Deaf people in Manchester march for the recognition of British Sign language as an official language of the country.*

25 **1916:** *Ishi, the last speaker of Yana, dies of tuberculosis in San Francisco.*

1930: *For the first time ever, the session of the Prague Linguistics circle is open to the public, who get to hear Roman Jakobson talk about "Linguistic questions in the work of Masaryk".*

2005: *Nederveld Associates, Inc. presents a plan to build a new town in South Dakota, designed specifically for sign language users.*

26 **2000:** *End of Provincial French Pride Week in New Brunswick, Canada.*

27 **1869:** *The Société de Linguistique de Paris decides to publish a newsletter.*

2001: *Eight people die in Belgium's worst railway crash for 25 years. Language difficulties are later shown to be the cause of the tragedy—a signalman had received warnings in French, but he himself spoke only Dutch.*

2004: *After a two-year illness, British-American historical linguist and Vasconist Larry Trask dies at the age of 59.*

28 *In 1954, this day marked the start of the Philippine Linggo ng Wika, or National Language Week. In 1955, the celebrations were moved to mid-August.*

1980: *Opening in Nijmegen of the Max Planck Institute for Psycholinguistics.*

29 **1955:** *A Dano-German convention on the linguistic rights of the German-speaking population in southern Denmark is signed.*

1997: Asialex *(Asian Association for Lexicography) is founded in Hong Kong.*

30 **1937:** *Otto Jespersen is widowed, as his wife Ane Marie dies.*

2000: *The Michif Working Group holds its first meeting in Saskatoon to discuss the possibilities of reviving this unique intertwined language.*

2000: *Alexandra Aikhenvald's typological survey of classifiers is published.*

2006: *The first (pre-publication) copy of Mikael Parkvall's Limits of Language is purchased by Oliver Wilke of Bad Arolsen in Germany.*

31 *Australia's "Assembly of First Nations" celebrates the "Official Aboriginal Language Day".*

1966: *The Haut Comité pour la défense et l'expansion de la langue française is created.*

1999: *Death of Yuri Knorosov, decipherer of the Maya script.*

2002: *A Swedish government-appointed commission reports on the possibilities of strengthening the position of Swedish vis-à-vis English in that country.*

APRIL

1 **1844:** *French linguist Pierre Étienne (a k a Peter Stephen) Duponceau, to whom we owe the term "polysynthetic", dies in Philadelphia.*

1886: *In Paris, a decision is taken to publish a small journal about phonetic transcription and the teaching of foreign languages. This journal is one of the forerunners of today's Journal of the International Phonetic Association.*

1887: *Leonard Bloomfield, who in his 1933 book Language set the standards of teaching in linguistics for decades to come, sees the light of day in Chicago.*

1936: *Orissa is recognized as a separate state—the first one in India to have its boundaries defined on linguistic grounds.*

1956: *Noam Chomsky completes the preface of his classic Syntactic Structures, although the book is not published until the following year.*

1993: *Ron Wardhaugh's textbook Investigating Language is published.*

1994: *Raymond Rising of the Summer Institute of Linguistics is kidnapped in Colombia by six members of the FARC guerrillas.*

2000: *The Enigma machine exhibited at the Bletchley Park Museum in south-eastern Britain is stolen. Work on cracking the German Enigma code involved plenty of linguists (and mathematicians) during the World War II, and their work contributed to the foundation of computational linguistics.*

2005: *Norwegian daily Bergens Tidende reports that the uvular realization of /r/ (which is common in the area where the paper is published) is harmful, and even capable of shortening one's life by 12 years! The amazing results derive from a study of 40 000 Frenchmen, published by Avril Premier in Journal of Linguistic Medicine. But then, this is the first of April . . .*

2 **1998:** *The constitutional court of Rwanda declares that the constitution should be in Rwanda, French, and English, and that in case of conflict, the Rwandian version should be given priority.*

3 **1952:** *British Mathematician Alan Turing, without whom computational linguistics might not be, is convicted of homosexuality.*

4 **1861:** *Paul Broca attends a talk by Ernest Aubertin at the Société d'Anthropologie which inspires him to research the localization of language in the brain.*

2001: *The Deputy Prime Minister of Singapore launches the "Speak Good English" campaign, aimed at eradicating the local variety, called "Singlish".*

5 **2001:** *Most of the pupils of a school in Tidaholm, Sweden, participate in a manifestation against foul language. After having written down the nastiest words they could think of, the pupils and their teachers set fire to them in the school yard.*

6 **1830:** *Thomas Gallaudet, who introduced of French sign language to the USA, resigns from as principal of the American School for the Deaf in Hartford.*

1921: *Death (in New York City) of Maximilian Berlitzheimer, founder of the Berlitz Language Schools.*

1990: *Canada's Northwest Territories' official language usage laws are revised.*

7 **1867:** *Danish linguist Holger Pedersen is born.*

1906: *A governmental decree is signed on modernizing Swedish spelling. Among its more notable features is <v> rather than <fv> for /v/.*

8 **1970:** *Czech Indo-Europeanist Julius Pokorny, mainly known for his voluminous etymological research, dies in Zurich.*

1982: *John Wells's four-volume Accents of English is published.*

2002: *The Algerian parliament decides to give official recognition to Tamazight, the language of its Berber minority.*

2002: *The first ever African-medium daily in South Africa is launched. Isolezwe ('the eye of the Nation') is entirely in Zulu.*

9 *Death of Michael Agricola (in 1557), the first to translate the Bible into Finnish, is celebrated as the Finnish Language Day—a public holiday. Elias Lönnrot, standardizer of this language, was also born this day in 1802.*

1955: *Ken Hale says "yes" to his Sara.*

1981: *Nature publishes a 207 000 letter description of the nucleotide links making up human mitochondrial DNA which later makes it into the Guinness Book of World Records as the longest word there is.*

10 **1982:** *New Mexico Governor Bruce King declares a Navajo Code Talkers Day. A little later , US President Reagan announces a nationwide counterpart.*

1991: *The MIT Press releases a paperback reprint of Chomsky & Halle's classic The Sound Pattern of English.*

11 **1797:** *British naval forces deported 2 248 Garifunas (or "Black Caribs") from St Vincent to Roatán island in present-day Honduras. So begins the presence in Central America of a black people speaking an Amerindian language.*

1861: *An aphasic patient named Leborgne, but better known as "Tan" (since that was pretty much the only syllable he was capable of uttering) is brought to Paul Broca. After the patient's death on April 17, Broca identifies the language center of the brain which still bears his name.*

1919: *Odense (Denmark) names a street after Rasmus Rask. He was born in Brændekilde, 15 km away but within the limits of the municipality.*

1980: *Legislation makes Norway officially bilingual in Bokmål and Nynorsk.*

12 *Feast day of St Zeno, patron saint of children with speech-learning difficulties.*

1950: *Joseph Stalin is convinced by a meeting with Armenian linguist Arnold Chikobava that Nikolai Marr's ideas on language evolution are wrong.*

1963: *Polish logician and semanticist Kazimierz Ajdukiewicz, also known as the inventor of Categorial Grammar, dies.*

1968: *The world's first international conference on pidgin and creole languages in Mona, Jamaica, closes.*

1993: *A new alphabet for the writing of Turkmen is adopted. Among the usual Latin character set, it also includes the curious symbols <$>, <£> and <¥>.*

13 **1814:** *A racehorse tastefully named Dr Syntax runs his first race. He subsequently wins the Preston Gold Cup for eight consecutive years—a record that remains unbeaten to this day.*

1897: *Otto Jespersen marries Ane Marie Døjrup.*

14 **1828:** *The first edition of Noah Webster's dictionary is published as The American Dictionary of the English Language.*

1852: *Birth (in Mühringen, Germany) of Maximilian Berlitzheimer, founder of the Berlitz Language Schools.*

1917: *Death of Ludwig Zamenhof, the creator of Esperanto.*

1925: *Birth of psycholinguist Roger Brown.*

15 **1755:** *Samuel Johnson's Dictionary of the English Language is published.*

1817: *The first American school for the deaf opens at Hartford, Connecticut. Thomas Gallaudet is its principal, and Laurent Clerc its only teacher. It is through this school that French Sign is introduced into the New World, where it eventually morphs into American Sign Language.*

1864: *The Russian administration in Lithuania plans to introduce the Cyrillic alphabet. In a letter to the governor-general of Vilnius, statesman Nikolai Miliutin writes that "Our alphabet will finish what our sword has begun".*

1958: *The European Community decides that all the official languages of the member states shall also be official languages of the Community.*

1966: *As one of the last institutions to surrender, the Swedish supreme court opts to no longer use plural forms of verbs, a feature which has been absent from spoken Swedish for centuries.*

16 **1890:** *Russian structuralist Nikolai Sergeyevich Trubetzkoy, one of the founders of the Prague school is born in Moscow.*

17 **1998:** *The First European NLP Forum Conference begins in Copenhagen.*

2001: *The idea of writing this very book is born.*

18 **1861:** *Paul Broca performs an autopsy on an aphasic who had died the previous day. He thus "discovers" the area in the brain in which much language processing is done, and which is now named after him.*

1949: *Leonard Bloomfield, who in his 1933 book "Language" set the standards of teaching in linguistics for decades to come, dies in New Haven.*

2002: *China announces that it plans to spend about 1m dollars on preserving the Nüshu script, unique to the Hunan province and used only by women.*

19 **1928:** *The last fascicle of the Oxford English Dictionary is completed. The entire work is not published until 1933.*

20 **1879:** *Jules Gilliéron submits his thesis on the dialect of Vionnez.*

2000: *Michael, partner of Koko, and one of the few gorillas to have learned American Sign Language, passes away at the age of 27.*

21 **1899:** *Otto Jespersen is elected to the Royal Danish Academy of Sciences.*

22 **1913:** *Birth of phonetician and Romanist Bertil Malmberg.*

1991: *Esperantists gather in the village of Kelmis in Western Belgium to honour the state of Amikejo. In the early 20th century, the former Neutral Territory of Moresnet, in which Kelmis is located, turned into the Free State of Amikejo—the only known state with Esperanto as its official language.*

23 **1801:** *Jean-Marc Itard publishes his book on Victor, the feral child of southern France. Disappointingly, Victor never learned to speak.*

1925: *British neo-Firthian linguist Michael A K Halliday is born in Leeds.*

24 **1869:** *A monsieur A Dufriche motions that the infamous second article of the constitution of the Société de Linguistique de Paris be revoked. The second article was the one which banned discussion on the origins of human language, as well as proposals for a new international auxiliary language. Dufriche's motion fails, and the article therefore remains in vigour.*

1897: *Benjamin Lee Whorf, who formulated the strong version of the notorious Sapir-Whorf hypothesis, is born in Massachusetts.*

25 **1925:** *Child language acquisitionist Roger Brown is born in Detroit.*

26 **1968:** *A government decree requires that all Algerian officials master Arabic.*

27 **1971:** *British police remove Welsh demonstrators from the entrance of a courtroom after they disrupt proceedings inside. Put on trial are eight members of the Welsh Language Society, accused of "conspiring to damage, remove or destroy" English-language road signs in Wales.*

1996: *The North American language Quinault becomes extinct with the death of its last speaker, Oliver Mason.*

1998: *In the first inter-species internet chat ever, Koko the gorilla answers questions from the curious public. Her performance disappoints many.*

28 **1789:** *Twelve of the crew members of HMS Bounty stage a mutiny that is to lead to the creation of a new language. They settle on the uninhabited Pacific island of Pitcairn, where their descendants still speak Pitcairnese.*

1908: *Foundation of the UEA, the Universal Esperanto Academy.*

29 **2006:** *The original edition of Mikael Parkvall's Limits of Language is published this day.*

30 **1943:** *Otto Jespersen, Danish linguist and Anglicist, and inventor of the artificial language Novial, passes away.*

1947: *In a reply to Warren Weaver's letter of March 4, Norbert Wiener replies that he is sceptical about the possibilities of machine translation.*

MAY

1 **1875:** *Karl Verner first presents the theory later known as Verner's law in a letter to Vilhelm Thomsen. It is published only the following year, as Eine Ausnahme der ersten Lautverschiebung.*

1893: *At the age of 33, Otto Jespersen becomes chair of English at the University of Copenhagen.*

1997: *David Crystal's impressive Cambridge Encyclopedia of Language is published by the Cambridge University Press.*

2 **1866:** *Birth of German Hellenist and comparative linguist Paul Kretschmer.*

3 **1806:** *Jean-Marc Itard delivers his second report on Victor the Wild Child.*

4 **1904:** *The Russian administration in Lithuania decides to allow the Lithuanian alphabet (and in practice, the Lithuanian language itself) in print.*

1919: *The so-called 'May-fourth movement' is founded among students in Beijing. Its main goal is to protest against Japanese imperialism, but the movement also plays a role in linguistic history in working for a writing reform. As a result Bái-huà ('colloquial language') is recognized as the standard written form of Chinese in 1992.*

1929: *Birth of Audrey Hepburn, who played the role of Eliza in the film My fair lady, one of the all too few films featuring a linguist hero.*

1943: *Otto Jespersen is buried at the Lundehave cemetery.*

1968: *American linguist Frederick Newmeyer presents his first public talk, "Durative keep in English" at the University of Illinois.*

5 **1539:** *French king Francis I signs the Ordonnance de Villers-Cotterêts, which makes French, rather than Latin, the official language of the kingdom.*

1998: *Ted Kaczynski is sentenced to four life terms for the terrorist attacks hitherto ascribed to the so-called Unabomber. Linguistic evidence played a major role in the Kaczynski case.*

6 **1911:** *During his third linguistics course at the University of Geneva, Ferdinand de Saussure runs short of time. In a letter to M L Gautier, Saussure complains that he has too many issues to discuss for the limited lecture time allotted to him. He also says that he basically has material for a textbook, only he cannot recall where the manuscript is. His course in general linguistics was eventually published posthumously, and was based on his students' lecture notes*

7 **2001:** *Joseph Greenberg, professor emeritus at Stanford, dies at the age of 85, of pancreatic cancer*

8 **1876:** *Ethnic and linguistic cleansing of Tasmania is completed, as Truganini, the last speaker of a Tasmanian language (also the last full-blooded Tasmanian) goes to meet her maker.*

1913: *In a letter to Edward Sapir, Alfred Kroeber reports that he believes to have found that Klamath-Modoc is related to one of the language families in California.*

1924: *Afrikaans becomes official in South Africa.*

2000: *Poland adopts the "Law concerning the Polish language", which, among other things, aims to "combat vulgar language use".*

9 **1753:** *In a letter to British member of parliament Peter Collinson, Benjamin Franklin expresses his worries about the future United States becoming German-speaking. Not only do the German immigrants not speak English, but they are also "generally the most ignorant Stupid Sort of their own Nation".*

1938: *Dictating for his wife from his sick bed, Nikolai Sergeyevich Trubetzkoy composes his last letter to Roman Jakobson.*

1950: *A S Chikobav criticizes "Marrism" in the Pravda. This is the beginning of a debate on the so-called Japhetic language family, a debate which rages until June 20th, when Stalin himself sides with the critics.*

1973: *Publication of Roger Brown's classic "The First Language: The Early Stages", which studies the language acquisition of Adam, Eve, and Sarah.*

10 **1839:** *For the first time, the Bible becomes available in Hawaiian.*

1917: *Birthday of phonetician Alvin Liberman.*

1986: *The Australian language Mangala becomes extinct as its last native speaker, Jack Butler, dies at the age of 85.*

11 **2001:** *Armenia signs the European minority language convention.*

12 *1891: Otto Jespersen defends his PhD thesis Studier over engelske kasus.*

1906: "Great name changing day"—24 800 Finns switch from Swedish to Finnish-sounding surnames.

1948: Andrew Booth's computer intended for machine translation experiments becomes operational.

2005: For the very first time, a British member of parliament swears allegiance to the Queen in Cornish. While Welsh and Scots Gaelic had been used in this context before, Andrew George of St Ives became the first to swear an oath ending in Ytho Dew re'm gweressa rather than So help me God.

13 *1876: Ferdinand de Saussure joins the Société de Linguistique de Paris.*

1942: Franz Boas gives his last public lecture.

1998: Founding of the linguistics association of Taiwan.

2000: First international conference on Kurdish linguistics kicks off at the University of Kiel, Germany.

14 *Sign Language Day in Sweden, commemorating the official recognition of Swedish Sign by the parliament in 1981.*

1978: The replacement of English he and she with an epicene third person pronoun is much discussed among the pages of the New York Times. Most noteworthy of today's contributions is that from Lawrence Ross of Huntington, New York, who offers sap (from homo sapiens).

15 *1848: Carl Wernicke—who later identifies "Wernicke's area", an important language center of the brain—is born.*

16 *1998: The first American "Linguistic Olympics" takes place in Eugene, Oregon. The competition had been held in Russia since 1965.*

17 *1996: Death of American linguist Mary Haas.*

18 *1842: At 1 p.m. in the rooms of the Statistical Society, 4 St Martin's Place, London, the Philological Society is founded 'for the investigation of the Structure, the Affinities, and the History of Languages; and the Philological Illustration of the Classical Writers of Greece and Rome'.*

2001: The "Plain language group"; appointed by the Swedish government, arranges a conference on the theme "Plain Language Opens Sweden".

19 *1859: Paul "Broca's area" Broca holds his first meeting together with the Société d'Anthropologie which he has just founded.*

1965: Publication of Chomsky's Aspects of the Theory of Syntax.

20 *Eliza Doolittle Day, encourages "proper use" of language.*

1980: Francophone Québec votes in favor of remaining a Canadian province.

1999: Opening of the first international conference on language teacher education at the University of Minnesota.

21 *1994: Solemn inauguration of the monument to the Estonian language in Kadrina, Estonia.*

2002: Joseph Mesa is convicted for the murder of two of his classmates. He is sentenced despite his plea of insanity, according to which the murders were inspired by voices in his head. Since Mesa is deaf, however, these were not literally speaking voices, but glove-clad hands urging him to kill—in American Sign.

22 *1992: Chomsky's mentor Zellig Harris dies.*

23 *1947: Typologist Bernard Comrie is born in Sunderland, Britain.*

1999: Closing of the first international conference on language teacher education at the University of Minnesota.

2002: The Australian language Gagadu vanishes as the only remaining speaker Big Bill Neidjie draws his last breath.

24 *The Day of Slavic Writing is a national holiday in Bulgaria, to commemorate the invention of St Cyril and St Method in the 9th century.*

1873: In a talk before the Société de Linguistique de Paris, A Dufriche-Desgenettes makes the first documented use of the word phonème.

1917: A Russian orthography reform is officially accepted by a Special Meeting of the Academy of Sciences in St. Petersburg.

1936: At the Shantok Burial Ground in Uncasville, Connecticut, a monument is erected to Fidelia Fielding (1827–1908), the last speaker of Pequot-Mohegan.

25 *1917: The town of Minsk in Belarus gives official recognition to Yiddish. The special status of Yiddish in the republic is later manifested in the coat-of-arms, which bears the inscription "Workers of the world, unite" in Russian, Belarusan, Polish, and Yiddish.*

1925: Otto Jespersen gives his last lecture at the University of Copenhagen.

1948: *Andrew Booth's computer intended for machine translation experiments is demonstrated to representatives of the Rockefeller foundation, which finances the project.*

26 **1828:** *The feral child Kaspar Hauser is discovered in Nuremberg, Germany.*

1998: *In a manifestation called the "National Sorry Day", Australia offers an apology to the Aboriginal population for the policy (lasting into the early 1970's) of removing children from Aboriginal families to Anglophone households. Among numerous other disastrous outcomes, this policy was responsible for the extinction of many Aboriginal languages.*

27 **1879:** *Birth of Karl Bühler, the German psychologist to present his "Organon" model of language in 1934.*

28 **1863:** *At Antoine d'Abbadie's place, messieurs de Chiaruluoj, d'Abbadie, Chodzko and Sentebel agree to found a linguistic society. This later develops into the famous Société de Linguistique de Paris.*

1915: *Birth of Joseph Greenberg in Brooklyn, New York.*

1945: *One of the last strongholds of number inflection in the Swedish verbal system falls, as the major Swedish news agency Tidningarnas Telegrambyrå begins using singular forms even with plural subjects.*

29 **1996:** *In a speech in Quimper, Brittany, French president Jacques Chirac admits that France might sign the European charter on minority languages.*

30 **1965:** *Death of Danish linguist Louis Hjelmslev.*

31 **2001:** *A new Bolivian penal law authorizes the use of an interpreter in cases where the defendant does not speak Spanish.*

JUNE

1 **1940:** *Evelyn Pike gives birth to a daughter, the first child of linguist Ken Pike.*

1952: *Michael Ventris produces the last of his Work Notes, where he first reveals his find that Linear B is a written form of Greek.*

1981: *The first English language daily newspaper in the People's Republic of China, the China Daily, begins publication.*

1987: *Stanford University Press publishes Joseph Greenberg's controversial Language in the Americas.*

1991: *Geoffrey Pullum's entertaining and oft-cited The Great Eskimo Vocabulary Hoax and Other Irreverent Essays on the Study of Language is published by the University of Chicago Press.*

1993: *Within the Lojban movement, a language reform known as The Great Rafsi Reallocation goes into effect.*

1999: *The Nepalese Supreme Court rules the use of minority languages in the country's administration "non-constitutional and illegal".*

2002: *For the first time since its inception in 1996, the Terralingua organization, promoter of linguistic and biological diversity, gets an office, located in Washington.*

2 **1915:** *Nikolai Sergeyevich Trubetzkoy and his wife Vera have their first child, a daughter named Elena.*

1989: *The French government issues a decree on the creation of the Conseil supérieur de la langue française.*

3 **1756:** *Death of the first known female Anglicist, Elizabeth Elstob, author of Rudiments of Grammar for the English-Saxon Tongue.*

1760: *Birth of French linguist Pierre Étienne (a k a Peter Stephen) Duponceau, to whom we owe the term "polysynthetic".*

4 **1992:** *A pregnant British woman named Paula Gilfoyle is found hanged in the garage of her home. On the basis of linguistic evidence, her husband is found guilty of having dictated the suicide note (undoubtedly in her own handwriting) to her. The case remains deeply controversial, though.*

5 **1956:** *Sri Lanka's Official Language Act declares Sinhala the only official language. This situation prevails until 1987, when Tamil is recognized as co-official.*

6 **1799:** *Russian national poet Alexander Pushkin is born in Moscow. He is widely acknowledged to have given standard Russian its current form.*

1829: *The last known speaker of Beothuk, a woman named Shanawdithit (a k a Nancy April) succumbs to tuberculosis in St John's, Newfoundland.*

7 *St Gotteschalk, official patron saint of linguists, was murdered on this day in 1066 in Pomerania, after having served as a translator in missionary work.*

1894: *William Dwight Whitney dies in New Haven, Connecticut.*

1934: *Wycliffe Bible Translators starts linguistics courses in Arkansas.*

1951: *Birthday of sociolinguist Deborah Tannen.*

1954: *Following his conviction for homosexuality, Alan Turing commits suicide.*

8   **1889:** *Ferdinand de Saussure gives a lecture on Lithuanian accent before the Société de Linguistique de Paris.*

2000: *The European Union Education Council adopts the decision of the Committee of Ministers to proclaim 2001 "European year of languages".*

2002: *A Japanese man turns himself in to the police after killing another person with his umbrella because he had not used the appropriate honorifics.*

9   **1912:** *Birth of Kenneth Lee Pike, the father of tagmemics.*

1977: *The new "Guidelines for Nonsexist Language in APA Journals" is published in The American Psychologist.*

2004: *In a historic liberalization move, Turkish state television makes its first broadcast in Kurdish, a language until recently banned not only from the media, but from all public life.*

10   **1898:** *The Dalmatian language becomes extinct as its last speaker Tuone Udaina (a k a Antonio Udina) accidentally steps on a land mine. He dies around 6:30 p.m. Fortunately, Udaina had acted as an informant prior to his death, but he was far from an ideal one—he was not technically a native speaker, had not used the language for 20 years, and was deaf and toothless.*

11   **1911:** *Death of James Curtis Hepburn, best known for Hepburn romanization system of Japanese.*

12   **1887:** *Czech Indo-Europeanist Julius Pokorny—mainly known for his voluminous etymological research—is born in Prague.*

1997: *Dragon Systems launches a new computer program for speech-recognition, which has a vocabulary of 30 000 words.*

13   **1972:** *Georg von Békésy, Hungarian-born auditory scientist, passes away.*

14   **1601:** *The Catholic church publicly burns Hebrew books and manuscripts in Rome.*

2001: *A new online edition of the Oxford English Dictionary becomes the first edition to contain important amounts of current slang terms.*

15   **1983:** *The local government of Galicia in Spain proclaims Galician the official language of the region.*

16   **1783:** *Lexicographer Samuel Johnson is hit by a stroke that leads temporarily to an aphasic condition. Fortunately, he quickly recovers.*

1902: *Bertrand Russell writes to Gottlob Frege for the first time.*

1911: *The Concise Oxford English Dictionary is published.*

1976: *After a decision that half of the school subjects be taught in Afrikaans, 15 000 South African students riot in what has become known as the Soweto Uprising. Nationwide, the riot causes hundreds of casualties. Since 1996, the day is celebrated as the South African Youth day.*

1998: *In a BBC poll, 63% of the (presumably mostly British) respondents would favor the use of English as the one and only official language of the European union.*

17   **1890:** *John Rupert Firth, originator of the "London school" of linguistics, is born.*

1996: *SIL field linguist Raymond Rising is released from captivity in Colombia, after being held hostage by a guerrilla movement for more than two years.*

18   **1816:** *Gallaudet and Clerc set sail from Le Havre (France) bound for New York to open a Deaf School, and thereby introduce French Sign in America.*

1928: *The "Terry expedition" sets out to chart some little-known territories in Australia. Among other things, it produces the first known documentation of the Warlpiri language.*

1936: *Mangei Gomango has a vision of an orthography, the Sorang Sompeng, for Sora, a Munda language of India. His orthography is still in use today.*

1977: *Marc Okrand, later of Klingon fame, defends his PhD thesis "Mutsun Grammar" at the University of California at Berkeley. The now extinct Mutsun was a variety of Costanoan once spoken just south of San Francisco*

1952: *Organized by pioneer Yehoshua Bar-Hillel, the first ever conference on machine translation kicks off at the Massachusetts Institute of Technology.*

1996: *Rwanda adopts English as its third official language. To the best of my knowledge, this is the first time that a country which has not been under Anglophone occupation does so.*

19   **1897:** *Irish estate manager Charles Cunningham Boycott is subject to protests from his tenants, and the incident establishes Boycott's family name as a new noun in the English language.*

20 **1913:** *Commenting on their own attempts to simplify John Wesley Powell's classification of American Indian languages, Alfred Kroeber writes to Edward Sapir that "we have finally got Powell's old fifty-eight families on the run, and the farther we can drive them into a heap, the more fun and profit"*

1938: *Andorra decides that official advertising must be in Catalan.*

1950: *In Pravda, Stalin publishes a piece which dismisses pretty much everything that Nikolai Yakovlevich Marr—until then the guru of Soviet linguistics—had ever said. As the column was graphically indistinguishable from other entries on the same page, it took an attentive reader to realize that what was claimed was the new Truth.*

1961: *Samuel Kirk and James McCarthy publish an experimental edition of the "Illinois Test of Psycholinguistic Abilities", used in diagnosing learning disabilities.*

21 **1928:** *The Putnam Patriot publishes Ken Pike's valedictory address, delivered upon his graduation (first in his class) from the Woodstock Academy.*

1966: *The chimpanzee Washoe is adopted by Allen and Beatrice Gardner, and begins her training in American Sign at the University of Nevada at Reno.*

22 **1767:** *Wilhelm Humboldt is born in Potsdam, Prussia.*

1902: *Gottlob Frege replies to Bertrand Russell's letter of June 16.*

1993: *A Slovakian stamp commemorates "150 Years of the Slovak Language".*

1994: *At the Annual Meeting of the International Society of Humor Studies in Ithaca, New York, the first ever symposium on "the linguistics of humour" takes place.*

23 **1916:** *Birth of historical linguist Winfred Lehmann in Surprise, Nebraska.*

1940: *Semanticist Barbara Partee is born in Englewood, New Jersey*

24 **1961:** *Following increasing tension between its two main language groups, Belgium abolishes its linguistic census.*

25 **1938:** *Russian structuralist Nikolai Sergeyevich Trubetzkoy, one of the founders of the Prague school goes to meet his maker.*

1992: *The International Association for Chinese Linguistics is founded in Singapore.*

1994: *The first Federation of Teachers of Languages in Latin America (FUPL) is founded, and the event is declared to be of national interest by the president of Uruguay.*

1998: *Indonesian official news agency Antara reports that two new languages—Vahudate and Aukedate—have been "discovered" in the Mamberamo river area of West Papua.*

26 **1992:** *Corsica's parliament adopts a motion giving official status to the local language. This decision is not approved by the French government.*

27 **1915:** *Germany annexes the village of Moresnet in present-day Belgium, and thereby puts an end to the only state with Esperanto as its official language.*

28 **1824:** *Birth of Paul Broca in Sainte-Foy-la-Grande in Dordogne (France), discoverer of one of the most important language centers in the brain.*

1996: *The Ukrainian parliament adopts a new constitution, which declares Ukrainian as the only state language.*

29 **1919:** *Death of Karl Brugmann, neo-grammarian and comparative linguist.*

30 **1921:** *The Californian language Tataviam becomes extinct with the passing away of its last speaker Juan José Fustero.*

1998: *British teenager Derek Bentley, hanged for killing a policeman in 1952, is posthumously pardoned, thanks to evidence from forensic linguistics.*

JULY

1 **1912:** *Nikolai Yakovlevich Marr becomes an ordinary academy member of the Russian Academy of Sciences.*

1952: *The BBC broadcasts Deciphering Europe's earliest scripts, in which Michael Ventris's cracking of the Linear B writing a month earlier is first announced to a wider audience.*

1966: *The department of linguistics at the University of California at Los Angeles is officially founded.*

1990: *Harvard University Press publishes Phil Lieberman's The Biology and Evolution of Language.*

1993: *Ken Pike is awarded the Doctor of Philosophy, honoris causa from Albert Ludwig University of Freiburg, Germany*

1997: *Hong Kong University gets a linguistics department.*

1999: *The Mauritius Broadcasting Corporation begins the first regular televised news broadcast in Creole, the only language understood by the entire population.*

2 **1907:** *Ferdinand de Saussure becomes professor of linguistics at the Université de Genève.*

1949: *Spanish Vasconist Koldo (Luís) Mitxelena marries Matilde de Ilarduya.*

3 **1997:** *Slovenia signs the European charter on regional or minority languages.*

2004: *This year's Finnish dialect speaking championship is held in Merikarvia.*

4 **1992:** *Death of David Abercrombie, a major figure in British phonetics.*

5 **1726:** *Peter, the Wild Boy of Hanover, is baptized in London.*

1998: *A new language law is passed in Algeria, emphasizing Arabic as the country's sole official language.*

2004: *In his farewell address as the chairman of the African Union, the Mozambican president creates quite a fuss by addressing the meeting in Swahili. Despite Swahili being the most widely understood African language, the official languages of the African Union are Arabic, French, English, and Portuguese.*

6 **1999:** *The language technology enterprise Ectaco releases an English-Yiddish Electronic Dictionary.*

7 **1969:** *Canada's House of Commons approves equality of French-English language across the country.*

1971: *The Californian confined child "Genie" moves in with her teacher, Jane Butler.*

8 **1840:** *German linguist August Leskien is born.*

9 **1858:** *Franz Boas is born in Germany.*

2001: *Idan Landau, Israeli syntactician and captain of the reserve, is imprisoned for 14 days for refusal to serve in the occupied territories.*

10 **1952:** *Michael Ventris announces his conclusion that the hitherto mysterious Linear B inscriptions represent a form of Greek.*

11 **1939:** *Azerbaijan officially adopts Cyrillic script for the writing of Azerbaijani.*

12 **1922:** *The English architect and decipherer of the Linear B writing, Michael Ventris, is born.*

1932: *Kemal Atatürk founds the Turkish Linguistic Society.*

13 **1900:** *A French government decree "accepts the use of pas alone [i.e. without an accompanying ne] as the general sentence negator".*

1933: *Birth of Beatrice Tugenhat Gardner, who, along with Allen Gardner, taught American Sign Language to the chimpanzee Washoe.*

1993: *Death of Madeline Tomer Shay, the last native speaker of Penobscot.*

14 **1937:** *Sino-Tibetanist James Matisoff is born in Boston.*

2001: *As a natural step towards full national independence, the Institute of Linguistics is officially inaugurated at the National University's new campus in Dili in East Timor.*

15 **1949:** *Warren Weaver issues a memorandum in 200 copies on the progress in machine translation made by Andrew Booth. This is the first time that the possibilities of machine translation reach anyone outside the innermost circles of this pioneer project.*

1997: *President Nazarbaev signs the new Kazakh language legislation, according to which Russian is not an official language of the republic, but that it nevertheless may be used as such (!).*

16 **1860:** *Otto Jespersen, Danish linguist and Anglicist, and inventor of the artificial language Novial, is born.*

17 **1915:** *Birth of Madeline Tomer Shay, to become the last native speaker of Penobscot.*

1996: *At a meeting in Lisbon, the Lusophone union Comunidade dos Países de Língua Portuguesa (C P L P) is formed by seven Portuguese-speaking nations.*

18 **1889:** *On a field trip to Mongolia, Nikolay Yadrincev discovers rock carvings which later prove to be an 8th century Turkic language. The discovery so-called Orkhon inscriptions mark the start of scientific comparative Turcology.*

1906: *American linguist and politician Samuel Ichiye Hayakawa is born.*

1966: *Belgium passes a law on the use of languages in national administration.*

1982: *Russian-American linguist Roman Jakobson deceases in Boston.*

19 **1799:** *The Rosetta Stone, an essential key to the decipherment of the Ancient Egyptian hieroglyphs, is discovered near the Nile.*

1973: *In the New York Review of Books, Noam Chomsky provides a reply to the criticism delivered a couple of months earlier by George Lakoff.*

20 **1794:** *The revolutionary government declares that official announcements in newly constituted French Republic must be made in French, and in no other language. The punishment for not abiding the law is six months of imprisonment.*

1913: *Edward Sapir writes in a letter to Paul Radin that he now "seriously believe[s] that Wishosk [=Wiyot] and Yurok are related to Algonkin".*

1946: *In New York, Andrew Booth meets Warren Weaver for the first time. Although they do not discuss the subject on this particular day, their contacts is later to lead to the first relatively functional machine translation systems.*

1967: *In Mexico City, Morris Swadesh passes away.*

1994: *The parliament of Tajikistan rejects a proposal to grant co-official status to Russian.*

21 **1877:** *Ferdinand de Saussure gives a lecture on Indo-European vowels before the Société de Linguistique de Paris.*

1890: *The First Annual Convention of North American Volapükists is announced.*

1918: *Upheaval of the Russian ban on Hebrew and Yiddish periodicals.*

2001: *Israeli syntactician and captain of the reserve, Idan Landau, again becomes a free man, after having been imprisoned as a result of his refusal to serve in the occupied territories.*

22 *Spooner's Day is said to be celebrated on this day, I'm just not sure by whom. In any case, it commemorates the birth of Reverend William Archibald Spooner, the king of slips-of-the-tongue.*

1922: *Nikolai Trubetzkoy writes a letter to Antoine Meillet about palatalization in proto-Slavic.*

1933: *The French-Armenian inventor Georges Artsrouni patents a translation machine.*

1960: *Mouton offers to publish Chomsky's The Logical Structure of Linguistic Theory, but the negotiations come to nothing.*

23 **1833:** *Jean-François Sudre, inventor of the artificial language Solrésol, presents his creation to the press and to the Royal Academy of Fine Arts*

1999: *The BBC reports that in a survey of more than 100 writers, actors and journalists, British Deputy Prime Minister John Prescott wins the title "The public figure who most mangles the English language". The poll respondents consider current English "riddled with misplaced apostrophes, split infinitives, clichés, American forms, and political correctness".*

24 **1986:** *In Mali, a decision is taken to establish the Direction nationale de l'alphabétization fonctionnelle et de la linguistique appliquée. Its goal is to make people literate in the mother tongues instead of—as has hitherto been the case—in French only.*

25 **1799:** *Three hunters come across the feral child Victor in a forest in southern France. They capture him, but he later manages to escape. Victor is one of the most well-known cases of a child growing up deprived of language.*

26 **1869:** *In England, the Disestablishment Bill was passed, officially dissolving the Church of Ireland. Organized opposition to this legislation by time coins a word widely believed to be the longest in the English language: anti-disestablishmentarianism.*

1887: *The first Esperanto textbook is released on this date.*

1941: *Benjamin Lee Whorf, who formulated the strong version of the notorious Sapir-Whorf hypothesis, dies in Connecticut.*

1950: *Upon his death, George Bernard Shaw leaves a will which devotes money to the design and propagation of a new English spelling. Shaw—who was incidentally also born on this day—also has another linguistic connection, in that he made Henry Higgins—the main character of his play Pygmalion—a phonetician.*

1999: *The first issue of Esperanto Studies is published by Bambu Publications in Bulgaria.*

27 **2001:** *The Gaelic League of Ohio inaugurates its local Irish Language Weekend.*

2001: *At his 80th birthday, Eugenio Coseriu is awarded the Gran Cruz de Alfonso X el Sabio, the highest Spanish cultural award.*

28 **1970:** *Geoff Pullum is awarded a Certificate of Proficiency in the Phonetics of English at University College London.*

29 **1987:** *Sri Lanka grants co-official status to Tamil.*

30 **1905:** *Ludwig Zamenhof, creator of Esperanto, enjoys a lunch in the Eiffel tower.*

31 **1896:** *A journalist of the Turkish newspaper Terakki writes an article in which he suggests that profane writing be in Latin, rather than Arabic script.*

AUGUST

1 *Beginning this day, the Welsh celebrate their one-week Welsh language festival called National Eisteddfod.*

National alphabet day in Azerbaijan, commemorating the replacement of Cyrillic with Latin script in 2001.

1996: *Merrit Ruhlen's opus on Proto-World,* The Origin of Language *is published.*

1998: *Introduction of the German spelling reform.*

1999: *The Chung-Yuan Christian University of Taiwan establishes a Department of Applied Linguistics and Language Studies.*

2005: *After a period of transition, the new German spelling officially replaces the old orthography.*

2 **1884:** *In* The Critic, *the word thon is proposed as a gender-neutral pronoun to replace the he and she of English.*

1894: *The Saussures are blessed with a boy child. The son, named Raymond, later becomes a renowned psychoanalyst.*

1972: *Creation of the Tahitian Academy, whose aim it is to "safeguard and enrich the Tahitian language".*

3 **1787:** *Horace-Bénédict de Saussure, Ferdinand's great-grandfather, ascends Europe's highest mountain, Mont-Blanc.*

2002: *The Turkish parliament votes to end the ban on the Kurdish language.*

4 **1994:** *France passes the much criticized so-called Loi Toubon, which regulates the use of foreign languages in France.*

5 **1813:** *Ivar Aasen, the creator of Nynorsk, is born in Ørsta.*

1890: *James Edwin Danelson sends out a circular regarding the formation of a Volapük club in New York.*

6 **2002:** *After a unanimous city council vote, the city of Moncton in New Brunswick, declares itself Canada's first officially bilingual city.*

7 **1973:** *Ugandan dictator Idi Amin proclaims Swahili as the "national language".*

2001: *The Japanese company Takara releases a device called "Bowlingual", which is said to translate dogspeak into human languages. Attached to the dog's collar, Bowlingual analyses the dog's barks and growls and delivers them to the owner clad in Japanese or English words.*

8 **1996:** *The South African* LANGTAG *(Language Plan Task Group) commission submits its final report the government. This results in the adoption of no less than eleven official languages in the following year.*

9 **1816:** *Thomas Gallaudet and Laurent Clerc arrive in the United States, where they subsequently lay the foundations for the American Sign Language.*

1896: *Birth of Swiss child language investigator Jean Piaget.*

1928: *Turkish leader Kemal Atatürk announces his decision to switch from Arabic to Latin script.*

1940: *Death of Rudolf Thurneysen, one of the first to apply the newly established principles of historical linguistics to Celtic languages.*

10 **1963:** *The Oregonian language Galice becomes extinct with the death of its last speaker Hoxie Simmons.*

11 **1628:** *Pidgin Delaware is attested for the first time, as the Dutch minister Jonas Michaëlius writes a letter from New Netherlands (now New York), saying that the natives seem to address Europeans in a reduced version of their own language.*

12 **2002:** *Ectaco, Inc. launches an English-Albanian bidirectional dictionary for use with the handheld Palm computers.*

13 *Since 1955, this day marks the beginning of the Philippine Linggo ng Wika, or National Language Week.*

1908: *At the Hôtel Bergerhoff in the Neutral Territory of Moresnet in eastern Belgium, the statehood of Amikejo, the world's first (and only) Esperanto-speaking country, is proclaimed.*

1971: *Jane Butler's application to adopt the 14-year old language-deprived child "Genie" is rejected, and instead, she is turned over to David and Marilyn Rigler, her new foster parents.*

1982: *The Comparative Syntax Festival begins at the Universität Salzburg, Austria.*

2003: *Amerindianist Marianne Mithun becomes an honorary doctor at La Trobe University, Australia.*

14 This is National Navajo Code Talkers Day in the United States, commemorating the Navajos who used their language as a weapon against the Japanese during World War 2.

2001: Ectaco, Inc. releases a speech translator. Weighing only 110 grams, the device is claimed to be able to translate spoken English into spoken French, Spanish or German.

15 **1877:** A letter from inventor Thomas Alva Edison to T B A David, president of Pittsburgh's Central District and Printing Telegraph Company includes the first written attestation of the word hello.

1975: In the search for a gender-neutral pronoun to replace he and she, H R Lee of Virginia proposes se ([si]) in Forbes.

1981: Phonologist and Bantuist Larry Hyman gets 5 000 American dollars to investigate the prosodic structure of Luganda.

16 **1800:** At 10 p.m. Victor the wild child arrives at the deaf school in Paris.

17 **1875:** Death (in Cape Town) of Wilhelm Bleek, the "father of Bantu philology".

1987: At the 8th World Congress of Applied Linguistics in Sydney, Michael Halliday is honoured with a two volume festschrift, Language Topics.

18 **1990:** Death (from leukaemia) of Burrhus Frederic Skinner, to whose work Chomsky's nativist theories was in part a reaction.

19 In New Zealand, this is "Aphasia and Language Disorders Awareness Day".

1922: Austrian-Australian linguist and polyglot Stephen Wurm is born.

1989: Opening of the IPA convention in Kiel. The association's centenary is celebrated by a revision of the International Phonetic Alphabet.

2000: The Constitutional Court of Bosnia and Herzegovina abolishes the constitutional articles declaring only Bosnian and Croatian official in the Federation and only Serbian in the Republika Srpska.

20 **1935:** SIL founder Kenneth Pike visits Mexico for the first time, together with his future wife.

1977: The Voyager II is launched. In an attempt at extraterrestrial communication, the spacecraft contains recordings in several human languages, and a metal plate with pictograms on it.

21 Feast day of Pius X, the patron saint of Esperantists.

1966: At an age of merely 32, Nostratist figurehead Vladislav Illich-Svitych dies in an automobile accident.

2002: Bror Rexed, the man held responsible for the introduction of du (T-form) rather than ni (V-form) in Swedish, passes away at the age of 88.

22 **1846:** The first attestation of the word folklore appears in a review by Ambrose Merton (a k a William John Thomas) in the Athenaeum. The work reviewed is one of the folktale collections by the Grimm brothers.

1915: Ishi, the last speaker of Yana, has to terminate work with linguist Edward Sapir, as he is hospitalized anew.

2001: The Michelin group of France receives WorldLingo's Multilingual Email Award. WorldLingo regularly tests various major companies' ability to reply to email sent in foreign languages, and Michelin managed to provide an answer in German in just one hour and 17 minutes.

2004: Christine Ohuruogu runs for Britain in the Athens Olympics. Being one of the world's fastest linguists, her 51-second dash gives her the fourth place in the women's 400m semi final.

2005: National Punctuation Day in the USA, initiated by Californian Jeff Rubin, who wants to "remind people that punctuation wasn't invented solely to put sideways smiley faces in e-mail".

23 **1975:** In the ongoing debate on epicene pronouns in English, Christine Elverson of Skokie, Illinois, in the Chicago Tribune suggests the forms ey, eir and em.

24 **1983:** In a letter to his former teachers Tom Wasow and Ivan Sag, Stanford linguistics graduate Christopher Culy reports from Mali that Bambara might match the description of a context-free language.

1995: The Uzbek alphabet is revised.

2000: Vanishing Voices, a book on the earth's decreasing linguistic diversity, is published by Daniel Nettle and Suzanne Romaine.

25 **1902:** The first Arabic-language daily newspaper of the USA begins publication.

1997: The BBC reports that the characters of the popular children's show The Teletubbies are to use a more adult-like language after complaints that their childish speech might influence or deteriorate that of their viewers.

26 **1977:** *The provincial parliament of Quebec adopts bill 101, which makes French the only official language of the province.*

27 **1987:** *A feral child, in this case a young girl raised by pigs, is reportedly encountered in China.*

28 **1922:** *The Department of Philippine Linguistics is founded at the University of the Philippines in Quezon City.*

1994: *In the newspaper Svenska Dagbladet, Hans Karlgren proposes the introduction of hen (from Finnish hän) into Swedish as a gender-neutral pronoun.*

1995: *At the University of Cenderawasih in Jayapura, the first International Conference on New Guinea Languages and Linguistics is held.*

29 *Telugu Language Day is celebrated in Telugu-speaking parts of India.*

1911: *A speaker of Yana, later known as Ishi, is encountered in Oroville, California. Until this date, the tribe and the language had been believed to be extinct for several decades.*

2005: *Probably the oldest linguist in the world, Murray Emeneau, dies in Berkeley, California, at the age of 101.*

30 **1800:** *Victor the feral child meets French minister of the interior, Lucien Bonaparte.*

31 *This is Limba Noastra (our language) day to Moldavians. Since 1989, it has been a national holiday to commemorate the reintroduction of the Latin script, which occurred in that year. August 31, 1989 was also the day when an amendment was added to the Moldavian constitution, recognizing the identity between Moldavian and Romanian. The Romanian dialect spoken in Moldavia was proclaimed a language in its own right during the Soviet régime, in order to minimize demands for independence or retrocession.*

1944: *This day marks the culmination of the Estonian Swedish exodus, as 632 individuals flee to Sweden. The Swedish-speaking population in Estonia, which has lived there since the 13th century, is virtually extinct by the time the world war is over.*

SEPTEMBER

1 **1904:** *Helen Keller graduates cum laude from Radcliffe College at age 24. She is, so far as I know, the first tactile signer to do so. Her reading was done through Braille script, and the lectures were spelt into her hand by her assistant. After graduation, Keller became a well-known socialist agitator.*

2000: *Randy LaPolla gets a grant to compile a dictionary of the Chinese language Rawang.*

2 **1957:** *Together with George Suci and Percy Tannenbaum, Charles Osgood publishes The Measurement of Meaning, in which the connotative meanings of words are investigated.*

1961: *Ken Hale fills the position of assistant professor of anthropology and linguistics at the University of Illinois in Urbana.*

1993: *A new alphabet for the writing of Uzbek is adopted.*

3 **1874:** *German linguist Hans Conon von der Gabelentz dies.*

1999: *In Moncton, New Brunswick, 52 heads-of-state are welcomed by secretary-general Boutros Boutros-Ghali to the Eighth Conference of the Francophonie, that is, the association of French-speaking countries. Or perhaps rather, more or less French-speaking countries, as Albania and Macedonia, desperate for international friends, are admitted as associate members.*

4 **1911:** *Ishi, the last speaker of Yana, who has miraculously survived the extermination of the rest of his people, is donated (sic) by the Bureau of Indian Affairs to the University of California Anthropology Museum.*

1930: *The first conference on Plains Indian Sign begins in Browning, Montana, attracting members from 14 different tribes. This is probably the world's first conference on a pidgin language.*

5 **1933:** *In Moscow, Petr Petrovich Smirnov-Troyanskii patents a translation machine.*

6 **1956:** *The English architect and decipherer of the Linear B writing, Michael Ventris, dies in a car crash, at a mere 34 years of age.*

7 **1999:** *American band "The Magnetic Fields" releases the album 69 Love Songs, featuring the song Death of Ferdinand de Saussure.*

2002: *Eugenio Coseriu passes away in Tübingen, Germany, at an age of 81.*

8 *Declared by UNESCO as the International Literacy Day.*

1865: *Mikhail Muraviev, governor-general of Vilnius officially outlaws the use of Latin characters in the printing of Lithuanian. In practice, this means a ban on Lithuanian print.*

1914: *In a letter to fellow lumper Edward Sapir, Alfred Kroeber wonders if there is no way of relating the extinct Beothuk to some existing family, so that the number of language families in North America can be reduced even further.*

1945: *The 26 500-page original draft of the Korean Big Joseon Language Dictionary resurfaces. It had been seized by the Japanese during World War II.*

9 **1945:** *The word "bug" gets a new application when U S Navy Lieutenant Grace Murray Hopper finds an actual bug stuck in a computer relay.*

1975: *English ethnographer Eric Thompson, who succeeded in deciphering the Maya hieroglyphs, dies.*

10 **1976:** *John Searle reviews Chomsky's Reflections on language in the Times Literary Supplement.*

11 **1956:** *This is the second day of a symposium at the Massachusetts Institute of Technology, organized by the Special Interest Group in Information Theory, and it is the event that Miller (2003:142) has referred to as the start of the "Cognitive Revolution". One of the participants is a certain N. Chomsky, who delivers the outline of his coming debut Syntactic Structures.*

12 **1869:** *Peter Mark Roget—after whom the Roget's Thesaurus is named—dies.*

13 **2004:** *Germany's Deutsche Welle adds one more language to the 30 already used for broadcasting— Klingon.*

14 *This is the birthday of two major figures of 19th century German and international linguists. In 1769, Friedrich Wilhelm Heinrich Alexander von Humboldt is born in Berlin, and in 1791, Franz Bopp is born in Mainz.*

1999: *The Nepalese capital Kathmandu is brought to a standstill by a strike provoked by a ban on the use of ethnic languages in official work.*

2005: *In Ho Chi Minh City, the first ever dictionary of Vietnamese Sign is published.*

15 **1845:** *Birth of Henry Sweet, English linguist and phonetician. Sweet was the real-life model for Henry Higgins of Pygmalion.*

1975: *In what is surely one of the more facetious attempts to coin an epicene pronoun to replace he and she, Joel Weiss of Northbrook, Illinois blends he, or, she and it into h'orsh'it.*

1999: *The Turkish government's Directorate General of Press and Information reports that Turkish is now spoken by no less than 200 million people, making it the 7th language of the world in terms of number of speakers. Most non-Turkish estimates put the number at slightly more than 60 million, putting it in 19th place among the world's languages.*

2002: *Parliamentary elections in Sweden. The liberal party Folkpartiet gets a surprisingly high percentage of the votes, due to their proposal that knowledge of Swedish be a prerequisite for citizenship.*

16 **1940:** *Benjamin Lee Whorf submits his article "Linguistics as an exact science" to Technological Review.*

1991: *George Miller is awarded the National Medal of Science by American President George Bush Sr.*

1994: *On the Linguist List, Dan Everett announces the discovery of a hitherto undocumented speech sound, a voiceless dental stop articulated simultaneously with a voiceless bilabial trill. He came across the sound in the Amazonian languages Wari' and Pirahã.*

17 *The saint of the day is St Hildegard of Bingen, who died on this date in 1179. She is one of the official patron saints of linguists.*

1774: *Birth of Cardinal Mezzofanti, legendary Italian polyglot.*

2005: *In Lautoka, Fiji, the first of a series of workshops are held whose goal is to produce the first dictionary of Fijian Sign.*

18 **1954:** *Steven "Language Instinct" Pinker is born in Montreal.*

19 **1921:** *Birth of psycholinguist Eric Lennenberg.*

1997: *During the International Congress of Esperantists in San Francisco, mayor Willie Brown declares an "Esperanto Day" in the city.*

2000: *The Municipal Assembly of Maputo, capital of Mozambique, decides to tolerate the use of the city's main vernacular, Ronga, both within the assembly itself, and in contacts with citizens. Hitherto, only Portuguese had been allowed.*

20 **1863:** *Death of Jakob Grimm.*

1884: *In The Current, Emma Carleton suggests ip as an epicene pronoun in place of he and she.*

1916: *German linguist August Leskien dies.*

1952: *The South Carolinian language Catawba, dies with its last speaker Sallie Brown Gordon.*

2004: *Yang Huanyi, the last competent user of Nüshu, dies in Changsha, China. Nüshu was a script used exclusively by women.*

21 **1936:** *Death at the age of 70 of Antoine Meillet in Châteaumeillant.*

1938: *In the Liverpool Echo, a Gregory Hynes proposes* se, sim *and* sis *as gender-neutral pronouns to replace* he, she *and their* variants. *Exactly half a century later, Eugene Wine of the Miami-Dade Community College in Florida suggests* e, *since other pronoun forms "have already been reduced to a single vowel sound".*

22 **1990:** *Steven Woodmore sets a new (though not uncontroversial) world record in speed talking. On the British TV show "Motor Mouth", he recites a piece of the "to be or not to be" soliloquy from Shakespeare's "Hamlet" in 56,01 seconds, yielding an average rate of 637,4 words per minute.*

23 **1989:** *The not yet independent Kyrgyzstan declares Kirghiz its one and only official language.*

24 **2000:** *Basil "restricted code" Bernstein dies at the age of 76.*

25 **1995:** *Hungary ratifies the European Charter for Regional and Minority Languages.*

2003: *Russophone Latvians protest outside the Palace of Europe in Strasbourg, seeking official recognition of the Russian language by the Latvian authorities.*

26 **2001:** *As a part of the European year of languages, the European Union organizes the European Day of Languages throughout its member states.*

27 **1790:** *Lexicographer Noah Webster is urged by his friend Daniel George to compile a dictionary.*

1998: *In a referendum, 56,4% of the voters in Schleswig-Holstein vote against the introduction of the new German orthography.*

28 **1995:** *The Minimalist Program becomes available in paperback.*

2001: *Eric Plunkett is found dead at Gallaudet University in Washington, where he was a student. Upon his arrest, the murderer Joseph Mesa later blames his action on voices in his head. Since Mesa is deaf, however, these were not literally speaking voices, but glove-clad hands urging him to kill—in American Sign.*

29 **1693:** *The first known female Anglicist, Elizabeth Elstob, later to write Rudiments of Grammar for the English-Saxon Tongue is born.*

30 **1920:** *In the wake of the First World War, Belgium abolishes the linguistic rights of its German-speaking minority. German regains its co-official status twelve years later.*

OCTOBER

1 **1928:** *All Turkish authorities are required to conduct their business using Latin, rather than Arabic, script.*

1953: *Andhra Pradesh becomes the second Indian state to be formed on the basis of linguistic frontiers.*

2 **1962:** *The East German government's post-war flirt with its Sorbian minority comes to an end, as German is imposed as the language of teaching in several subjects.*

3 **2001:** *Media all over the world report the finding of the "language gene". The truth behind the claim is that a group of British scientists under the leadership of Anthony Monaco had found that a gene called FOXP2 causes certain verbal dysfunctions when mutated.*

4 **1914:** *Nikolai Sergeyevich Trubetzkoy gets married in Moscow.*

1957: *The first man-made satellite is launched. For two reasons, this event is often mentioned in linguistics textbooks. First, overnight, it introduced the word Sputnik in scores of languages. This word is therefore mentioned as one of the rare examples where the appearance of a certain word can be dated. On October 3, few people had heard it, the next day it was part of the vocabulary of most westerners. Secondly, the shock experienced by Americans when realizing that other nations were as technologically advanced as theirs is often said to have provided the real impetus for the start of computational linguistics and machine translation—few American scientists knew any Russian, and could thus not keep themselves updated on the developments in Soviet research.*

2001: *Turkey announces constitutional changes, which, among other things, are to lead to an end to the ban on Kurdish language usage in media.*

5 **2000:** *The Swedish government appoints a commission intended to investigate the possibilities of protecting the Swedish language against the onslaught of English.*

6 **1926:** *"Der europäische Sprachgeist" by Henrik Becker becomes the first ever lecture to be delivered at the Prague Linguistics Circle.*

1999: *The governor of Mardin state, Turkey, issues an official memo insisting that teaching of the Syriac language in the local monasteries' boarding facilities be put to an end, since they violate Turkish law.*

7 **1992:** *Tevfik Esenç, the last speaker of Ubykh, dies in Istanbul. Ubykh is known mainly for its awe-inspiring phoneme system, consisting of two vowels and about 80 consonants. As it happens, Esenç died on the very same day that linguistic fieldworker Ole Stig Andersen arrived in order to interview him.*

2002: *The N|u language dies with the passing away of Elsie Vaalbooi, born some time around 1900.*

8 **1868:** *Preaching in Salt Lake City, Mormon leader Brigham Young proposes a new phonetic alphabet to be used among his followers. The alphabet is devised, but little used, and later abandoned.*

1991: *Peter Bakker of Amsterdam defends his thesis on Michif, the unique French-Cree mixed language of USA and Canada.*

1994: *Swedish phonetician and Romanist Bertil Malmberg dies at the age of 81.*

2001: *Death of Ken Hale.*

9 *The launching of the Han'gŭl alphabet in 1446 is commemorated in Korea as the "Korean Alphabet Day"—until recently a national public holiday.*

1940: *Nazi representative Rudolf Schlichting writes home to Germany from occupied France, suggesting that the allegedly positive Breton attitude vis-à-vis Germans could be exploited in the eradication of their language. "In one generation, Brittany will be a predominately German country", Schlichting notes not without satisfaction.*

1947: *Publication of the first volume of the monumental Joseon Language Big Dictionary, the first large dictionary of Korean.*

10 **1922:** *The British authorities in Palestine define the three official languages of the League of Nations mandate as Arabic, Hebrew and English.*

11 **1896:** *Russian-American linguist Roman Jakobson is born in Moscow.*

2002: *Two members of the Center party propose that the Swedish government includes Swedish Sign among the country's officially recognized minority languages.*

12 **1967:** *Noam Chomsky publishes a "call to resist illegitimate authority" in the New York Review of Books. It is signed by thousands. The demonstrations following eventually lead to Chomsky's arrest.*

13 **1807:** *German linguist Hans Conon von der Gabelentz is born.*

1881: *The Hebrew language is officially revived as Eliezer Ben-Yehuda and his friends agree to only use Hebrew in their conversations.*

1971: *Susan Curtiss notes that "Genie" for the first time really reacts to the stories that are being read to her.*

14 *In British Columbia, Canada, this is "Aboriginal Language Day".*

15 **1997:** *The Crimean parliament votes to make Russian the peninsula's official language in place of Ukrainian. 56 of the parliament's 96 deputies approved the motion and four voted against it.*

16 **1913:** *George Bernard Shaw's Pygmalion, with a phonetician as one of the leading characters is premiered in Vienna. Only the year later does it hit a London stage.*

1936: *A 14-year old Michael Ventris gets to hear about Linear B for the first time.*

1997: *Release of Steven Pinker's How the Mind Works.*

2000: *The band Jega (actually a pseudonym for Dylan Nathan), which plays instrumental electronic music, releases the album Geometry, which is remarkable for containing a song called Syntax Tree.*

17 **1920:** *The Indian feral children Amala and Kamala are discovered by a Reverend Singh.*

1979: *American creolist David DeCamp dies, at a mere 52 years of age.*

18 **1994:** *Geoff Pullum joins the Editorial Board for Oxford Textbooks in Linguistics.*

1994: *The film Secret of the Wild Child, a documentary on "Genie" and Victor, two of the best documented cases of first language deprivation is aired in the USA on the PBS network.*

19 **1983:** *A milestone in linguistic oppression: Turkey adopts law no. 2932 on "publishing in other languages than Turkish". Not surprisingly, such publishing is declared strictly forbidden. More amazingly, its third article states that "The native tongue of Turkish citizens is Turkish" and that speaking any other language natively is illegal!*

20 **1997:** *For his 25 years of linguistic service, the University of Connecticut honours Howard Lasnik. A symposium is organized, and a Festschrift is presented to the veteran generativist.*

21 **1989:** *An amendment to the constitution of Uzbekistan makes Uzbek the only official language.*

22 *International Stuttering Awareness Day (ISAD) is celebrated this day since 1998. Among the organizations behind the event are the seemingly incompatible International Fluency Association and the International Stuttering Association.*

1793: *The city of Strasbourg orders the burning of all literature in Hebrew.*

1978: *In the Unites States, the Court Interpreters Act is passed. Hereby, even long-time citizens of the country are allowed a certified interpreter if necessary.*

23 **1867:** *German linguist and Sanskritist Franz Bopp dies.*

1909: *Zellig Harris is born in Balta, Ukraine.*

1930: *Czech authorities accept and acknowledge the articles of the Prague Linguistics Circle.*

1980: *Birth of Kanzi, the most talking ape there is.*

24 **2004:** *In collaboration with the Goetheinstitut, the Deutscher Sprachrat (German language council) decides that Habseligkeiten 'belongings' is the most beautiful German word among the thousands submitted.*

25 **1937:** *Louis Hjelmslev makes his first and only guest appearance at the Prague Linguistics Circle, presenting the paper "Forme et substance dans la langue".*

1953: *Danish linguist Holger Pedersen passes away.*

26 *Countries in which French-lexicon creoles are spoken celebrate the Jounen Kweyol Entenaysonnal (International Creole Day).*

1492: *The word "canoe" is attested for the first time in a European language (under the form "canoa") in the writings of none other than Christopher Columbus.*

1789: *Lexicographer Noah Webster marries Miss Rebecca Greenleaf.*

1925: *David Premack is born. Among other things, he is known for having done language research with the chimpanzee Sarah.*

1967: *The Gardners deliver their first report on the chimpanzee Washoe's language acquisition progress to the Psychonomic Society.*

1973: *Ken Pike of the Summer Institute of Linguistics is awarded an honorary doctorate degree by the University of Chicago.*

27 **1995:** *In Washington, the American National Zoo unveils its Orangutan Language Project, led by biologist Rob Shumaker.*

28 **1910:** *Saussure begins his third course in general linguistics at the University of Geneva. The notes from this course made by one of his students, Émile Constantin, are later edited and published by Roy Harris and Eisuke Komatsu.*

1999: *The domain name pneumonoultramicroscopic-silicovolcanoconiosis.com, including what is the longest word in many English dictionaries, is registered by a commercial company selling . . . domain names.*

29 **1675:** *Gottfried Wilhelm von Leibniz makes the first use of the symbol ∫ for integral. This symbol was later adopted as the IPA symbol for a voiceless postalveolar fricative.*

30 **1990:** *The congress in Washington adopts the Native American Languages Act, which aims at a better protection of native American languages.*

31 *This day each year, the Conseil de la langue française must submit a report of its activities during the past year to the French government.*

1996: *Creation of Teilifís na Gaeilge, a TV channel broadcasting entirely in Irish.*

NOVEMBER

1 **1928:** *The Turkish parliament passes law 1353 on the use of the Latin alphabet in Turkey. This is actually but a recognition of the state of affairs—Turkish authorities have in fact used Latin script for more than a month.*

1941: *The American Defense Language Institute Foreign Language Center begins teaching. The institute subsequently developed into the world's largest foreign language institute.*

1997: *The most extensive description ever of the artificial language Lojban, The Complete Lojban Language, by John Woldemar Cowan is published.*

2004: *The Michel Thomas Language Center reports—not unexpectedly—that multilinguals are better paid than monolinguals. More interestingly, it also suggests that speakers of more than one language are perceived as sexier.*

2 *For Croatians, this is the Anniversary of the Croatian Language, commemo-rating the orthography of Ivan Broz.*

1949: *Timothy Evans of London "confesses" to having murdered his wife and child, for which crime he was hanged. Linguistic evidence later casts doubt on the confession leading ultimately to a posthumous pardon.*

2003: McDonald's demands that 'McJob' be removed from the 11th edition of Merriam-Webster's Collegiate Dictionary. The word has come to be applied to low-paid, unqualified employment, but McDonald's claims copyright, having registered McJobs as the name of its internal training program.

3 **1929:** Death of Polish linguist Jan Baudouin de Courtenay, forerunner of the structuralist school, and accredited with launching the term "phoneme".

1967: A young Háj Ross, clad hippie-style, protests against napalm production, a picture of which winds up in Time Magazine.

1998: Alaska makes English its official language of government despite protests.

2000: Death of Charles Hockett.

4 **1970:** At the age of 13, the most well-documented language-deprived child, "Genie", is discovered and taken care of in Arcadia, California.

1992: A new Lithuanian regulation states that place-names in the country should be in Lithuanian.

1994: First public preview of the Human Language trilogy—a film series on lin-guistics intended for laymen (but with a heavy Chomskyan bias!). On this day, the first part, called Colorless Green Ideas, is shown at Boston University.

5 **1881:** Ferdinand de Saussure starts teaching Comparative Germanistics at the École des Hautes-Études in Paris.

1891: Louis-Lucien Bonaparte, amateur linguist and Prince of France dies.

1896: Lev Semenovich Vygotsky is born. Vygotsky left a remarkable imprint on the study of child language acquisition.

1995: The Kasbe (Luo) language of Cameroon falls into obsolescence, as its last speaker, an old man known as Bogon, dies.

6 Finland Swedish day: Finland's Swedish-speaking minority celebrates itself.

7 **1942:** A US president gives a speech in a language other than English for the first time. Franklin D Roosevelt addresses the Vichy troops in North Africa in French, urging them not to resist allied landings. and to fight the Nazis.

1970: At a Phnom Penh conference, it is suggested that the "excellent linguistic rules" of Khmer are far superior to those of any other human language.

8 **1923:** Welsh is broadcast for the first time by 5WA in Cardiff.

1962: Belgium defines its four linguistic zones: Flanders (Dutch), Walloonia (French), Brussels, (bilingual), and a tiny German-speaking area in the east..

9 **1883:** Death of François Lenormant, the first (in quite some time, that is) to understand the Akkadian inscriptions from Mesopotamia.

1943: Lebanon launches a new constitution, in which both French and Arabic are recognized as co-official. The situation lasts for less than a month, when Arabic alone is declared the official language of the country.

1984: In the continuing debate on the need for a gender-neutral third-person singular pronoun in English-speaking, linguist Steven Schaufele of the University of Illinois suggests borrowing hann from Old Norse (which has already contributed they and them to English).

2003: Clinton Neakeahamuck "Lightning Foot" Wixon dies in Massachusetts. Wixon is thought to have been the last native speaker of Wampanoag.

10 **1944:** British-American historical linguist and Vasconist Larry Trask is born in upstate New York.

1993: While not an EU member state, Norway promises that it will give its Saami-speaking minority the same rights as minorities within the EU.

2003: After demands from a certain fast food chain, the word 'McJob' is deleted from the web edition of Merriam-Webster's dictionary.

11 **1866:** Birth of Antoine Meillet.

2003: After an exchange of letters, Merriam-Webster (see Nov. 2) responds that 'McJob' will indeed be included in the next printed edition of its dictionary.

12 **1912:** The colonial authorities in Oubangui-Chari (now the Central African Republic) forbid the use of native languages in schools, since it is thought that this might interfere with their acquisition of French.

13 **1952:** Patricia Curran's dead body is found in The Glen, in Northern Ireland. A confession, which a linguistic analysis later found to be false, imprisons Iain Hay Gordon for 48 years, until he is declared innocent in 2000.

1991: The new Ukrainian citizen law makes knowledge of Ukrainian a prerequisite of citizenship.

14 **1832:** A week before his 45th birthday, Rasmus Rask dies of tuberculosis.

1993: *Field linguist Charles Watson is kidnapped by the Islamic Abu Sayyaf guerrilla on the Philippine island of Pangutaran.*

1998: *Congo-Kinshasa presents a suggested new constitution, in which not only French, but also English, is recognized as an official language.*

2002: *Despite its unwillingness to include Swedish Sign among the country's officially recognized minority languages, Sweden's parliament today laun-ches a new version of its web site, in which parts are translated into Sign.*

15 **1969:** *Janis Joplin is arrested for using vulgar and indecent language onstage.*

16 **1974:** *A puzzle for future Alien linguists to solve, a message containing information on mankind and the planet we inhabit, is broadcast to the M13 star cluster, 50 000 light-years from us.*

17 **1794:** *The revolutionary government of France decrees that all education in the republic be in French only—at least in theory. Recourse to local language is tolerated when necessary.*

1985: *Birth of Panbanisha, the equally language-apt sister of Kanzi the Bonobo.*

1999: *The UNESCO decides to make February 21st the official "International Mother Language Day".*

18 **1988:** *Lithuanian is declared the only official language of the not yet independent Soviet Republic of Lithuania.*

1997: *Liechtenstein signs the European Charter on Regional and Minority Languages, but declares that it does not have any minority languages.*

19 **1992:** *Copenhagen University gives phonetician John Ohala an honorary PhD.*

1998: *A new minority language is officially born in previously monolingual Portugal, as its national assembly recognizes the status of Mirandese.*

2002: *The applicant countries participate in a debate in the European Parliament in Strasbourg, and for the first time in the history of the European Union, simultaneous interpreting is provided in 23 languages.*

20 **1629:** *In a letter to Pierre Mersenne, René Descartes describes his idea of assigning a number code to all concepts. This would allow translation where two persons don't share a common language. The writer's message, converted into numbers would allow the receiver to simply substitute for the number the lexical item in his own language.*

1889: *Ferdinand de Saussure takes a sabbatical from Sorbonne, and is replaced by Antoine Meillet.*

1916: *Birth of Charles Osgood, inventor of semantic differential technique.*

1975: *The International Circle of Korean Linguistics is founded.*

21 **1800:** *The Société des Observateurs de l'Homme releases its psychological verdict on Victor the feral child: "enfant idiot".*

1918: *Edward Sapir writes to convince Alfred Kroeber that Salish must be related to other languages of North America, although no suitable relative has been found as of yet.*

1991: *Closing of the fourth Sommet de la Francophonie in Paris, which was attended by 50 more or—in many cases—less French-speaking countries.*

22 **2001:** *John McCarthy's book A Thematic Guide to Optimality Theory is published.*

2002: *At the NATO summit in Prague, the organization's other official language, French, is used for once. The reason is that the French names of the participating countries permits the unwanted guest, Ukrainian president Kuchma to be placed further away from the representatives of Britain and the USA, the countries most opposed to his participation.*

23 **1964:** *Latin is abolished as the official language of Roman Catholic liturgy.*

24 **1916:** *Birth of Frank Mihalic, compiler of the first Tok Pisin dictionary.*

1967: *Alvin Liberman, Franklin Cooper, Donald Shankweiler, and Michael Studdert-Kennedy publish their classic article "Perception of the Speech Code" in Psychological Review.*

1982: *Basque and Spanish are both recognized as "official" languages of the Basque country, while giving only the former the status of "proper language of the Basque country".*

25 **1842:** *The British Philological Society holds its first meeting.*

1850: *Birth of Eduard Sievers, German phonetician and philologist.*

26 **1857:** *Birth in Geneva of Ferdinand de Saussure, "father of modern linguistics", just in case you didn't know. Not celebrating this is not an option.*

27 **1948:** *Ken Pike's third child and first son is born in Santa Ana, California.*

28 **1915:** *A disappointed Alfred Kroeber reports to Edward Sapir that he cannot find any relationship between Zuni and other American Indian languages.*

1980: *Tahitian is for the first time recognized as the official language (along with French) of French Polynesia.*

29 **1922:** *The British mandate authorities recognize Hebrew as the official language of the Jews in Palestine.*

30 **1950:** *Abraham Kaplan of the Rand Corporation in Santa Monica, California, completes a seminal study on the role of context in machine translation.*

1976: *A Mexican law bans non-Spanish advertising in the capital area.*

1991: *Phil Resnik and five of his colleagues are granted American patent no. 5 267 345 for a "Speech recognition apparatus which predicts word classes from context and words from word classes".*

2001: *Linguistics enter the world of sports equipment manufacturing as Adidas in Pusan (South Korea) unveils what is claimed to be the fastest football ever made. Its spectacular speed is said to be due to its "syntactic surface".*

DECEMBER

1 **1930:** *The Prague Linguistics Circle is formally founded by Roman Jakobson and fourteen of his colleagues.*

1998: *Dutch and Flemish lexicographers publicly present the final and complete version of the Woerdeboek van de Nederlandse Taal, the biggest ever Dutch dictionary. It has taken a century and a half to produce.*

2 **1906:** *Antoine Meillet becomes a Corresponding Member of the Russian Academy of Sciences.*

1985: *The Summer Institute of Linguistics this day publishes Desmond Derbyshire's extensive treatment of the Amazonian language Hixkaryána.*

1999: *The Swedish parliament gives official recognition to five minority lan-guages: Standard Finnish, Meänkieli Finnish, Saami, Romani, and Yiddish.*

3 *Celebrated as the Day of the Basque language (Euskararen Eguna) since 1947.*

1876: *August Leskien becomes a Corresponding Member of the Russian Academy of Sciences, as does Elias Lönnrot, standardizer of Finnish.*

1993: *A new law is adopted by the Italian government, intended to protect the Ladino-speaking minority of the Trento province.*

2002: *The South African government announces that, to facilitate things, each department should choose one of the eleven official languages as its one and only working language. Critics believe that this is a first step towards an English-only policy.*

4 **1880:** *Having been a member for a few years, but only a recent immigrant to France, Ferdinand de Saussure starts taking active part in the activities of the Socété de linguistique de Paris.*

1893: *German linguist Friedrich Karl Brugmann becomes a Corresponding Member of the Russian Academy of Sciences.*

1927: *Birth of William Labov.*

5 **1858:** *Louis-Lucien Bonaparte, amateur linguist and prince of France becomes an honorary member of the Russian Academy of Sciences.*

1948: *A church service interpreted into a sign language is televised for the first time (from St Matthew's Lutheran Church for the Deaf on Long Island).*

1996: *A new law passed by the Iranian parliament bans the use of non-Persian words and names in the country.*

6 *Declared "Plain English Day" by the "Plain English Network", a British group which aims to improve communication from the government to the public.*

1868: *Death of August Schleicher, the man behind the Stammbaumtheorie.*

1877: *The first sound recording of human language is made, as Thomas Alva Edison recites 'Mary Had a Little Lamb' into his phonograph.*

1995: *Press Secretary Mike McCurry in a White House Press Briefing uses an exceptionally long word: floccinaucinihili-pilification.*

7 **1928:** *Birthday of none other than Noam Chomsky.*

1993: *The Philippine Islamic Abu Sayyaf guerrilla releases field linguist Charles Watson in Manila. He had been kidnapped three weeks earlier on the island of Pangutaran.*

8 **1966:** *The first linguistics class in Bolivia is held at the Instituto Nacional de Estudios Lingüísticos in La Paz.*

2001: *Death of Frank Mihalic, compiler of the first Tok Pisin dictionary.*

9 1853: *German linguist and Sanskritist Franz Bopp becomes a corresponding member of the Russian Academy of Sciences.*

1986: *The Swiss Canton of Fribourg decides that real estate ownership registers be in the language of the municipality concerned.*

10 1904: *With the ban on printing in Lithuanian recently lifted, the first daily newspaper in the language, the Vilnius Žinios begins publication.*

1929: *Birth of psycholinguist and language acquisitionist Lila Gleitman.*

1996: *A Unicode standard is proposed for writing Solrésol, one of the most eccentric artificial languages there is.*

11 1990: *A resolution of the European Parliament establishes the status of the Community languages and Catalan.*

1997: *Death of American child language acquisitionist Roger Brown.*

12 1857: *German linguist August Schleicher becomes a corresponding member of the Russian Academy of Sciences.*

1890: *Logician and semanticist Kazimierz Ajdukiewicz, also known as the inventor of Categorial Grammar, is born in Poland.*

1913: *First official use of Hebrew as a language of instruction in Palestinian schools.*

13 1897: *Jan Baudouin de Courtenay and Hans Conon von der Gabelentz become corresponding members of the Russian Academy of Sciences.*

1949: *The Public Health and Local Government Act of Northern Ireland forbids street signs in Irish.*

1989: *The first ever (according to the choir) concert sung in sign language is performed at the Gwyn Town Hall in West Glamorgan, Wales.*

14 1921: *Birth of James Deese, author of Psycholinguistics (1970).*

1951: *Norway's parliament decides to create a Norwegian Language Council.*

1960: *Britain's first Professor of General Linguistics, John Rupert Firth, dies.*

15 Esperantists all over the world celebrate in memory of *Ludwig Zamenhof, the creator of Esperanto, born on this date in 1859.*

1893: *Danish linguist Vilhelm Thomsen announces that he has deciphered the Orkhon inscriptions, making it the oldest known Turkic text fragment.*

1990: *Inauguration of the Linguist List.*

16 1843: *Italian cardinal and polyglot Guiseppe Gaspare Mezzofanti becomes an honorary member of the Russian Academy of Sciences.*

1882: *Ferdinand de Saussure becomes assistant secretary of the Société de Linguistique de Paris.*

1999: *Andorra promulgates the Law on the organization of the usage of the Official Language, that is, Catalan.*

2003: *Joseph Mesa is arrested for two murders. He pleads insanity, blaming the murders on voices in his head. Since Mesa is deaf, these were not literally speaking voices, but glovecl hands urging him to kill—in American Sign.*

17 1832: *After a brief exposure to a language of Tierra del Fuego, Charles Darwin comments that it "barely merits classification as an articulated language".*

1962: *A new constitution of Monaco declares French as its official language.*

18 1987: *The Perl programming language (developed by a linguist) is born.*

1995: *Andrew Spencer's Phonology is published by Blackwell.*

1996: *The school board of Oakland, California, votes to recognize "Ebonics" as a minority language. Thus begins a heated debate in the USA on whether African-American Vernacular English is a language in its own right, or simply a dialect of English.*

2002: *The "International Language Week" begins today. It occurs annually in the third week of December.*

19 1927: *Language usage in the Finnish parliament is fixed by law, and deputies are allowed to use either Finnish or Swedish.*

20 1934: *Death of Russian/Soviet linguist Nikolai Yakovlevich Marr.*

2000: *After examining linguistic evidence, the British Court of Appeal overturns the conviction of Iain Hay Gordon, sentenced for murder in 1953.*

21 1940: *The Société Genevoise de Linguistique is founded in Geneva, Saussure's home town.*

1996: *Algeria's law n° 96-30 declares that all communication with authorities, companies and associations be in Arabic, although the use of French or other languages is permitted in international contacts.*

2000: *Through the journal Nature, phoneticians of Australia's Macquarie University let the world know that British Queen Elizabeth II's speech has, over the past 20 years, drawn closer to colloquial London English and further away from Received Pronunciation.*

22 **1845:** *The voice synthesizer Euphonium is demonstrated to the public in Philadelphia. Using reeds, bellows and chambers to simulate the anatomy of the human speech organs, it is said that it could produce 16 syllables.*

1942: *Franz Boas dies.*

2000: *Vietnam announces that different 11 minority languages will be broadcast on National Television in addition to Vietnamese.*

23 **1790:** *Birth of Jean-François Champollion, who played a major role in the deciphering of Egyptian hieroglyphics.*

24 **1949:** *Noam Chomsky marries Carol Schatz.*

1974: *Edward "Ned" Maddrell, the last native speaker of Manx, dies.*

2004: *Frisian is recognized as co-official on Germany's Heligoland island.*

25 **1932:** *Ken Pike applies to the China Inland Mission, but is turned down.*

2000: *Death of Willard Van Orman Quine.*

26 **1992:** *Niger's new constitution declares French the country's official language.*

2001: *The web site yourdictionary.com publishes its word-of-the-year list, including the first ever "suffix of the year", -stan (as in Afghanistan).*

27 **1942:** *Cognitive grammarian Ron Langacker is born in Fond du Lac, Wisconsin.*

1945: *A couple of months after the devastation of Hiroshima and Nagasaki, spelling reform advocate George Bernard Shaw writes to the Times claiming that the omission of the final, silent <b> in bomb, and similar reforms, would save a lot of time and bring major economical benefits.*

1996: *The Catalan government decides to support the use of Catalan in communities outside of Catalonia.*

28 **1989:** *Publication of Colin Renfrew's Archaeology and Language in paperback.*

29 **1975:** *In Britain, Sex Discrimination and Equal Pay acts are passed. Their consequences include the replacement of "firemen" by "fire fighters".*

1995: *Within two years of its introduction, the Karakalpak alphabet is revised.*

1996: *The civil war in Guatemala ends with a peace treaty which specifies, among other things, that 23 different indigenous languages be used in education along with Spanish.*

30 **1997:** *Yugoslav riot police are called upon to disperse students demanding Albanian language rights in Kosovo.*

2001: *The peace treaty in Afghanistan after the fall of the Talibans is delayed, because of problems with translating it into Persian, the second biggest language of the country.*

31 **1937:** *President Quezon proclaims Tagalog the official language of the not yet independent Philippines.*

1975: *France passes a new language law, the Loi du 31 décembre 1975 relative à l'emploi de la langue française.*

1997: *The United Bible Societies report, that "at least a Portion of the Bible" has now been translated into 2 197 languages.*

2000: *SIL International President Emeritus Kenneth Lee Pike dies in Dallas.*

Some days, there just isn't much going on

PICTURE CREDITS

The majority of the illustrations in this book are either free of copyright or were produced—drawn, photographed, or otherwise—by the author. Exceptionally, the following are reproduced with the kind permission of their copyright holders.

REFERENCES

In order to fit internet addresses conveniently into the available space, they have sometimes been split between two lines. Such splits are only made either at a dot or a slash. Note that internet addresses are normally followed by the date at which they were accessed.

Aarseth, Espen (1997): *Cybertext: Perspectives on Ergodic Literature*. Baltimore: Johns Hopkins University Press.

Abondolo, Daniel (1998): Khanty. Abondolo (ed.), pp 358-86.

—— (ed.) (1998): *The Uralic languages*. London: Routledge.

Abou, Antoine (1992): Les enfants de St-Domingue à St-Martin. Martin, Michel, François Vellas & Alain Yacou (eds): *La République Dominicaine, la Guadeloupe et la Caraïbe*, pp 187-206. Paris: Center des Études et de Recherches Caraïbéennes & Economica.

Abraham, Werner & Robert Binnick (eds) (1972): *Generative Semantik*. Frankfurt: Athenaum Verlag.

Adam, L & V Henry (1880): *Arte y Vocabulario de la Lengua Chiquita con algunos textos traducidos y explicados compuestos sobre manuscritos inéditos del XVIIIo siglo*. Paris: Librairie-Éditeur J Maisonneuve.

Adams, Douglas & John Lloyd (1983): *The Meaning of Liff*. London: Pan Books.

—— & —— (1990): *The Deeper Meaning of Liff*. London: Pan Books.

Adelaar, Willem (2004): *The languages of the Andes*. Cambridge: Cambridge University Press.

Aikhenvald, Alexandra (1999a): The Arawak language family. Dixon & Aikhenvald (eds), pp 65-106.

—— (2000): *Classifiers. A typology of noun categorization devices*. Oxford: Oxford University Press.

—— (2001): Areal Diffusion, Genetic Inheritance and Problems of Subgrouping: A North Arawak Case Study. In Aikhenvald & Dixon (eds), pp 167-94.

—— (2003a): Evidentiality in typological perspective. In: Aikhenvald & Dixon (eds), pp 1-31.

—— (2003b): Multilingualism and ethnic stereotypes: The Tariana of northwest Amazonia. *Language in Society* 32: 1-21.

—— (2004): Grammars in contact: a cross-linguistic perspective. MS.

Aikhenvald, Alexandra & Bob Dixon (1998): Dependencies between grammatical systems. *Language* 74: 56-80.

—— & —— (1999): Other small families and isolates. In: Dixon & Aikhenvald (eds), pp 341-83.

—— & —— (2001): *Areal diffusion and genetic inheritance*. Oxford: Oxford University Press.

—— & —— (eds) (2003): *Studies in evidentiality*. Amsterdam: Benjamins.

Aissen, Judith (1997): On the syntax of obviation. *Language* 73: 705-50.

Aleksov, Bojan (2000): The Evolution of the Anthroponymic System in Belgrade over the Course of the Twentieth Century as a Reflection of Popular Mentalité. Paper presented at the Socrates Kokkalis Graduate Student Workshop on Southeastern Europe, February 11-12, 2000, Harvard University.

Alici, D M (1996): The role of culture, history and language in Turkish national identity building: an overemphasis on Central Asian roots. *Central Asian Survey* 15.2: 217-31.

Allan, Jim (ed.) (1978): *An Introduction to Elvish*. Hayes: Bran's Head.

Allen, W S (1965): On one-vowel systems. *Lingua* 13: 111-24.

Alrabaa, Sami (1985): The use of address pronouns by Egyptian adults. A sociolinguistic study. *Journal of Pragmatics* 9.5: 645-57.

Amunts, Katrin, Axel Schleicher & Karl Zilles (2004): Outstanding language competence and cyto-architecture in Broca's speech region. *Brain and Language* 89: 346-33.

Andersen, Ole Stig (1996): Guds eget modersmål. http://www.olestig.dk/klummer/jesus.eng.html. 2002-02-14.

Anon. (1994): Streboj al internacia mono. *Eventoj* 50.

Anonby, Stan (1999): Reversing Language Shift: Can Kwak'wala Be Revived? Reyhner, Jon, Gina Cantoni, Robert St Clair & Evangeline Parsons Yazzie (eds): *Revitalizing Indigenous Languages*, pp 33-52. Flagstaff: Northern Arizona University.

Antoine Philippe & Claude Herry (1982): *Enquête démographique à passage répétés agglomération d'Abidjan*. Abidjan & Petit-Bassam: Direction de la Statistique & ORSTOM.

—— & —— (1983): La population d'Abidjan dans ses murs. *Cahiers de l'ORSTOM, série Sciences Humaines* 19.4: 371-95.

Anttila, Raimo (1972): *An introduction to historical and comparative linguistics*. New York: Macmillan.

Aoun, Joseph, Norbet Hornstein & Dominique Sportiche (1981): Some aspects of wide scope quantification. *Journal of Linguistic Research* 1: 69–95.

Arnott, D W (1974): Some Aspects of the Study of Fula Dialects. *Bulletin of the School of Oriental and African Studies* 37: 8-18.

Asher, R E & J M Y Simpson (1994): *The Encyclopedia of Language and Linguistics*. Oxford: Pergamon Press.

Atchia-Emmerich, Bilkiss (2005): *La situation linguistique à l'île Maurice. Les développements récents à la lumière d'une enquête empirique*. Nuremberg: PhD thesis, Friedrich-Alexander-Universität.

Aulestia, Gorka (1990): Luis Mitxelena: A Basque of International Fame. *Basque Studies Program Newsletter* 41.

Austin, J L (1962): *How to do things with words*. Oxford: Clarendon Press.

Bach, Emmon & Robert Harms (eds) (1968): *Universals in Linguistic Theory*. New York.

Bahgat, Gawdat (2003): Oil and militant Islam: strains on US-Saudi relations. *World Affairs*, winter 2003.

Baker, Philip (1993): Australian influence on Melanesian Pidgin English. *Te Reo* 36: 3-67.

Bakker, Peter (1997): *A language of our own. The Genesis of Michif, the Mixed Cree-French Language of the Canadian Métis*. Oxford: Oxford University Press.

Bakker, Peter & Maarten Mous (eds) (1994): *Mixed Languages. 15 Case Studies in Language Intertwining*. Studies of language and language use, 13. Amsterdam: IFFOT (Institute for Functional Research into Language and Language Use).

Balçık, Mehmet Berk (2000): Politics of National Identity and Language: Turkey, a Case Study. MSc disser-tation, University of Bristol.

Balcom, Patricia & Sandra Clarke (2004): Academic Career Paths in Linguistics: A Report on the CLA Questi-onnaire. *Canadian Journal of Linguistics* 49: 73-105.

Baldi, Philip (1983): *An introduction to the Indo-European languages*. Carbondale & Edwardsville: Southern Illinois University.

Bar-Adon, Aaron (1975): *The rise and decline of a dialect*. Paris/ The Hague: Mouton.

Barger, Jorn (1993): The Policeman's Beard was largely Prefab! *Journal of Computer Game Design*, August 1993.

Barnes, Janet (1999): Tucano. Dixon & Aikhenvald (eds), pp 207-26.

Baron, Dennis (1981): The Epicene Pronoun: The Word That Failed. *American Speech* 56: 83-97

—— (1982): *Grammar and good taste: Reforming the American Language*. New Haven: Yale University Press.

—— (1986): *Grammar and Gender*. New Haven: Yale University Press.

—— (1990): *The English Only Question: an official language for Americans?* New Haven: Yale University Press.

Bartens, Angela (1996): *Der Kreolische Raum. Geschichte und Gegenwart*. Helsinki: Suomalainen Tiedeakatemia.

Bates, Elizabeth & Laura Benigni (1975): Rules of address in Italy: a sociological survey. *Language in Society* 4.3: 271-88.

Baudoin de Courtenay, Jan (1895): *Versuch einer Theorie der phonetischen Alternationen*. Strasbourg.

Bauer, Laurie & Peter Trudgill (eds) (1998): *Language myths*. London: Penguin.

Bauman, R & J Sherzer (1974): *Explorations in the ethnography of speaking*. Cambridge: Cambridge University Press.

Bavin, Edith (1995): Language acquisition in crosslinguistic perspective. *Annual Review of Anthropology* 24, pp 373-96.

Bekerie, Ayele (2003): A writing system of the Edo people. http://www.library.cornell.edu/africana/Writing_Systems/ Edo.html. 2003-08-16.

Bella, L de Sousa (1946): Apontamentos sôbre a língua dos balantas de Jabadá. *Boletim Cultural da Guiné Portuguesa* 1: 729-65.

Bentley, Holman (1887): *Dictionary and Grammar of the Kongo Language as spoken at San Salvador, the Ancient Capital of the Old Kongo Empire, West Africa*. London: Baptist Missionary Society/Trübner & Co.

Bergen, Benjamin (2001): Nativization processes in L1 Esperanto. *Journal of Child Language* 28: 575-95.

Bergman, Gösta (1954): Nämnden för svensk språkvård. *Språkvård. Redogörelser och studier utgivna till språkvårdsnämndens tioårsdag 1954*, pp 1-31. Stockholm: Svenska Bokförlaget & Norstedts.

Bergsland, Knut & Hans Vogt (1962): On the validity of glottochronology. *Current Anthropology* 3: 115-53.

Berko, Jean (1958): The Child's Learning of English Morphology. *Word* 14, pp 150-177.

Berko, Jean & Roger Brown (1960): Psycholinguistic research methods. Mussen, P H (ed.): *Handbook of research methods in child development*, pp 515-57. New York: Wiley.

Berlin, Brent & Paul Kay (1969): *Basic color terms: their universality and evolution*. Berkreley: University of California Press.

Bernus, Edmond (1962): Abidjan: note sur l'agglomération d'Abidjan et sa population. Bulletin de l'IFAN B24: 54-85.

Berreby, David (1992): Kids, Creoles, and the Coconuts. *Discover Magazine*, April 1992, p 44.

Berry, Christopher (1974): Adam Smith's considerations on language. *Journal of the History of Ideas* 35: 130-38.

Bever, Thomas (1970): The cognitive basis for linguistic structure. Hayes, J R (ed.): *Cognitive development of language*, pp 278-352. New York: John Wiley.

Bhat, Darbhe Narayana Shankara (2004): *Pronouns*. Oxford: Oxford University Press.

Bielenstein, August (1892): *Die Grenzen des lettischen Volkstammes und der lettischen Sprache in der Gegenwart und im 13. Jahrhundert. Ein Beitrag zur ethnologischen Geographie und Geschichte Russlands*. St Petersburg: Kaiserliche Akademie der Wissen-schaften.

Bird, Charles & Timothy Shopen (1979): Maninka. Shopen (ed.) (1979b) pp 59-111.

Bisang, Walter (1996): Areal typology and grammati-calization. *Studies in language* 20: 519-97.

Blake, Barry (2001): *Case*. Port Chester: Cambridge University Press.

Blevins, Juliette (2004): *Evolutionary Phonology*. Cambridge: Cambridge University Press.

Bloom, Lois (1973): *One Word at a Time*. The Hague: Mouton.

Bloom, Paul (2004): Can a Dog Learn a Word? *Science* 304, pp 1605-06.

Bloomfield, Leonard (1933): *Language*. New York: Holt, Reinhart & Winston.

Boeder, Winfried (2005): The South Caucasian languages. *Lingua* 115: 5-89.

Bolinger, Dwight (1978): Intonation Across Languages. Greenberg (ed.) (1978b), pp 471-525.

Boretzky, Norbert (1991): Contact Induced Sound Change. *Diachronica* 8: 1-16.

Borkin, Ann (1984): *Problems in form and function*. Norwood: Albex.

Botha, Rudolf (2000): How much of language, if any, came about in the same sort of way as the brooding chamber in snails? *Stellenbosch Papers in linguistics* 33: 21-48.

Bowern, Claire (2002): Nhirrpi Data. http://www.people.fas. harvard.edu/~bowern/Nhirrpi. 2003-10-19. [=web vers-ion of Stephen Wurm's 1958 field notes, and the only preserved data there is on this now extinct language].

Bowern, Claire & Gül at Aygen-Tosun (2000): Titan's Tensed Prepositions. Paper presented at the Chicago Linguistic Society's Annual Conference (CLS36), 27-29 April 2000.

Braine, M (1963): The ontogeny of English phrase structure: the first phase. *Language* 39: 1-13.

Bréal, Michel (1864): *De la méthode comparative appliquée à l'étude des langues: leçon d'ouverture du cours de grammaire comparée au Collége de France*. Paris: Germer Baillière.

—— (1883): Les lois intellectuelles du langage. *L'annuaire de l'association pour l'encouragement des études grecques en France*.

Breton, Roland (2000): Can English be dethroned? *The UNESCO Courier*, April 2000, pp 23-24.

Bright, William (1997): A language is a dialect with an army and a navy. *Language in Society* 26: 469.

Brincat, Joseph (2001): Purism and neologisms in contemporary Maltese. Paper presented at the symposium *Purismus im Zeitalter der Globalisierung*, Universität Bremen, 18-21 September 2001.

Bruce, Les (1984): *The Alamblak Language of Papua New Guinea (East Sepik)*. Canberra: Australian National University Press.

Brush, Beaumont (1995): The Status of Coronal in the Historical Development of Lhasa Tibetan Rhymes. Paper presented at the 24th Annual Meeting of the Linguistic Association of the Southwest, University of New Mexico at Las Cruces, October 6-8, 1995.

Bulitta, A (1942): *Russisch-Ukrainischer Sprachführer: Taschenbuch für den Gebrauch im russisch-ukrainischen Sprachgebiet—geeignet für militärische und zivile Stellen*. Stuttgart: Franckh'sche Verlagshandlung.

Burenhult, Niclas (1996): Deep linguistic prehistory with particular reference to Andamanese. *Lund Working Papers in Linguistics* 45: 5-24.

Burung, Wiem (2000): A Brief Note on Elseng. http://www.sil. org/silesr/2000/2000-001/silesr2000-001. pdf. 2003-07-31.

Caldwell, Robert (1856): *A Comparative Grammar of the Dravidian or South-Indian Family of Languages*. Madras: University of Madras.

Calvet, Louis-Jean & Robert Chaudenson (1998): *Saint-Barthélemy: une énigme linguistique*. Paris: CIRELFA - Agence de la Francophonie.

Campbell, George (1991): *Compendium of the World's Languages*. London & New York: Routledge (2 vols).

Campbell, Lyle (1997): *American Indian languages: the historical linguistics of Native America*. Oxford: Oxford University Press.

—— (1998): *Historical linguistics – an introduction*. Edinburgh: Edinburgh University Press.

Capell, Arthur (1962): Oceanic linguistics today. *Current Anthropology* 3: 371-428.

Carroll, Paul (2003): Tristan da Cunha. http://www. btinternet. com/~sa_sa/tristan_da_cunha. 2003-08-14.

Carroll, Robert Todd (2001): Speed Reading. http:// www. skepdic. com/speedreading.html. 2001-05-22.

Čekmonas, Valeriy (2001): Russian varieties in the southeastern Baltic area: Urban Russian of the 19th century. Dahl, Östen & Maria Koptjevskaja-Tamm (eds): *Circum-Baltic Languages. Volume 1: Past and Present*, pp 81-99. Philadelphia: Benjamins.

Chambers, Jack (1998): TV makes people sound the same. Bauer & Trudgill (eds), pp 123-31.

Chan, Marjorie (1987): Tone and melody in Cantonese. Proceedings of the Thirteenth Annual Meeting of the Berkeley Linguistic Society, pp 26-37.

—— (1998): Gender differences in the chinese language: a preliminary report. Lin, Hua (ed.): *Proceedings of the Ninth North American Conference on Chinese Linguistics*, vol. 2, pp 35-52. Los Angeles: GSIL Publications, University of Southern California.

Charles, Alobwede d'Epie (1998): Banning Pidgin English in Cameroon? *English Today* 14: 54-60.

Chaudenson, Robert (2001): *Creolization of language and culture*. London: Routledge.

Chen, Ping (1999): *Modern Chinese: History & Socio-linguistics*. Cambridge: Cambridge University Press.

Choi, S & Gopnik, A (1995): Early acquisition of verbs in Korean: a cross-linguistic study. *Journal of Child language* 22: 497-529.

Chomsky, Noam (1957): *Syntactic Structures*. The Hague: Mouton.

—— (1959): On certain formal properties of grammars. *Information and Control* 2: 137-67.

—— (1964): *Current Issues in Linguistic Theory*. The Hague: Mouton.

—— (1965): *Aspects of the Theory of Syntax*. Cambridge: MIT Press.

—— (1975): Questions of form and interpretation. *Linguistic Analysis* 1: 75-109.

—— (1980): On binding. *Linguistic Inquiry* 11: 1-46.

—— (1986): *Barriers*. Cambridge: MIT Press.

Chomsky, Noam & Morris Halle (1968): *The sound pattern of English*. New York: Harper & Row.

Churchward, Clerk Maxwell (1940): *Rotuman grammar and dictionary*. Sydney: Australasian Medical Publishing Co.

Cienciala, Anna (1996): *The Rise and Fall of Communist Nations, 1917-1994*. Lawrence: Department of History, University of Kansas.

Ciscel, Matthew, Richard Hallett & Angie Green (2002): Language Attitude and Identity in the European Republics of the Former Soviet Union. *Texas Linguistic Forum* 44: 48-61.

Clark, Julia (1988): Tasmanian Aborigines. Jupp, James (ed.): *The Australian People*, pp 140-44. North Ryde: Angus & Robertson.

Clark, Katerina & Michael Holquist (1984): *Mikhail Bakhtin*. Cambridge: Harvard University Press.

Clark, Ross (1990): Austronesian languages. Comrie (ed.), pp 171-84.

Clements, George (1985): The geometry of phonological features. Phonology Yearbook 2: 225-52.

Clouse, Duane (1997): Towards a reconstruction and reclassification of the Lakes Plain languages of Irian Jaya. Franklin, Karl (ed.): *Papers in Papuan linguistics* 2: 133-236. Canberra: Research School of Pacific and Asian Studies, Australian National University.

Cole, Chris (1989): The biggest hoax. *Word Ways*, pp 205-06.

Coleman, John (2001): The phonetics and phonology of Tashlhiyt Berber syllabic consonants. *Transactions of the Philological Society* 99: 29-64.

Colin Masica (1991): *The Indo-Aryan Languages*. Cambridge: Cambridge University Press.

Collins, Paul (2001): Prophet of sound. *Fortean Times* 145: 40-45.

Comrie, Bernard (1981): *The languages of the Soviet Union*. Cambridge: Cambridge University Press.

—— (1992): Balto-Slavonic. Gvozdanovi , Jadranka (ed.): *Indo-European Numerals*, pp 717-833. Berlin: Mouton de Gruyter.

—— (ed.) (1990): *The major languages of South Asia, the Middle East, and Africa*. London: Routledge.

Comrie, Bernard & Maria Polinsky (1998): The great Daghestanian case hoax. Siewierska, Anna & Jae Jung Song (eds): *Case, typology and grammar: In honor of Barry J Blake*, pp 95-114. Amsterdam: Benjamins.

Conniff, Richard (1993): Easter Island Unveiled. *National Geographic* 183.3: 54-79.

—— (1996): What's in a Name? *Smithsonian Magazine*, December 1996.

Cook, Guy (2001): 'The philosopher pulled the lower jaw of the hen'. Ludicrous invented sentences in language teaching. *Applied linguistics* 22: 366-87.

Coon, Brad (1995): *Proto-Wakashan Roots: recons-tructions, phonologies, and implications for external relations*. Master of Liberal Studies, Indiana University.

Corbett, Greville (2000): *Number*. Cambridge: Cambridge University Press.

Corliss, William (1991): Killer trees that talk among themselves. *Science Frontiers* 73: Jan-Feb 1991.

Corne, Chris (1990): Tayo pronouns: A sketch of the pronominal system of a French-lexicon Creole language of the South Pacific. Te Reo 33: 3-24.

Corsetti, Renato (2002): Majstri la anglan per langoperacio. *Esperanto Revuo* 95.5: 104.

Corsetti, Renato, Maria Antonietta Pinto & Maria Tolomeo (2004): Regularizing the regular: The phenomenon of overregularization in Esperanto-speaking children. *Language Problems & Language Planning* 28.3: 261–82.

Cortazzi, Hugh (1987): *Victorians in Japan in and around the Treaty Ports*. Atlantic Highlands: Athlone Press.

Couturat, Louis & Léopold Léau (1903): *Histoire de la langue universelle*. Paris: Hachette.

Crawford, James (1996): Seven hypotheses on Language Loss: Causes and Cures. Cantoni, G (ed.): *Stabilizing Indigenous Languages*. Flagstaff: Center for Excellence in Education, Northern Arizona University.

Croke, Vicki (1999): Thorns of plenty. *International Wildlife*, November/December 1999, p 34.

Crombie, David (2000): *I lovens favm – Latterlige lover fra hele verden. Hvad de dog siger i retten. Om advokater og dommere og den slags*. Copenhagen: P Haase & Søns Forlag.

Crothers, John (1978): Typology and Universals of Vowel Systems. Greenberg, Joseph (ed.): *Universals of Human Language*, vol. 2, pp. 93-152. Stanford: Stanford University Press.

Crowley, Terry (1997): *An introduction to historical linguistics*. 3rd edition. Auckland: Oxford University Press.

Crystal, David (1987): *The Cambridge Encyclopedia of Language*. Cambridge: Cambridge University Press.

—— (1997): Vanishing Languages. *Civilization: The Magazine of the Library of Congress*, February-March, 1997.

Cunningham, Kristina (2001): Translating for a larger Union – can we cope with more than 11 languages?. http:// europa. eu.int/comm/translation/en/eyl/speech.pdf. 2001-07-25.

Cuoq, Jean-André (1866): *Études philologiques sur quelques langues suvages de l'Amérique*. Montreal: Dawson Brothers.

Curnow, Timothy (2001): What Language Features can be 'Borrowed'? Aikhenvald & Dixon (eds), pp 412-36.

Currie, Haver (1952): A projection of sociolinguistics: the relationship of speech to social status. *Southern Speech Journal* 18: 28-37.

Cysouw, Michael (2004): On the distribution of rare characteristics. Paper presented at the workshop *Interpreting Typological Distributions: Using the World Atlas of Language Structures (WALS)*, 11-12 December 2004, Max Planck-Institut für Evolutionäre Anthropologie, Leipzig.

Dahl, Östen (2005): Measuring linguistic distance. Paper presented at Sling 2005, Lund 28-29 April, 2005.

Dalby, Andrew (1998): *Dictionary of languages*. London: Bloomsbury Publishing.

—— (2002): *Language in Danger*. London: Penguin Books.

Dalby David (1999): *The Linguasphere Register of the World's Languages and Speech Communities* (2 vols). Hebron: Linguasphere Press.

Damen, Cees (2003): Neutraal Moresnet. http://home. hccnet. nl/c.damen/nederlands/index_nl.htm. 2003-09-11.

Daniels, Peter & William Bright (1996): *The World's Writing Systems*. New York: Oxford University Press.

Davies, Ian, Tat'jana Sosenskaja & Greville Corbett (1999): Colours in Tsakhur: First account of the basic colour terms of a Nakh-Daghestanian language. *Linguistic Typology* 3: 179-207.

Davies, John (1981): *Kobon*. Amsterdam: North Holland.

Davison, Alice (1970): Causal Adverbs and Performative Verbs. *Papers from the 6th Regional Meeting of the Chicago Linguistic Society*, pp 190-201.

de Ruiter, Jan Peter & David Wilkins (1997): Max-Planck-Institut für Psycholinguistik. Annual report 1996. http:// www.mpi. nl/ world/ann/ 96/ar509.htm. 2002-03-30.

Delafosse, Maurice (1914): *Esquisse générale des langues de l'Afrique et plus particulièrement de l'Afrique française*. Paris: Masson.

Dell, François & Mohamed Elmedlaoui (1988): Syllabic Consonants in Berber: Some New Evidence. *Journal of African Languages and Linguistics* 10: 1-18.

Delpech, Bernard (1983): Les nouveaux Abidjanais et leurs racines. *Cahiers de l'ORSTOM, série sciences humaines* 19.4: 567-83.

Dench, Alan (1995): *Martuthunira: A language of the Pilbara region of Western Australia*. Canberra: Pacific Linguistics.

Dench, Alan & Nicholas Evans (1988): Multiple case-marking in Australian languages. *Australian Journal of Linguistics* 8: 1-47.

Derbyshire, Desmond (1961): Hixkaryana (Carib) syntax structure. *International Journal of American Linguistics* 27: 125-42, 226-36.

Dickens, Patrick (1992): *Ju|'hoan grammar*. Windhoek: Nyae Nyae Development Foundation.

Dimmendaal, Gerrit (2000): Morphology. Heine & Nurse (eds), pp 161-93.

Disterheft, Dorothy (1990): Women in linguistics: Recent trends. Davison, Alice & Penelope Eckert (eds): *The Cornell Lectures: Women in the linguistics profession*, pp 89-110. Washington:

The Committee on the Status of Women in Linguistics of the Linguistic Society of America.

Dixon, Bob (1980): *The languages of Australia*. Cambridge: Cambridge University Press.

—— (1997): *The Rise and Fall of Languages*. Cambridge: Cambridge University Press.

—— (2003a): A program for linguistics. *Turkic languages* 7: 157-80.

—— (2003b): Demonstratives and cross-linguistic typology. *Studies in Language* 27: 61-112.

Dixon, Bob & Aikhenvald, Alexandra (1999): Introduction. Dixon & Aikhenvald (eds), pp 1-21.

—— & —— (eds) (1999): *The Amazonian languages*. Cambridge: Cambridge University Press.

Dixon, R M W (1977): Where have all the adjectives gone? *Studies in Language* 1: 19-80.

—— (1994): Adjectives. Asher, R E (ed.): *The encyclopedia of language and linguistics*, vol. 1, pp 29-35. Oxford: Pergamon Press.

Dixon, Roland & Alfred Kroeber (1913): Relationship of the Indian Languages of California. *Science* 37: 225.

Dolgopolsky, Aaron (1986): A probabilistic hypothesis concerning the oldest relationships among the language families of northern Eurasia. Shevoroshkin, V V & T L Markey (eds): *Typology, Relationship and Time: A Collection of Papers on Language Change and Relationship by Soviet Linguists*, pp. 27-50. Ann Arbor: Karoma.

Dong, Quang Phuc [=Jim McCawley] (1971): The Applicability of Transformations to Idioms. *Papers from the 7th Regional Meeting of the Chicago Linguistic Society*, pp 206-22.

Dunér, David (2002): Talsystem på kunglig befallning. *Forskning och Framsteg* 8-2002, pp 44-48.

Duponceau, Peter (1819): Report of the Corresponding Secretary to the Committee, of his Progress in the Investigation committed to him of the General Character and Forms of the Languages of the American Indians. *Transactions of the Historical and Literary Committee of the American Philosophical Society*, vol. 1, pp xvii-xlvi. Philadelphia: Abraham Small.

Dutton, Tom (1985): Police Motu: iena sivarai. Port Moresby: University of Papua New Guinea Press.

Dyen, I, J Kruskal & P Black (1997a: IE-TIME95. http://www. ldc.upenn.edu/ldc/service/comp-ie/IET)IME95. Downloaded 1997-10-30.

——, & —— (1997b): IE-RATE1. http://www.ldc. upenn. edu/ldc/service/comp-ie/IE-RATE1. Downloaded 1997-10-30.

Eckler, Ross (1992): The Ugliest Words in English. *Word Ways* pp 224-25.

Edwards, Gavin (1996): Dejpu'bogh Hov rur Qabllj! *Wired* 4.8: 84-93

—— (1999): Babble On Revisited. *Wired* 7 (8), p 66.

Edwards, John (1994): *Multilingualism*. Londen: Penguin.

Ehret, Christopher (2000): Language and History. Heine & Nurse (eds), pp 272-97.

Eichhorn, Johann Gottfried (1781): *Repertorium für biblische und morgenländische Literatur*, vol. 8. Leipzig.

Einarsson, Jan (1978): *Talad och skriven svenska*. Lund: Studentlitteratur.

Elbert, Samuel (1965): The 127 Rennellese possessives. In: *Acta Linguistica Hafniensia* 9: 16-24. Copenhagen. Nordisk Sprog- og Kulturforlag.

Elert, Claes-Christian & Britta Hammarberg (1991): Regionala variationer i röstkvalitet. Berge, Kjell Lars & Ulla-Britt Kotsinas (eds): *Storstadsspråk och storstadskultur i Norden*, pp 213-16. Stockholm: Institutionen för nordiska språk, Stockholms Universitet.

Elgin, Suzette Haden (1986): Hush my mouth. Waugh, Charles

& Martin Greenberg (eds): *Alternative Histories: Eleven Stories of the World As It Might Have Been*, pp 231-238. New York: Garland.

Emeneau, Murray (1939): The vowels of the Badaga language. *Language* 15: 43-47.

Endo, Orie (1999): World of Nüshu. http://www2.ttcn. ne.jp/ ~orie/. 2001-07-23.

Enfield, Nick (2005): Areal linguistics and mainland south-east Asia. *Annual Review of Anthropology* 34: 181-206.

Enwall, Joakim (1994-95): *A Myth Become Reality: History and Development of the Miao Written Language* (2 vols). Stockholm: Institute of Oriental Languages.

Europeiska kommissionens översättningstjänst (2001a): Europeiska kommissionens översättningstjänst. http://europa.eu.int/translation/en/eyl/sv.pdf. 2001-07-25.

—— (2001b): "EC Systran" – kommissionens system för maskinöversättning.http://europa.eu.int/comm/translation/en/eyl/ecmtsvsumm.pdf. 2001-07-25.

Evans, Nicholas (1998): Aborigines speak a primitive language. Bauer & Trudgill (eds), pp 159-68.

Evans, Nicholas & Toshiki Osad (2005): Mundari: The myth of a language without word classes. *Linguistic Typology* 9: 351-90.

Everett, Dan & Barbara Kern (1997): *Wari'*. London: Routledge.

Everett, Daniel (2004): Cultural Constraints on Grammar and Cognition in Pirahã: Another Look at the *Design Features of Human Language*. http://lings.ln.man.ac.uk/ info/staff/DE/ cultgram.pdf. 2004-07-22.

Faltz, Leonard (1998): *The Navajo verb*. Albuquerque: University of New Mexico Press.

Farfán, José Antonio Flores (2001): Nahuatl Purism: Between language innovation, maintenance and shift. Paper presented at the symposium *Purismus im Zeitalter der Globalisierung*, Universität Bremen, 18-21 September 2001.

Finegan, Edward (1999): *Language: Its Structure and Use*. Harcourt Brace.

Flournoy, Théodore (1983): Des Indes à la planète Mars. Paris: Le Seuil. (Original edition published in 1900.)

Foley, William (1986): *The Papuan Languages of New Guinea*. Cambridge: Cambridge University Press.

—— (1997): Anthropological linguistics. Oxford: Blackwell.

—— (2000): The languages of New Guinea. *Annual Review of Anthropology* 29: 357-404.

Foo, Yuck [=Jim McCawley] (1970): A Selectional Restriction Involving Pronoun Choice. Zwicky, Salus, Binnick & Vanek (eds).

Frank, Wright Jay (1999): *Nuer noun morphology*. MA thesis, University of New York at Buffalo.

Frege, Gottlob (1892): Über Sinn und Bedeutung. *Zeitschrift für Philosophie und philosophische Kritik* 100: 25-50.

Friedman, Victor (1996): Observing the Observers: Language, Ethnicity and Power in the 1994 Macedonian Census and Beyond. Rubin, Barnett (ed.): *Toward Comprehensive Peace in Southeastern Europe: Conflict Prevention in the South Balkans*. New York: Twentieth Century Fund Press, pp 81-105.

Friedrich, Paul (1970): Shape in grammar. *Language* 46: 379-407.

Fronval, George & Daniel Dubois (1978): *Indian signals and sign language*. New York: Wings Books.

Gair, James & Bruce Cain (1996): Dhivehi Writing. Daniel, Peter & William Bright (eds): *The World's writing systems*, pp 564-68. New York & Oxford: Oxford University Press.

Gajewski, Boleslas (1902): *Grammaire du Solrésol, ou langue universelle*. Paris.

Gallatin, Albert (1836): *A synopsis of the Indian tribes within the United States east of the Rocky Mountains, and in the British and Russian possessions in North America*. Cambridge: American Antiquarian Society.

Gant, Nathan (1997): More on Poliespo and its creator. *SSILA Bulletin* 58: 9.

Gardner, Allen & Beatrice Gardner (1969): Teaching sign language to a chimpanzee. *Science* 165: 664-72.

Gardner, Allen, Beatrice Gardner & Tomas van Cantfort (eds) (1989): Teaching Sign Language to Chim-panzees. Albany: State University of New York Press.

Garey, H B (1957): Verbal aspect in French. *Language* 33: 91-110.

Geach, Peter (1962): Reference and Generality. Ithaca: Cornell University Press.

George, Ken & George Broderick (1993): The Revived languages: Modern Cornish and Modern Manx. Ball, Martin & James Fife, pp 644-63.

Gibbons, John (2003): *Forensic linguistics*. Oxford: Blackwell.

Giles, Howard & Nacy Niedzelski (1998): Italian is beautiful, German is ugly. Bauer & Trudgill (eds), pp 85-93.

Gilley, Leoma (1992): *An Autosegmental Approach to Shilluk Phonology*. Dallas: International Academic Bookstore.

Githiora, Chege (2002): Sheng: Peer language, Swahili dialect or emerging creole? *Journal of African Cultural Studies* 15: 159-81.

Givón, Talmy (1971): Historical syntax and synchronic morphology: an archaeologist's field trip. *Proceedings of the Annual Meeting of the Chicago Linguistics Society* 7: 394-415.

Glebov, Sergei (2003): Science, Culture, and Empire: Eurasianism as a Modernist Movement. Chebotarev, Tanya & Jared Ingersoll (eds): *Russian and East European Books and Manuscripts in the United States*, pp 13-31. New York: Haworth Press.

Goldsmith, John (1976): An overview of autosegmental phonology. *Linguistic Analysis* 2: 23-68.

Golovko, Evgenij (1996): A case of nongenetic development in the Arctic area: The contribution of Aleut and Russian to the formation of Copper Island Aleut. Jahr & Broch (eds), pp 63-77.

Gomez-Imbert, E (1991): Force des langues vernaculaires en situation d'exogamie linguistique: le cas du Vaupès colombien, Nord-Ouest amazonien. *Cahiers des Sciences Humaines* 27: 535-59.

Gonçalves, Jorge & Maria Alexandra Peixoto (2001): *O menino selvagem*. Ms, Universidade de Lisboa.

Gordon, Matthew, Pamela Munro & Peter Ladefoged (2000): Some Phonetic Structures of Chickasaw. *Anthropological Linguistics* 42: 366-400.

Gove, Philip (1954): The History of Dord. *American Speech* 29: 136-38.

Graddol, David (1997): *The Future of English?* London: The British Council.

Grant, Anthony (1995a): The Development of Functional Categories in Grand Ronde Chinook Jargon. *Paper presented at the 2nd Westminster Creole Workshop, April 1995*.

—— (1996a): The evolution of functional categories in Grand Ronde Chinook Jargon: Ethnolinguistic and grammatical considerations. Baker & Syea (eds), *Changing meanings, changing functions*, pp 225-42, London: University of Westminster Press.

—— (1996b): Chinook Jargon and its distribution in the Pacific Northwest and beyond. Wurm et al. (eds), pp 1185-208.

Grau, Susan, Michael Robb & Anthony Cacace (1995): Acoustic Correlates of Inspiratory Phonation During Infant Cry. *Journal of Speech and Hearing Research* 38: 373-81.

Green, Diana (1997): Diferenças entre termos numéricos em algumas línguas indígenas do Brasil. *Boletim do Museu Paraense Emílio Goeldi, Série Antropologia* 12.2: 179-207.

—— (2001): Palikúr numerals. http://www.sil.org/americas/ brasil/ PUBLCNS/LING/EnglPLNB.pdf. 2002-09-08.

Green, Georgia (1972): Some Observations on the Syntax and Semantics of Instrumental Verbs. *Papers from the 8th Regional Meeting of the Chicago Linguistic Society*, pp 83-97.

Green, M M & G E Igwe (1963): *A descriptive grammar of Igbo*. Berlin: Akademienverlag.

Greenberg, Joseph (1956): The Measurement of Linguistic Diversity. *Language* 32: 109-15.

—— (1963): Some universals of grammar with particular reference to the order of meaningful elements. Greenberg, Joseph (ed.): *Universals of Grammar*, pp 73-113. Cambridge: MIT Press.

—— (ed.) (1978b): *Universals of Human Language*, vol. 2, Stanford: Stanford University Press.

Gregersen, Frans & Inge Lise Pedersen (2001): À la Recherche du Word Order Not Quite Perdu. Herring, Susan (ed.): *Textual Parameters in Older Languages*, pp 393-431. Philadelphia: Benjamins.

Grice, Paul (1975): Logic and conversation. Cole, Peter & Jerry Morgan (eds): *Syntax and Semantics*, vol. 3,   pp 41-58. New York: Academic Press.

Grimes, Charles & Kenneth Maryott (1994): Named speech registers in Austronesian languages. Dutton, Tom & Darrell Tryon (eds): *Language Contact and Change in the Austronesian World*, pp 275-319. Berlin & New York: Mouton de Gruyter.

Groce, Nora Ellen (1985): *Everyone Here Spoke Sign Language*. Cambridge: Harvard University Press.

Gruber, Jeffrey (1965): Studies in lexical relations. PhD thesis, MIT.

Gruzdeva, Ekaterina (2004): Numeral classifiers in Nivkh. *Sprachtypologie und Universalienforschung* 57: 300-29.

Guelke, Leonard (1988): The anatomy of a colonial settler population: Cape Colony 1657-1750. *International Journal of African Historical Studies* 21: 453-73.

Gunnemark, Erik (2000): Donald Kenrick as polyglot: could he be replaced by a machine? Acton, Thomas (ed.): *Scholarship and the gypsy struggle: commitment in Romani studies*. Hatfield: University of Hertfordshire Press.

Gustafson-äapková, Sofia (2005): *Integrating prosody into an account of discourse structure*. Stockholm: PhD dissertation, Stockholms Universitet.

Guthrie, Malcolm (1953): *The Bantu Languages of Western Equatorial Africa*. Oxford: Oxford University Press.

Guyot, Xavier (1997): Noms Révolutionnaires des communes de France. http://www.geneaguide.com/ onomastique/ revolution/k-nomrevol-generalites.htm. 2002-03-23.

Hagège, Claude (1974). Les pronoms logophoriques. *Bulletin de la Société de Linguistique de Paris* 69: 287-310.

Haiman, John (1979): Hua: a Papuan language of New Guinea. Shopen (ed.) (1979a), pp 35-89.

—— (1995): Grammatical signs of the divided self. A study of language and culture. Abraham, Werner, Talmy Givón & Sandra Thompson (eds): Discourse Grammar and Typology, pp 213-33. Amsterdam: Benjamins.

Hajek, John (2000): From Melanesia to the Deepest Darkest Africa: rare sounds, typology and distant convergence. Paper presented at the Research Center for Linguistic Typology, LaTrobe University, Melbourne, Australia, 2000-12-13.

Hajiãová, Eva, Petr Sgall, Jiãí Hana & Tomáš Hoskovec (2002): *Travaux du Cercle Linguistique de Prague*, vol. 4. Amsterdam & Philadelphia: John Benjamins.

Hale, Kenneth (1964): Classification of Northern Paman Languages, Cape York Peninsula, Australia. *Oceanic Linguistics* 3: 248-264.

—— (1973): Deep-surface disparities in relation to analysis and change: an Australian example. Sebeok (ed.): pp 401-58..

—— (1981): *On the position of Walbiri in a Typology of the Base*. Bloomington: University of Indiana.

—— (1991): Remarks on Sander's "Leveling in the history of the Polynesian passive formations. *Journal of the Polynesian Society* 100: 99-101.

Halle, Morris (1970): Is Kabardian a vowel-less language? *Foundations of Language* 10.6: 95-103.

Hamm, Cameron (2003): Sociolinguistic survey of the Kabalay langauge of Chad. http://www.sil.org/silesr/ 2003/silesr2003-008.pdf. 2003-07-31.

Hammarström, Göran (1971): The problem of nonsense linguistics. *Acta Societatis linguisticae Upsaliensis* 2.4: 99-109.

Hammarström, Harald (2002): The three-way quantity contrast of Estonian. Ms.

Hansegård, Nils Erik (1968): *Tvåspråkighet eller Halvspråkighet?* Stockholm: Aldus/Bonnier.

Hardman, Martha (1981): Jaqaru color terms. *International Journal of American Linguistics* 47: 66-68.

—— (2001): *Aymara*. Munich & Newcastle: LINCOM Europa.

Harley, Heidi (2002): WCO, ACD and QR of DPs. *Linguistic Inquiry* 33: 659-64.

Harman, Danna (2002): In Kabary, the Point Is to Avoid the Point. *Christian Science Monitor* 2002-03-09.

Harris, Allen (1993): Generative Semantics: Secret Handshakes, Anarchy Notes, and the Implosion of Ethos. *Rhetoric Review* 12: 125-159.

Harris, Zelig (1951): *Methods in structural lingustics*. Chicago: University of Chicago Press.

—— (1952): Discourse analysis. *Language* 28: 1-30, 474-94.

Haspelmath, M, M Dryer, D Gil & B Comrie (eds) (2005): *The World Atlas of Language Structures*. Oxford: Oxford University Press

Hausenberg, Anu-Reet (1998): Komi. Abondolo (ed.),   pp 305-26.

Haviland, John (1979): How to talk to your brother-in-law in Guugu Yimidhirr. Shopen (ed.) (1979b), pp 161-239.

Havlik, Ernst (1981): *Lexikon der Onomatopöien – Die lautimitierenden Wörter im Comic*. Frankfurt-am-Main: Verlag Dieter Fricke.

Hawes, Alex (1995): Machiavellian Monkeys & Shakespearean Apes: The Question of Primate Language. *ZooGoer* 24 (6).

Hayward, Richard (2000): Afroasiatic. Heine & Nurse (eds), pp 74-98.

Heath, Jeffrey (1981): A Case of Intensive Lexical Diffusion: Arnhem Land, Australia. *Language* 57: 335-67.

Heath, Shirley & Frederick Mandabach (1983): Language status decisions and the law in the United States. Cobarrubias, Juan & Joshua Fishman (eds): *Progress in language planning: international perspectives*, pp 87-105. Berlin: Mouton.

Heine, Bernd (1973): *Pidgin-Sprachen im Bantu-Bereich*. Berlin: Dietrich Riemer.

—— (1982): *The Nubi language of Kibera – an Arabic creole*. Berlin: Dietrich Reimer Verlag.

Heine, B, T Güldemann, C Kilian-Hatz, D Lessau, H Roberg, M Schladt, & T Stolz (1993): *Conceptual Shift. A lexicon of grammaticalization processes in African languages*. Cologne: Institut für Afrikanistik, Universität zu Köln.

Heine, Bernd & Derek Nurse (eds): *African Languages: an introduction*, pp 298-347. Cambridge: Cambridge University Press.

Helimski, Eugene (1998b): Selkup. Abondolo (ed.), pp 548-79.

Héran, François, Alexandra Filhon & Christine Deprez (2002): La dynamique des langues en France au fil du XXe siècle. *Population et Sociétés* 376.

Hermans, Judith (1999): *Klingon and it users: a socio-linguistic profile*. Tilburg: MA thesis, Universiteit van Tilburg.

Herodotus (1966): *The Histories by Herodotus*, book 2. Harmondsworth: Penguin Classics.

Hetzron, Robert (1967): Agaw numerals and incongruence in

Semitic. *Journal of Semitic Studies* 12: 169-97.

—— (1990b): Semitic languages. Comrie (ed.), pp 160-69.

—— (1990c): Hebrew. Comrie (ed.), pp 192-210.

Heurlin, Kaj & Ignacio Olagüe (1968): *Mundo hispano. Pequeño manual de civilización*. Lund: Gleerups förlag.

Hewitt, George (2005): North West Caucasian. *Lingua* 115: 91-145.

Higgins, John (2000): The Effle page. http://www.marlodge. supanet.com/museum/effle.html. 2003-11-28.

Himmelmann, Nikolaus (1997): Voice in two northern Sulawesi languages. Wouk, Fay & Malcolm Ross (eds): Proceedings of the Focus-Workshop at the 8th International Conference on Austronesian Linguistics. Taipei: Academia Sinica.

Hjelmslev, Louis (1935-37): La catégorie des cas. *Acta Jutlandica* 7.1: 1-184, and 7.2: 1-78.

Hock, Hans Heinrich (1991): *Principles of historical linguistics*. 2nd revised and updated edition. Berlin: Mouton de Gruyter.

Hockett, Charles (1947): Problems of morphemic analysis. *Language* 23: 321-43.

—— (1954): Two models of grammatical description. *Word* 10: 210-33.

—— (1955): *A manual of Phonology*. Baltimore: Indiana University.

—— (1958): A course in modern linguistics. New York: Macmillan.

Hoff, Berend (1994): Island Carib, an Arawakan language which incorporated a lexical register of Cariban origin, used to address men. Bakker & Mous (eds), pp 161-68.

Hoffman, Margit (1991): "Världsspråkens rötter". Om August Strindbergs hebreiska ABC-bok och språklära för nybörjare. *Judisk Krönika* 4-1991, pp 19-21.

Holden, Constance (2004): Life Without Numbers in the Amazon. *Science* 305 (5687), p 1093.

Holm, John (1989): Pidgins and Creoles. Vol. 2. Cambridge: Cambridge University Press.

Honan, William (1997): To Masters of Language, a Long Overdue Toast. *New York Times* 1997-12-31, p C21.

Honti, László (1993): *Die Grundzahlwörter der Uralischen Sprachen*. Budapest: Akadémiai Kiadó.

—— (1996): 9=9!. Ein Beitrag zur Lösung des Ratsels der 'neur' im Nordsamojedischen. *Linguistica Uralica* 32: 124-27.

Huber, Magnus (1998a): The origin and development of Krio: new linguistic and sociohistorical evidence. *Paper presented at the meeting for the Society for Pidgin and Creole linguistics*, New York, January 9-10, 1998.

—— (1998b): Restructuring in vitro: Evidence from early Krio. *Paper presented at the conference "Degrees of Restructuring in Creole languages"*, Regensburg, June 1998.

—— (1998c): Ghanaian Pidgin English. A sociohistorical and structural analysis. PhD thesis, Universität Essen.

Hudak, John (1990): Thai. Comrie (ed.), pp 29-47.

Hunkin, Galumaleman Afeleti (1988): *Gagana Samoa: A Samoan language course book*. Auckland. Polynesian Press.

Hurford, James (2003): The Neural Basis of Predicate-Argument Structure. *Behavioral and Brain Sciences* 23.6: 261-83.

Hutchins, John (1995): Machine Translation: a brief history. Koerner, E F K & R E Asher (eds): *Concise history of the language sciences: from the Sumerians to the cognitivists*, pp 431-45. Oxford: Pergamon Press

—— (1997): First steps in mechanical translation. Teller, Virginia & Beth Sundheim (eds): *MT Summit VI: past, present, future*, pp 14-23. Washington: Association for Machine Translation in the Americas.

Hyltenstam, Kenneth (1997): Om begreppen språk och dialekt och meänkielis status som eget språk. Westergren, Eva & Hans Åhl (eds): Mer än ett språk. Stockholm: Norstedts Förlag.

Hyman, Larry (2001): On phonological weight. Kreidler, Charles (ed.): *Phonology: Critical concepts*, vol 3., pp 143-95. London: Routledge.

Igué, Mamoud Akanni & Raphaël Windali N'Ouéni (1993): The politics of language in Bénin. Fardon, Richard (ed.): *African Languages: Development and the State*, pp 55-61. London: Routledge.

Inoue, Kyoko (1979): Japanese: A story of language and people. Shopen (ed.) (1979b), pp 241-300.

Inouye, Sakae (2003): SARS transmission: language and droplet production. *The Lancet* 362, p 370.

Irvine, Judith (1974): Strategies of status manipulation in the Wolof greeting. Bauman & Sherzer (eds), pp 167-91.

—— (2001): "Style" as distinctiveness: the culture and ideology of linguistic differentiation. Eckert, Penelope & John Rickrod (eds): *Style and sociolinguistic variation*, pp 21-43. Cambridge: Cambridge University Press.

Isaak, Mark (2001): Curiosities of Biological Nomenclature. http://www.best.com/~atta/taxonomy.html. 2001-05-17.

Izre'el, Shlomo (2000): The Emergence of Spoken Israeli Hebrew. Paper presented at the syposium *Corpus Linguistics and the Study of Modern Hebrew*, Emory University, Atlanta, February 3-4, 2000.

Jackendoff, Ray (1972): *Semantic Interpretation in Generative Grammar*. Cambridge: MIT Press.

Jacobsen, William (1967): Switch-reference in Hokan-Coahuiltecan. Hymes, Dell & William Bittle (eds): *Studies in Southwestern ethnolinguistics*, pp 238-63. The Hague: Mouton.

—— (1979): Noun and Verb in Nootkan. Efrat, Barbara (ed.): *The Victoria Conference on Northwestern Languages*, pp 83-155. Victoria: British Columbia Provincial Museum.

—— (1986): The heterogeneity of evidentials in Makah. Chafe, Wallace & Johanna Nichols (eds): *Evidentiality: The linguistic coding of epistemology*, pp 159-67. Norwood: Ablex.

Jacottet, E (1906): A practical method to learn Sesuto with exercises and a short vocabulary. Morija: Sesuto Book Depot.

Jahr, Ernst Håkon (1996): On the pidgin status of Russenorsk. Jahr & Broch (eds), pp 107-22.

Jahr, E H & I Broch (eds) (1996): *Language contact in the Arctic. Northern pidgins and contact languages*. Berlin: Mouton de Gruyter.

Jakobson, Roman (1929): Remarques sur l'évolution phonologique du russe comparée à celle des autres langues slaves. *Travaux du cercle linguistique de Prague* 2.

—— (1959): On Linguistic Aspects of Translation. Brower, Reuben (ed.): *On translation*, pp 232-39. Cambridge: Harvard University Press.

Jankowski, Hans (1994): *Esperantomono: ilustrita historio pri universala monsistemo*. [n pl]: Libera Esperanto-Asocio.

Janson, Tore (1997): *Språken och historien*. Stockholm: Norstedts Förlag.

Jespersen, Otto (1933): *Essentials of English Grammar*. London: Allen & Unwin.

—— (1937): *Analytic Syntax*. London: Allen & Unwin.

Jesse, C (1956): *Outlines of St Lucia's history*. Castries: The Voice Publishing Co.

Johannisson, Ture (1973): *Ett språkligt signalement*. Gothemburg: Göteborgs Universitet.

Johansson, Ulf & Mona Neppenström (1991): *Det visste du inte!* Stockholm: Det Bästa.

Johnson, Samuel Victor (1978): *Chinook Jargon: A computer assisted analysis of variation in an American Indian Pidgin*. PhD thesis, University of Kansas.

Johnston, Judith & Dan Slobin (1979): The development of locative expressions in English, Italian, Serbo-Croatian and Turkish. *Journal of Child Language* 6: 529-45.

Jones, Alan (1996): Privately owned Mekeo-based trade

languages. Wurm et al. (eds), pp 219-24.

Jones, Daniel (1950): *The phoneme: its nature and use.* Cambridge: W. Heffner.

Jones, Mari (2001): *Jersey Norman French. A Linguistic Study of an Obsolescent Dialect.* Oxford: Blackwell.

Joseph, Brian (2003): Evidentials: Summation, questions, prospects. Aikhenvald & Dixon (eds), pp 308-27.

Joseph, Brian & Arnold Zwicky (eds) (1990): *When verbs collide: Papers from the 1990 Ohio State Mini-Conference on Serial Verbs.* Columbus: Ohio State University.

Judd, Elizabeth (1980): Hallucinogens and the Origin of Language. *Sociolinguistics Newsletter* 11.2: 7-12.

Kaminski, Juliane, Josep Call & Julia Fischer (2004): Word Learning in a Domestic Dog: Evidence for "Fast Mapping". *Science* 304, pp 1682-83.

Kaminski, Robert & Raymond Bore (2002): Z E O – Zamenhof / Esperanto-objektoj. http://www.ikki.com. pl/esperant/zeo/. 2002-06-27.

Kanazawa, Makoto (1993): *Weak vs. strong readings of donkey sentences and monotonicity inference in a dynamic setting.* Amsterdam: Institute for Logic, Language and Computation.

Karimova, Nigar & Edward Deverell (2001): *Minorities in Turkey.* Stockholm: Utrikespolitiska institutet

Karlsson, Fred (1994): Linguistics in the light of citation analysis. *Publications of the Department of General Linguistics of the University of Helsinki,* no. 23.

Katamba, Francis (1983): *An introduction to phonology.* London & New York: Longman.

Katzner, Kenneth (1994): *Languages of the world* (3rd revised edition). London: Routledge.

Kay, Martin (1979): Functional Grammar. *Proceedings of the Fifth Berkley Linguistics Society Meeting,* pp 142-58.

Keenan, Edward & Ellinor Ochs (1979): Becoming a competent speaker of Malagasy. In: Shopen (ed.) (1979b), pp 113-59.

Kegl, Judy, Ann Senghas & Marie Coppola (2001): Creation through Contact: Language Emergence and Sign Language Change in Nicaragua. DeGraff, Michel (ed.), *Language creation and language change. Creolization, diachrony, and development,* pp 179–238, Cambridge: MIT Press,.

Kelley, Walter & Tony McGregor (2001): Keresan Pueblo Indian Sign Language. Paper Presented at the Deaf Studies 7 Conference, Orlando, Florida, April 2001.

Kellnerova, Stanislava & Melvyn Clarke (1997): The Czechs have a word for it. http://www.geocities. com/Athens/ Forum/7953/ word.html. 2002-12-31.

Kelz, Heinrich (2001): Sprachpolitik auf den Philippinen. Paper presented at the symposium *Purismus im Zeitalter der Globalisierung,* Universität Bremen, 18-21 September 2001.

Kibrik, āleksandr ävgenevich (1997): Beyond subject and object: Toward a comprehensive relational typology. *Linguistic Typology* 1: 279-346.

Kim, Nam-Kil (1990): Korean. Comrie (ed.), pp 153-70.

King, Gareth (1993): *Modern Welsh: A comparative grammar.* London & New York: Routledge.

Kiparsky, Paul (1965): Phonological change. PhD dissertation, MIT.

Kite, B (2002): Slips of the Tongue: English as a Really Foreign Language. *The Village Voice,* Education Supplement, 2002-08-07.

Klima, Edward (1964): Negation in English. Fodor, Jerry & Jerrold Katz (eds): *The structure of language,* pp 246-323. Englewood Cliffs: Prentice-Hall.

Klomp, Ank (1993): The Legitimacy of the Cacique, the 1989 Municipal Elections on St Martin, F W I. *Annales des Pays d'Amérique latine et des Caraïbes* 11-12, pp 249-74.

Kluge, T (1955): Über eine bisher übersehene Sprachen-gruppe mit Knacklauten (Schnalzen, click). *Orbis* 4: 432-51.

Koerner, Konrad (1989): *Practicing Linguistic Historio-graphy.* Amsterdam: Benjamins.

—— (1999): *Linguistic Historiography: Projects and Prospects.* Amsterdam: Benjamins.

Köhler, Wolfgang (1929): *Gestalt Psychology.* New York: Liveright.

Kolin, Philip (1979): *Successful Writing at Work.* Boston: Houghton Mifflin Company.

Konstantin, Phil (2002): Tribal Names and their meanings. http://www.americanindian.net/names.html. 2002-02-28.

Koon, Jeff, Andy Powell & Ward Schumaker (2002): *You May Not Tie an Alligator to a Fire Hydrant: 101 Real Dumb Laws.* [n pl]: Free Press.

Kornoussova, Bossia (2001): Language policy in Russia: focus on Kalmyckia. Paper presented at the symposium *Purismus im Zeitalter der Globalisierung,* Universität Bremen, 18-21 September 2001.

Kouwenberg, Silvia & Pieter Muysken (1994): Papiamento. Arends, J, P Muysken & N Smith (eds), *Pidgins and Creoles. An introduction,* Amsterdam: Benjamins, pp 205-18.

Krakovska, Violetta (2004): Lithuanian language policy. Paper presented at the conference *The Baltic States: New Europe or Old?,* University of Glasgow 22-23 January 2004.

Krashen, Stephen & Natalie Kiss (1996): Notes on a Polyglot: Kato Lomb. *System* 24.2: 207-10.

Krauss, Michael (1973a): Eskimo-Aleut. Sebeok (ed.), pp 796-902..

—— (1973b): Eskimo-Aleut. Sebeok (ed.), pp 903-78.

Krier, Fernande (1999): Obituary on André Martinet (1908-1999). *The Phonetician* 80.2: 13-14.

Kristof, Nicholas (1995): Japanese women begin to find their own voices. *Vancouver Sun* 1995-12-23, p B5.

Kube, Sabine (2005): *La francophonie vécue en Côte d'Ivoire.* Paris: l'Harmattan.

Kudryavtsev, Eduard & Louis-Dominique Ouedraogo (2003): *Le multilinguisme dans le système des Nations Unies.* Geneva: United Nations.

Kuipers, Aert (1960): *Phoneme and Morpheme in Kabardian (Eastern Adyghe).* The Hague: Mouton.

—— (1968): Unique types and typological universals. Heesterman, J C et al. (eds): *Pratidanam: Indian, Iranian and Indo-European studies presented to F B J Kuipers,* pp 68–88. The Hague: Mouton.

Kumakhov, M A (1973): Teorija monovokalizma i zapadno-kavkazskie jazyki. *Boprosy Jazykoznanija* 6: 54-67.

Kuschel, Rolf (1973): The Silent Inventor: The Creation of a Sign Language by the Only Deaf-Mute on a Polynesian Island. *Sign Language Studies* 3: 1-28.

—— (1974): *A Lexicon of Signs from a Polynesian Outlier Island. A Description of 217 Signs as Developed and Used by Kagobai, the only Deaf-Mute on Rennell Island.* Copenhagen: Akademisk Forlag.

Kutscher, Eduard Yechezkel (1984): *A history of the Hebrew language.* 2nd edition. Jerusalem: The Magnes Press.

Laakso, Johanna (2001): The Finnic languages. Dahl, Östen & Maria Koptjevskaja-Tamm (eds): *Circum-Baltic Languages.* Vol. 1: *Past and Present,* pp 179-212. Philadelphia: Benjamins.

Labov, William (1966): *The social stratification of English in New York City.* Washington: Center for Applied Linguistics.

—— (1970): The study of language in its social context. *Studium generale* 23: 30-87.

—— (1972): *Language in the Inner City: Studies in the Black English Vernacular.* Philadelphia: University of Pennsylvania Press.

Ladefoged, Peter & Dan Everett (1996): The status of phonetic rarities. *Language* 72: 794-800.

Lafage, Suzanne (1985): *Français écrit et parlé en pays éwé (Sud-*

Togo). Paris: SÉLAF.

Lakoff, George (1968): Instrumental Adverbs and the Concept of Deep Structure. *Foundations of Language* 4: 4-29.

—— (1972): Linguistics and natural logic. Davidson, Donald & Gilbert Harman (eds): *Semantics of Natural Language*, pp 545-65. Dordrecht: D Reidel.

—— (1987): *Women, Fire, and Dangerous Things*. Chicago: University of Chicago Press.

Lakoff, Robin T (1971): Passive Resistance. *Papers from the 7th Regional Meeting of the Chicago Linguistic Society*, pp 149-61.

—— (1977): What You can do with Words: Politeness, Pragmatics and Performatives. Rogers, Andy, Robert Wall & J P Murphy (eds): *Proceedings of the Texas Conference on Performatives, Presupposition and Implicature*, pp 78-106. Arlington: Center for Applied Linguistics.

—— (1989): The way we were; or, The Real Truth about Generative Semantics: A memoir. *Journal of Pragmatics* 13: 939-88.

Laman, K E (1912): *Lärobok i Kongospråket (Kikongo)*. Stockholm: Svenska Missionsförbundets expedition.

Lamb, Sydney (1971): The Crooked Path of Progress in Cognitive Linguistics. *Georgetown University Monograph Series on Languages and Linguistics* 24: 99-123.

Lambert, Richard (1999): The Winds of Change in Foreign Language Instruction. *International Educator* 8 (2).

Lapenna, Ivo (1960): *Memorlibro eldonita okaze de la centjara datreveno de la naski o de D-ro L Zamenhof*. London: Universala Esperanto-Asocio.

LaPolla, Randy (2005): Typology and complexity. Minett, James & William Wang (eds): *Language Acquisition, Change and Emergence: Essays in evolutionary linguistics*. Hong Kong: City University of Hong Kong Press. [pagination refers to pre-print version]

Lareau, Paul (2003): Who's who on Pitcairn. http://www.lareau. org/pitcres.html. 2003-08-14.

Large, Andrew (1985): *The artificial language movement*. Oxford: Blackwell.

Lasersohn, Peter (2000): Top Ten Linguists Who Were Famous for Other Things, or Famous People Who Were Also Linguists. http://www.linguistics.uiuc.edu/lasersoh/famous. html. 2002-12-27.

Laubenberger, Franz & Steven Rowan (1982): The Naming of America. *Sixteenth Century Journal* 13.4: 91-113.

Laver, John (1994): *Principles of Phonetics*. Cambridge: Cambridge University Press.

Laycock, Donald (1987): Stephen Wurm: a linguistic migration. Laycock & Winter (eds), pp 3-14.

Laycock, Donald & Werner Winter (eds): *A World of Language: Papers Presented to Professor S A Wurm on His 65th Birthday*. Canberra: Department of Linguistics, Australian National University.

Leclerc, Jacques (2000-2006): L'aménagement linguistique dans le monde. http://www.ciral.ulaval.ca/alx/ amlxmonde/ monde.htm. Accessed at various times from 2001-06-05 onwards.

Lees, R B (1960): A Multiply Ambiguous Adjectival Construction in English. *Language* 36: 207-21.

Lee-Smith, Mei W & Stephen A Wurm (1996): The Wutun language. Wurm et al. (eds), pp 883-97.

Lestienne, Cécile & Denise Péricard-Méa (eds) (1997): *Nya fakta om världens mysterier*. Stockholm: Det Bästa.

Lewis, Geoffrey (1967): *Turkish Grammar*. Oxford: Oxford University Press.

Li, Charles & Sandra Thompson (1979): Chinese: Dialect variation and language reform. Shopen (ed.) (1979a), pp 295-335.

—— & —— (1990): Chinese. Comrie (ed.), pp 83-105.

Li, Xueqin, Garman Harbottle, Juzhong Zhang & Changsui Wang (2003): The earliest writing? Sign use in the seventh millennium BC at Jiahu, Henan Province, China. *Antiquity* 77: 31-43.

Lichtenberk, Frantisek (2005): On the Notion "Adjective" in Toqabaqita. *Oceanic Linguistics* 44: 113-44.

Liming, Wei (1998): Découverte du foyer d'origine des Yao. *Beijing Information* 41 (48), Novermber 20, 1998.

Lins, Ulrich (1988): *La Dan era Lingvo*. Gerlingen: Bleicher Eldonejo.

Lisker, L & A S Abramson (1964): A cross-language study of voicing in initial stops: acoustic measurements. *Word* 20: 384-422.

Lithgow, David (1973): Language change on Woodlark Island. *Oceania* 44: 101-08.

—— (1987): Language change and relationships in Tubetube and adjacent languages. Laycock & Winter (eds), pp 393-410.

Lodge, Anthony (1993): *French: From Dialect to Standard*. Florence: Routledge

Loos, Eugene (1999): Pano. Dixon & Aikhenvald (eds), pp 227-50.

Loutkotka, āestmír (1955): Les Indiens Botocudo et leur Langue. *Lingua Posnaniensis* 5: 112-35.

Lorcduy, L (1981): Pitch, politeness, and sexual role: an exploratory investigation. *Language and Speech* 24: 71-88.

Lowe, Ivan (1999): Nambiquara. Dixon & Aikhenvald (eds), pp 268-91.

Luxardo, Hervé (1994): Quand les communes de France se débaptisent. *Historia* 572: 62-67.

Lynch, John (1998): *Pacific Languages*. Honolulu: University of Hawai'i Press.

Lyons, Christopher (1998): *Definiteness*. Cambridge University Press.

Lyovin, Anatole V (1997): *An Introduction to the Languages of the World*. New York: Oxford University Press.

Mac Eoin, Gearóid (1993): Irish. Ball, Martin & James Fife, pp 101-44.

MacLaury, Robert (2001): Color Terms. Haspelmath, Martin, Ekkehard König, Wulf Oesterreicher & Wolfgang Raible (eds): *Language Typology and Language Universals: An International Handbook*, pp 1227-52. Berlin: de Gruyter.

Maddieson, Ian (1978): Universals of Tone. Greenberg (ed.) (1978b), pp 335-65.

—— (1984): *Patterns of Sounds*. Cambridge: Cambridge University Press.

Maher, Julianne (1997b): French and Creole on St. Barthélemy and St Thomas. Valdman, A (ed.), *French and Creole in Louisiana*, pp 237-53, New York: Plenum Press.

Malkiel, Yakov (1993): *Etymology*. Cambridge: Cambridge University Press.

Malkiel, Yakov & Marvin Herzog (1967): Uriel Weinreich (1926-1967). *Language* 43: 605-10.

Manaris, Bill (1998): Natural Language Processing: A Human–Computer Interaction Perspective. Marvin Zelkowitz (ed.): *Advances in Computers* 47: 1-66. San Diego: Academic Press.

Manavit, Augustin (1853): *Esquisse historique sur le cardinal Mezzofanti*. Paris: Sagnier et Bray.

Marçais, W (1930): La diglossie arabe. *L'enseignement public* 97: 401-09.

Mardin, S (1962): *The Genesis of Young Ottoman Thought. A Study in the Modernization of Turkish Political Ideas*. Princeton: Princeton University Press.

Mariscal, Antonio (1996): Multilinguality/Mezzofanti. *Linguist List* 7.1129.

Martin, Laura (1986): Eskimo words for snow: A case study in the genesis and decay of an anthropological example. *American Anthropologist* 88: 418-23.

dumblaws.com/. 2002-11-24.

Premack, David (1971): Language in a chimpanzee? *Science* 172: 808-22.

Prokosch, Erich (1986): *Arabische Kontaktsprachen (Pidgin- und Kreolsprachen) in Afrika*. Graz: Universität Graz.

Pullum, Geoff (1991): *The great Eskimo vocabulary hoax and other irreverent essays on the study of languages*. Chicago: University of Chicago Press.

Racter, William Chamberlain & Thomas Etter (1984): *The Policeman's Beard is Half Constructed*. New York: Warner Books.

Ramsey, Robert (1987): *The languages of China*. Princeton: Princeton University Press.

Ramsland, Katherine (2000): Literary Forensics. http://www.crimelibrary.com/forensics/literary/. 2002-08-18.

—— (2001): Forensic Voiceprints. http://www.crimelibrary.com/forensics/voice/. 2002-08-18.

Rao, Giridhar (1999): La plej frua skribo? *Monato* 8/1999, p 12.

Rea, Joy (1964): On the naming of America. *American Speech* 39: 42-50.

Reap, Simon (2002): Derek Bentley Page. http://web1.pipemedia.net/~sar/bentley/db_main.html. 2002-07-13.

Reed, Jan (1995): Theory of linguistic derivation. http://www.tc.umn.edu/~reed0180/page3.html. 2002-08-23.

Reisman, Karl (1974): Contrapuntal conversations in an Antiguan village. Bauman & Sherzer (eds), pp 110-24.

Remijsen, Bert (2002): Lexically contrastive stress accent and lexical tone in Ma'ya. Gussenhoven, Carlos & Natasha Warner (eds): *Laboratory Phonology* 7, pp.585–614. Berlin: Mouton de Gruyter.

Renfrew, Colin (1987): *Archaeology and Language: The Puzzle of the Indo-European Origins*. London: Jonothan Cape.

Ridouane, Rachid (2002a): Le statut du schwa en berbère chleuh. *XXIVèmes Journées d'Étude sur la Parole, Nancy, 24-27 juin 2002*, pp 29-32.

—— (2002b): Words without Vowels: Phonetic and Phonological Evidence from Tashlhiyt Berber. *ZAS Papers in Linguistics* 28: 93-110.

—— (2004): Les mots sourds en berbère chleuh: analyses fibroscopiques et photoglottographiques. *XXVèmes Journées d'Étude sur la Parole, Fès (Maroc), 19-22 avril 2004*. (no pagination)

Rischel, Jørgen (1995): *Minor Mlabri: A Hunter-Gatherer Language of Northern Indochina*. Copenhagen: Museum Tusculanum Press, University of Copenhagen.

Rivarol, Antoine de (1783) [1991]: *L'Universalité de la langue française*. 1991 edition: Paris: Arléa.

Rivera-Castillo, Yolanda (1998): Tone and stress in Papiamentu: The contribution of a constraint-based analysis to the problem of creole genesis. *Journal of Pidgin and Creole Languages* 13: 297-334.

Rivers, Napoleon (1934): Why Negroes Should Study Romance Languages and Literatures. *Journal of Negro History* 19: 118-36.

Robinson, Andrew (1998): *Skrivkonsten: uppkomst och historia*. Stockholm: Forum.

Rodrigues, Aryon (1999a): Tupí.Dixon & Aikhenvald (eds), pp 107-24.

—— (1999b): Macro-Jê. Dixon & Aikhenvald (eds), pp 164-206.

Röllinger, Hugo (1997): *Monumente pri Esperanto. Ilustrita dokumentaro pri 1044 Zamenhof/Esperanto-objektoj en 54 landoj*. Rotterdam: Universala Esperanto-Asocio.

Romey, Kristin & Mark Rose (2001): Saga of the Persian Princess. *Archaeology* 54: 24-25.

Rosen, Robert, Marshall Singer & Patricia Digh (2000): *Global Literacies: Lessons on Business Leadership and National Cultures*. London: Simon & Schuster.

Rosenbaum, Peter (1967): *The grammar of English Predicate Complement Constructions*. Cambridge: MIT Press.

Rosenfelder, Mark (2001): *Language Family Information for the Numbers List*. http://www.zompist.com/families.htm. 2001-07-09.

—— (2002): They Thought You'd Say This: Unlikely phrases from real phrasebooks. http://www.zompist.com/thought.html. 2002-08-19

Ross, John Robert (1967): Constraints on variables in syntax. PhD thesis, MIT.

Ross, Nigel (1995): Dubbing American in Italy. *English Today* 41: 45-48.

Rowlands, E. C. (1959): *A Grammar of Gambian Mandinka*. London: School of Oriental and African Studies.

Rumbaugh, Duane (1977): The Emergence and State of Ape Language Research. Bourne, Geoffrey (ed.): *Progress in Ape Research*, pp. 75-83. New York: Academic Press.

Rumbaugh, D M, H Warner & E von Glasersfeld (1977): The LANA Project: Origins and Tactics. In: Rumbaugh, Duane (ed.): Language Learning by a Chimpanzee: The Lana Project, pp 87-90. New York: Academic Press.

Russell, Bertrand (1905): On Denoting. *Mind* 14: 479-93.

—— (1948): *Human Knowledge - Its Scope And Limits*. London: George Allen and Unwin.

Russell, Charles William (1858): *The life of Cardinal Mezzofanti; with an introductory memoir of eminent linguists, ancient and modern*. London, Longmann.

Saarelma-Maunumaa, Minna (2003): *Edhina ekogidho – Names as links. The encounter between African and European anthroponymic systems among the Ambo people in Namibia*. Helsinki: PhD thesis, University of Helsinki.

Sadock, Jerold (1974): Read at Your Own Risk: Syntactic and Semantic Horrors You Can Find in Your Medicine Chest. Papers from the 10th Regional Meeting of the Chicago Linguistic Society, pp 599-607.

Sagan, Carl (1979): *Broca's Brain*. Random House: New York.

Sallabank, Julia (2003): "It won't be the Guernsey French we know": identity issues and language endangerment. *Reading Working Papers in Linguistics* 7: 181-209.

Salverda, Reinier (1990): Linguistics and the Dutch. Inaugural Lecture delivered at University College London, 26 November 1990.

Samarin, William (1982): Colonization and Pidginization of the Ubangi River. *Journal of African Languages and Linguistics* 4: 1-42.

Samb, Amar (1983): *Initiation à la grammaire wolof*. Initiations et études africaines 33. Dakar: Institut Fondamental d'Afrique Noire.

Sammallahti, Pekka (1998): Saamic. Abondolo (ed.), pp 43-95.

Sampson, Geoffrey (1985): *Writing systems*. London: Hutchinson.

San Martin, Itziar (1999): Notes on obviation. Paper presented at the University of Maryland Linguistics Student Conference, College Park, November 11-12, 1999.

Sanders, Gerald (1990): On the analysis and implications of Maori verb alternations. *Lingua* 80: 150-98.

—— (1991): Levelling and reanalysis in the history of Polynesian passive formations. *Journal of the Polynesian Society* 100: 71-90.

Sandfeld, Kristian (1930): *Linguistique balkanique*. Paris: Champion.

Sandler, Wendy, Irit Meir, Carol Padden & Mark Aronoff (2005): *The emergence of grammar: Systematic structure in a new language*. Proceedings of the National Academy of Sciences 102.7: 2661-65.

Sapir, Edward (1915): *Abnormal types of speech in Nootka*. Ottawa: Government Printing Bureau.

—— (1921): *Language: An Introduction to the Study of Speech*. New York: Harcourt & Brace.

—— (1929): Male and Female Forms of Speech in Yana. Teeuwen, S W J (ed.): *Donum Natalicium Schrijnen*, pp. 79-85. Nijmegen-Utrecht: Dekker en Van De Vegt.

Saussure, Ferdinand de (1916): *Cours de linguistique générale*. Paris: Payot

Savage-Rumbaugh, Sue & Lewin, Roger (1994): *Kanzi: The Ape at the Brink of the Human Mind*. New York: John Wiley.

Savage-Rumbaugh, S, D Rumbaugh & S Boysen (1978): *Symbolic Communication Between Two Chimpanzees* (Pan troglodytes). *Science* 201: 641-44.

Schiffman, Harold (1995): Language shift in the Tamil communities of Malaysia and Singapore: The paradox of egalitarian language policy. *Southwest Journal of Linguistics* 14: 151-65.

Schlegel, August Wilhelm von (1818): *Observations sur la langue et la littérature provençales*. Paris: Librairie grecque-latin-allemande.

Schlobinski, Peter (2001): Knuddel-zurückknuddel-dich ganzdollknuddel. Inflectives and Inflective Construc-tions in German. *Zeitschrift für germanistische Linguistik* 29. 192 010.

Schlyter, Birgit (2003): Sociolinguistic changes in transformed Central Asian societies. Maurais, Jacques (ed.): *Languages in a Globalising World*. West Nyack: Cambridge University Press, pp 157-87.

Schmerling, Susan (1971): Presupposition and the Notion of Normal Stress. *Papers from the 7th Regional Meeting of the Chicago Linguistic Society*, pp 242-53.

Schmidt, Gerhard (1955): Thinking and language. *Orbis* 4: 66-73.

Schultze, Leonhart (1928): *Zur Kenntis des Körpers der Hottentotten und Buschmänner*. Jena: G Fischer.

Scott, N C (1941): Broad Transcription. *Le Maître Phonétique* 76: 48-51.

Seaman, David (1996): *Hopi dictionary*. Flagstaff: Department of Anthropology, Northern Arizona University.

Searle, John (1975): Indirect speech acts. Cole, P & J L Morgan (eds): *Speech Acts*, pp 59-82. New York: Academic Press.

Sebeok, Thomas (ed.) (1966): *Portraits of Linguists: A Biographical Sourcebook for the History of Western Linguistics 1746-1963*. Bloomington: Indiana University Press.

—— (ed.) (1973): *Current Trends in Linguistics*, vol. 10. The Hague: Mouton.

Seguin, Edward (1907): *Idiocy: And Its Treatment By The Physiological Method*. New York: Teachers' College, Columbia University

Seibicke, Wilfried (1991): *Vornamen*. Frankfurt am Main: Verlag für Standesamtswesen.

Seiler, Walter (1985): *Imonda, a Papuan Language*. Canberra: Pacific Linguistics.

Sekerina, Irina (1994): Copper Island (Mednyj) Aleut (CIA): A Mixed Language. *Languages of the World* 8: 14-31.

Selinker, Larry (1972): Interlanguage. *International Review of Applied Linguistics* 10: 209-31.

Selkirk, Elisabeth (1982): The syllable. Hulst, H van der & N Smith (eds): *The Structure of Phonological Representations*, vol. 2, pp 337-83.

Senft, Gunter (1996): *Classificatory Particles in Kilivila*. Oxford: Oxford University Press.

Senghor, Léopold Sédar (1944a): Les classes nominales en wolof et les substantifs à initiale nasale. *Journal de la Société des Africanistes* 14: 109-22.

—— (1944b): L'harmonie vocalique en Sérère (dialecte du Dyéguème). *Journal de la Société des Africanistes* 14: 17-23.

—— (1947): L'article conjonctif en Wolof. *Journal de la société des africanistes* 17: 19-22.

Seuren, Pieter (1998): *Western Linguistics. An Historical Introduction*. Oxford: Blackwell Publishers.

Shaul, David Leedom (2002): In the Last Days of Living Latin: The Dynamic and Realities of Twilight Linguistics. *Texas Linguistic Forum* 44.2: 401-12.

Shaw, Karen (1993): Somewhere between the word and the sentence: The great apres and the acquisition of language. Ms.

Sherzer, Jori (1973): Areal linguistics in North America. Sebeok, Thomas (ed.), pp 749-95.

Shevoroshkin, Vitaly (1995): Genetic relatedness of languages. Figge, Udo (ed.): *Language in the Würm Glaciation*, pp 167-76. Bochum: Brockmeyer.

Shibatani, Masayoshi (1990a): Japanese. Comrie (ed.), pp 127-52.

—— (1990b): *The languages of Japan*. Cambridge: Cambridge University Press.

Shopen, T (ed.) (1979a): *Languages and their status*. Cambridge: Winthrop Publishers.

—— (ed.) (1979b): *Languages and their speakers*. Philadelphia: University of Philadelphia Press.

Siegel, Jeff (1987): *Language contact in a plantation environment*. Cambridge: Cambridge University Press.

Silverman, Franklin (1988): The "monster" study. *Journal of Fluency Disorders* 13: 225-31.

Silverstein, Michael (1976): Hierarchy of features and ergativity. Dixon, Robert (ed.): *Grammatical Categories in Australian Languages*, pp 112-71. Canberra: AIAS.

Sinclair, Kevin & Iris Po-Yee Wong (1991): *Culture Shock: China*. Portland: Graphic Arts Center Publishing Company.

Singh, Simon (1999): *Kodboken*. Stockholm: Norstedts. [Swedish translation of the British original *The Code Book*].

Slezkine, Yuri (1996): N Ia Marr and the national origins of Soviet ethnogenesis. *Slavic Review* 55: 826-62.

Slobin, Dan (1982): Universal and particular in the acquisition of language. Wanner, Eric & Lila Gleitman (eds): *Language acquisition: The state of the art*,   pp 128-70. Cambridge: Cambridge University Press.

Smith, Neil (1996): Colourful language. *Glot International* 2.6: 9.

—— (1999): *Noam Chomsky: Ideas and Ideals*. Cambridge: Cambridge University Press.

Smith, Neil & Ianthi Maria Tsimpli (1991): Linguistic Modularity? A Case Study of a 'Savant' Linguist. *Lingua* 84: 315-51.

—— & —— (1995): *The Mind of a Savant: language, learning and modularity*. Oxford: Blackwell.

Smith, Neil, Ianthi-Maria Tsimpli & Jamal Ouhalla (1993): Learning the Impossible: The Acquisition of Possible and Impossible Languages by a Polyglot Savant. *Lingua* 91: 279-347.

Snyman, Jan (1970): *An introduction to the !X (!Kung) language*. Cape Town: School of African Studies, University of Cape Town.

Söderberg, Bertil & Ragnar Widman (1966): *Kikongo*. Nordiska Afrikainstitutets Språkhandböcker 2. Stockholm: Svenska Bokförlaget.

Sohn, Ho-Min (1999): *The Korean language*. Cambridge: Cambridge University Press.

Sokal, Alan (1996): Transgressing the Boundaries: Toward a Transformative Hermeneutics of Quantum Gravity. *Social Text* 46/47: 217-52.

Sorensen, Arthur (1967): Multilingualism in the Northwest Amazon. *American Anthropologist* 69: 670-84.

Spears, Richard (1967): *Basic Course in Mende*. Chicago:

Northwestern University.

Spence, N C W (1993): *A Brief History of Jèrriais.* Jersey: The author.

Spencer, Andrew (1999): Chukchee Homepage. http://privatewww.essex.ac.uk/~spena/Chukchee/CHUKCHEE_HOMEPAGE.html. 2001-07-27.

Sperry, Roger (1968): Mental unity following surgical disconnection of the cerebral hemispheres. *Harvey lectures* 62. New York: Academic Press.

Spolsky, Bernard & Elana Shohamy (1999): *The languages of Israel.* Clevedon: Multilingual Matters.

Sridhar, S. N. (1990): *Kannada.* London: Routledge.

Stampe, David (1972): How I spent my summer vacation. University of Chicago, PhD dissertation.

Steever, Sanford (1990): Tamil and the Dravidian languages. Comrie (ed.), pp 231-52.

—— (1998): Introduction to the Dravidian languages. Steever, Sanford (ed.): *The Dravidian languages,* pp 1-39. London & New York: Routledge.

Stein, Peter (1982): *Connaissance et emploi des langues à l'Île Maurice.* Hamburg: Helmut Buske Verlag.

Stewart, J M (1963): Some restrictions on objects in Twi. *Journal of African Languages* 2: 145-49.

Stewart, William (1962): Creole languages in the Caribbean. Rice, Frank (ed.) Study of the role of second languages in Asia, Africa and Latin America, pp 34-53, Washington: Center for Applied Linguistics,.

Stirke, D E C & A W Thomas (1916): *A Sikololo Phrase Book.* London: John Bale, Sons & Danielsson.

Street, Warren (1994): *A chronology of noteworthy events in American psychology.* Washington: American Psychological Association.

Suárez, Jorge (1983): *The Mesoamerican Indian languages.* Cambridge: Cambridge University Press.

Sudbury, Andrea (2000): Dialect contact and koineisation in the Falkland islands: Development of a southern hemisphere English? PhD thesis, University of Essex.

Svartvik, Jan (1968): *The Evans statements: a case for forensic linguistics.* Stockholm: Almqvist & Wiksell.

Svensén, Emil (1879): Från Aspelands härad i Kalmar län. *Svenska landsmål ock svenskt folkliv* 1, pp 636-640.

Swadesh, Morris (1939): Nootka Internal Syntax. *International Journal of American Linguistics* 9: 78-102.

Sweet, Henry (1900): *The history of language.* London: J M Dent.

Szemerényi, O (1967): The new look of Indo-European: reconstruction and typology. Phonetica 17.2: 65-99.

Talmy, Leonard (1978): Figure and ground in complex sentences. IGreenberg, Joseph (ed.): *Universals of Human Language,* vol. 4, pp 625-49. Stanford: Stanford University Press.

—— (1985): Lexicalization Patterns: Semantic Structure in Lexical Forms. Shopen, Timothy (ed.): *Language Typology and Syntactic Description,* vol. 3, pp 57-149. Cambridge: Cambridge University Press.

Tandefelt, Marika (ed.) (2002): Viborgs fyra språk under sju sekel. Helsinki: Schildts.

Tappolet, Ernst (1977 [1905]): Phonetik und Semantik in der etymologischen Forschung. Schitt, Rüdiger (ed.): *Etymologie,* pp 74-102. Darmstadt: Wissenschaft.

Tardif, Susan Gelman Twila & Fan Xu (1999): Putting the "Noun Bias" in Context: A Comparison of English and Mandarin. *Child Development* 70: 620-35.

Tarski, Alfred (1944). The semantic conception of truth. *Philosophy and Phenomenological Research* 4: 341-75.

Taub, Sarah (2001): *Language from the Body: Iconicity and Metaphor in American*

Taylor, Douglas (1977): *Languages of the West Indies.* Baltimore: The John Hopkins University Press.

Taylor, Douglas & Berend Hoff (1980): The linguistic repertory of the Island-Carib in the seventeenth century: The men's language – A Carib Pidgin? *International Journal of American Linguistics* 46: 301-12.

Terrace, Herbert (1979). Nim. New York: Knopf.

Terrace, H S, L A Petitto, R J Sanders & T G Bever (1979). Can an ape create a sentence? *Science* 206: 891-902.

Tesnière, Lucien (1959): *Éléments de syntaxe structurale.* Paris: Klincksieck.

Thijs, Roger (2000): What a border can do. http://home-13.tiscalibusiness.nl/~tpm09245/lang/lg/nl_b/baarle.htm. 2005-06-30.

Thomason, Sarah (1983): Chinook Jargon in areal and historical context. *Language* 59: 820-70.

—— (1996b): Mednyj Aleut. Thomason (ed.), pp 449-68.

—— (ed.) (1996): *Contact languages: a wider perspective.* Amsterdam: Benjamin.

Thomason, Sarah & Everett, Daniel (2001): Pronoun borrowing. MS.

Thurber, James (1957): *Alarms and diversions.* New York: Harper & Row.

Tilque, Dan (1998): Reversed Placenames. *Word Ways,* November 1998.

—— (2001): Common placenames. *Word Ways* pp 97-99.

Tirvassen, Rada (1999): La problématique du choix des langues d'enseignement dans des pays indépendants: l'anglais dans la politique de l'école mauricienne. *DiversCité Langues* 4.

Tomlin, Russell (1986): *Basic word order: Functional principles.* London: Croom Helm.

Trager, George & Bernard Bloch (1941): The syllabic phonemes of English. *Language* 17: 223-46.

Trask, Larry (1993): *A Dictionary of Grammatical Terms in Linguistics.* London & New York: Routledge.

—— (1996): *Historical linguistics.* London: Arnold.

—— (1996b): *A dictionary of Phonetics and Phonology.* London: Routledge.

—— (1997): *The History of Basque.* London: Routledge.

Traunmüller, Hartmut (1991): Conversational Maxims and Principles of Language Planning. *Perilus* 12: 25-47.

—— (forthcoming): *The International Vocabulary.*

Traunmüller, Hartmut & Anders Eriksson (1993): The frequency range of the voice fundamental in the speech of male and female adults. http://www.ling.su.se/ staff/hartmut/f0_m&f.pdf.

Tricoche, Georges Nestler (1929): *Terre-Neuve et alentours; Îles de la Madeleine, Labrador, Saint-Pierre et Miquelon.* Paris: Éditions Pierre Roger.

Trousseau, Armand (1864): De l'aphasie, maladie décrite récemment sous le nom impropre d'aphémie. *Gazette des Hopitaux* 37: 13-14.

Trubetzkoy, Nikolai (1928): Établissement et délimination des termes techniques. *Acte du premier congrès de linguistes, tenu à la Haye du 10-15 avril 1928,* pp 17-18. Leiden: Sijthoff.

—— (1931): Die phonologischen Systeme. *Travaux du Crecle Linguistique de Prague* 4: 96-116.

—— (1939): *Grundzüge der Phonologie.* Prague: Cercle Linguistique de Prague.

Truchot, Claude (2002): *Key aspects of the use of English in Europe.* Strasbourg: Council of Europe.

Trudgill, Peter (1994): Language contact and dialect contact in linguistic change. Kotsinas, Ulla-Britt & John Helgander (eds): *Dialektkontakt, språkkontakt och språkförändring i Norden,* pp 13-22. Stockholm: Institutionen för nordiska språk, Stockholms Universitet.

Tsujii, Jun-ichi (1988): *Reasons why I do not care grammar formalism.* Coling Budapest: Proceedings of the 12th International Conference on Computational Linguistics.

Budapest: John von Neumann Society for Computing Sciences.

Tuite, Kevin (2003): Of phonemes, fossils and webs of meaning: The interpretation of language variation and change. Jourdan, Christine & Kevin Tuite (eds): *Ethnolinguistics and Anthropological Theory*, pp 441-500. Montréal: Éditions Fides

U S Department of the Interior (1997): *Plains Indian Sign Language: A Memorial to the Conference September 4 - 6, 1930, Browning, Montana*. [No place].

Usnadze, D (1924) Ein experimentelle Beitrag zum Probleme des psychologischen Grundlagen der Namengebung. *Psychologischen Forschungen* 5: 24-43.

van Beek, Pieta (1999): "Het Babel van haar tijd": Anna Maria van Schurman (1607-1678) en haar kennis van (oosterse) talen. *Tydskrif vir Nederlands en Afrikaans*, June 1999.

Van den Berg, Helma (2005): The East Caucasian language family. *Lingua* 115: 147-190.

Van Driem, George (1993): The Proto-Tibeto-Burman Verbal Agreement System. *Bulletin of the School of Oriental and African Studies* 56: 292-334.

Van Valin, Robert (1985): Case marking and the structure of the Lakhota clause. Nichols, Johanna & Anthony Woodbury (eds): *Grammar Inside and Outside the Clause*, pp 363-413. Cambridge: Cambridge University Press

Veditz, George (2002): The Preservation of the Sign Language. http://www.sscnet.ucla.edu/polisci/faculty/ boneill/veditz.html. 2002-06-17.

Venneman, Theo (1972a): Rule inversion. *Lingua* 29: 209-42.

Venter, Dawid (1999): A global perspective on racial and linguistic integration in South African Christian congregations. *Journal of World-Systems Research* 5: 619-50.

Versteegh, Kees (1984): Piĝingado, kreoligado kaj esperanto. *Hungara Vivo* 24.4: 127-29.

—— (1993b): Esperanto as a first language: language acquisition with a restricted input. *Linguistics* 31-3 (325), pp 539-55

Veselinona, Ljuba (2003): *Suppletion in verb paradigms*. PhD dissertation, University of Stockholm.

Vihman, Virve-Anneli (2004): Valency Reduction in Estonian. PhD thesis, University of Edinburgh.

Voß, Christian (2000): Die Integration von International-ismen als puristischer Zug der makedonischen Standardsprache. *Die Welt der Slaven* 45: 27-48.

Waerden, B. L. van der & Graham Flegg (1975): *Counting I: Primitive and More Developed Counting Systems*. Milton Keynes: The Open University Press.

Wahlgren, Yens (2004): *Klingon as Linguistic Capital. A Sociologic Study of Nineteen Advanced Klingonists*. Lund: BA thesis (sociology), Lund University.

Wallace, Amy (1986): *The Prodigy: Biography of William Sidis*. London: Macmillan.

Wallechinsky, David, Irving Wallace, Amy Wallace, Per-Erik Lindorm & Sten Söderberg (1979): *Första Listboken*. [n pl]: Askild & Kärnekull.

Walter, Henriette (1988): *Le français dans tous les sens*. Paris: Robert Lafont.

Wangkheimayum, Bharati & Anjani Kumar Sinha (1997): Tense and agreement in Nagamese. Paper presented at the Annual Meeting of the Society for Pidgin and Creole Linguistics, London, June 27, 1997.

Ward, Andrew (2005): *Feral children*. http://www. feralchildren.com. 2005-07-26.

Wartburg, Walther von (1969): *Évolution et structure de la langue française*. 9th edition. Bern: Éditions A Francke.

Wassman, Jürg & Pierre Dasen (1994): Yupno Number System and Counting. *Journal of Cross-Cultural Psychology* 25: 78-94.

Watkins, Arwyn (1993): Welsh. Ball, Martin & James Fife (eds): *The Celtic languages*, pp 289-348. London: Routledge.

Watkins, Laurel (1984): *A Grammar of Kiowa*. Lincoln: University of Nebraska Press.

Watterson, Bill (1994): *Homicidal psycho jungle cat*. London: Warner Books.

Weber, George (1997): The World's ten Most Influential Languages. *Language Today* 2.

Weijnen, A. (1957): De Rijksgrens tussen België en Nederland als taalgrens. *Bijdragen en Mededelingen der Dialectencommissie van de Koninklijke Nederlandse Academie van Wetenschappen te Amsterdam* 18. Amsterdam: Noord-Hollandsche Uitgeversmaatschappij.

Weinreich, Max (1945): Der YIVO un di problemen fun undzer tsayt. *Yivo-bleter* 25: 3-18.

Weinreich, Uriel (1954): Is a structural dialectology possible? *Word* 10: 388-400.

Welmers, William (1959): Tonemics, morphotonemics, and tonal morphemes. *General Linguistics* 4: 1-9.

—— (1976): *A Grammar of Vai*. Berkeley: University of California Press.

Westrum, Peter (1988): A grammatical sketch of Berik. *Irian* 16: 133-87.

Wettenhovi-Aspa, Sigurd (1935): *Fenno-ägyptischer Kulturursprung der Alten Welt. Kommentare zu den vorhistorischen Völkerwanderungen*. Leipzig: Genius-Verlag.

Wheatley, Julian (1990): Burmese. Comrie (ed.), pp 106-26.

Whorf, Benjamin Lee (1936): The Punctual and Segmentative Aspects of Verbs in Hopi. *Language* 12: 127-31.

—— (1938): Language: plan and conception of agreement. Unpublished until 1956, when it appeared in Carrol, J B (ed.): *Language, Thought and Reality: Selected Writings of Benjamin Lee Whorf*, pp 125-33. Cambridge: MIT Press.

—— (1938b): Some Verbal Categories of Hopi. *Language* 14: 275-86.

Willerman, Raquel (1994): The phonetics of pronouns: Articulatory bases of markedness. PhD dissertation, University of Texas at Austin.

Williams, Robert (1997): The Ebonics Controversy. *The Journal of Black Psychology* 23.3: 208-14.

WIPO (2000): *Use of Portuguese as a working language of WIPO*. World Intellectual Property Organization document WO/GA/ 26/1. http://www.wipo.org/eng/ document/govbody/ wo_gb_ga/ pdf/ga26_1.pdf. 2002-04-03.

Wise, Mary Ruth (1999): Small language families and isolates in Peru. Dixon & Aikhenvald (eds), pp 307-40.

Witte, Jörg (2000): English as a global language: the case of the European Union. *Erfurt electronic studies in English* 6-2000. http://webdoc.sub.gwdg.de/edoc/ia/ eese/artic20/witte/6_2000.html. 2004-04-12.

Wolff, Ekkehard (2000): Language and society. Heine & Nurse (eds), pp 298-347.

Wonderly, William, Lorna Gibson & Paul Kirk (1954): Number in Kiowa: nouns, demonstratives, and adjectives. *International Journal of American Linguistics* 20: 1-7.

Woods, David (1998): The education variable in language patterns in Republic of Congo [sic]. Maddieson, Ian & Thomas Hinnebusch (eds): *Language history and linguistic description in Africa*, pp 307-316. Trenton & Asmara: Africa World Press.

World Health Organisation (1999): *Atteindre le plus grand nombre: les langues et la communication à l'OMS*. Report no. EB105/20, 24 November 1999.

World Lingo (2001): The WorldLingo Quarterly Email Survey – August 2001. http://www.worldlingo.com/ en/downloads/ aug_email_survey.zip. 2002-09-01.

Wurm, Stephen (1996a): North China: Intercultural communication involving indigenous languages other than Chinese. Wurm et al. (eds) pp 815-25.

—— (1996b): The Taimyr Peninsula Russian-based pidgin. Jahr & Broch (eds), pp 79-90.

Wurm, S, P Mühlhäusler & D Tryon (eds) (1996): *Atlas of languages of intercultural communication in the Pacific, Asia, and the Americas*. 3 vols, Berlin: Mouton de Gruyter.

Wynne, Clive (2004): *Do Animals Think?* Princeton: Princeton University Press.

Yadav, Ramawater (1996): *A reference grammar of Maithili*. Berlin: Mouton de Gruyter.

Yanega, Douglas (2001): Curious Scientific Names. http://entmuseum9.ucr.edu/staff/yanega.html. 2001-05-17.

Yigezu, Moges (2001): Articulatory and acoustic effects of lip-plate speech in Chai and its implications for phonological theory. *Journal of the International Phonetic Association* 31: 203-21.

Yukita, Hiroyuki (2003): An overview of the TEFL situation in various countries. http://www.asahi-net.or.jp/~nx6h-ykt/overview.html. 2003-07-20.

Zenk, Henry (1988): Chinook Jargon in the speech economy of Grand Ronde Reservation, Oregon: an ethnography-of-speaking approach to an historical case of creolization in process. *International Journal of the Sociology of Language* 1: 107-24.

Zhao, L, K Kipper, W Schuler, C Vogler, N Badler & M Palmer (2000): A Machine Translation System from English to American Sign Language. White, J S (ed.): *Envisioning Machine Translation in the Information Future*, pp 54-67. Heidelberg: Springer.

Zubiri, Jesús Olza & Miguel Angel Jusayú (1986): *Gramática de la Lengua Guajira (morphosintaxis)*. San Cristóbal: Universidad Católica del Tachira.

Zürcher, E J (1993): *Turkey: A Modern History*. London: I B Tauris.

Zwicky, A, P Salus, R Binnick & A Vanek (eds) (1970): *Studies out in the Left Field: Defamatory Essays Presented to James D McCawley (on the occasion of his 33rd or 34th birthday)*. Edmonton: Linguistic Research.

INDEX

Entries are arranged in strictly alphabetical order. Roman letters accompanied by a diacritic (accent) are not distinguished alphabetically from the same letters without a diacritic, e.g. **é** is not distinguished from **e**, **ç** is not distinguished from **c**, etc. Somewhat similarly, **ø** is treated as a variant of **o**. Non-alphabetical elements which occur in the names of several "click" languages are disregarded for the purposes of alphabeticization so that, e.g. !Xū is listed under X.

All entries such as Algonquian languages, African languages, Romance languages, etc. indicate those pages where there is reference to these languages as a group. There are also separate entries in the index for each of the languages belonging to these groups which are mentioned in the text.